JUDY
CASSAB

Australia Council
for the Arts

This project has been assisted by the Commonwealth Government through the Australia Council, its arts funding and advisory body.

Random House Australia Pty Ltd
20 Alfred Street, Milsons Point, NSW 2061

Sydney New York Toronto
London Auckland
and agencies throughout the world

First published in 1995

National Library of Australia
Cataloguing-in-Publication Data

Cassab, Judy, 1920–
    Judy Cassab Diaries

    ISBN 0 09 183102 4

    1. Cassab, Judy, 1920– –Diaries. 2. Artists, Australian–20th century–Diaries. 3. Women artists–Australia–Diaries. 4. Immigrants–Australia–Diaries, 5. Holocaust, Jewish (1939–1945)–Hungary–Personal narratives. I. Title.

    759.994

Designed by Reno Design Group 14758
Typeset by Midlands Typesetters, Maryborough
Printed by Griffin Paperbacks, Adelaide
Production by Vantage Graphics, Sydney

10 9 8 7 6 5 4 3 2 1

Most of the photographs taken in the 1960s and '70s are by Jim Fitzpatrick.
Those taken in the '80s and '90s are by Robert Walker.

JUDY CASSAB

D I A R I E S

ALFRED A. KNOPF SYDNEY 1995

To Bernie Leser who first suggested the idea.
  'When are you going to do something with your diaries?'
  'When I am old.'
And then I realised that I *am* old.

To Elizabeth Riddell who sifted through the pages saving the interesting anecdotes, facts, dreams and events of over fifty years of my diary. A labour of love.

To Lynne Segal for her sensitive and creative editing and advice.

In 1941, when Jancsi was sent to a forced-labour camp in Russia, we'd only been married for two years. We knew there would be no contact. So, before he left, we chose a star on which to meet. We both kept this nightly appointment. Jancsi says this kept him alive.

I dedicate this book to my best friend—my husband of fifty-six years. To Jancsi, who preferred a happy wife for ten months of the year to a frustrated one for twelve.

Foreword

Reading a diary is rather like watching a pointillist painter creating a landscape out of coloured dots. Unless the design is already laid on the canvas, the thousands of tiny elements bear no relation to the final product. Trying to guess what the completed image will look like is a tedious and frustrating process.

In the same fashion, to enjoy a diary you must have some knowledge, past or present, of the diarist.

Judy Cassab has a very public persona. She is a fine painter. She is a portraitist of singular skill who counts many famous men and women among her subjects. She has been for many years a well-known and generously supportive member of the art community in Sydney. She is respected as an artist; she is loved as a woman.

However, the Judy Cassab revealed in the pages of these journals is a far more complex, more various personage than one might expect. The diaries are a chronicle of fifty years from 1944 to 1994. The twenty years of her youth were recorded too, but the volumes have been lost. As Judy herself puts it:

> The beginning is not really the beginning. I was born in Vienna in 1920 . . . My first journal had a deep-blue velvet cover with a gold lock. I was twelve years old. I wrote about the seasons, of my enchantment with the first snow, the buds on the cherry trees . . .

This record begins in 1944 with a chilling simplicity:

> The Germans are in Hungary. Jancsi has returned from Russia after three years of forced labour. We think the end is near. Jews have to wear the yellow Star of David.

That's the first thing you notice in these pages. This is life seen under naked light, caught as the visual artist is forced to catch it, in swift impressions, curt sketches which one day hopefully will form themselves into a canvas, whole and intelligible.

The story unfolds itself by fits and starts on a variety of levels. It records her obsession—a life-saving, reason-saving obsession with painting. It tells of the love-affair which has coloured her whole life: her attachment to and her dependence upon her husband, Jancsi Kaempfner.

His portrait, in many variations of mood, is present in many pages of the diaries. His judgment of her work was the final Court of Appeal against the discordant verdicts of critics and the inevitable jealousies of her professional peers. He is the point of union between herself and her children, who like all offspring of talented people are both enriched and deprived by their parents' gifts.

All this being said, the golden threads which run through this very personal record of Judy Cassab's life are passion and love. She is passionate about everything she does, about her failures as about her successes, about questions she asks as about the answers she has painfully discovered both in her life and in the practice of her art.

Let me say it plainly: every art makes tyrannous demands upon those who practise it. Every art makes cruel revelations of every artist's shortcomings.

One of the things I admire most in Judy Cassab is the craftsman's discipline which underlies all her work. She confesses frankly what she has done ill. She is jubilant, as every artist has a right to be, when a painting comes off or when the sitter is happy with the image she has created, or when—more rarely—the critics and the colleagues are gracious.

However, the diaries reveal more than this. They reveal the tensions which drive every creative life—the tensions between harsh reality and the ideal world to which the creative spirit is born, the tensions between brutal memories of survival in a mad time and the desperate wish to enjoy the passing present and the promised future in a new land.

All these aspects of Judy Cassab the reader will discover in the diaries.

They are vivid with joy, shadowed at times by hidden griefs and cyclical depressions, but they are a true record of the life of a brave lady and her gallant consort through a long and adventurous lifetime.

There is one passage which has remained engraved in my memory:

God knows, I have weathered more abysms than most. I have been torn away from my husband for years when I was young. I suffered not knowing where he was nor how cold or hungry he felt in the snows of Russia. I was an outcast with my maid's identity, persecuted, hiding, alert for my life. I went through the unspeakable agony of knowing my mother was gassed in the ovens of Auschwitz. I lost my home three times. I starved. And I floated above all this horror with dulled innocence, and survived without going insane. I kept a sense of adventure of the young, retained details of the holocaust without daring to file it into its historical, sociological, psychological entity.

I would be strongly tempted to submit to analysis to search for lost traumas, to dig them up to make me a better artist if I were not scared of the exact opposite. Of finally having all in the conscious mind, and then not being able to paint at all. Paradoxically, I am not really involved with the art world. I am an onlooker, a bystander. Not terribly passionate either. I belong to a migrant, Jewish, middle-class family where even established families are looking and acting nouveau riche, living the pleasant empty life. (June 1964)

Such sustained and tragic eloquence is rare in the diaries. They reflect all the moods of the lady herself: gossipy, enthusiastic, clubbish, humorous, resentful sometimes, but curiously lacking in malice.

This is a woman who invokes often the memory of love and the name of God and who, in spite of all the horrors to which she was witness, has never surrendered to bitterness or despair. One cannot write everyday about oneself without some revelation of the creature who lives in one's skin. What these diaries reveal is a gallant and loving lady, dedicated to the hardest of all vocations, that of a painter.

Morris L West
Sydney
July 1995

The beginning is not really the beginning . . .

I was born in Vienna on 15 August 1920. My father longed to be a poet and a playwright, but instead carried on the family tradition of business—not very successfully. When I was nine, my mother and father separated. She and I went to live with my grandmother in Beregszász, a small town in Hungary, where the family owned the local brick factory.

My first journal had a deep blue velvet cover with a gold lock. I was twelve years old. I wrote about the seasons; of my enchantment with the first snow, the buds on the cherry trees, the fiercely hot summers and rainy autumns. I wrote about my teachers and classmates.

And later, I recorded every detail of my meeting and eventual marriage to Jancsi, a man double my age. He assured me this would change in time. Our wedding was austere. The Second World War was moving closer to our doorstep. Jancsi was sent to a forced-labour camp in Russia. He said if we had to be separated, I might as well take the opportunity to go study art in Budapest.

All the while I wrote. I recorded the horror of being Jewish in a world consumed with the annihilation of all Jews. Everything began breaking down around us. In the chaos of moving from Jancsi and my first home in Munkács, the first volumes of my diary were lost.

April 1944

Budapest

The Germans are in Hungary. Jancsi has returned from Russia after three years in forced labour. We think the end of the war is near. Jews have to wear the yellow Star of David.

We are living in a boarding house. We share one room not knowing, of course, for how long. The chestnut trees are in bud outside. My easel stands in the corner, neglected. The art school has closed.

In Beregszász the Jews are in ghettos. Anyu [my mother] is fighting to keep the spirits of the family up. Neurotic as she is, she always blossoms in a crisis. They took Pista away. I don't know where.

The latest order instructs Jews to declare their assets. The proverb says 'The wanderer with the empty pocket smiles'. We don't have much money, but we declared the Persian rugs and the silver. This doesn't matter. What hurts is that when our furniture was moved from the flat in Munkács, my diaries got lost. I started to write thirteen years ago. My childhood, my school years, my engagement and marriage to Jancsi were in it.

Jancsi has become a labourer in a suitcase factory.

August 1944

In the middle of May, Anyu (Mother), Grandmother, Pista, Sanyi [Anyu's husband], Jancsi's mother, brother and his family, were all deported. During the last few days we made desperate attempts to save them. We sent a Gestapo car with a bribed officer to bring them to Budapest. He took their last pengö and abandoned them.

Feri, a close friend of Jancsi, went to his office, carefully placed his yellow star on his desk and shot himself.

Witnesses saw the family at the railway station being herded into cattle trains. Women were separated from men, young from old. Some were beaten, identification cards taken away. Eighty locked in a wagon without food, only a bucket of water.

The day we found this out Jancsi decided we would be safer if we separated. He made me take the yellow star off. So, four months ago I shed my old self. I now live as Mária Koperdák. I have taken on the identity of Mariska, my old maid. I have her papers. I moved into a room advertised in the paper. As I put my suitcase down I realised that I have to sleep in the same room as the landlady and her 21-year-old son. They asked questions. I answered, guilty and frightened. I lay in the dark listening to the beat of my heart and the alarm clock. Around morning, still palpitating and awake, I thought I cannot stand this, not even for a day. At first I felt I was being watched on the street. I combed my hair back, put dark glasses on and stood ready to jump on the tram.

I'm becoming used to it. I lie fluently about being a dressmaker. Just now I'm making lampshades. I have also worked in a chemical plant where I handled poisonous digitalis for eight hours. I kept a shawl around my nose and mouth. The fire had to be kept going under the powder, so in the mornings I cut wood in the cellar to feed the oven. The saddest part of the day, perhaps even now, is to leave Manyi and Gyuszi's flat after dinner, coffee, cigarettes, light and warmth, and go down the dark stairs alone.

I meet Jancsi in the Jewish house with the yellow star, secretly. Once we met in the street and we had to pass as strangers for he wears the star and I now don't.

Since the Allies are closer there are bombings every night. People don't take it very well. I feel more alienated than usual as I don't feel afraid at all, or rather only afraid when the planes fail to come. Sometimes it starts at 8 p.m. and as the trams stop I sleep in Manyi's cellar. After the all-clear we go on the roof. A gruesome sight. The whole town in flames.

September 1944

On average we spend four hours in the bomb shelter in the morning and four in the evening. Electricity fails, or water or transport. The other day I walked 45 minutes in black nothing to what I call 'home'. I got the shivers and I think some fever. Next day I became ill. Manyi made up a bed for me in her flat and left me alone as she had to go out. I cried and cried until the doorbell rang. It was Jancsi. He has never been here before and we know how dangerous it is. It is exactly as when I was once bogged with the car in the snow in Munkács and he received the message and felt he had to go. He saved me then, and he saves me now.

I am not panicking over these depressions though. I know them well, they are old acquaintances. There is no cure but the knowledge that it passes. What I suffer most from, perhaps, is the naked crudeness, the rudeness of the crowd. For weeks one doesn't meet a Western European face. In the milieu I have chosen as a refuge for myself there is spitting, sweating, the smell of garlic. I am melting in with the rags I wear, but somehow it becomes more important than ever before to have clean underwear.

I cry often nowadays with or without tears. As it's getting colder and I wear a pullover, the thought nags in me that Anyu might be cold. And I think of Grandmother, whom one can't visualise without her checked scarf. And all the others. They only had what they were wearing when they were taken away. I make my body work the eight hours and try to work out where the Allies are. Refugees pour into Budapest from Transylvania by the thousands. They come in carriages and on trucks. I'm terrified that I feel no pity for them. Not in comparison.

October 1944

Jancsi and I met on the street, on my way to his place. I walked ten steps behind. A stranger came running towards him, shouting something I didn't hear and, as he embraced Jancsi, with the same movement tore the yellow star off his coat. Jancsi flew to me, his eyes brimming over. 'Jucókám, the governor just announced on the radio, we surrendered. The war is over.'

Euphoria all day. Trying to guess whether the Russians will reach Budapest from Szolnok tonight or only by tomorrow. We ran up to Manyi together, drank and kissed and held our swimming heads.

Towards evening, news of a different nature invaded our joy. The radio suddenly started playing German marches. Rumours held that a Nazi group occupied the station, shot the speaker and commandeered the microphone. There had been a coup.

Jancsi insisted he return to the Jewish house to look after his landlady and her child, perhaps there would be atrocities going on there. I had no choice but to agree. Half an hour later, however, we became so anxious that Gyuszi and I followed and begged him to return to Manyi's place. He yielded, but only if he could bring the child with him. All right, the child can sleep in the bathtub. By the time we got back to Manyi's there was another woman and another child. They slept on the floor.

Next morning we understood that the Germans took the governor prisoner. The Hungarian Nazi leader, Szálasi, has taken over the government of the country. The fight for Budapest goes on.

Immediately there followed the evacuation of the Jews from the Jewish houses. Even those wives who had Christian husbands in the army were taken away.

Next day I went to work (the plant works for the army now). Missing a day is impossible and considered treason. On the tram looking out the window I felt icy terror. Along Rákóczy út the Jews were being herded like cattle, carrying bundles on their backs. Some old people sat on carts, their feet dangling over the side. They looked like grandparents who should rest in easychairs. Now they rattled the cobblestones with fear in their eyes.

If my journal is found, my life will be in danger. So I write on this zigzag toilet paper without dates.

In the factory I pack dextrose in pink tissue paper. The mechanical movements are soothing. I look at the park through the window and see swirling smoke. The others see it too and guess what it might be. Eventually the delivery boy goes out to explore. From far away, machine-gun fire. The delivery boy comes back and announces that the smoke comes from bodies being burned.

'What bodies?'

'Jewish bodies.'

In the evening I go up to Gabi's flat. Gabi Izsák, from Beregszász and now an active member of the small Jewish underground. He wears the Nazi uniform, works in a shoemaker's shop and I help him fake documents for Jews. I roll a hot hard-boiled egg over an original document and duplicate it on false papers. I also deliver stolen medicine for the underground's hospital. I smuggled it in my bra.

'What's happening to Jancsi?' he asks as soon as he opens the door. I tell him Jancsi is at Manyi's at the moment but can't stay there. It's dangerous for her to even hide her husband, my uncle, Gyuszi.

'Bring him here,' he says.

No one is allowed to be on the streets after 5 p.m.

I knew a Hungarian officer, a major, who was not a Jew-hater. I asked for his help. He escorted Jancsi and me to Gabi's flat. His uniform meant safety for us. But at Gabi's we found 23 Jews in a darkened room. Gabi was hiding them.

Jancsi pressed my arm and repeated over and over: 'Let's get out of here, let's get out of here.' The major was still there. It was four thirty and no place to go. 'Let's go to my place,' I said. 'If they capture you, they capture me. We shall tell the caretaker you just returned from the forced-labour camp. Perhaps they will leave us be.' But Jancsi wouldn't. We took a tram and went back to Manyi's flat.

After work the next day Jancsi told me he has decided to move into the ghetto. Better than this furtive existence, this trembling uncertainty.

I argued, begged, cajoled, but he wouldn't budge. Then the doorbell rang, Kati and Frici, his old friends. 'Now you are coming to us and we will hide you,' they said.

Kati was an actress before the war, and Frici a film director. Their friendship goes back long before Jancsi met me. Jancsi strongly resisted, saying that people who are hiding Jews are being treated as Jews. He can't risk their lives.

'For God's sake,' said Kati, 'what is friendship for?' And we took Jancsi to Róna ucca, in Zugló.

Jancsi spent three months there. Whenever a stranger came to the door he hid in a wardrobe. Not only did Kati and Frici risk their lives, they also risked their family which had escaped to Budapest from Debrecen before the Russians occupied it.

I only work four hours now because of electricity restrictions. We wait for the Russians with feverish impatience.

I spent Christmas at Kati's. As I arrived in the afternoon I found Frici working on a manger. I painted cut outs of the holy family which we placed on real sand and straw. Then we lit two yellow candles. Good dinner and wine, black coffee and a small tree. We tried very hard not to think of other Christmases.

The cannons started next morning. The trams stopped. I started walking and signalled to a car. The young man opened the door for me politely, yes, he knows there are no trams. He wore a leather jacket. Only later did I see the swastika on his sleeve. He assured me too, that if they stop us he will say he's taking me to headquarters as he is a detective anyway. I almost laughed at the irony. We were stopped at a checkpoint, but nowhere would I have felt safer than in the Nazi car. My driver saluted with the Hitler gesture and the other answered 'Long live Szálasi'.

On New Year's Eve we became subterranean creatures.

The siege of Budapest has begun. As soon as I reached Manyi's place there was such thunder that we ran into the bomb shelter. During the first few days, we sneaked upstairs to the flat during the mornings, where we washed and cooked, before we got stuck in the cellar completely. I sleep on a stretcher in my clothes. Manyi brought her bed down and some food and tins. The coal cellar has become the kitchen and also the latrine. When one has to go, one either asks the cooks to leave or sits between the petroleum cooker and the table. At night one can only go if the lock of the three iron doors is open.

We have eight children under the age of two, they cry all night.

The interior looks like this: Manyi's bed, around it two tanks with water, a radio which doesn't work, four sandbags, a water jug, a basket with dried bread, books and teapots. All round there are hooks with winter coats.

Today there was a tremendous blast, the earth was shaking and we thought the house was hit. There are no sirens any more, the place is a battlefield. Under the arcades in front of the house there are trucks, tanks and cannons. Occasionally they bring in wounded soldiers.

During the lull we went out to look. There wasn't a glass window left. When we went up to the flat we could see into the next apartment which got hit by a bomb.

Three days later gas, electricity and water supplies ceased. We burned candles all day. The block had four new hits. We started to ration food. Each meal consisted of one piece of dried bread with bacon. No more cooking. One evening the doctor made some pies on his spirit cooker and as it was the last of his flour everybody received a slice along with a glass of wine. The opera singer sang an aria.

One can hardly move from all the stretchers. Lately I share mine with another girl. We took the latrine from the coal cellar into the lift shaft. Washing is a luxury of the past. No fresh underwear.

We sit huddled in blankets. This morning a deafening explosion threw us from our seats.

As I turned in the direction of the fire I saw the bomb had blasted the wall away, and the fuel from the burning tank rushed in like a flaming river. There were screams and panic. I ran with Gyuszi and Manyi towards the exit through the smoke and debris pressing my shawl against my face. The vestibule was aglow. At the gate two trucks were blazing. For one petrified moment I thought we would be burned inside. There was no choice but to make a run through the square. Manyi fell and glass pieces went through her knee. Overhead the planes were dropping bombs. The bomb shelter where we fled was occupied by the army. The soldiers were touchingly gentle. They dressed Manyi's wound and covered us with blankets.

Gyuszi and some other men ran back to our burning building to save the children. Everybody came out alive. They brought some of our scorched belongings over, but the food was gone.

The square is littered with the skeleton-trucks and the houses are in ruins. The soldiers got hot coffee for breakfast and we were given some too. For lunch we got a cupful of soup.

It's too dark to read so we play games. We have become utterly shameless. We wash with the soldiers looking on. They keep feeding us, and giving us wine and cigarettes. They tiptoe at night so as not to disturb the little sleep we snatch.

Everything is deteriorating. There is shit on the parquet floors of apartments. Shops are wide open. When there is a lull in the bombing, people loot even the most unnecessary objects.

The air in the shelter makes us cough and when sometimes we ascend into the daylight, we recoil from each other's faces.

I am feeling quite apathetic and try not to think if Jancsi survived the bombs locked in the wardrobe. There is no way to know if he is alive or if we shall ever meet again. Human and animal carcasses lie around us. It's been three weeks now since the siege began.

The corporal rests with his boots pressed against the wall. A kerosene lamp casts its weak yellow light. I am wondering whether—after this great wind which has blown us apart—some of us will find each other again. If not, I know I shall be like a hollow tree. I know I won't be able to feel joy or sorrow. Strangely I am still longing for my painting.

The soldiers have to go over to the Buda side. The shelter has become very depressing since they've left.

The house next door was hit and two storeys are burning. I crossed the square to fetch water. Several women were cutting out the flesh of dead horses. The sight repelled me. Little did I guess that I shall be lucky to do the same when I get hungry enough. In the evening we all had to help quench the fires. It was pitch dark as we climbed up to the fourth floor with buckets of water. We climbed, stumbling and wheezing and trembling. When the fire was under control we fell on our stretchers exhausted. Our cellar seemed like a haven. We drank tea with dried bread and waited for tomorrow.

Rumours are that the Russians are in Zugló. Zugló is where Jancsi is. The Russians occupy the eastern railway. In our part of the city the German cannons are blasting away.

Then the day that was true hell. From 5 a.m. the planes attacked relentlessly. Four or five bombs fell every minute. The ground shook convulsively. Our house got hit. The first floor is entirely gone. We have no idea where the military front is. Paris, Belgrade, Bucharest,

Rome—none have experienced this. The wall to the next house fell in. A Russian tank shot it down. Gyuszi came with the news that the Russians have reached the town hall.

A group of Nazis burst into our cellar with hand grenades. 'Stay calm,' they said. 'We just want some volunteers to clear the ruins in Buda so our reinforcements can advance.'

With the Russians so close there were no volunteers.

Then they grabbed us and pointed their guns at us and herded us upstairs. A bomb fell nearby, killing one of them. They let us go, promising to be back in the morning.

There was silence in the morning.

The first Russian to come into our cellar was polite and calm. He was looking for Germans and weapons. Somehow I felt that this was a historic moment, but could not realise it.

The second group was wilder. They took all the watches and torches. The third wave was drunk and wanton.

Then two Jews arrived from the ghetto. They were terribly thin and almost unrecognisable. We gave them food and tried to stop them eating too fast. A little later Jancsi arrived.

I leaned against him to stop myself from fainting. We clasped each other. It was unreal, unbelievable, to fill my eyes with the sight of him.

Zugló was taken eleven days before the Russians reached us. Jancsi stuck with them for eleven days, to reach me and to take us back to Zugló before the looting and the raping start.

We were worried about how Manyi would stand up to the long trip after her illness, but she wouldn't hear of being left behind.

The walk through the city was an agonising experience. Houses were still burning on both sides of the street, the skyline punctured with telegraph poles. Their broken wires crisscrossed the snowy ground and had to be stepped over. We stepped over fallen bricks and dead bodies. Surrealistic objects littered the urban landscape; discarded dolls, gramophones and sewing machines.

Now we sit in Zugló. Too many people in Kati's small flat. We wait for the war to finish.

I crawl around like a shadow. When I hear the word 'Juci'. I don't react. I feel tricked, deceived, the victim of a terrifying hoax. I can't feel any pleasure on any level and I don't understand this. I am longing to return to Beregszász at least until water, gas, electricity and food supplies will be available here again. I am longing for home, some home and know that the meaning of home is lost. I expect the little town to be deserted and hopeless and that an awful reality will confront me, something I don't dare to think of.

Jancsi, Gyuszi and Csura go on expeditions. They steal wood from fences to heat the stove. Jancsi visited the ghetto and said he found starving wrecks of humanity, looking like lepers. Every few steps dying people are sitting in the snow. Later we went together to the city.

I took him to my room, the scene of eight months of my life as Mária Koperdák. It was empty. Not a stocking, not even the old suitcase.

The face of the street is abominable. Suddenly everybody sports a red armband and calls each other comrade. The dirt floats to the top again.

At Kati's we live ten in a room as only this one room can be heated. On the same iron stove we cook whatever our men steal. Each person can wash every third day. The men bring water from a well in buckets. We are constantly hungry and amuse ourselves reciting recipes.

If only the trains would start.

February 1945

Budapest

We moved back to the city as the daily twenty-kilometre walks proved too much for us. Our base for life is a book of tickets to the relief kitchens where we wait for our daily dish of beans. We are so undernourished that even though we fill our stomachs with beans it doesn't satisfy us. Almost every night I have dreams about roast dinners and white glasses of milk. Gyuszi hikes into nearby villages to barter cigarettes for food. Food means carrots and maize from which we bake small tasteless cakes. Jancsi stole sulphurous apples from a tin factory which we swallow like medicine.

We live on Rákóczy út in a lawyer's draughty shabby office, the only room available in the apartment where four other families live with us, all using the same kitchen. When water is available we carry it to our rooms and wash in near freezing temperatures. The windows are shot out and it's bitter cold. We burn the lawyer's documents in the stove to give the illusion of fire, perhaps heat. We took the velvet drapes off the windows and use them as blankets. The desk is our bed. There are broken chairs, framed diplomas and brass Buddhas.

On the streets there is still shooting. Mines explode and the Russians go on with raping. Yesterday an army truck arrived from Beregszász with the mayor of the town and took a few friends home. Ukrainians are governing now and they have taken all the property.

Buda has fallen.

Life has more swing now. In the backlash of the war, people search and often find each other. Peasants come to Budapest to exchange geese for diamonds. A Courbet was found serving as a ceiling for a pigsty. There are no shops, no transport, no window glass, no machinery and no raw materials.

The director of the Dreher brewery invited Jancsi for a meeting. He introduced him as his right-hand man. Now, we can't decide whether to take the offer, or go home to Beregszász or emigrate. From where, and where to?

I visited the old caretaker. His wife remarked: 'We knew you lived here with false papers, you know.'

'You knew? But how?'

'You never showed us photographs of your parents,' she said.

A schoolmate of Gyuszi's, Béla Illés, who left Hungary in the 1920s as a committed communist, came back to Budapest with the advancing Red Army and is now commandant of the city. He is a writer. He spent a few days en route in Beregszász and saw my paintings. He found his 84-year-old mother in the ghetto, established her in a flat and searched for me to paint a portrait of her. In payment I got two kilos of bacon, a bag of potatoes, two eggs, two apples and a loaf of bread. We shared the treasure with friends. Most of it went to Kati's.

Since I'm painting Béla Illés's mother I feel more alive. After the first sitting in over a year, I looked at the eyes in the portrait and our eyes lock. Mine and the painted ones. I think I will never let this happen again, this parting from paint and brush.

19 March 1945

Theatres open. There is no gas, electricity nor transport. Anybody who desires can open one of the empty shops. One merchant put out a notice: 'Food? No. But available are bicarbonate of soda, a block of paper, a prayer book and condoms.' The black market flourishes. One can get five kilos of flour and lard for a pair of trousers.

Exactly a year ago the Germans occupied the country. Black flags are on all the houses.

25 March 1945

Beregszász

Transport has started. So at 7 a.m. we went to the railway station. Until noon no one could tell us which train to take.

The crowd sits on the roof of the train, others shove in through windows. The war has not changed people for the better. A young man who sat on the floor at my feet blocking the way to the lavatory wouldn't budge all night. I thought my bladder would burst.

We ate a can of food. I wrapped a blanket around me and urinated in the empty container. It was a little better than some other passengers who held bottoms out the window of the moving train.

In Miskolc we submitted to a lice-searching procedure. This is because of a spot-typhus epidemic.

From then on we travelled in a cattle train another whole night through. Next evening we arrived in Munkács. We didn't recognise the station. The old one had been bombed and in front of the new one there were fifty aeroplanes waiting to be transported.

The well-known streets, the unharmed houses, every stone and blade of grass screamed in our ears: 'Nothing happened. Nothing changed.' But the soul of the town is missing; not one of our friends lives in these houses. This is stage decor, a Potemkin village and nothing I see is true. At every turn, every step a recognition flooded over me to disappear the next moment. I was very disturbed by the time we reached the Hotel Csillag. My state of mind can't understand this either. That there is no home to go home to. Why go to a hotel?—asked my memory—I should go home.

I was almost angry with Jancsi for whom all this is easier, because of the warmth and affection which greeted and welcomed him.

That same night we went to see Vali and met Olga who had just returned from the concentration camp in Auschwitz. They were deported the same time as Anyu and the rest of our family, and here they are. They came home. And so do others, in great numbers. But no one brings news of Anyu. For the first time I hear of the crematoriums and how, to the tune of Dr Mengele's *J'attendrais*, Jews were selected to be gassed to death. Mercy, God.

One can only get to Beregszász, 25 kilometres away from Munkács, if one hitchhikes on a Russian truck. We weren't so lucky, we got a horse-drawn carriage and I remembered how many times I made this trip by car, sitting between Anyu and Pista.

I unfroze a bit in Beregszász. Didn't feel that strangeness in the Grand Hotel where a small group congregated among those who survived deportation. New skeletons arrive every day, and every day I wait for my mother.

I went to Grandmother's house, the house of my childhood. All the doors have been torn out; door handles, the copper door of the stove, straw and horse manure are scattered on the parquet floor. The chandeliers are hanging in the trees in the garden. They took the bathtub and the piano. The storeroom, the terrace, the chicken house, the wood bin, all empty.

When Mariska arrived she showed me things she guarded. A camera and bicycle, silverware and a stamp collection. There is only me. If only they would come back, we could all use the linen and the clothes. The clothes of Anyu still smell of her cigarettes and eau-de-cologne.

31 March 1945

I didn't count on this. I can't stay here and I don't feel like going back to Budapest. The comforts of the country have corrupted me. One switch and the light is on. To have a bath and to have as much meat and cake as I can eat. I don't belong anywhere. I am strangely disturbed. I sit in the coffee house waiting for Jancsi or for Gyuszi. I stare at the door. And every minute I seem to see Anyu coming in with her brown travel bag. I can't understand that I may be waiting in vain. I feel old and bitter. I am ill. My grasp on life is weak.

But I don't know whether she is alive somewhere. If she is, does she suffer? And if she died I don't know how. Was it in the gas chamber? Was she electrocuted on a wire fence in the extermination camp?

6 April 1945

The ones who reach Munkács describe Auschwitz. When they arrived there the Germans divided the Jews into groups. Old people, children and the sick were ushered to the left, told they were to be disinfected. Younger women who wanted to stay with their mothers or with their babies were allowed to do so. They had to undress and go to the shower with soap and towels. Then the Germans pressed the gas through. It took about three minutes.

Someone told me Pista died in Kraków. The ones in the same train with Anyu said she didn't arrive in camp at all.

If it wasn't for Jancsi who is warm and dear I really wouldn't know how to carry on.

May 1945

Budapest

I visited my old teacher from the art school. Aurél Bernáth. I asked for advice. He couldn't give any. He himself doesn't paint now. There is nowhere to work. Nothing to work with. No mood. No peace. What will happen to art and artists?

When we came back from Munkács Jancsi declined the offer of a position in the Dreher brewery. Jancsi can't start building a life for us, he says, while there is no organisation to care for the deportees who come back half-starved and without clothes.

Not having any money we went to a friend who lent us four Napoleon gold coins. Jancsi went to Bucharest where the centre for the International Red Cross is and came back with a cheque for one million Swiss francs.

First we went to Béla Illés, commandant of Budapest, who could give him a letter to the Ukranian government in the Ukraine. Béla says he doesn't give a hoot whether it's for Jews or not, it's American money and as such no communist would allow it into this region. Besides, two expeditions tried it before and both are in jail.

'I was a prisoner for three years,' Jancsi said, 'and I didn't know why. If I become one now, at least I will know it happened for a cause.'

Then we went to Sas ucca, where the Budapest Joint had their offices. The Swiss francs were changed into pengö and stuffed into two potato sacks and off Jancsi went in a taxi at night through the fields crossing over the Russian border. As I heard later he bribed the minister and set up seventy kitchens. Meanwhile he lived off Vozáry's Napoleonic gold as he wouldn't take a salary.

Gyuszi and Manyi opened an espresso bar on Madách Square amid burned houses and broken windows. But the espresso has a sign with its name, 'Black and White', freshly painted and people come in and think, that's life. Not me. I lost the war. I miss Jancsi like a drowning man the saving hand.

28 May 1945

I went to the doctor today. I am pregnant. God willing, I want it, I want it. Jancsi doesn't know yet. How I'm longing to tell him.

Today a group came back from Germany with the news that Anyu is on her way home. She is still in Karlsbad, where she is a nurse. She is well (or so they say).

I have the shakes and I cry.

June 1945

Jancsi was here for a few days and went back to Munkács. The joy about the child, that joy. He only speaks of us in plural.

I have begun to study painting again in Lipót Hermann's studio. I finished an interior and started a still life with paint so thick it's squandering.

My slender hope for Anyu is broken. A different person with the same name.

On the weekend Kati and Frici took me out to Leányfalu on the banks of the Danube River. It was wonderful to just lie in the grass, watch the clouds, the leaves above and the river. To visit the goat and play with the rabbit.

I have rented a simple clean room in the city. I'm still alone. Painting all day I don't feel it as badly as at night. With my baby no discomfort at all except I'm hungry more often and crave for meat which I can't afford.

Jancsi unexpectedly returned at 7 a.m. and the world filled with light. Now that his volunteer work is done he has decided to take the job at the brewery. He is manager of the yeast and chocolate factory as well.

4 July 1945

Painting, I mean the searching and growing work, fills my life again. It's not the hand which loses touch. I have to learn to see again. This is what I lost in that year. I gather momentum like a heavy wheel. God, it's hard to turn that wheel. I'm painting a tall grey building, and placed roses on the windowsill. How rich grey can be; yellowish, opal, greenish hues.

19 July 1945

Stories of 'sightings' of Anyu keep coming in, often via Gyuszi's espresso bar. I'm certain Anyu is sick, that's why she can't come. I sent a telegram to the American Joint trying to track her down. I didn't eat or sleep for two days waiting for their reply: 'No one under that name here.'

A breakdown worse than any before. I wanted to drink myself into a stupor. I am losing all hope.

We call the baby Juja, for Juci and Jancsi.

In the mornings I study with Hermann. In the afternoons I have a nude at home. Just now while I wait for my model a chicken is cooking on the stove. A rare occasion as it's horribly expensive, but Juja doesn't leave me in peace. Juja wants chicken.

1 August 1945

I think Juja moved. It was an infinitesimal movement but I am very happy. And very exhausted. I get up at 6 a.m., I press Jancsi's shirt, clean his shoes, wash his razor. When he leaves I do the shopping before going over to the studio. I am taking French lessons and studying art history. Then I go home and cook dinner. We argue about emigration. Jancsi doesn't want to start off with me pregnant. But I would much rather have the baby outside this country.

To my horror I find that I have resigned myself to the thought of my mother's death. I no longer believe she is alive. The wound I carry inside bleeds on.

In my life with Jancsi I am more conscious every day of sharing, of having a splendid companion. We both are expecting, not only me. 'I bought you both peaches,' Jancsi says.

16 August 1945

My second birthday without Anyu my dear mother. I am thinking of her with longing and grief. Gyuszi said just the other day that the island of life where one could always return for love and help is gone. We lost a whole world. The poor souls who survived go back to their empty houses. They wander between borders. The saddest wandering history ever produced.

20 August 1945

God willing, we have a furnished flat. It costs a fortune, true, but it's worth a fortune just to have a home after so many years. It's one room, a hall, a kitchenette and a bathroom without hot water. Not easy to get documents to show we live in an inadequate place, documents to prove that I'm expecting a baby. There is a danger that someone else will grab it.

My growing tummy is very useful. Sometimes I get a seat on the tram. I don't have to queue for bread.

They took Korláth (a member of parliament who helped me get Jancsi out of forced labour) before the people's court as a war criminal. He helped many other Jews as well. We were witnesses for the defence. He is now free.

15 September 1945

It's very difficult to paint and cook at the same time. I mix a colour, turn the chicken over, peel potatoes. And I must cook because we can eat three meals for the cost of an inferior lunch in a restaurant.

20 September 1945

Jancsi is in Prague. I follow him with my imagination. He wants us to become Czech citizens if we can.

10 October 1945

In the flat at last. No painting as I am busy all day queuing for lard, sugar and other food for the winter. You can't get potatoes for any amount, we haven't seen one for three weeks.

I was very lucky to get a housekeeper. Mrs Dános sent me a widow who cleans and cooks very well. I am amused how much richer she is than me. The first day she looked around in my bare room and brought me a tablecloth.

20 October 1945

A telegram arrived from Egypt from Amika. It churned up everything and I cried. The wound is bleeding again.

The government has fixed the prices. Jancsi got a few kilos of sugar from Dreher's and we took Kati and Béla Molnár and my old caretaker some of it. We have cognac from the brewery, a luxury supreme. We can't afford shoes though.

Glass is unavailable so we have pergameneous paper on the windows. A good thing too, I don't see the people opposite and they can't see us.

We have a wrought-iron chandelier with candles, two glass bowls with flowers. The little flat starts to look like us. Even a piano on which I often play. If only I get a chance to work on my painting.

6 November 1945

I painted Persian miniatures all over the pergameneous windows and the doors with aniline, contoured with Indian ink and gold, so it can be seen on both sides. Trees with pink blossoms, red birds, slit-eyed angels with flaming urns. On the ground black horses with long necks, antelopes, plants and eastern faces.

15 November 1945

Sometimes I'm frightened how Jancsi fills my whole being. Perhaps it's unsound to build all I am on one man. Often as we sit reading in the light of the lamp, I glance up at him and want to cry, I love him that much.

He doesn't sleep well at night. When I hear him sigh after a nightmare I take him in my arms and he dozes off in a few minutes. He tells me my nearness is so soothing it dissolves the cramp in his soul.

16 November 1945

Jancsi is in Prague and I am ill for the lack of him. I also have appalling dreams. The place is desolate without him.

6 December 1945

The first letter from Amika in Egypt. Maya writes too. When I last saw her in Beregszász she couldn't yet speak. Amika writes like Anyu. She somehow takes her place in my mind.

I have approximately three weeks till the birth. Strange to think that Juja is alive in me, all ready to arrive and I can touch its head under my skin. Unfortunately it doesn't behave as it should and lies upside down. The doctor says it won't be easy but I'm not afraid. I am in God's hands.

17 December 1945

I have two more weeks to wait. I still paint and run around and feel well. Recurring nightmares disturb me night after night. Mainly our loved ones appear often, and all day I'm under their spell. I also dream that they misplaced my baby in hospital; that I'm running with my pursuers gaining on me; that I'm swimming in infinite water and my clothes pull me down; that the tram in which I'm travelling overturns.

I have no clear image of the child. I feel enveloping, tender joy without contours. Sometimes I imagine something warm in the crook of my arm.

24 December 1945

I have discovered the theory of the bluebird anew. Contentment isn't an outside thing, we harbour it in ourselves. Jancsi and I are alone this evening, without a tree and presents, and never before have I felt such festiveness.

We hear Christmas carols on the radio. Jancsi drew me to him in silence and intimacy. We had tea and salami for dinner and afterwards Jancsi brought two glasses and poured us a brandy. He toasted me alone. So sweetly and beautifully, our tears fell in the brandy. I said this was the best Christmas I've ever had.

I haven't written yet about my miracle: Jancsi made his first business trip to Vienna since the war, he went with the brewery truck. I was still worrying about nappies and towels and shirts for the baby which were unobtainable in Budapest. Next evening the doorbell rang and there stood the driver of the truck with two large suitcases. 'Your husband sent these from Vienna,' he said. I couldn't imagine what it was. As I opened the first one I saw baby shirts, nappies, towels and realised that these used to be mine.

When Anyu divorced Apu in 1929, I knew she left a lot of things in Vienna but had not given them a thought for all these years. As it came and when it came was, to me, simply a parcel that Anyu sent, because I'm expecting and she knew what I needed. I cried all night. When Jancsi returned he said Count Schönborn took them out of storage thinking they would be in a better place in the cellar of his palace in the Renngasse. 'There are a few more cases coming with the brewery truck.' But a few days passed and I wasn't thinking of them when a friend, who lent us our pillows and blankets, announced she is getting married and could she have them back. 'Of course,' I said and tramped all over the city trying to borrow or buy others, with no result. I came home in the evening, utterly exhausted, and saw these three big cases in the foyer. The caretaker opened them for me. The first one had pillows, eiderdowns, blankets and sheets with a J.K. monogram. It used to be Ilus Kaszab, but it could be Juci Kampfner.

9 January 1946

Our son was born on New Year's Eve. It was already getting dark. He weighs three kilos, his name is Jánoska, and he is the greatest wonder in the world.

The birth wasn't without complications. I had a high temperature for a day. I imagined myself dead and Jancsi a widower. And when they took the stitches out they didn't heal and hurt like hell.

I only started to realise I'm a mother since I feed Jánoska. I can go home soon now.

12 January 1946

I am still in hospital. I must write about something, but only briefly, because if I dwell on it I will shake the bed in fury. I mustn't despair now, or I will lose my milk. It's Anyu. She will never see my child. I'm starting to believe that deportee who returned. They said they saw Anyu in the group who were sent to the 'showers'. The gas chamber.

14 January 1946

I'm at home, I have to be in bed for one more week. Jánoska is beside me in a basket. I fret when he cries. He is so tiny and breakable. Like a small frog.

24 January 1946

Beside me the palette, paint and brushes. Behind the Persian miniatures on the paper door the nappies are drying on a rope. The room is not warm enough for Jánoska so we put him in the basket on the bathtub. It is covered with timber. Beside the basket is a baby scale where I measure whether he gets enough milk.

Jancsi was waiting for a car to fetch him. The radio played dance music. He asked me for a dance. He in snowboots, me in slippers and dressing-gown, dancing.

15 February 1946

I don't dare tell this to anyone, but I feel one day I am going to paint better portraits than anyone. I don't intend to stop at that point where portraitists usually stop. I am painting seriously and I think I've improved.

Jancsi has a wonderful instinct for criticism. He not only knows what not to do, but also what it is that should be done. He said yesterday it's not enough to attack the picture and to paint what I see, I should know what the painting should look like when it's completed.

24 February 1946

Once again the desire to become a good artist is stretching and pulling me. I want to improve as a painter, and the way I live now combined with this rotten and stagnant city forces it to remain nothing but desire.

22 May 1946

I have rented a place in Szentendre, an artists' colony on the banks of the Danube. I take Mrs Beck with us to keep house. Perhaps this will help get out of the rut.

12 June 1946

Szentendre

Jánoska is now eight kilos. He is in his cot on the terrace. There is a large garden. The rooms are smallish, crowded with Biedermeier furniture, and there is a picture of Kaiser Franz Joseph. We have a pendulum clock, tiled stove and lace curtains.

7 July 1946

Now I'm in my element. I rise at 6 a.m., feed, paint, eat, sleep after lunch, feed, walk, paint, go to bed.

After the ten paintings I've painted in three weeks I find another five subjects, but the best thing is I don't have to struggle.

Jancsi brings me money once a week which I spend at the market on Saturday. Food for the whole week is stored in the cellar in the sand to keep it cool.

17 July 1946

Last night we walked in the dark with only the highway curving lighter and the trees whispered and the Danube flows swollen, encircling their trunks. There is fragrance in the air and the moment should be captured.

26 July 1946

Czóbel is painting me. Such a great artist and how limited. Nothing interests him but his painting and food. He looks far away with his blue sailor's eyes and puffs on his pipe, he scratches his poodle's head and nods quietly.

He lends me books about Matisse, Picasso, Rouault, Derain. I hadn't even heard of them in Beregszász. I learn a lot by watching how my portrait develops after each sitting. He has completely overpainted it for the eighth time and therefore keeps it as fresh as after the first sitting.

I bought a new sketchbook and I draw. In the evenings I either go to one of the artists at the colony or they come to me. We sit on the terrace, without a lamp because of the mosquitoes and talk. This is what's been lacking, this atmosphere. I drink it in, my thirst seems unquenchable. Sometimes I feel frightened by how much I demand of life.

We want to migrate, but when I think of this my head spins. For not only must it be more expensive overseas to get help, but I hear it's near impossible. I never wished to be a man. Not even when I screamed from the pain of childbirth. I only wish to be a man when I see the men painters for whom all domesticity is taken over by their wives.

Jánoska can kneel now and has one tooth.

19 September 1946

Budapest

Soon we shall move into a two-room flat. The stay in Szentendre was really good for my painting. I can now construct my picture in a cubist way. It's a new road to travel. The painters were wonderful. Hatvany gave me a pastel as a farewell present, and Mrs Czóbel a little oil painting.

24 October 1946

I take lessons from 10 to 12 noon from Kmetty, and then work on my own from 2 to 3.30 p.m. That's all the time I get. Art is like sport, one should be in constant training; sketch at night even when one has company, talk about it, read about it, and always have the easel and the paint in the room.

30 October 1946

I am painting a nude with my colleague, Galitzer. It's almost impossible though because if Jánoska cries I can't ignore him. If somebody rings the bell or if the soup is too thick, Mrs Beck calls me to the kitchen. No matter, I paint. I study composition now. It's like mathematics. I find it boring but necessary.

3 December 1946

On Saturdays we keep an open house for artists. Even painters we don't know.

Kmetty came to see what I have painted since Szentendre. There are three still lifes, a nude, a few watercolours and lots of sketches. Trembling, I show the portraits too. The analysis he gives doesn't relate to drawing or to colour any more, it's philosophy, rather, and everything is hard to define.

They stole the car of a minister from Parliament House. Pedestrians are stripped on the streets again. On Sunday we went for a drive, and in a small village, parked our car in front of the pub. When we came out, no car. We found it in the field where they pushed it and it had become bogged.

12 December 1946

Kmetty, who comes regularly to teach me, asked not to be paid for it, though he is very poor. He wants two young and talented students to get the money so that they shouldn't know it comes from him, nor that it comes from us. It has to be deposited somewhere neutral so they needn't show gratitude to anyone. I felt ashamed to think we are generous when giving away only what we don't need.

30 December 1946

We spent Christmas Eve at Gyuszi's with Jánoska. A great tree, many presents. Jánoska clapped, and looked amazed. He didn't play with the teddy bear but rather with the wrapping papers. One has to get acquainted with one's child just as with anyone else. When it is born one is like an animal, protecting the vulnerable and defenceless baby. Today, he is not 'a baby', he is Jánoska Kampfner, doubtless an individual.

We wanted to enlarge and spread our abundance of love like a wing under which more children can nestle. I am two months pregnant, ecstatically happy, forever hungry and don't know what I wish to eat. Meanwhile I paint all morning while Jánoska is alone in his room. I take English and singing lessons. We go to the theatre often.

4 February 1947

I attend Aurél Bernáth's lecture at a club for artists and bohemians. He was my first teacher and greatest influence. They know me already, greet me, although I have a long, long road until I am allowed to exhibit. Bernáth talked about styles in the history of art logically following each other. Abstract is the first trend which started fresh rather than as a development.

Apu [my father] is here. I didn't lose him in the war, but then I never had him either. He is a pal, not a father. Still, now that he is gravely ill I'm riddled with guilt. He sits on the edge of his bed, that's the only position in which breathing is possible.

24 March 1947

The doctors say that Apu won't get better. I sit with him. I dip my hand into cold water, stroke it over his head, neck and swollen feet. I used to be repelled by illness, but it doesn't disgust me now.

Two of my paintings were exhibited at the Károlyi Palace in the spring show. There are so many shows now, so many painters and they're not bad either. Jancsi is convinced that I will grow out of mediocrity through my portraits. The way I can paint still lifes, five hundred others can too. But only two perhaps can paint a portrait like I do. I argued against easy success, and at which time in my life should I think positively if not when I'm young?

27 March 1947

Today was Apu's funeral. His last wish was to be buried in the Jewish cemetery. This gave me a bigger shock than his death. He gave up religion before I was born. All his life he was an atheist. The roots are very deep.

12 May 1947

Szentendre

We moved to Szentendre in a taxi truck, to a leased two-bedroom house with a terrace and a garden. I am not painting to full capacity. My new baby has established itself not only in my body but in my mind and soul. I am lazy. I like to lounge in a garden chair and just follow the clouds and gaze at the trees. I sketch a bit, out of duty, and think that perhaps it really will be the portraits where I can be better than average.

16 May 1947

Czóbel's just arrived from Paris. Persona grata that he and his wife get passports. The only Hungarian painter well known in France. I made dinner for them. He talked about his visit to Matisse, an old friend who has been bedridden for two years. Matisse works lying on his back with a brush tied to the end of a bamboo pole on a canvas stretched on the ceiling. Czóbel also visited Braque. Names of art history.

5 July 1947

I had two paintings exhibited in Budapest, one in the National Salon and the other at the Szinyei exhibition. After fifteen new paintings, I still don't feel like doing abstracts. There is so much beauty in nature I don't need to search for the invisible. In any case my foundation is sound, and if I arrive at the abstract one day it must happen without prompting.

17 July 1947

I am searching for subjects nearby so that I can keep an eye on János. I want to go back to the city soon as I don't wish to have my baby in a taxi. There are a lot of things I would like in the flat if we had the money, such as a corner for my canvases and tools, hidden behind a curtain.

Barcsai came to see me today and we had an exciting discussion. He is an abstract painter. He initially worked from nature. As soon as he waved this possibility before me, I was willing to accept all his arguments. He thinks one shouldn't weigh each problem, one should let go. I am talented, he said, and I shall find my own way. He prophesied that I shall be satiated with what I do—like eating too many sweets—and I shall then struggle and eventually embark on a different plane.

All these artists here with their theories are like yeast. This year I breathe Czóbel as easily as air, while the avant-garde rubs me from the other side. Sometimes I despair that someone so young should be so conservative.

24 July 1947

Kmetty is terribly depressed, as if he has lost his will to live. He is a cubist and a committed communist, and the two are clashing. He doesn't paint at all.

Dénes Diener has no such problem. He is a Dionysian and his pictures roar with life. According to Lipót Hermann, Dénes is the one Hungarian who knows how a good picture should be constructed. One has to climb a rope ladder into the tree where his studio is. He has a shock of white hair, a black beret and a smile of a bohemian of a past era.

Every morning as I wake up a wave of happiness flows through my body. The baby should be born soon. I start the day landscaping, then go down to the Danube with Jánoska. We are alone on the bank and nobody can see that I just about fit into Jancsi's underpants. After lunch I have a long siesta with Jánoska and by the time we are both washed and dressed, Jancsi arrives. Then the three of us go for a drive.

The artists come round in the evening. Mrs Czóbel gathers spinach from her garden for János, the Dieners bring us homemade butter and they like to keep János company when he is in his bath.

9 September 1947

Budapest

On the fifth of September at 5 a.m. Péterke arrived at last. We now have two sons. Thank God.

17 September 1947

I am in bed at home, but this is only an illusion because I am constantly on the move, like the pendulum of a clock, between my two sons.

Poor Péterke is not three kilos yet. He vomits a lot. He is so tiny, particularly beside Jánoska, one hardly dares to touch him. In the mornings I feed and bath the little one and take János to the park. It's a full-time job the whole day, but as soon as a routine is established I will start painting again.

30 September 1947

Sometimes I marvel at this man whom my good fortune let me have. It's amazing how my feeling isn't blunt, didn't decline, neither is it habit nor taken for granted. At noon, without reason, as he speaks on the phone, I realised that I couldn't live without him. I watched all those details, features, sounds, which form that unique phenomenon which is Jancsi. The whole room takes on a shining aura when he steps into it.

28 November 1947

I work every day. Dénes Diener comes to give me lessons. He says, things like 'Juci, paint a lemon on the spot,' and, 'Take a rag dipped in turpentine and wipe the picture off, however much you like it. Next day, if you paint what you wiped off again, you can be sure it belongs.'

I painted János in twenty minutes and it's good though I didn't use the obligatory portrait colours. I painted Péterke in his pram before the window, blue afternoon light outside and the yellow of the lamp light inside. Painting the children is my present preoccupation. They are very intimate paintings.

25 January 1948

My passport application was refused with no explanation. It's most difficult to get one. The government likes to keep the families where one member can travel hostage. So Jancsi goes west again without me.

I am longing to bring up the children somewhere where they can feel they belong. We shall migrate. Jancsi says, 'These are the people who killed our families and I can't live and work among killers'. He is a hurt man who can't forgive. On this coming trip Jancsi will look into how we can leave and live somewhere else where we can give freedom to the children.

The fashionable places to migrate to, like Venezuela or Chile, don't tempt us at all. On the contrary. We've already lived through one revolution, so why go to a place where the social structure is unjust? We would rather choose a country where there are no giant differences.

31 March 1948

Businesses employing more than a hundred people were taken over by the state. It's like a coup. Hundreds of people who went to work this morning, to places which they founded and owned, were turned back from the gates by communists. They were told that as from today nothing belongs to them. If there was money in the till, bad luck. If they kept their car in the garage on the premises, that was gone too.

Jancsi had an argument with the new leaders of the brewery. He isn't afraid to speak his mind. He told them that the situation reminds him of the Hitler regime. Not enough to take a life's work away, but to kick them out of employment as well? It causes more damage than gain. Where is the know-how and international connections? 'I don't see the difference,' Jancsi said, 'between what you are doing now and the persecution I suffered because I was a Jew.'

23 July 1948

A great French exhibition in the Museum of Budapest. It completely confuses me. Some former students who studied with me at Bernáth's school, came home with the French train and stood around Bernáth who castigated a Léger. 'Well, what is this? Is this art for you? This is a pathetic soap advertisement. Please compare it with a Courbet and then judge!'

My complaint is that beside Picasso, Matisse, Braque and here Barcsai, Czóbel, Bernáth,—I don't see other than epigons. To me, the two Czóbels in the exhibition were like a breath of fresh air.

I feel as if all my life I would be doomed to commute between Budapest and Szentendre and I'm hot with anger when I think that I want to be a painter and have never ever seen an original van Gogh.

However the time has come to describe Szentendre, to fix it in my mind, to preserve it as I preserve the fresh summer taste of peaches and strawberries. So I can take it out of the larder one day and taste it again. Our rooms are Victorian with carved brown sideboards and marble tops, and we only use them to sleep in. There is a glassed-in balcony and the garden where we read and eat and entertain.

I start cooking breakfast in the kitchen for Péterke at 4.45 a.m. It's still dark, but by the time the milk boils I see reds on the horizon. I look out on the fairytale trees, the white walls of houses and gulp the morning air.

Péterke opens his mouth and swallows the warm liquid, he makes a quiet noise in the early morning silence. I change his nappy and he falls asleep, content. Then I take the easel, paintbox, canvas and camp chair, and set off to paint in one of the old streets. I don't meet a soul. I work until eight and hardly notice the time. I catch the bus on the main square and get off at the old saint's shrine. The children are still asleep. I eat breakfast, light a cigarette and look at the morning's results.

I painted only about ten pictures this summer and perhaps two of them are acceptable. I don't mind if my output is small, if only it is constant. Many women painters who marry and have babies say: 'Oh yes, I used to paint too, when I was young. I must take it up some day again.' And they never do. I pray every night not to lose this passion.

28 January 1949

Painting is rolling from the brush again and I leave the stylistic problems alone for the time being. The Centre of Art Politics printed a memorandum condemning abstract art as the product of a decaying bourgeois world. All those who only a year ago preached about abstract being the only salvation have turned full circle and now only talk and practise social realism.

20 July 1949

We wanted it, we were prepared, we thought, but now that we hold a migrant passport in our hands, the change in our life is enormous.

Four years ago we opted for Czechoslovakian citizenship. In Hungary it's impossible to get a Hungarian passport. It is just as difficult to get a Czech passport in Prague. But somehow, our combination worked. I kept hearing the way some of our friends escaped. They swam the Danube, jumped the trains, paid Russian trucks or simply walked through the border with its mines, barbed wire fences and police dogs.

Our passport is valid for Israel where Jancsi's niece, Irénke, is. At present, one link in the chain of bureaucracy is missing. We hang in limbo between here and Vienna, our first stop on the other side.

We sent the children to Szentendre with Ilonka and go out there every day. Here the heat is devastating. My every thought is stuck to an incomprehensible future. Is this immense drive justified?

The answer came one night at 4 a.m. The doorbell rang. Two men stood there wearing communist armbands. They announced that Mr Kampfner is expected at headquarters at 8 a.m. The psychology of the night call being that one loses a few hours sleep after that.

'Do you travel often to the west, director?'

'Yes.'

'Did you meet Mr X, Y and Z? We would be grateful if, next time you go you would bring us information . . . '

'Listen,' Jancsi interrupted with quick anger, 'I am selling malt. I don't sell people.'

Next day he had no job. Neither was it probable that he could get one again in Hungary.

25 August 1949

Vienna

I had no time to write in my diary during the last weeks in Budapest. Visas, tickets, permission to leave, and what to take out. It seemed so many almost insurmountable obstacles. The Conservatory of Music had to give permission to take the piano. The state library had to approve our books. They blew open every page to discover hidden dollars. We had to get permission from the national gallery to take my own pictures. The museum determined what furniture we could take. The national bank made a prevaluation, then a postvaluation. We lived in the empty flat and slept on the floor in borrowed bedding for a fortnight. We brought the children in from Szentendre only on the last day.

Gyuszi and Manyi were at the station to welcome us and so was the Count Schönborn's director, Ernst Rassl.

Next day Schönborn recommended us to a woman who was his cook for thirty years, and she rented us two rooms, and cooked and cleaned for us. Jancsi hired a nanny for the children so I could start painting.

28 August 1949

The Naglergasse, where we live, is in the inner city, dark and narrow with cobblestones. A few steps further however there is a beautiful square with baroque palaces and on the other end of the street is the Graben. I felt at home at once.

Yesterday I got permission from the Kunsthistorisches Museum to copy Brueghel's peasant dance. I could hardly sleep at night from the excitement this picture gives me. When I started it I thought one can't penetrate a masterpiece thoroughly without doing such a copy. I wonder, will I persevere? It can't be done under, I would say, six weeks. The copy. What must it have been like to do the original?

The morning I arrived to start the copy, someone came with me to the Brueghel room where they prepared a large studio easel for me, a big table and a ladder. They brought me a ruler and drawing-pins.

27 September 1949

Brueghel proves to be the best teacher I could have, even if he died 400 years ago. Though I work about five hours a day and my back aches, I can only cover a tiny bit and that has to be painted over again. It teaches me discipline and humility.

I also look at Botticelli, Perugino and Cranach. I was taken to the restoration room and this is fascinating too. On a Dutch master's landscape where two hounds run from left to right, they speculate that the hounds must have a reason to do so. Cleaning the right side they discover a boat on the river with figures.

28 September 1949

Something incredible happened again. My parents had a house in Vienna in which I was born. It was confiscated during the Hitler regime and our claim has been going on since the war finished. And just now, when we needed it, the new owners decided to pay. Not its full price, but still a small fortune.

29 November 1949

I became pregnant again, but as a displaced person on the way to the unknown I can't afford the luxury. I have an abortion. I woke up in the hospital, terribly depressed.

I don't really want a nanny any more. They seem to be very good at putting powder on bottoms, but have no idea of the child as a person. As a matter of fact I am horrified to see what sort of inanity pervades the very air here in matters of bringing up children.

These difficulties, plus my present illness after the abortion broke my optimism about migration considerably. I feel the lack of having a home, and unfortunately the letters from Israel are getting worse and worse. Irénke, Jancsi's niece wrote that we are too old for this country, she advises us not to come.

30 December 1949

I found out what it is that is so depressing in Vienna. Since we don't want to stay in Austria we are sitting on a highway waiting for God knows what. We meet almost exclusively other migrants, whose stay, like ours, is temporary. And all of us become confused, for one week Canada is fashionable, the next week it's Chile. Then a letter arrives from a brother-in-law of a great-aunt in Chile who writes that a cousin has rheumatics in his right leg. And everyone switches to Australia.

The other oppressing thing is that Vienna is still a four-nation city. There is an American, English, French and Russian sector.

20 January 1950

Reichenau

It's a joy to watch the children speeding down the hill in the sleigh. They jump off and roll in the powdery, glittering snow.

2 February 1950

Jancsi was asked to act as consultant for the breweries and left for Switzerland, Germany and Belgium. We are alone in Reichenau and there is peace and whiteness and silence. We have breakfast together, and when the children leave on their skis, I start painting. A local peasant girl is my model. She is willing to pose in the nude and I do sketches and watercolours. I work sitting so my back doesn't ache so much.

The three of us ride the sleigh together in the afternoon and play until evening. Manyi and little Gyuszi are here and we look like a kindergarten.

6 February 1950

The valley and the peak of the Rax are standing in sharp light. The rocks on the other side are like a background of Persian miniatures, pinkish-grey, and the black dwarf pines hug each other. I stand before the spectacle in silence and paint with my eyes. My feet would freeze if I should attempt to paint outside. So I paint Manyi knitting beside little Gyuszi, and our children playing with Helga.

12 May 1950

Vienna

Nine months have passed and we have just received the first reply from Australia that we are now being considered as migrants. If everything goes smoothly, as nothing ever does, it will be another six months.

Jancsi is working in Germany for the breweries. He wants to earn as much as he can as we are spending a lot to live here in transit. The word 'if' seems to grin at us. If we would have asked for the permit as soon as we arrived in Vienna, we could already be on a ship. If we would have spent the money we spent here over there instead, by now we would be acclimatised and would have learnt English. Meanwhile, I feel joy with the children and Jancsi, and I paint.

I keep thinking that there was a time when people arranged high school reunions. I think of my class. Two of them were killed in Auschwitz. Zsuzsi Vincze stayed in Budapest. Two are married in New York. One is a bank clerk in Venezuela. And Erzsi Hartmann who sat on the same bench as me for eight years has just arrived in the Rothschild Hospital to have her baby. I visit her every day and take what I can for her and the baby.

The Rothschild, as one calls it in short, is a world on its own. Polish, Czech and Hungarian Jews stand in the courtyard and read letters from those already overseas. Some trade meagre belongings. There is constant congestion in the offices as people wait for medical examinations, or for clothes and money. In Erzsi's room there are twenty beds and twenty cots. Some, who find the food boring, cook on a small burner in the corridor. There are rows of tubs full of soiled nappies. Clothes hang on nails.

17 May 1950

Salzburg

We are a family of four and we have to come from Vienna to Salzburg three different ways. We decided to move into the American sector, away from the Russians. As I have no passport I had to get the Red Cross bus (which is in fact a Rothschild transport), the only vehicle which the Russians cannot stop at the Enz-zone. Jancsi has travelling papers, so he will fly to Munich in Germany and then on to Salzburg.

The children will take the train with Helga as they don't need identification.

The busload was deposited in a huge camp in Salzburg, a dismal landing place where people are numbers with no identity. We felt lucky indeed to be able to call a taxi and just leave, and guilty at the same time because, but for the grace of God, it could be us who remain.

19 May 1950

What a magical place this is, the fourteenth-century streets nestling at the foot of majestic mountains. One can go to the top in a lift and within minutes, the scene changes from city to forest. In the middle of town I found the most beautiful, soothing and friendly cemetery I have ever seen. The graves are stuck to the rock, decorated with reliefs and murals. There are flowers on the resting places of six hundred years of dead butchers and bakers. The town is preparing for the music festival and there is a babel of languages.

28 May 1950

St Gilgen

Considering the shortage and the high price of accommodation in Salzburg, I took the bus to the country. I got off in St Gilgen and found two rooms with a telephone and garden. The Wolfgangsee, a lake, is a three-minute walk away. I sent a telegram to Vienna and was it wonderful to see the two red caps in the window of the train.

Helga wanted to hang a blanket on the window so the children shouldn't wake too early, and crashed down with the curtain rod. While we tried to place the provisions in a dry place, our suitcases swam in the corner. We dried the clothes on the stove and moved things into the room where it wasn't raining. I bought a kerosene cooker and established a separate kitchen on the balcony.

Salzburg and the whole district behave now like a hostess who expects guests at a party.

17 June 1950

Jancsi arrived yesterday from Munich.

22 June 1950

My first commission in St Gilgen comes from the hairdresser. Would I be so good to repair the mannequin because the sun bleached it in the shop window. When I returned from the milk-fetching walk I almost collapsed of fright. There was a lemon-yellow monster on the couch which grinned and had a bald skull. The wig was just being washed. I carried it on the balcony, now it frightens the villagers.

Jancsi had to go to Frankfurt. I have to have shortwaves for the rotten inflammation of my ovaries, and try saltbaths in Ischl, near us. I find it most unseemly that a grown-up person should be constantly preoccupied with her own tummy.

Jancsi said, perhaps others don't have that trouble but can't paint pictures. And when I said I don't feel it makes much sense to do landscapes which only creates more unwanted possessions to have to pack and carry, he quoted in Latin: '*Navigare necesse est.*' It's necessary to sail. 'Throw them out, give them away, burn them, but make them,' he said.

27 August 1950

The Sekers, English Hungarians, who rented rooms in the same house as us, turned out to be just the kind of people who give one back one's faith in humanity. They went back home to England today and left a gaping gap behind them, we loved them so much.

It started with them giving us tickets to the festival's *Don Giovanni*, because for some reason they couldn't go. I think they knew we wouldn't spend that much on tickets. Then followed an invitation to Yehudi Menuhin's concert. Miki Sekers commissioned me to paint his three children. He thought my fee ridiculous and paid me double.

30 August 1950

I feel the portraits are getting good. I could be like an athlete who knows he can run one second better than the record. The brush is an extension and as it works quickly and precisely I almost watch from outside me and feel grateful for the gift. But I want to be more than a craftsman. I want to be a good artist.

13 September 1950

Salzburg

I no longer consider us refugees. I look at our life here as an adventure, a travelogue, a newsreel, and I feel happy in it. When we get to Australia only the frame will have changed because the core remains my love for Jancsi, the children and painting.

Our permit arrived two days ago. Funny, it looks like any other document. It has a photograph of the four of us and it opens the door to the opposite end of the globe.

30 September 1950

I painted the Haffnergasse, a narrow old street with a white tower in the background. The Kapucinerberg with the cloister.

Preparations go on for the trip to Australia.

When I cook all three boys love to keep me company in the kitchen. Péterke likes to turn the gas on, János looks into the meat grinder and Jancsi (who heard that in Australia husbands are domesticated) wants to beat the eggs. When this gets boring he wants me to beat eggs while he boils the milk. While he boils the milk he burns his fingers, so he lets me boil the milk while he beats the eggs.

2 November 1950

It's very lucky that we don't even feel that there are nine of us living in the one flat which we rent in Salzburg. Mrs Kletzmayr directs the traffic. By 8 a.m. Edith, Franzi and Mr Kletzmayr are gone and the bathroom is ours.

The first snow has fallen. It's too cold to paint the street scenes. I'm painting Edith and Franzi with a flute and harmonica.

2 January 1951

The pre-visa arrived from Australia and threw us into excited confusion. We have no idea as yet how long it will take until we really are allowed to go. As we talked about the unknown world, Jancsi told me 'You know, I feel safe with you. Like a child, protected in its mother's arms.'

God is good to me in letting me find the bluebird in my own cage.

I was daydreaming about having a studio one day. Here I have to place the chair with the sitter on a certain flower in the pattern of the carpet because that's the only tolerable light in the room. And then I don't have enough room to step back and look at it. I would love to have a table one day, like a carpenter's table, where I can leave my tools, and not to have to tidy up because the table is needed to have dinner on.

23 January 1951

En route to Bruxelles

What a fantastic change, I am on my way to Paris. I must have been most suspicious to the French consul. I have a passport to Australia, I go to Paris because I can only get our boat tickets there, besides, I am an artist and have never seen the Louvre. He told me straight to my face that he doesn't like my story, and it's not so easy to get a French transit visa.

'Look, this is an Argentine passport on my desk and I gave it only three days in France. And he is Argentine and not a DP [displaced person] like you.'

He finally decided not to give me the visa. So I asked for a German transit visa to Bruxelles, from where I hope to get the French visa on the way back to Austria. It is very complicated for a refugee to travel.

25 January 1951

Bruxelles

Sanyi Goldstein, our old friend who now lives in Bruxelles, was at the station to welcome me. I stay with them. They made me go to bed after the two-day journey while Sanyi went to the consulate to get my French visa.

Miraculous thing, to go through a border in Europe, five years after the war. The landscape in Germany was a surreal picture of lonely chimneys. Suddenly this ends along with the sound of the German language. The houses turn to red Flemish oblongs and people speak French. On the train at night I use my raincoat as a pillow and my winter coat as a blanket. I only stay one day in Bruxelles.

26 January 1951

Paris

Lilly Brody, my friend, an artist, picked me up from the station and found me a hotel. I am on the third floor. The screen—which modestly hides the bidet—must have been Chinese silk a long time ago. Now it looks like the worn dressing-gown of a coquette. The sheets on the double bed don't look too clean either. The washstand is definitely filthy and the electric bulb hanging from the ceiling like a lidless eye plunging me into a Baudelairean mood.

Lili lives near the Seine, we walked and walked. I think I have a fever.

I thought three or four mornings will be spent with official errands and eighteen mornings in galleries. It is the other way round. I spent six days so far to get permission to stay in Paris for three weeks. Still, I did get my first look at the impressionists. I make notes. I gobble up gallery after gallery.

2 March 1951

Salzburg

The boat-ticket affair is settled, we can get our money back. Jancsi and the children at the station, euphoria.

20 May 1951

Miki Sekers telephoned from London. The three portraits of the children were a great success and if I would consider going to London I would have some commissions which would provide useful contacts in Australia. He would get us a visitor's visa. Please come.

25 June 1951

Blue airletters from Egypt were all I knew for years, and I had no idea how Amika, Anyu's sister, will look. The night before they were due, Gyuszi and his family arrived from Vienna. We cooked a goose and baked a cake. When they came, I found myself in Ami's arms, we were not strangers. Gyuszi and Jancsi cried and I looked at Maya who wears my fifteen-year-old face. Two weeks is all. They go back tomorrow.

5 July 1951

Helga has changed her mind about migrating with us. As a farewell gesture she will mind the children while we go to London.

9 July 1951

London

Twenty-eight hours on trains and a boat.

No one but Jancsi would arrive like we did, at festival time, without sending a telegram to anybody, without a hotel booking, at 8 p.m.

We put the suitcase in a locker and took the bus to Queensway where Ibi, an old friend, lives. Ibi hauls out a basket with coffee, tea, eggs, and ham. Not easy to get in London where everything is rationed.

The Sekers were expecting us and had portrait appointments all set up. They also had tickets to Covent Garden. What's really wonderful is we have a large studio with a skylight where we stay, and where I paint.

I painted Valerie Hobson (Mrs Profumo), Lady Richardson, Lord Wilmot, who gave us a letter of introduction to Charles Lloyd Jones in Sydney, and two of Hugh Gaitskell's children. We spent a weekend in Whitehaven, in the north of England, with the Sekers. Miki Sekers offered to pay our fare to Sydney. We declined, but it's another kind thing one never forgets.

17 September 1951

Zurich

One doesn't want to become sentimental. Still, one feels poised as if on a high point above the pool below, just before diving in head first. I also feel unreal and disoriented.

It's difficult to describe what a mad scramble the last day was ... Anyway, we were finally on the train and saw the magnificent stage decor of Salzburg and the mountains fading back into what will become the past. A chapter closed.

19 September 1951

Lugano

We bought a little Austin in Zurich as Elek Kálmán wrote from Sydney that it's difficult to buy cars there. So now we are on our way by car towards Genoa, and as we climbed up St Gotthard I felt we were a consolidated family and not, as the French consul said, DPs—which is what we really are.

21 September 1951

Genoa

It's very strange to know that this is our last evening in Europe. The car and the suitcases are on the boat. I don't feel a thing. I went to the beach with the children this afternoon and I feel blessedly tired. We admired shiny stones smoothly polished in the surf, and fishing boats. I scanned the horizon beyond which my dreams cannot reach.

22 September 1951

Early rise, nervous breakfast. Milling crowd at the wharf. Babies scream. Ours are restless, like fillies before a storm. We proceed awfully slowly.

I have palpitations. Like before exams, or before a birth, when things are irreversible.

At last someone looks at our passports and then we wait another hour. I can hardly believe we are sailing.

25 September 1951

Tonight the sea was choppy. The dining room was empty. We sat on deckchairs outside eating sandwiches and fruit.

27 September 1951

Port Said

The police board the ship at 7 a.m. Only those passengers whose passports get stamped are allowed on shore. We showed our DP papers. 'Sorry,' they said.

Never mind, I thought, Ami and Jacques will come to see us instead. At breakfast a letter arrived from Amika. They have not got permission to board the ship. Jancsi cursed Egypt, declaring that it's a Nazi state if someone who lives here for fifty years isn't allowed to board a ship. A steward comes with a note. Five storeys below, on the water, Ami and Maya sit in a small boat, waving. I'm waving. We can't hear each other's voices. The power in the fez takes pity on us. He lets them come up on the rope ladder. We stay where the fez can see us.

29 September 1951

Suez

We are moving on the Suez Canal. We see camels in the desert. Tents. We sit on deckchairs watching the two sides gliding by. I imagined the canal as something narrow. I had no idea about the number of great ships that come and go.

30 September 1951

Salzburg, Vienna and what used to be before that, Budapest; and what used to be a hundred years before that, Beregszász, is not real at all. Australia isn't real either. We live in the middle of a circle of blue and eat and sleep. This is reality.

11 October 1951

Another five days on this not very gracious seahorse before Fremantle. Today the sea is unkempt, like a woman in the morning.

17 October 1951

Fremantle

Thin line on the horizon: Australia.

Quick medical examination and passport control. A letter from Elek Kálmán. 'Welcome to Australia. We greet you with joy and love, with the hope and wish that you should find a home here with your children and live in peace.'

18 October 1951

We see the gardens and white houses of Perth. It could be Lugano, the way one can see the sea and the bays and white sailing boats. Palms in abundance. The city is like a provincial town in Hungary.

'Ten days stretch before us on the ship,' Jancsi says.

Elek writes that we must pay for our room in the boarding house for the ten days we are not there. That makes the airfare that much cheaper. We fly to Sydney. Jancsi's logic in this case is typically mine. 'We start earning money ten days earlier.'

21 October 1951

Sydney

Things happen with great speed now. One is buffeted with new impressions.

Anku, Elek and Médi, who we know from Beregszász, are standing at Sydney's airport.

Things which don't usually occur in the same place, occur in Sydney. Palm trees and fir trees. Long, slim cypress and cactus. Geraniums and mimosa.

We pay ten pounds a week for one room in a boarding house. Everybody cooks separately. There is a frigidaire, and one can wash and dry things in the courtyard.

Médi took me and the children to a kindergarten where Lili and Peter also go. I was reluctant, it's too early, but Médi is resolute. 'You will see,' she said, 'this is not a European type kindergarten, they love it and can't be dragged away.' In the garden are shovels, toys, swings, slippery dips, and the teacher speaks German.

I was apprehensive. I was prepared for tears and clinging, but there were none.

This boarding house is like an island of Hungarians. Some have been here for five months. Some were Nazis and some Jews from concentration camps. Everyone is equal.

Tibor Galdi who owned the fastest BMW car in Budapest is a house painter, and Janó Halmi, who was a landowner, now works in a wine cellar. The women do all sorts of strange jobs which do not require language. They string pearls, address envelopes, make sandwiches, sew neckties.

Ili Kalina, who sells cakes at David Jones, says: 'Isn't it the same whether I wear my white coat in the cake shop or the chemist shop?' And Pali told us a story about the place where he works as a cleaner. One of the Australian cleaners asked him what he used to be in the old country. 'I didn't want to tell him that I was a lawyer, so I told him I was a labourer.' 'Good boy,' the cleaner said happily, 'all the other reffos say they used to be lawyers.'

Emil, Médi's husband, who started the same way three years ago is now manufacturing raincoats.

People buy fridges, gramophones, cars. They don't seem to worry about it. It's just that most women think that money doesn't buy them the comfort they used to have in Europe.

I haven't met an artist yet.

Jancsi takes the children to kindergarten while I wash, every day, so the dirty laundry doesn't pile up. I cook dinner while the gas ring on the one communal stove is free. I find it very strange that suburbs have no shops, and shopping centres have nothing else but the butcher, the chemist, the grocer, etc. Although the shops are hideous, everything is very reasonable except apartments.

1 November 1951

Jancsi hopes to get a position in a brewery which should pay well with his experience and qualifications. We don't have much money and have to be careful not to make a mistake.

I go to my first art exhibition at the Contemporary Art Society. The paintings are rather weak and amateurish, four or five good ones, perhaps. The rest: imitations. The audience is the same everywhere; uncombed young, a few collectors, several survivors, intellectuals and ladies in hats.

I heard such derogatory remarks about the Art Gallery of NSW that I was pleasantly surprised. After all, one doesn't have to look at the eyesores, there is a Monet, a Pissarro and a Dobell.

14 November 1951

When I asked our landlord, Mr Rozsnyai, who Charles Lloyd Jones is he must have thought I suffer delusions of grandeur. I sent off Lord Wilmot's letter and got an appointment immediately. On the desk before him was the newspaper article and the photos the *Herald* had taken of the children and me, and the letter of introduction. He asked me what he could do to help. 'Let me paint you,' I said. He couldn't because he is being painted by Dobell. In Budapest that would have meant rejection. However, he rang, and said he would be very pleased if I would paint his wife.

When their son comes to pick me up from the boarding house in a Rolls Royce everybody hangs out the window in disbelief.

János (known in Australia as John) goes to Bellevue Hill School and Péterke (now Peter) to Aunty Gerda's kindergarten.

26 November 1951

Nervous, transition days. In Salzburg or Vienna this was the legitimate way of existence. Here, it's a drawn-out, insecure situation. As long as we are in a boarding house where I can't possibly establish a studio, my chance of painting, to help Jancsi make a living is non-existent. And as long as I can't earn at least a little, painting as art is an unjustified pursuit, which doesn't warrant the help of a housekeeper. Keeping house means repetitive, unproductive, stupefying drudgery for me, at the end of which I only see the things which are not done. It makes me weary and this is not the healing, satisfied tiredness which envelops the artist after creating. This is angry and frustrated tiredness.

The weekend was terrifying. Peter got a high temperature. We called a doctor who thought it was an inflammation of the middle ear. While I was nursing him, Jancsi took János to the beach where he fell off the merry-go-round and came home bleeding profusely. We called the doctor. His hair had to be shaved to get at the wound and he was screaming.

Peter has been ill now for three days and in spite of my efforts to tidy up, the one room looks like a battlefield. One has to clean and cook and wash dishes and Peter wants attention and calls constantly and I rush upstairs for the umpteenth time.

Jancsi isn't at his best in squalid situations. He looks grim, he doesn't want to go out, but since he isn't the domestic type he only makes things worse. He combs the *Sydney Morning Herald* to find a job. Dear God, stay with me in Australia too.

Meanwhile I console myself with the thought that the kids are growing and they won't always have hundreds and thousands of questions between the laundry and the sink.

15 December 1951

What bliss. We found a flat, a sunny, light, new flat in Weeroona Avenue in Woollahra; It's not finished yet.

31 December 1951

Anyu, my dear, if you could see us, how amazed you would be.

And Elek Kálmán, the brilliant lawyer, now has a tobacco shop in Sydney, about one metre square. And Ági Friedmann's new child is called Vivienne. She never talks about the other one. The one who was killed in the gas chamber. I have just found out that Médi's baby was also killed. How lucky we were not to have had children before the war.

6 January 1952

We comfort ourselves by going to see how the building in Weeroona Avenue is progressing. I have the same sort of feelings as I used to have when I moved with false papers into another life. I was a guest in that life, I visited it. And while living in the slum, working in the factory, I said: 'Thank you, God, for the experience.' Although it was hard, it was fascinating too. I was younger then and more pliable.

So I turn for help to this younger self. I want to acknowledge life in the boarding house as an adventure. I have a lovely flat waiting, a space in which I can create beauty.

My first rainy day here in Australia and I feel sad. The rain is strange and different, not at all like at home. It's primeval and it soaks right into my sunny nature, forcing me to look into the pit where problems sleep. I ponder our friendship with our own children and where it will lead.

16 January 1952

My first theatre. Amateurs who make an heroic effort. It seems like a country charity performance. Quite in contrast to the luxurious cinemas which import American films and have a special crying room for babies.

It seems nobody wants to achieve immortality by financing real theatre. I find people generally selfish and materialistic here. Europeans are picking up the bad example. I hear stories of parents sent for, who very soon have to take jobs and move into rented rooms while the child accumulates money in a bank account.

I feel as if I am sitting in a boat in the ocean. This boat isn't moored yet.

19 January 1952

Jancsi is still trying to get into a brewery.

Unskilled labour seems to be paid better than expertise. Meanwhile money dwindles. I should take a job. Painting here is considered a hobby, not a profession. This would be unfair to the children. Jancsi is against it in any case. 'You are an artist,' he says, 'and you will paint.'

21 January 1952

Jancsi is thinking about buying a milk bar. I don't paint at all. Peter's kindergarten started today. János is running a temperature. The Kletzmayrs wrote from Salzburg, they want a permit to migrate.

They have started to paint the flat in Weeroona Avenue but there is no water connected yet. It's like a slow-motion camera.

9 March 1952

As soon as we moved into the most beautiful flat in the world, we employed a woman with a baby as housekeeper, and I could have started to paint. I became disturbed and confused and consequently panicked.

It's very strange. One stands firm as long as one must. Then I broke down. Migrants know that this will happen in some form, after the first few months. That there comes a crisis when firm ground below slides and disappears. I don't know. I think what happens is this: the roots which still suck sustenance from the old soil of Europe dry out, wither and die. The desire to cling on by correspondence wanes. One's body rebels against the steam and inertia of the climate. And new roots are not yet grown.

I worry about my art, if I can't sell it, if no one wants what I do, this sacred striving, this leitmotif of a whole life shrinks to a hobby, an idea *fixée*, useless hours not to be accounted for.

I have no higher aspiration but to pay my housekeeper. I don't want to be a burden on Jancsi who still doesn't earn any money. Both of us are worrying about this every day. We live above our means.

5 April 1952

The first commission fell from the sky. Meanwhile I spent an evening drawing portraits for charity, joined the Contemporary Art Society, and went to a lecture by Lloyd Rees.

Sheila McDonald, an artist and patron of artists, invited me to join a sketch club.

I try to nestle, to find a niche. But I am still afraid to open my eyes in the morning.

18 April 1952

I got highly commended on the first picture I sent for an exhibition. It was the one I painted of Franzi and Edith in Salzburg, playing harmonica and flute. I met Michael Kmit, a Ukrainian painter whose Byzantine style and use of colour attracted me.

We drove to the Blue Mountains. The road keeps climbing but there are no peaks. When one arrives one looks down, not up, at mountains with their heads cut off. The hotels are primitive. Australian native trees aren't green, but greyish blue, as if dust has covered them and they have been bleached by the sun. The trunks aren't brown and covered with moss, but white and tortured like ghosts.

I visited Orban, an old Hungarian painter. He said he developed more, in the vacuum of Australia, than under all the influences of Paris. 'You are talented,' he told me, 'but you stopped somewhere in impressionism. You must forget that a table has four legs, only use what is essential to your picture. Forget the object.' I sense that Orban is right but I feel that I have to hide my construction underneath all I have to say. Otherwise I shall just imitate what every mediocre student does to hide how mediocre they are.

8 June 1952

Jancsi bought a general outfitting shop with a partner in Leichhardt. I promised myself to give up smoking for a month if Jancsi starts working. I still can't believe that Jancsi will go to work every morning as in Budapest. Even though it's not at a brewery.

Orban tells me lots of new things, like what the difference is between harmonious colours and colour harmony. The first is like a recipe everybody can learn. The latter has to be my own discovery; composition can be learned, design has to be found. All this will help me, he said, to find my own style.

I paint a flower I have never seen before. It has a head like a reindeer, its neck is silver and alizarin.

24 June 1952

I have been commissioned to paint David Luber. He has a brain tumour. He is paralysed, has double vision and sits in a wheelchair. I have always felt repelled by sickness, so it is a lesson for me to realise that this man still enjoys living. 'It doesn't matter. Life was perfect,' he said.

He introduced me to every bird on the tree outside his window. There is a mirror behind me so he can watch what I do. I have never painted a laughing portrait before. His smile remains delighted and happy.

6 July 1952

Orban invited us over along with the art critic of the *Sydney Morning Herald*, Paul Haefliger, and his wife, Jean Bellette. Orban's Friday nights are stimulating. I discover a very important thing: to use nature as a raw material.

14 July 1952

I haven't painted for a fortnight because Peter had a bad attack of measles.

15 August 52

I am 32 years old. How strange. Jancsi bought me something unpractical, which I was longing for. Schubert's songs and Chopin's ballades. Today I sit at the piano and sing the songs Anyu used to sing. I sit in the living room. There are yellow narcissuses in the vase. I can't really understand that my birthday is now in spring and not in autumn as it used to be.

7 September 1952

The spring exhibition of the Society of Artists. Three exhibits of mine. A picture of a kerosene lamp before an open window in the artists' colony in Szentendre; one of Johnny at breakfast; one of my Australian birds of paradise. Haefliger, who has a pretty poisonous pen, called my lamp 'charming', like Aladdin's. He only mentioned eleven out of 120 painters, and as Jancsi and I read it in bed in the morning, I jumped so high the bed almost collapsed. There were 800 people at the opening and everybody looked for my Aladdin's lamp, and my picture of Johnny had a red spot which meant that somebody bought it.

I have finished a portrait of Andrea who writes in the *Telegraph*. She is cosmopolitan, very witty and still very beautiful. She was a prisoner of war in Hong Kong.

At a dinner I met a man there who said, 'Isn't it a coincidence? In half an hour I'm going to talk about you on the radio.' It was Jeff Smart, art critic of the ABC. We listened to the broadcast and for the first time in my life I heard my name when he said, 'The standard this year was very high. Beside the well-known names there was a surprise, a big still life by Judy Cassab.' He went on to describe it.

The dinner led to four commissions for portraits: Collins, Owen, the Haege children and Mr Justice Maxwell. We were invited to Fay Coppleson's twenty-first birthday and I was photographed in the paper with her portrait. And Sheila McDonald, my friend in the sketch club, writes me a letter every week, addressed 'To the kindest little girl I know', just to make sure I come along to the meetings.

17 September 1952

I still search for explanations why life here is so different. There are facts one simply has to accept, like for instance the need for more sleep than in Europe. I think with incredulity at the nightlife in Budapest, night after night, and how in Paris life begins at the end of the working day. It seems that because of my profession we go out often at night here too, but if we don't have a break twice or three times a week, we are half-dozing the next day.

Frames are only available in rough timber: I have to paint them with glue and gold dust, and then with a colour to antiquate the gaudy look. If, after this it's still garish, I daub it, glaze it, and scratch it with razor blades. Not to mention that masonite (the cheapest surface on which to paint) comes only in prefabricated sizes, so I saw it to the size I want. All very time consuming. I should kiss Agnes's hands who takes on washing, ironing, cleaning and cooking.

What this soil produces in flowers is incredible. In Hungary I saw azalias only in pots. Here whole streets bloom with all sorts of shrubs, orchids, and mimosa.

I paint Justice Maxwell in robes and wig. I haven't seen anything like this before, except in Shakespeare's plays. I became enthusiastic.

Lady Effingham rang, she would like to bring her friend, the ambassador for Brazil, to lunch. 'Don't go to any trouble, my dear,' she said. 'Perhaps a bit of fish, because José is on a diet.' As I had no car, I spent half an hour travelling to buy the fish but no matter, lunch was good. Since the children have just broken my last glass I went to a neighbour to borrow three glasses.

The ABC rang Jancsi in the shop, they want to interview me. He told me smiling, 'I think they want to make a great painter out of you. It's about time you painted a good picture.'

Justice Maxwell is very happy with the portrait, only complaining that the robes are more interesting than him. His head starts to merge from a lion's head into the death mask of Beethoven.

I discover that it's not important that the fur should be fur, the hair hair, the skin skin coloured.

2 October 1952

I started a new commission. Mr McKerihan, president of the Rural Bank.

31 October 1952

I know one has to pay, and the way I pay for the exciting last few weeks is by having dysentery. It's disgusting how sorry I can be for myself. Dr Orban said it must be a nervous diarrhoea. I said I have no reason for nerves. She said 'except for the household, the children, the daily repetitions'. Don't I get up at night to cover the children? Don't I bend down to them because, after all, they are still children? How about the insecurity and danger of the last ten or so years? I don't want to only be my husband's wife but an artist as well, and I have to stand firmly because they lean on me. Anyway, she gave me a tranquilliser and kaolin.

My young friend Fay Coppleson stopped at the door with a big black car, we took painting gear and a small suitcase and left for Palm Beach. Our room has a balcony, and the balcony overlooks the sea. We eat outside, sleep a lot and go to the beach to swim.

Andrea wrote a long article about me with a picture of Maxwell's portrait. I went to his place for the last sitting, carrying the canvas and the rest of the gear. Everybody on the tram recognised Maxwell, they wished me luck and handed the gear down. Two policemen on the corner stopped me and exclaimed, 'Hi, girl, this is a good job.' I was reminded of the day I matriculated when the beggar on the corner of the main street congratulated me, 'Little miss, I hear you have matured.'

24 November 1952

I am glad we have made our decision to reverse our initial lapse of faith. In Hungary it seemed to me that either we go to Israel or, if we do not, we don't want the children to grow up as Jews. It needed a year in Australia to partly lose the terror of persecution and realise that Jews are just one of the many minorities. It's important to recognise that one is and remains what one was born to be.

2 January 1953

I entered my first two pictures in the Archibald Prize: Andrea and Justice Maxwell.

The French exhibition is opening next month. The ship which brings it sits on a sandbank at the moment, but I hope it arrives without a hitch.

I painted a Madonna and child for the Blake Prize. It's twice life-size, blue and mysterious. The child's cheek half-covers the face of the mother, the mother's hand covers the child's head.

12 January 1953

Deep gratitude in me now that I see that Jancsi, for the first time since our arrival, is cheerful again. It's Sunday and he luxuriated for a long while in the bathtub and read the paper in the sunny living room with Pasa the cat, around his neck. Afternoon in Vaucluse. Cards and black coffee while the children play in the garden. Evening, when they fell asleep he dictated letters to me, because he has a phobia of writing. This happens pacing up and down like a captive lion and every five minutes or so he utters one word.

28 January 1953

William Dargie won the Archibald Prize for the seventh time. It's a second-rate picture of a stiff sitter on a red velvet chair. The reviews were ghastly. Only four painters were praised, I among them. In spite of this I am rather sorry my two paintings are not among the rejects, because there will be something like the Salon des Refusés where better pictures will be exhibited than most of those which hang in the Art Gallery of NSW.

I had a bad day. We have money worries again. I only have one commission, the portrait of the wife of the Israeli consul. When I get paid there's the electricity bill, some frames, and the radio needs repair. Doctor and chemist was a fortune.

I have awful diarrhoea again. My knees are like jelly and I can't keep food down. I woke up at 2 a.m. with the strangest sensation that I can't breathe properly. Jancsi held me up in front of the open window till 6 a.m.

2 February 1953

University students are demonstrating on the steps of the gallery. They have posters which say: 'Don't hang Dargie, hang the judges.' They brought a dog, with a sign, 'First prize, William Dogie.' Since then, a record-breaking crowd of viewers.

We read Arthur Koestler's *The Age of Longing*. It captures the essence of our time.

I have no home and no roots but I am not on swampy ground. I strongly sense the presence of a higher power.

12 March 1953

The French exhibition is here. I go almost every day. I learn and enjoy. It's interesting how much closer I feel to the paintings here than I did in Paris. When I come home, my colours seem murky, my figures photographic and if not, then they are Matisse-like or Bonnardish. Nothing yet I could call my own. And in this quandary no one can help me but myself. Orban remarked acidly that I should give up being The Artist for six months and try to paint abstracts, for if I try, I shall feel them. I have tried doing an abstract. It's easy and I hate it. I would prefer to attempt a surrealistic experiment, but have no imagination.

29 March 1953

My Madonna was accepted at the Blake Prize, and Haefliger gave it a good mention. Michael Kmit won the prize which made me very happy because he really deserved it.

I saw the printed catalogue of my first one-man show. I have terrible stage fright.

According to Jancsi, my Madonna can't be really good because there is no Christian background behind it. No conviction. To illustrate this he told me a story: in a Catholic religion lesson a teacher promises one crown to the student who best answers the question, who has done the greatest good in the history of mankind? One child says, 'The American president'. Another says, 'Einstein'. The third says, 'Jesus Christ'.

'You win the crown, my son,' says the teacher. 'But I don't know you. What's your name?'

'Moricz Kohn.'

'How come you are in the Catholic religion lesson?'

'I heard one can win a crown.'

On Easter Monday McKerihan picked us up to greet the Kletzmayrs' ship. They have never been close to us, but in this whole continent they don't know anyone but us, from their letters I sense how frightened they are. So they sobbed and trembled as they embraced us. They just can't believe that we really found them a job and a flat, and that the president of the Rural Bank personally came to fetch them. The customs took them first and none of their luggage was opened. We took them to the McKerihans' where Emily will work as housekeeper, and all four of them can live. Frank already has a job in the Rural Bank. I had them for dinner that night.

20 May 1953

I am planning to go to Alice Springs on a painting trip. July would be the right month, not as hot as usual. My Australian friends tell me I won't be able to wash for a month. They advise me to take a revolver with me. Jancsi differs. He says if I can't wash for a month, I won't need the revolver.

20 June 1953

Money is a serious problem. How I will ever get to Alice Springs is a mystery. There is no doubt that next time I am invited somewhere I will have to decline.

3 July 1953

I was supposed to arrive in Alice Springs today. I did exactly what small children do when they boast, show off, play hero, then shit in their pants. I wasn't aware that I'm doing just that, but after getting the ticket I had violent diarrhoea and could not even think of boarding a plane. I immediately ran to Dr Goulston who, last time, miraculously cured me in one visit.

'Of course,' said Dr Goulston, 'it's understandable excitement before the trip.' And prescribed medicines and assured me this will stop diarrhoea. But he doesn't know my tummy. What with the tamine, bismuth, and opium drops. However I had the shakes, fluttering and vibrating limbs, an inability to hold down food and for good measure, severe depression.

I postpone the flight.

Meanwhile I have my conversations with God. I promise that if I have help in getting over this, I will not squander my strength. I will have fewer late nights and I won't smoke for a week and I won't forget to light the candles on Friday nights.

I can't function and I hate myself. I hate myself because when Jancsi comes home after the day's work he has to do everything for the children, because I am in bed with the shakes. And later he has to attend to me, he takes me in a tight embrace to try to stop me shaking. I moan and all I want is a sleeping pill to knock me out.

So we have bought canvases, a lot of paint and the flight tickets, and we have two pounds left. And all this for nothing.

6 July 1953

I am in bed still. I went to see Bandi Peto, a psychoanalyst, a friend, a wise and educated man. Surely he'll know what's wrong with me, and after an hour's talk with him I shall calm down.

The first thing I found out was that treatment will take many months. I could ill afford this single visit. So I thought, it's simply guilt which drives me to such despair and confusion. If I wasn't an artist, I wouldn't cost Jancsi so much.

While we talked, Bandi quickly and cruelly demolished all the false beauty I built around myself. Children, he said, are not angelic. Life is not a breeze. Art isn't a blessing, it's a lifelong fight. The question is only how one copes.

I don't know how I got home on the right tram. The shakes are persistent, the tranquillisers don't help. I get insulin now to induce appetite, but it doesn't work.

Fay came with a hot-water bottle. I crawled into bed and it somehow stopped the shakes and melted my obstinate limbs. I feel better for a day. I eat a bit. Okay, I think, I'm going to get out of this.

I have a long talk with Jancsi that night and a good, healing cry.

Jancsi in a crisis is understanding, accepting, intuitive and spiritual. He interprets and deciphers all the reasons which could have caused a nervous breakdown. I can't describe how I feel towards Jancsi, how close and sheltered. 'You will surface again, Jucókám,' he says.

3 August 1953

My newest commission is a prostitute. I like her. Decency is relative; she is talking about it strictly on a business basis. When she arrived from Romania she worked in a factory for a year. She realised she would have to work there for ten years to save a bit of money. She changed jobs and the next year she bought herself a home unit and had a thousand pounds in the bank.

'You know,' she said, 'I work at the Cross, but I never get into a Cadillac or a Jaguar. They don't pay properly.'

I feel better. I wonder if one of the reasons which drives me to despair is that in Sydney I have to feed spiritually on myself. I mean nothing outside like antiquity or sculpture or architecture or human warmth rushes at you.

While I was so ill, I started the day (I suppose just to drown in some activity) by doing little Christmas cards, a bit like stained-glass windows. All 'hand painted' as one would say here. I sell them for one guinea a piece.

I wonder how I will look back at this period of my life. I only know at present that I have changed, this is not the same self which rejoiced even during the famine when I found a bit of horsemeat on the street.

I am always afraid that my depressions will return. They descend upon me unexpectedly, and for no reason. They may hit so hard that I cannot function. I console myself with the knowledge that they do pass, although at the time, one thinks they never will.

Jancsi sold his share in the business, and now he sits and reads the advertisements in the *Herald*. We are in limbo. Thank God, I have portraits to do and we haven't started eating up our small savings yet.

I went out with Jeff Smart to La Perouse. I'm interested in the red trees, blue sea and brown people. He stops before the gas works. 'Look at it,' he says, 'isn't it magnificent?'

As I try to analyse myself looking back into my young self, I recognise the fact that I didn't see any shadows beside the light. Maybe these suppressed darknesses are coming to the surface now. I confront this silly, shallow Juci. Sure, there were desperations and pain, but always with reason. The reasons always existed outside. I grow up very late and pay now for this tardiness.

7 October 1953

The *Telegraph* interviewed me. I felt completely well, then in the evening we had to go out and a terrible fear and anxiety welled up in me. I am aware that I must help myself, nobody can do it for me, not even Jancsi. I look at myself with repugnance.

What helps me most is painting. I think I have four good pictures which could go into a one-man show. I did a few oil sketches in La Perouse, and at home, Chagall gave me the courage to do a purple sky. I painted the figures over and over until the crust was too thick and then scraped it off with a razor blade and then glazed them with umber. They seemed to acquire a quality different to the old Szentendre ones. The trees became mine. A bluish-green house has a shocking-pink window. The Aboriginal figure sitting in the foreground is mauve. The other one a deep green. I play and create.

15 October 1953

It's exactly a year now since I had diarrhoea and I thought I ought to celebrate this anniversary by seeing a new doctor.

Dr Huth reminded me of my old Sanyi Mandel. Not only a medical man but a human being. He examined me first, found nothing physically wrong, and said: 'Have you heard of delayed shock? Don't you think that after all those things you lived through without, as you say, feeling afraid at the time, your psyche retained the suppressed panic? You should have gone to a psychoanalyst a year ago. There is no doctor on earth who can help you if you don't help yourself. You have to learn to live with yourself.'

2 November 1953

Glenowrie

Andrea got me a commission. I must go to a sheep station, 40 miles from Sydney. Isabel Viney looks as if she stepped out of Vogue, elegant and frail. They spend six months every year in Europe. We have to hurry as she has to milk the cows and he has to feed the pigs. I like it very much when Vogue's pages metamorphose into jeans, and Sullivan Viney into overalls.

It's a lovely homestead in Glenowrie. The rooms form the core and they are surrounded by wide verandahs and a great park. My verandah is enclosed by a mosquito net.

We cooked dinner together, I was responsible for the toast.

3 November 1953

The Vineys went to Sydney for a party, and I go with them to celebrate Jancsi's birthday.

Jancsi has great news, he put a deposit on a new business.

After three sittings I spoiled the portrait so badly, I have to start another one. First, the light in the living room is dispersed with no sharp shadows, and Sullivan was behind my back, talking. I was too shy to tell him to get the hell out of there. The maid then came in and brought the farmer and his mother-in-law to look at the painting lady. Isabel has a boneless, charming, ageing baby face. I started with bold brushwork, and it was difficult to correct the features in the impasto. It was painful to confess my failure as this meant prolonging my guest status. We moved the studio into a small room with only one window. I started drawing cautiously, which may kill the painting, but will perhaps help the likeness.

Isabel picks flowers in the garden and arranges them with great artistry. In the evening they take their farm clothes off and dress elegantly for dinner. We sit at the table around red roses and four mellow candles. It interests me greatly to see how these people live here, and how differently the gentry lived in Hungary.

28 December 1953

Sydney

Preparations in Sydney for the Queen's visit. I am asked to contribute a sketch to a book by Australian painters which she will be presented with. I was invited to a meeting of artists where, among other things, this book was on the agenda. The president speaks. The secretary speaks. The treasurer speaks. A member thanks the president, the secretary and the treasurer for speaking. The president then proceeds to read all the telegrams from those who were unable to come.

Our third Australian Christmas has passed. Hot, humid and frantic.

6 January 1954

Another country commission: a portrait of Mavis McPherson.

She lives on a giant, arid, sheep station, the backbone of the country's wealth.

In the morning I have diarrhoea. Tension, disorientation, as I sat in the black Jaguar and Jancsi and the children wave goodbye. Jim and Mavis point out the beauty of the landscape, lost on me as it's the same for hours. A parched, ancient continent. If one gets used to it one would concede that one's eyes don't have such scope and space in Europe. No house, no man, no beast. Only fences cutting through the emptiness. After eight hours of this, on excellent roads, we arrived at the homestead.

The shortness of staff is insurmountable. A rich woman like Mavis works physically harder than the average housekeeper does in Hungary. The house is a shambles. Parcels half-unpacked from Sydney are pushed under the beds. There is a dead frog on the verandah. Dirty laundry on the floor of every bathroom. There is tennis and golf equipment, abandoned prams, a sewing machine left open. There is an obsolete deep-freeze which was bought without regard for the frequency of the kilowatts. A bread-cutting machine in the kitchen is surrounded by shavings of yesterday's bread. What goes to waste is fantastic. We drink powdered milk because there is nobody to milk the cow.

22 January 1954

Sydney

One morning at 8.30, McKerihan stopped at Weeroona Avenue with his chauffeur-driven black car. 'Do you still look for premises? I know of a place where you can put your new knitting machines. There are premises available in Bathurst Street, in the house of the Rural Bank. Would that suit you?' So Jancsi started his factory with second-hand machines, in a place found for us by McKerihan.

3 April 1954

My painting develops in leaps. My Archibald entry was chosen out of eighty to go to the Adelaide Art Gallery.

30 April 1954

It's our fifteenth wedding anniversary and I'm crying.

People magazine interviewed me; a sort of life story. Luckily, before the catastrophe was irreversible, I told Jancsi that among the photos there was one of us together. He became violently angry: 'You know how I feel about publicity, how could you do this to me?' I immediately telephoned the editor, withdrew the photo, apologised about thinking that since he is the centre of my life I thought he wouldn't mind. No forgiveness. He can be merciless.

22 May 1954

It is Saturday afternoon and we are alone in the house. Black coffee steams and there is no painting work.

Mr Sisa, who lives downstairs and who makes all my frames, is hammering in the garage, I have many new paintings and buy old frames in a junk shop which can then be altered.

A big portrait of Michael Kmit stares at me, unfinished, with simplified limbs, primary colours. I transform nature at last from inner necessity and I use nature as a raw material.

Hanna Peto stands in another corner, with mauve face and hands, yellow background, yellow dress and somehow it's right that it should be so.

26 June 1954

The National Gallery bought a painting.

There was a three-page article in *People* about me.

1 July 1954

I'm painting the largest picture of my life: *Serenade*. It's of the courtyard in Sheila's sketch club. On the left a black and white winding staircase, on the right an enormous red cello leaning against the wall. At a window there is a tall thin figure in black playing the violin. Everything leans, but they all balance each other.

27 July 1954

Without realising it we have come through a crisis in our marriage. I know one thing: nothing and no one is as important to me as Jancsi, and it's up to me to keep him balanced. The small and seemingly unconnected differences all fall into a pattern. Troubles about invitations. My guilt about being a financial burden. His out-of-proportion hatred of publicity.

In the end the festering sore burst when Jancsi said: 'I am a humble man and I have a famous wife. I don't sleep and I am troubled because at home things are going the wrong way.'

That shook me. Jancsi started anew when he was fifty. He had to struggle alone so I could be an artist. I leaped ahead because he made it possible. I had a prop, a support, a hold. He stayed in the background because of me. I am young and well-known and he lost his confidence in himself, which he needs to remain the man I love.

He is the patriarch, the head of the family, and felt his position threatened. He is sometimes called Mr Cassab at parties. His sense of humour and his wisdom do not stretch this far.

The newspapers mention me frequently, it's unavoidable. While he works so I can have a car and a housekeeper and comes home exhausted and doesn't have the stamina to play with the children. It's a crooked, shifting situation.

I told him: 'Jancsi, let's face the situation which may have changed. I haven't changed. If we stand by each other there isn't a problem we cannot come to grips with.'

2 October 1954

I have a few students now and this is marvellous. Jancsi doesn't think I should teach. He said I get 75 guineas for a portrait, for this I have to teach for 75 hours. But that's not how it works. I haven't had a commission for three months. And so the good old guilt comes to haunt me.

Now it means four or five pounds each week, and I only have four students, which isn't hard. One of my students is the Norwegian consul who is afraid of retirement and boredom. Another is the Austrian commercial attaché.

1 November 1954

The sketch club nights are a feature of my life. It's good, hard work. I do hundreds of studies. Kmit and Olszanski also draw there, together with the hobby painters.

Jancsi has discovered a new type of nylon and elastic stocking, and it's a great success. Suddenly the machine-knitted old stockings have become a sideline. He has to employ another woman, and now feels much more optimistic. So do I. More than I do about myself.

16 November 1954

I painted Warwick Fairfax for the Archibald. It took twelve sittings.

After I finished his portrait, he took me and the children to show us the dachshund puppy he wants to give us. In his car Johnny asked, 'Gee, what sort of car is this? I wish we would have a car like you instead of the old Austin.' We turned into Fairfax Road. 'Gee,' Johnny said, 'is that road named after you?' And when we got there, 'Gee, is that a hotel?' 'No, this is my house.' 'How many families living here?' asked my son. 'Only us,' Warwick answered, but he was quite red by then. There were three cars in the garage. 'Whose cars are these?' 'Mine.'

8 December 1954

Christmas party at the Macquarie Galleries. Paul Haefliger tells a story about Kmit. 'I saw him at the Cross, painting a street in a mixture of Byzantine and Chagall. He asked me, "Do you think I captured the Australian spirit?"'

'Judy, I gave you good advice up to now, I trust. You got rid of baby pinks and sweetness. My advice for the new year is, disintegrate the forms and look for new colour relations.'

Jeff Smart interrupted, 'Why can't you leave Judy alone?'

'Because she shows promise.'

Jeff stares at a Fairweather behind us and says, in a broad Australian accent, 'Tell me, Mr Haefliger, because you know, I don't know much about art, what is this picture supposed to be? Is that what you call form disintegration?'

'Of course,' Paul said, '*You* wouldn't know what disintegration means.'

Touché. Everybody knows how Jeff got stuck within the contours, making hard outlines. The photographers took about twenty shots of everybody, but next morning only my picture appeared in the *Herald*. Jancsi said he will divorce me if I get any more publicity.

24 January 1955

Stayed at the Ritz, in Leura. Patches of paint were dancing behind my closed eyelids like circling dancers after a ball. The portraits had to be taken in for the Archibald before the holidays and of course were not finished. I never worked so hard before. Started early in the morning and went on all day.

There was a spot behind Kmit's head which wasn't a colour at all. In desperation I covered it with a strong bluish-green. It jumped. I repeated it in the lower left-hand corner for balance. It left the rest for dead. So I climbed upwards from square-inch to inch, scraping, glazing, rubbing. I had to overpaint a stronger yellow, then a red. Jancsi didn't go in to work. He stood behind me like a slave driver all day. I cried but painted. We forgot to eat lunch.

28 March 1955

Fairfax bought his portrait and commissioned me to paint his daughter, Caroline.

1 May 1955

My one-man show opens at the Macquarie Galleries in a month.

23 July 1955

Blackheath for the weekend. I went by train. The Australian ghost trees in the dusk skating along the window looked like Watteau trees. Jancsi bought me a *Women's Weekly* for the journey. I read some inane love story. I stared at the advertisements for tinned foods. I fell into bed, arguing with myself about the background of Judy Barraclough's portrait.

Great strain before the exhibition. I hung the finished pictures to see them all together, and then took them down again to change bits. Since I learned how to disintegrate forms, a new avenue has opened. I can connect two things which don't belong together in the literary sense, or I can cut through an object if the composition requires it.

Johnny loves fishing. I went to pick him up at the Rose Bay wharf as darkness fell. There was no one on the pier but an old man and Johnny, and my heart ached as I saw his small solitary figure. His silhouette dark before the sea. He showed real pleasure as he saw me coming, holding up the fish he caught. I asked him to show me how to cast a line. In a while I was quite absorbed wondering if there would be a bite.

'I never knew, Mummy, that you were interested in my fishing.' I felt ashamed.

I am almost ready for the show. Pat, the ballerina, sits with an elongated neck in red stockings. Another has a red background. In another, Hanna, in yellow dress and yellow background. Hanna, as a young girl, one half of the face is light with dark eyes, the other half-light eyes, dark face. A profile. A little bit of Nefertiti. She leans forward, almost jumping off the canvas. Birds of paradise lie horizontally on black. Paul said it's like watching a ping-pong match. Why not put a yellow accent in the centre to connect the two halves. All his advice is sound. He says, after the middle European misty colours of the first show, I now use too much out of the tube—a reaction. Tube colour is no colour. And just the way there are major or minor keys in music, so there are in painting. After this remark I started to repaint lots of pictures I thought were finished. I demolished a great deal of tube colours and, miraculously, less was more.

On Monday I took the 26 paintings by taxi truck to the Macquarie Galleries and had the same feeling one experiences on the first day of summer holidays. I walked in the city, something I haven't done for six months, window shopping. I went to see the Italian exhibition. Bought two ashtrays and placed them on a new black table. I bought some sheet music and played the piano. I took the children to the Australian Museum, and after two hours collapsed at the foot of a whale's skeleton under Maori decorations while my children discovered the fauna.

I painted Judy Barraclough, a top Australian fashion model, in a pyramid shape, like a queen. It turned into a dead queen and I started afresh. The experience of the first attempt is in it without the torture.

On Wednesday I went to the Macquarie Galleries before the opening. Soon there was a crowd of people. Keith Smith, socialites, artists, Hungarians, telegrams. Judy Barraclough, Kmit, Wallace Thornton, Jean Bellette, Elaine Haxton. 'A great personal tribute', said Lucy Swanton. An hour passed with not one red spot.

I saw Andrea panic-stricken rushing to and fro like a hen. She placed herself before Warwick Fairfax and said 'I have just bought a beautiful painting'. She is a friend and a fighter. And although she lives off a salary, and not so well either; and though all those millionaires buy hats and not paintings, she spent 35 guineas on a picture I would have given her for nothing. It all fairly choked me but I couldn't have butted in. She faced Warwick aggressively. 'And how do you like my choice, Mr Fairfax? Do you approve of my purchase, Mr Fairfax?' Within five minutes he bought the birds of paradise. But that was all. During the fortnight two more pictures were sold.

11 August 1955

On Tuesday the bell rang at 10 p.m. There was a telegram. 'Congratulations, winning open oil prize. For portrait of Michael Kmit. Perth Prize Committee.' It's the first time I ever won a prize. I had such a positive feeling of joy.

12 September 1955

I won the *Women's Weekly* Prize with the portrait of Judy Barraclough. I was waiting for the result of the competition knowing it would be published in the Thursday edition. On Wednesday the Vineys called from Glenowrie. 'Congratulations, Judy. We just read in the *Women's Weekly*, that you won the prize with Judy Barraclough.'

I rang the *Weekly* to check and was switched to the editor. She rudely said, 'You are not supposed to know. And the newsagents in the country are not supposed to sell the paper before tomorrow. We worked very hard on this competition and we have to keep it secret. We can't tell you yes or no, and please don't mention it to anybody.'

I almost suffocated on this. Mr Malley, who was sitting for his portrait that day, had no idea that all I did was background. He will give me a washing machine in exchange for this portrait.

Next morning Jancsi rushed out to get the papers. I am in the clouds. There were champagne toasts in the Art Gallery of NSW. The director, Hal Missingham, told me, 'Judy, come in one day and I shall point out to you, not the virtues, but the faults the judges found in your picture.' I thought, that's great.

The guard at the Art Gallery of NSW told me he and the other guards bet on me. The greengrocer on Queen Street was particularly proud of me as he always stops to look at what I'm painting as he passes through the living room with the box of oranges and vegetables on his shoulder. And when I took the prize money to the bank, the teller grinned and said he had been expecting me.

12 January 1956

School holidays, beach season. I am at Redleaf pool with the children at eight every morning. This is punishment because my phobia of the water only gets worse as time passes. I watch Johnny diving and have palpitations. I keep losing sight of Peter.

I drive Jancsi to the city every morning and do the shopping on the way back. The children count the number of Holdens or Austins.

Before Christmas I finished the Archibald entry; Chips Rafferty whose freckled, pudgy hands do not match his lanky, angular body, so I substituted the hands of Leslie Keller.

20 March 1956

I hate Sydney just now. I am so tired from unproductive household chores and as much painting as can be fitted in, that I feel ten years of my life will pass without trace.

Tropical rain falls for six weeks. Sometimes I have diarrhoea and other nervous symptoms but the secret I learned is to be friends with one's neuroses.

I am painting Elaine Haxton for this year's *Women's Weekly* competition. It's like a harlequin, with a patchwork smock, young face and snow-white hair.

The Archibald reviews mention me again. Ivor Hele wins it for the fourth time.

I had a three-man show in Brisbane, at the Johnston Gallery, and sold nothing. Luckily there is a portrait of a chairman to finance this luxury of being an artist.

29 March 1956

Since we came to Australia I have become quite grey. I have some wrinkles too. I will be 36 years old this year. Perhaps in Europe age would also tell a bit but not as much, of that I am sure. The strain of a new life and the thousand changes in it certainly rob one of a slice of youth.

A sign of getting older: I like my bed. I develop small habits, sort of rituals like a glass of milk, cream on my face, the book I read. Today is Good Friday and I am a lion tamer, keeping the kids quiet so Jancsi can sleep longer. I made a dozen ham pancakes for breakfast and had great difficulties to keep three for Jancsi.

6 April 1956

Annette came with Paul Haefliger and I was criticised cruelly. I needed it. I deserved it. It was the truth. For all three reasons it hurt.

Paul said I retrogressed, I am sweetish, slimy and this still life here is for a boudoir. He is sure I will sell it as most people's taste is abominable. And this one, with that clever technique, of course it's no more than a trick. It's easy, isn't it?

'If this is what you decide to do,' he said, 'you will win another prize or two, no doubt, and repeating this sort of performance you will melt into oblivion. Make a decision: Is this what you want? Do you want to be a fashionable portraitist or do you want to be an artist? I wouldn't even bother telling you all this if I didn't know how talented you are. I expect more of you. Self-discipline, girl. Kick a hole through these still lifes. Don't exhibit for a few months. And try something you haven't tried before, for God's sake. Try abstract.'

'I can't feel abstract, Paul. I think, furthermore, that we may be past the abstract stage and we don't know what the new frontier is that we are supposed to be pushing.'

'This is true,' Paul said. And as he had already had a few brandies he became a fountain of knowledge, a firework of words that something came alive in me which took me away from Polish housekeepers and spinach. But while I welcomed and nursed the little newborn flame another part of me felt deep despair that such rare moments happen only perhaps, twice a year. There still are no coffee houses for artists to meet and people live far from each other. There is no artist colony, there is no salt and no yeast, only a climate that makes you heavy as lead. And one is lonely.

'Judy,' Paul implores, 'don't try to be a success. Strive for failure. Aim so high that it is inaccessible. Only this way will you be able to ruin experiment after experiment and find yourself. What Cézanne strained for, fell into Picasso's lap. Like a gift. But Picasso was a genius and knew how to use it. The past fifty years was Picasso and decoration. Enough of the decorative. Let's turn against Picasso.'

'You preach easily,' I tell Paul.

11 April 1956

Sheila has opened the sketch club again after the summer break.

There is the violin maker and his sign: a violin hanging from the tree. The smell of cats wafts through the doorway. One climbs up the wooden stairs into the studio with its great arch, old brick walls and candlelight. Few artists come. Mostly it's the hobby painters who need this to balance the grey and barren sameness of their jobs. Four of my students come, and a director of the railways who likes to look at the nudes and fiddles with watercolour and precision.

There is an exhibition of French tapestries at the Art Gallery of NSW. Apart from the Victorian monstrosities, there are Matisse, Dominguez, Corbusier, woven in Aubusson.

19 April 1956

I had a telephone call from Canberra today about doing a portrait of Lady Slim, wife of the governor-general.

Picnicking with the Halmis and the Kochs. We light a fire and Johnny and Peter collect wood. We barbecue meat and sausages. Johnny, who always wants to want something, wants to hire a boat. We don't let Peter join him because he can't swim, so he wails and cries.

30 April 1956

For our seventeenth wedding-anniversary Jancsi bought me a leather-bound diary with lots of good quality paper. What a treat after four years of school exercise books. I love to touch it.

Jancsi is good and kind and wise and easy to talk to. He has grey hair at the temples and wears glasses. I accept this now. I don't want to conjure time as it used to be. There is what is. And as it is so it is dear to me and so he is someone to treasure. The core of my shaky universe.

2 May 1956

I did a sketch for the portrait of Lady Slim. The footmen, the butlers, the secretary, the two policemen at the gate, intimidated me a bit. I said. 'Your Excellency, when I'm painting I can't keep my mind on saying "your excellency" all the time so I just call you "you".' She laughed and said that will be a nice change, do, by all means.

In my own time I paint with white tempera on white paper, pour black Indian ink on it when it's dry and wash it under the tap. Delightful accidents happen which I use to tickle my imagination. Two came out quite well: *Joseph is sold by his brothers* and *The Dream of Jacob*.

Meanwhile my meatloaf cooks in the oven, and my cabbage in tomato sauce bubbles over the stove. No housekeeper.

12 May 1956

A letter came from the Art Gallery of NSW. A London magazine, *The Studio*, wants to do an article about young Australian artists and they want me to bring in a painting to be reproduced.

In the exhibition of the Society of Artists the papers mention only five of 132 painters exhibited, my *Blue room* is praised.

I painted a gouache of Lot and his wife who turned into a pillar of salt. It was exhibited at the Macquarie Galleries and the Art Gallery of NSW bought it.

30 June 1956

This week I'll send in my entry for the *Women's Weekly* Prize.

This year saw the Hungarian uprising and the Suez crisis. It touched our life in a very big way. Amika, Jacques and Maya are immigrating to Australia, boarding a ship in two weeks time. They are finally leaving Egypt. It must be unpleasant to be called Kohn in Cairo just now.

Tomorrow the Salk vaccine will be used for the first time in the schools. One can hardly believe that polio, this monstrous threat, will really be eliminated.

Things that happen regularly here: the drycleaner, the grocer with the weekend order, the garbagemen, all come on certain days and make the fabric of life seem monotonous. Only painting, books and music are events.

20 July 1956

There isn't an hour when I don't think of Amika. We are so alone, no family around us as I once had. I like it that we are importing a grandmother substitute.

Paul attacked me again about the *Women's Weekly* portraits. He thinks I should give up portraits altogether. 'You try to make it contemporary but you won't succeed because your faces are hopelessly academic and therefore anonymous. You could attempt it in a classical way, the only other solution is expressionism like Kokoschka.' I know he is right but I can't give up something that has been my aim since childhood and I know, I just know, that I will solve the problem one day.

Still no housekeeper and I find it not only exhausting, but also unfair that I work all day, as Jancsi does, but at 6 p.m. when he sits down in his armchair with the newspaper, I still have three extra hours to cook, wash the dishes, make the beds.

30 July 1956

I entered Elaine Haxton's portrait in the *Women's Weekly* Prize. I have tried to break through this awful wall of the human face. It's impossible to explain to anybody who does not paint and can't understand why I am not satisfied with my success as a portraitist. I could perhaps best compare it to a singer trying to hit a certain note in a certain way.

Paul Haefliger proposed an interesting experiment. At Annette's, I painted her daughter, Sima, and got a likeness in half an hour. Paul then took over and transformed it into a classical head. He eliminated all the shadows, made it smooth as an old master, and kept some of the likeness. Only by not touching my eyes, of course, which stay and burn alive in an otherwise pretty dead head. This doesn't strike a chord in me as I have no inclination for distortion. Expressionism is as timeless as the primitive, I think, and one has to be born with it. Besides, neither of these styles has anything to do with the disintegration of form—which I am leaning towards at present.

Paul seems like a clever pianist who can play a pop tune in the style of Chopin or Mozart or Rachmaninov.

The living room is cluttered with coffee cups and brandy glasses and newspapers on the floor because Paul spills oil with elegant carelessness over the carpet and flicks cigarette ash on top of it. Annette and I take turns to scrub on all fours with turpentine.

Meanwhile the children come home. Johnny spills ink. Peter tries a scout's knot on the tail of the cat. I put dinner on the stove. While I chop onions, Paul explains about Soutine. I wash the brushes (he used about twelve). The doorbell rings. While I pay the dry-cleaner, I burn the rice. Annette and Paul leave, I sauté vegetables.

Amika and her family are on the boat. I cross my fingers to get them the furnished flat which we have waited two months for.

2 August 1956

Johnny sits in the sunroom in a woollen dressing-gown and writes an essay in the circle of the lamp's light. Peter sits on the floor and plays general with his armies. When I'm not too harassed I enjoy not having a housekeeper. There is an atavistic female satisfaction in cooking for the family.

Amika and family are due in Perth on 13 August. I sent them a note to Perth. 'Welcome home.' And then I cried. Ah, to have a big family again. It's them I think of as I wake and not whether I win the *Women's Weekly* Prize or not.

16 August 1956

I won the prize.

My birthday yesterday was lovely. Jancsi bought champagne, flowers and a dozen stockings. Peter bought flowers from his pocket-money. Johnny locked himself in the sunroom, and with a knife and some matches made me a bunch of flowers out of coloured plastics.

The prize is £500. For an hour I felt quite numb. Jancsi hugged me, the children ordered records, paints and soldiers.

The newspaper people were already here at 8 a.m. I was notified that at the opening I would be sitting at the table with Menzies, and the gallery and magazine people. Last year's prize winner which was bought by the Art Gallery of NSW will be hung behind us.

I now have some experience concerning such good news. Euphoria for a day or two. Then emptiness. That's all right.

10 September 1956

The big event became quite insignificant the day Amika's ship docked.
We were at Pyrmont at eight in the morning. Tears, hugs, kisses. Jacques
is sixty-five and his usual cheerful self. Maya is exotic. Ami looks like
Anyu.

The day passed with oysters and paprika chicken. We took them over
to the holiday flat we rented for them in Edgecliff Road. It's nicer than
our own. I packed the flat full of flowers and the fridge full of food.

In the evening it became clear that as a consequence of the Suez
crisis, almost all their money is lost in Egypt. All they have now is the
amount Maya didn't spend while she was in boarding school in
Switzerland.

Ami's state of mind and nerves are terrible. I think she would like to
go back to her villa in Meadi with the servants, Nasser and all. I use
all my strength and persuasion to explain that in Australia nobody has
starved to death yet. It is in vain.

Jancsi shows once more how great he is. He told Jacques, 'I was
waiting for you with a business proposition just in case you have no
other plans. I intended to put five thousand pounds into it and you
could have put in the same amount and we would have been partners.
Now, just because Nasser chose to take your life savings doesn't mean
we can't do it. I simply take that much more overdraft on Elasco and
we shall be fifty-fifty partners. We will manage together, somehow.'

Jancsi of course doesn't take a penny out of whatever they are going
to earn in the new venture. Jacques will, because they have to live on
it, Jancsi says. Maya will get a job, without trouble. Ami, if she wants
to, can work in Elasco and earn a living too.

There is turmoil, relief, pity, all mixed up in me. Relief that the
family will be able to live, and a deep, emotional appreciation for this
dear, dear man of mine who has struggled so hard for five years and
who takes all the weight of my family on his shoulders.

They know it too, which makes things even harder.

2 October 1956

Taubman paints commissioned me to paint their founder, Henry
George Taubman. When the portrait was finished, they took it home
until the frame was ready. They rang me. Mrs Taubman doesn't want
to part with the picture, could I do another. For another hundred

guineas and on top of it Mr Taubman brings me flowers from his garden every day.

More unpleasantly, the wife of the German ambassador commissioned me to do decorations for a ball. Naturally I didn't refuse as I had already done three pictures for them. Naturally, the Jewish community protested. Anyway, instead of paper they had an enormous sheet of plastic delivered to the flat which not only covered the whole wall but stretched all the way to the sunroom. I painted the Rhine with its castles, and dancers in the foreground. When it dried and I took it off, I turned it around so that the painting showed through the wrong side which was the right side of course, looking like a glass painting.

Ever since I have been aware of abstract art, I've never felt tempted by it. It's too geometric, calculated and cold. Recently, though, there is a new wave of abstract. It is juicy, emotional, lyrical and imaginative. Hartung and Mannessier slowly dissolved my conviction that the lack of subject matter takes the artist's personality away.

Paul is still storming and fighting about my portraits. The soil is becoming fertile. I feel that the direction I have taken for the past three years leads nowhere. I want to run elsewhere. Yes, but where?

'Why not try?' he asked. 'Even if you discard it, surely you can't leave a world movement unexplored if you want to be a painter.' (This is true.) 'I warn you,' he said, 'it will be hard. There is nothing but the canvas and you. Why did you paint apples lately, and jugs? Did the apple interest you or the apple's colour and form?' (Colour and form, of course.) 'You see, you used it purely as an excuse for painting.' (Also true.) 'Throw away the crutches, throw away the excuses. Everything you ever learned, everything you know, you are, you lived through, will emerge from your paintings, and be expressed better than they ever can be in apples and jugs. Don't be afraid to lose something. You can only win. Everything will be used: your sensitivity of line, your sense of proportion, your flair for composition, your colour sense and your emotions. Don't you think this has been your approach anyway, for a long time now, without you realising it? Why do you turn the picture upside down when you really want to see? Because the subject is only distracting you. You try to achieve balance and wasn't an arm, or a table or an explanation only in your way?'

Before I decide to jump into cold water, I feel I need a new vehicle to help me change. I went into the paint shop, bought powder colour, screw-top jars and moved down to the garage.

I got a rude jolt when I went to see the big Australian exhibition on the liner *Orcades* which is taking contemporary art to Honolulu and

San Francisco. The idea is great; it's time to show that Australia is not only a country of footballers, swimmers, kangaroos and sheep. They don't need to hire a gallery, it's on the ship.

They were all there. Eric Smith, Passmore, Olsen, all of them with abstract expressionist work. The rest beside these were all so bloodless and boring. My ballerina, poor thing, with all her disintegration, seemed to say: '*Ich will, aber ich kann nicht.*' I want to but I can't. She also said, 'Yes, but. Yes, but.'

What impressed me most in the abstracts was that they were all recognisable. Eric Smith's could be Christ, without Christ, with its Gothic composition and his personal texture and colour. Passmore's soft greys with the one spot of rose d'oré in the corner could have been one of his bald-headed people.

I went home and broke eggs for tempera and let go. It was decorative and stiff and it wasn't me. I shall try to paint on top of one of my old pictures. Perhaps nature will help.

The Fairfaxes have a farewell party for James Gleeson who will accompany the floating exhibition to San Francisco. Ferrar, the French violinist is there and so is the Katherine Dunham Company who are dancing at the Tivoli.

I am having dinner in the library with Passmore and Donald Friend who clowns and says 'If I had a Rembrandt I would probably sell it and buy a second-rate Goya and yes, and I would buy a new hood for my car.' Passmore jumps up, leaves his dinner uneaten and says, 'Shut up, you fool. You don't know what you are talking about.'

This doesn't disturb Donald who launches into another story: 'I bought a wonderful book in Italy by Roberto Luigi Stevenson.' He recites some poetry which goes, 'Ohoho', and explains how ingenious this is as it would mean something entirely different if it would be 'Ahaha'. About Passmore he says, 'He is too bloody profound.'

By the way, Passmore looks like a textile merchant who isn't doing very well. Only his eyes are real painter's eyes. How many of those I have observed; blue, childish, innocent, but sharp as a sailor's, used to scan distances. Donald always looks like he needs a haircut. His teeth are long and protruding, his eyes register one drink more than he can stand.

My new commission is the portrait of Bishop Burgmann. I was flown to Canberra. It's almost a holiday. I work two hours in the morning in the bishop's house and am free the rest of the day. He is a kind, wise, humble man, tall, powerful and white. He has a swinging nose, bushy eyebrows and a quick, disarming smile. I am surprised at how broadminded he is. He spoke about Australia's geographical position and that we can't shut Asia out, how we belong much more to Asia than to England. He said: 'I would much rather have half-yellow great-grandchildren, you know, than no great-grandchildren at all.'

He took me to a smorgasbord lunch in the university's great hall, very impressive; before the glass entrance a Henry Moore. The waterways inside the courtyard make it look like the Taj Mahal. The dining room could be a cathedral, but the coffee room beside has an Italian espresso machine. I was invited for dinner at Hess's, the German ambassador where I had a joyous reunion with my first housekeeper, Agnes.

At intervals, Bishop Burgmann and I go into the kitchen to have a cup of tea. He allows me a cigarette ('Your ration for the day'). In Hungary a bishop making tea in the kitchen would be unheard of.

The new building where the picture is going to hang is very contemporary and I try to persuade him to buy one of Eric Smith's Christs and to place a Dadswell sculpture before the entrance.

28 October 1956

Today Lady Slim rang. She wants to buy her portrait. But mainly, 'I didn't forget, you know, what you have told me, about starting a contemporary Australian collection in Government House. I would like to buy a few paintings now, before the Duke of Edinburgh comes to open the Olympic Games, for our dining room in Canberra. Could you help me?' I asked Hal Missingham to take her to a few galleries to choose.

20 November 1956

I am painting Frank Packer for the Archibald.

Paul Haefliger wrote a shattering review of James Gleeson's one-man show. In consequence only two paintings were sold. He should save his vitriol for 'gum tree' painters and not spend it on a good artist, like Gleeson, just because he is a surrealist and not an abstract expressionist. Paul behaves like Savonarola.

At the Christmas show in the Macquarie, Cedric Flower exhibited *Paul's governess*. Paul is clearly recognisable. He screams, his pants are slipping, tummy showing, a yellow straw hat on his big head. The governess slaps him with a *Sydney Morning Herald*. And because Paul has a sense of humour, he mentions the picture: 'Paul, clearly an intelligent lad who discovers that it's not easy to be a critic.'

20 January 1957

For the first time in five years none of the three critics mentioned my Archibald entry. I confess I take it badly.

3 February 1957

I am painting for the Blake, *Joseph is sold by his brothers*. After several months, it has started to come alive. Two figures have an inner illumination quality. All eight figures are barefoot and the feet form a separate pattern. I also work on *Lot* which is more dramatic. The two women running in the foreground are lit like Vlaminck's houses in the storm. I have never used as much brown, rust and ochre as I do here. I am at peace when I'm immersed in these canvases.

12 February 1957

Juliska and I decided that instead of gazing at one another's walls we shall go to Georges, a brand new espresso bar in Double Bay. They open up like mushrooms now. This one is modern and elegant. We tried to analyse why it isn't anything like the European coffee houses. Not only is this one different, everything is. One can't create a past. Relive past feelings. There is no stimulus. And we slowly change into creatures like the ones we spat upon when we first arrived. That the life of each one of us is in fact not ours—we lost our identity. Without the familiar background no one is quite themselves, not in the eyes of the other or in their own. If one rebels too strongly one destroys one's soul. If one gives in one stops living. Is there a solution at all? Most pathetic are those migrants who conjure up the past. Whose eyes sparkle when they talk of what sort of people they used to be. Of what the gypsy band used to play when they entered, of how many servants they used to have, and how many rooms, decorated just so. I ask myself whether this was beautiful because it simply was, or because we were ten years younger.

Again another show at the Macquarie Galleries. Again no mention in the reviews. Was I mentioned too much when I did not paint half as well as I do now? They spoiled me and now I'm sulking.

21 February 1957

Jancsi wouldn't let me paint for a fortnight. He says I have to unwind. So I painted the corridor, ceiling and all. Passionately.

Elwyn Lynn won the Blake Prize with a rooster. I applaud.

Kmit deserved at least one of the three prizes with a picture that looked like a jewel from Byzance. Paul mentioned me in his review this time.

7 March 1957

I painted the living room. It seems that hard labour suits me at the moment. It resolves all tension.

We became Australian citizens. McKerihan was the first speaker and he praised us until I thought Jancsi would disappear under the carpet. Abstract expressionism seems to be the paradise of every dilettante. One vomits on the canvas and calls it one's innermost soul. I think that established artists who sit on the bandwagon lose their personality. If they create something 'new', it's only in a provincial sense. It looks like a version of a Mannessier.

I am experimenting with it. It's simply impossible to hold oneself back because it's overpowering. Perhaps there is something behind it that I may reach. I don't know. I am at a low point. I have a few abstracts now, but I loathe them. I overpaint them one by one, and lovely figures emerge with an underlying abstract pattern. I discover that one doesn't have to wait for a used canvas. I can make it deliberately so. What happens on top will almost surely be fresh.

31 May 1957

I'm losing my Hungarian. We begin to have real conversation with the children, in English, of course. And in all shoptalk about painting I express myself in English.

The Art Gallery of NSW has a new library, open every Thursday. I look at art magazines from New York, Belgium, France, Germany and Japan. The whole world has turned abstract expressionist. The best ones I would call calligraphic but can't see how I could fit in.

It's as if yet unborn generations should be graphologists and we should all paint exaggerated handwritings for them to solve. That the apple is only an excuse for painting, I already know. I don't know how to replace the apple. I need to explore what's happening in Europe and America.

4 June 1957

Diana Field, an actress, commissioned her portrait. She said, 'My boyfriend in Melbourne wants me to have it done in a particular evening gown, with a special hairdo, in memory of a special night.' I said, 'If he thinks I'm going to paint a chocolate box he is mistaken.' I trembled at the thought of pink lace.

I drew it first and covered each pattern with white tempera, then smeared it all over with black Indian ink and washed it down with the garden hose. I got a pattern, black and white, like a woodcut, well balanced and very exciting in design. On top of it I avoid the danger of flimsiness.

I'm planning to travel in September.

11 June 1957

I try not to think of my trip. I go over the preparations in a matter-of-fact way. Passport, American visa, French visa, writing to friends and hotels.

11 September 1957

En route to Honolulu

I am finally sitting on a plane. This is the first leg of my trip which will eventually take me around the world. I am confused because I can't believe it is happening. The last ten days were hell. My own private, secret hell. Everything I have been longing for—Paris, New York, Rome—shrank to the size of a pinpoint. Jancsi and the children grew to the height of the Empire State building and all I wanted was to stay with them.

During a crying fit, Jancsi, who is staying behind with the children, said: 'After all, we are only half of your life. Stop being such a coward. Jump into the water and swim.'

We are one hour from Fiji. It will be 6 p.m. at home now, but this plane is in such a hurry it stole two hours from the night.

It's black ink outside and the propeller spits red flames. Mostly I sit with my eyes closed. I'm not yet used to relying on a machine which pretends to be a bird.

Dinner in Fiji. Black people in white skirts waited on the tables. Two large ventilators substituted for air. Very hot. Very humid.

12 September 1957

Honolulu

Day and night and night and day the Hawaiian guitars strum so that the tourists will know where they are. One never is sure if what is happening here is happening as a tourist attraction or something that would just happen anyway.

I couldn't fall asleep till 2 a.m. I felt desperately lonely without Jancsi and the children, and indescribably sad. The sea sang, the guitars played, the bamboo curtains whispered.

Sheila gave me an address of a painter who has an art shop here. I went to the shop where a small Chinese man sat behind the desk and said: 'You are Judy Cassab.' It sounded strange. He showed me carved figures from 700 BC, pre-Columbian and Aztec art, and his own modern paintings.

13 September 1957

San Francisco

Andrea's friends were at the airport to meet me. They are lovely and kind, and I am tense and desperate. Tears choke and constrict my throat. I try to live through this never-ending long day. My system is so confused that I'm not hungry when they eat, but in the afternoon I'm starving. My diarrhoea has flared up so badly that I have to take my opium drops.

I miss Jancsi like an arm or a leg and pray to God to give me the health to go through with this trip.

15 September 1957

New York

My appetite has improved. I enjoy a meal of cold chicken and sleep till noon.

This city is so different to what I've imagined. The glass facades of the skyscrapers reflect other sights and it's visually staggering. I lunch in the Metropolitan Museum.

Hanna and Bandi took me to Greenwich Village which is like the Montmartre. Thousands of paintings are exhibited on the pavements, stuck on the walls, standing on easels. Every few steps a figure on the ground sits and is gazed at by a crowd. Some have beards, some are black, some yellow wanting to be Parisian in an American way, and it's like Luna Park.

16 September 1957

To spend the entire day in the Metropolitan is like leafing through the pages of a well-known and much-loved book. The most marvellous Cézannes are here. There are Manets and Renoirs. The intensity of the city, and my immersion in the work is so strong that I go to bed early with no strength left.

I spend whole days in the Metropolitan Museum and the Museum of Modern Art.

The more I see of New York, the happier I feel that we didn't immigrate to America. It's a merciless race. And though opportunity seems to be greater, if there is a casualty who drops by the wayside, nobody picks them up, nor can they rise for a second chance.

Very often I have lonely and anxious hours. For everything I learn and for all I experience I pay. I drag my dizzy, palpitating, badly-functioning body with me everywhere while my brain makes photocopies of the kaleidoscope.

This seems to be my destiny, this double meaning of a life. I have come so far for this side now and for it I have left the other and so, at the moment, I only have half a life.

Dear God, let me have peace of mind through these beautiful and horrible few months.

18 September 1957

Hal Missingham gave me a letter to Monroe Wheeler, director of the Museum of Modern Art. He took me for lunch and around the gallery, had a look at my coloured slides and some of the portraits and because I happen to live on the periphery he could understand my difficulties in longing to have a springboard to the art centres of the world. He gave me a letter to 'Portrait Incorporated'. The letter was fine but wonder of wonders, they had the two covers of my winning portraits of the *Women's Weekly*. Mrs Appleton Reed said, 'We haven't many painters here who can paint such portraits.' She suggested I paint a portrait while in New York and leave it on exhibition with them. Then, by the time I pass through on my way back, they may have a commission for me.

So I started to paint Cyril Ritchard (an actor on Broadway) who gave me five sittings. The picture is good.

There are five thousand times as many painters as in Australia, but mainly eclectics, following Pollock or De Kooning. I see the chaos of swirling brushstrokes and thick paint behind my closed eyelids at night.

23 September 1957

At last a letter from Jancsi! I feel his love even more than when he sits beside me. The boys sleep in the same room as him and they have written too. Peter advises me that he has formed a navy club, and for some unknown reason he is the electrical engineer. Johnny writes about the quality of the stamps I sent him from Fiji.

24 September 1957

Amsterdam

Crossing the ocean towards Amsterdam, I think that I would be less disoriented if I flew shorter distances.

At the airport the first face I see belongs to my Uncle Gyuszi who flew over from Vienna to greet me on European soil. He came with a bunch of flowers and tears.

We saw the Rijksmuseum with those Rembrandts which glow from inside. Walked on the cobblestones and then the Stedelijk Museum. I forgot that the material was so vast. The current exhibition is called 'Europe 1907'. I have a book on the Fauves but had no idea that from Kandinsky to Dufy, Matisse to Monet, everyone painted the same in this epoch.

Monet's waterlilies and the paintings of Odilon Redon, strange poet, are pure examples of abstract expressionism.

Mondrian slashes away at trees, mountains, and the sun. How on earth did he distil his pure geometry? Even Rouault showed promise in those dark contours. This exhibition is a bit like an academy, where one doesn't know who will turn into what. Here Derain is still as soft as Vuillard, and I already know that those who are clumsiest here will be the greatest, because I am fifty years wiser than 1907.

Picasso is the only one in this period who differs. He is painting his Negro sculptures.

Modigliani is more beautiful than ever. The decorative doesn't interest me now, I crave for more.

Chagall. I am prejudiced. Nothing seems strange to me in his world closed in by the frame. I greet the goat which plays the violin, the rooster with the bunch of flowers, and the fiddler on the roof. How much love one needs to bring dreams like this. Is it true one shouldn't paint what one loves? The portrait of Madame Chagall is done with devotion, but is almost dilettantish and vulgar. She obviously wears her Saturday best, a green velvet affair with écru lace and her hair freshly out of rollers. In the background on one side of her face is a bunch of lilacs, on the other side, an angel flies. If I didn't know who painted this picture, I would find it comical.

Walking through rooms full of abstracts I find it hard to see their value. Is there no talent, no genius perhaps, who by sheer force, could reach over to me? This isn't painting, for heaven's sake, this is cuisine. Scratched, dripped, cunningly tricked, there seems to be effort in it but I don't feel the inspiration. Oh, I know, I shall recognise the genius when I see one.

There are no words I can write about the van Gogh room. I let his mad and gentle melody play through my soul.

1 October 1957

Rome

I reached the hotel in the late afternoon. I washed and sat down at a streetside cafe on the Via Veneto. I did not go anywhere else. I'm learning that it's better not to become exhausted and then have to deal with the diarrhoea. So I just sat and looked at the people and the contemporariness which moves among the beauty of ancient buildings.

I walk and walk and walk with a dictionary. I know how to buy ham and bread, and peaches and cheese.

The fountain de Trevi left me speechless. How would it feel to be at home in such a city? The yellow-red of houses is a colour impossible to describe, even to paint. The bridges of the Tiber, St Peter's, life with so many Volkswagens and Fiats, barbers and holy pictures.

Every stone lives.

No words can describe Michelangelo's *Pieta*, nor details like St Peter's foot, worn from the kisses of ten centuries. The marble on which Charlemagne knelt. The Colosseum, Forum, Michelangelo's *Moses*. I don't even sketch. Ego seems so unimportant.

One would need a year in the Vatican Museum alone.

Before today I could not get past the past. Two things seem closer to me. The first is surrealism. Why not hang the head of a Roman sculpture in the sky above a city? The second is the classically-drawn figure.

I was thinking that my study trip is good for more than studying. With no friends, no amusements, no duties, no responsibilities to distract me, I submerge in the fact that I AM A PAINTER. I make sacred resolutions that when I go home I shall dig myself into inexhaustible material. But I know after a while this resolution will be deflated. But perhaps not ... if God takes my hand.

Slowly something starts to emerge. It's undefined, but takes a form, a direction that I could follow. For ages I searched for something and didn't know what it was. It's not a certain artist, neither is it a certain style. It's not that bellowing, shouting, gesticulating, vulgar abstraction. There is something else. It's difficult to define but it originates from nature. It has no connection with geometric forms. It's something to do with the atoms of life. There is a place in it for poetry and mystery. The image is unresolved, but there is time to think it through.

Florence

I travel like a poor student, third class, on wooden benches. My eyes see the same things that they would in first class. The October summer day is like a gift.

I climb the filthy stairs of the pensione on the Piazza Annuziata tired and sweating. There is no water to wash in. The texture of the walls is like the basilica in Assisi, but without Giotto's murals. I discover the Ponte Vecchio. Donatello's *Magdalena*. Michelangelo's *Gate of Paradise* and his third *Pieta*, which he sculpted at eight-two. *David* is such perfection, one despairs. His dignity is indescribable, his superiority as he stares into eternity, ready to vanquish Goliath. The unfinished works call Genesis to mind.

The Palazzo Pitti. The Uffizi Gallery. Giotto and Botticelli move me most. Both are simple and pure and devoted. I keep searching for a solution to the contemporary figure. Signorelli, Filippino Lippi, Piero di Cosimo, Perugino. Treasures. Giorgione. Giovanni Bellini. Cranach.

A Sydney couple drive me to Siena and San Gimignano. On the road yellow leaves, brilliant sunshine, pink houses on the hills, vineyards and villagers. Black and white marble dome in Siena, mosaics and sculpture and murals.

The world is a picture in everyone's mind reflected in one's own reality. My mirror receives beauty, art, yes, but this is a fable, this is a stage and I sit in the audience by myself. Reality, my reality is Jancsi, and the children, so I shall always be alone no matter how many people I meet.

In Italy one can only look, mute and humble and discover it. It's like childbirth but one can't really write about it. Only point.

Invited for lunch to the Volterras. He is a famous pianist, she an Australian. They have three Canalettos, a Piero di Cosimo, and a garden where the trees are trimmed exactly as they appear in Leonardo's canvases.

Vienna

The first day I only had eyes for Vienna and for the family. Manyi said she is sorry not to have ten eyes, with all ten she would look only at me. I took in the Kärtnerstrasse, the Stephansdome and the Graben, and the coffee houses—the placidity with which the people read the newspapers on the small marbletop tables with their glasses of water beside them. For hours.

Whole new rows of houses on the Ring. The old lady had a good facelift. Grinzing, lunch on the Kobenzl.

In the Kunsthistorisches Museum I visited my friends, the Bruegels, the *Peasant Dance* which I spent four months copying in that room. I saw Shakespeare in German. Went to the Auersperg Palace for supper. The waiters are gliding with the trays under the Titian, the pianist plays 'Wien, Wien, nur Du allein' under fifteenth-century Gobelins. We sat among palm trees and fountains and giant birdcages.

Vienna is like an island containing a fragment of our old way of life. It wasn't the coffee houses I envied, but the pace. No one hurries. When I say that I live in Australia they look at me as if I have been deported. Gosh, we are far from Europe.

5 November 1957

Paris

My first day in Paris in the Musée d'Art Moderne.

I feel somehow that the classics belong to one's general education. I accumulated and put in store all I saw in Amsterdam, Rome and Florence, it will stew inside me.

I see Paul Haefliger who is deeply depressed. This is exile for him. He lives for the remote possibility that Annette will eventually leave her husband and children and join him. He left his wife, Jean, as soon as they arrived. He doesn't want to see anyone, lives in a furnished room in Montparnasse where he doesn't paint, only writes agonised letters to Annette who never answers. He seems to hate Paris, he is critical of filth and the rain. I only see the leaves of the chestnut trees glistening from the drizzle, the shiny pavement reflecting the light of the terraces. He crosses the road with blinkers hoping a car would do for him what he can't do to himself.

A letter from Jancsi, at last. It's been a fortnight. Every line warms me. It relieves my anxiety. Namely that we feel like stray cats who are abandoned in a strange place. I only hope the artist in me reaps some benefit.

No nation handles paint as appetisingly as the French.

Galerie Charpentier, École des Paris. It's stimulating. The tips of my fingers itch. Contemporary, yes, but distilled from nature. What a comfort. The new I see here and saw in Italy demonstrates abstractions that are not rigid and controlled, sliced and calculated, but free-flowing and personal. There is anarchy here too, but there is Hartung. Soulages, Mannessier, so subtle in colour they almost whisper like a breeze.

I pray that what I admire will take root in me.

On the rue Napoleon and rue des Seine every door opens to a gallery. Paul says: 'You can have Paris. It's raining. It's grey. It's dirty. These are not fifteenth-century houses, dear girl, they are only twenty-seven years old but no one paints over them.'

'What else is wrong with Paris?'

'Annette isn't here.'

I am lonely. One can't look at pictures twelve hours a day. It's raining and every drop which depresses me also gives me a feeling of joy about living in Sydney in the sun.

I am not a tourist, I have friends who live in squalor, who climb five flights in almost complete darkness to reach their rooms, and I have relatives in Maisons-Lafitte where I take the bus on Sundays. One has to face life. One can't only meet people who are clever and rich and beautiful.

At home they think I am having the time of my life in this city of light. But the light is only what I learn and experience. The light does not exist without shadow. Oh, these grey mornings. Mondays when the galleries are closed. I went to the flea market. Antiques. Iron bedstands. Altmoser glasses above old bidets. African sculpture, grandfather clocks and mosaic fragments from the thirteenth century.

Moya Dyring asked me for lunch. Cosy studio flat on the Quai d'Anjou. A bar, a dog, easels, north light and a view of the Seine. Moya who is about forty-five says 'In Australia I'm made to feel like a castrated cat. Here I am a woman.' She paints Paris, and every three years or so sells the paintings in Australia.

My cousin, Eva Kepes, came to my hotel room. We sat on the bed and she talked about how we live either in the past or in the future, when the only time is really NOW.

Paul and I have a silent pact, almost a barter. He comes with me to exhibitions and helps tremendously with his great range of comparisons. He places my impressions into ages, styles, movements and lets me find the connection. My part of the deal is to sit in coffee houses and listen to his desperate love for Annette. After three months he still waits for mail.

A letter from Jancsi. Every word drops on my soul with comfort and joy. He writes exactly what I had in my mind at that moment. There has always been a telepathy between us, and it now extends from Sydney to Paris. He writes that feelings get dusty in an old marriage, nebulous, taken for granted, and shine again after separation. His love helps me ignore the cold, the wind and the fog. I read and reread the letter when I'm freezing and lonely.

Paul is deteriorating. He jokes about his suicide plans.

17 January 1958

London

London is more like New York than Paris. It's vast, hostile, foggy, noisy, and the first day is depressing.

My cousin, Zsuzsi Roboz, had a one-man show in Bond Street. Her teacher, Pietro Annigoni, wrote the introduction to the catalogue. Zsuszi is beautiful and talented.

The galleries, after Paris, seem well-behaved and lukewarm.

Judy Barraclough's friend, the famous model, Barbara Goalen, sits for a portrait.

Mingi (Beregszász again) took me to René, Princess Margaret's hairdresser. I mean, he is a hairdresser like Dior is a tailor. Margaret takes him to Jamaica. On my right, under the dryer, sits the Maharani of Baroda, and the Duchess of Westminster on the left. Hanging on the wall are two Marie Laurencins and a Cocteau drawing signed, 'For the great artist, René'.

While he sculptured my hair, Barbara Goalen sang my praises, Mingi pushed reproductions under his nose and we talked of Modigliani. René broke his leg skiing in Zurs, leaps in the plaster like a dancer, yells 'But this is fantastic' and commissions me to paint a portrait of his wife, Hugette.

Mingi and Jirka took me for dinner where his clients gave me another commission. After three weeks of failure in London and three more weeks to go, suddenly this rush. I feel the necessity to grab a foothold again in Europe and somehow justify myself and my long absence.

I stay with Ibi in Queensway.

The telephone rings and says: 'Mrs Cassab? This is Peter Thorneycroft speaking.' The chancellor of the exchequer who has just resigned. 'Barbara Goalen was raving about you, and if you would paint me I would be delighted. I have time now, you see, as I am unemployed.' Five minutes later Hugh Gaitskell rang to arrange a sitting time.

This is four yet unpainted commissions. I won't paint any more, except of course for money. I wrote to Jancsi: 'My first three weeks were squandered. However, I've now cancelled America on the way home because I shall need the two weeks here to finish the portraits. What should happen if I get any more commissions? It's possible. While I wait for your answer I'll take what comes my way. If you write that I should not prolong, I will cancel them. Maybe the sequence of the fantastic events of the last few days will stop. However, three portraits are lots of Australian pounds. There is an agonising feeling of emptiness in my body and soul. I miss you. I yearn for the children. You are me and I am you and you must feel out of all this how confused I am.'

Ibi forced me to go to bed. She nurses me and feeds me and I need rest. Though I try to think methodically and to consider every day as only one day, still it is a tremendous effort physically and psychologically.

The talks with Hugh Gaitskell are fantastic. Even men in such high positions like to talk about themselves as private people. He told me how he changed from a university professor to a politician. My impression of the Gaitskells is of a middle-class family who have moved into a house too big for them. Dora cooks, the floor is grey, the carpet threadbare. Chrysida, the younger girl, studies in the dining room.

Thorneycroft's background is quite different. An elegant townhouse in Chester Square. His wife, Carli, is an Italian countess, very beautiful, polished, elegant. He sits in a white pullover with his arms crossed.

The longer I am separated from Jancsi and the children, the clearer I experience living in solitary confinement. There are no other humans on earth who can share my life except those three.

At the Gaitskells' for lunch. Interesting guests, the American missile boss, sentences like 'Mr Khrushchev told me' and 'No, Malik didn't tell me.' Gaitskell introduces me to Mr Pringle, former editor of the *Sydney Morning Herald* and now editor of the *Observer*.

Mr Pringle says, 'Not *the* Miss Judy Cassab?'

'Not *the* Mr Pringle?'

'You know each other?' Gaitskell asked.

'We have never met,' said Pringle, 'but of course, who doesn't know Miss Cassab in Sydney?'

I wrote to Jancsi: 'It would be my greatest wish for you to come over next time, because one can't sense the difference between the two worlds until one has returned to Europe. I won't make your life more difficult. But I would like you to make a trip too and look around because this much I see: here you can count on me too to earn a living.'

Lady Beatty told me about her life during the sittings. One of the most beautiful women in the country, she is divorced and desperately unhappy. She was in hospital in Switzerland for two years with a nervous rash which took almost her whole skin leaving the flesh raw. They saved her life with cortisone. 'I would like to work,' she said. 'I am tired of being a decoration.'

Jancsi's reply arrived. 'For one or two more commissions, do not stay. True, we could use the money but the children need you. If you think it's important for your career to stay longer, that I leave to your own judgement. I can't advise you from this distance.'

The problem is solved. I shall go home according to the original itinerary.

Jancsi's letter also says that if I have more commissions I should return in a year. The run of good happenings cannot just be luck. Once can be a coincidence, or two, or three, but such a number of coincidences doesn't occur. Maybe I am better than I thought.

Cancelling three more commissions, I simply had to accept another, which I finished in five sittings, in five days. It's Rixi Marcus, bridge champion of England.

Incredible last days, incredible things happen.

I am sitting in the plane at last, going home. I can't quite grasp the fact that soon I will fill my arms with my children and Jancsi. I feel very happy and very excited.

Sydney

The trip home takes fifty-six hours.

Sydney is beautiful. A thousand bays and a thousand hills and a thousand ships and the end of the world.

Dazed, I stumble down the stairs, see only the crowd in the dark, sense the direction of my family from wild shouts of 'Mum, Mum'. The children are hanging on my neck, tears are falling down my face. A bit to the side, silently, stands Jancsi. Just like when he returned from Russia after three years, he does not seem happy to see me. I only realise after a few days what he went through. He says, 'Jucókám. I dry out without you. No one to share with. I crave your love.'

I forced Annette to write to Paul. The first letter after two months. Annette plans to marry George Olszanski.

I haven't started work yet, and after a week I feel less at home than on the first day. Love and gratitude streams towards my selfless man, though it's a bit of a surprise to lose my independence. I get scolded for buying five *Heralds* with a big photo of me and the children in it. I had to cancel an ABC interview. 'Work,' Jancsi said, 'and don't live on the surface.'

I don't want to get old here.

14 April 1958

I go with Johnny to the Royal Easter Show. It is frightening how fiercely he wants to conform. We meet Australian kids, and his language instantly metamorphosed to slang. I sit on a bench surrounded by the waste of the showground and microphones selling the best washing powder and the latest hi-fi system.

It is a very rare occasion. Australia is to be represented at the Venice Biennale. They send twenty Percivals and ten Boyds. No one knows of Fairweather or Passmore.

Feuerring exhibition. To shout is good. But to shout in all forty-eight pictures is not. Every painting has a purple frame within a frame and he dribbles yellow through a hypodermic needle.

I wrote an article about the artistic climate in Paris. Took catalogues and books to the sketch club, and talked, and gathering my courage by hearing myself talk, I realise again that for myself, forms without any meaning are a very limited field of expression.

After the traditional cup of tea, I drive home. As I get out of the car, the smell of frangipani trees greets me. I like Sydney now. It's a lovely village.

12 May 1958

My life is lovely and satisfying. Sydney is the ideal place for executing germinating ideas. I am quite happy to live here when I see how they are fighting on the Champs-Elysées on television.

2 June 1958

Andrea took me to see the New York City Ballet. The music was Bach's *Violin Concerto*, Debussy's *Prelude to the Afternoon of a Faun* and Stravinsky's *Firebird*. Chagall designed the stage sets. His presence is in the Overture—the woman with the body of the bird, the bird itself, and the moon and trees, the upside-down face in the trunk of the tree. The audience giggled at this. In the second part there was a self-portrait of Chagall hidden in an orange-coloured tree. A Russian wedding. Chagall's bride, white veil, the menorah, the goat and the explosive bunch of flowers suspended in the sky above the sleeping village.

On the way home we were invited by Sir Charles Lloyd Jones to come home for a drink. So we drove up the driveway of Rosemont in the rickety Austin. Lady Lloyd Jones and Andrea discussed how it would be possible to collect fifty Chinese lanterns for the Hordern wedding. Sir Charles remarked it would be wiser to give the young couple a house instead.

Andrea said the newspaper might send her to Japan.

'Oh, don't go,' said Lady Lloyd Jones, 'it's so dirty.'

Her son: 'You didn't see the dirt, mother. You stayed in luxury hotels.'

15 July 1958

Daniel Barenboim, a fifteen-year-old prodigy, gave a concert. Brilliant. The Australian Opera's *Carmen*. Two singers from Covent Garden, the rest are young and talented Australians. Feuerring's decor.

I was introduced to Dr Evatt.

'Just this morning we were talking about you,' said the leader of the opposition. 'We liked your portrait of Frank Packer enormously. Where is it now?'

'In the garage.'

'Why didn't he buy it?'

'He probably couldn't afford it.'

Since I have begun work on abstract paintings, my favourite enemy, Oscar Edwards, became a supporter. He invited us to dinner and we saw the best private collection in Sydney. Pre-Columbian sculpture, Greek, Ming, African, Aboriginal bark paintings. Sketches, Toulouse-Lautrec, Cézanne, Klee, Rembrandt, Campigli, Kito, and fifty more. There were also two weak pictures. One was brown and white anarchy, the other purple line in an orange circle. 'Which of the two do you like better?' Oscar asked. Without hesitation I pointed at the brown muddle.

Oscar expressed a mixture of deep disappointment and elation. The orange circle was done by Hofmann and the other by a chimpanzee from the London Zoo. 'I am very sorry, Oscar,' I said, 'I like the ape better.'

5 August 1958

Jancsi is holidaying in Surfers. I shall sleep longer, and I shall have more time to think. But I miss him and feel restless.

I am painting the children's rooms, always a sign of escaping serious painting.

I am thirty-eight years old.

I panic again because I am going to England. Bronchitis, diarrhoea, fright. Nothing I can do about it. I'm mixed up. I love them, I love them. And still have this drive to go.

27 August 1958

London

The older I get the more my belief grows. Dear God, hold my hand. I started to feel pleasure the last two days. The trip won't be as long, and the world towards which I travel is more familiar than the first time.

Jancsi and I had a long talk on our last night. He is even more lucid, great, wise and good than other times before other events.

'You want much, Jucókám,' he said. 'You are a good mother, a good partner a decent human being. I want you to run your course. You don't go to earn money. If that was it, I wouldn't let you go—not for £600 and not for £6000. "Wouldn't let you" is the wrong expression, forgive me. Within your ambition, you have two ambitions. You want to be a good artist and study. And you want to be seen and to be known. Your vehicle is the portrait. It's not sufficient for you to be known in Weeroona Avenue. That's why you have to go. I support the foible in you, if one can call it a foible, because this is you within your other yous. It's your father in you, who could never make it. I want you to be a whole person, I want your life to be a full life. Whether you will come home with money and glory is irrelevant to me. Don't worry, control your anxieties, you are free as a bird.'

It's this freedom which makes me Jancsi's slave.

I enjoy and savour the voyage.

On my fourth day in London I got the commission from the Slotovers to paint Mrs Slotover. When I went to Hampstead to see them I felt honoured to be asked into the company of four Renoirs, van Gogh, Dufy, Picasso and Seurat. We had tea in the garden beside the pool. It seems as in a film, manicured and beautiful. She is fortyish, blonde and groomed, he about the same age. Three children, the oldest fifteen. They mentioned that the Israeli ambassador in Sydney is a cousin, and invited me for dinner on the eve of Yom Kippur.

Lunch at the Gaitskells. Dora hesitates, then asks me to come back on Friday to decide if she should sit in yellow. One week out of the eight is already gone but of course no one is in a hurry but me.

I was really downhearted yesterday. Will I be able to justify the hopes for which I flew across half the globe again? I would be more than happy to earn just the ticket and expenses.

I cheered up a bit in the evening because I went to René's to have my hair done and he offered me their flat which they keep for their Paris guests. I only pay the rent they pay. It's a lovely flat on the seventh floor, spacious and light, in Kensington. I feel lonely, things stagnate, I have diarrhoea. The days go by mercilessly and the decisive factor on which everything depends is luck. I painted René on Sunday. This is a present. I haven't been to the theatre yet. Zsuzsi Roboz took me around the galleries.

My main joy is to see old masters. English artists: considering how much more the sheer number of them is from which they can select, and especially if one views it without local bias, internationally, I think Australia has more talent than they have. And I saw mainly mixed shows with a lot of Sutherlands, Ben Nicholsons, Matthew Smiths, Pipers.

The first letter arrived from home, and suddenly London has changed. So has the weather. The diarrhoea has stopped and the tension lessened. It's frightening how dependent I am on them. I am less impatient. I walk through Piccadilly like a tourist. I look at the cashmere and silver of Burlington Arcade. I notice the red buses. I buy toys for the children.

Barbara Goalen is on summer holidays, the Leicester Gallery's Mr Brown is in Paris, and the Redfern's Mr Miller in Majorca. And my eight weeks melt away without miracles.

Zsuzsi takes me to a party at the home of the director of the Tate Gallery, Mr Rothenstein. He looks like Bartok's miraculous mandarin. In spite of a crowd and candlelight, the house feels chilly. Under mellow pictures, people sit on the stairs with their own bottles of drink. An excellent trio is playing. The mandarin dances with a good-looking woman of about twenty. Pseudo, quasi, bluff, spoof, everyone seems to show false colours.

Mrs Gaitskell's third sitting.

Peter Thorneycroft came up to see the few abstracts I brought with me. He liked them. His portrait hangs in his study and looks good. A letter from the Teachers' College in Sydney. When I get home they would like me to paint Miss Skinner, the principal, who is now eighty.

I showed those few paintings I brought with me to Harry Miller at the Redfern. I feel terrible, like selling electrical appliances or something. I feel hot and red and humiliated as I unpack them.

I took it into my hard head to get a show in London, and it's lunacy. They are booked out for years, and anyway, there are hundreds of better-known painters than me.

Harry Miller sent me to Waddingtons. If Picasso came himself in person, no vacancy, sorry. And then to Roland Browse's. I got home so depressed that a less tenacious bulldog would have given up. He, for a change, did not even like the work, it was too abstract for him. He was brisk and rude. Didn't wait to see all twelve, interrupted after five: 'I like it but I don't like it enough. No, no, I am sorry. You have to excuse me but I have an American client upstairs.' And disappeared.

Harry Miller sent me to the Crane Kalman Gallery after that but added: 'I told you it's a heartbreaking business, this, but what do you expect? Painters here wait for years and years and you want to do it in a month?'

He is right but I won't give in.

29 September 1958

This morning I went to the Crane Kalman Gallery with the folder under my arm. André Kalman already told me on the phone that he is booked out for years, but was willing to have a look at my work.

And it happened!

'Are you from Budapest?'

'No, from Beregszász.'

'I am from Mátészalka.'

'I have been to Mátészalka once, and I was invited to a chemist for dinner whose name was Kalman. He had three sons.'

'I am one of them.'

We were both so delighted about it (his whole family perished in Auschwitz) that as a matter of course, since he liked my paintings, he agreed to give me a one-man show in October 1959.

I got what I wanted. I earned my trip and had a show booked. I thanked God.

1 October 1958

I am pacing up and down in the flat talking to myself. I received a message from the Maharani of Jaipur. She wants to have her portrait painted. She flew home today, but wants me to drop in on my way home to Australia.

Jaipur is a place that only existed in a romantic drawer of my brain where it rested with the knights of Malta and Camelot.

One of her secretaries picked me up this afternoon, and took me to the apartment in Grosvenor Square. I raised my fee to £200 with fifty for expenses, taking into account the extra fare to Delhi.

Sitting in the train to Cardiff where the incredible Mingi got a new commission for me, I'm biting my nails wondering if I asked too much. There are both of them to paint, the maharaja too, and £450 seems an awful lot of money. Will they think I'm taking advantage of their wealth? However, I was thinking of raising the fee anyway, and what better place to start than Jaipur?

I worked on the Cardiff portrait and waited for the maharani's response. The secretary rang, 'Her Royal Highness accepts your offer of £450,' he said, 'and is looking forward to seeing you in Jaipur at the royal palace.' Unbelievable. I sent Jancsi a telegram: 'Commissioned to paint Maharaja and Maharani of Jaipur. Should I take it on or postpone?' While I painted in Cardiff Jancsi's answer came: 'Hurry up. They won't last much longer.'

30 October 1958

New Delhi

Two hours in Delhi where the sidewalks are sand. There are as many people as flies. It's as if I am watching a film of colonial times. New buildings neglected, oxen and Cadillacs, bicycles and saris, a mosque, a red temple. I watch a shouter as he dangles his feet from the end of a cart, beating an ancient drum.

31 October 1958

Jaipur

I have the feeling on the plane which takes me to Jaipur that this can't be happening to me. The plane looks like a car. There is a pilot and copilot, both bearded and turbaned. My suitcase and some parcels are sitting on the front seat, and this provides the only sense of reality. The stewardess wears a blue muslin sari, her navel is uncovered and she offers chewing gum.

A secretary and a driver meet me and whisk me to the palace. My room is of giant proportions. I have a marble bathroom and a ventilator above the bed goes round and round sharing my loneliness. Her Royal Highness gave me a studio where three people rush to supply me with newspapers, rags and coca-cola. She has been listed as one of the ten most beautiful women in the world and she seems bored.

While choosing her sari, I was able to see the bedroom of a maharani, and her dressing-table on which every object was gold. Everything is oversized, cream coloured, upholstered and fragrant. She drove me herself to a club, the sort of club which I thought existed only in Somerset Maugham's short stories. Moorish windows, embroidered ceilings, red leather bar.

We sit with Sir Frances and Lady Beak under framed photographs of the maharaja playing polo, the maharaja shaking hands with the king, the maharaja with his tiger trophy. 'I simply hate sapphires, they look black at night, don't you think? We bought the most gorgeous emerald in Delhi. I don't like the setting but I will have it remade in Bombay.'

1 November 1958

Breakfast on the marble terrace, fountain playing. Three servants serve me, a fourth brings a rose. My second sitting begins at ten, and in the afternoon I start the maharaja's portrait. He decided to sit in a polo shirt.

His majesty invited me to swim in the new palace, in the open swimming pool. Meanwhile I wash brushes, prepare the palette. Wherever I go a guard follows me. At lunch one slides the chair back for me, another puts a serviette in my lap, the third brings food, the fourth brings drinks. All wear white gloves and orange turbans.

A driver shows me Jaipur. Maybe the stench is reduced in a Rolls Royce, but it's still there. Pink palaces, hovels, cows, bazaars, dust.

Sitting in my studio I wait for Her Highness who is always half an hour late before she appears in a turquoise sari.

The maharaja told me how many children he has. They have a European education, speak English without an accent. He lived with a harem till the age of forty when he married his present wife and renounced all his other spouses. She wouldn't have tolerated them, he said. However, their religion doesn't allow divorce, so the women can't remarry.

2 November 1958

The hunting lodge where I am invited for a tiger hunt is another palace. Rambling, irregular, terraced, it dominates a lake full of crocodiles.

The interior has stuffed lions and tigers, bad animal pictures, and a billiard table. On the adjoining terrace are comfortable rocking chairs. The terrace below has a pool and a lawn.

The villagers were alerted that the ruler had arrived. As we drove into the park a crowd stood under the cacti, with camels and goats. People bowed before the approaching vehicle. Behind us two convertibles and two jeeps carrying a staff of pages, waiters, valets, grooms, maids and cooks.

Whisky on the terrace before lunch. I opened my mouth maybe twice, to say 'really', or 'ha ha'. Gossip about the Aga Khan, Duff Cooper's last party, a mad Lady Ashley who would not allow the architect to build a staircase in her double-storey house, Lady Mountbatten, African safaris, and what type of gun is best for shooting leopards.

The maharaja's motor boat was moored at the pier. It has to be silent so as not to disturb the animals. It is completely covered in blue velvet. A barefoot captain stands at the helm. There is a shooting tower on the other shore, five storeys high. Crocodiles pop up out of the lake.

By the time we had lunched, the stage was set for the hunt. At the back of the palace, where the mountainside falls deep into a ravine, there is an arena where a buffalo is tied to a pole. Spotlights are directed at him, until a tiger is lured by his smell into the brilliant circle. The tedious job of laying in wait is left to the servants, who will sound the alarm for us who sit eating a five-course dinner in the garden at a table loaded with crystal and silver. I found myself praying that the tiger would not make an appearance. We waited till 11 p.m. and he didn't come. Nobody knew I willed him not to.

3 November 1958

I worry about the maharani's portrait. She is too aloof. I don't make contact with her. Consequently the picture is stiff. It doesn't help that they think it's marvellous. Today she said: 'It's better already than Annigoni.'

At dinner, the maharaja said: 'You seem to enjoy our Indian delicacies so much. I enjoyed your paprika chicken very much too, when I was in Budapest at the Ritz. Wouldn't you like to cook us a paprika chicken one night?' I said I would be delighted and I was. After the sitting a cook-official came into the studio to ask me what ingredients I needed. During my siesta a knock on the door. The cook-official. How many pounds should the chicken weigh? How many pounds of flour for the nokkies? How many onions? 'For how many people?' I asked him.

'Twenty four,' he said.

How many onions do I need? How many capsicums? I never was too good at arithmetic and never did I cook for so many. 'Are you the cook?' I asked him. Oh no, he is the royal kitchen official and everything is locked, that's why he has to have exact details.

I wonder how this manoeuvre will work tomorrow.

4 November 1958

After working all day on the portraits I decided to go to the indoor swimming pool. A guard came with me.

The maharani's car came in the evening (his numberplate a golden sun in a red field) to take me to the kitchens. Rather to the catacombs. The chef is a eunuch and the only one who speaks English. Seven boys stood in a row, the ingredients were prepared on a medieval wooden table. I realised that to do things myself just isn't done so I told the eunuch to cut the chickens, a boy to cut the onions, another to melt the butter and boil water. I stirred the nokkies, gave it to a boy to work until it bubbled. Finally, all of them stood in a circle around me while I was cutting the nokkies into boiling water. By the time I finished this task for twenty-four people, the chicken was ready. I changed and washed and joined the guests.

A great number of sisters-in-law from Nepal (freshly out of the harem) sat like sparrows on a telegraph wire. They ate with their fingers, red gravy trickling down the wide sleeves to their elbows. I must say it was more successful than the portraits, and certainly more appreciated.

I bade goodbye to the palace and the airport which reminded me of the railway station in Beregszász. The tiny plane was familiar now. As I arrived in Delhi, the maharani, in a pink muslin sari, was waiting for me with a cheque.

22 December 1958

Blackheath

We have rented a cottage in Blackheath. We have three bedrooms, a large living room, an open fire, a piano, a radio and a good kitchen. Johnny has brought his friend, Peter Kadar, along. The boys play, great logs burn in the fireplace, it's raining outside and the fog makes the night white.

I am alone with the boys and they are wonderful company. I enjoy cooking.

24 December 1958

It's 11 a.m. and I haven't yet had time for a shower. If anybody calls this a holiday, I'll kick them in the shins. I can't grumble because all three children are angelically happy in spite of the cold weather. There is cocoa for breakfast, coffee, orange juice, bacon and eggs, toast. While I wash the dishes, Johnny and his friend play chess. While they have a bath, I clean the cottage. Peter wakes up. I start breakfast again. I lug heavy boxes from the shopping centre with coca-cola and watermelons. I wash a lot of clothes. I dry yesterday's wet shoes in the oven. I make the beds. Perhaps a hotel would be better, after all. Peter has a cold and a sore ear. We don't have enough warm clothes.

31 December 1958

Peter Thorneycroft came to us straight from Ben Gurion and Nehru, en route to Khrushchev. Being New Year's Eve we started with caviar on toast followed by paprika chicken. We showed him where Govett's Leap would be if one could see it for the fog. Then I did a still life, gave him paints and he settled down to paint happily.

26 February 1959

Sydney

No energy. I give birth to every picture amidst pain. No stimulus. February is steaming. Though I think I've improved over the last three years, reviews don't mention me. I have a one-track mind in which nothing else has place but the family and the pictures. No lunches with friends, no beach.

There is only the furious, nauseating, wet, killing heat.

I painted the steps of Victoria Street at the Cross with Ilse Tauber. I painted a lot of cranes and bridges and steel constructions and skeletons, and it isn't me. Me is vacant.

No commissions for months.

Invited for lunch to Barry Stern who decides he is a painter too. I hardly know what art is any more. My friends have all left and live abroad. The new ones, Gleghorn, Coburn are good but don't exchange ideas. There is a woman at Barry's who writes serials for the radio. It's depressing.

I go to the junk shop every week. It is much cheaper, and thrilling, to buy grandfather's photograph in a gold frame for sixpence or a horrible sunset in pink. I take it to pieces in the garage, give the picture a coat of paint (it's usually fine quality paper) and paint over the frame. Then I use the foundation and when the picture is finished nail it in the frame.

Mornings I teach now. Leslie Pockley comes and Phil Cullen. Only two or three at one time. It means three pounds.

I paint trees in Centennial Park. Something mysterious has happened. Perhaps I will find my way home. This place, this place. It still strangles me. In spite of what I think is a full life, sometimes I feel my soul starving and my spirit crushed. It's not possible to feed constantly on one's own self and mostly nothing comes from the outside. Perhaps it can't, because of the steamy heat. The city, the streets, the same every year. The same policeman stands on the corner of Park Street. His white helmet clearly visible beside the same palm tree and the walls of William Street.

I feel rebellion. I want to grow.

12 March 1959

I sent my pictures *Kon-Tiki* and *Composition* to the Contemporary's autumn show. The review said: 'Judy Cassab probes deeper than ever before in two gouache paintings. The special relationships of the shapes marks a considerable advance in her approach to painting.'

20 March 1959

I don't exactly know when this feeling began, but I realised I'm not good enough as an artist. How could I be good enough for London? It's agony to know that the figure—my forte—can't be placed in the style I'm developing. To know that six months are gone and I haven't created anything worthwhile.

I am tired.

12 April 1959

A glimmer on the horizon. I recognised something in connection with the paintings. My work doesn't fit into any category. It's not abstract enough for abstract and it isn't really figurative. I am jaded and bored with the accepted and official trends and their limitations. The great contrasts and the gestures seem to be from muscles I don't possess. But I have lyricism, mysticism and femininity.

To describe the way I work just now: the painting is built up in three layers. There is a very freely painted abstract foundation. The second layer is the theme, and the third phase seems to be the connecting work which interests me most: the planes which form space.

11 May 1959

I don't know how I paint, I don't know if what I paint is good or bad, but it's really painting—that much I know. The colours, like independent groups. The forms, moods take my brush away from me, they rule me, and when I want to force them into an object, they protest.

28 May 1959

Alice Springs

Finally on my way to Alice Springs. At Adelaide airport I meet Beryl Foster, a budding painter whose mother lives in Alice. She offers me a lift into town which is just what I wished for.

Alice Springs itself is where the bitumen dies and the hills breathe.

I sit on a chair on the pavement in front of the hotel. When I close my eyes the air feels like Semmering air. When I open them I see groups of Aborigines, the occasional Land Rover or station wagon crawling slowly along. Obviously no one is in any hurry.

I rang Rex Battarbee, the artist, and he immediately invited me over. He is *the* painter of the territory—which doesn't mean he is a good painter, but he taught Albert Namatjira and others. His house is a gallery open to tourists. His wife used to be a missionary, and is prim and proper. Rex has deep-set, blue, child-like eyes under bushy eyebrows.

He told me at what time I should go where, to catch the right light and how to approach the Aborigines.

Beryl came along and invited Rex to join us on a painting trip. I am so glad to have him, he knows all the tracks.

I borrowed a hammer, bought masonite and stretched six canvases. Now I sit in the 'ladies parlour' from where I have a good view into the pub. Marvellous characters.

Dinner in the dining room near the window. A young Aboriginal girl presses her nose against the glass. One can feel that this represents the 'big life' for her—the plastic tablecloth and roses, and the waitress who brings the inedible Irish stew.

I'm looking forward to the trip with Beryl and Rex.

We travel for hours and everything is gently red and pale emerald. The landscape envelops and embraces my spirit.

My first picture is of Standley Chasm reaching over the sky, burning orange. Another is a U-shaped trunk with little palms growing on both branches. Rex painted a tree with watercolours—meticulous. Beryl painted a photograph. At noon we lit a fire and barbecued some chops. I can hardly wait to go back and paint more. Of course it's thirty miles away and the road is corrugated by the wind. All around are strange mountains. Their sides are pinkish orange and dotted, and they have flat hats on top of ochre rocks. Sometimes, as if out of nowhere, there appears an Aboriginal stockman. He and his horse are deep purple. We see lots of kangaroos. They skip with grace.

I feel like Ali Baba discovering the treasure cave—or like a child in front of an enormous box of chocolates. I feel so greedy. I want it all. I have begun fourteen pictures in a week. On my first day I painted Mount Gillen four times, and each time I see different totemic designs. At Bitter Spring Gorge, a hundred miles away, I see hills which are like striped lollies, round green and pink ones. I painted a windmill with a kangaroo. I painted the dead trees which look like bodies after a battle.

The velvet darkness of the night is soothing. My eyes burn from the vivid colours of the day. I have never experienced this. Colour has always been something which pops up here and there in spots and hues, something on which the painter's glance focuses. Here, it's a physical force, hitting you not only frontally but sideways and from the back.

Beryl stopped the car and touched the ground. She rolled the red dust between her thumb and fingers. 'God, how I love this country.' I understand, for the first time since arriving in Australia, that one can love the soil.

At the local airport I was squeezed with six other tourists into a single-motor plane the size of a taxi. A boy stood beside the plane with a fire extinguisher in case we exploded. An ambulance stood in readiness and to make matters really simple, the cemetery is right beside the airstrip.

After an hour and a half we arrived at Ayers Rock. A small bus was expecting us and our guide, Howard. The shed where we were taken has plywood cubicles. There is a barrel on the roof to catch rainwater if it rains and there is a tap for us, for show.

We sat around a table waiting for the kettle to boil. I adore the place. Ayers Rock is a wonder like the Taj Mahal or Niagara Falls but this place doesn't advertise. The awe, marvel, fascination it inspired in me was like my first look at the Louvre. It's indescribable and impossible to reproduce. Full with legends, caves, murals, ponds. The surface resembles the back of a fish—the forms recall Henry Moore. I found the face of the Sphinx and Lady Godiva, and from further away at sunset it burns with such an intense orange I had to catch my breath.

I visited Bill Harney the guardian of the rock, who lives in a tent, writes books and cooks on an open fire under the trees.

We drove to Mount Olga thirty miles away. It hurts me that all these heavenly sights have pedestrian names like Emily's Gap, obscene to boot. They should be renamed something like Kilimanjaro, exotic and spiritual. Mount Olga looks like hundreds of cupolas and domes thrown into a mountain. A magic castle. It's not sandstone like Ayers Rock, but a conglomeration of coloured pebbles as if stuck together with cement.

We are waiting for the little plane which will take us back to the Alice. No such thing as a schedule. When we hear the noise, we go out to the airstrip.

When I tell about the happiness I knew in that shed which only has walls for the sake of elegance, but no ceiling, where a throbbing little motor generates electricity for a few hours, where the toilet is outside, most people will call me mad. I smile at my prejudice which made me imagine that this is some unfriendly or dangerous place, like dark jungle, wild creatures.

I understand Bill Harney better now. He looked at my pictures and, recognisingly, said: 'That's the valley of the great serpent' and 'That's the knee-knife', and immediately this was a reality.

Beryl took me to Simpson's Gap and Glen Helen, another phenomenon. First a three-hour car trip through desert country, alive with colour and form. At the river we continued in a jeep, which Bert Gardener, our guide, pushed till it found its way in the groove of the sand. We reached rocky country after that and a shallow pool. We left our jeep on one shore and waded through to the other where another jeep was waiting. Bert lugged a petrol tank from one vehicle to the other on the Glen Helen side. There is no other fuel supply.

I am not too happy in Glen Helen. A bloke called Jack cooks, washes dishes and told us to make our own beds with the sheets we brought with us. The shower is outside. You can see the bare feet of people showering (as in a Parisian *pissoir*) and it is freezing cold. I went out to have a shower. I took off my shoes and hung my coat on a nail and proceeded to turn the tap. It wouldn't budge. So I put my coat and shoes back on and went to Bert for help. He looked at me as if I was an idiot and said: 'Didn't you see the pliers?'

Back inside the shower, took the coat off, hung it on the nail, turned the tap with the pliers—no warm water. I let it run for a while, hopefully, little finger extended under the cold, but nothing. I gave up and returned, coat slightly moist.

Jack whistles in the kitchen, like the murderer in a thriller.

Next day we went to Ormiston Gorge, another miracle. I didn't even look at the majestic rock walls on both sides of this dry riverbed. Around me were surreal shapes in purple and pink and giant pebbles of the same hue. My eyes watered from the brilliance of the stripes and dots on those marble rocks, washed and polished smooth by a water that disappeared thousands of years ago. Let me add that the verticals and horizontals are so shifted that, although I knew I was straight, it gave the optical illusion of being crooked, and added to the unreality of the walk. Everything stretches around in abundance and magnitude and volume and quantity, massive, intense, noble, extravagant, like every part of the Territory.

July 1959

Sydney

I work on the Alice pictures. They have so much to say that I don't even stop to apply techniques, the brush is all I need. A new world opened up, not a limited one any more, a treasure house to which it is possible to return for inspiration and suddenly my immigration made sense, from a visual, artistic point of view as well.

The paintings catch the eye with their abstractness but looking into them, they make sense as objects, too. There they are, the dry fallen-soldier trees, shifting rocks, burning colours. And for the first time the figure is there without being conspicuous.

September 1959

London

I am here for my show. I arrived at 5.30 a.m., no one to welcome me of course, only a letter from Bridget Blundell to please go to a hotel, there is no flat available as yet. The customs agent telephoned three times, the pictures are in Liverpool and can't be moved without my signature. I head first to René. Of course I can have his flat again, but this time there is no china, cutlery or sheets.

'Does it matter, cherie?'

'No, no it doesn't matter at all.'

Bridget gives me sheets and blankets, Ági all the rest. The flat is a pigsty. I clean and call the plumber to fix the toilet, and shop, and arrange a carrier for the paintings.

I feel nervous, unsure, full of doubt. It's different to be a well-known artist in Sydney or a nobody in this giant city. Is it worth the whole effort, the strain and the risk?

The date of my one-man show falls at a bad time. It opens on 6 October and (something one couldn't guess last year) the elections are being held two days later. It will be difficult to get space in the papers, even should the critics come—which is pretty unlikely.

Since I arrived I need a sleeping pill, but pill or not, my brain switches into gear at 4 a.m. like a kaleidoscope married to a tape recorder. I worry about money. How much will the drinks cost at the opening? I have to share the cost of the catalogue. Will my pictures arrive in time? Will my famous sitters attend? Will the critics come and why should they when there are twenty-eight other exhibitions the same week. Will I have other commissions? I write about twelve letters a day—one doesn't ring people up after a year's absence.

4 October 1959

I finished the portrait of Jacqueline Siddeley. My feeling towards her and her husband, John, an interior-decorator and one of the most handsome men I ever met, is of special warmth. Knowing that it's by considerable sacrifice that I make the big jump here from Sydney, and seeing the way I try to make ends meet, they appeared one day with two cups and saucers and spoons. I can now serve coffee to my sitters in style. Very sweet. On weekends, I paint children, half-price.

Lady Beatty brought a commission: Stanley Donen, the film director. He has his sittings at 8 a.m. Ochre complexion, oily skin, slender, humble.

Henry Moore's *King and queen* at the Tate. Hands and feet beautifully modelled while his usual forms sit where the heads ought to be. Dualism and still convincing.

13 October 1959

On Monday I went to the gallery to see my paintings hanging and would have liked to tear them off the walls. Two characters came strolling in, critics I felt sure. I caught sentences like: 'First I was dazed with the colour, but one gets used to one's surroundings. There is no shape whatsoever.'

I struggled over the Brompton Road for a cup of coffee and felt like I was sitting at the bottom of a dark cave. What conceit, to exhibit in London, what did I need this for? I could see the bad reviews already. Horrible.

I don't remember much about the opening. There were two hundred people and either I am stupid or senile but I can't memorise names. It's different from Sydney as the critics come on the same day and reviews might appear a week or a fortnight later. Two pictures were sold at the opening.

Next day Eric Newton's review appeared in the *Manchester Guardian*. The incredible thrill of it. Though he writes about another woman in the same article, he writes about me: 'Her paint is positively rapturous.' He reserved a picture for himself. He actually wants to buy my picture!

The Rugby Museum bought *Chasm*.

London is slow. After the cool beginning, a few critics (all good) and articles here and there, the ball begins to roll. The Nuffield Foundation bought a picture for Oxford University.

Reviews in the *Times*, the *Observer*, papers in Glasgow and Newcastle, *Evening News*, *Daily Sketch*, and others. Then the television. The publicity helped enormously. I finally sold nineteen paintings.

They were sold rather in spite of the gallery, not because of it. It seemed to me like a brothel where they serve coffee in the foyer. I was the coffee. While Kalman sold his Matisses and Marquets downstairs.

A Mr Servaes, who bought *The green lady*, is one of the directors of Orient Line. He introduced me to Sir Colin Anderson, president of Orient Line. Sir Colin said I would be just right to paint the portrait of Princess Alexandra for the *Oriana* which she launched. Reproductions of my portraits (obviously from André Kalman) were displayed on a desk.

'Would you be able to undertake such a commission?' asked Sir Colin.

'Yes.'

'How do I know that I can trust you?'

'You don't.'

He smiled. And told me not to be disappointed if it doesn't materialise. The duchess has to give her permission and it has to pass the palace. If it passes, could I come in July? My fare will be paid, of course. Only one more thing: it's a secret. Talking about it would jeopardise the whole project. So I walked away, stunned, as if I had a bomb in my handbag. God, it's too good to be true.

30 November 1959

Sydney

I have learnt not to look for reasons for either depression or for happiness. Sydney is sleepy and passive and parochial, but I am happy.

I am painting the Lord Mayor and I don't care whether they kick it out of the Archibald. I just paint his triple gold chain and hope something ripens in me with portraiture. Maybe I can't carry it through in the Lord Mayor but I started the foundation which is worked with abstract form and I want to superimpose the figure linearly. Then integrate it.

I finished a large painting, *Arcades*.

A gallery in Rome and another in Paris want me to send in paintings regularly. Looking at it from here it will be impossible. I can't open a painting factory, what with a one-man show coming up at the Newcastle City Art Gallery.

The Orient Line wants some 'rough sketches' because the Duchess of Kent can't imagine my concept of underlying abstract shapes.

I never did so many studies for a portrait before. I did three pastel foundations, striving upwards. It's lyrical and mysterious. I did them on cardboard with enamels, then on top of that I glazed and printed. I asked the director of the Sydney office of the line, to please get me standing photos of Princess Alexandra. I then have a tall model stand in for me. I have to post this by airmail.

Last night I dreamed that the picture towered above me. I stretched and strained but could not reach the face.

14 December 1959

Peter broke his wrist. They gave him an anaesthetic to set it. No swimming all summer.

22 December 1959

The fact that the Contemporary Art Society left me out of their exhibition sent to London created such publicity that more notice was taken than if they included me. All three reviews of the show mentioned my absence. Others were left out too, and the reviews asked, 'Why do they send second-rate paintings?' A letter in the *Herald* answered that Cassab and Plate had successful one-man shows in London anyway, they are known there, that's why they were not included. The critic responded by asking whether success means an artist should be excluded? Isn't the standard of the exhibition the first consideration?

January 1960

The *Sydney Morning Herald* rang to know whether I am painting Princess Alexandra for the *Oriana*. 'Irresponsible gossip,' I said, and wrote to

London about it. I took a Goya book out of the public library to study his royal portraits. Started the large foundations. I am afraid.

The heat is unbearable and my brain is melting. The secret is oppressing.

February 1960

I try to analyse why I write so little when I am at home. Partly because 'I' is not so important to me now as when I was young. Partly because 'I' expresses itself more and more in paint and as this matures and deepens, so other forms of expression: talk, writing, even memory seem to become shallow.

Too many newspapers and magazines. The telephone rings too many times.

I'm reading Anne Lindbergh's *Gift from the sea*. She writes about women being the spoke of the wheel, life as the wheel, with centrifugal motion in which one splinters away if one doesn't consciously stop.

I have this struggle. Constantly wanting to decrease activities and even social arrangements in order to have more in common with the spoke of me. And as I do this, so comes the well-known feeling of guilt. Because if the 'I' takes more time it's neglecting something or someone else and one feels selfish.

Jancsi and I made a big decision. We declared that the television is our servant and not the other way round and it's forbidden now, Monday to Friday.

7 March 1960

New York

I walked along Madison Avenue, among grey heaps of snow shovelled aside and forgotten.

I woke at 6 a.m. and sleep fled as I remembered all the love I left at home, and as I projected forward into a pregnant, unknown strangeness— Alexandra's picture which nobody knows of. I pray for it to succeed.

12 March 1960

London

It's spring. I'm staying in Chelsea in a large house of serviced flats, among small houses with colourful doors and boxes full with hyacinths, violets, and narcissuses.

I went to the Tate to see Sargents, Reynolds and Renoirs, and to the National Gallery to see Gainsboroughs. There may be inspiration but nothing is a help. My canvas is my canvas. Servaes rings me every day to tell me to take care of myself. They worry I will break like a vase.

As I stepped into the large office of the Orient Line I saw the six-foot canvas which I'd prepared in Weeroona Avenue with its sunny background. When Sir Colin first saw it, he said he would keep it as an abstract.

The situation, however, seemed to be reversed. They were the ones who were excited. Servaes kept mopping his brow and Sir Colin said: 'Now just let's pray nobody gets ill,' and started behaving as if I were the star around whose person they have built a scenario.

On Monday we go to Kensington Palace, Tuesday I move into Buckingham Palace. The reason I have to stop working in the yellow drawing room by April is because General de Gaulle is moving in. Looking at it from Beregszász this is very strange.

21 March 1960

The office of the Duchess of Kent has the same atmosphere, even the same smell, as the Count Schönborn's castle in Beregvár and I didn't feel out of place. The smell is slightly musty, like old lace put away in attics, apples in winter, perfume and smoke.

23 March 1960

The sun is shining. I got there early to move into the yellow drawing room. I felt funny, standing in the crowd before the palace gate.

As I arrived a truck brought the canvas, a monstrosity of an easel and a soapbox for me to stand on. I was taken along a corridor which seemed to be miles long with pictures on both sides. Then we took the lift and started walking more miles on another corridor with red carpet. Queen Marys, Queen Victorias and battle scenes accompanied us to the yellow drawing room. How yellow the room really is was difficult to determine as dustsheets covered the furniture.

Three footmen helped me to redecorate my studio. The carpet was already concealed by a drop sheet, held in place with drawing-pins. They must have suspected I am a tachist who throws paint around. A screen was covered with hessian, a blessing, as it put the many objects out of sight.

There was a large easel, a moveable upright mirror, a table with paint spots (Annigoni used it). I was given a second soapbox, presumably so I shouldn't fall off the first if stepping backwards. There was a dais for Alexandra to rest on, a chair if she tired of the standing position. I closed two shutters on the south side because the sun shone in, and asked one of the pages to sit down so I could study the light. Below the window, just then, three golden carriages with six horses each drove out, a rehearsal for de Gaulle's visit.

My canvas in Buckingham Palace looked like a green man from Mars but I hoped that is why it will fit on the *Oriana*.

In Kensington Palace, Lady Moyra took me upstairs and introduced me to the Duchess of Kent. One could still see her great beauty. Her eyes were a sienna colour. She wore a brown dress. She extended her hand and I curtsied as I was told.

'I suppose you speak German,' she said. '*Ich spreche auch aber nicht so gut.*'

Alexandra looks younger than I thought she would. She has beautiful green eyes and a complexion like milk and roses. She is not quite as tall as I imagined and her nose is fine, not like in the photographs. I curtsied again.

They took me into the bedroom to choose the dress. Alas, the one I used for the underpainting was not there so I have to paint the apron from memory and cut the length a bit. Her only crinoline (which I need, again, to fill in the space) is pink. That has to be transposed into greys and blues and yellows. I asked her to wear her Biedermeier hairstyle.

Alexandra didn't want to wear jewels, her mother wanted her to. I explained that whatever she will wear will be only a blob of paint anyway on which I draw with a thin brush, like Dufy. They nodded that they understood.

'This is the first time I have ever been painted,' Alexandra said.

'I hope you won't mind if I come to look,' said the Duchess, 'as I paint myself and I am very interested.'

They didn't offer me a seat so I guessed this audience was meant to be a short one and took my leave.

My next appointment was with Professor Misha Black in the Research Unit Organisation of the Orient Line. He is doing the decor of the *Oriana*, He is Jewish, has an accent, is small, likeable, self-assured, puffs on his pipe and wears horn-rimmed glasses. I took my sketch, he pinned it on a wall with drawing-pins. They liked it. They discussed the frame which should be a thin rim of gold leaf. 'And what happens if a child puts his foot through the canvas?' someone asked. 'Surely,' Servaes said, 'not first-class children?'

Anyway, they decided the picture has to be sent to Paris to be stuck on board and the wood panelling around it has to have a different colour, and above, the light has to be crystal. They decided that if the royal family agrees, then Monitor Television should film me with the painting and Pathe Newsreel too, and the thing isn't even started.

24 March 1960

I went to Buckingham Palace at 10 a.m. to get into the mood of the place. I slipped on my painting shoes and waited. Alexandra was late, then we chose jewels. I couldn't care less but it's not every day I see fifty big diamonds. She changed into the dress and I was nervous. However, no young woman of twenty-two could have been more cooperative.

'May I talk?' she asked.

'Of course. I wish you would.'

'Do you smoke? My mother puffs away when she draws. Please do.'

We talked about everything from immigration to music, from the centre of Australia to Salzburg. The work went well; the only thing that disturbed me was stepping on and off the soapbox. She said at the end of the sitting: 'I used to think sittings were a waste of time. Now I see that I can help in creating something.'

Second sitting. I am waiting for her and I scrutinise the picture. I woke up at dawn and couldn't remember whether it had started well or not. Even now I can't judge if I did a lot, or not enough yesterday, and partly I wish she would be late and partly I can hardly wait to start and I know that I have to get the expression right before I can think of the hands holding the flowers and only then start on the real problem: to bring the same spirit into both. I feel I am terribly alone and only God will determine if I do something good.

Under my window there is the changing of the guard. A red circle and the avenue and a big crowd outside, looking in.

Critics as well as royal-watchers will tear the picture to pieces and I must not think of it.

The strain I feel is enormous. The tranquilliser is in my handbag but I don't dare take it lest it dulls my sensibility.

Alexandra asked me: 'How did you imagine I would be?'

'I was scared to death,' I said, 'that I'd only be allowed to speak when spoken to.'

'How did you get this commission?'

I told her the story.

'I didn't tell anyone and I choked on it.'

'I wonder why this is?' Alexandra mused. Is she really so naive? Does she really not know what her secretaries do?

'Maybe it's the Orient Line,' she said, 'who do not want to release anything before it's finished.'

'Maybe.'

It is Sunday. I have not seen the picture since Friday and I am going mad. Of course I have diarrhoea and a rash. I also sneeze a lot and worry. Disgusting hypochondriac.

I remember the part in Delacroix's diary where he states that the last brushstroke is always done by God. Dear God, please do the last brushstroke.

28 March 1960

The third sitting.

It was duly reported at the door of the privy purse that the flowers sent by the Orient Line wilted, and they want instructions as to what kind of a bunch the gardener should pick in the palace garden.

'Oh,' I say, 'just anything. A few irises, perhaps, spring flowers.'

I march on down the corridor, have a better look at *The crowning of King George*. What a horrid painting. Now I know where all the gifts are which the royal family has received through the centuries. There are glass cupboards, with ivory elephants, Buddhas, sailing boats and overwhelmingly, a tremendous number of clocks. A court clock winder winds them each morning as I arrive.

As I squeeze out new paint and work on my stage fright, a page comes in with the gardener to say that the irises are only buds, would tulips and narcissuses do? Princess Alexandra drops in fifteen minutes early.

I think the portrait is alive. I think the likeness is good. For the first time today, after realising this, I dared to neglect the face and concentrate on the arms and hands, shoulders, skirt, background. I darkened it a bit, consequently the figure is more prominent, and thus more academic. But the face is a face, isn't it?

I mentioned to her last time how attractive it would be to paint a thin line above her eyes with an eyeliner. I brought the tiny bottle and the brush and showed her how on my eyes.

'Oh, thank you, Miss Cassab, what a difference it makes.' Could she please try it? And where does she buy such an eyeliner?

'I'll give it to you,' I said. 'But then, first, let's wash the brush.'

'What for?' said the Princess. 'Spit will do.'

About the picture: 'But how can you do it? In so little time and no apparent effort.'

'The effort is there. Before and after. But if I want you to look relaxed I have to look relaxed.'

'You do. And it is a pleasure to sit for you. Are you sure five sittings wil be enough? Do you want me to stay all day on Friday? I could bring some cheese and we could have lunch together.'

30 March 1960

The night before the grand unveiling I only slept three hours and for the rest I scratched an itchy rash and ran to the loo. The Duchess of Kent was coming to inspect the portrait.

It was raining, and no taxis. I stood there with three small Alice Springs paintings which Alexandra wanted to see. It was almost 10 a.m. and still no taxi. I told the porter. He asked, 'Where to?'

'To Buckingham Palace.'

Three porters took the three paintings out for me, looking at me as if I dropped from the moon. The hire car cost a lot but it got me there on time.

Alexandra was sleepy. She went to change. While I prepared the palette, one of the older pages came in.

'I came to tell you, Miss Cassab,' he said, 'that we all think the picture is marvellous.'

At 11.45 a.m. the Duchess of Kent swept in, followed by the Duke of Kent and Philip Hay. I watched the duchess. No need for those sleepless nights. She said: 'Yes, oh, yes, but this is excellent. This is you.' Philip Hay echoed: 'God, this is exciting.' I almost cried with relief. 'Even the flowers,' said the duchess, 'are like the flowers they are holding. The expression is wonderful. May I say one thing? Couldn't the colour of the skin be a bit warmer? Sort of flesh colour?'

'Mam, try to visualise a Gainsborough or a Renoir skin. It has to go with the rest, you see.'

Hay butted in: 'I wouldn't touch it. It is perfect as it is, it would spoil it. This is the most unusual portrait I have seen—a very contemporary picture and such likeness.'

'Wouldn't it be a pity,' said Princess Marina, 'if this picture would not be shown before it goes on the ship?'

They whispered about it.

When I went home, I thought, this is too much for one day, too much for one person. And that wasn't the end of it. Mrs Fay, who took her portrait home yesterday, rang and said: 'My husband is delighted. He would like you to paint his portrait too.'

1 April 1960

Today was our last sitting. The duchess mentioned the triple portrait— perhaps we could start on 18 April when all three are together? And continue at the end of October when Alexandra returns from her tour of Nigeria.

In the meantime Alexandra's portrait is taken to the offices of the Orient Line. On Tuesday photographers come to photograph me with the painting. On Wednesday they make a print of it, order a temporary frame. We shall see. I hope my nerves can stick it out. This and the many commissions. Thank you, God.

6 April 1960

Alexandra is upside down as I work on the background and connect fragmented forms. The yellows are riper, more golden, and my inclination to paint a frame within the frame comes out in greyish mauves and blues, and forces the figure closer. I realised suddenly that into those freely-painted crystalline shapes the timid spring flowers don't fit in. I overpaint them.

Today I bought birds of paradise. And as nothing in the picture is truly realistic, why should the flowers be? So they are grey, white, blue strelitzias. I hope I finish it tomorrow. The frame is finished.

9 April 1960

For the very first time I talked with Sydney on the phone. It was 8 a.m. here and 6 p.m. there, but at least it was Sunday in both cities. Instead of feeling joyous and easy now, I am sad. I had their voices with me in bed, in my ear, touching me like a physical contact, in the present, and not hours away. The click came and Australia slipped back to the other end of the earth, and here there is London.

11 April 1960

I was invited to Kensington Palace. The Duchess of Kent greeted me. On the main wall, in a place of honour, there was my picture. She told me, a friend was startled as he thought Alexandra will step out from the wall. She added: 'Only Miss Cassab, why did you change the lovely flowers?'

'After I finished the painting, they just didn't fit in. They looked like poor relations.'

She laughed: 'You couldn't possibly change them again?'

'I am afraid not. I could, of course, but it wouldn't be right.'

They are going to let me know about sittings for the triple portrait.

13 April 1960

Jancsi's last letter is concerned lest I get swollen-headed now that success surrounds me, and he is not with me to counteract its effects. He wrote: 'I realised that I also am impressed by titles. Only, to me you are a duchess, a princess, a lady-in-waiting and a lady of pleasure in one person and for this I honour and love you.'

'Lady in waiting I really am' I wrote to him, 'as I wait for you year in year out on the corner of Bathurst Street. But still, I prefer the last mentioned role of lady of pleasure.'

I feel painted out. I sweat on the picture of the Panke children. I finished John Siddeley and that is a good one. Underpainted blue abstract pattern. Started Jocelyn Stevens yesterday on orange yellow grey shapes, while he speaks about gossip writers and scandalmongers.

During the sitting, with the permission of the Orient Line, I told Jocelyn that I painted Alexandra. He rang them, got reproduction rights for *Queen* magazine, which will feature a full page in the 27 April issue.

An evening at Wilfrid Thomas's, an Australian who became famous at the BBC. Theatre and radio people, cultured, pleasant. Diplomats from Geneva, from UNO and NATO, a few beatniks, and Josh White, the black singer with his guitar. He coaxed human sounds out of the instrument and sang well into the next day while we all sat on the floor around him, spellbound.

19 April 1960

Easter Monday. There can't be anything more lonely than a holiday, alone, in London. I worked on the foundation of the triple Kent portrait and it looks like the three kings, spiced with a bit of Byzantine. I walked in Hyde Park.

After a gallery tour in the afternoon, messages and telephone numbers galore from the press who probably got the release today. The *Star*, *Daily Mirror*, *Times*, *News Chronicle* and a newsreel which wants to film me next Wednesday. The Orient Line phoned to ask me not to move from home.

Five minutes ago Princess Alexandra telephoned that all three of them could sit for me on Friday. Could I come to Kensington Palace tomorrow afternoon? 'Have a look at the light in my room,' she said, 'and I will help you to push the furniture out of your way.'

Tomorrow I have to rush to Qantas (after Jocelyn's sitting) to change the booking so I won't feel hurried.

20 April 1960

There is a big photo in the *Times* and there are articles in *News Chronicle*, *Daily Sketch*, *Telegraph* and *Express*. Tomorrow at the BBC television at 9 a.m. and Pathe Newsreel at noon. Everything is so busy, I don't even feel excited. The BBC phoned that they will broadcast on shortwave to Budapest.

At 2 p.m. I carry the foundation of my *Three kings* in wrapping paper to Kensington Palace, and an easel too. Alexandra radiates goodwill, they all look for the best light and giggle. The Duke of Kent gives me a lift home.

22 April 1960

I had to get to Lady Beatty's early as at 6.15 there was a program on TV about Stanley Donen and after that, about me. As the only TV set she has is in the kitchen, we descended underground, where there was a Siamese kitten and the Duchess of Westminster.

After the program we returned to the upper regions, filled with orchids, pâté de foie gras, smoked salmon. Among the guests there were Margot Fonteyn and her husband, Dr Arias, Moira Lister, the actress, and the richest man in the world, Jean Paul Getty. Moira Lister's French aristocrat husband told me the reason they didn't go to Australia was that they heard there is nobody to clean your shoes there. He wanted to take his butler but was advised against it.

At Kensington Palace, Prince Michael and Prince Edward are pushing the heavy couch, Michael dropping it on his brother's foot. They are undisciplined this time, their mother goes in and out of the room, I can only block in their heights and colours. I return at 2 p.m. for Prince Michael, a nice, shy eighteen year old. I have to try hard to expel the worried frown from his brow.

26 April 1960

I spent the weekend in Switzerland.

Today I went to Kensington Palace for Prince Michael's second sitting and Alexandra's first. She starts by commissioning a portrait of her mother. 'There were many painted of her, but none really her. You must paint one that will be so good that I can take it into my own home when I marry.'

Agnews will show the picture on Monday.

28 April 1960

Hairdresser in the morning. René and the staff open champagne in my honour. *Queen* magazine appeared with my photo on the first page and a full page with Alexandra's portrait and the story.

My final booking is for 10 May. I wrote to Jancsi and the boys that from then on, princesses can drop from the sky, I'm coming home.

In Piccadilly and Oxford Circus in front of the cinemas there are huge photographs of me painting Alexandra's picture. On Bond Street, before Agnews, there are posters of it.

6 May 1960

I paint the Duke of Kent in my room in the Nell Gwynn House. I ask him about Germany where he is enlisted. He doesn't react much, except when I played some music on the radio. That cheered him a bit.

Yesterday Atalanta Fairey came with her picture which I have just finished, saying that she usually has her mouth open and it's closed in the portrait. Could I open it? While I tried to do this, they commissioned me to paint Richard Fairey. I can't do it this time, as I'm going home next Tuesday, but in October . . .

They went, Prince Michael came. Sweet kid, he is friendly and talkative now, tells me about the fantastic ball they had in Buckingham Palace last night. 'But I didn't know anybody there.'

To the Thorneycrofts to watch the wedding of Princess Margaret to Lord Snowdon. The strange experience was that these people in this room spoke about Margaret and Tony the way I would comment on Mrs Schwarz or Juliska, should I see them in a home movie.

We watch Margaret making her way slowly towards the altar. She doesn't dare to tilt her head. René has built a tower of hair on which rests the crown. Like eastern women carrying water jugs.

18 May 1960

On the plane

I know, things can't go all smoothly, but I feel I spoilt the third sitting of Alexandra's portrait. I shouldn't have painted her en-face as her chin is weak that way. I tried to correct my mistake and now it looks tortured. This sitting was postponed twice and finally she came one day before my departure, which is not the best psychological moment. I told her previously that I would like to take the picture to Sydney with me to work on it. It presented a problem in protocol. This could only be allowed if, for example, the face was to be embedded into the structure— like a virgin oval emptiness. Like I have done in the large portrait.

Philip Hay rang me on Tuesday. The Duchess of Kent decided I could take the picture with me. She would like me to take time with this and not to do it under pressure. As long as I keep it quiet.

On the last day I took the triple portrait off the stretcher and rolled it up. I behave with that narrow roll like a detective, peeping behind the curtain in the plane every hour to check whether the roll is safe.

I don't feel at all. I am so tired from these last few days. The only thing I know for certain is that it will be good to embrace Jancsi and the boys, and it will be good to live ordinary days and be happy with each one. One can't live in such high tension for long.

20 May 1960

Sydney

Warmth, light, belonging. The telephone rings. Letters, telegrams, orchids, oysters, black coffee. Friends, sleep. Changes of plans. I cancelled the one-man show in August as I hardly have any paintings left.

Jancsi promises he will come with me to Alice Springs in August. I can paint plenty then for the one-man shows in Sydney and London.

10 June 1960

Stagnating. No inspiration. Jancsi says it's because I don't paint from nature. He is right. Desperately, racking my brain, I stand in front of the empty canvas and feel defeated. Though I have my own forms, colours and style, they only fill with excitement if I transform something not when I invent.

I get my ticket to Alice Springs. Jancsi can't make it but insists I go.

I intend to do the future Alice Springs paintings differently to last time when I approached them with a white canvas and poured on riotous colour, unplanned. I now plan. The subject will come on top of existing constructions and all that which I know would gain new direction. But what I'm doing now, and what most painters would consider the final aim, the abstract recipe, the cottonwoolly dark forms running out at the edges with some strong emphasis of brilliance at strategic points, my long triangles which somersault on top of each other in a veiled, transparent manner, it all seems like woodchopping to me now. I need the subject to come from outside. Surrounding subjects, the vase, the flowers in a room, fruit, guitar, don't interest me now.

13 June 1960

Painting two portraits, in Canberra again. I work all day and it's still restful. Before and after sittings there is nothing but books and country. One can't even hear the children as they kick a ball about half a mile in the distance. The only event is a horse opens a tap under the barrel and the drinking water spilled on the grass. And a bird got caught in the telephone wire.

It's almost frightening how easily the portraits paint themselves. Too much routine. The Dutch chargé d'affaires was here and commissioned me to paint his wife and three children.

15 June 1960

Last night Peter, dear soul, gave me a piece of his mind.

'You have an obligation as a parent, and I think you leave us too often.'

Today, in bed with a cold, feeling sorry for myself, I search deeply. Peter may be right.

I feel like dry soil waiting for rain. For something to return which seems to have gone. I don't paint. Perhaps this way the vessel fills.

18 June 1960

Peter's problem with my travels came up again last night.

'You know,' I said, 'lives are different. I can't help it that I was born an artist, and that this leads to a different way of life than the average family.'

'Mum,' said Peter, 'I didn't mean what I told you. But what is so frightening is that I'm getting used to you not being home. Sometimes I don't even miss you.'

'Peter,' I said, 'you must not see me as a flighty apparition ready to disappear at any moment. You have to know I am like a rock and I shall be here for you until the day I die.'

'I know, Mum. I guess I say these things because I want to hurt you.'

'That's natural and human. You want to punish me for my absences.'

25 June 1960

I think about painting. Ten years ago it was comparatively easy. One painted fruit or landscape.

It is hellishly difficult to make the breakthrough into abstract but once one is in it and found one's handwriting, this becomes easy, too. It's really hard *now*. I want to amalgamate the two. And I don't want semiabstract. I want an organic whole where nothing dominates, where the millions of molecules I collected are one. I know it's in me. But it is formless and I have not the power to give birth to it.

7 July 1960

I imagine I'm Greta Garbo. I want to be left alone to concentrate on my family. Partly I have a slight case of paranoia because nobody leaves me alone and I'm going to Alice Springs in a few days time. Since I returned from London I have not painted anything but portraits.

Jancsi has never been more loving, the children are so wonderful. Do I have to be impatient with *them* because bored socialites, the home for the aged, the synagogue, the Albury Art Society and a new gallery all want something from me?

17 July 1960

Alice Springs

I was afraid that this visit to the Alice might turn into a soppy love story. Will I find her the way she lived in my memory? Will she generate the same excitement in my tired head as last year? Will I be able to paint again?

I've no idea what it is about this country, but after two days I recharged and no matter where the bus takes me, the subject is waiting. It's not the impact, shock, wonder, rather a friendly welcoming. In two days I have painted two large canvases and two paintings on paper, and I can hardly wait for tomorrow.

I'm happy to live at Cloudy's. I had my first glimpse of her at the airport, the humour in her myopic eyes behind the thick lenses, her tall bony frame and thin white hair—I wouldn't have changed her for a luxury hotel. Although I can't imagine anyone of my crowd living here. Thank God I'm not spoiled by palaces.

Evenings, after work, we sit in the kitchen around the table, with Cloudy's other tenants. A road builder, a stone cutter and my friend of last year, Frank, who owns the local garage. I wash dishes for Cloudy then head for the shower which I can only start by climbing on a chair. The loo is in the garden.

In the mornings, as I put foundation on the canvases, chickens run around my feet and James, the dog, keeps me company. Lance Rust calls for me in the little truck and I paint Standley Chasm for the second time. (The first was bought by the Rugby Museum in England.) We have steak and billy tea, cooked in the aroma of gum leaves.

I don't know what day it is, only that I have four pictures and four sketches and there is nothing else only kangaroos and red dust and the beauty of the land.

I don't know what or how I'm painting but images crowd on me and long triangles appear and they are juicy.

Towards Santa Theresa Mission, sitting beside Lance Rust in my usual place. His bride's photograph is under the steering wheel. Unlimited variations of visual wonders. White cockatoos fly in droves, the underside of their wings pink. The mission itself is one of the most depressing sights I've ever seen. Cement cubes for houses. Aborigines are not able to shift and take to the bush. It is awful how they force this nomadic tribe into concrete. I find it painfully wrong that they have a horrid place near Alice where they live and where nobody is given the dignity of work. They will raise a generation expecting handouts. We might just have our own Mau Mau problem in another decade.

Frank took Cloudy and me to Glen Helen for the weekend in a Holden station wagon. We started off last night and drove in the bush for three hours on the red track. Kangaroos jumped through the black backdrop, and mulga trees alternated with emptiness. Frank was a drover here for twenty years and I felt safe, knowing he navigates by the stars like Winnetou from the stories of my childhood.

Later he lifted the back seat out of the Holden. It had five gallons of water, seventeen gallons of petrol, an esky with cold beer, a case of food, lots of blankets, a mattress, and my canvases and gear.

At the foot of Mount Sonda he drove off the track to camp for the night. Cloudy and I even got pillows. We stretched out and slept.

I woke to a glorious morning. I know that to sleep under the stars in a forest in Europe would be just as wonderful, but who lives like this? The difference is that since we left we haven't seen one human being, and that for a hundred miles ahead and a hundred miles behind there is not a single house.

Yesterday as we drove with Mona I stopped her before an erosion. It was neither beautiful nor green nor red, only fantastic forms. As I slashed it on canvas it became grandiose and abstract and expressionist. Gigantic, because there was nothing in scale beside it to indicate its actual size.

At 10 a.m. we reached a road sign which said Glen Helen but failed to point into any one direction.

The road got worse. In parts it disappeared completely with no trace of tracks, then it was dry creek bed up and down again. For two hours we thought we were lost. Cloudy said: 'Frank, this is not a bloody endurance test. If you don't know where you are, let's turn back on our own tracks before the wind erases them.'

Suddenly I saw a rocky hill on our right, just as Frank took a sharp left turn. And I, who get lost in Pitt Street, yelled, 'Stop. Let me see what is over the hill.' I jumped out of the car, climbed the hill. There was a jeep. 'Isn't that Bert Gardener's place?' I asked the driver.

'That's it,' he said.

I never felt less like painting than I did at that moment, but since the only reason they both came was for me to paint the rocks at Glen Helen, I sat down in the cruel sun and started to work.

I was scared to drive back on the same route, like a mountaineer who doesn't dare go forward or back. We camped for the night, and the next morning was bathed in gold. It was cool and I painted. White grass, deep crimson earth, mauve Picasso shapes, black trees.

I could have cried in the late afternoon when I had no strength left, and no daylight. We passed ant hills, a fantastic sculpture gallery larger than life-size. There were female figures and lovers and whole family groups, and it was all in the pink of Roman houses. My eyes hurt from the colours.

Two rock abstracts were born there, and a sketch. With these I have fourteen paintings now. As I only brought eleven canvases from Sydney, I bought the only existing roll in Alice and paid double. To make sure I don't run out of material I underpainted two masonites as well because Mona and Des are taking me by jeep to see new hunting grounds.

I got up at 5 a.m. yesterday. Mona took me to Corroboree Rock. It was still starry. It's a sacred place of the Aborigines. Twenty-five miles only, Mona said. Sleepy and freezing, I blessed each minute. The rising sun picked out orange peaks like a great conductor pointing at various musical instruments. Desert trees were etched on the sky. Instead of exhausting the subject it keeps growing. I'd like to return to the ant hills. I'd like to return to the trees. Corroboree Rock is smoothly terraced, deep grey and pink.

We drink our coffee, I work and teach till lunchtime.

While I make new foundations in the afternoon, I hear Cloudy communicating with her different animals.

Mona is busy so I order a taxi, and Cloudy and I go out to the Wigly. The Wigly sounds like a harmless Swiss picnic spot. It has a waterhole, with no water. And it looks like the photographs sputnik sent down. I am painting it in mauves and browns, keeping in mind not to explode oranges as on the last trip, but it's almost impossible. And irresistible. Guiltily I dab in one glowing spot.

Danger somehow lurks in the background everywhere, as in a thriller. One knows it's fiction and it's still hair-raising. The driver says he will take us home on another route, and as he turns the car into hairpin curves, moonscape, stones, rocks, he tells us that this is the old road. No one uses it nowadays. Very soon he proves it. We get bogged in a dry creek in deep sand. We get out and push. The taxi won't budge.

The driver lets the air out of the back wheels with a hiss. 'She will be gripping better,' he says. Indeed she does and clutches the road to firmer ground. He then pumps the air back with a bicycle pump. We progress dead slowly, tilting, falling on our noses, hitting our heads on top, stuck in sand again. Air out again. There I stand, in my thriller, a cream-coloured Holden, like a hundred others. And still, I have palpitations.

Around us the Devil's Marbles, Mount Gillen shocking pink, blue giants on the right and on our left hundreds of empty beer cans.

29 July 1960

I hired a comfortable large old Land Rover. Des and Mona brought all
the rest. How ignorant I was to think that sleeping in the bush would
be uncomfortable.

As we camped for the night, everything was planned with terrific
know-how. Des found a place with as few ants as possible, plenty of
wood to light the fire, soft sand to put down our sleeping bags, and the
Land Rover served as a windbreak. The fire lit up the landscape around
us. We grilled our steaks and drank icy beer.

I fell asleep with the largest firmament and closest stars I have ever
seen and woke up when the dawn painted my eyelids pink. Incredible
peace. This time of day is called 'piccaninny daylight' in the Northern
Territory.

Mona had no difficulty getting permission to enter Hermannsburg
Mission. Her father was a stockman there, and she was born there. The
missionary is a kind young man. How he stands the stench, the filth,
the dust and the despair, I don't know. Painting is out.

On the way to Palm Valley we met black lovers on a pony, their feet
almost touching the ground.

We reached the amphitheatre by noon. Round, terraced, crimson, tall
and fantastic. No roads at all, but Des cranked the magic button and
the Land Rover mastered gullies, steep rocks, like a charm.

We painted, I taught Mona. We reached Ellery Creek and settled
down for the night in sand as white as Bondi Beach. Fire, grill, hot
black coffee, whisky, snuggled into the swag under the stars.

5 November 1960

Sydney

I received a telegam from Buckingham Palace to say that Alexandra is
free from the fourteenth.

Jancsi said that I should go, even if there are no other commissions.
Even if I only go for two weeks.

11 November 1960

Cairo

The pilot's window is broken and we spend twenty-four hours waiting for a new one. I am delighted because I would probably never have had the opportunity to see Cairo otherwise. I have a corner room in the Nile Hilton, with a terrace on the river. Qantas rented a bus and took us to the pyramids and around the city. Fantastic dinner, piano in the bar, and walk on the shore of the Nile. Thank you, God.

I have painted two portraits for the Archibald—Rapotec the artist with his two butcher-like hands on his chest as if saying '*mea culpa*', browns, blacks, blues. And Cyril Ritchard, the actor, gesticulating as if reciting, his feet like a ballet dancer's before the jump. This painting started well, the velvet jacket played. Then I overworked the face and now there is the usual schism.

Ritchard behaved like a prima donna. Would I put a record on? He stands easier with music. Not this one. The other one. I bring coffee. Could I shut the music off? He can't drink with the music on. Could we eat our lunch on the verandah? The sun is so nice. In order to get onto our balcony one has to cross a long corridor, our bedroom, and Johnny's room. Bother. With trays and food.

Since I bought a projector I often screen a slide on canvas and draw on it with black and white. I can do this with artificial light. Next morning I give it a layer of Indian ink and use the hose on it like a brush, spraying where I want a pearly grey, putting pressure on where I want white. Where I have left the paper out the previous night, the Indian ink remains black. It's easy to forget what it was that made me start it. A rock formation can look like the last judgement.

I suppose it's necessary for everyone and good for the soul, but I received a terrific blow. John Reed, director of the Museum of Modern Art in Melbourne, arrived in Sydney. Elwyn Lynn wrote to him some time ago that I was planning to have a show in Melbourne. He replied that my fame there is one of a fashionable society portrait painter. Elwyn made me send him three reproductions. He replied that these were very good, he would like to see them in colour, and wanted a meeting. I invited him for dinner with the Lynns.

When I spread out the paintings in the other room, there wasn't one, not a single one which would have won, not his approval, but even his forgiveness. He talked down to me as if I were a beginner. 'Why do you paint?' he asked. 'What is it that you want to convey to the world? What is it that no one painted before you?'

A Savonarola. My stomach turned over I fell into such gloom. It's quite true, I don't want to convey anything to the world. Why do I paint? Because I have to. Because there was never anything else I wanted.

I think a lot about it. Perhaps it's not enough that I draw well and that I have good colour sense and have found my own handwriting. I have no direction. I am schizophrenic with my portraits and my rocks.

Dear God, please make me a better artist. I am afraid that as a human being I'm not deep enough. I have no philosophy. I am superficial and want to enjoy life.

Of course by Reed's standards (Drysdale and others are waved away with a flick of the wrist) everybody can drop dead. Still, I am depressed. No doubt I thought myself a better artist than I am.

13 November 1960

London

I am in London with only 100 pounds, counting on getting paid here by my client in Cardiff. They don't have the money because they are building a house.

I start painting Mme René, as a present. *Navigare necesse est.* Alexandra comes on Friday.

Mathieu exhibition. Tremendous impact. It is impossible to judge or value Mathieu by one painting. But a one-man show is his statement. It is the first western calligraphy I've seen. Even if I was unaware of his exhibitionism (he painted publicly in Tokyo for instance, major canvases in fifteen minutes) it's evident that these pictures could only have been painted with urgency and fury. They are rather like clashes with the haste and confusion of everyday life. The catalogue explains that it is a kind of braille for the benefit of those who are able to see. However, that speed should be essential and that it requires utter concentration, while the conscious mind is blank, is a theory which one painter or a group of painters built for themselves and which isn't necessarily valid for others. There is altogether too much background talk.

The wind is blowing furiously outside, it rains, it's hostile and grey and heavy as lead. What is happening to me? Am I corrupted by last time's success?

22 November 1960

Alexandra's second sitting is going well and we found our way back to that amiable atmosphere interrupted in May. She fell asleep three times, her eyes are unfocused on the picture and I'm getting cramp when I touch it.

I am mortally lonely, can only pray. Why am I such a coward just now, not daring to make vital changes? It's too sweet, too pretty, not enough character. Now I can't complain of not feeling. As if woken from a faint, my self returned and so did my palpitations. Her mother dropped in, wasn't enchanted, said Alexandra's head is too large beside the boys' heads. God, help me.

I bargained for one more sitting with Alexandra. On the fourth I thought I got it, and felt deep relief, and later I was dissatisfied again. Torture. It's too overworked by now to be able to take even tiny changes. I discovered in the night that, to my horror, all the features tend to concentrate towards the mouth which makes it look like a goat. Maybe I had a nightmare though because Mme René is enchanted. I have three days until the next sitting and keep it turned to the wall. It's my only chance to see it fresh on Tuesday.

I get the *Express* in the mornings. I look excitedly into the horoscope which I know is a fraud.

The publicity question worries me. I paint half for nothing and if I don't even get the benefit of public relations, why on earth did I come? When Alexandra and her mother left the other day I took them as far as the lift. I met a lady who remarked what distinguished visitors I have. The porter also knows and asked me which one of the two I paint. I mentioned it to Alexandra.

'I hope it won't get into the newspapers,' she said. 'For your sake.'

It almost sounded like a threat.

The Royal Society of Portrait Painters exhibition is much worse than our Archibald. Waxen images out of Madame Tussaud, *Esquire* title pages, a few weak imitation Renoirs.

27 November 1960

Against my principles, I took a tranquilliser this morning to help me through the Duchess of Kent's first sitting. She came with Alexandra and the duke who needed one more sitting. Prince Edward was in better spirits, his eyes were open, I put a tie on him and made his hair looser— to the satisfaction of all. Alexandra left early while the duchess whiled away time with crossword puzzles. Then she sat and the duke continued the puzzle. It was a bit disturbing to my concentration—'what is a siege with three syllables?'—and I think the sketching was too cautious again and it disturbed me to have only one hour. But it looks a good beginning. She is a charming woman, and wise. Under the bone structure there is great beauty. I have to be careful not to paint her young. This was a Sunday. I spent the rest of the day being lonely.

1 December 1960

The second sitting of the duchess became old, hard, elegant, and can't be left as it is. For this I have to wait till the eighth. Prince Michael arrives on the thirteenth. Mme René's portrait is finished. It's very good. I started Jill Slotover in turquoise and burnt sienna.

Meanwhile I'm kept humble by the fact that no one thought of inviting me to a gala lunch on the *Oriana* before her maiden voyage.

Unexpectedly, I heard that someone on television had talked about my paintings, about my composition and colour sense. I was told that it was Sir Kenneth Clark, one of the most important critics in England. It definitely soothed the loss of self-confidence.

Lady Beatty married Stanly Donen, the film director. They invited me to their country house for the weekend. It has a thatched roof and was built in the fifteenth century. It has many bathrooms, central heating and a butler, a maid, a cook, a driver, a Rolls Royce, a station wagon, two sheepdogs, a great dane, a fox terrier and two children for the weekend only, of course.

8 December 1960

Third sitting of Princess Marina. Trembling, but I did not follow Jancsi's advice: 'Paint her beautiful.' If ever this picture is exhibited somewhere, it will not be a Madame Tussaud for which I have nothing but contempt. Kokoschka is less kind to his duchess than I am to her, and even for this small concession I am sorry. At least the bitterness is there, the ruins of her beauty, the elegance, the half-smile. I hope, oh I hope it's really good.

It's only light enough for painting at 9.30 a.m. and the sun goes down at 3 p.m. and I panic about whether I can finish everything on time.

Two new commissions: Mr Wilder through René, and Ronny Driver through the Siddeleys. In September, I said.

The last glimpse of London before Christmas. The city is dressed like a bride. Large illuminated snowflakes hang along Oxford Street, and on Regent Street there are angels which catch the rain and as they overflow they pee on the throng.

I shall reach home in the deluge.

Middle East airlines takes me to Beirut.

I am dead tired, have an awful cold, and not for one minute have I felt such happiness in the past month as I feel now, approaching Sydney and my three boys. I feel warm and secure.

1 January 1961

Blackheath

We are here for ten days. Exhaustion shows in not being able to sleep. I am so lazy the whole day that I don't read or write or move out of the park. Jancsi brings me breakfast in bed. It's 11 a.m. before I venture out to the easychair near the pool.

6 January 1961

Oriana

I am on the *Oriana* for a cruise with my painting of Alexandra and my friend, Tubi. Tubi and I share a cabin. We stood out on the deck, seeing the Harbour Bridge on our left and the Opera House under construction on our right. It held the magic of a first happening. There are rich graziers and our Hungarian crowd, saying: 'Well, it's not the *Mariposa*.'

Having been invited because of Alexandra's picture, I am interviewed in each port. People get photographed in front of it like they do in Venice in front of St Mark's.

28 January 1961

Sydney

I teach the new housekeeper to cook.

Another great change in the family is two new front-door keys, cut specially for the boys. Sometimes they come home from the dance later than we do.

We are now 'not wanted' on Bondi Beach because, they say, it's only for young people. I think of Bondi Beach now with some nostalgia and some relief—when I had to take them every day and watch which wet head popping up from under a wave belonged to them.

10 February 1961

I won the Archibald on 27 January. Jim McDougall of the *Sun* telephoned the night before. 'Judy,' he said, 'how do you spell Rapotec?'

'Why? Are you gazing into your crystal ball?'

'I can tell you this much: there are two finalists. Pidgeon and you.'

I had no special hopes till now, because I haven't won for nine years, so why now? After the call I got excited. The radio usually announces the winner on the midday news. Nothing. At 12.30 p.m. the radio announced the jury had postponed the decision for one hour. They were quarrelling over us.

I was sitting on the verandah in shorts and a bra under the umbrella, for it was a hot day, and typed a letter. At 12.40 p.m. Daniel Thomas rang from the Art Gallery of NSW.

'Judy,' he said, 'you have just won the Archibald Prize.'

I screamed and sat on the floor. Peter fell on top of me and we rolled on the carpet.

Champagne, then we went to the opening at the gallery. Positioned in a semicircle around my picture were television cameras, film cameras, photographers, cables, wires, electricians, spotlights and a great crowd and suddenly I stood in the centre, not believing it.

When I came home, the flat was full of flowers and telegrams. Everybody who ever bought a picture from me sent a letter. I did nothing but answer each one for two weeks.

A Gladys Archibald wrote: 'My uncle would have been so pleased.'

I got commissions from the minister for the navy, the synagogue and Dr Williams, in New Zealand. I have to be easy on the portrait sittings now, because the Sydney show opens on 26 April and I was invited to send in to Brazil's Biennale.

I paint more than I ever painted. Two things emerge. One flows naturally like a river, the other is torture. First, I no longer feel the necessity, no, more than that, every fibre in my body resists the use of objects for straight painting. I sketch from nature and use the sketches instead. Since doing this, I think, my best side emerges. Before, if the picture didn't work on the first sitting, I nagged it, bothered it, crowded it.

The size of the paintings has grown. I throw them on masonite in the garage with big splashes, and a pair of rubber gloves help me psychologically to become ever filthier and messier. Marvellous for the pictures.

Next issue: the portraits. I had a few bad reviews. They write that the Rapotec is a compromise, which is true. Thirty years routine is at my fingertips, it comes so easily, it can't be good. I decided to paint commissioned work the way I painted the Rapotec. In other words, what I considered a development will now become the conservative approach. Even so, it's blood-chillingly bold but one can't experiment on other people's money. And a saint I am not, to refuse commissions.

The trouble is I studied other painters' approaches to portraiture so thoroughly that whatever I do, I see the debt I owe to others. To Soutine or to Matisse, to Villon or to Bacon or Kokoschka.

25 February 1961

Rapotec won the Blake Prize. For thirteen years he was a so-called 'neglected' painter. The Art Gallery of NSW didn't buy from him, neither did anyone else. In my opinion, the Archibald noise brought him to attention, and they discovered he is a good artist. We were at the Lynns that night when we heard it over the radio. Jancsi stopped at a pub, bought a bottle of champagne and we went to his house but didn't find him home.

His winning entry is *Meditation on Good Friday*, and Jancsi says the nuns will have a problem explaining it to little girls. It's totally abstract and not necessarily a religious picture. Dark despair starting in the left corner going through fifteen feet dissolving in yellow rays of hope.

My own personal ray of hope keeps me working in the garage like someone possessed, till sore eyes and trembling knees say stop to my body. The time my body allows me seems so inadequate.

My Alice Springs *Never-never* which is subtle and pale, a desert diminishing into bizarre shapes in the distance, becomes something entirely different in my new handwriting.

2 March 1961

The body of work grows. I don't answer the telephone and paint till exhausted. I even draw at night.

I stopped painting for two days as I felt I would go crazy, dreaming forms all night. The abstracts which do not represent anything, which somehow smuggled themselves in, are not me, but a recipe. There must be times when one lives without a brush in hand. The trouble is when

I emerge from under the colour spots, there is no inspiration to talk of in the outside world. Only a pleasant vacuum.

24 April 1961

They're hanging the pictures for my one-man show today. They look so strange on the strange walls, but they stand on their feet. A Melbourne collector reserved one. So did Bob Shaw. Olsen chose *Mirage* for his 'Picture of the Week' column in the *Sunday Mirror*, and wrote an excellent review.

The only picture in the show which is marked NFS (not for sale) is *Mother and child*. Peter says, 'Mum, please don't sell this picture. When I grow up and have enough money, I want to buy it.'

1 May 1961

Robert Hughes, art critic for *Nation*, rang me, congratulated me on the exhibition and invited me to see his paintings.

The Trees for Israel Society's gala evening. Isaac Stern plays the violin. A book was published and each page cost £50 or £100. My painting *Drift* is on the title page.

20 May 1961

Alice Springs

After the one-man show, Jancsi dispatched me to Alice Springs to paint for the London show. I will only stay ten days. No long journeys hunting for subjects this time. All the missing pieces of the mosaic are nearby.

The way I live reminds me of the saying of a famous singer, 'I am nothing but the box of my voice.' And me, the container of visual notes.

Alice still means peace. Dry, cool breeze blowing fine red dust, cheeky flies, orange smile of ancient geological miracles. Evenings I guzzle beer with the others, then climb on a chair to reach the tap of the tin barrel for a shower. I read in my birdcage (there are no windows, only a mosquito net) and fall asleep at eight.

Yesterday, unexpectedly, a new hill introduced itself. Looked like a sugarloaf or the hat of a magician. It told me not to take any notice of its cinnamon-coloured side, only Greco's *Toledo* intruded.

Smoky steak for lunch with Mona, smelling of gum leaves just where the erosion was that became *Never-never* and *Drift*. Conveniently the sand drift had changed its mountain ranges and blue cavities and flowing depths. One only had to sit down and plunge into its sienna sides and ghostly sheen to have it emerge into another vast desert landscape. I have no means of knowing what I do, no time for reflection, it has to wait for Weeroona Avenue. But it is what I came for. Not to sweat it, nudge it, tickle it, pull it out of a tired painted-out mind along with old slides and sketches from dusty drawers. The impact is as before and I greedily exploit it and rob the treasures. The round giant pebbles on the old road towards the abandoned Aboriginal settlement became skipping objects. The Gap, which used to be a majestic orange-blue mountain, is now an excited tumble of dark hues. And then there are the sketches spat out sinking into the pages of the large map like half-formed thoughts, forgotten before reaching a meaning.

I work like one possessed, a pace quite hard to achieve in a place where no one else is in any hurry.

Mona was busy so I took Cloudy by taxi to the erosion and she just sat and smoked and looked. Mona was late and I got palpitations fearing I might miss the sun's last deep-rose diagonal rays.

15 July 1961

Sydney

Sydney seems to be a barren rock for my writing self, but fortunately humus for the painting one. I even start thinking I am in the right place. A place on earth where I can paint in peace. As I read what I wrote about the Toledo Hill. That one has changed from being vertical, into a horizontal amphitheatre. When I worked on Toledo Hill I felt as if I were in the centre of the landscape. As if the canvas would have ceased to be three-dimensional, but it was not the third dimension stepping in its place, but a fourth. Whatever triggered off the starting point becomes irrelevant, I can only see within this world now.

I had a real shock when I unpacked the canvases in Sydney. As the ropes fell away, and the newspaper peeled off, and the FRAGILE was removed, something astonishingly and entirely different emerged than the pictures of last year. *Erosion* is something of storm and passion.

The wonder I felt last year was diminished as one doesn't feel the same for the third time round. It raves in the pictures instead. Beside them, the previous harvest looks elegant, smooth and polished. I use more paint and less control.

A big Australian exhibition opened in Whitechapel in London and I was left out. Bryan Robertson, the director, was in Sydney at the time when I was painting Alexandra in London and there was no one apparently to draw his attention to an absentee. Even if my next London show is good, how can one not be influenced by the fact that I wasn't considered good enough in my own land to be represented abroad?

25 July 1961

Peter is fencing every week at the All Nations Club. I sit in the car waiting for him, radio playing.

We are worried about Johnny. Nothing interests him at the moment but sloppy pullovers, a bodgie hairstyle, more pocket-money and rock and roll. He considers us old fools.

3 August 1961

Paul Haefliger wrote from Majorca.

> Dear Judy,
>
> Thank you for your letter and photographs. But what am I going to say now? (How poor old Sali Herman hated that BUT.) That your paintings are very nice, that you should go on with it, that you should do some more living, that you should come out of your shell? Your handwriting already reveals that you are accustomed to disguising your feelings, possibly you are not even aware of them, or do not know what your feelings are. A little self-examination, then.
>
> For God's sake, remember that you are Jewish, a nostalgic race if ever there was one, and that you have had some experiences during the war— remember them, they are material for your painting.
>
> I don't mean that you should do miserable depressed paintings but that you should learn to use the stresses of your life. Your paintings look well enough and are well enough painted but (here it is again) they remind me of other painters, that is, a real character is missing and with it, frankly, their justification except as exercises in the modern mode. I don't mind that as a groundwork but as a means to self-expression this is not even a beginning.
>
> Thus I am not concerned with their excellence as paintings or their technical improvement—indeed, I would prefer worse paintings which yet fumble, however painfully, for some truth, some aspect which you have discovered within yourself (remember Gauguin's 'Nothing so resembles a

daub than a masterpiece'). If you say: 'But I have done this,' then there is nothing further to be said and I cannot help you. If you say: 'All right, I will try to do this and then send you a photo,'—don't. Give it at least three years. A painting done a week later has at best only a week's improvement. Even the simplest individual aspect reveals itself with the greatest difficulty. That is why I say that you have been playing. Please, forgive me my detachment. How else could I make it clear to you?

I would say this of contemporary art, that while it is the outcome of tradition, tradition cannot help the practitioner. For the first time, absolute originality (and I don't mean novelty) is the very hallmark of its expression, precisely because no two people are alike. This is quite different from the individual commentary on some universal theme of other ages. The works of those who resemble others are still commentaries, and while they still may have poetic content, invalidate themselves quite basically, as true expressions of this new art form. No wonder there are so few painters of even passable ability.

After all, you are dealing with the internal, not the external, with the subjective, not the visual. That the subjective is made visual by you, and that your surrounding in all its visual aspects in your subconscious, makes no difference to my original contention that the approach is subjective. It is, of course, not 'abstract', either which is, like most terms of convenience, quite erroneous.

Artists understand all this, dealers do not: they still talk about 'direction', that is 'school'. Now, there is a certain tendency towards a kind of realism in Paris, as in Dubuffet, but it is bound up with the realisation that our internal world is connected with the external world, that the external world does make a journey through our subconscious where it mixes and amalgamates with our deepest desires and instincts. You see at once what difference then divides the visual experience of studied forms and the emergence of a realism imbued with subjective half-realisation.

The surrealists understood this but could only think of a contrived symbolism to express it—in certain recognised and universal forms. In this aspect even Leonardo da Vinci was far ahead of them. (The point of course is, they were deliberate, but was he even conscious of it. I think that he was but it doesn't matter.) There it is, the forward step into realism, not a 'going back to realism' of which the idiots talk. The two are entirely different. The approach is different and diametrically opposed. For myself, I live in the half-world, real to me, but only sometimes discerned by others, and sometimes not.

What I just briefly wrote about is the main element of present-day painting. If you wish to follow this painting you had better know what is involved.

But is there any reason that you should follow this course? You can be a perfectly good painter in the traditional course—better so, perhaps, as you are not prepared to start all over again, like a child, and thus you will merely achieve decoration of less value than your former painting.

An introspective and instinctive art form might not suit you at all. (Have I once advised you to the contrary? If so, this is how I feel now.) You may of course ask, 'How do I realise something that I do not know? How do I commence?' Well . . . you might start painting, saying to yourself. 'I know nothing at all.' And when you do paint thus, remember, there are no marks for beauty of composition or beauty of form. If you genuinely continue you may find that certain elements, certain shapes not of your conscious devising, repeat themselves—those are yours though you may dislike them.

Remember: empty your mind and know nothing. If you are an artist it will manifest itself whether you know it or not. As a matter of fact a little reading of Zen philosophy might help you. I don't ask you to become a Zen Buddhist, on the contrary. But there are to be found in Zen many hints of tremendous value to the contemporary artist. (Get Suzuki's Zen and its influence on Japanese culture *and Herrigel's* Zen and the art of archery.*)*

Well, this is as far as I go for a beginning, no use for red herrings.

You can tell me your problems as you go along.

My reply:

Dear Paul,

Thank you for your letter and criticism and detachment and your time and seriousness. This was an act of friendship. You seem to think 'Judy spent a lot of time and money on these glossy photos, she must think they are wonderful. What a painful task to tell her the truth.' It was only natural I sent them as you were still here in 1955 at my last show and I couldn't imagine this one without you. Of course, you are still Savonarola and I am still superficial, although less so than five years ago.

I know that this is but a beginning.

You know that all my life I made a snail's slow progress. However, I feel that, from sweet, pink babies through semiabstracts there was progress just the same. And I don't mean technical progress either. You are right in setting such high standards. One gets dizzy and feels as small as a flea. When you say I should try and give it three years I considered it a compliment.

Nevertheless the things you wrote about are not new to me. It doesn't matter much what is visible as long as I know that I have a direction. It is an inner one through which pass outer experiences and will come out (I hope) as my own realism.

I have my half-world too, which is real but very far away.

I don't care what anybody thinks, even you! I shall eventually find it, solve it, and I don't care if that happens when I am seventy. I might have more of a chance then, than I have now, anyway.

What you did not consider is women's position in society, combined in my case, with a strong sense of duty and responsibility. At present I am more involved with Peter's broken arm than with painting, and place Zen and self-expression in the shadows.

You didn't consider immigration either which, in my opinion, causes a setback of at least many years. Unfortunately, life has its practical sides and countless little hurdles which make it difficult to dig into my Central European and Jewish past and my subconscious, and make them work. I know I have not discovered much yet. I am searching.

Does this sound like a schoolgirl's apology: 'This page, teacher, was torn out from my historybook'?

I took your advice and read Zen and the art of archery. *Can see the connection clearly.*

Where I disagree with you, is not the estimation of the stage of the road I'm at. The 'Make your mind a blank—return to childhood' can't be applied like a recipe. We are, as you say, not the same and everything in me rebels against the uncontrolled. The appearance of certain returning shapes which are your own can happen whether your mind was blank at the time or not, as long as your mind isn't bound to the visible and the external. I don't believe in vomiting on the picture, to me this is the easy way out.

It's almost as if you would give me a choice whether to follow present-day painting or a more traditional course. As if I would have a choice.

To exchange letters with Paul is good for pausing in and regrouping one's thoughts. No doubt it is easier for Paul to think, dangling his feet on the isle of Majorca. He lives like a hermit with a difference: hermits have to wipe their noses sometimes but I'm sure Jean wipes it for Paul. Whereas the atmosphere I am living in can't do any artist good.

When I started to read *Zen and the art of archery*, I thought Paul is pulling my leg. The revelation came when—after years of training—the Zen master told Professor Herrigel: 'And now, don't shoot. Let it shoot.' (Don't paint. Let it paint.)

Still, Dubuffet, Orban, all those who advocate the superfluousness of art training are wrong to begin with. Because one has to master the trade before one can begin to forget what one has learned.

And Paul is wrong because we Jews have wandered for 5000 years while the easterners have spent 10,000 years contemplating their navels.

Still the book fascinates me in very important ways. It teaches me to concentrate and to relax, both of which I seem to be able to do only rarely.

My brain consists of mosaics and little drawers. Perhaps most western brains behave like mine, but my mosaics seem to skip and jump, and my drawers pop open unsolicited.

My soul needs peace for creativeness—not mosaics and open drawers.

22 September 1961

En route to London

A circle completed. Ten months since my last trip and the same symptoms, except this time I made it without the doctor's help. I planned it so I could spend Yom Kippur with my family.

I don't long to live in Europe any more. Perhaps it is right that it should be so. Perhaps we are far, not only from colours and tastes and smells, but also from the Berlin crisis and atomic radiation.

I will stay in Paris with Anne Sumners, who wants a portrait. It's 7 a.m. as I write on a terrace above the Etoile in a garden swing. She came to Orly with her small bug-car and took me straight to the Louvre courtyard where there is a special chapel to house Chagall's stained-glass windows before they go to Jerusalem.

I suffocate in paintings. Saw a Hartung show, spent two days on the biennale where the age limit is thirty-five. I borrowed a tripod and shot three coloured films. Perhaps because they're young, one can't tell the difference between nations. China uses the same idioms as Brazil, Spain as America and Iran, Morocco and Chile are the same. The size is part of the work.

5 October 1961

London

A telegram from Carla Thorneycroft that they expect me for lunch on the fourth. A man in the lift said, 'You must be Judy Cassab. I am Kenneth Clark and this is Jane, my wife.' Sir Kenneth asked me at lunch: 'Do you really think academic training is important today?'

'After all,' I answered, 'it's such a small fragment of the trade. And if art—such a changing thing—takes a turn towards nature, which I believe it does, the artist without training doesn't have anything to turn back to.'

'I agree wholeheartedly.' I felt he was testing me.

'And did you give up portrait painting?'

'I don't intend to. I intend to find a solution if it takes me thirty years.' I explained my experiments. 'You see, I wasn't born with a distorting eye like Soutine or Greco so I can't force that. I paint an abstract before I superimpose a portrait on it.'

By the end of lunch we had established contact and he made a note in his diary to see my show.

I went to see Sidney Nolan's exhibition at the American embassy. He went to the United States on a Harkness scholarship to sketch. Same impression as the one I had at the Tate years ago. I don't care how he paints. He is a man with a unique vision. So much so, that the exhibited photos are Nolan pictures too. The choice, the way he cuts that choice. He finds the same desolate nightmare landscape in Arizona as at home. Instead of a bird, a helicopter is hanging upside down, like an insect. Instead of carcasses of sheep, there are carcasses of cars. Rodeo could be Ned Kelly. The sketches are black Indian ink wash painting and Rötl sketching on top. Or it is Rötl pastel, rough sketch on smooth paper, cut through with thumb or rag, creating eerie smooth areas.

A sitting with the Marquess of Hertford. First he seemed just blond and milky, but he changes during the work. His cheekbones are prominent, his nose wrinkly when he smiles, and he talks about his 100-room castle being open to the public. He sells the entry tickets and his wife makes tea.

18 October 1961

I have a whale of a hangover after the opening and is it worth it? The exhibition looks crowded. There were at least 200 people. The Gaitskells, the Thorneycrofts, Jocelyn Stevens, the Siddeleys and the Hertfords came. Not one red spot. Waiters, drinks, sandwiches, dizzy turns, telegrams. I have no idea if critics came or not.

The gallery seems hostile somehow. Bryan Senior on the telephone about a Corot. Kalman runs up and down the stairs selling his stock. I wait, like a beggar, for them to take notice of me. They don't give anything but the walls.

I am painting Andor Foldes, the pianist, and his wife. I call it a sketch but work on it a lot. I go to the gallery to see how my show goes, and feel impotent. The Duchess of Kent and Princess Alexandra come 'for a quiet look', so I don't tell anyone. Eric Newton was there and liked it.

However, this exhibition doesn't take off as well as the first one, and this is not nerves, this is serious worry. I wish something would happen just to save face. I really doubt whether it's worth working so hard on all those portraits just to sweat out the airfare.

22 October 1961

Bryan Senior told me about the opening of the show of contemporary portrait painting. Every good portraitist from Kokoschka to Bryan Senior exhibits. The last day to enter was 5 October, and he didn't tell me. I start to work myself into a nice fat persecution complex.

Went out to Whitechapel to see the Mark Rothko exhibition, Bryan Robertson (who left me out of the big Australian exhibition) has no time to say hello to me. Mark Rothko, however, is trying to tell me in deep-colour sound not to care about little humiliations as long as there is art like this. I didn't think I would and could be as enthusiastic about him as I am. Here is an example of what cannot be taken in by reproductions and slides, maybe even not by seeing a single painting. The size is essential. It envelops, descends, opens windows, sometimes rejects. But one never rejects it. Mostly it lets one in. It reminds me of Tàpies, without the texture. Rothko is more an inventor. Fabulous painter.

At last two pictures are sold in the exhibition. They bargain them down but I happily comply, for Kalman's sake as well as for mine.

25 October 1961

I am lonely and a heavy stone sits on my heart. Around me there seems to be nothing but negativity. I can't fight it. I did my best. I know my paintings are good, there they shout, on Brompton Road, only nobody hears them.

28 October 1961

Orders start to come when I am not able to stay any longer. I am almost ashamed how many pictures I am able to manufacture in four weeks. My values start shifting, unfortunately. I shouldn't have turned down O'Hana Gallery last year out of loyalty to Kalman.

2 *November 1961*

Princess Marina came for a sitting because she didn't like the way I have painted her mouth, a bit lopsided, which of course it is. During the painting session I said: 'Mam, I don't know much about etiquette but I would like to ask you something. You remember when I finished the portrait of Princess Alexandra, you said "Wouldn't it be a pity if nobody sees this picture until it hangs on the boat?" Now, I want to say the same. Wouldn't it be a pity if nobody would see yours?'

'But of course. By all means, Miss Cassab, do exhibit it. We just have to fix the month.'

This morning she rang. 'Princess Marina speaking. The duchess will ring for an appointment.'

Yesterday *Campfire* was sold at the gallery.

I couldn't sleep until four. Woke at six, sick with worry because I'm starting the duchess, and how will I place the three Hagenbach sisters in the blue-yellow field which dries on the table? I shall be late in Milano, and Rica bought the canvas already. The three most important people I have in this world all waiting for me at home. But what's another week if something important pops up after a succession of failures?

When will I have time to go to the hairdresser?

Jocelyn Stevens comes in the morning to have a look at Princess Marina's portrait. He advises me to send the portrait in to the Royal Academy. He needs six weeks to do a coloured reproduction for *Queen* magazine. By then, however, I shall be watching 'Six O'Clock Rock' in Weeroona Avenue, and will they really lend the portrait for the exhibition? And will it be picked up in time? And I have to order a frame and without a good frame I can't send it in. I have to make sure that both portraits will be delivered to the palace afterwards.

Too much. Too much.

I suffer with the three sisters. The canvas is too large for the small room and casts a shadow on the models. Three sittings a day are too much. The exhibition closed. That's it.

Gaitskell phoned and invited me for lunch.

The Duchess of Kent phoned and made an appointment.

I woke at 4 a.m. desperate about coping with three sitters, lunch at the Gaitskells and an evening at Wilfrid Thomas.

Blessed London taxis. En route to Gaitskells I put my feet up, driving or rather feeling like floating in a boat across half the city, resting. Hugh took me for a walk in Hampstead Park while Dora cooked.

I am lucky in my relationships. With this brilliant scholar strolling beside me, his talk pleasant and relaxed and friendly, it seemed quite secondary that this was the leader of the opposition. The rest of the guests started to arrive around one.

Dora served the pea soup in a saucepan, and we just reached the pudding when I had to telephone for a taxi, not to be late for my 2.30 sitting.

Princess Marina comes to sit on Tuesday. I request permission to exhibit her portrait at the Royal Academy. She says, 'It will be an honour.' Even bows, jokingly.

Jocelyn comes to take the coloured slide.

The young Duchess of Kent is coming next week. I postponed my flight for a week.

Rosemary Cooper of *Vogue* wants portrait sketches of Isaac Stern and Yehudi Menuhin and others. I've been in London for six weeks, and now it happens. My pattern.

O'Hana wants me to send paintings for his spring and autumn show. Rose invites me for dinner with Lajos Lederer from the *Observer*. He theorises that the critics have not come to my show because of all the publicity I had about the royal commissions. They don't know what is genuine and what is phoney. I would need years to establish myself in my schizophrenic painter existence to be accepted.

According to Lederer, I should have approached Princess Marina to get me Princess Margaret. He thinks Marina is astounded that I did not ask her any such favour.

My poor confused chicken brain finds it difficult to digest all these happenings. I take tranquillisers and suffer from diarrhoea.

11 November 1961

I feel ugly, old and overworked.

London *Vogue* rings to know if I would paint a portrait of Laurence Olivier. Not this time. No more time. Sorry.

Strenuous work on the triple portrait. Sometimes I have half the canvas hanging out the window above the Pont Street church and half the time it balances on two chairs behind. But it looks good. I was sent a ticket to a concert in the Tate Gallery and took Ron Russell with me. Bach and Schubert among the masterpieces.

One and a half more weeks in which to finish the duchess's portrait and do Robert Helpmann's. I see a lot of people. Work, work all through the week-end.

15 November 1961

The duchess is a charming young girl. She doesn't mind if I exhibit the picture at the Academy. She doesn't mind publicity. The only thing she doesn't want is for people to know when she has her sittings.

I paint Helpmann in wild colours, had two excellent sittings. The duchess, who is enthusiastic after her second sitting, asks whether she could bring the duke next time in his lunch hour. 'Of course. We could have a sandwich here.'

'And Nescafe?'

'Sure.'

'Could we really do that?'

It was worthwhile agonising over the triple portrait of the sisters. The parents cried when they saw it. Mrs Hagenbach even forgot to consider whether it will fit over the tudor fireplace. The sun-yellow and blue background swims through arms and hair, making everything transparent.

I managed to achieve a similar effect in the portrait of the duchess— as if there are country, cornfields, green grass and air *under* it all.

Princess Marina is bowled over with the portrait of the duchess. Really a piece of luck that it turned out to be that good.

Next day is the last sitting, we wrap the canvas, the duchess drives her Jaguar up on the pavement, we open the boot.

'You must come and see it hanging next time you're here,' she says.

30 November 1961

Sydney

I arrived at 7 a.m. in Sydney. My two boys and I stood wrapped around one another. Jancsi was excited and couldn't really believe I was home. Talk talk talk until exhaustion took over.

I don't desire painting, but I'm impatient for the desire. A feeling of unreality. The first few mornings when I opened my eyes, I didn't recognise the curtains.

A few swims in the sea improves my health.

18 January 1962

It's Archibald time again. It doesn't interest me very much. Nothing does. Elwyn Lynn talked to Daniel Thomas.

'And how is Judy Cassab's portrait?'
'Much better than last year.'
'Will she win?'
'No.'
Of course not. One doesn't win two years running.

7 February 1962

It seems to me that we have changed a lot. Many of our friends have not assimilated. On the contrary, increasingly they tend to take refuge in a past which gets more and more glorious with the passing years.

I found it difficult to settle this time. I had to grab hold of Sydney and squeeze it for a bit of juice, or rather stamp it under bare feet like grapes in our vineyard. The only advantage of summer is the beach. Camp Cove, my favourite bay, has lost some of its lure since there is a danger of sharks. A shark swam into knee-deep water in Brisbane and ate the arms and a leg of a bride. I am braver on Sundays when many swimmers are further out than me, and I use them as bait. On weekdays I opt for Parsley Bay which has a net. However, I still have a phobia about swimming in deep water.

The paintings paint themselves. Later on, I suppose, I will catch them by the tail. Saturday morning I started a portrait of Bob King, the handyman. He used to be a wrestler, loves beer but art too. He sits in a singlet, thick-set arms hanging down. I find it too realistic.

Sundays are different. The children now make their own plans. We buy fish and chips at Watsons Bay and eat in the car.

26 February 1962

I had two pictures in the Brazil Biennale. I just received a form to fill out for the archives of the Museum of Modern Art. Amazing how the reviews of both the Brazilian and the Pittsburgh shows agree about modern art being totally uniform. That two directions have crystallised, the international and the individualistic. I am convinced that the international branch is a blind alley. It starts to become such a bore, and although I still have not found my figures, I feel remote from all the sprinklings, dashings, dribblings, and graffiti which thousands use in the wake of Pollock. It's not bold. Bold is *not* doing it.

6 March 1962

I painted Luisillo and I don't know whether it's brilliant or kitsch. He is one of the great dancers of this age, and Andrea introduced us. When I saw the ballet, the picture was finished in my mind. I prepared the ground with transparent geranium red, on top I placed cadmium red shapes. I superimposed Luisillo with blacks, white sleeves. He bought it and took it to Madrid.

26 March 1962

Jocelyn Stevens wrote: 'We put a publishing date forward to 17 April as we believe that the *Sunday Times* has it, too.' Since nobody else had a coloured transparency, we could only think that Anthony Armstrong-Jones went out to Coppins and took one.

The first invitation from Melbourne, after ten years in Australia. The Argus Gallery wants me to put on a one-man show. These are exterior happenings. But, thank God, things are happening inside me too. Two of the paintings started to talk. Waiting, waiting, painting, they dropped out of me like a child, it's independent from me now.

My orange–brown period is over. The long triangles will peep out from under this new thing. How did it come about? I sketched as usual on white paper with white tempera, then decided to use not only black, but coloured inks. Then I washed it down. When it dried I started working on top, with oil. Then I bought large sheets of masonite and painted the foundation with a polyvinyl acetate mixed with pumice, sugar or simply thick white powderpaint, for texture. Later I tried using Ripolin, which was partly absorbed in wood, and became wrinkled where it wanted. Then I glazed it with colours on top of which I'm going to paint. It takes several days, of course, to get to the beginning of a new painting. And here comes the discovery, and each discovery is like an unknown continent. I keep my eyes glued on the sketch and, not looking at the canvas, the lines become awkward and searching, dropping my thirty-year-old habits. And the Something emerges.

Only after this exercise did I realise that I'm doing what Haefliger was talking about, and what I read in the Zen book. I don't paint. I let *it* paint. The subconscious is given a chance. As I trace the rhythm of the paint, my brushstrokes get more and more excited and the image is romantic and poetic.

The same process opened up a track which had eluded me: to do the figure in the same way. But I haven't touched that yet. Haven't dared to hit through *that* wall. The image exists in me only.

Meanwhile I'm reading Marcel Brion's *Geschichte der abstracten Malerei*. One of his remarks hit me in the face. Psychologists suspect that painters who crowd every inch of a canvas are anxiety-ridden. As this is one of my failings I try to leave large areas free. Is it possible that by doing this I address my anxiety?

I paint the portrait of Dr Morgan, an orthopaedic surgeon. Charming man.

'Tell me,' he said, 'what is it that you miss in this country? What is different from Europe? Culture?'

'No, I don't think so. I wish I could go to all the events which are on in Sydney at the moment. There are books, there are records. No. What I think is most different is that in Europe I feel alive and here I don't.'

We had a long debate about the definition. How materialistic people are. That we get flatter and less enthusiastic. How few the number of those there are with whom one can fence with words.

'You see,' Dr Morgan said, 'it is Sunday today. I'm going to visit a friend, an eminent surgeon who has a lovely home and four children whom I love. We shall talk about oil shares, sit in the sun and drink beer. And what's wrong with that?'

According to Morgan, the European system which keeps professors working to the age of eighty is most unhealthy. Let them tend their roses and make place for the young.

'That's another thing I don't like here,' I said. 'As long as a person isn't senile, how can one kick them aside? Such a person has immeasurable wealth of wisdom and experience. And talking of stamina, well, Renoir painted his best pictures with a brush tied to his arthritic wrists.' Jancsi and I and Morgan all shouted at once.

He is tall, lean, elegant, around sixty, with vague watery eyes under eyebrows like moustaches. 'I see now what you mean about enthusiasm. I go now. I leave you happy.'

31 March 1962

Not only was I left out of the exhibition to the Tate Gallery, but Rapotec, Hessing and Rose were left out too. This stinks of injustice so strongly that in this case I am only one of a group of neglected.

What I didn't know, is that Rapotec sent a hundred-word telegram to the Adelaide Festival, where they chose the pictures. I only just heard that Drysdale was chosen as a member of the Art Advisory Board which, up till now, consisted mainly of public servants, and that Drysdale finally succeeded in squeezing in Rapotec, Hessing and Rose.

They must hate my royal commissions. (Is it more harmful than useful?)

Tuesday a telegram from Jocelyn: 'Kents will not give permission for paintings to be published. Have informed *Women's Weekly* they have no right to publish. Apparently they have decided on their own to go ahead. Have withheld publication in *Queen*. Will contact you when situation clears. Jocelyn.'

London telegram about both duchesses hanging in the Royal Academy. People congratulate me as it was in the papers but I can't feel a shade of pleasure. It starts with a nervous shudder as soon as I see a telegram.

The other and more serious soul searching is about portraits and the schizophrenic pictorial existence this causes. But we need the money. Portraits like Bob King and Helpmann, yes, of course. But what do I do when Mrs Smith, whose face is like a pancake, commissions me? I also torture myself by trying to place the figure into the abstract, and once it's there it's either too elegant or it's the childish point-point-dash which isn't me either. In the end it's a relief when the last traces of the figure are blotted out.

The London press-cuttings are all about royalty and not of any of the artistic merits. It turns the pictures into society gossip. And it does me no end of harm.

Bob Hughes was here. He is writing a book on Australian art for Penguin and asked me for a reproduction. Then he left me out of the book. It is fashionable, it seems, to leave Cassab out.

He went to Queensland to interview artists and Jon Molvig took him to see Ian Fairweather. Molvig has a vintage Chevrolet which must keep the engine running otherwise it stalls. So it kept idling on the ferry on the way to Bribie Island and passengers suffered massive carbon dioxide poisoning. The island really used to be uninhabited but to Fairweather's chagrin, tourists discovered it. He lives deep within the bush and only a few sticks point that way. It's difficult to distinguish between the gum trees and the sticks. The hut is built of grass and mud. The artist wore a pyjama top and dirty jeans, a thong on one foot while the other was wrapped in rags.

'One gets pretty lonely,' he confessed, blushing, 'and I have a pet goanna. We play a game where I place pieces of cheese between my toes and the goanna picks them out. The other day it mistook one of my toes for cheese. Anyway, it got infected so I went to the chemist, he gave me a shot of penicillin.'

Fairweather is seventy-six. He carries water on his back in petrol cans. When he has enough material for a show, he stacks the paintings (painted on cardboard), drives a long nail through them and kicks them to the post office. (Let the restoration experts at the Art Gallery worry about it.)

11 May 1962

Press-cuttings are still flooding in, and my ears are burning with shame for imagining that the Royal Academy was a barricade to conquer. It only hurts my integrity.

Sydney's art market has gone through a change. Difficult to say how it began. Perhaps with Sotheby's auction last year where a Cézanne was sold for £80,000 and a Rembrandt for £150,000.

Schurek, the collector, died. At the auction there was mass hysteria. The Dobells went for £4000. Since then it's not unheard of for others to put £200 on their pictures. People buy. A Passmore jumped from £100 to £200 at Terry Clune's. A Kmit from £300 to £400. Collecting has become an investment.

Rudy Komon has an exhibition: The Imitation Realists. It was said that it's a renewal of Dadaism. We were delighted and surprised, we laughed and enjoyed the show. A few youngsters have produced much vulgarity out of discarded objects with Luna Park associations regrouped, used as tools for art, that I gained new respect for Rudy who let them paint over his ceiling, his bathrub and wash basin.

10 June 1962

Above the Hungry Horse restaurant, a new gallery. Major Rubin opened it, a legendary madman, keeps the press busy, gives £300,000 to St Vincent's Hospital. Adopts an Italian baby. Why he came no one knows. He is in an awful hurry, looks like he lives on borrowed time. There is a weak single globe on the ceiling and the Picassos, Riopelles and Dobells and a couple of hundred other paintings are on the floor. Major Rubin warmly thanks me for the pink giraffes I did not paint.

3 August 1962

The Australian government commissioned me to paint Queen Sirikit of Thailand, but she doesn't want to be painted in Australia. Prime Minister Menzies wants me to come to Canberra to meet her.

The news of Sirikit's portrait was officially announced on Monday night. It's an exchange of gifts between the two countries.

Queen Sirikit was in plain dark blue. We sat on a couch discussing her dress for the painting and the details. I shall go to Bangkok.

22 September 1962

Thank God my bluebird flew back. I can paint again. It was pretty awful having been impotent for three months, with a one-man show booked in London for April next year. The painting for this ought to be on the ship by February. November, a one-man show in Melbourne. And in October, Sirikit.

As a consequence of the Sirikit commission, my picture was rejected from the Transfield Prize and I was left out yet again from the Commonwealth exhibition organised by my friend Eric Newton. One has to take it.

23 October 1962

Bangkok

How lucky can you get? Once a year there is a procession of the Royal barges on the river and today is the day.

The masonite arrived from the airport, was loaded into a station wagon together with me, and I was taken to the palace which is surrounded by a moat and tropical shrubs. We drove through a great park and were greeted by Tula Bunnag, master of the household, and Narawadi Davivongse, the diminutive lady-in-waiting, whom I met in Canberra.

The room I was shown to was more French than Thai with its Aubusson carpet and gilded empire chairs. The lady-in-waiting ushered me into another room, to lovely Sirikit. While I curtsied, flashlights popped. We discussed the details. She prefers sitting in the afternoons, as in the morning her eyelids feel heavy. We arrange to meet the following afternoon.

Two servants, walking on their knees, entered with tea. Then she led the way to the studio. People fell on their knees. She kept her head straight up. We stepped into an air-conditioned room full of books, with large windows. The dais was set up and my easel was there. A small table, two palettes and a bottle of turps.

Queen Sirikit told me that this is King Poumiphon's study. She showed me the gold dress she wants to wear, and then left. They will send a car from the palace to pick me up tomorrow.

The royal Mercedes comes, with master of the household, Tula Bunnag.

The light in the studio is wrong.

'Can we push the dais to the other side?'

'Yes.'

'Come on then.'

'No, no.'

He claps.

The servants come in and push it.

'Would you be so kind and sit on the chair, so I can see if the six-foot canvas casts a shadow on the sitter?'

He claps, servants come in. They take the chair off the dais and put another chair on. Even though Tula Bunnag is a prince, he can't sit on the chair the queen is going to sit on. The servants comb the fringes of the Persian carpet under the chair. I squeeze the paint and realise with a sinking heart that I forgot to bring black. I have to use Prussian blue instead. Tula shows me the bathroom. It's black marble with pale blue walls and a gold settee. I hardly dare to pee.

Three ladies-in-waiting, two servants, we all wait.

Sirikit enters in gold silk. Her hair, with a tiara with diamonds the size of walnuts, is towering on her head.

'Should the court stay in, Miss Cassab,' Sirikit asks, 'or would you rather they leave?'

'I would rather they leave, Your Majesty.'

'Could I listen to the radio, Miss Cassab?'

'No, Your Majesty.'

She is a bit surprised.

The foundation was planned for her height, and the tall hairdo is ruining my plan. Sirikit stood the whole time. She said she would like to give me a dinner party and asked whether I would prefer a formal dinner in the palace or a real Thai dinner in an old Thai house. I chose the latter.

As conversation wasn't easy, the Kents were a great help. Sirikit wanted to know about the new Duchess of Kent. So, the first sitting was quite pleasant, except my stage fright was worse than usual because I had to step on a stepladder to reach the top of the canvas.

When the queen left, Tula came in and told me that not all the windows look out on the garden, some open on the corridor and the king was peeping. The king sent a message. Would I, please, not paint his wife's eyes so Chinese. Now, this being my first eastern face, I couldn't tell the difference between Chinese, Malaysian or Thai eyes. I sent a message to the king. 'Please don't peep any more.'

By the time the Mercedes delivered me home to the hotel, my knees were shaking.

It is like an oversized villa on the French Riviera. Let's say thirty times as large. But there are yellow canvas awnings and pink ceramic tiles in the white wall and I step in to the palace through an enormous door. Tula doesn't leave me alone—it must be for security reasons.

Sirikit sails in, steps on the dais and we start. She is friendly. Do I think her face is wide as the moon? Could I please give her nose a little bridge? ('No, Your Majesty.')

As I progress to her shoulders, arms and wrists I realise that the figure I used for the foundation (and for which a thin-boned girl posed) relates to Queen Sirikit's fragility as a fleshy Rubens would to a Modigliani.

An embassy employee takes me on a boat trip. The boat is very long but so narrow that we sit behind each other. I'm in front, under a linen canopy. I stretch my legs, take my shoes off and stare. The small motor almost idles, and as we glide over the smooth yellow river I remember the fairytale caves of my childhood.

Everything happens on the river. The people wash in it, bath babies in it, brush their teeth in it, urinate in it and it's the commercial centre.

I don't even sketch lest I miss something. The fishing nets, the rich man's buffalo, Siamese coffee houses, thousands of flowerpots hanging on strings, laughing people in straw hats.

I have a positive feeling of happiness to be here.

On royal command I was shown the Grand Palace. Tula fetched me and I saw things no tourist is allowed to see. Like the throne room. The throne is pure gold with a round baldachin above, everything is mother-of-pearl and Italian marble transported from Carrara. It is so incredible. Hundreds must have toiled for a hundred years to create it. The Venetian chandeliers, the lapis lazuli and jade.

Journalists from *Der Stern*, a German magazine, take photos of me painting the portrait. Sirikit tells them I am a famous painter whom the prime minister of Australia sent to paint her. All this is time consuming and I fear there won't be enough time left for the sitting.

Since being in Bangkok I have quite a different concept of this picture. It's contemporariness must not be a western one. I want to introduce gold leaf in patches, and repeat the Siamese embroidery on her gown. A solution could be a sort of iconic, Byzantine look. But that has to wait till Sydney.

My dinner party is arranged for Monday and the queen has the old palace—the old Thai house—prepared for the occasion. We shall eat sitting on the floor, lanterns will be lit and there will be Thai dancers. The Australian ambassador, who has never seen this, will be invited in my honour.

While I work on Sirikit's hands, she tells me: 'My husband is upstairs with the children. You know, Miss Cassab, my husband is a very shy man. And to cover it, he acts stern.'

Tula reminisced about the royal world tour. When the Duke of Edinburgh, in Buckingham Palace, whispered to King Poumiphon, 'My wife is nervous. She has to make a speech.'

'My wife is very nervous too,' replied the king, 'she has to reply.'

When the men's turn came, Philip said to Poumiphon, 'Now, you better not make a mess of it. Otherwise I'll make a mess of mine.' I also learnt that queens have the same tummy trouble on trips as I do. Sirikit lost a stone on the Australian trip.

It's the last sitting. Sirikit tells me the king is coming to have a look at the painting. He arrives, looking like a university student. I curtsy, he shakes my hand. He loves the portrait.

'We have a court painter,' he tells me, 'President Sukarno sent him and he does nothing else but portraits of us. He paints a bit more bones into my wife's nose and straightens her eyes. But he doesn't get a likeness.' No wonder.

'I asked Miss Cassab,' Sirikit said, 'to give my nose a little bridge but she didn't want to do it.'

'Right so,' said the king. 'That's why this one looks like you. Why, it almost talks. And it has a smile. But it still looks dignified.'

'And,' Sirikit said, 'look. It looks tall and it's only my size.'

'An optical illusion,' said the king. But since he also paints (often using his wife as a model) he found things to criticise. That shadow on the forehead is larger. 'I think we have to leave Miss Cassab now,' Sirikit said, 'after all she is going to a big dinner party tonight.' And laughed.

'I would just like her to meet our court painter' the king said 'and see his portraits. Then for him to see hers.'

He looks like Dénes Diener, an affable rogue with thick eyebrows and tiny teeth. I saw that my large picture is small to his which is twice the size. It has to be as the throne is depicted, the mother-of-pearl door, the gold brocade curtain and of course Sirikit whom I recognised from her necklace. This cheered me up so much that I became generous and told him he paints like the old masters.

LEFT: My father in 1917
BELOW: My mother and me, aged five, 1925.

ABOVE: My first portrait, a charcoal drawing of my grandmother, 1932.

RIGHT: Jancsi's brother, Sandor Kampfner, his wife Erzsi, daughter Irene and mother Gisella, 1927. She and Sandor were killed at Auschwitz; so was Irene's young brother Ocsi.

My father visiting my mother and me in Beregszasz, 1934.

My portrait of Judy Barraclough, 1955.

JUDY CASSAB

Judy Cassab, besides being Australia's leading woman portrait painter, can hold her own against most men competitors here in this field. She has recently, as shown in her Sydney exhibition of last May, achieved a new coherence of theme and expression in her abstractions of landscapes.

Johnny and Peter help me carry my portrait of Rapotec to the car to take to the Art Gallery of NSW as my entry in the 1959 Archibald Prize.

Winning the Archibald Prize with
Stan Rapotec, 1959.

My portrait of the Maharani
of Jaipur, 1961.

LEFT: Painting
Queen Sirikit of
Thailand, 1962.
The first sitting.

BELOW: Winning
the Charles Lloyd
Jones Prize with
Sir Charles Moses,
1970.

ABOVE: Johnny and Greta, 1972.

LEFT: My portrait of John Laws won the Sir Charles Lloyd Jones Prize in 1972.

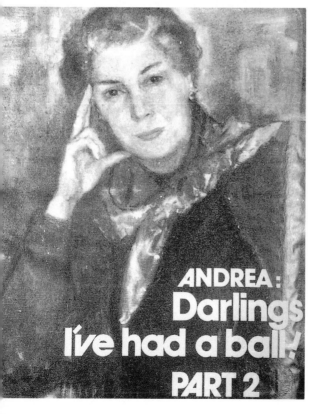

ABOVE: The Power Foundation Inaugural dinner, 1972. From left, Dr Nugget Coombs, me, Elwyn Lynn (curator), Rose Skinner (Skinner Gallery, Perth) and Bruce Williams, vice chancellor of Sydney University.

LEFT: My portrait of Andrea in the *Australian Women's Weekly*, 1975.

ABOVE: Greta and Johnny, 1979.
BELOW: Greta and my grandson, Bodhi, 1978.

ABOVE: Members of the Australian Award Council, meeting for the first time at Government House, Canberra. From left, Keith Spann, Sir David Brand, Major General Kenneth David Green, John Holland, Andrew Grimwade, Raymond Briley Ward, me, Admiral Sir Victor Smith, the Governor General Sir John Kerr, Sir James Vernon, Sir Garfield Barwick, Peter James Lawler, Frank Stewart.

LEFT: Poster of my exhibition at the Australian Embassy in Paris, 1981.

ABOVE: At the launching of *Ten Famous Australians*, a portfolio of lithographs, 1984. From left, Thomas Keneally, Donald Friend, Lloyd Rees, Lou Klepac, Morris West, me, Sir Robert Helpmann, Peter Sculthorpe, Rosemary Dobson.

BELOW: Lou Klepac and Brett Whiteley at my 'Artists and Friends' Exhibition at the S. H. Ervin Gallery, 1988.

With Peter (above) and Johnny, 1994.

ABOVE: Jancsi and me at lunch with our family to celebrate his 92nd birthday, 1994.
BELOW: Jancsi's 92nd birthday. From left, Johnny, seventeen-year-old Bodhi, Peter, Shayne and Jancsi.

'Yes,' he answered, 'but we live in the twentieth century, don't we? But you see, this is meant to hang in the grand palace, beside all the other queens and kings.'

'I see,' I said, while my roving gaze discovered enlarged photos of eyes, which he copies.

Then we went up to my studio. I was surprised how much he liked the portrait. He wagged his head right and left saying how lucky I was to get such a likeness. He went close and touched the texture and worried that I may spoil it if I do anything more.

I got back to the hotel at six, changed into a short evening dress and went to the old Thai house which is built on three levels. The royal household provided an orgy of colour. There was the prime minister and his son, and the women in orange, sky blue, and plum silks. The king in a white dinner suit, the queen in purple robes. I sat with them and the servants, on their knees, started serving cocktails. The king tells the ambassador that Thai beer is better than Australian beer. Anyway, it has a higher alcohol content.

The master of ceremonies calls us for dinner. Sirikit is barefoot. She tells me to take off my sandals to be comfortable. The photographers from *Der Stern* click wildly as the procession files in. The king and queen sat down on the upper level. Beside them are triangular pillows over which they place their arms. I was seated below them so I had a few inches over which I could hang my feet to the next level but even so it was an unusual position. On the left side of the great room was the orchestra. On the right sat the singers, a level lower. The ladies-in-waiting were kneeling. The servants also knelt, with their elbows on the floor. The servants, one to each guest, brought low tables (one for each guest). The plates were gold.

The son of the prime minister, who sat at my feet, one level lower, whispered to me not to eat it all because it was only the first course. And throughout the night we were entertained by the ballet.

Sirikit gave me presents and signed photographs.

9 December 1962

Sydney

Since my return, an avalanche of people. Looking at Sirikit, wanting to hear about Thailand. I project slides, make coffee, and only a few days till the Melbourne show.

Jancsi, God bless him, turned sixty in November.

I flew to Melbourne for the opening of my exhibition at the Argus Gallery. Nine pictures were sold.

Peter Burns took me to John Perceval's studio. His ceramic angels are wonderful, diabolical, disgusting little cherubs. He took me to the Museum of Modern Art. Luckily, John Reed isn't in. I still resent him not wanting to give me a show.

Melbourne critics failed to read my curriculum vitae and write about Judy Cassab leaving portraiture and exploring the world of abstraction. Besides, Leonard French published a book of his painting and the book launch is in the Argus. Some of his glowing enamelled paintings hang near mine and kill them stone dead.

Now came *my* restoring job. First, I gave it a foundation. Then a coat of enamel. When it dried I overpainted it with Wyngell, which forms a thick texture and dries into a firm layer. When this dried, I applied the colour, and after that the gold leaf I bought in Bangkok.

My queen slowly becomes richer and more graceful, the folds of the piece of golden Thai silk I bought, draped on. The delivery date draws near. It's King Poumiphon's birthday.

Sundays Jancsi stands behind me and paints the picture with words. Sometimes I really am like the extension of his mind as he coaxes, dictates, drives, praises. Our collaboration is as magic, suddenly the fable is born. The pattern of the stone-rubbing from the temple gets scratched into the gold leaf. The picture now looks as if Queen Sirikit is stepping from a twilight-blue garden with its leaves and twigs, through an arch, into a well-lit room.

Bill Rose, the artist, who took over Drysdale's framing, makes a gold leaf frame. Telephone calls with Jim McCusker in Canberra who sends a truck from the department of supply. They hover over Bill Rose until he finishes his work and brings the picture back. I don't believe I have painted it at all. God finished it during the night.

The Contemporary Art Society wants premises of its own. Members donate pictures to be raffled. I myself sold nine lottery tickets. Every fourth ticket wins and the auction is exciting. A Blackman, donated by Rudy Komon, is won by the Macquarie Galleries, and Barry Stern, who bought four tickets, won two paintings, which he sold at once for £200.

The consul of Thailand comes. McCusker brings Russell Drysdale in his official capacity as member of the Art Advisory Board.

'All right,' Drysdale says, 'I know you can paint a portrait. But the skirt. It's sculptural. The painting is a wonderful painting.' And adds humbly, 'I couldn't have done it.'

Peter prepares for his Intermediate. He stays up till midnight studying and then wants to be woken at 6 a.m. He is so gentle and thoughtful and loving and wise. It's as if someone much older and wiser inhabits the frame of a seedling tree that he is.

10 December 1962

Dante's hell commences in Sydney. The pre-Christmas hard-pressure sales, the sweating rushing drunken people. A crowd billows in the city, silent desperation in their eyes. We go to parties. We are always sleepy.

In the meantime Sirikit's painting was flown by special plane to Canberra because it never fitted in a commercial airline. A secretary rang to say Menzies was delighted and invited me to attend the celebrations for the Thai king's birthday.

Harold Holt asks me why I don't paint from sketches, like Dobell.

'Because my temperament is different,' I said. 'I need the electric contact of the person.'

He replied, 'I'd love to have an electric contact with you.'

2 January 1963

Johnny passed his driving test. Peter is ecstatic. Now he can ask Johnny for lifts. He takes the car in the morning, goes to the beach, and in the afternoons he fetches Jancsi. I feel blessedly peaceful without a car. I have started painting again.

We heard so much about Hill End, we went there on the weekend, with Jack and Lily Lynn. The only life to be found is in the pub, but one can't stay overnight, so we drove another twenty-three miles to Sofala. The loo is in the backyard, there is no shower, but we love it. Jancsi and I walked on the main street in the early morning. Only one inhabitant is visible. An old man who sits on the porch wearing a hat, smoking a pipe, and he doesn't acknowledge our greeting.

The night before we had dinner in the Sofala pub at a communal table where women had rollers in their hair, presumably in preparation for a dance. When we asked where the road leading to the river was, nobody knew. But we found it. It's a steep track and I worried because Lily is seven months pregnant. We had an esky in the boot and drank cold beer after sketching.

23 January 1963

In Bangkok I had to sketch with great speed as the boat was gliding away from the subject, so I didn't look at the paper while I drew. Suddenly I found that I was able to make distortions and 'mistakes' which I couldn't before. Now I transpose those nervous, trembly lines onto shiny carton paper. When the paint dries somewhat, I break through the lines with a rag dipped in turps to give the movement an even greater feeling of speed. I'm longing to find my own figures.

16 February 1963

I am painting the chief justice, Sir Charles Lowe, in Canberra. He is eighty-three, straight and tall. Under bushy eyebrows small myopic wise blue eyes. Find nose far above his lips, a moustache. He moves in the Supreme Court like a king. The picture progressed without a hitch. The skin over his temples is stretched smooth and it's transparent, almost blue. The rest of his face is yellowish brown like parchment. Menzies said, 'Nobody can be as wise as Sir Charles looks.'

I bent down yesterday and couldn't get up. When I did, the pain was excruciating. I now walk like an old general. I'm quite crooked as I paint.

24 February 1963

Since I can't bend, I drop everything. Yesterday I dropped the alarm clock and my toothbrush fell out the window.

Jancsi asks, 'Does it hurt?'

'Only when I move.'

2 March 1963

My back isn't well. I have to see a specialist.

12 March 1963

Sir Douglas Miller looked at my x-ray and said that two discs have slipped badly and are pressing on a nerve. In order to have absolute rest, it's best to put me in plaster.

Now I'm in a barrel from my armpits to my bottom. Jancsi called me a marble bride. No dress fits and it's hard to sit as the plaster pushes upwards. But the pain has stopped and the doctor assures me I can go to London.

Johnny woke us up late last night. He was booked for speeding. One can't give children one's experience. Miserable parents may talk till they're blue in the face, but children have to make their own mistakes. We are just happy to see he's not hurt.

22 March 1963

I resigned myself to the fact that we can't have the house we want with the money we have. Last Saturday Jancsi and I kept looking and either there is no place for a studio or it's damp and dismal. The agent mentioned a house on Victoria Road, Bellevue Hill, but it's two storeys which we don't want.

'Look,' Jancsi said, 'now we are here, at least have a look at it.'

So I heaved the plaster barrel out of the car, took the hike up and suddenly we both cried out: 'That's it.'

It's a dream. Only too big. The atmosphere is European. The children will have a separate wing, three rooms, and the upper terrace has its own entrance. A sunroom upstairs and down, and another large room opening to this will be ideal for a studio with a south light and three enormous built-in wardrobes. The whole wonderful house is so cheap that I keep pinching myself.

12 April 1963

I am very involved with Bernard Smith's *Australian painting*, tracing the various capillaries of styles. The Melbourne painters, who call themselves the Antipodeans, always remained figuratives. In Sydney only Jeff Smart has stuck to the figure persistently, and also Robert Dickerson. I gave the figure up for four years, because I could not find its place within the abstract. Now that I want to return to it, there is a foundation I can lean on. Many of Sydney's abstract artists can't draw and are therefore antifigure. My major limitation is that, as yet, I have no image of my own. After countless sketches, I finally painted *Flight*. The figures are running, moving, the abstract experience is there, but is there a Me?

Since my back is bad I haven't painted large canvases. I only transfer the Bangkok sketches to a larger page. Where is the next one-man show? It will come in one huge breath, that I know.

Reading keeps me in touch with art, and resting in bed, I have plenty of time to do it. Jack Lynn keeps me in touch.

Since I can now look forward to having a studio I realise how many disturbances I have put up with for these past eleven years. Now I find it an irritation when the greengrocer sails through the living room with the box on his shoulder while I paint, that the drycleaner and the butcher ring the bell.

Will outer circumstances be able to change me?

Sir Douglas Miller rang. How am I? Very well. Then I should sit in the bathtub and when the plaster softens, cut it off with scissors. What? Me? Sure.

I have a comical fantasy of sitting in the water, the plaster refusing to budge. Or cutting into my skin with a kitchen knife. But it did come off quite easily.

He said it will be all right but to wear a surgical corset when I go to London. It's difficult to get used to but it gives me a feeling of security. I booked the trip, coming back on 15 June when we can move into the house in Victoria Road.

14 April 1963

London

Beryl Whiteley took me to Serge Poliakoff's opening at the Whitechapel. I'm not impressed, he is a routine painter. I climb the three storeys to Beryl's Knightsbridge flat cautiously in my corset. Brett, her son, is an enormously talented twenty-three year old who paints pink bottoms into landscapes. Wendy, his wife, is twenty-one, wears false eyelashes and a pale lipstick and her breasts are pushed even higher than they already are. There are two Persian princes in the room. One is Soraya's brother. He doesn't like modern art but it's his chauffeur-driven motor boat that takes us on the Thames to Whitechapel.

I meet more Australian painters here than in Australia—Charles Blackman, John Perceval and Leonard French.

I started the portrait of Lady Rosemary Muir, a niece of Winston Churchill. Tall, gangling, nice young girl with prominent eyes, her temples a bit too wide, chin a bit too small. Easy prey.

For Alexandra's wedding I borrowed a chinchilla scarf to wear with a deep-blue Thai-silk suit (Queen Sirikit gave me the silk and Tubi and Juli made it.)

I am the only mortal not to arrive in a Rolls Royce, but a good black London cab. I go to my seat, as in a cinema. Luckily the seats are straight and hard so I fit in with the corset. It's only 11 a.m. but the abbey is full. Lady Rosemary's husband is an usher. Each great column has a television set as one can't see from the south aisle to the north. While one waits, one watches the procession start from Buckingham Palace, coaches in which the queen sits and Princess Margaret and the Kents.

Meanwhile, Lord Attlee and Anthony Eden sit opposite me, and Thorneycroft beside Attlee.

When it's over, I go out to Westminster Place which is like a camp city of thousands, and stand for half an hour in a queue till I reach the underground.

The portrait of Robert Helpmann was accepted in the Royal Academy.

I walked along Bond Street for the first time, saw a Ben Nicholson retrospective, poetry in geometric shapes. My picture of Rapotec is exhibited at Agnews.

Sidney Nolan's African Journey exhibition opened at the Marlborough. They are still unmistakeably sketches in big format. It isn't the simplification of a great artist, rather the assured manner of the successful artist who knows what his signature is worth. The images are like blown-up shorthand; each being 4 x 5 feet.

Eric Newton unkindly said it's *National Geographic* combined with Baron Münchhausen and Walt Disney.

I see Asher Bilu who lives in London now with his wife and baby. He rang Nolan and Cynthia shouted: 'Who gave you our telephone number? No, you can't talk to him!'

24 April 1963

I am churning out portraits. I feel like a dentist. Next please. It's not an easy way to make money.

I take care of my back. I lie flat on the floor between sittings. I am beginning to suspect that I swindle when I talk about art seriously while manufacturing so many portraits. Brett Whiteley lives in self-chosen poverty, creating a great triptych and measuring the whisky very meanly.

4 May 1963

Robert Helpmann took me to the Academy to look at his picture. I have never seen a summer exhibition, it's a nightmare. There are good paintings, I suspect, but one can't see them as they hang in triple rows from the ceiling to the floor, screaming abstracts indiscriminately jumbled with velvety kitsch still lifes. Helpmann, I think, would love to become the director of the Sydney Opera House. Not only does he want to import the famous from overseas, but he wants to bring up a new generation of Australian performers.

I can't understand why they have not invited him to do just that. He's just returned from New York where he directed his new ballet, *Electra* (Arthur Boyd's stage designs are brilliant), and next week he's flying to Moscow and then Leningrad to produce *Swan Lake*.

10 May 1963

When I don't have portrait sittings, and when I feel physically capable, I trot to exhibitions. London is full of pop art. Donaldson at the Rowan Gallery shows sharp-edged repetitive figures, like squares on movie film.

Johnny has done marvellously in his exams. He writes that he now wants to do his honours in maths. Peter writes protectively: 'Take care of that back.' Jancsi's letters are as they were twenty-four years ago. I feel happy and am looking forward to moving into our new house.

15 May 1963

I invited John Perceval, Asher Bilu, Brett Whiteley, Ron Russell and Len French over. Two bottles of whisky are consumed. Perceval leaves me two sketches on which he writes 'Portrait of Cassab'. It's a gossip-only night. No one talks art.

26 May 1963

I went to the Festival Hall to hear Callas in concert. Great experience to hear one of the best sopranos of the century, though on the podium she can't show how good an actress she is. Tibor Dery, the giant of Hungarian literature, came along. He was imprisoned for three and a half years (after the revolution). His wife was only allowed to visit him twice a year, and he could write to her every three months, no more than thirty-two lines. Although he is celebrated and feted now, his eyes show the terror of the soul.

Anne meets me in Nice and takes me to Cannes and Monte Carlo. I cannot believe I'm here on the Riviera, which I have heard and read so much about. I really see it. Anne rents the main flat in her house, and stays in the downstairs bachelor flat. She occupies two tiny rooms, a shower and a kitchenette, and a door to the garden which has thirty-two orange and lemon trees, and a corner of the blue sea.

She takes me in her small Fiat on long excursions to the Musée Léger, on a hill above an enchanting sleepy village. This fantastic mixture everywhere. The Cocteau chapel in Villefranche, and at noon we sip red wine on the square as we wait for the siesta to end so we can enter Picasso's chapel of war and peace.

Anne burns insect repellents in her bedroom lest a mosquito mars her skin, but to make doubly sure she covers her face with black muslin. She has to look well as Tom, an American, arrives the day I leave. When the American goes, she's due to meet a chap in Istanbul.

Charles sends red roses and telegrams every day. The famous violinist, (who bought her the house) will meet her at the Edinburgh Festival in September, but by October she has to be in Africa on a safari, and she's going skiing in November in Negève.

She says she adores her life,. for few women are born whores but she was. She tells me about techniques no untrained wife has heard of nor can compete with. She has an arsenal of sex aids as a dentist has drills. 'A wife,' she tells me, 'expects to get satisfaction. I don't. I'm selfless in sex. That's why I'm such a good whore.'

We go to Vallauris, a potters' village placed on the map by Picasso where I buy lamp bases for the new house, and on to Grasse to see the ancient olive press, masses of roses in the process of becoming perfumes, miles of hothouses full of carnations.

I enjoy the few days of my holiday in spite of my strange friend who breaks three crystal glasses, combs a blonde wig as lovingly as Lorelei would her own, reads six newspapers from London and New York. Inexplicably the atmosphere turns hostile. As a consequence I break the fourth crystal glass, and two nails, and I cut my finger and spoil one roll of film in my camera. After confiding in me about a cure she had to take for alcoholism, I get frightened when she drinks one whisky after another while we wait for the steak on the barbecue in the garden. She gets so drunk that she falls and breaks the fifth crystal glass.

Next morning she tells me she was so drunk she soiled the bed.

'It's my bed,' she declares angrily, 'I soil it if I want to.' And as she woke with a headache and a hangover, she starts drinking beer for breakfast. I try to dissuade her unsuccessfully as she prepares to take me to San Remo on the Italian side.

'I don't want to go to San Remo,' I tell her, 'go sleep it off.'

No use arguing with a drunk. I know I risk my life as the little Fiat takes curves at too great a speed. Anne lets go of the steering wheel and I grab it just in time. She drives through red lights, and smears lipsticks on at crossroads while impatient French horns hoot behind.

Luckily, we find out at the Italian border that she left her handbag at home including her passport. They would not let us through without documents. Suffering such indignity, we turn back tearfully and for lunch she has more alcohol, sending a chill down my back. A swim sobers her up a bit and we go to a museum (in a bikini, alas as she lost her dress on the beach). Never mind, the scarf covers her front and the paintings cover her back even though one can't see paintings that way. Nothing can spoil the Picasso sculptures gazing out of plate-glass windows over the Antibes roofs and the blue blue sea.

Next day, vowing to stay sober, we drive to Vence. When she is sober she is like a soldier, wanting only to serve.

22 June 1963

Sydney

I am painting still lifes again after many years. While Mautner Ur, the house painter, filed into the new house with an army of Hungarians who bellow folk songs above the harbour view and tear down the old wallpaper.

I started a portrait of Elwyn Lynn.

28 November 1963

No diary for months.

We moved into the house. It is strange, enormous, lonely. It took months for our souls to move in with our bodies. It is beautiful. I gaze at the harbour every morning, or at the ocean on the other side.

We went to Cairns for a holiday. The little Mini we rented swallowed the canvases, the paint, the easel and us, and Jancsi did all the driving while I searched for the subject. We did a thousand miles in two weeks, exploring rainforests, sugarcane fields, towns, mountains and sea. By 6 a.m. we had already found our spot where I painted and Jancsi read his book. The block disappeared in a day as the new colours, the lush and soft and rotting and growing world around me sneaked onto the canvas. I don't think I know peace greater than painting *in* the landscape.

It seems I can only bring a show together this way, in one, long, strong burst.

All is familiar now. The monument with the clock. The neon of the pub. The Aborigines on the streets, the wet heat, and the red, purple and orange poinciana trees.

A telephone call out of the blue. Lord de L'Isle, the governor-general, would like a portrait of his daughter before Christmas, could I come to Canberra? They rang me again in the motel in Cairns. Could I come for a drink at Admiralty House in Sydney on Sunday (the day I arrive), have the first sitting in my studio on Monday, and come on their plane on Tuesday and continue in Government House. Bring my Cairns canvases to work on (I told them I have to work for my show), a studio will be prepared for me. Meantime I have another week. Jancsi has gone home.

In the evenings I go out alone. And at the end of my stay I found Yorkey's Knob which signifies the essence of all that Cairns means to me. The swamp is breathtaking. Things which look like bristle brushes stand stiffly in the squashy morass, small alluvial lakes, petrified mangroves. A jungle bursting out of slush.

I have forty paintings. Thank you, dear God. No doubt He held my hand as, for two years, I didn't have five paintings which mattered. I hope this is better than Alice.

18 December 1963

Buying painting materials, finishing Elwyn Lynn's portrait for the Archibald.

Government House is a good hotel with three chefs. Vichyssoise, duck stuffed with chestnut, excellent pastry, a waiter for each guest. The lady's maid not only unpacked my suitcase and ironed my dress, but each time I return to my room she has changed the towel and folded the toiletpaper back at a sharp angle.

After painting in the afternoon, Lord de L'Isle showed me his painting and was so delighted with the lesson I gave him, he was annoyed when we were disturbed by the secretary who asked him about a cable to be sent to the queen. For, that morning, five new ministers were sworn in. And after, there was the unveiling of Dargie's copy of Dargie's portrait of Her Majesty. I found myself beside Menzies and Holt, and Senator Spooner.

There was a gala that night for which Mrs Colthurst (Lord de L'Isle's daughter) lent me long white gloves. After dinner the ladies had to leave and the men stayed with a glass of port. A yawning night.

20 December 1963

The governor-general commissioned me to paint all four of his daughters together. He even asked me not to make it academic. I taught him well.

16 January 1964

I opened the Sydney Morning Herald this morning, and there it was, in black and white: J. G. Kampfner has won a scholarship to Sydney University. I burst into tears.

7 April 1964

The show is done, for better, for worse, there it stands in the living room and stares back at me.

There is a postal strike and thirteen million letters are now piled up. The invitations for my show are among them.

19 April 1964

En route to London

It was the most awful wrench to part from the family.

The show was a disaster.

Wallace Thornton started by saying that after all those royal commissions and after all those prizes, look at her.

Gleeson wrote: 'Judy Cassab has a difficult problem. She is in the unfortunate position of having a remarkable talent for setting down likenesses at a time when the setting down of likeness is barely regarded as an artistic activity at all. A hundred years ago Miss Cassab's ability would have earned her the highest praise. Today it is an anachronism and, conscious of this fact, the artist has sought to change her natural talents to suit the times. Unfortunately her attempts to date have rarely been satisfactory.'

29 April 1964

London

After Athens and Vienna, I go to London's Tate Gallery, into the most important exhibition I have seen in years. 54–64: Painting and Sculpture of a Decade, sponsored by the Gulbenkian Foundation. I bought myself a season ticket to let it soak in. There are 300 paintings from twenty-six countries. It's like seeing 100 one-man shows. Five Tàpies, five Appels, four Sugais, five Soulages, three Motherwells, four Burris, five de Staels, five Jorns, six Rauschenbergs, three Mannessiers, five Klines, five Bacons, five Vasarélys, five de Koonings, five Hartungs, five Rothkos, six Giacomettis, six Dubuffets, etc. The Tate is redesigned into intimate bays. In the natural chaos of such diverse material as over the last ten years, there is sufficient order in the hanging.

Another exhibition at the Whitechapel (Stuyvesant Foundation, twelve British painters), the new generation left me stone cold, except Brett Whiteley's bathroom paintings. The 'statements' in the catalogue are so pretentious I shudder.

I write my letters sometimes to Jancsi, sometimes to Peter or to Johnny. I wrote that I feel like a student on a scholarship to the Tate University. All along those walls whether figurative or not there are marvellous empty areas encouraging me to clutter less. I wrote them that these absences of mine are like bitter medicine. I'm out in cold exile. I mean that. However, these withdrawals are necessary. I am forced to think, a faculty which rusts a bit in everyday living. I weigh my values, looking back at those young men I left behind, longing to keep them as friends, always.

I am now in Hever Castle where Henry VIII lived with Anne Boleyn. I'm painting the Astors. Gavin, owns the *Times*, and Lady Irene is the daughter of Field Marshal Haig.

I paint portraits in the music room and my easel shares the company of a harp, a harpsichord and a ping-pong table.

Gavin's stepbrother, Lord Landsdown, came today and Lord Rupert from the *Times*. There is roast beef, Yorkshire pudding and on the wall a Delacroix and a Renoir. Corot is in the corridor. I pass Holbein's Henry VIII on my way to the dining room. Afternoons I walk in the Italian garden where every stone is ancient, pillars from Rome, Etruscan vessels with flowers, the lake. There are chess figures sculpted out of shrubs in Anne Boleyn's Garden. There are eight gardeners. The castle is surrounded by a moat and the drawbridge still works. So do the secret doors leading to the torture chamber.

20 May 1964

Tony Underhill analysed my problem in painting. He thinks Australian painters are involved with the landscape while Europeans focus on contact with the human element. 'You are ready now,' he told me. 'You have all the equipment you need, starting with colour-sense, which very few painters in Australia have, and with your emotion and poetry and your knowledge. Just now the "human" is repressed because you have the need to search for new roots in a new country, and you found it in the landscape. Our generation, who went through the war and through shattering changes, has a more difficult task. The question is, which one of us and in which phase of our life, will discover the childhood seed?' I feel I have not found the seed yet.

12 June 1964

I have earned a lot in six weeks with the portraits. I deserved to rest on my laurels and my exhaustion, enjoying the mild sunshine of London, looking at shop windows in Knightsbridge. This was the day that O'Hana chose to look at the two Cairns paintings I brought with me. I wanted to show him the direction I'm taking, and which he hasn't had time to see for the previous five weeks. If I do not fit in with the art politics of his gallery, I would rather not exhibit.

However, the most important fact I face is that the Cairns pictures really are not good enough. I must have known that the two paintings I hurriedly packed for London are anaemic, pale and too naturalistic.

When I reached my room in Chesham Place I trembled and wheezed as if one just escaped a sordid, ugly adventure. I opened the two telegrams waiting on the table. One was: 'Congratulations. Won Perth Prize. Love Daddy, John, Peter.' The other: 'Darling, congratulations, you did it again. Juliska, Manci, Edith, Nelly.' I couldn't stop laughing. It was the Rubinstein Prize. I sent in the portrait of Oscar Edwards. Am I only outstanding in portraiture?

16 June 1964

Alitalia is on strike. There is no service on the plane, but it's deliciously empty and I stretched out and sleep all night. A 'short' journey home.

27 June 1964

Melbourne

Rudy Komon took the whole one-man show to Melbourne, including the pieces already sold. The Georges Gallery is spacious, stark white, black ceiling, spotlight on each painting, two bays as well. It looks much better than in Sydney and we added all the Cairns paintings which didn't fit in Rudy's small wall space; forty-two altogether. We flew over Friday morning, dumped the luggage at the Windsor and hung the show all day. I don't know about them any more. Might be that the blow of Sydney's reviews sapped my confidence or the distance in time elapsed. I wish I could overpaint each single one except the gouaches, which I think are unique and point to the future.

I know now what is was I tried to do with the Cairns oils. I felt I tended to overwork things, that they are too congested and that I ought to be more simple. I made the mistake of leaving them thin and underdone. And so, in fact, they are just as congested, instead of leaving larger areas for simplicity, and then work on them longer. Not for technical or textural reasons, but because this is how I achieve depth, and ultimately this is what I think I can do better than most painters.

Only Europeans know about surface and *matière* and I threw it away in this show. Wanting to bring the colour back into my paintings, getting sick of greys, muddy browns and black, I ran wild without spending enough time achieving subtlety. So I sit here in the Windsor Hotel waiting for the Melbourne axe to chop me down to size. I know, of course, that my whole life should be changed. That I never really shut that studio door, except in theory. It's not drawing or painting I should work on now. I have to work on my inside which is shallow and superficial. I should read all those books I bought in London: Rosenberg's *The tradition of the new*, and the study of composition with dissects everything from Botticelli to Rembrandt. A weak point. Philosophy. Not bestsellers. Only from a valley where I have to dig deeper into the self can come painting with something to say. With more aim than to please. Others, or myself.

God knows, I have weathered more abysms than most. I have been torn away from my husband for years when I was young. I suffered not knowing where he was nor how cold or hungry he felt in the snows of Russia. I was an outcast with my maid's identity, persecuted, hiding, alert for my life. I went through the unspeakable agony of knowing my mother was gassed in the ovens of Auschwitz. I lost my home three times, I starved. And I floated above all this horror with dulled innocence, and survived without going insane. I kept a sense of adventure of the young, retained details of the holocaust without daring to file it into its historical, sociological, psychological entity.

I would be strongly tempted to submit to analysis to search for lost traumas, to dig them up to make me a better artist if I were not scared of the exact opposite. Of finally having all in the conscious mind, and then not being able to paint at all. Paradoxically, I am not really involved with the art world. I am an onlooker, a bystander. Not terribly passionate either. I belong to a migrant, Jewish, middle-class family where even established families are looking and acting nouveau riche, living the pleasant empty life.

The only real value in me is I am a good wife and a loving mother. And even there I have made mistakes. In this whole mess, Jancsi emerges as my anchor, the selfless love, security, wisdom and the only balancer of values I know.

Len French's studio is in a factory building. He is boyish-looking with a sly smile. He likes to appear a simple working-class boy, as he sits in the corner pub. Under the deceptively gentle boyishness there is a professional who knows his trade as well as art. The factory suits him. It's echoing, empty, vast, austere. In it the *Genesis* glows. Enamels, PVA, chalks, inks, aquarelles, rollers, tools, concrete, hessian. He employs a boy who makes frames, cuts glass, mixes pigment. In comparison I feel like an eighteenth-century gentlewoman who dabbles.

Why did I give up trying to solve the technical problem of working in larger sizes and different materials? What have I achieved in gouache and ink? Surely there is a way. When did I last boil wax, fight the inanimate object? I just sit with Windsor and Newton, comfortably on my bum. Blast it. On the other hand, I like comfort. I like luxury. I like to preserve my looks. I go for massages to keep my figure and to the hairdresser. I like to cook good food too, and time is running through my fingers.

1 July 1964

My love for my three nearest and dearest starts to drag and drain and pain and worry me again.

Peter's diet includes a Veganin a day. He has headaches and feels tired. I sent him for a check-up. Dr Whealy thinks it's nothing to worry about—just growing pains.

Johnny is never home. It's more like having a boarder than a son. Two hundred students demonstrated for equal rights for Aborigines. Johnny was among them. We caught a glimpse of him on television.

10 July 1964

Seasoned as I am in the art world's neglect, it's hard for me to take the fact that Rudy Komon left me out of the anniversary show. Not that there was anything good enough to show, and I know it now. I'll start working on Monday (like losing weight on Monday). I'll lock myself in and start training my mind. Mental gymnastics.

Am I intolerant and impatient with people lately?

18 July 1964

Our new baby arrived. He is a three-month-old boxer. We call him Cassy, short for Picasso. He is delightful to watch, wobbly walk, worried frown, white socks and all. He sleeps with each of us in turn until he gets used to the place. When left alone he collects shoes, bathroom mats and generally misbehaves. He wags his tail at Kitty, our cat, wanting to make friends. But she is hostile or terrified and has to be hand fed.

5 August 1964

I'm not committed to any show and it's a delight to spoil pictures. 'Painting pretty pictures' in the well-trodden path won't get me further. I have a nude model, and the black and white torsos are better than the oils which still shimmer in all colours of the rainbow, instead of two or three well-chosen, well-thought-out spaces. But then, if one would know beforehand how a picture should look when finished where would the creative search be? The tentative and the instinctive? I think that with the great artists, it's the stumbling upon that gives them direction. So I throw one after the other on canvas and on paper and wait, patiently, for what I will stumble upon. One day.

26 August 1964

The nudes don't work. Neither do the enormous heads. I experiment now with the 'foundations', my excuse for a pure abstract. If I had an image, it's gone. The abstracts are suggestive, evocative and inspiring. A marvellous way of tickling one's fantasy. I place unstretched canvas on the table, mix oil colours with varnish and turps, and pour. Not touching it with the brush. Direct its flow with my hand under the canvas. Coincidence? Perhaps. But it's I who directs it.

Tony Underhill's exhibition opens today. I arranged it for him with

Rudy Komon. Last week I restored the peeled-off edges and cracks which showed, after the parcels were opened. It's my baby now, and I envy him the good criticism today which he fully deserves. Because he did it, he did what I'm trying to do and can't. The figures are torsos, emerging from a wonderfully integrated abstract surrounding.

A new television program, 'The Lively Arts', compared by Laurie Thomas. Leonard French, walking through the park, hands in the pockets of his short jacket. A simple bloke on the way to his factory building. Juxtaposed, his voice on tape answering questions which are wiped off the tape so it reads like a monologue, a sort of thinking out loud.

Laurie praises Molvig for always being different, and Fairweather for always being the same.

Colin Lanceley makes collages out of discarded objects. He calls them the scars of living. My only objection is that they're perishable. If Michelangelo would have chosen a broomstick instead of Carrara marble he would have created masterpieces. But, noble materials stand up better to time.

When Lanceley started his assemblages with the Annandale imitation realists, he was vulgar and amusing and himself. In these piano bowels and Victorian table legs he is one more page of art gloss, and much like what can be seen at the Tate.

Andrew Sibley came for a beer and offered valuable criticism about the Cairns paintings. The trouble with them, he thinks, is not so much how congested they are, but rather the areas of colour cancel each other out. It's true. If I would stick the blue and the yellow patches together by the square-inch they would be equal. I would have seen it in anyone else's paintings but my own.

The Newcastle one-man show was an utter flop. The reviews were better than anywhere else and *one* picture was sold in the three weeks. I was mainly upset because the van Bertouchs are fighting a losing battle in Newcastle. I gave them the painting they liked best as a gift.

I am painting Andrea for the second time.

'Paint me yellow or purple,' she said, 'I don't care.'

I painted an umber canvas with two large ribbons of green running across. The shocking-pink hat and face crisp over the green.

We bought a ceramic table for the living room, and went out to Gerard Havekes, the Dutch sculptor, to choose the tiles for it. He was always eccentric. He bought a deserted nightclub and sleeps, eats, cooks and works in the one large room. Chimneys sticking through the roof. The television sits on a beer barrel. Car-tyre lamps, fishing nets. The place sits in twenty-eight acres of bush. In one glade, a white goat. In another, a pink baby and four boxers.

Kaldors commissioned me to paint a mural on the wall of the new Sekers building. Clever as I am, I looked at the recesses which seemed small. When the masonite arrived I realised I have to paint five enormous panels and the price shrank as the job grew. Lucky that my old astonishment prevails. How much I enjoy doing my work, and amazement that people actually *pay* for it. I worked it into one panel. They can cut it into five for all I care. I built the texture up with PVA and pumice stone. Used eggshell varnish, powder colour, and oil in the end. Glazed and scratched, bent and lifted and turned, and it glows.

31 October 1964

Friday was Peter's last day of school. Celebration pranks all day, and a party with lots of boys and girls at our place. We 'old ones' went to bed, complying with a request to please not look in.

At 12.30 a.m. we were woken up. 'Don't be alarmed,' said Peter, 'I have been in a car crash.' We turned the light on and saw Peter standing with blood all over his face and shirt.

I dressed and took him to hospital. Pouring rain. Joe Glass stepped on the gas instead of the brakes. Peter had two stitches for the gash in his forehead. Next day both knees swelled up. Today one eye closed. Peter slept a lot and had to stay in bed. One week before exams.

I am very tired because our housekeeper is sick and I nurse her, cook and clean and wash and iron.

As always I'm terrified of losing the bluebird.

Johnny seems to lose all sense of purpose. One day he wants to go to New Guinea with a group of university students to build a school. Next day the group is no good. He wants to drive a truck to Melbourne. He wants to earn money for a new gearbox for the Sprite. He needs money to go to Surfers Paradise.

I am tired.

8 November 1964

After nursing my housekeeper back to health she decides to leave. I advertise in the *Sydney Morning Herald*. This means a month of no painting.

This lovely, enchanting house sits on me like a golem. Subconsciously I must feel angry as I dropped a bottle of wine on the glass table and it shattered into thousands of pieces. I burnt a hole in Peter's shirt while ironing. I have beds, dishes, garbage, animals, garden, laundry, drycleaner, flowers, plants, shopping. No bluebird.

12 January 1965

Johnny failed his exams. Of course he could have passed, but he didn't work to capacity. I feel desperately sad for him. It's hard, but I have no idea what goes on inside him.

Communication? I don't know how any more.

14 January 1965

John took a job as a postman today. He starts at 6 a.m.

Peter failed his matriculation.

The fault must be ours. I am shaky, weak and depressed.

23 January 1965

I went to North Sydney where one can request a re-mark if the failure in the matriculation is under five marks. Peter's was six under.

We book him into a coaching college. He works from morning to night. Jancsi promises that if he makes the effort he can go to London and study at RADA (Royal Academy of Dramatic Art).

20 March 1965

I welcome the return of routine. I am happy when the boys take the car making me a prisoner. There is nothing then that I can do but paint. I have a roll of unprimed canvas from England. Beautiful Irish canvas which gets only a coat of glue and then I pour diluted oil paint on it, unstretched as it is, and I direct its flow with my hand underneath. When it's dry I pour and direct the second layer. It's pure transparency and gives me such pleasure that I find other ways of painting at the moment boring in comparison.

I started a portrait of Desiderius Orban. I saw him the other day and said: 'Mr Orban, I asked you ten years ago to sit for me. You said you never do. It's a principle. Do you still hold it?'

He did not. I picked him up in his studio on Bronte Beach, a converted garage as tidy as a chemist-shop. Orban, at eighty-one, does geometrical abstract collages with plastic shapes stuck on a board.

All during the sitting he was amusing, witty, full of information and anecdotes. We argued for and against the portrait as an art form. When he saw the end of the first sitting, he said: 'That's amazing. Absolutely amazing. You can still spoil it next time.'

'I won't.'

I painted him very old and ugly.

18 May 1965

I took a bold step. I asked Orban to help me out of the rut. It's fantastic how he helps. I told him about the portrait routine, about a desire but inability to distort. He thinks I shouldn't step back while I paint. Stepping back means looking with the eyes of a spectator, not an artist. Also, looking at the sitter from a close-up gives a caricature sort of vision. Besides, Orban has such an amazing critical eye that he asked me, surprisingly, whether I always start my composition from the centre.

'Yes. I always do. Does it show?'

'Of course it shows. The edges are mostly unresolved. Try composing from the edges, inward.'

It's hard, even when it's a still life. But for a portrait, it's so incredibly difficult, I can't get over the delight of my misery.

For the first time in my life, I look for the pure-form relationship. I drew a self-portrait with charcoal. I started at a line of the background in the upper-right corner. Then I did the outline of the left arm. The right collarbone. The left top of the head. The right of the neck. The left eyebrow in connection with a corresponding form. Which, by this time, ceased to read: 'background'. And as I was not allowing myself to focus my attention on any part of my anatomy without looking somewhere else, the thing went along unoiled, creaking, clumsy, and the end product looked, I thought, like the first steps of a dilettante. I was exuberant.

Orban, on the other hand, used to teaching middle-aged housewives for forty years, thought he was watching the most exciting thriller. Or, as he said, watching a precision instrument sensitive to the lightest touch.

Coming in from the edges means, among other things, that by the time I reach the centre, it must be distorted. A thing which I envied in others, forced, tried, fell down on, or simply produced someone else's distortion. A Modigliani elongation. Kokoschka arthritis. Giacometti-like fish bones. This way I distort my own way because I can't help it. It's inevitable. If we would win the lottery, I know I would not paint another portrait for money. I plod on with my new exercises which produce no pictures.

10 June 1965

Rudy's new gallery looks slightly antiseptic with virgin white walls, a terrazzo floor, moss-green carpet and a roof garden. How the wheel turns. Last year I exhibited in a crummy old gallery, now I belong in a metropolitan place.

I exhibited the new, empty, clear, transparent abstracts. All critics mentioned them though they look tiny beside my neighbour, a ten-foot Daws.

23 June 1965

1965 finds us in an English-speaking, queen-curtsying island in the middle of the Asiatic sea. In other words, after the war we ran as far as we could to bring our children up in peace, away from the centre of danger. The centre seems to have slid over now. Australia is sending troops to Vietnam and John is twenty.

3 July 1965

I have won the Helena Rubinstein portrait prize for the second time. They failed to send a telegram. The news burst from a small newspaper article in the *Telegraph*.

7 July 1965

I'm on to something new. I discovered that I can use my gouache–Indian ink techniques on unprimed canvas. This is the only successful way for me to paint figures now, and since they started to occupy the studio, they are so much more alive than everything else.

7 November 1965

A friend wrote from London introducing Shan Hailey who is coming to Sydney. Into our life walked a stunningly beautiful girl and Johnny is in love.

3 January 1966

Johnny went to Europe. As I watched him walk towards the jet I thought it right now to cut the umbilical cord. The small boy with two teeth missing who arrived on the other side of the world travels in a suit with traveller's cheques in his pocket. Shan was at the airport with Nick and Romy Waterlow. Peter is going next year. Right now he is a waiter in the mountains during the holidays.

I ponder about us often and how unfair it is that Jancsi who, in his previous life, handled breweries, wineries, properties, loved his work, made it thrive, and lost it all. Like so many migrants, he couldn't find a place in his field and the work with which he supports us is repetitive and boring. Our elastic stockings are excellent but what a narrow lane for a first-rate mind.

10 March 1966

Johnny moved in with Shan. Jancsi wants to sell the house.

We are planning a trip together.

11 April 1966

New York

New York is the world of the merchant-Medicis, who built the Lincoln Center in a few years—like a couple of Sydney Opera Houses—with Henry Moore in the centre court.

Another great experience is a Max Ernst retrospective in the Jewish Museum. *Dayenu*, as we say on Passover night. One such experience would have been plenty. I drag my sketchbook along and try to hold it, jot it down, scribble; my eyes popping.

The museum itself displays *torahs*, *menorahs*, and silver emblems and treasures of Jewry in such a way as to elevate it, and exhibit the pride of a great race.

Three hundred people stood in the queue in the Museum of Modern Art to see Turner. I saw a Leonard French among the new acquisitions.

I dropped into the opening of Andy Warhol's show. Silver-foil pillows filled with helium gas are floating in the room. The well-dressed audience is flicking at them. I looked around the bare walls. There is nothing else. Only pillows. The receptionist wears a silver-foil tie.

Lilly Brody, my painter friend of Szentendre, takes me to visit Lucas Samaras in his studio. Fifth floor, no lift. An iron stove, a bed, and objects. There are boxes. A box, stuck with coloured wool. It's like grandmother's Gobelin, but not stitched. Stuck. On it sits a stuffed bird. One can open a tiny drawer in the box. There are marbles in it. There is a box in which an embryo's heart swims in a test tube which is placed into a dirty tennis shoe. A pin-cushion with a plastic breast protruding, pink nipple. A lady's shoe inlaid with imitation jewellery. It has two heels. There is an x-ray of his own skull, bordered with nails which cast their shadows onto the thing. Very inventive.

Is painting out of fashion?

I went to Theodor Stamos's studio. This is the old school. At least ten years old. He is a friend of Mark Rothko and Robert Motherwell. All three are famous enough to be shown all over the world except in New York. Only objects will do.

Stamos bought himself a four-storey house on the West Side which is a 'bad address'. People get mugged there. But he likes it.

29 April 1966

At long last Jancsi is with me on a trip.

We are in Tel Aviv. I am still astounded that the advertisements are written right to left, in Hebrew, and that the customs official is a Jew. No wonder one says that this is a country with two million presidents. To a Jew, another Jew doesn't seem to be an authority.

Jancsi's nephew, Garai, who was twelve when I last saw him in Losonc, is director of the Sheraton Hotel.

I haven't seen Ági for 24 years. We lived together for a year in Budapest while our husbands were in labour camp. She studied sculpture, I studied painting. She is married to a professor and a colonel in the army. They took us to Akko, a delightful Arab town on the shore of the Mediterranean. Behind a Camp Cove-like beach is a crusader's fort which is 5000 years old.

After the first week we rented a Volkswagen (part of the German *Wiedergutmachung*) and moved to the Holy Land Hotel in Jerusalem. It overlooks a valley and lovely Arab villages. No wonder this was the birthplace of great religions. The mountains slope into terraces and everything has this indescribable tender orange colour like a pale blush, striped with green. It all swings in semicircles and there are the cypress trees for verticals like exclamation marks.

We drove from Jerusalem to Lidda Airport and boarded a plane to Rome. After a short and violent love affair with the eternal city, we took a bus tour to Naples, Pompeii, Sorrento, Positano, Amalfi and Capri.

We flew to Geneva. We rented a Volkswagen and started driving through Switzerland. We stayed in Gstaad in a sweet Posthotel, got drunk from all those lakes, snowy giants, lilacs, the smell of milk and manure, unceasing beauty. I don't think I could live here.

After seventeen years we are on our way to Budapest. When I last saw the border I nursed two little children and fed them spinach from a thermos. I don't recognise anything. Every street name is changed and the cars are scrap metal. There are only four hotels in Budapest, and out of those one just collapsed as the Danube flooded the Margaret Island.

We stay at the Royal in a dark hole of a room. The orchestra playing for afternoon tea just underneath our window is drowned out by the clanking of the trams. I tried to close the window but couldn't live with the stench. The smell pervades all Budapest. The state is the landlord, and the landlord has not painted the houses for twenty years, and the odour of the cabbage cooked in them for twenty years mingles with badly-ventilated toilets. The houses are dark grey and shabby, and so are the people. Only a sense of humour remains.

In the National Gallery the youngest painter visible is over seventy. No new generation. They must be somewhere, but one can't find them.

Laci Gerend drives us to Szentendre, the artists' colony where we spent four summers. I wanted to see the Danube again, the curve with the willows and elms which I painted so often. We go for lunch at a little inn near Leányfalu. At last, a real memory, vivid recognition, a souvenir to keep. Danube smell. Tisza smell. Bread and butter smell with green paprika.

Russian soldiers patrol the shore.

It's raining in Salzburg. We are walking in the stage decor under an umbrella, in the jewelbox which is even more beautiful than I remember. I have three favourite towns. Jerusalem, Salzburg and Venice. We drive to St Gilgen in the wet. We almost don't recognise Frau Elmauer's house where we stayed with the children for a year.

The best part of the trip leads through the Grossglockner to Cortina d'Ampezzo. The Dolomites are not at all pink as I was told, not after Alice Springs. But unique. And Verona and then Venice.

12 August 1966

Sydney

We are invited for dinner to John and Shan. They serve warm sake in ceramic cups made by John. Hungarian chilled white wine for dinner. Shan cooks in jeans and a red pullover. Her cheeks are red and flushed as she serves. I totter up the winding stairs to see the bookshelf Johnny built.

Peter likes to be there and Jancsi is mellow. While we listen to Bob Dylan I am aware of the irony that since Johnny moved from home he is the good boy, and now Peter is the one who gets up late, comes home late and doesn't study.

20 January 1967

Canberra

I paint Sir John Eccles for the Australian National University. I know he won the Nobel Prize, but for what? Last night he greeted me stiffly, in a dark suit. In his lab this morning, in his own environment, his eyes spark fire at the adventures of every day. He is sixty-three years old and six feet tall. He moves so fast his white smock flies. His assistants are from Tokyo and Pisa. Retiring from the ANU, he will be welcome in Chicago.

Would I like to view one of the experiments after the sitting? Yes.

An anaesthetised cat lies on the table, head open, brain showing, electrodes connected to nerve centres and as they receive the electric stimulus, a closed-circuit television screen shows the secret signs as each zigzag represents a message of the animal's brain.

26 February 1967

Sydney

We are invited to a cocktail party by Princess Alexandra and her husband, Angus Ogilvy. It's been six years since I painted her. The Royal Blind Society rang. They would like to reproduce *Three kings*, for their Christmas card next year. It's in a convent in Adelaide. Could they possibly fly it to Sydney for the reproduction? I have to get Father Scott's number in Melbourne. He knows the telephone number of the

Adelaide convent. I ring the mother superior. Which one I don't know. Mother Superior doesn't know who Judy Cassab is. The *Three kings?* She has never seen it. Perhaps Sister Cecilia will know. Sister Cecilia tells me the *Three kings* is their prized possession but they will lend it to me.

16 March 1967

Princess Alexandra's cocktail party was enjoyable. We are standing in a queue. Men go first. Mr John Kampfner. Four handshakes. Mrs Kampfner. I am almost past when Alexandra suddenly exclaims, 'Judy, my dear, it's you.' She calls to Jancsi, 'Come back.' Ogilvy asks Jancsi, 'How does it feel to have a famous wife?' 'You must know,' Jancsi told him. 'You have one too.'

As we stood around in the multitude, a secretary came over. 'Mr Kampfner, Sir, could I borrow your wife for a while?' And ushered me to Alexandra who asked me what I am painting and when I will be in London again.

Later, I saw Sir Frank Packer, whom I painted in 1956 for the Archibald. I had not heard from him since he announced at the time that he wanted to buy the portrait.

'I feel guilty.'

'Why?'

'I should have bought that portrait.'

'Yes, you should have.'

'Who bought it?'

'No one. I still have it.'

'Good. Then consider it sold.'

'The price has gone up.'

'It doesn't matter.' Then he added, 'How much was the price eleven years ago?' I didn't tell him. He laughed.

The next day I read in the paper that Packer was in hospital with pneumonia.

19 April 1967

Hal Missingham and his wife, Esther, came to dinner. His blond curls are snow white now, his face is incredibly young underneath the hairline. William Wright, a young expatriate Australian painter who has a show with Rudy Komon, also came.

Missingham projects his photographs of rocks, birds, shells and other natural abstracts through an artistic lens.

Prue and Eric Penn wrote asking me if their son, David, could stay with us when he comes to be jackaroo. I painted all three of them. Eric is comptroller of the queen's household, and the office of the Lord Chamberlain.

We picked David up at the ship terminal, with Peter. Since his arrival there are more underpants to wash, of course, and more breakfasts and less painting but I'm glad I can help Prue.

I received a letter from them today about the Shah of Persia looking for a portrait painter for himself and the empress. The ambassador loved the three Penn portraits and recommended me. Would be another adventure. The world is pretty grey just now.

21 May 1967

I work on titles for my paintings. First, I gave them names like 'Red' and 'Green' but this sounds too clean-cut and cool. Concrete terms like 'Landscape' would be false. The recurring shapes in these last eighteen months are sort of pyramids and everything floats. I bought a *Roget's Thesaurus*. I look up the commonplace word which covers it, open the corresponding page and a new world of words opened up for me. I hover over them as if with a Geiger counter until I find the music for the painting.

It's the irony of life that just when I arrived at my abstract expression, three abstract painters in Sydney returned to representation. Rapotec got hold of his exploding, frolicking, saturnine circles, and hung them on Gothic cathedrals. Olsen has more Klee midgets and animals than before. And Eric Smith exhibited a show of portraits to glowing reviews and I wonder whether I am so critical because of jealousy? The portraits are painted from photographs, of Chagall, Rouault, Bonnard and Picasso and (among the Australians) of French, Drysdale, Nolan and others. They are contemporary paintings without a doubt. He frames his usual uncontrolled expressionist strokes into Rauschenberg-like boxes which gives a first impression of pop art. This is reinforced by the lettering, whole lines of them.

Besides, Bonnard's portrait is painted in the manner of Bonnard. Mattisse sits beside a Matisse-like table in Matisse's pure colour. Where there isn't a painting style to borrow from, as in the case of Patrick White, for instance, he is depicted in red, like a comic strip. Tucker has a Tucker-like bird sitting on his head. Not in good taste, but appropriate to pop's illustrative character.

I have no commissions and very little money.

6 June 1967

War broke out in Israel.

We are amazed about the emotion this war awakens, not only in us. We sit near the radio from dawn to dusk as in the 1940s.

17 June 1967

A miracle of biblical proportions happened. Israel achieved victory in one week. It was the first time in our crippled life that we felt proud to be Jews. The Star of David, which was stamped on our clothes and our houses as a symbol of shame and humiliation in 1943 is now on the victorious flags of battle in Jerusalem and Jericho.

Shan says after Johnny's exams they want to go work on a kibbutz.

1 July 1967

After four years, my one-man show is opening next week. Jancsi is very angry at the thought of the publicity intruding into our lives once again. So I answer telephone calls from the press secretly and with feelings of guilt.

16 August 1967

Nineteen pictures are sold. One was bought by the Art Gallery of NSW, one by the Commonwealth Art Advisory Board. The show was a success and more importantly, God has shown me my own personal way of expression. The material itself took me on a road into the unknown and when, after years of searching and experimenting, I finally created an object which is my own, I feel that I have hardly scratched the surface. I have so much to say.

11 September 1967

A one-man show at the Skinner Gallery in Perth. I went ten days before the opening as I had commissions. One is Margaret Hohnen, whose husband is chairman of Rio Tinto.

I sold fourteen paintings at the opening. The National Gallery of Western Australia bought one.

It so happened that the conference of the gallery directors was in Perth this year, and Hal Missingham who was present, opened my show. He said, 'We watched her development and this is the sixth painting we acquired. I must say that not only is she an excellent artist but that she is a true professional. There are those who congregate in pubs and talk about all the wonderful things they are going to do next week, or next year. She doesn't talk about it. She just gets it done. How she does it, I don't know. What with two whacking big sons and a delectable husband to take care of. She also cooks the best apple strudel I have ever had. Many people told me tonight, if only I could afford one, I'd love to buy one. Well, I'm telling you. You *can* afford it. Buy it. Think about paying the butcher afterwards.'

I could hardly believe it but I received another three commissions. It seems I can crawl out of financial embarrassment at last.

3 December 1967

My disc slipped and I'm encased in a steel corset. It hurts.

The pound sterling is devalued.

The war in Vietnam is raging.

Smiling girls in bikinis on the front pages.

David returned from Cairns with seven pennies to his name. He washes cars and saves for his fare to Perth. He plays the gramophone in his room.

Johnny passed his exams and welds candelabras in the garage.

The washing machine and the dryer are both turning with their laundry. Shan rings from England where she's gone to visit her parents.

Saturday afternoon. Peter and Julie watch television. The Maharishi who taught the Beatles to meditate is talking about meditation. Peter is impressed. He hasn't read my Zen books. I've been practising deep breathing for a long time now. The centre of the universe is the centre of our body, ourself. If one learns how to concentrate and dive deep down into the self, that's the only place to find peace of mind.

21 December 1967

The Friday program is to pick up the Orbans. Originally it was to be just Orban and me, but Alice has got into the habit of joining us. There she sat, rouge and wrinkles, like a spider in her web while I analysed his new paintings. If we go out, we have to stop at the delicatessen for her to shop. We go to the galleries together. She has become an annex and I am used to her.

30 December 1967

I sigh at the end of every day.

I don't write. I don't read. I try but can't concentrate. The life of Benvenuto Cellini doesn't interest me.

It is ninety degrees and I choke. Everybody is irritable.

9 January 1968

I never know whether it's Thursday or Monday. I have nothing to say in painting.

Visit Orban. Alice fell off the bed last night and broke a shoulder. Orban helps her in the shower each morning.

'The Zen Buddhists are right,' he says. 'Our kind of love chains us to each other. One shouldn't have such bondage. Meanwhile, because a human is extremely cruel, I am thinking, that after fifty-three years of marriage, at last I can do what I want.'

15 February 1968

My portrait of Margo Lewers won the Archibald Prize.

Two television channels, the radio, the newspaper headlines, hundreds of telegrams, telephone calls, flowers.

Johnny and Shan have decided to get married.

'I realised,' Johnny said, 'I not only love her. I like her.'

We feel terribly happy.

Meanwhile there are thorns. I am not pleased that he wants to go to the wedding in a fire-engine, resplendent in fancy dress.

Beryl Foster, my Alice Springs friend and pupil, asked me to go to Lightning Ridge for a long weekend. While we were on the road I didn't think of anything but how the car gulped the miles. We took turns driving every hour, barbecued the steak with gum leaves, drank cold beer and sketched.

It's a bizarre world with hundreds of molehills on the surface and the corresponding mini-mines under it. Ancient motors hang on strange poles and ropes. People live in makeshift hovels, and the only hotel is a tram.

10 March 1968

The first exhibition of the Power Bequest opened. It's too one-sided. All kinetic. It lights up, moves, glitters. The human element is missing.

12 March 1968

Happiness for three days. Peter finally got a job—at the ABC. It's boring and bureaucratic but he has to wrestle with reality. I pray he will keep it for a while.

The Kampfner restaurant is in full swing. The Astors arrived. Gavin is president of Commonwealth Press. They spend one day in Sydney and have lunch with us on the patio. The two boys are present and Mrs Vincent Fairfax is there, the atmosphere is pleasant.

The Hagenbachs arrived from London and Tony Woods, the artist, from Tasmania.

20 April 1968

Peter got a promotion.

Johnny and Shan have set off in their Land Rover on honeymoon. They plan to go around Australia for five months. The Land Rover is splendid. It's like a house or a boat. It has a compass and a radio.

The *Sydney Morning Herald*'s new art critic, Donald Brook, is a gentle-looking young intellectual which, it seems, is a characteristic of bloodthirsty arbiters of taste.

14 May 1968

Johnny and Shan are in Katherine where it hasn't rained so much in eighty years. All right, nothing worse ever should befall them, but it *is* miserable on a honeymoon, in a Land Rover in the rain.

I want Jancsi to accept the children's invitation to fly to Alice Springs for a week. He will see.

'What does it depend on?'

'I have to discuss it.'

'With whom?'

'With myself.'

Wrong person.

I was invited to a reception of the third Commonwealth Study Conference (I never knew of the first two) which was opened in Australia

Square by the Duke of Edinburgh. Only artists, film, theatre, design and music people, and some academics. No wives or husbands. It was a swinging affair.

The duke's speech was very amusing. He said, after leaving the exhibition, everyone will feel fit. Only for the life of him he couldn't guess why this round tower is called a square. Afterwards, dinner on the forty-seventh floor in the Summit restaurant which revolves dead slow and all the bays, harbours, ships, skyscrapers, lights, bridges flow by in majestic procession.

I finished a portrait of Mungo MacCallum. 'Survey', his critical program on television started again after a long break (Elwyn Lynn is part of it now). He said the ABC is almost bankrupt mainly because 'This Day Tonight' eats up such a lot of money.

27 May 1968

Hectic week. UNESCO seminar, a conference of international art critics. Clement Greenberg, world-famous authority from New York, flits from Pittsburgh to Amsterdam to Venice to judge competitions. His Contemporary Art Society lecture was a disappointment as he covered the narrow field of minimal art, which repeats the picture within the picture. It has to be empty everywhere except if cutting into the edges of the square. Frank Stella does it as a third dimension. This is the taste of the moment. Fear of the moment is to ruffle the surface in any way. It's the furthest point to which art can go. They guarantee the picture's integrity by making it uniform.

After abstract expressionism, where the obvious brushstroke kept the picture together, it was a process of weaving. Pollock's trickles were woven. With tighter unity there was space left at the edges and the configuration floats. Greenberg talked about elementary issues introduced as revelations. Like Clyfford Still discovered that if you keep your values close together you can be bolder in your drawing. That Barnett Newman discovered (with his stripe down the centre) that symmetry will assure the unity and integrity of the picture. That concentric circles in Jasper Johns (who at least is painterly) and in Kenneth Noland have symmetry as well as all-overness. It is impossible for the informed New Yorker, he said, *not* to like such a picture. He talked about playing it safe. How sad. Jules Olitski is considered a rebel violating the accepted taste simply by a squiggle of a brushstroke at the edge. The tendency really works like Dior's hemlines.

We were invited to Harry Seidler. The Seidlers took everyone around the house, but no one was introduced to Greenberg. He sat guru-like in the centre of Central Gallery people and I didn't feel like squeezing in. They are the hard-edge and colourfield people and therefore were crestfallen when Greenberg considered their work derivative.

Second time I met Greenberg, at Oscar Edwards. A different man there—relieved to give a prize to little old ladies' flowerpieces. He actually liked Pro Hart, but dislikes Michelangelo.

I am quite sure eminence has a lot to do with geography. Should Lynn live in New York ...

About pop art he said: 'Heavens, how wonderful. No need for knowledge.'

All pop art is good because the standard is so low.

6 June 1968

What a violent world to be born in. Student revolts in Germany, America, France, triggered off ten million workers striking. The whole country paralysed, no railway, airport, electricity, petrol, post. Old Caesaromaniac de Gaulle does it again. He won't abdicate and order is restored. Disgusting election campaign in the US. Robert Kennedy sings pop songs with a comedian. Next day he is assassinated like his brother. Unspeakably horrible.

Malcolm Muggeridge writes, 'There is so much power, so little strength, so much wealth and so little ease, so much information and so little knowledge.'

During the international art critics' seminar I devoted a day to drive three critics around the Paddington galleries. Professor Hutchings and Dr Salek Mink from Perth, and Gertrude Langer from Brisbane. When we arrived at Rudy Komon's, they were shown Leonard French, Fred Williams, Clifton Pugh and Charles Blackman. None of mine. This was upstairs. Downstairs he pulled out Sibley, Molvig, Moriarty—none of mine. I was sickened by this, got red and chilly.

At Oscar Edwards's dinner Greenberg said, 'Miss Cassab, I haven't seen any of yours.' Professor Bernard Smith said, 'Judy, we went to Rudy's but he didn't show us any.'

That was it. I decided to leave his gallery. To have a one-man show in two years, I don't need him. Any gallery in Sydney will be glad to give me one.

When I saw him two weeks later my anger had evaporated, but not my decision. However, after 'It's my fault', 'I am to blame' and 'Give me another chance' my soft heart got the better of me.

A. Alvarez, a critic from England, held a seminar at the association for cultural freedom. He called pop art 'capitalist realism'. Witty and true. I considered social realism pop two years ago. He talked more of poetry than painting but the analogy was surprising. He called the 'contemporary poem' a fragment with both ends open.

I've gotten into the habit of visiting John Olsen's art school on Wednesdays. It's the nearest there is to Parisian coffee houses. He encourages artists to talk to the students. I grabbed a charcoal myself and demonstrated what I had to say about the nude. Olsen cooks green prawns in garlic and we lunch together, drink red wine and talk some more about art.

Last Wednesday night I was invited to a party for Alvarez. The old bakery swings. Drysdale, Blackman, Fred Williams, and Bill Rose are there, as well as students, it was tremendous. I felt like Cinderella at midnight, as usual.

4 July 1968

Western Australia

An invitation from a stranger, Rachel Blythe, to stay at Mount House station.

I took the plane at 11 p.m. in Perth (there is no day flight to the north) and reached Derby at 5.30 a.m. It stopped at small sheds every hour. In Derby the motels did not open till seven, and then there was no room. So I sit around in Derby half-dead. The mail plane leaves at ten. It can't land at the airstrip at Mount House because it's a DC3 so we flew to Glen Roy station where an old truck carted me fifty miles back.

Rachel is Lord Reynolds' daughter, and I simply cannot comprehend how she settled here where news comes only every two weeks, the flying doctor every six weeks, and as Richard is gone mustering cattle, she has no company but the farm labourers and the Aboriginal maid. Certainly, the English are colonising stock, I can't see a Jewish woman doing this however much in love.

Got into a bit of a panic on the first day without a car to borrow for sketching. When the truck took me out at six this morning (it's flying doctor day so I climbed on) it was uncertain when it would pick me up again. In any case it meant that I had to choose my subjects within walking distance.

None of the enchantment, weirdness and harshness of the Alice. No sight new to the eyes. When one talks of the fabulous north-west, one can't mean this corner of the Kimberleys. I try to inject imagination in tall yellow grass, gum trees and stone, and hope something better turns up. Luck had it that the man who had come to do the fences was a hobby painter. (They turn up everywhere, don't they?) As I help him along, he helps me carry and cart, and at least I'm not alone in the bush.

5 July 1968

It's not a country that rushes at you showing itself. The second morning the fencer and I got a truck, and all the things worth painting were less than ten-inches high. Yellow spinifex bumps, and stripes of dusty pink and greyish green with fluff on their heads. I'm not *thinking* about art. I'm not approaching it intellectually. There is no time for that in the shadow of the truck, spraying fly repellent all over myself, it starts pouring out on bits of paper while all the carefully prepared canvases remain empty. But there is plenty of material for later.

At the end of the day Rachel and I go over to the old house to have a beer with Brack, the manager of the station. John Roulston is there, the pilot who does the aerial mustering. He flies up, searches for cattle, twenty cows here, ten bullocks there, dives down on them, scaring them and driving them to the station in a red cloud of dust. Terribly dangerous profession. He already has two stations of his own. Rachel asks, as he flies to Derby on Friday, would he give me a lift?

'Well,' he says, 'the aircraft is not as it should be. I wouldn't want the responsibility. Let's put it this way, if Judy was my wife, I wouldn't take her.'

That's that, let's wait for the cattle train. When? Maybe tonight, maybe in three days. Next day I offer to cook Hungarian goulash with nokkies, Richard Blythe is coming home.

Lights at Mount House station go out at ten minutes past eight, after that it's one candle for each room and a torch for the outside loo.

Richard is late and when he bursts into the room, I understand what Lord Reynolds' daughter is doing under these desperately primitive circumstances. He is the most beautiful man I have ever seen off the screen. Very young, brown, perfect teeth; life and life-giving happiness surround him. One can see it.

When the candles come on, Brack comes in and says, 'Judy, John Roulston says he patched up the plane a bit and he *will* take you tomorrow morning.' I took the candle and packed, and said a prayer for the plane.

Bacon and eggs at 4 a.m. The truck took us to the airstrip. We climbed in through the wing and John pushed the starter several times. It was a smooth beautiful flight and in an hour we landed at Derby and while waiting for a taxi, I looked on as John Roulston opened up the hood. 'What a small engine,' I marvelled. He said, 'And you know we flew over on half an engine.'

A pretty young woman came out of the next room. I remembered her from Glen Roy. She is Mary List, a photojournalist married to John Selsmark, pilot of the DC3. She persuaded me not to leave Derby next morning because she knows the place and will be my guide.

Mary took me to the clearing among the baobab trees, and I made four sketches of that incredibly beautiful, mysterious bush. Then she took lots of photos with me looking like a scarecrow in my sunhat and dirty slacks. I realised she was using me as material, heaven knows for what magazine, just as I used the baobab tree.

After dinner we went to see the Kununurra Kid, an old Aborigine we met in the pub this morning. He explained that if he sings so early, the police will think he is drunk and put him in jail.

As it turned out he didn't sing in the evening either because, his wife explained, he drank a bit too much. We sat down in the lounge while Mary projected some slides of the country I'm going to paint in Broome, Port Hedland and Roebourne.

We left at 7 a.m. for Fitzroy Crossing.

I do five sketches, drive 150 miles, refuse to go to the mission to paint Aborigines.

My first trip this morning (with a rented car) was the Japanese cemetery. There among the tall yellow Kimberley grass stands a forest of obelisks. Each stone is hewn out of some lovely rock, rather flat and tall and elegant. There are two beer bottles each on every grave which serve as urns.

By now all my judgement of what is called 'the situation' is gone. If I paint an abstract Broome, I could have stayed in Paddington. In Broome the roofs are slanted and taller than the houses and look like sails or Gauguin's Normandy women.

13 July 1968

I flew from Broome to Roebourne, then got a lift to Wittenoom with Andrew Macintosh. The mud was twenty-inches high, the water equally deep. It took six and a half hours to go 150 miles.

The pub, the only civilised place, had no room for me.

The town administrator arranged for me to stay with an 'artistic couple' for the night. He works in the geology department, teaches pottery at night, and she is a music teacher. (The visit to the mission in Broome was useful after all. I left one drawing for them, gave one to each of my drivers, left a colour one for Rachel and gave John Roulston one for flying me to Derby.)

After lunch we drove to Wittenoom and there I decided not to travel any further south. It looks like Alice Springs and is very beautiful, except that here the really beautiful sight comes every 400 miles, and the 399 one has to drive to get there are terribly boring.

I rented a Holden station wagon, made a cosy little studio in it, drove slowly and stopped and painted red hills and yellow spinifex.

23 July 1968

Sydney

Very happy being at home. Everything is intoxicating. Real coffee, fresh toast, an electric blanket, the studio, and being loved.

16 November 1968

Jancsi is overseas. The first week I felt relief. No one to ask who I'm calling on the phone. Again?

By the second week my freedom felt unnecessary. Then, a burden. Now, loneliness. Strange that love works again, after thirty years. I remember only tenderness and wisdom.

Sydney is becoming like other international cities; there is hardly a moment without someone arriving from interstate or overseas.

I sold two portraits; a doctor from Adelaide bought Peter O'Shaughnessy, and after eleven years, Frank Packer's portrait was sold to David McNicoll.

24 November 1968

Jancsi is coming home next Tuesday. At last! John and Shan are only waiting to see him before flying off to England on Saturday. John got lots of sculpting commissions after his exhibition—even one from Kym Bonython.

I painted Robert Askin, the premier.

I have started working on lithographs at Gallery A's print shop. I want to tackle the unknown virgin plate, to achieve texture with my fingers dipped in black printer's ink, use sponge, toothbrush, wax, two-colour plates, cut precisely with a blade for blue and ochre.

The Transfield Prize was $5000 this year. The judges, that naughty pup, Lansell, and Donald Brook from the *Sydney Morning Herald*. They hung *Autumn*, a painting of gold-grey texture alternating with dense browns and strong, flat yellows. It's very large but looked like a small old master hanging as it was beside a screaming giant of purple stripes.

31 December 1968

Johnny and Shan have left. It is blissfully quiet. I know I shall start missing them soon, and after a while I shall start loving them again and forget the nervous strain of them living here over the past few weeks.

10 February 1969

I feel the isolation of Australia again. Nothing seems to be exciting and *Art International*, edited in Lugano and showing only American art, bores me.

I am hoping a trip to Greece and Spain will bring inspiration.

The Archibald was won by Willie Pidgeon, and I got praised.

We are alarmed by our finances. I have to pay taxes. No money. It means we spent too much last year.

24 February 1969

Painting is dormant with such worries and with February humidity, heat and wet upholstery.

I do portraits for which I thank God, though there is no pleasure to be had from the money. I have taxes to pay.

29 April 1969

Côte d'Azur

Eze village empty of tourists, all mine. St Paul de Vence, perched on a rock. I don't use my camera. It's been postcarded too often, I'm afraid of turning into Mrs Average. But I bought a small box of chalks to use when I can't lug oils with me. Not satisfactory as an artist's medium, but how lucky I am to have them. It was cold and raining last week and I used the chalks while sitting in a car looking through the windscreen wipers.

We drove through Aix-en-Provence. Vineyards with little tortured stems. The closer I looked at them, the more I saw van Gogh's trees with their tortured trunks and the same swirling twining repetition in the brushstrokes of the sky, the sun, and the cypresses.

I found Sisley, Seurat and Monet in the transparent, lacy, trembling, whispering forms of the plane trees in spring.

We lose all sense of time and only know it's Monday because the bakers are shut.

We drove to Arles and saw a Picasso drawing exhibition. I saw someone taking a black labrador for a walk. I thought of Jancsi and Cassy.

Lilac, tamarisk and wisteria, we head for a village in the Pyrenees near the Spanish border. Hairpin curves in the road. Foggy, rainy and cold. Rooms primitive but clean and warm.

8 May 1969

There is a lull. I enjoy it less. Violent cold, hankies, aspirin.

I am in a bus now. I hate crowds. I enjoy looking out the window, but not queuing before lavatories with faulty plumbing. At Costa del Sol dreamy fishing villages are surrounded by hotels and apartment blocks.

At Algeciras part of our group leaves for Morocco and Portugal. They really work us hard. After the eleven-hour drive and a quick dinner we are packed into fiacres and shown an illuminated Seville. It's dream-like and unreal. The cathedral swims in the night sky, one of its towers a minaret. Flamenco and cognac and late nights. I suffer poisoning.

11 May 1969

In Madrid I rush to the Prado and see Goya first. There are acres of commissioned portraits of kings and queens which are not very good. They make me feel better.

Goya is not at ease in idyllic scenes. A loving mother smiling at her child on a swing turns sinister.

One can clearly see Picasso's debt in the circus people.

The Grecos are a sea of joy. *The burial of Count Orgaz* is as unforgettable as Rembrandt's *Night watch*.

In the bullfighter's church the Madonna has two diamond teardrops on her mannequin cheeks. She looks as if she came from Madame Tussaud's dressed in a Spanish costume with a halo.

It's a disgrace how rich the church is and how poor the cave-dwellers are. One emerald out of the thirty-six on the Madonna's dress could relieve much misery.

15 May 1969

Cuenca is a highlight. As the taxi ascended I got my first breathtaking view of the hanging houses. Built in the twelfth century, they hang on the top of the rock, poised to throw themselves down.

Today, my last day in Spain, I'm in the Prado again, revisiting the paintings I admired most.

1 June 1969

London

John and Shan gave a party in my honour. Old painter friends. New friends of John's. The flat has paintings, herbs in the kitchen, furniture built by John. They are in love.

It's a strain meeting strangers who are now close relatives. I try very hard not to try very hard. Johnny is under pressure too. He gets up from the dinner table and dries the dishes—something I could never make him do.

Government House rang to tell me I was to be awarded a CBE. I immediately rang Jancsi.

'I got the CBE.'

'What's that?'

'Commander of the British Empire.'
'Oh,' said Jancsi. I laughed.
'I won't commandeer you!'

10 June 1969

Stella Oceania

London behind me and what a trip to crown a trip this is! Sharing a cabin with Tubi who flew from Sydney, and we met on the ship.

Crete and Heraklion, Santorini unbelievably beautiful. Symbols everywhere—the bull, the snake, the lion, the fish. One and a half hours by bus to Lindos to see the Acropolis which is older than Athens, and has a wall that was built in medieval times. There is not enough time for any one sketch so I combine two or three elements on one page and discover it works.

In old Rhodes I become exhausted by information, history and heat. We sit in a seaside cafe looking beyond the yachts at the fort and three windmills.

Two days in Istanbul. Magnificent mosques, the Aya Sofia with Byzantine mosaics and the Topkapi Palace. Otherwise dirty, disintegrating, drab and disorganised.

24 July 1969

Sydney

Home was beautiful and sunny and warm. The sketches grow better as I gain distance from their source.

When I arrived Jancsi said, 'Sit down, I read you the telegrams.' More than a hundred, and only then did I start to realise what the CBE means. I engaged a secretary to cope with the thank you letters.

Johnny writes that he doesn't feel like sculpting. I wonder when he will start on something seriously. Peter wants to leave the ABC.

Maria, the Yugoslav housekeeper, leaves. I am teaching the new Swiss girl to cook inbetween painting for the Adelaide show.

Got involved with the first step on the moon. Finally the first picture. A foot. A hesitant, white, awkward, clumsy foot dangling over the moon. It was one of the greatest sights of my life.

11 August 1969

Friend of seventeen years, champion of my early career, Andrea, is getting more and more difficult. In the car, I am instructed, cajoled, warned and policed. She says, 'That portrait of Ken Myer was a real chocolate box.'

I say, 'Mmmmm.'

'You know, you can't really take criticism. And when an artist can't take criticism, that's the end.'

John and Shan telephoned. He has taken a traineeship with IBM in London. The interview must have gone well, it's difficult to get in. He was always good at mathematics.

15 August 1969

My eighteen-year-old self which feels delight at birthdays is still with me. I love my birthday. I don't mind age. Jancsi bought me a new, small, lovely piano.

This was a restless week.

Now that I find that I need more solitude, people become an intrusion, an annoyance, with the exception of twenty-year-old Caroline Williams. She works in Sydney and is an artist.

13 October 1969

André Kalman from the Kalman Galleries, where I had my two London shows, is here. He flew in from Tokyo where he attended a Sotheby auction. Incredible! All the way from London to Tokyo for London's Sotheby! He asked me to lend him two small paintings for a show he is going to have around April for expatriate Hungarian painters, and that means pretty good company for me, what with Vasarély and Moholy Nagy.

All afternoon I drove him around galleries. He was most impressed with the exteriors, less with what was on. Like Greenberg before him, he liked Clifton Pugh and Fred Williams. It seems that international talk notwithstanding, one looks for the regional.

Meanwhile Christo is wrapping Little Bay in plastic, and one would think he is climbing Mount Everest what with all the communiques about rock falls, climbers, sprained ankles as the plastic fabric smoothly conceals holes and gaps.

Little Bay locals are interviewed. Mrs Mavis Smith says, 'As long as he hasn't wrapped up my husband's favourite fishing spot.'

A corgi keeps coming into the courtyard to drink Cassy's milk. We now keep the milk in the laundry. This morning, Sunday, we are having breakfast in the kitchen when Cassy walks in with the corgi, leads him to the laundry, first puts his own nose in to show him what to do, then stands aside and lets the corgi drink.

29 January 1970

Peter wants to move from home. The time is right. He says, 'There is no lack of love. But I irritate you with my way of life and you irritate me by showing it.'

Much will change. This great beautiful house is a burden to me now. I want to sell it.

7 February 1970

John wrote that when he finishes his computer training he and Shan want to study ecology. This is the first time I ever heard the word.

Suddenly I'm aware that the sweet air is befouled with carbon monoxide, hydrocarbons, lead compounds, sulphur dioxide, nitrogen dioxide, ash, and countless other poisonous substances.

The greatest need, as I understand it, is for a change in values. The environmental problem stems from a dedication to infinite growth on a finite planet.

14 February 1970

I gave the portrait of Sir Lorimer Dods to his research foundation. Jancsi and I decided it was a better place than my storeroom.

22 February 1970

One more of those nightmare first nights with Andrea. The Arthur Miller play, *The price*, was excellent. After the play we mingled with the cast. Stewart Ginn, who played the Jewish merchant, was addressed: 'Daaarling you were superb. Of course only someone Jewish could have played that part!'

Stewart Ginn: 'Madame, I have Scottish, Irish and Yorkshire blood. I wish I had some Jewish blood, they are such marvellous entertainers.'

No painting.

4 April 1970

We have booked a trip. Even the hotels are booked.

15 July 1970

I haven't written in this journal for a long time.

Before we left for the trip, a Chinese man came to the studio and bought two major pictures from the Alice Springs period. In Hong Kong he invited us for drinks at his home in Deep Water Bay. A beautiful house, with plate-glass windows looking out on the bay. Gardens, swimming pool, music, servants, and a fat old wife. We went to a floating restaurant for dinner with the head of Hong Kong intelligence and his wife. He, as well as our millionaire, praises communist China and wouldn't mind if their children would want to go there. 'America,' he says, 'is an old new country. China is a new old country.'

Next day he provided an air-conditioned Cadillac and a driver. When I tap the driver on the shoulder, he stops and I sketch.

Coincidences are fantastic. We met Ivan and Jutka Lorentz on the Kowloon ferry and Ken Myer (whom I painted) in the lift at the Peninsula Hotel. We have drinks in their room and dinner on the summit. On the flight to Rome, we sat in the same row as the Felekis.

John and Shan were at Rome airport. One day of euphoria. We sat together eating pasta and drinking red wine at Bernini's fountain, and Jancsi is witty. Johnny says, 'To hear your humour again, Dad! I forgot!'

But now Johnny isn't sure he can finish his computer course. He doesn't mind the research, but that's only offered outside London and they don't want to move. He still doesn't know whether he wants to sculpt or go back to university.

In Peggy Guggenheim's museum in Venice, we met the Thorneycrofts.

(In the garden of the museum is a Marino Marini horse and rider sculpture. The rider has an erection. Peggy Guggenheim has a key to that penis which screws off. Inside is a safe for jewellery and cash.)

On the Piazza St Mark we ran into my cousin, Zsuzsi Roboz and her husband, Teddy.

Prague

Jancsi's cousin, Dezsö, and Jóska's daughter Margot meet us at the airport. The Alcron, which used to be *the* luxury hotel is now fifth-rate, with threadbare carpets, railway clocks on landings and the *smell*. They can only give us a suite—we may move tomorrow.

Margot is divorced. So was Dezsö's daughter Dulinka. Fifty per cent of all young marrieds get divorced for the same reason—they have to move in with their in-laws. Dulinka has remarried. She is a doctor, beautiful, charming. Her husband is a waiter and earns more than she does in tips from American tourists. He has a flat in a housing settlement. Dezsö is a lawyer, and has a responsible position. Anci, his wife, is manager of an art gallery. In spite of their social standing, Dezsö has to do translations to make ends meet.

Jóska, also a lawyer, works in a chicken hatchery. He gets up at 4.30 a.m. to be there by seven. In the socialist system white-collar workers must not arrive later than the labourers. Marcsa, his wife, is a teacher. Jóska also does translations.

The hotel is horrid so we drink straight gin at Dezsö's four-roomed luxury flat. The light bulbs are very small and cast a cold light. They show us old photographs from when Anci was still elegant. They holiday in Yugoslavia in a tent, and take salami and tins. They are only allowed five dollars a week.

Memories return. The old city is beautiful. There is no rabbi in the whole of Prague.

Budapest

The Hotel Duna in Budapest is not just a hotel, it's a haven in a city where one escapes from misery and drabness.

Kati, who saved Jancsi's life in 1945 by hiding him at the risk of her life, is wiser than ever. We have sent her money every year since Frici died. She says, 'Okay, you give me bread and butter. But why caviar?' She enjoys the theatre, and is the most sunny ageing philosopher in the world.

Johnny and Shan plan to leave their jobs and head off for six months through Spain, Morocco, Ethiopia and Somaliland. On motorcycles.

We are relieved to leave for Mexico.

Mexico

They sell iguanas. Wonderful real faces everywhere, repeated in the Museum of Modern Art. It's a different visual climate. Diego Rivera, David Siqueiros, José Orozco, Rufino Tamayo dominate. They depict the human condition.

Seeing the young Mexican contemporaries one comes down with a jolt to Noland stripes, Warhol pops.

There is a change coming. Incorporating the figure into a shell which awaits it. Something which may be hollow and lost and lonely, but human.

10 October 1970

Sydney

Two of my contemporaries died recently. Dobell suddenly from a heart attack, and Molvig after a kidney transplant.

I'm fully occupied now. Time too, because we are in the red again at the bank. The house was up for auction. Inspections twice a week, but it wasn't sold. We were overjoyed. However, it will sell, sooner or later, it has outgrown us.

I had five paintings in the exhibition of expatriate Hungarians in the Budapest Musée Des Beaux Arts in September. My picture was hung beside Moholy Nagy's. They wanted to purchase another one of mine, but I donated it.

Rupert Murdoch telephoned. He wants me to paint a portrait of his mother, Dame Elizabeth Murdoch, who lives on Cruden Farm.

My days on Cruden Farm are pleasant and peaceful. I paint Dame Elizabeth in the mornings. In the afternoons I sit with her, and her ninety-three-year-old mother who's in a wheelchair. I read and write, and walk among calves and sheep and trees. What a gift it is to make intimate and close friends during such a painting session.

In Sydney many portraits.

A few weeks ago I flew to Melbourne to paint Sir Colin Syme, one of the industrial barons of Australia. He is at first reluctant, then enthusiastic. When I finished he said he didn't doubt I would get a likeness, what he was afraid of was that it would be just another boring portrait. However, it isn't.

Spent ten days in Perth, painting. Jancsi told me Johnny rang. He and Shan have separated. We rang London. They behave as if there's no crisis. No heartbreak. Whether they ease themselves and us into this new situation, or whether this ends their love or improves their relationship, I don't know.

The Transfield this year was by invitation. There was no doubt in anybody's mind that it's for the younger generation only, and mainly those connected with Central Street. That is to say, hard-edged, colourfield, kinetic and everything mechanical. The effect was much like in previous years, it looked stunning with primary colours, optical effects and didn't hold me for longer than five minutes.

The saddest exhibit was a sketch of an empty wall, with 'walk along this line' printed on both sides. Donald Brook raved about this piece, how tactile a sensation it is to walk along this line with one's back pressed to the wall. He apparently did not think Fairweather's new show at the Macquarie or Leonard French's at the Holdsworth were worth a mention.

27 January 1971

We've just had ten blissful days in Fiji, so remote and removed from reality that coming home was a jolt.

The lagoon was like Lake Balaton, our room opened onto a patio and Jancsi slipped out at dawn, crossed the lawn with the coconut palms and swam. We had breakfast on the patio, fed the birds and then swam. Maureen arranges the flowers. They are all in the ginger family. Giant things and so heavy that they need to be reinforced with sticks and wire. She made an arrangement for me to paint, and I did her a sketch of it and took it to Suva. I saw vanilla creeping up the trunk of a tree and learned that it has to be artificially inseminated because the bloom is too deep for the insect to reach. So they pick up the pollen with pincers and put it in by hand. Another rare tropical tree can only be planted by a bird which eats the seed, digests it, and with its droppings, plants it. No other way to do it.

There was a debate of critics at the university. One said that there is an atmosphere of unease, confusion and uncertainty among up-and-coming artists. He put this down to their being at a loss, not knowing which direction to take, waiting for a lead. If this is so, heaven help them. If they are waiting around to find out what the next mainstream will be instead of digging it out of their own guts, they should just as well stop being artists. Up till now, nobody ever suggested that a new advance was the death of all that had gone before.

12 February 1971

There's a postal strike in England and we've had no communication with John. The last letter came a month ago. He is active in encounter groups and some of the leaders want him to take over. God only knows what he will eventually do. Sculpting or encounter groups?

20 *February 1971*

Problems of art criticism. The age is overcrowded. There are too many artists, working too fast, and reproduced too widely for historians and critics to keep track of them without jamming them together into conveniently labelled packages.

When I look at my present work, the abstracts, the ones which satisfy me more are those with some recognisable element. The portraits. And lately, the hollow figures which aren't pop, aren't realism, aren't expressionism. I'm a bad girl. Where do I fit? And yet everything I touch, is me.

14 *March 1971*

Peter is showing great perseverance in his search for a job. It amazes me. He needs a break.

16 *March 1971*

Finally! Two letters from John. Absorbing, frank, candid, trying to communicate, get through to us. I try to open up, to receive, to accept. I am wondering if he is sane, or if he takes drugs? Is he a hippie? Will he be a man with a place in the world? Will he be a writer, a sculptor or nothing? Will he return to reality or will he sink?

24 *March 1971*

I find myself becoming more disciplined and tidy as I grow older. I would like life to be a great continuity, and if threads are hanging loose I try to untangle them and place them where they belong. It is a battle which life constantly conspires against. The telephone rings. Masses of cares, duties, the house, the garden, the friends, the needs of those in Hungary and Czechoslovakia. Parcels are packed and money is sent. I fight hasty, casual contacts. Life is creative work too, and when I'm interrupted I try to keep the thread unbroken.

I feel like a magnet which pulls scattered pieces into its centre. The only way I can do it is in solitude. I call it my siestas and expect my surroundings to respect these when I withdraw into my own guts. Days when this becomes impossible, leave me weak and vulnerable and confused.

7 April 1971

I'm reading Anais Nin's first journal, Spy in the house of love; poetic and beautiful. Something that interested me, she went into psychoanalysis with Dr Rank who told her the journal is like her opium, and while she pours herself into the journal, not enough remains to go into her book.

I worry about how often I neglect my journal. Now I realise that perhaps one's capacity for self-expression is finite, and by writing less, perhaps more goes into the painting. But does it?

An interesting remark about Rank. He wanted to work in New York because there aren't enough neurotics in Paris. Mainly because Paris is a city where people nicely divide their marriage and their love affairs without guilt.

Johnny writes: 'It was nice to get your letter, parents, and to realise that I don't have to be the same as you, or even be something you approve of before you'll accept me. I feel this would not always have been so, and I am particularly thankful that I am able to write to you about my life, and not about what I think you'd like to hear.' He writes that Shan is now working as a gardener along the embankment for approximately half of what she earnt as a journalist.

I went to a lecture by Anthony Caro, a leading sculptor. He was unpretentious, simple and humble, with none of the nonsense one is used to. Just an artisan who explained his craft. As he showed the slides he told how he picked up his aircraft propellers in the scrapyards and how a young apprentice helps him weld things together. After the early 1960s, his works became more baroque and freer. He was the first to take sculpture off the pedestal and put it on the ground. As his followers started doing the same, he lifted the sculpture up on the pedestal again.

Peter got a job in real estate. I promised myself that when Peter started work I'd give up smoking for a week, as a sort of thanksgiving. I miss it like hell.

14 April 1971

Is this all getting too detached? Either the art situation, or the children. I won the Sir Charles Lloyd Jones Memorial Prize in the Easter Show, which I forgot to mention. The Duke of Edinburgh opened the show. Next day Rudy Komon rang me to say that the duke returned to his gallery, and, seeing one of my pictures, sent his regards to me. 'He mentioned you painted one of his sons. Which one did you paint?' Rudy doesn't know anything.

29 April 1971

John writes beautifully. He is now living with an American girl, Greta. Candelabras, flowers and a few sculptures are sprouting, getting better and better all the time, he thinks. He wants me to read *The Tibetan book of the dead* and Timothy Leary's book on the psychedelic experience. None of them are available in Sydney. I will buy them on my trip to gain insight into what my son wants to experience and why.

I think most people's ability to read, to listen, to see, to smell, is lost, that all doors of the world are shut. What a world to be an artist in.

7 May 1971

News about painting the Duchess of Kent's children leaked on radio and in the newspapers. I will be surprised if after all this I get the commission. But I am going to London to see John anyway.

10 May 1971

New York

Elwyn Lynn wrote to Patrick McCaughey, the Melbourne critic, who is in New York on a Harkness scholarship. I meet him under the Washington Arch in Greenwich Village. It's good to have a guide. We go to wayout downtown galleries where, for example, two cameras are whirring simultaneously projecting common happenings. It's entertainment, not art, and boring at that.

We go to Sydney Ball's warehouse loft. Packing cases, sewing machine, mirrors, clothes on nails. No daylight, only neon. He paints fourteen-foot-high stained canvases which are supposed to be vertical, but the studio ceiling is only eleven-foot high. He's never seen his pictures other than horizontally.

There is Robert Jacks from Melbourne who puts white paper on white walls and cuts pockets in them. The flaps hang limp. It's avant-garde above all.

Patrick moves in and out like a master of ceremonies. Down on the street, enormous trucks, industrial landscapes, urinating tramps and glorious bales of textiles and old wooden crates to inspire artists to pick them up and place them in galleries.

The contempt of those working in the lofts of Greenwich Village towards the established, polished, Fifth Avenue, Fifty-Seventh Street establishments reminds me of the woman who finds the ten-carat diamond ring on her friend's finger vulgar. The friend says, 'Yes, so did I before I owned one.'

Andy Warhol retrospective at the Whitney. Campbell soup cans, all the same size, all ordinary, all 'hand painted'. If he did them all himself, without assistants, it must have been a bore and so deserves recognition for endurance. Not for art. No, not for art.

17 May 1971

London

I arrived and expected the worst, so that whatever I saw wouldn't have been a disappointment.

Johnny has long curly hair but no beard. His eyes are smiling and sweet and crinkly and he kissed me with a warmth I haven't experienced since he was six.

His studio is something. On big big windows he pasted plastic so the outer world remains outside, and hung his lovely iron wheels on the light. The sculpture is good and inventive. And he worked so much. Greta is delicate with long, blonde hair.

22 May 1971

I contact friends and go for lunch and drinks and dinner. And my diarrhoea is bad, and I swallow pills all day. I feel in exile, homesick, lonely, longing for Jancsi.

27 May 1971

I have an appointment with the Duchess of Kent's secretary, Commander Richard Buckley, who combines a smooth man-of-the-world attitude with the lecturing of a schoolmaster and the harshness of Rasputin.

The letter I received in Sydney from the agent general said: 'The Duchess will be pleased to see you middle of May.' I saw the press-cuttings on his desk. I said, 'I know from experience that the best way to lose such a commission is to talk about it.'

In any case, I was the one who was penalised. I did not leak it. The boy I was going to paint has holidays until July. I hastened to say at this point that I wouldn't wait until July. Perhaps next year, at Easter. When I left I felt I had been humiliated.

Johnny came to my flat and we went to buy books for me to take back to Sydney. He wants me to understand him and the group he lives with. There are acres of books about drugs and drug culture, and the psychedelic experience, and Thoreau, and Buckminster Fuller's designs for utopia or oblivion.

My heart is turning round in my chest because I love him, and another part of me wants to get out of London to escape.

13 June 1971

Last night Johnny invited me for dinner. I am very glad and interested to get to know all his friends which he mentions so often in his letters.

We sit around, on the floor, on sacks of foam rubber. We eat brown rice with vegetables and salad—very tasty. There is apple juice and *vin rosé*.

I would state that they are without exception, the gentlest, most intelligent people. Still, I wish Johnny wouldn't have met them. They have all opted out of society, and reality.

A marijuana cigarette begins its circling. Each takes a puff and hands it to the next one. When it comes to me it's impossible to reject it. I take a puff. It tastes pleasant. They ask me how I like it and whether I got high. I said I did, not wanting to disappoint them, but I felt completely sober.

17 June 1971

Paris

With Johnny in Paris visiting my cousin Vera Székely, a sculptor, who teaches art to children. Vera says van Gogh's cut-off ear and Dali's antenna moustache do not matter. All that matters is the object which remains. Therefore it's ridiculous to consider it important whether one wears long hair or short, it doesn't make the artist. The only thing which makes her really angry is the cult of personality.

The conversation continued the next morning at the Exhibition de Jeune Sculpture, where Giacometti stands in a lake, ducks waddle around Calder, and children climb upon Vera's red arches.

I don't contact any of my acquaintances in Paris. I suffer from a poisoning of friends and company. I need to be anonymous and alone.

I wallow in emptiness as I walk in the rain and the cold. (London and Paris in June are having a severe winter and the only thing I have to wear is a thick black dress with a thick black coat.)

I sit down at one of the terraces, partly protected by a glass wall to drink a Campari and buy a paperback. I have finished my whodunnit. Then walk some more, soaked through. If only the weather would be kind, I could take Paris in. I have a snack, go back and ring Jancsi and Peter and fall asleep with their loved voices.

2 July 1971

Tel Aviv

I am here with Anku. We hired a car to see the old city of Jerusalem. I felt an atavistic, strong emotion on touching the Eastern Wall for the first time, and prayed. I felt the wonder of it when our guide explained that archeologists dig beside the wailing wall because deep underneath lies the city of Herod. We went to see the newly dug-out proof. It costs the government sweat and blood in diplomacy as the orthodox sector consider it sacrilege to disturb the holy place.

10 July 1971

Sydney

Exactly one week at home. Jancsi is as much me as anyone is able to be another person, and I am him, while allowing each other to be ourselves. Thirty-two years together, and growing to be like this is a gift of God. Also, to endure through the bad passages, and to labour and fight for such a relationship is no small matter.

How many thousands of faces love can have. There is no doubt in my mind that this is still love, or again love, or simply love. Pure luck, the chemistry of our skins still works. Maybe these realisations come to me now because for eight weeks, without him, I suffered deprivation. But I can be in the present and feel alive in it.

Orban, the indestructible, at the age of eighty-seven has a one-man show at the Holdsworth Gallery. Gleeson writes: 'If Orban would have stopped painting fifteen years ago, he would have had his honourable place in Australian art. But it's only in the last six years that his creative talent turned into genius.' According to him, as the body declined, Orban's soul took flight into these upper regions.

Orban tells me he can thank me for all this. Without me, he would never have enlarged the small pieces into big paintings, he would have never have thought of using the underpainted coincidences for feeding his imagination.

21 August 1971

Life falls back into a routine, repeating itself weekly. I pick up Jancsi at the bridge club every Saturday and Sunday evening. It is an island where Europeans revert to life as it was thirty years ago. As I sit and wait for 'the last round' in the poker cubicle, I see four enormously fat ladies, flesh gently reverberating as they utter the same inane, teasing remarks they have been saying for years. Consuming potatoes and chicken liver which makes them fatter.

21 September 1971

Today John's one-man show opens in London. He sent us the poster.

A large real estate agency has offered Peter a job, which will pay him far more than he's earning now.

He looks the exact opposite of his brother. Groomed, clean, suave.

Hal Missingham retired as director of the Art Gallery of NSW, after twenty-six years. As a present Mary de Teliga, of the Rudy Komon Gallery, and the Bonython Gallery arranged a book for him, with an artist's work on each page. The farewell party was at Wallace Thornton.

I painted Wallace about fifteen years ago when he still painted. Not having enough money for canvases at the time when I exhibited it, I painted another painting on top, which I now regret. He became a critic, then resigned. Nothing in his career prepared me for the kind of world he created for himself. He bought twenty-five acres near Hornsby.

Cars were guided to their parking place by yellow cravats hanging on gum trees, the kind of cravats Hal likes to wear. From the parking spot we walked ten minutes on a bush track into a great valley where the house stands. He built it himself of natural stone. As far as the eye can see there isn't another human being, only virgin bush.

And in this setting the 250 artists mingled. No crowd. No party feeling. A happening. People lit little fires all over the valley for barbecues (everyone brought their own food and drink), and children and dogs didn't disturb us. It was probably the last of the parties where all the old and young artists congregated.

I started Jung's *Memories, dreams, reflections*, which was a revelation to me. I was thunderstruck when he related how he woke up at the age of twelve to the realisation that an 'I' exists. I remember such a revelation in my own life, and how exhilarating it was.

19 October 1971

The Leonard French exhibition last week was a marriage between his old symbols and figures which don't connect.

Donald Friend romps and frolics and gave me the idea of using coloured paper for my black and white gouaches. They can't be coloured afterwards, but I could leave out the paper along the lines and introduce another colour.

The hard edge has disappeared into thin air suddenly, and the figure is coming back, if not here, in the Biennale in Brazil. I had to laugh as I read that Aspden, who only last year was the most avant-garde painter, looked old hat in the Biennale with his colourfield.

15 November 1971

John came home from London. He thinks we should set aside one evening a week in which the four of us, as a family, will sit down and talk. I was very pleased about it, but we haven't had such an evening yet.

My eagle brought the car home for me at noon, and I dropped him in front of the macrobiotic restaurant in Bondi Junction, right beside the kosher butcher. He has found a yoga place, an encounter group, and bought several records. He exercises in the afternoons to the beat of African music played at full volume.

My dove returns from his estate agency as immaculately as he leaves. In cufflinks, tie and a business shirt.

Ever the twain shall meet?

27 November 1971

Christmas is approaching with parties one can't always avoid.

16 December 1971

At the Bonython Christmas party, Carl Plate said that art always draws its full circle; perhaps the portrait will come back one day. Not in my lifetime, I think, but it remains my absorbing interest.

Brett Whiteley says he is involved in portraiture. We start an animated conversation. His hair looks permed, grubby velvet coat, eyes unfocused. When he mentions 'extraterrestial forces' while painting a portrait, I say, 'Brett, they are words. You mean the current between the sitter and the artist . . .'

'Yes, yes. The current.'

14 January 1972

We go out for dinner to celebrate Johnny's birthday. John invited a friend who looks like a guru. In the middle of dinner Jancsi started to laugh. 'We need a photographer,' he said. 'Look at us.' Peter, immaculately groomed, John looking like Jesus Christ, and the guru. Jancsi says he is learning from his children. He is not interested in what anybody thinks of them, only in what we think.

4 February 1972

We went to the opening of John's exhibition. It looked fabulous. The black mandalas on the stark white walls looked like lace, and the thin metal sculptures danced in the breeze. He sold seven and got four commissions.

I want to create situations the way I create paintings. Not accepting the situation that *is*, rather the one *I wish it to be*. My concept of family, in which all four love each other equally, just isn't reality. Relationships shift and change, and this has to be faced.

My portrait of Rose Skinner was rejected from the Archibald. As usual, my first thought was to look for excuses in defence of those who kicked me. Rose said she told everyone that she withdew the portrait so as not to damage my 'image'. Humiliating business.

So, things aren't going my way now. No commissions over the past four months and no sales.

Painting is in the doldrums. I feel dried up. Rudy Komon pressed me for a date for a one-man show as I have not exhibited in Sydney since 1967. Tentatively I said yes, and my stomach has been in knots ever since.

The sketches of Western Australia and the Snowy Mountains are very good, but as soon as I enlarge and transpose them, they fail. All the figure paintings I tried to transpose from black and white drawings are shocking. Why not do what I used to do before my abstract period? Go for another sketching trip (because I am no good if not using nature) and instead of sketchbook-sized small things take canvases again.

27 March 1972

I won the Charles Lloyd Jones Memorial Prize with a portrait of John Laws.

Allen Ginsberg came on to Sydney from the Adelaide Festival. He was described as 'a scrotum with glasses'. He was meditating in the nude in his hotel room with a flower in his ear when the maid walked in. She got such a fright she dropped his macrobiotic breakfast. During Ginsberg's lecture Brett Whiteley started stripping. When a policeman interfered, he bit him.

The Power Bequest, in a fundraising effort, organised a dinner at the Hunters Lodge only for professionals. No spouses. Dr Nugget Coombs told me he has been in Budapest and found they had one of the best film schools in the world. On his way there, he came across an English magazine with an article on famous Hungarians. It had my name in it and made him feel at home.

19 April 1972

What a spineless, ugly, murderous world we were born into.

We lounge in bed in Bellevue Hill, munching grapes, while the silver flicker of television shows untold misery of North Vietnamese people escaping with bundles and infants on the roads.

American planes bomb the north, while China sends ping-pong players to New York.

Bombs explode daily in Ireland. *Apollo 16* is on its way to the moon.

10 May 1972

Alice Springs

Jancsi and I came to Alice Springs for a holiday. It served a double purpose: to unwind (we were both very tired), and to get me out of the deadlock with my painting. The place exerts the same magic as ten years ago. It's still the clearest, cleanest, widest landscape in the world; unique, majestic, invigorating. Mona brought us two collapsible aluminium chairs, an esky, a soft board for pinning canvases on, and lots of citrus fruits from her garden. We hired a station wagon which became our studio and our dining room.

The first few days I worried that I would repeat what I painted ten years ago. Three or so of my first canvases were timid and colourless and I was tense. The sketches went well, but they only exist on small pieces of paper. Slowly, I discovered that sitting in the car with the orange roundness of the horizon, or lying in the sands of a creek with rocks embracing me in a circle, that I am the centre of the painting. Why not paint the landscape around me, as it really seemed to be? Now, that is exciting. I turned the canvas and surrounded the empty (orange or blue or green centre) with either the bush or the mountains on all four sides until a new object appeared. It was mine.

For lunch we packed our bread, capsicum, ham, cheese, cold beer, hot coffee, and it was absolute bliss. The material grew and we were very happy and tired from all day in the air.

We spent three days in Ormiston Gorge. It's indescribable.

This morning we set off on the Ross River Road. Corroboree Rocks are just off the main highway and further on is Trephina Gorge.

We started on the road to Todd River, and the car got hopelessly bogged. I suppose we dug in deeper by trying to drive out. We made the mistake one should never make in Australia. We had not told anyone where we were headed. Nobody knew where to look for us. The car sat waist-deep in the sand. No sign of life anywhere except for flies and three wasps.

I wondered whether there was such a place as Todd River. I mean whether it's a township at all. Sometimes I thought I heard an engine, but it was only the wind in the trees. I observed the tune a bird sang above on a branch and whistled a reply. The bird answered. It was comforting.

I sat alone in the sand as Jancsi set off for help. He made me promise not to move.

After five hours, shadows fell over almost the whole wide riverbed where I sat. The car was gleaming in the last rays of the sun. I prayed that Jancsi was somewhere waiting for a truck to pull me out. He must have been as worried about me as I was about him. Where was he? An apple was all he took.

After six hours, I moved back into the car. At that moment a yellow straw hat popped up behind the hill. A brown face with black rimmed glasses and a blue shirt. It was the most heavenly blue I have ever feasted my eyes on. Jancsi came with springy steps, a wide grin, and said, '*That* was a good hike'. I started to weep.

He knew from the map that Todd River was twenty-eight miles and our speedometer showed we had done twenty-one. That left seven miles to walk, wherever that was. He thought he could do it slowly. He arrived at a station with several buildings, dogs, chickens, a camel and a kangaroo. Not a soul on the property.

He went to the telephone and called the motel to send out a tow truck, with exact instructions. He sat on an empty barrel for a while to rest, but had to get back to me. It was marvellous. He was justly pleased about his feat and we opened the beer and waited for the tow truck.

15 June 1972

Sydney

Peter made his first really important sale. And just before his round-the-world trip, other negotiations become ripe. It's an irony of fate that he might have to leave before these deals reach contract stage. He will probably pick up the thread easily when he returns.

Just now we are poring over the map of Europe. We plan his trip with him with such joy. Hong Kong, Athens, the Greek islands, Rome, Amalfi, Positano, Capri, Venice, and because Peter is interested in where he was born, Budapest.

In the meantime John has given up his studio, bakes his own bread, meditates for an hour and a half and has taken to cycling all over London. He goes for acupuncture to rebalance his energy, and has given up marijuana for a couple of weeks to do transcendental meditation.

The problems facing the contemporary artists are the disturbing events occurring in our society. Although this has been a problem for artists in any age, we are now dealing with problems being force-fed to us through the media.

What is the artist to do? Should they try to absorb all the world events as food for a creative belly, for regurgitation? Or should the artist seek oblivion and escape into themselves in order to bring out the poetry or mysticism that dwells below the conscious level?

After my honest, but dismal attempt at painting student revolutions and other crowd compositions, I ended up with seven-foot landscapes which look like giant watercolours.

1 July 1972

I just saw Clifton Pugh on 'This Day Tonight'. He was commissioned to paint Golda Meir and flies off to Israel. This is a hard one to swallow. Our Jewish community uses me many times a year, requesting I donate pictures to be auctioned for different groups: the Hebrew University, the Jewish National Fund etc.

Bob Hughes, the enfant terrible of Sydney's art world ten years ago, returned home for a series of lectures for the Art Gallery Society. Heaven and Hell in Western Art; Postwar American Art; Leonardo da Vinci. Not scholarly, although that was there; showbiz, personal charisma, bad taste, and a delightful shower of words. There were 700 or 800 people at each lecture, whereas the Society for Cultural Freedom invited Patrick McCaughey and Noel Hutchinson to speak on Art and Progress, and about twenty people showed up.

20 July 1972

John gives me more homework than I ever gave him. For sure. We should read Gurdjieff's *Meetings with remarkable men*. And Ouspensky's *Search for the miraculous*. It's a trend among the young I know, but I also have to remember my father was always interested in these things. Like a conscientious schoolgirl, I get the books to try to keep up with the workings of my son's mind. Gurdjieff, strangely, is easily readable and reminiscent of one of my favourites, Joseph Kessel's *The horsemen*.

The family meetings John insisted upon are the most fascinating experience. He says families are the most uncommunicative units. 'We come home, say Hi, go to the phone or read the newspaper. We swallow our dinner, say Bye.' We religiously keep Mondays free. We sit in a circle. So strong is the current, we are sucked in. Since their aggression is allowed to come out, there has never been so much love in the air. It's like a whodunnit where the killer is someone nobody thought of.

It was on one of these Mondays that the boys asked me to translate my journals from Hungarian. 'We are so lucky to have a mother who kept a journal all her life. We want to know about the time before we were born. About our childhood, immigration, the first years in the new country.'

Since then, the evenings always begin with about eight typewritten pages of the journal, translated that week.

Johnny said: 'Can't you see, Peter, it fits like a jigsaw puzzle. Where one of us bulges out the other caves in. We could both change our attitudes.'

27 July 1972

There is a petrol strike. We hang my show tomorrow at Rudy Komon's and Saturday is preview day. Next Tuesday is critics' day and next Thursday is drinks with the artist.

Complete and utter silence around me. No newspapers ring, no one asks for an interview. I think it's the result of four years of Jancsi's 'say no' to all such approaches. We succeeded admirably. If nobody has petrol next week, there won't be any reviews either. Or sales.

I had my first portrait commission for many a month this morning. Jim Foots, chairman of Mt Isa Mines. If he can't fly in, I lose the amount which we are now counting on for our trip. We are in the red in the bank.

If only this wretched great house would sell. It's been up for sale for almost six months.

30 July 1972

A bad day. After the Foots sitting I drove to the gallery and waited for Ian McKay's show to be disassembled.

Rapotec came to help with the hanging and John Olsen dropped in. We discussed Michael Brown's exhibition at Watters. Dr Donald Brook wrote 'Though it's the worst show in town, it has to be taken seriously as it shows contempt for the gallery as well as the buying public.' Brook is going to be at Watters tomorrow to discuss Brown's statement, and if necessary to sling mudpies on the pictures.

Meanwhile, petrol supplies are dwindling, with milk, meat and bread deliveries, bus and taxi services in jeopardy. It's insignificant that I have a show.

At our last family meeting before Johnny left for London, Peter said: 'It could be he is destined for great things. He certainly has the capacity. He could also throw it away and become a hippie. It's all in him.'

10 August 1972

Gleeson gave me a lovely review on Wednesday. Big headlines. 'Judy Cassab's step forward'. On Thursday Donald Brook wrote, 'No beating about the bush'. He writes, 'Do you seriously deny that you feel a warm, inner glow in the presence of those Judy Cassabs at the Komon Gallery, that are the epitome of Australian culture-kitsch? Come now, admit your taste for muddy, complicated, stained and textured romantic semiabstracts with just a hint of landscape and a hint of symbolism, ready-made for interior decoration. Confess!'

Jamie Boyd didn't fare much better. 'Ah yes, these Boyds. How many art-Boyds are there by birth, by marriage, by association and no doubt by deed poll? And every one a genius ... etc.

16 August 1972

Dr Brook did a good job. I only sold three small pictures in the three weeks of the show.

20 August 1972

Bangkok

Jancsi and I are a marvellous team on holiday when we are alone. We were served three dinners on the plane. Next day I couldn't eat lunch, hungry at 3.30 p.m. and gobbled down a French loaf with butter, and then couldn't touch dinner which the Bunnags gave in our honour, with the Australian and Portuguese ambassadors, and their blonde appendices.

Jancsi rented a motor boat and that was blissful and I sketched. The klongs are as I remembered them, only one is more aware now of the pollution.

Sunday I took the oil paints on the motor boat, and as it chug-chugged along the klong, I threw figures around. The river moves like a film, one only has to sit and gaze. The heat isn't too bad, except when Tula invited us to see the royal palace. It was the first time for Jancsi. Impressive, though slightly gaudy. An army of 'restorers' is at work on the peeling murals. No masterpieces to begin with, they gained some dignity by patina, mildew and age. Now they look spick and span and horrible.

We had permission to visit 'Chitla-da-Palace', the royals' private residence, to see my portrait of Queen Sirikit.

2 September 1972

Austria

We stepped off the plane in Klagenfurt, a smallish town in the south of Austria, looked up and saw John's black beard and waving leather coat and in a minute Peter's raised arms. What a rendezvous! Greta's blonde hair is tied in a bun. John's hair is miraculously trimmed short. He looked distinguished. Peter oozes *joi de vivre*.

We grew very fond of Greta during this week. She is placid and even tempered.

Our family problems shrink this morning as we hear over the radio that Palestinians have murdered eleven Israeli athletes in Munich. The world holds its breath. It's horrible.

When Peter and John left, we had two peaceful days all to ourselves. We went on to Vienna, laughed and called it a lull.

When we arrived at the ancient Hotel Post on the Fleischmarkt, we discovered that it was the only room available in a radius of thirty miles. It's the 400th anniversary of the Spanish Riding School, and there was an exhibition covering five centuries of horses and riders in art, from Dürer to Picasso.

20 September 1972

London

Sandwiched between dinners of high living and fathomless pits of misery. The Slotovers ask us over. We bathe in Vlaminck, Utrillo, Matisse, a pre-Columbian collection; a tree grown out of a thin marble hall. There is an atmosphere of culture, taste and wealth combined with Jewish family feelings.

We have a flat in Buckingham Gate. Our window, which has the advantage of north light, overlooks the back of Buckingham Palace where the band practises all day long. Sometimes it's the bagpipes, sometimes the trumpets. On the whole the orchestra repeats a passage twenty times.

It takes two weeks to finish Rosenheim's portrait, so little time has he to come and sit. His friend from Rhodesia comes to have a look at the finished painting. Rosenheim leaves and Louis Black stays to discuss details.

I feel a bit happier now that I have a second commission.

As I have sittings mostly at noon or after, the mornings are more or less a waste. I am tense and don't dare tire myself out visiting galleries. So we go to the bank, we find Andrea's slippers that she likes to wear. We walk in Soho, gaze at hippies and a one-man band's entertaining long queues at movies, strip joints and porn shops.

I met Allanah Coleman who has left Bonython's and opened a gallery in Canterbury. And Perla Hessing, who came to London to be near Leonard, only exhibits in America and Europe.

The Tutankhamen exhibition at the British Museum is a great experience. It has already been on for six months, and the queues are still long. We went after five, got in after ten minutes. We bought hot chestnuts and warmed our hands on them. The taste brought back childhood memories. It was pitch dark inside, walls covered with felt, and the spotlighted treasures appeared to float, golden and perfect and full of mystery.

8 November 1972

The Alitalia flight from Rome to Hong Kong was pretty sinister. Much talk of Palestinian skyjackers. In Athens we were not allowed to disembark. We settled down to a six-hour stretch to New Delhi. We reached there at dawn. Not allowed to disembark.

12 November 1972

Sydney

Objects feel estranged. The house has no soul, and still isn't sold. The dog has a sore eye. The sink seeps water into the cupboard and the dishwasher is kaput.

20 November 1972

Sorted out two bags of letters, bought a new car (can't believe it!).

Lipót Hermann, my former teacher, died. He was eighty-eight. Like me, Lipi kept a diary for fifty years, only his was illustrated. He did a self-portrait every day during his illness, and each day as we leafed through the pages we followed the deterioration of his features until the end. On the last page he wrote: 'It is finished'. Signed it, dated it and died.

I put foundation on canvases today, but I'm not itching to paint.

Peter's back. He is warm, trusting, loving and old patterns reveal themselves in five shirts sprawled on the floor (for me to pick up?). After all those months away, he seems happy to live in Sydney. He works hard, goes swimming, looks tanned.

3 February 1973

It's over a hundred degrees and so humid, the sweat hangs on our skin like dew.

Not one portrait commission. Not one good painting since I started work.

'Gift to the nation.' Lady Gaitskell gave my portrait of her husband, Hugh, to the National Portrait Gallery on the tenth anniversary of his death. As it was a considerable sacrifice, she had two copies of it made for her daughters.

12 March 1973

Robert Morley arrived with his daughter, Annabelle, to show her my portrait of him. 'Someone really ought to buy this, it's so good.'

We invited Andrea to celebrate her birthday, and suggested she invite her own friends. This way we don't care who she insults. Except she insulted me. I bought her a salmon-pink wool shawl with tassels, imported from Paris, the sort of thing I would like to get for my birthday. She threw it back like a discus champion. 'I won't have it. This is for old ladies, not me! I wouldn't be seen dead in it in the Macleay Regis.'

25 March 1973

At eighty-nine, Orban has written his third book.

We've decided to stay in the house a while longer. So we put in a new kitchen. Everything is demolished. I looked at the toaster in a spot where I'd never seen a toaster before. I saw my reflection, all beautifully distorted on the concave surface.

I drew a larger-than-life toaster with charcoal and pencil, and there it stood: a presence, a new avenue. Then I drew the thermos. I am planning to pour acrylics on canvas and see what happens. But what next?

I got two commissions, at last. One was Charles Walton, husband of Nancy Bird, the aviator. Charles is fairly tall, middle aged, a bit shy and wears blue-tinted glasses. He used to be a textile manufacturer and knows many Hungarians, and even a few words of the language. He gave up his business and became a researcher for the Smithsonian Institute of Washington.

They invited us to St Ives for Sunday lunch, and as usual I went without Jancsi. Acres of rare trees, shrubs, salmon mornay and champagne beside the pool.

Nugget Coombs was there, very much in the public eye as economic adviser for the new government, and director of Aboriginal affairs and the Council of the Arts. He is small, has tiny hands and feet, and a keen, witty face with piercing eyes. There was a former head of British information service who now records Australian birds.

Instead of a staple diet of Hungarian conversation, I learn that the name budgerigar for the bird is an Aboriginal word meaning wave, named for the formation in which they fly. I learn of a composer who wrote music inspired by an Aboriginal melody played on the didgeridoo, but isn't allowed to use it as the player's spirit has to be on the spot.

Marcel Seidler, the architect's brother, gave up making shirts after twenty years, got his MA in psychology and now conducts group therapy. He also teaches photography. He came to see if I have any paintings suitable to be woven for tapestry at Aubusson.

So many who, in middle age, choose more creative and less lucrative professions.

5 April 1973

The new kitchen is still being built. No one wanted the old gas stove. Workmen hammering and drilling, but I manage to paint inbetween. The canvases which have been rotting on the rack since Alice Springs suddenly matured, and as I knew exactly what to do, grew into good paintings.

Suddenly everything sells.

8 April 1973

Yehudi Menuhin concert. He seems to have left ego-trippings, ratings, success, behind long ago. Seeing him in the Town Hall was more like watching a saint. A reviewer writes that normal critical values no longer seem to apply to him. Some critics pounced on slips of the fingers. They are scarcely more important than the momentary flicker of a brilliant light.

Picasso died. For a whole century almost, critics wrote about him in the present indicative. When the tense changed to 'was' instead of 'is', it seemed like a malfunction of the language itself. The most generous display of creative exuberance in several hundred years has come to an end.

8 June 1973

Andrea is not satisfied with the corsets Jancsi had made for her, so returned the gifts for the third time. I picked her up, took her to Elasco, where she addresses Mrs Malloy as Mrs Winnipeg. Three double cognacs later we have fish with lemon sauce and go to see Vittorio de Sica's film, *The garden of the Finzi Continis*. For thirty years we have seen films and plays and novels about our tragic past. Why de Sica chose to open those wounds again, I wouldn't know.

Mr Raynor (after whom a room is named at the National Gallery of Victoria) rang to say he wants to buy a painting. I cancelled the chiropractor and the hairdresser and for two hours showed him paintings. He took three.

Next, Ken Thomas of TNT for a sitting. This is an important commission. The portrait will hang in a magnificent new building. I drew on a foundation of burnt orange outback and we had a fabulous first sitting. He came at 9 the next morning for the second sitting.

The Reid Gallery phoned from Brisbane. The Queensland Art Gallery bought my portrait of Robert Morley.

10 June 1973

John writes that Greta longs for our bathroom and says how nice it would be to sleep in a clean bed. I had a premonition that it would not be long before they arrive. I felt like my grandmother; buying new pillows, fresh sheets and blankets. We gave the spare room a big cleaning and made up the bed.

12 June 1973

We woke at midnight when the doorbell rang. I sat up in bed and said, 'That's John.' We rushed downstairs, and there he stood, my guru, long hair, long beard, Indian shirt. Greta, long blonde hair, poncho. Warmth, embraces, kisses. John ran to Peter's room. The two brothers hugging.

Next evening our dinner table is like a Fellini movie. Peter wears his brand new grey suit, Pucci tie and his hair is fashionably trimmed. He brought Vicky who was once Abigail, the sex symbol from television's 'No. 96'. Margaret and Maria, the two housekeepers, a guru, Greta, and two middle-aged, middle-class Jews.

15 June 1973

Life is tranquil in the house on the hill. Bondi Beach from my studio window, Rose Bay with the small island on sparkling water when I pull the blind up in the morning. Days are mostly busy and sometimes hectic but this is self-inflicted, I still haven't learnt to say no.

Most afternoons I manage an hour or two to be alone, ease the tension, pray for the children, for us, for becoming a good artist, for peace of mind. Then I empty my mind and just breathe and drift off, usually until Jancsi comes home. I answer the telephone calls I don't take while I paint, read the newspaper like homework for school. Maria calls us for dinner. Cassy sits unobtrusively while Jancsi smuggles a bite to him under the table.

The ritual of taking Cassy for a grand tour. The leash, my ancient jersey cap against the southerly wind, Cassy collects the mail on every tree leaving messages at strategic points. We know the entire dog population. The white labrador on the corner of Birriga Road is a sworn enemy, the newsagent's black spaniel is scared and sidles away. Cassy, the gentle lamb, turns into a tiger under our protection.

John and Greta have settled into the room. They put the mattress on the floor, carried the table and armchair out. Under the window is an altar. Sacred objects we are unfamiliar with. Burning incense, a small candle. Is this religious mania?

We have only one week together before we leave for New Guinea. One more family evening.

When the four of us are in the same place, we continue our family evenings. It's a breath of fresh pure oxygen. It causes a stream of wisdom (in Jancsi), of goodwill (in John), no inhibitions (in me), and naked truth and intelligence (in Peter). Greta is silent. A new member.

I find myself looking forward to the next occasion. It's a high court before which one may vent any grievance or problem of adjustment.

18 June 1973

New Guinea

We are in Port Moresby, taken care of by the administrator's secretary. After the letter Dr Coombs wrote for us, we are given VIP treatment. Beautiful orchids in the hotel, a typed itinerary. Lady Cleland sent her driver for us, and we had tea in an old-fashioned, open, colonial-style, tropical house, on a terrace above the sea, hills, storm clouds, bougainvillea, palms.

In the hotel we turned the radio on and listened to the Papua New Guinean news which was amazing. It sounded like a kindergarten lesson. The church should not speak in a foreign language called 'Latin' we were told, and why have a European-type religion? Jesus Christ was not a European. And those who want to believe in their old gods should be allowed to do so. Other times: a policeman was fined $20 because he gave some man a driver's licence without an exam.

Mr Johnson, the administrator, and his wife (romantically called Dulciana), gave us a dinner party. Exceptional people: a couple who are friends of the Haefligers, a Papuan author, Vincent Eri, the secretary, Chris Van Lieshont who used to be a patrol officer, Tom Craig and his wife Margaret, both from Scotland. He is an art teacher in the creative art centre.

They all seem to love this country fiercely, none of them have grown rich on the fat of the land, they are idealists and long to be useful. No one knows what their fate will be after independence.

Tom Craig says he doesn't really teach, he just provides the tools, the setting, atmosphere and encouragement. Only educated people need training, he said, to peel off their education to make them creative. These people *are* creative and shouldn't be taught, it would spoil their art. Akis, an exciting New Guinean artist, whose drawings, Indian ink, fine brushline, sensitive thin line with a fine nib, depicting figures which have sometimes six toes, sometimes seven fingers, and whenever there is a negative form he fills it with a crocodile or, alternately, a mosquito. Amazing drawing, Jancsi bought it.

The museum in Port Moresby has a Sepik Giacometti, ten-foot tall and magical. It possessed something which reminded me of the Tutankhamen exhibition in London. I would like to come back here and paint a particular presence—a Sepik Chagall in cedarwood.

Twenty-four hours crammed full of fantastic visual experiences and interesting people paved our way from Lae to Goroka to Hagen to

Wewak, telephoning the district commissioners at each place.

At last arrived in Goroka, settled into a large room with a sigh of relief, no people, no appointments, no invitations, just ourselves.

Not the slightest idea what I am doing, except that the sketches look alive. Jancsi suggests I should paint each one again to develop the copy freely. I will be surprised I think, when I unpack this material in Sydney.

23 June 1973

Kundiawa

I prepared paint and paper in the morning. They stuck a big umbrella on the lawn and brought me three chairs. For me, for the palette, and for the sketchbook. I couldn't quite believe my eyes when two black beauties appeared. My models. They had cadmium red painted on their cheekbones and a blue dotted pattern on their cheeks. Across their foreheads was an embroidered band holding a headdress of red-orange-pink feathers. Bare breasts, embroidered bands on their arms, a woven belt with strips of lambs wool hanging down the front. I filled the whole page with nothing but the face; first it was almost a portrait, then it became free and loose. I painted a sitting figure, light lines on dark background, the reds behaving differently. Worked till noon.

I was to have a male model in the afternoon. Siesta, dead tired. At 3 p.m. my man appeared. He looked savage. A real warrior. He wore plumage like a peacock, and palm leaves around his waist. When I finished work, suddenly and unexpectedly an old man came in, in full regalia, uninvited. The news probably spread. I couldn't disappoint him, or myself. He wore a copper coin on his head and from that a proud, enormous white feather. Most artistically he surrounded that feather with dry leaves. His face became unimportant, such was his abstract quality.

24 June 1973

It is Sunday, the mountains are grand in the mist. We were told the church in the next village is an experience not to be missed. We drove nine miles, found the church, and made as quick a turnabout as was possible in the onrushing crowd. To see hundreds of warriors is really frightening. There wasn't a single white person for miles.

The models kept coming. I worked like fury.

The evenings are beautiful. Around 6 p.m., like an express train, the storm comes. We sit inside the Chimbu Lodge with a drink.

A very tense two-hour drive to Mt Hagen in the morning. I never exceeded thirty miles an hour. Hundreds of squatters, children and pigs, in the middle of the road.

Phoned Peter. John and Greta have left for Nimbin.

26 June 1973

Mt Hagen

The Hagen Park Hotel is impressive, with low buildings around a giant park, but the room is a slum.

We float in the landscape, like two innocents.

Hagen looks like a frontier town, complete with beer-bellied six-footers drinking at the bar.

Madang

Madang, the only step in the whole trip which wasn't planned, is a delight, a holiday, a rest. We feel we needed just that. Badly. Alien, strange, fantastic impressions battered us. Here is peace, beauty, a slow-going, warm little spot. It is not typical or unique in the painterly sense. I can't pick out anything I haven't painted before.

The owner of our hotel, the Smugglers Inn, John Bestow, looks like a Frans Hals painting, complete with reddish beard and moustache. He just sold this enormous compound (the land, the hotel), and will move with his wife and daughter to Carrara to work in the quarry and learn about marble before launching into his new life as a sculptor.

10 July 1973

Sydney

From such heat into Sydney's bleak winter.

Jancsi broke his arm first day in the factory. I help him shave and dress but he is back at work with a sling.

Started to work on the New Guinea paintings. There is so much: forty-nine sketches. A rigid schedule. In the morning I cut canvas and make a gesso foundation. On yesterday's dry one I pour a layer of thin acrylic. Placed a piece of perspex on one of the pages (they are from a block and therefore the same size), squared the perspex with a felt pen and can now place it on any of those I want to enlarge. Every move away from home is a small sacrifice.

John writes from Nimbin. He wants to buy land in a commune. Nepal was exotic, far away and temporary. Perhaps I'll get used to it in time. Peter says there are many middle-class parents whose children are hippies. He thinks John is as happy as he has ever been. He goes on to say, 'With me, everything is material. I never searched for my soul. With John everything is soul, and nothing is material.'

4 August 1973

Lynn's 1973 acquisition for the Power Bequest opened in the new National Gallery with a bang and a fanfare. Radio, television, all papers, at last he is rewarded for his hard work.

I am commissioned by Sydney University to paint Bruce Williams, the vice-chancellor. An official portrait in his robes. This is the second time I've painted him. He is very reserved, dignified and shy in a boyish way and we get on very well.

Lynn told me that the vice-chancellor talked about the new portrait. He thinks his eyes are too hooded. Lynn told him, 'It's time the emphasis is on the picture, not the portrait. People who come to the university should say, "Where is that Cassab portrait of what's his name?"'

A grave responsibility. I underpainted the background and face with greys and blues, and the robe with mottled reds. Now it glows from under the black folds. And the gold stripes are rubbed in softly. No uniform chancellor for me, I hope.

There are now six New Guinea canvases painted and stretched. Compared to the original working sketches which are, let's say, 'A', the canvases are 'Z'. They work the same way as the abstracts, texture, the use of the accidental, a figure, hallelujah, which could have been painted by no one but me. The news of my painting a series of figures spread like wildfire. This has never happened to me before. The canvases have to be kept in the bedroom, as I don't want to sell those. With God's help they will become a one-man show. Four of the small ones are sold, but not before I translated them to another page. It's not a copy but different in background colour, movement of the limbs—still, I can't afford to lose them. Especially not before they are enlarged.

Orban left for Japan!

19 August 1973

My vision of Nimbin (as a symbol) undergoes change. Vernon Treweeke, a talented painter who painted every house in the village, creating a Christo-like happening, was here. We talked about putting Nimbin on the map. They are looking for crafts to do so that the community can support itself. John orders materials for candlemaking. I feel a bit better now that he talks about sculpting. If he gives everything he might earn to the community, that's *his* business.

14 September 1973

I arrived in Mt Isa for the presentation of my portrait of Jim Foots. Sir Asher Joel, who owns the Mt Isa paper, telephoned, and there were a journalist and a photographer at the airport. The picture and article appeared on the front page.

The local art group helped with unpacking and hanging in one of the reception rooms of the hotel. They had catalogues printed, numbers ready, 'sold' signs, everything.

Next morning I spoke on the radio, later met 200 invited guests and Jim Foots' portrait was unveiled. Six of my paintings were sold at the opening.

A long article in the *Australian* came out on the same day as the Mt Isa cover story. It was part of a series, 'Hungarians in Australia'. I am sandwiched between the millionaires.

Jancsi was angry. Tim Dare who wrote these articles spent an hour and a half interviewing me.

The first piece was on Sir Paul Strasser. The second on John Kaldor, the third Erwin Graf, another property developer. At the end of the page it said, ominously, 'Tomorrow Judy Cassab'.

We have received two invitations which I am terribly pleased about. Both for 20 October, the day the Queen opens the Opera House. The first is for 2.30 p.m., the official opening, and the second for the opening concert. Tickets can't be bought for this.

2 October 1973

Everything is selling. Almost all the large seven-foot canvases from last year's one-man show. *Crossing* was bought by Jim Foots, *Red desert* was bought by the National Bank in Melbourne. *Night flower* was bought from the Reid Gallery in Brisbane.

Dr Coombs took me to lunch. He wanted to hear all about New Guinea. He's an economic adviser for the new Whitlam government, and is going to China with the prime minister. A sensitive, cultured, deep-thinking man, with a sense of humour and charm.

Started to paint John Olsen who is jovial, baby-faced, grinning. He is a sad clown after the second sitting.

Today, at Margaret Olley's opening, Charles Blackman said: 'I would so much like you to paint Barbara, but I can't afford your prices.'

'Charles, for heaven's sake, I would gladly make an exchange with you.'

'It would be a challenge for you. Have you ever painted a blind person before?'

5 October 1973

Lunching with Sir Peter Abeles in his office at TNT at Macquarie Street, right opposite the Opera House. The chairman, Mr Millar, comes in. As I turn from my avocado to shake hands with him I caught sight of a Renoir reproduction behind me. 'Now I know why I was allocated *this* chair: so I wouldn't see that you've hung a reproduction instead of an original.'

Peter tells me he is going to China in February with Bob Hawke, president of the ACTU.

14 October 1973

In a country which used to do nothing for its artists at home or abroad, we have suddenly made international headlines as the country which spends more on artists at present than any other.

James Mollison, young director of the not-yet-built National Gallery in Canberra, was said to have been taken for a ride up the Hudson. How does he explain the two million for the Pollock? He is said to be negotiating for Picasso's *Guernica* irrespective of cost. He just wants to get masterpieces and of course, in a hundred years he will be proved right!

Unexpectedly I also felt a breeze of the spending spree. Canberra commissioned me to paint Mr Cope, the Speaker of the House of Representatives. The voice informed me of the regulation measurement for the King's Hall, and added, 'You will receive $3500 for the painting.' Which is $1000 more than I would have charged if I had been asked.

Orban came last week and I started a new portrait of him. The first hangs in the Budapest National Gallery. I had this picture in my head for the last year. We sit, have lunch in the courtyard, his beret on his head, on the garden chair, gesticulating.

One sitting and almost not to be touched. It's translucent, the orange greens of the landscape foundation breaking through the whole of the figure. The head is also transparent. Please God, it should be true, but I think it's the most successful portrait since I painted Margo Lewers.

18 October 1973

Had a disastrous one-man show in Perth. I am a seasoned exhibitor by now, and not quite as depressed as I would have been a few years ago. But it was a stinging rebuke. Thank you, dear God, for keeping me humble. I deserved it. I would never have shown this melange in Sydney, so why should I inflict it on Perth?

Not one picture sold.

21 October 1973

To be one of only 2500 at the opening of the Sydney Opera House is really a privilege, and the afternoon was spectacular. Sixty thousand coloured balloons flew up. Hundreds of pigeons. Streamers poured out in the breeze. Tugboats pulled giant pink ribbons away from the Opera House 'sails'.

The night was positively the most glamorous I have ever seen. Premiers of each state, the famous, the titled, the rich, seated strictly by protocol. Beethoven's Ninth conducted by Willem van Otterloo.

After the concert, champagne, a buffet of goose liver, smoked salmon, seafood. Outside the harbour and the shores glittering, the ships illuminated.

7 November 1973

John writes from Nimbin. Two monks are holding meditation courses, and busloads arrive from all over the country.

> Got a few minutes off from the kitchen. Up at 4.15 a.m. preparing warm water in buckets, light the fire, sweep, ring the gong, meditate for half an hour, prepare breakfast, serve it, wash up, start cooking lunch, empty toilets, fix tents, do the shopping, get flowers for the shrine, join the group meditation for an hour, make tea, hear the monks' discourse. I do

notice a calm vibration when I return from Nimbin that surrounds the house like sweet perfume, and both Greta and I feel stimulated. Now, back to work.

Love love love John.

It's good that Peter is here tonight to talk to us, because my first, bourgeois reaction (and Jancsi's) is a sense of waste (his talent, his brains and he slaves all day in lowly tasks). Emptying toilets instead of creating sculptures.

'It's *his* turn,' says Peter 'and when he meditates for ten days it's someone else's turn to serve meals and clean. What can be more creative than helping others achieve peace of mind? He is unselfish, he works terribly hard and not for money and not for fame. You should be proud to have such a son.'

Thank you, Peter.

12 November 1973

I am working on seven-foot canvases of the Mt Isa sketches. Good for New Guinea to lose impetus and good for me to stand again in the centre of the unstretched canvas on the floor with a brush tied to the broomstick, swinging. Simultaneously I paint Mr Cope for Canberra and Olsen for myself. Olsen is overworked after three sittings and I decide to start a new one and paint the face (at least) in one sitting only. So it won't be tonal but linear with the red ground coming through.

John Olsen sits for my next attempt. I'm painting him on a red-green foundation with Olsenish squiggles, and watch what happens to the colour when I draw the face in with blues and greens upon red. It looks kitsch. And more academic than the first one which looks like an eighteenth-century composer. Romantic. Schumann.

26 November 1973

Belgiorno (of Transfield) organised the first Sydney Biennale of paintings in the exhibition room of the Opera House. Robert Haines did the hanging, acres of black on which the spotlit paintings float beautifully.

Pick up the Lynns in full evening dress. Pick up Rose Skinner who arrived from Perth with her secretary, Suzanne. Directors of all the state galleries, critics from all states. Champagne flows. Whitlam opens it. Announces $38,000 worth of grants to artists. Dr Coombs introduces me to Yevtushenko, the poet from Russia. James Fitzsimmons arrived from Lugano. He is the editor of *Art International*. Jack Lynn is the Australian editor. We go to the Hungry Horse, where Rose booked a special room for us, Don Gazzard and Ray Crooke.

On Monday morning Jack Lynn and I took Jim Fitzsimmons to artists' studios. Lynn took him to galleries all Saturday. He is on a kind of talent-hunt choosing, I think, artists to be reproduced in the magazine. I was to drive and lunch was planned for our place, where Jack wanted him to see my paintings. He seems to favour poetic, lyrical things.

It was a long day. I was taut as a string what with writing out routes and directions from a map. We didn't want to get lost in small back lanes and waste time with a very heavy schedule.

Actually it was a treat. All the artists being closer to John's age, I seldom get invited over, and I was very interested.

Brett Whiteley lives in the gas works on the North Shore. We drove through bumper-to-bumper traffic on the Harbour Bridge, into a strange landscape of shiny aluminium gas drums at the edge of the harbour, boats being built, bulldozers crawling, and on one of the identical houses saw a large Chinese sign painted by Brett.

We climbed up on crates, pulled the iron door aside and found Brett still asleep in his studio. He pulled on a sweater. Drawings were scattered all over the enormous area, some erotic, some social commentary, a series of Bacon portraits, planes shifted, drawings of Fiji, of a beach, of Hitler, of Queenie in the bathtub, of lovers. Undoubtedly an artist and first-rate craftsman.

Next, back to the east, to Peter Powditch's studio. He has painted on the same pink background for three years now, nudes with and without bikinis. Lately there is a vase of flowers between their open legs.

Over to Ron Robertson-Swann who is a member of the Visual Arts Council. He selected the pictures for the Biennale and included himself as well. Two enormous workshops, one for sculpture, the other for painting.

Then we drove to the new Hogarth Galleries. Same old scene, twenty sacks filled with earth, a yellow picture frame on the floor kissing a bicycle. Oscar has two small collages, they look good.

Next a visit to Alan Oldfield whose house looks like an architect's, the studio, a courtyard with a swimming pool, on the other side a pool room. He is a good realist painter, squinting at Caravaggio.

At home, whisky. Two new large paintings in the living room which he seemed to like, going close to look at the texture. Upstairs one on the easel, a lemonish-greeny one, he talks about the canvas breathing. Looking at paintings of 1970, he remarks, 'You've made great leaps since then.'

Jack and Lily love my painting of Orban.

We have lunch. Fitzsimmons visibly enjoys the European surroundings and taste. His wife is Hungarian, and she is a painter too. He thinks women are still discriminated against. Also, he finds it ridiculous that youth should be favoured against mature painters.

Next we drove to the Art Gallery of NSW. I stay in the car, tired, pretending there is no parking-space.

Jack says, 'Judy, please drop us at the hotel.'

Fitzsimmons: 'We want to discuss the things we went to see today. Thank you for the excellent driving and the delicious lunch. Also I am grateful Mr Lynn took me to Madame Cassab's studio because that's where I have seen some of the best paintings in Sydney.'

He didn't have to say this. He wasn't complimentary or polite anywhere.

This was Monday. Today, Thursday, Jack Lynn rang me. 'Fitzsimmons wants me to write an article about you,' he announces in his dry manner. 'Have three-inch transparencies made of Orban's portrait and the old one of Vice-Chancellor Williams. Also, of the three new large ones and a couple more you can paint in the next few weeks. Also, black and whites of the same.'

'That's the best news I've heard for years!'

'Nothing to do with me. I only write the article.'

I thank God on my knees. It is one of the most important things which has happened to me.

3 December 1973

The invasion goes on. Jeff Smart arrives from Rome. John Siddeley and his wife from Japan. They want to spend tomorrow evening with us. Great joy, we love them. If only it wasn't the Christmas rush.

28 December 1973

New Zealand

Catapulted out of it. We are on a lazy conducted tour of New Zealand. Only fourteen in the bus, all shaken together after three days, no driving, planning, caring for suitcases. We are limp and boring and it's a cure.

In Sydney, before Christmas, incredibly more was added to our load. Hedy Goldstein arrived from Madrid. Could she spend ten days with us?

'You are very welcome for one weekend,' I said.

After the visit I had flu and diarrhoea, entered the two Archibald portraits and two large landscapes for the Wynne Prize, distributed Christmas presents, wrote hundreds of cards.

31 December 1973

The tour gets more and more beautiful in spite of two days of rain and fog which covered up the Franz Joseph glacier. We stopped at Queenstown which, from the tall mountains, looks like the view from the Schafsberg looking at Wolfgangsee but strangely without a sign of human habitation. Strange also, the way subtropical vegetation almost kisses the glaciers.

15 January 1974

Sydney

Settling back is as difficult as ever. Took me three days to unpack.

A letter from John Siddeley.

Couldn't you arrange your wonderful New Guinea exhibition while we're there? I hesitate to say that I would like to open it, because that seems a trifle arrogant, but being a lord has a certain value and if that value can help you then I'm at your command because Bernard (Leser) and Charles Lloyd Jones would back the idea with all their force.

27 January 1974

Our family meetings are becoming deep and loving, abrasive and healing, and as fascinating as fireworks.

Jancsi talks about having been insecure all his life. That's why he abhors debt, though he acknowledges it's better business to owe money. We try to understand why he transfers his insecurity to his sons. We talk about pulling in only one direction.

'You think,' Johnny says 'if I sculpt for long enough I will become famous or rich. Or if I concentrate on being a healer, the same will happen. Dad, what if Freud's father had wished him to become a nose and throat specialist instead of following those crazy ideas nobody even heard of? I know I am on the right track.'

I continue reading my journal translations in each family meeting.

John is twelve and already in trouble at Sydney High School. The reading acts like a tuning fork. The tone reverberates in the room and John starts to talk about the school years which, he accuses, crippled them for life.

They talk about a prison sentence and opening cages and finally illness as escape. It was painful talking about this phase of their life as if one was projected backwards, knowing the future as now we know the past, something inevitable. And while illnesses in the future are brewing there I am with my drive and thirst and trips to London.

I don't know if we solve anything, but it is a catalyst. Perhaps Peter will grow to be less bitter, perhaps John will find a path.

7 February 1974

Cassy died of a heart attack. He was pure love, and now he has gone. Twelve years old, a very old gentleman indeed, getting slower and more dependent. Jancsi walked him before breakfast every day.

Maria, the housekeeper, shaking, white-faced told us, 'Cassy is dead.' She took him for a walk and he was so happy, dancing on the grass, sniffling, pulling on the leash, and then he just collapsed. My reaction was, how wonderful. He was happy on the grass, he didn't suffer, didn't even know.

I rang Jancsi who said, 'He died as gallantly as he lived.' And then I just cried and cried. In the evening we went for the usual walk, without Cassy. Next morning Jancsi went to the bathroom while it was still dark and, returning to bed, he left the door of the bedroom slightly ajar. For Cassy. We shall miss him for a long time.

10 February 1974

Townsville

I am in Townsville for the unveiling of the vice-chancellor's portrait. I sketched this morning from an air-conditioned car. It's incredibly hot and steamy, and the rain which caused such floods in Queensland still hangs above or pours down.

Attitudes and artifacts in all categories have replaced line, colour, and form as ingredients of art. But although the work of art has diminished in importance, there has been no corresponding decline in public interest in artists or in the ambition of individuals to become artists.

The changed relation between the artist and the product has radically altered art criticism. The critic has a theory about where art is going and a conviction about where it ought to go. The firmer the critic's outlook, the less likely they are to be satisfied with art that has matured without the benefit of the critic's collaboration.

In traditional art, the canvas is the key to the painter's experience. In postobject art, the artist is the key to what is offered to their audience. In an earth work, for example, the artist may be the only factor that distinguishes it from farming.

The first screening of artist-performers is conducted by dealers (or impresarios and collaborators).

The critic who wishes to remain a critic ought to give way before these representatives of these mysterious powers of money, fashion and institutions.

I had to smile. John went to a Nimbin meeting. There was concern, he said, about hippies who come to the cooperative, smoke dope and step on the vegetable garden. 'But if we want to be different to the existing system, we can't just put a sign out—Keep Off.'

13 February 1974

Dr Back, the vice-chancellor, took me by ferry to Magnetic Island. Then we rented a Mini-Moke and he drove and read while I sketched.

Boarding the plane for Brisbane I got caught in a torrential storm which drenched me. The stewardess took my dripping dress, packed me in blankets and hung my clothes up to dry.

22 February 1974

Sydney

I enlarged two of my New Guinea pictures to 7 x 6 foot. Strange how when growing to that size, they become so much more spiritual and free. They continue to appear as 'lyrical abstracts' with nothing fixed. Limbs, movements are ambiguous, and can be read by the spectator as they choose. It's still only a beginning.

1 April 1974

Nimbin

We flew to Casino, and took a bus to Lismore where John and Greta fetched us in the old Morris made roadworthy. At last we saw Nimbin. Each facade—the butcher's, the newsagent's, the baker's—has been painted by the community. On Sunday it looked like Luna Park when it's closed, when the merry-go-round has stopped.

John and Greta don't live in a commune. They have a little cottage near a farmhouse. They don't pay rent, but work for the owner three days a week for the cottage and their share of the vegetable garden. On the other days they work in the commune.

They cut wood for the stove. There is a small machine which they use to grind the wheat into flour. They bake their own bread. Greta is responsible for the chickens and geese. Guavas boil in a large pot. John peels and cleans jam melon to add to it. Jars are sterilised. They take what they need and barter with the rest. Money is used only rarely.

The kitchen water is supplied from a tank of rainwater. There is another tank outside on the verandah where they wash. There is a box for rotting fruit peels, vegetables, and ashes for compost. John is planting new seedlings in the garden. It's a nice garden with herbs and flowers.

The life we see here resembles the life of a Hungarian peasant before the war.

2 April 1974

John and Greta take us to Tuntable, the commune. Like the Garden of Eden, in a way. A thousand acres of lush green valley, a river and mountains and woods, and beautifully cultivated vegetable gardens. Some of the young people are nudists, and it's somehow natural here for a naked man to work with a pickaxe, while an equally naked girl emerges from the river.

Domes are being built everywhere, some coated with plastic, some with canvas or wood. The only existing old-type building is what they call the White House, the centre of the cooperative.

There's a library, a tool room, a carpenter's workshop, a music room. In the evenings there are meetings, lectures. The tribe, the big family— a fantastic spirit pervades the whole place, and I breathe easier. The experiment justifies John's being here.

Then John takes us to his 'construction', a sculpture in which one will be able to live. The site he chose embraces some trees around which wire mesh is sculpted and cement is then poured on it. There are two windows which are made from abandoned car windscreens. The door is Gothic, and leads to a clear little waterfall. This will be the bathroom. Inside the dwelling is a large, round rock which is being chipped away to form a bench.

We feel relieved to have found something to be genuinely delighted about.

He tells us that Greta doesn't want to live in the commune. He talks about perhaps going back to India without her.

Sculpture, farming, building, counselling, India, communes—I feel he is still fragmenting himself. He says he isn't interested in the future. Only today exists.

15 April 1974

I started Barbara Blackman's portrait. Open, unseeing eyes, blonde hair sleek over shoulders, framing a tragic face.

The whole country is in a turmoil. Strikes, inflation, insecurity.

Jancsi said Whitlam is a bad driver. He switched into the wrong gear. Now there will be a double dissolution of parliament and new elections.

A week of the Power Bequest. Dr Jim Golding, who wrote a book about cubism, and is a lecturer at the Courtauld Institute (and artist), came to deliver this year's lecture on Malevich and the Black Square. Slides show how he is influenced by cubism, by Léger and Kandinsky. He is not a major artist, but he reached the black square as an emblem or symbol in 1920, to reappear in the late 1960s. That makes him an important figure in art history.

The moral of the fable seems to me that when he arrived at this conclusion, he stopped painting altogether.

8 June 1974

Peter made his biggest sale. He worked on it for five months. He now has money in the bank. He was shining with happiness.

Greta moved out of the farmhouse. Have they split up? No letter from John in weeks. Jancsi telephoned the White House, and left a message. Nothing. We telegrammed. Greta rang. John is on another commune.

At long last he phoned. 'I have become a hippie again. I've hit the road.'

'What do you mean, hippie?' asked Jancsi.

'Someone who doesn't know where he sleeps tomorrow.'
Jancsi tried to joke. 'Come home and be a hippie in Bellevue Hill.'
My son, my son. When will God help him to stop running?

14 June 1974

At last a letter from John.

*Wrote a long letter but everything had changed before I got to the post
office. Centre of the cyclone. Change, change, change. Have spent some
time on different roads, breathing freedom and the dust of cars. Carefully
and methodically I strip myself back to the bone, prune myself down to the
roots.*

*I feel the start again of that awareness of that incredible cosmic dance
which becomes apparent when I let go of my desires and lower myself into
chaos, purposelessness, here and now. Everything that happens becomes
relevant, just right, just so. The universe, when we let go of what we want,
gracefully provides for our every need, and everything is illuminated by a
simple grace.*

22 June 1974

Charles Blackman came over to see Barbara's portrait. The picture went
through many phases in colour. The yellow sofa on which she sat partly
disappeared on the right side of the square canvas, leaving on the left
a suggestion of an armrest on which she leant her elbow. Hair plays
greenish blonde, I played a fine ochreish grey over the dark-blue
background, as well as over the yellows. The darkness permeates
everywhere, mainly in her white frock which came through as transparent
as a spiderweb—crystal, but anchored firmly.
Blackman said, 'It is tender, it is gentle, it's like a waterfall.'
'Waterfall?'
'Yes, the hair flows into the fingers of the hand. The hand into the
arm, the arm into the cascade of the dress.'
He liked it. 'It's a swap,' he said. 'Come to my studio and choose
something.'
Barbara is very keen about school for children who don't fit easily
into regimentation. As a fundraising idea, she wanted to auction
manuscripts. She told me that Judith Wright sent her a poem, painters

wrote her letters with sketches. Would I, perhaps, write her a page of my diary? I said I would.

I found a charcoal sketch of a rather pale and gentle face of a man and on top of it, across it, I wrote down the page of the diary of January 1945 when the first Russian soldier entered our cellar in Budapest on Madách tér.

Blackman gave me a choice of three major works. One was a double image (as he called it), two paintings, one below the other horizontally in a vertical canvas. The other had two heads on a dark brown ground, three legs each. The third was one of the best Blackmans I have ever seen, one that struck a chord in me immediately. On strong blues and pitch black, a table with flowers and a teapot on the left. The blind face of his wife on the right with both hands raised to the chin, horizontal, monumental. I was dumbfounded when I pointed at it. I said, 'But Charles, this is too much. It's worth so much more than what I gave you.'

'We are not counting in inches, are we?' he said. Next morning he had it delivered.

I know we don't count in money, but this was so extremely generous, the painting (which hangs where the Bruegel copy used to, the only wall wide enough to take it) is great.

9 July 1974

Charles had a party celebrating my picture of Barbara. It looks fabulous in a floating frame, twice as large, airy, shimmery as I remembered. It stood on an easel in the middle of the room and Charles told everyone, 'Take your time, it's a slow picture, let it talk to you.' People said it looks inwards (which it does).

Charles took me aside. 'When we saw it on the easel, a few friends and I cried and cried, the tears streaming down our faces, that Barbara can't see this.'

Barbara moved easily among the food, the dishes, the glasses. Two enormous casseroles of hot soup simmered on the stove. The kitchen is part of the room, covered by curved arcades. Barry Humphries told me he spent ten days in Budapest, walking in Buda and listening to Hungarian gypsy songs every night.

14 July 1974

John writes that he has renounced all personal desire, has shaved his hair and beard, and become a monk.

Roughly my thoughts are: it's better than having a heroin addict. Or an alcoholic. But then, how many middle-class Jews do we know whose sons have become Buddhist monks?

I do what I have to do to protect myself. I take half a Valium and go to bed and pray. I know that in a few days' time this pain will be dulled and that I will get on with the business of life.

We have booked to leave on 7 August. We have no set itinerary.

28 July 1974

Oscar, without knowing that Jack Lynn wrote an article about me for *Art International*, sent off two colour transparencies to Clement Greenberg (one of the most influential critics in America) adding, with prejudice no doubt, that in his opinion these are among the best paintings currently done in Australia.

Yesterday Oscar rang. Greenberg wrote, 'I remember Mrs Cassab. *Figures* is very good. *Cascade* is too ornamental. But one can't judge too well from slides. However, there is no question about it, Mrs Cassab is a real painter.'

1 August 1974

We had three family meetings this week. Peter finally got the money owed to him and wants to earn more. John thinks he should do something creative, like making candles or cooking.

'John,' Peter says, 'whatever you choose to do I respect and accept you. I should get the same acceptance from you.'

'It's not that I don't accept you, Peter, I do. I'ts just that I'm concerned for you. I'd like you to see the real values in life. The realities. Money is fiction.'

'Not for me. We have different realities.'

12 August 1974

Switzerland

It was a long twenty-four hours to Vienna, but still a miracle. We had marvellous seats, with the emergency door on our left and the toilets on our right, and yards of room in front.

The Kärtnerstrasse has become a pedestrian mall, with public benches and new trees and red umbrellas and cobblestones. Between the Stephanskirche and the Graben the earth is shattered into a bottomless canyon, a new underground one day. Meanwhile, it ruins businesses in the neighbourhood.

We had a beautiful trip on the transalpine express, through Salzburg and the Arlberg to Zurich.

We rented a car and started our journey in Switzerland. In Bad Raggaz we lost our way for a minute, and who did we see walking from the Schlucht? Zsuzsi Gardos from Sydney! She almost fainted, such a surprise! The Strassers are here in the Quellenhof. The Jakobys were there from Spain. They asked us to come to Torremolinos and commissioned a portrait. We were ecstatic! With so much easy and unexpected money we can take a plane from Zurich to Malaga, then fly to Madrid. From Madrid to Budapest, then Prague to London. There I can meet the Duchess of Kent who wrote that she wants her three children painted in the Easter holidays. Everything went like a dream.

We stopped in Flims to have smoked trout and fresh raspberries. As we drove on the villages became browner and poorer, and I felt a sense of something sinister.

I stopped before a majestic view of a dam. Jancsi got out of the car to look out and fell into a shallow ravine. I heard his cry of pain and saw him lying on his back, his right leg at an angle. I ran after a young couple, calling for help. The man left his wife and two children and drove off to call an ambulance from the Lukmanier Pass telephone.

Another car pulled up with a French couple who supplied an eiderdown. The young man returned. The ambulance was on its way, he said, but first a doctor had to see Jancsi. It took an hour. The French couple brought a gas cooker to make us tea. The doctor arrived in a Jaguar, cut Jancsi's trousers off and wrenched the broken leg into position. Jancsi yelled with pain.

Another hour before the ambulance arrived and set off for Chur. 'That's the centre of the ski world. The Kanton Spital has the best specialists for broken bones,' the doctor said.

The Swiss and French couples helped to load all our overseas luggage in the ambulance. I lay down on the other stretcher. We were like two mummies.

They wheeled Jancsi in for blood tests, a cardiogram, and x-rays. The nurse telephoned a hotel, and booked me in. The ambulance driver offered to take me there, with the suitcases. But at the hospital, Jancsi was still in casualty. They couldn't find the Herr Professor (it being a Sunday) but anyway the operation would not be until the next morning. I was not to come in until after ten.

At last Jancsi was put in a bed, drowsy from the drugs, glucose and salt dripping into his veins, his leg fixed and stretched with a weight hanging at the foot of the bed.

The professor wanted to wait at least five days before operating, because there is some danger of clotting.

After the operation Jancsi must stay in hospital for three weeks, they are going to put a steel plate and screws into the bone. Then he can fly back to Sydney, but it will take another three months to heal. After a year or two, the steel plate will be removed.

20 August 1974

The shock starts to wear off a bit. I settled down to four weeks of hospital in Chur. Jancsi holds my hand while I read the *Zuricher Tagblatt*. Professor Schumann visits once a day. Jancsi gets four pints of blood to counteract the internal bleeding.

I made cold compresses sprinkled with 4711 to cool him. I shave him in the mornings, I feed him. The leg is stretched in such a way he can't move at all. After his lunch I do the shopping, stretch out on the bed, then go back.

Later I sit on the terrace and sip red wine. A row of lights hang between the chestnuts.

Jancsi was operated on yesterday. He is out of intensive care, no more oxygen, much fresher, no pain, but he is running a temperature.

It's one week now since the accident. His leg is swathed in a tight dressing, because of the bleeding.

In the dark, exhausted and depressed, I can only go to the hotel's restaurant which is hideously expensive. All is cultured and polished and humming, except in place of a heart there is a cash register ticking.

4 September 1974

It's a horrid thought: Jancsi could be a stretcher case on the aeroplane home. Perhaps something should be done to bolster up Jancsi's general health, nerves, perhaps more vitamin shots. Good God, Switzerland is famous for its rejuvenation treatments.

6 September 1974

Peter writes. He tells me that he has had all the necessary inoculations and is ready to fly over at a moment's notice.

> Mum, I know what a strain you are going through. Dad can get pretty difficult sometimes, particularly when he is sick. Try to be strong, because now your strength is needed. Do not let money be a worry. I know it is expensive. I have money sitting in the bank. You know whatever I have is yours. I know you are holding Dad's hand, but in a way, I wish I was there holding yours.

11 September 1974

I remember when we first came to Australia I felt the doctors were impersonal. They are definitely chummy and warmhearted compared to these.

18 September 1974

I rang Sanyi Mandel in Budapest, our old doctor from Beregszász. I told him about our predicament, and that Jancsi longs to recuperate in Budapest. What does he advise us to do? Go straight home to Sydney, or stop at the Gellért, with its physiotherapy and medical supervision, without the hated atmosphere of being in a hospital? He said, 'Come, by all means, I will alert a bone specialist, a urologist, you couldn't be in better care.'

I almost fainted when I saw the hospital bill.

24 September 1974

Budapest

Jancsi felt he couldn't bear another weekend with sergeant-major nurses and cold fish doctors, so we phoned Kati. We would like to stay for the weekend and she should send an ambulance to the plane. The Swiss ambulance picked Jancsi up from the hospital, and we went to Zurich.

In Budapest the Harsányis were waiting.

It was pouring with rain and the city was dark and the staircase smelly, but Kati was there. Jancsi slept well for the first time in weeks. So did I.

18 October 1974

Sydney

Jancsi went to the plane by ambulance. The next twenty-five hours were not too bad. I kept the medicines on European time until we touched down in Sydney. Jancsi was carried home on a stretcher, and checked into St Vincent's Hospital the next day. The catheter was removed, a few cups of tea and some liquid and without any pain or difficulty, Jancsi pissed like a fountain for the first time in eight weeks. They x-rayed the leg, took him off anticoagulants.

The days go by quite easily at home. Jancsi is going downstairs on his bottom, sits in the courtyard in the sun among Oscar's flowering orchids, eats well, goes upstairs on his bottom too, only backwards . . . I couldn't believe it.

People came in droves, flowers and books are sent, and by now bridge parties have begun.

15 November 1974

We are still housebound. It's been four months, and Jancsi can now walk up and down the stairs.

Meanwhile I paint Sir Roden Cutler, the governor of NSW.

John Kenilworth asked me to do a portrait of him, but only about ten-inches tall. First I refused, then I tried, and then did it in one sitting. I wouldn't take any money. Next day a parcel arrived and from layers of tissue paper and foam rubber a Khmer head emerged; beautiful, beautiful! His note: 'One good head deserves another.'

3 December 1974

Asked to lecture on portrait painting for the Art Gallery of NSW. Refused. Asked to be councillor in the Power Foundation. Refused.

29 December 1974

We've just spent ten days in New Zealand. We pulled ourselves out of the season's festivities like an aching tooth, and returned to Wairakei on the North Island amidst pine forests and thermal pools.

In good light, what really is simply boiling mud changes into molten silver with amethyst castles. Dali would have a ball.

Completely in the dark about what I'm doing.

The owners of the kiosk in Waiotapu won't charge me the entry fee, they are so proud that I return each day to what they advertise in crude rainbow colours as 'Wonderland'.

18 January 1975

We hardly noticed stepping into the New Year. The Vienna Philharmonic played Strauss on television, and we drank champagne in bed.

I drive Jancsi to work and pick him up at 2 p.m. almost every day. I still manage to paint.

Unemployment has reached an unprecedented level of 300,000. Cyclone Tracy demolished Darwin. I hate the sight of newspapers, disasters, bombings, and an atmosphere of general hate.

I sent in two of my seven-foot landscapes to the Wynne, two figure compositions to the Sulman, and two to the Archibald. Eric Smith won the Wynne, Keith Looby the Sulman, and Sam Fullbrook the Archibald. Not even a mention. Jancsi says I shouldn't send in to any more competitions. I can't afford not to win.

10 March 1975

On 28 February I had a one-man show of twenty-eight paintings in Newcastle. It was the inauguration of Anne von Bertouch's new gallery, and the invitation said, '... to mark International Women's Year.' That's the reason why the catalogue referred to a 'One-painter show' (not *man*!).

It was a delightful weekend, not only because ten paintings were sold, although that helped! Newcastle's Lord Mayor (a woman, aptly) opened my exhibition.

28 March 1975

I am expected in England to paint the Duchess of Kent's children. I booked my flight to arrive three days earlier. Canvas (sent by air to be stretched), paints, easel, the usual.

5 April 1975

London

It snowed yesterday and it affects me like a tropical flower. I shrivel and wilt, and feel depressed. Is it worth it?

So I went on a gallery tour with Zsuzsi. Augustus John retrospective. Didn't teach me anything I couldn't teach myself. It was good to meet my own 'Gaitskell' in the National Portrait Gallery. By popping into a dozen galleries does one learn about 'trend'? It's all either super or photo realism, or minor examples of masters, enshrined, entombed, hushed.

London seems to represent the culmination of my masochism for which, as far as one can know oneself, I think I have a tendency.

10 April 1975

Sitting in the train I thought, what do I need this for? Sitting in a train, in a sad, industrial, foggy, semidetached, rainy landscape with a heavy suitcase and a heavy parcel, 3 x 4 foot, neither of which I'm able to lift without help.

I was the last passenger to reach the exit where her Royal Highness stood, patiently waiting. We placed everything in the back of the station wagon and Dido, the black labrador, was allowed into the back seat. He licked my hand as an introduction.

I have pampered comfort, hot-water bottle under my satin eider-down. The children are beautiful. I hope I will do a good painting, please God.

12 April 1975

Feeling a bit more at ease now that I have sketched the three figures into the composition. Anmer Hall is like other English country houses. My bathroom has an emerald green carpet and the towelling armchair matches the towels, embroidered in emerald green. I have two kinds of bath salts and three different bath oils to choose from and Roger Gallet carnation soap.

There is also that English phenomenon—the nanny—who came when the first child was born. When Nicholas is eight and goes to boarding school she will become obsolete.

The afternoons are desperately long because I only paint in the morning. I dress in boots and a warm woollen cap and go walking around the park. Dido, the labrador, wants a bone to be thrown. George and Nicholas join me. They show me the sandpit, the swings and the daffodils.

By now I have a tight knot of anxiety in my guts. So there I toil away, smiling sweetly and praying, dear God, help me out of this predicament, help me do a good job.

15 April 1975

I still don't know my capacity for progress. The picture makes giant strides, and I think it's only the sixth day and there isn't much left to do. Everybody is terribly pleased.

The duke left for London yesterday, taking a labrador puppy for King Constantine of Greece.

Georgy is a near genius, I would say. One forgets he is only twelve. He knows about classical music, and Jung and Freud, and economics, and more about art movements than the average grown-up. His thirst for learning is unquenchable. They have to curb him all the time. Are they lucky? How did they do it?

17 April 1975

Incredibly, the triple portrait is finished, the likenesses are good, and, by changing the yellow couch into a gentle curve stretching horizontally over the upper third of the canvas it became something left to the viewer's imagination.

I suffered loneliness on my trips without Jancsi before. But it always had redeeming compensations. But now they are extremely rare. One of the things that will illuminate the darkness of this one is the drawings of Michelangelo at the British Museum.

Not like the sculptures, the crushing genius at the Accademia in Florence. Not like the Sistine Chapel. The drawings are intimate and personal and, as I glided along the glass cases, brightly lit in the dark room with my spectacles on my nose, inches from the probing, running, searching lines, his hand almost touched me over the centuries.

And, even more than his genius, perhaps, I was touched by his miserable weaknesses in the 'presentation drawings', some of which he did for his boyfriends. There, in a corner, in his own handwriting (translated below) he says, 'Let me know if you like it' (*The rape of Ganymede*). 'If you don't I'll make another one by tonight.'

The drawings for someone else are overworked, losing his freedom, without the play of racing lines, of men with three arms or divine double lines, and separate studies of shoulders or knees or buttocks or feminine heads, small and tender on muscular torsos.

I became a student again. Learned a lot about two profiles with the same solution. The first was the head of *The sick child* by Edvard Munch, in the Tate, where the outline is completely lost, merging into the background of the pillow. The other was in the Graham Sutherland exhibition where, in a portrait of Kenneth Clark (in profile), the contour is hardly visible, as the colour of the face and the background have the same tonal value.

15 May 1975

Sydney

Home again after two days in Singapore to break the journey.

The news that I was *appointed* by the governor-general as a member of the council which decides the new Australian honour, elevated me more in the public eye than the Archibald did fifteen years ago.

At the first meeting, there were twelve men around the long green table. Sir Garfield Barwick is the chairman. Almost all the others are politicians, former politicians, and two industrialists, Arthur Grimwade and Sir James Vernon. Clearly, I was the only one there who knows about art.

The meeting started and for two hours Sir Garfield made the rules known to us: this is not an honour of patronage but of merit; that the highest one 'Companion', is only for international merits. 'Officer' is the equivalent of being a knight, 'Member' is higher than the OBE.

'Chairman,' I asked, 'are members of the council allowed to recommend?'

'No, Miss Cassab, they are not. However the council as a whole can take up the recommendation. Who do you have in mind?'

'Sidney Nolan for one. It's an incredible omission that he is not on the list, as well as people like Patrick White and Joan Sutherland. He donated twenty-five paintings to Lanyon House and twenty-six to the Art Gallery of South Australia. In the 1950s, when Australia exported nothing but sport and beef, Nolan was our only cultural ambassador.

'And Elwyn Lynn was president of the Contemporary Art Society for sixteen years, editor of the broadsheet for fifteen. He is a good artist, won the Blake Prize, among others, has written several books, is advisory editor for *Art International*, critic for *Quadrant*, curator for the Power Bequest. He gives at least two free lectures after each of his purchasing trips, judges innumerable competitions, helps young artists.'

Arthur Grimwade supported me. During the course of the day I got seven names in.

'I am a migrant,' I said, 'and when one doesn't speak English, one still has cultural needs.'

Sir Garfield looked at me sideways and remarked, 'You are a most persuasive lady.'

On Saturday, the question of the actual emblem came up. I suggested Douglas Annand, but they want someone else.

'May I suggest that it should not look like a tourist souvenir. No kangaroos, emus, or koalas.' The minister from Canberra said a boomerang would be more Australian. Someone else said the boomerang is a weapon. Besides, how would it look if we took an Aboriginal symbol, considering that he haven't given them a single honour?

Not having sat on any committee for twenty-two years, I am now on two. The day I arrived from London I had to go to the Town Hall as one of the artistic advisers for the Lord Mayor. The first thing I glimpsed as I stepped out of the lift was my portrait of him.

John and Greta are staying with us at the moment. Greta is flying to Minnesota to visit her parents. She also wants to divorce her husband.

Peter has left his job. He lives at home and comes home late.

27 May 1975

Peter started a job this morning. No retainer, but a desk, an office, a secretary and regimentation.

23 June 1975

Greta, now in America, has to wait six months for her divorce. John wants to go to India next week.

The new honours list is out. Nolan wasn't on it. Obviously he refused, and so did Judith Wright, the poet.

12 July 1975

Bali

Jancsi and I are in Bali and I don't know the date or the day of the week. There are no newspapers or radio, and if there were, we wouldn't have time to read them.

After a busy week and thirty-five sketches, this is the first time I could induce myself to write in the diary.

The charm and magic of the island are incomparable. Festivals are so common in Bali that they certainly come under the category of everyday activities. Lovely dancers and celebrations are rendered more poignant by the contrast of brutal cockfights.

People seem to have abundant time for their art, woodcarving, painting, decorations.

24 July 1975

I have more than fifty sketches of Bali now. We take the car for six hours every day, the moving studio. I don't come back without at least four studies. We stopped at Tampaksiring to paint rice paddies, Bedugul and Bratan Lake. Tanah Lot with its temple in the sea, and Klungkung with its holy springs. We stop near Sanur, where our hotel is. Open the boot, get out the gear. Astin, our guide, gets me a chair from a house and as I sit down and open the sketchbook we are surrounded by curious Balinese. Group after group emerges, until noon.

As we put on weight the first week, eating sandwiches at the pool, now we have bananas and pineapple on our terrace, then we swim. Plenty of hard work in the afternoon. Jancsi cuts a roll of paper we bought in Denpasar. I prepare foundations for the next day, wash brushes, have a bath. Honestly, we hardly have time for reading.

16 *August 1975*

Sydney

Greta was at the airport. She can stay in Australia until her divorce is through, and then apply for a resident's visa.

She is the most pleasant guest I have ever had. Softly gliding, she smiles and knows when to join us, and seemed happy in her room devouring a book a day. She planted flowers and vegetables in the garden and helped me paint simple designs on the flowerpots.

John writes that every day he walks several miles in the mountains in Dalhousie, above Delhi. He has learnt to fly kites and is looking around for musical instruments. What he does and why, God knows.

The economic situation is a disaster. Everything seems to have doubled in price. No portraits. If I want to sell at all, I dare not raise my fee.

My joy and salvation are my Balinese pictures. After New Guinea, the idea of squaring on a perspex instead of directly on the sketch, for enlarging, seems to save a lot of time. Peter bought me a little electric calculator which makes it easy to estimate how many centimetres each square should be. But with all that ease, I still had to square in the large canvases with charcoal, and after enlarging the drawing, had to painstakingly rub out the auxiliary lines.

After Bali, I wanted to put all sixty sketches on slides. And now, in the evenings, I can project the paintings I choose into any size. The drawings I do in the dark, and the result and quality of those drawings are a source of wonder to me. I work constantly. I first place a layer of acrylics on canvases 3 x 4 foot, not larger. Yet. This acts as a large watercolour. As I use a lot of water, in order for the colours not to obscure the design, I leave a thin wedge of the canvas out. This developed into a kind of trademark, though later on I either glaze over the white or break it through from both sides, leaving it in a staccato-like rhythm.

23 *August 1975*

Alice Springs

We arrived at midnight, utterly worn out. We rented a car and rolled through the empty desert landscape which I love. The first thing that strikes me is the silence. Only birds. I draw with pastels.

The magic has gone. Jancsi says the paintings I do are like forced love. I don't want rocks any more. Fifteen years ago, they were a springboard for my abstracts. I don't want circumvisions, which after the initial discovery would now be a gimmick, repeated. 'There are no bad subjects,' Orban says, 'only better ones.' So I paint one or two a day, and file them away in the black suitcase with the well-worn red and green stripe.

I feel we're in exile. We're both depressed. Routine keeps us busy: squeezing orange juice for breakfast. Filling the esky with our lunch. Filling the car with the palette, the paints. Shadows seem to evade the Territory. Red dust, flies, ants. Little waterholes in Simpson's Gap and Trephina Gorge have disappeared.

The visit is cloudy.

A detective story. A sleeping pill.

1 September 1975

Mona planned an excursion into Rainbow Valley. 'It's a place we keep secret. Buses can't reach it because the track is too narrow, and cars can't get through, only Land Rovers.' Looking at the downpour we tentatively booked a flight home, not wanting to spend another day in Alice.

Miraculously, Sunday morning was bright and sunny. Three Land Rovers drove in convoy.

No wonder Rainbow Valley is a well-kept secret! *Voila!* There was the magic I was missing. It's a fragile place, so old that it would make the Greek ruins look young. The character of the rock is like nothing I have ever seen. We ate lunch in a cave where the rock ceiling looked like three waves of a Chinese scroll, meeting gracefully, reflecting the orange glow and the ivory sheen of the walls. Amazing. Enchanting.

The drive home was equally breathtaking. The land produced the burning orange and the soft pale yellow trees against the dark purple sky I remembered.

29 September 1975

Sydney

John arrived in the morning. He unpacked at least a dozen musical instruments from Indonesia, woodcarving tools, and can hardly wait to get back to the country. Greta is expected tomorrow.

2 October 1975

Gray's Auctioneers rang me on a Sunday morning. 'Miss Cassab, there is a painting of yours put up for auction which we think is a fake. Could we bring it along to show you?'

I was thrilled. The first fake Cassab.

He arrived with a monstrosity. A view of Rose Bay. Jancsi and I both decided that it couldn't be mine. But what if it was? We asked him to find out who was selling it. The next day a very refined Australian woman visited me, bringing the picture with her. She told me, her sister had commissioned me to paint the view from her garden. 'Do you remember? You painted the Captain Cook into the picture and then erased it.'

I did not remember at all, but told her that this is such a criminally bad picture, I would give her a new one instead. Fair enough.

Jancsi and I simultaneously thought of the story of Bródy Sándor, the Hungarian author, who was sitting in a circle of his admirers, holding forth about how disgusting it was for men to wear long underpants. When one man exclaimed, 'But master, your long underpants are showing!' Bródy Sándor looked down and remarked, 'Those are not my legs.'

18 October 1975

I have survived a bad patch without the help of a psychiatrist. Always, when there are problems not in my power to solve, I make a sort of sacrifice to God. Not as a bribe, but only to feel that I, too, am doing something, even if it's only giving up sweets for a month. Things have started to change.

Peter was chosen out of eighty-four applicants, and now works in a commercial real estate company in the city. He gets a salary, a car allowance and a parking space.

Sydney Legacy wants to buy the portrait of Sir Roden Cutler. And Clare came to sit for a new one. Sir Peter Abeles sat for a boardroom portrait for TNT. Max Taylor of Trinity Grammar School sells amazingly well. Fred Gardiner, in Toowoomba, also. The unlikely places. Rudy sells nothing.

What is best of all, I feel I have made progress in some of the enlarged Bali canvases. I skate on thin ice indeed, as I've never seen anyone else attempt to do what I'm doing. I grope and feel my way and the figures melt into the landscape like waves. Orban says it's like an x-ray of a

Dürer. Lynn thinks it's like ancient Chinese art. Oscar said it reminds him of Giotto.

What's important however, is that they belong in *this* century. *And*, that I am on to a new experience without copying myself.

Andrea's book is out and we feature prominently in it. Jancsi cringes because she got all the facts wrong.

2 November 1975

Paul Haefliger and Jean Bellette came to dinner. Paul's approval of my new pictures means more to me than all the critics could give me.

I started a charcoal drawing and left it as such. It's dark in the room, the charcoal flies and flutters, and as I don't draw lines, the effect is exactly as mottled as when I pour the liquid acrylic on unstretched canvas where it forms pools and rivulets.

All across Australia the political temperature is rising at an unparalleled pace. Whitlam and Fraser clawing each other daily in parliament.

14 November 1975

Orban's retrospective at the Art Gallery of NSW. The first picture done in 1900, the latest, but not the last in 1975. And because he is so old, the good vibrations from all those people warmed the air until it seemed a true celebration.

The governor-general, Sir John Kerr, sacked Whitlam, dismissed the government, and placed the opposition as caretakers until the elections on 13 December.

22 November 1975

Some artists are arranging an exhibition in Paddington in support of Labor. I always believed artists should be apolitical. Luckily, I wasn't approached. I would have said no.

Charles Blackman sawed one of his paintings in half in protest at his name being used for political purposes.

7 December 1975

The second meeting of the Council for the Australian Honours met in Canberra last week, the week before the elections.

There were more than 900 recommendations to work through and the whole system is somehow wrong. If any Tom, Dick and Harry can write in, one finds very few worthwhile appointees, and it creates a lopsided mirror achievement. Some weird ones: a woman who was a fruit fly baiter in Queensland: a rodeo organiser: someone who repairs bicycles; women on school committees and bowling clubs cutting sandwiches for thirty years.

There was not sufficient publicity about the honours, someone suggested. When one of the names recommended was an abortionist, Major-General Green remarked, 'Give it to him and there will be *such* publicity!' And Sir Garfield Barwick: 'He calls it fertility control. Give it to him and there will be no need for honours in future generations.'

There were only two recommendations for artists. Is it because painters don't recommend each other? Both over eighty-five. Grace Cossington Smith and Grace Crowley. If I were not sitting there, even these two would not have got in.

We worked from morning till midnight. The governor-general and Lady Kerr invited us for lunch. I sat beside Sir John. 'How do you feel, Miss Cassab,' he asked 'about art and politics?'

'That they shouldn't mix,' I answered. 'That was one of the reasons I left Hungary. Art is a fragile thing which could be crushed in a power struggle. When Blackman cut his picture in half, I sent him a note. "Congratulations, Solomon couldn't have done better." '

The governor-general told me that Clifton Pugh had asked him to sit for a portrait for the Archibald. 'Then, when I sacked Whitlam,' he recalled, 'Pugh called me a traitor and added an ugly snarl to my portrait.'

12 January 1976

I should have read Proust when I read Thomas Mann, Tolstoy and Selma Lagerlöff.

Swann's way is a source of incredible enjoyment. My love for the garden also grows. After the afternoon's siesta, I usually work in the vegetable patch. We have a steady crop of tomatoes and cucumbers, and the beans are on their way. Capsicums grow inbetween flowers and there are pots on the terrace upstairs where new petunias grow.

27 January 1976

Alan McCulloch declared in the Melbourne *Herald* that the Archibald Prize, given to a twenty-five-year-old schoolteacher, John Bloomfield, for a picture which used a photograph, is invalid because the conditions clearly state it has to be 'painted from life'. I said, when Archibald made his bequest, nothing like photographic blow-ups existed, and it's now a worldwide trend. But I was still the only one who didn't wish to deprive him. Clifton Pugh and Eric Smith both said it was against the rules and Rudy thought, 'It's a technique for painters who can't draw.'

The winning portrait is, in fact, a compelling presence, though I don't like photo realism (which, when photographed, and scaled down, become photos again).

12 February 1976

Experimenting with a variety of papers, paints, stains and inks. Jim Fitzpatrick photographed my line drawings of Greta and John in Nimbin, and the dancing holy men in Batur Temple in Bali. They are now slides where the black and white are reversed, and when I project them, only white lines can be seen in the dark room—a magic and inspiring trigger. The lines I draw in the dark are fluid and free. I used good, coarse, grained blocks of paper and a thin nib, others with white poster paint, using beige Japanese rice paper which acts as a blotter. Then I use a hose. I let the water touch it with a fine spray. After drying I get a greyish-fawn result.

8 March 1976

Some people may think paintings are good investments in a time of inflation. I am selling well.

Have had a month or two of incessant visitors. Claire and Freddy Wadsworth arrived from Hong Kong, boisterous, tall, explosive, loud, drinking, charming. Patrick Hutchings and Susan stay in Sydney on their way to Perth. I invited Paul Haefliger and Jean Bellette. It was a bit like inviting Isaac Stern with Yehudi Menuhin, a brilliant fencing match of exceptional brains.

Unfortunately, the night moved on and on with two bottles of cognac and whisky spirited away among Irish brogue, French quotations, politics, philosophy, art, Jewish jokes and delight.

For some unknown reason, I have kept my Hungarian friends apart from the 'others'. Suddenly I realised that over the past twenty-five years they have all learned English (though they behave as if they hate it, and lapse into their mother-tongue in mixed company. A reprehensible habit, socially.) Asking the Totis and Gréti Pallai last night with the Hagenbachs was quite successful.

25 March 1976

After months of no commissions, portraits now come in droves. They seem to all come from the heavy-industry sector.

Australian Consolidated Industries want to have their chairman painted. He is Sir James Forrest, who is also director of the National Bank and Western Mining. He looks an elegant man of the world, bushy eyebrows, sudden chuckle, a lawyer.

Next, Sir John Austen, chairman of Blue Metal Industries. Short, stocky, ugly, interesting. More interesting, if less lucrative, the Sydney Opera House Trust commissioned me to paint Joan Sutherland when she is here in July and now, Robert Helpmann. Both will be hung in the building.

30 March 1976

Nimbin

The sadness building up within me culminated in seeing John and Greta. It should have been a joyous occasion but wasn't. It's very difficult to analyse my melancholy, and why a Jewish middle-class mother should gaze at her suntanned, athletic, brilliant young son and think 'What a waste'. No ambition. No money. No sculpting, except for three beautiful new mandalas. Where is his future? What will he be like at forty?

Is my depression partly culture shock?

Our bed is clean and comfortable. We have a mosquito net, but it's difficult to get up from the mattress on the floor and go out into the dark, wet, cold garden during the night. The toilet is now an elevated box with a white seat. So one looks at the lush valley, over-looking a luminous cloud, which spreads over the vista like a Japanese screen with some of the treetops breaking through the fog. Inside the sleeping house, a kerosene lamp is left burning. In its light the new silver mandala levitates and looks as spiritual and mysterious as the luminous cloud.

John now calls himself John Seed. I don't know why, but I find it difficult to accept this, and still address him as John Kampfner.

5 April 1976

Sydney

Magdalena Abakanowitz has an exhibition at the Art Gallery of NSW. Orban said it was his greatest experience since seeing the rock gardens in Kyoto. Woven sculpture, hanging from the high ceiling, a dark forest of organic shapes, soft Giacomettis, twelve human figures sitting naked in a row of chairs without heads. What a formidable show to come out of Poland.

Meanwhile a woman with bare breasts, covered in chocolate, is playing the cello at a Paddington gallery. I didn't go.

We were invited to the Australia Council by Dr Jean Battersby, for dinner. Partly in honour of Roger Chapman, here from England for the Adelaide Festival, partly to celebrate Dr Coombs's seventieth birthday. I went alone and was seated next to Patrick White, opposite Nugget, beside Roger Chapman.

Patrick White looked stiff, bored, self-conscious. But he melted when I talked about the unfinished paintings turned to the wall, and what Delacroix wrote about the last brushstroke being done by God. He said, 'But it's the same with writing. First I always write in longhand. It looks totally different when typed, and again, when printed. Then again different when I reread it. You know, on rare occasions when there is a flow of inspiration, it never comes out as well as it does with hard work.'

We found that we are both mean with time. That our best energy comes in the mornings, that we both take a siesta in the afternoon and resent intrusions of the outside world. He lives with Manoli. A long-lasting marriage of males.

29 April 1976

We went to Noumea for Easter. It wasn't a good holiday. We returned the rented car on the first day. The landscape was boring. Little hills with gum trees. One unusual but unpaintable feature is the miles of cobwebs all along the wires of telegraph poles.

On our thirty-seventh wedding anniversary, Peter wrote,

To Mum and Dad,
With all the love that I can give to two beautiful lovebirds. You have taught me how important the love for one to another can be.
Love Peter.

The two birds he bought us (one dark grey, the other pearl grey) sit on the television set, under Paul Haefliger's *Elles*.

21 June 1976

Jack Lynn is the new chairman of the Visual Arts Board of the Australia Council. At last, the right man in the right place. Suddenly, he has lots of friends. They came for dinner and he mentioned that Violet Dulieu of Melbourne's South Yarra Gallery wants me to have a show. She had a cancellation for October. Melbourne Cup time, could I do it?

After Purvis not bothering to ring back. After Reality Gallery being booked out for two years, South Yarra is still the best gallery and I'm thrilled.

Violet came on Saturday morning. We chose twenty-five pictures and it's only June. Strangely, I need more larger-sized pictures to make the exhibition balanced. Now I get up in the morning with a new incentive and purpose.

4 July 1976

I was invited to a dress rehearsal of *Lakmé*, in the Opera House, where Joan Sutherland wore the costume she has chosen to be painted in. The auditorium is buzzing with a television crew. I hold the sketchbook. I draw in the darkness, write down Prussian blue and emerald, for background; alizarin, brown madder and rose d'oré for the dress. The director, interrupting La Stupenda several times. We meet in her dressing-room, discuss sittings.

At Midge McAuleff's physiotherapy rooms. I'm early as usual. I wait, sitting in the car. It's my space capsule. Wipers cleaning the raindrops, the heater blowing, radio playing. I sit protected from the rain and the traffic outside.

Midge says we are building a surgical corset out of muscles. Lucky I am persevering like a bulldog, for this has to be done twice a day, every day. As soon as Jancsi starts the little transistor radio to hear the morning news, I exercise.

5 July 1976

A week ago a French airliner flying from Tel Aviv was hijacked and forced to land in Uganda. The Palestinian captors threatened to blow up the 100 Israelis they kept as hostages.

Well, two El Al jets and a Hercules flew 3500 kilometres into the centre of Africa, freed the hostages and killed the terrorists.

We felt seven-foot high and terribly emotional about this unprecedented act of daring. In Sydney the Jews are proud (as all over this globe), but instead of feeling pride we should give more. After all, all we give is money. They take risks, they die for us.

9 July 1976

I sweat over my 7 x 4 foot figure painting, realising again that the more I leave, after having poured liquid acrylics on unpainted canvas, to complete with oils on the stretched picture, the deeper the water I swim in. Wanting to keep the original texture of rivulets and blobs, I have to combine the technique of a restorer with that of a painter. Not only must I keep the rhythm of the waves through background and figures, now a face disappears, now a hand grows too explicit and the logic creeps in. If there are fingers, after all, why no eyes? Besides, one figure is blue and the other red. Now I have to push the yellows back, as they cancel out the rest.

6 August 1976

Andree Rapotec killed herself, at her sister's farm in Dural. In the middle of shredding lettuce for lunch, she ran into the garage and cut her throat with the kitchen knife.

I went to see Rapo at his mother-in-law's place in Double Bay. Drysdale came from Gosford, Olsen from Dural. There was cake, coffee, drinks and lively discussion. How can one survive such a tragedy?

On my first sitting with Joan Sutherland she opened the letter box, brought up the mail, and cheerfully announced 'the postman is here'. She was a delight throughout. The world's best soprano sat humming a private concert for me.

Sandy, the wardrobe mistress, arrives ahead of her to unpack the complicated edifice with the wig, tiara, jewelled belt, an arsenal of trinkets.

Orban, who is usually hostile to portraits, said, 'It's a renaissance portrait. Really beautiful in colour.'

Frank Barnes came yesterday on his way home. Very pleased. 'You must have these for your Melbourne show,' he said. I looked at him. 'They will be a permanent fixture, hard to remove.'

He shrugged. 'No matter.'

15 August 1976

I still like my birthdays, although I don't really believe I am fifty-six. Zsuzsi Rogers and Joan Sutherland both invited us for a birthday lunch. We went to both. A crystal lion from Joan.

It was a colourful gathering. Pianists, voice coaches, two world-famous singers, conductors, directors, Desmond Digby who designed the sets and costumes, a view of Sydney Harbour, warm embraces from Joan.

We went to Ági Yoeli's opening in Melbourne. She is a terrific ceramic sculptor, transforming (just for a comparison) the way Claes Oldenburg transforms a soft car or a cardboard bathtub. Agi did a three-foot, snow-white peanut, a giant walnut, and witty animals. Her lion's mane has a red glistening glaze which is more glass than stoneware. The impact was tremendous.

30 August 1976

A couple of days ago, Andrea, on her way from a television interview with Don Dunstan, was in an ugly car crash. I rushed to the telephone, expecting her to be in deep shock. The young man died instantly, the van driver is in a bad way. Andrea, however, was very much alive: 'Four reporters were here already,' she announced. The police, the ambulance, all recognised her and onlookers mobbed her, demanding autographs which she diligently gave in the midst of all the blood.

11 September 1976

Nimbin

For reasons of his own, John still insists it's easier for us to come to Nimbin than it is for them to go to Sydney. I've grown used to the sounds of the night—mice scurrying across the floor, the creaking of the gate, and the mandalas moving in the gale. Branches of trees tapping on the iron roof. I'm glad to be sharing their life.

There is a meeting in one of the houses to discuss the coming 'Festival of Light'. Everyone brings food. Home-baked bread, freshly picked vegetables, rice and sauces. We eat. I listen and sketch. I am introduced as Judy, John Seed's mother.

It's amazing how the babies and young children fit in. No whingeing or crying. They seem to toddle from arm to arm and from love to love.

Fifteen of us meditating in the morning. Picnic lunches on the grass near the creek. As Tan Achaan talked, the parallel between creation and meditation clicked into place.

On my last afternoon, a brother found his way to the cowbales. He is a stranger but not a stranger, easily distinguishable by the sitar he carried from India and by the oval bag containing his sleeping bag and earthly belongings, by the clothes he wears and the gentleness he radiates. He was greeted with an interest that was concentrated and whole. He is on his way to Cairns, to visit his mother. 'Would you like to spend the night?'

He is given a kerosene lamp and (because I'm occupying the living room) taken to the banana shed where there is a mattress.

Then they come down for dinner. Greta spreads a chequered tablecloth on the floor on the straw mat. Then they go out into the moonlit garden to pick radishes, shallots, celery. A big chunk of cheese is added, and tea. Roman, the boy, adds bananas, apples and dates to the dinner. Then he plays the sitar in the candlelight. Greta plays Haydn on the flute. I never heard her do this before and am amazed how accomplished a player she is.

Syd, the taxi driver, picks me up early the next morning. We take Roman to the highway to hitch a ride towards Queensland. Syd calls the hippies 'the ones with the alternative lifestyle'. He gets this from newspapers, obviously. 'Oh, it's good, the change they brought to Nimbin. Property values jumped!' His only consideration. Spiritual values don't make sense to him.

As soon as I got home, we bought a six-gallon cooking pot and donated it to the meditation centre. I also sent Tan Achaan some x-ray film for printing, and some Japanese rice paper.

14 September 1976

Sydney

Mao Tse Tung is dead. It has been long anticipated but still, it comes as a shock.

18 September 1976

There is an ethnic radio station, and every Saturday morning there is a Hungarian broadcast with enchanting kitsch and gypsy music. 'Sziv küldi szivnek.' Ezt a dalt Erzsikének küldi örök imádója, férje, Lackó.

Sentimental, pathetic and slightly ridiculous, but it still has the power to touch a deep, deep chord that can never be touched in quite the same way by anything else.

28 October 1976

The Melbourne show looks lovely. Jeff Smart flew in from Italy and came to the opening. Old, dear friend, he admired the work. Seven are sold.

Back in Sydney, a review (rather an assault) appeared by Graham Sturgeon: '... and in the South Yarra Gallery an exhibition by Judy Cassab which is awe-inspiringly awful. She paints a mish-mash and trying to combine figuration with abstraction she gets badly unstuck, producing a show that has neither quality nor interest.'

If he wrote this about an antique shop or a new-line clothing label, he could be sued for damages. However, being an artist, one has to take it.

I couldn't sleep the next night. I'm still depressed.

10 November 1976

Depleted, I am waiting like dry earth for the rain to fall. No word from Violet, no press-cuttings in the post. I spend my days painting new portrait commissions. Have lost heart about my planned exhibition of drawings. As usual in such times, time rushes into crevices like foaming surf and fills them with Christmas presents and letters to distant friends and dinners I owe for years. Having our smallpox and cholera shots for Bali.

4 December 1976

The Biennale, sculpture only, opened at the Art Gallery of NSW, costing $100,000, while Jack Lynn has to juggle with $30,000. And even the few things he bought in New York had to be cancelled since the devaluation of our dollar. I was disgusted with the Biennale. Pieces of string, pencilled circles scribbled on the wall, earth on the floor and such rubbish. The photos of the 'artist' who hung himself up with fishhooks through his skin are sickening.

6 December 1976

Looks like we might have bought ourselves a piece of land. Or, rather, Greta and I may be shareholders in the Bodhi Farm Company. One hundred and forty acres of forest and creek, with maybe twenty acres which is suitable for agriculture.

Now, however, a further piece of news. It seems likely that Greta is pregnant. Amazing, eh? Anyway, the pregnancy is not confirmed yet, so I'm not supposed to tell anyone. But yippee!

The thought of our first grandchild makes me incredibly happy.

12 December 1976

I had a letter from a London art gallery called the New Art Centre. It is owned by Michael Servaes. His father, Bill, was instrumental in getting me the Princess Alexandra commission for the *Oriana*. Michael had seen *Valley*, the large picture Lord Kenilworth bought at my Sydney show, and would like me to exhibit at his gallery in London.

18 December 1976

Bali

I wondered if my memory of Bali would let me down. It didn't. We arrive at harvest time. The women hold a small machete hidden in their palm so as not to frighten Brother Rice. They have done this for 2000 years. I brought a book of Kokoschka drawings with me. He teaches me to get away from elegant lines and *Vogue* magazinish faces.

Donald Friend's place is on Sanur Beach, near the great hotels. One drives through a maze of old compounds, shell walls, fragrant gardens, to be greeted by typical Donald Friend boys, who usher us into the living room to wait for their master. The living room is a separate building. One goes up steep steps without banisters, to find an open space without walls, Indonesian style. Surrounded by deer, gargoyles, foliage, the vista of poinsettia trees in full bloom and frangipanis scenting the tropical air.

Donald Friend looks like a Buddha in a skirt with a protruding tummy.

Which of the many buildings is his studio? Wherever the mood takes him, he says. Underneath us (where he keeps his collection, which he's going to show us on Monday) he is working on an eighteen-foot painting for a university in Perth. He drew the design, and then glued down transparent Tibetan paper, on top of it he puts colour. But, for instance, this morning he painted in the house on the lagoon. He got up at 4.30 a.m. and swam out, no one in sight except two fishermen in a long boat. He returned just as the sky turned pale yellow, to breakfast and work.

On Monday, Donald showed us his collection. Eleventh-century doors are built into thick alcoves, shelves in apricot blush house Ming dynasty china, a pig stands in a corner, life-size, white and black dotted, with drawers to hide treasures. His own mural has nice sections where the Tibetan paper makes it look like Giotto sky. But Adam, in striped trousers, and Eve with a death skull, and cruel black boots occupy too much space and look hideous. The small figures look better. Hieronymus Boschish, but crawling, like pink crabs. He uses gold leaf which is good. There is a helicopter in the middle of medieval groups. I make intelligent noises, after all it isn't finished and he is a master draftsman.

31 December 1976

Sydney

John accepted a commission to make a gate and create a sculpture for a house in Palm Beach. When we returned from Bali we found four of them in the house. So, the hotel is full, once more.

I look at Greta and I'm overflowing with love, thinking 'There is the mother of our grandchild'. They prepare for the baby with care and tenderness. I pray to God for a smooth and healthy delivery.

I started meditating with John. He wakes me at 6.30 a.m. I am very keen to learn. The fact is so simple, the techniques so well-known.

At 7 a.m. we drive to Camp Cove Beach every morning for a vigorous swim in very cold waves. No parking problem at that hour and only a few seagulls, dogs and joggers for company. I rub my body dry and slip the wet costume off under Jancsi's dressing-gown. Home to a hot shower and then breakfast in the garden. How lovely. Which big city can one do that in?

28 January 1977

Brett Whiteley won the Archibald and the Sulman competition. There is no doubt that both pictures left the others behind. Although the portrait is but a tiny part of a large interior, it's the best painting in the show, and as John Olsen, John Coburn and Ken Myer are among the new trustees who judge the show, they dared to make the decision. My portrait of Orban was a finalist and was bought by the National Gallery of Rockhampton.

I'm longing now for more colour. I have become almost monochrome lately, largely Orban's influence. Being a tonal painter, however, I stand before a monumental riddle: how to break pure colour down? Easy enough to reproduce in nonrepresentative work. But, figuratively, only Matisse really solved it.

25 February 1977

Melbourne

I am in the middle of painting the three commissions Violet Dulieu arranged for at my November show. It means manufacturing, next please. I let anybody believe that what I'm doing is preparing sketches as all think it's impossible to paint three portraits in twelve days in a hotel room. What it costs me is another matter. Tension, strain, nerves, doubts, loneliness, knowing I am exercising my craft, and hoping the divine spark will move in and transform it to art.

I didn't find it easy in England twenty years ago. It's harder now.

I prepared a canvas for the Diana Gibson picture in layers of emerald green, greyish blue. Her dress has shades of yellowish green and bluish mauve which was thrilling in a way while I blocked the figure in (thinking of what Matisse could do with evening gowns), but then I neutralised the background so it was almost monochrome. She was easy, with intelligent yellow eyes and a cupid bow mouth. Today I start Dame Jacobina, her grandmother.

My third sitter is Jeff Donaldson, stockbroker, millionaire, six-foot eight, and he is the (by now) well-known mixture of the Aussie who can chop a tree down on the farm, cosmopolitan traveller and local aristocrat. Strangely, *his* face gives me more difficulties.

1 March 1977

Still in Melbourne, feeling a bit more relaxed in my second week. Jancsi has joined me. He is my better eyes. Pinpointed Jeff's long neck. 'It has a goatee. That sienna colour makes it protrude, push it back with blue.' Delighted about Diana and raving about Dame Jacobina, as good a beginning as the last Orban portrait. The mauves and blues in the underpainting look like a pond with waterlilies, and the drawing sweeps and curves in sure lines on top. A grand old lady, transparent with age.

Jancsi seriously plans to close Elasco in June. He contacted the only other manufacturer who makes elastics in the country to see if he wants to take over the machinery.

Violet asked us for a drink Saturday morning. I had a second look at Leonard French's exhibition, Death of the Generals. Three bought by the state galleries, no private sales. People don't want to hang death, skulls, scorpions, war and guns. He painted the series after a South American trip, a brave effort after Rivera, Orozco and Siqueiros.

Freddy Williams on his way soon to New York where he is the first Australian to have an exhibition at the Museum of Modern Art. He is more rotund and worried than ever, eyes bulging under a frown. Cupid lips. Humble and lovable. Violet gave him a grand farewell dinner. Jim Mollison came and Michael Shannon. John Brack can't get over the fact that I paint portraits in a hotel room as he needs about eighty sittings, and the portraits are usually rejected. He was recently commissioned to paint the official portrait of Sir John Kerr, the governor-general, but declined, mainly because he is afraid his windows will be broken by militant Whitlam supporters.

Freddy told me that he loved my exhibition, that I'm on the right track, they come closer in tone and flow beautifully. Somehow, I feel that exhibition far behind, I don't think I'm keen on the Bali sketches any more and don't know what to do next.

Violet's house has leopard-patterned couches on which two shaggy Afghans flop gracefully, a superb Venetian mirror, Aubusson pillows, a louvred muslin ceiling with spotlights, and birdcages and lemon trees around the pool. A rambling house of a collector.

Alone with Jancsi, we were young again and everything seemed new in a strange city.

After the day-long 'forced labour', not daring to put a foot outside in case I should be too tired for the next sitter—old friends every night. I manage to accumulate them to such a degree ('Some people collect stamps,' Jancsi says) that there are still lots I don't even ring up.

Met Andrew Sibley after ten years. He invited me for dinner. He and his wife, Irena, have two sons and live a settled life in a charming terrace house. Since Andrew spent a year in West Germany it seems to be his spiritual home (as Italy is Jeff Smart's), his pictures have become more acceptable to me. Bit of George Grosz, bit of expressionism, on two or three sheets of perspex placed on top of each other, which works rather well.

Another night at Louis Kahan. Best things I have seen by him. The etchings are so inspiring, I'm thinking of trying out the medium myself. Charles Blackman is here at the moment too, having *his* printed.

12 March 1977

Sydney

I sleep badly. Bad cosmic rays all around. Everybody going broke.

Jancsi slaves over my taxation. I find it impossible to paint. The portraits arrived from Melbourne a week ago and I haven't touched them.

I flew to Canberra for the first investiture by the Queen of the Order of Australia. I borrowed a hat from Clare Dan.

The Queen appeared on the dot of ten. David Smith, the secretary of the Council, read the names and achievements of the recipients. Only afterwards did I see the stopwatch taped to David's book. Twenty-seven seconds for each person.

20 March 1977

It is like climbing uphill all the time. Every small decision is a worry. Nature warns: stop.

While all this goes on, I finish the three Melbourne portraits and phone all my lame ducks, the ones who are sick, or down. Until I realise that *I* am down. Check up with the doctor. Blood pressure normal. Heart normal. Slow down.

28 March 1977

It continues.

Jean Bellette and Paul Haefliger came for a lunch which lasted until 7 p.m.

It is as if painting is an inbetween activity. The sheer quantity of interruptions wears me down.

18 April 1977

We went to Michael Kmit's opening at the Holdsworth. Another terribly depressing, pathetic happening. All those unused champagne glasses, the quiet waiter. About ten people in the huge space. Where were all the artists? Only the Haefligers and I took the trouble to come. Kmit used to be an important painter in the 1950s. Now the younger generation does not know his name.

3 May 1977

En route to Broken Hill

With Beryl Foster, my friend of Alice Springs twenty years ago, and Lightning Ridge ten years ago, we are on our way to Broken Hill. Growing up in a tent left her with the instincts of an Aborigine, the mechanical skills of an engineer and the needs of a bush creature. She now owns a kombivan.

As we drove towards our first stop, Wellington, we listened to Tchaikovsky and Dvořák on two hi-fi speakers situated under our feet. One can easily step from the cabin into the belly of the van, have a siesta in the back seat, or stop and convert the space into a dinette. There is a fridge, and on top of it a gas cooker. Under the seat, facing the back seat, is a toilet with septic system. On the side are kitchen cupboards with toaster, jug, salt, pepper, coffee and so on. All this converts into two beds. The top of the kombi can be raised so one can stand up comfortably. We pull a trailer with our suitcases, canvases, easels and paints. I marvel and admire.

I still have to remind myself after twenty-five years that May is autumn. The elms and birches shimmer gold and red.

Second night in Cobar. We pull up at a caravan park. We collect wood on the roadside, make a fire and barbecue lamb. While the flames build up, we sit on our collapsible chairs, drink whisky, notice the clouds, moon, stars and the shape of trees, unaware of our neighbours.

Nothing paintable so far, but the problems are far away. We stopped before an old pub and two sketches were born, after all.

6 May 1977

The sameness of country towns. The road is a long, grey ribbon. Leaving Cobar it rains heavily, but the colour of the land is splendid. Cosy studio inside, drawing the dark orange, pale yellow and the dark shrubs grown into the shape of praying hands. Near Wilcannia locusts hit us, thumping like hail. The windscreen guard holds hundreds of them, crucified against the wire by the force of the wind. This is emu and kangaroo country and there are wild pigs.

In the next pub there is a plaster bust of Menzies. Someone has placed their felt hat on his head, using him as a hat stand. The inevitable mural on the wall frames Menzies in the curve of a gum tree. A yellow T-shirt advertising 'Silverton Pub' has a $5.50 price tag. Underneath a Pro Hart framed in gold for sale. 'He has a collection of paintings worth millions,' the publican informed us. 'A Cézanne, a Braque, Boyds, Nolans. He is part of some new, crook religion. Forbids him to drink. But he has dispensation from God for a good port.'

7 May 1977

Broken Hill

Dinner at the house of two lesbian nurses born and bred in Broken Hill. Must have taken some courage before the advent of sexual liberation.

I ring Pro Hart. It's as unimaginable not to see him in Broken Hill, as not to visit Donald Friend in Bali.

Next morning our van stopped in front of a cluster of buildings, and a wall decorated with sculpture of scrap iron. Inside there was more. Huge iron sculptures and a jeep. Cages of parrots, rabbits, two poodles, five children. We stepped into the main gallery which is three storeys high, and truly, has one of the most impressive collections of Australian painters I have ever seen, with Len French, Charles Blackman, John Perceval, Asher Bilu, Aspden, Robert Juniper, Russell Drysdale, Sidney Nolan. Twenty-four Dobells are in the strongroom. There really are original lithographs by Dali, Picasso, Matisse. There is Howard Ashton, Tom Roberts. A thousand I would say. They are not for sale, but probably help selling his own, which also hang in profusion. Not only did I gain respect for the man who created his environment, I even liked some of his paintings. He poured tea for about ten of us, answering questions from his six year old, and ushering us from one studio to the other (he has six). In one of them, he throws a bit of plaster of paris on his new sculpture, a six-foot grasshopper.

Suddenly, as I registered a weak chocolate-box portrait on the floor, I turned back to find that was one of my own, painted in 1952 of a blond child with an open picture book in its lap. I couldn't remember anything about who it was. Pro bought it at an auction. Who on earth is selling this child? I found a small Corot, and a mural by Pro covering three walls.

In the main building there is a huge organ, a sauna, a collection of old silver baby's rattles, of paperweights, of excellent Sung dynasty china, a Louis XV table, his portrait on oval enamel in the centre, and a dozen miniatures surrounding it with portraits of his mistresses.

And I only caught a glimpse.

We drove off towards Menindee, listening to Rubinstein playing Chopin, watching emus. I have painted weeping willows on the river's shore, a bridge with naked trees standing in water.

8 May 1977

Menindee

Beryl decided to spend a day in Menindee. I feel more caravan parkish than ever. The shower is covered with bugs, dead and alive, and the airbrick is thick with cobwebs. There doesn't seem to be a spot on which to place the overnight bag, except between a frog (trying hard to be the same colour as the wall) and a grasshopper.

In the morning we drove into the village.

Beryl's subject: the pub and dear little old houses. I placed one building far down into one corner, crushed by weighty trees. The second sketch I followed and traced into the paper's crevices and rivulets, using some shrubs as a trigger. Then we stopped before a windmill broken down so long ago that its broken crookedness makes it magnetically paintable. It's surrounded by trees. I have never been very good at trees.

9 May 1977

So we are on the road again which is, of course, the subject. Worked well today, on erosions and red earth. Going through the locust patch I painted three, looming large against the landscape.

There is so much of everything in this land. So many miles, so much road, kangaroos, emus, galahs flying in ribbon-like formations, and as they turn the ribbon changes from pearl grey to pink.

10 May 1977

How well I know the van by now. Beryl paints outside but I stay in my small cubicle studio. I lean back on a comfortable couch, placing all my tools on newspaper. I lean the sketchbook on the server against the gas stove and place the palette in front of it. A tape plays Bach and I feel more contented than in Cannes.

13 May 1977

Sydney

Home from my trip, I accepted Ernest Kirby's invitation to have dinner with Dr Fritz Koreny, the curator of the Albertina Gallery in Vienna. He is thirty-five years old, and looks ten years younger. The conversation flowed in German. But what an international language art is! I sat beside him during dinner and he talked of the levels of comprehension as *ebene*, and called the cerebral and intuitive *kalte und heisse kunst*—but we understood each other perfectly. He didn't agree that creativeness means that one has to let the picture speak. One merely has to weld it in constant white heat so the cerebral doesn't cool the emotional. 'Poussin is a good example,' he said. 'Painterly and full of feeling, but perfectly balanced architecturally.' When I expressed resistance to blown-up photographs appearing meticulously on canvas he said, 'If Leonardo da Vinci were alive today, wouldn't he be at it like a flash?'

15 May 1977

I'm in several new publications. Elwyn Lynn's splendid *Australian landscape and its artists*, and Hamlyn's *Australia's heritage*. And Angus & Robertson's anthology of the Australian mother—poetry, short stories and paintings.

24 May 1977

The Power Institute's lecture this year was given by Bryan Robertson of the Whitechapel Gallery in London. Picked up Lynn, sat through two hours of delight, wit and civilised opinions. One of the more remarkable theories was that an artist doesn't have to 'develop' after every show.

'Scott Fitzgerald,' he said, 'sent a manuscript for Gertrude Stein to read. It was The great Gatsby. "I hope," he wrote, "it's better than my last book." When Gertrude Stein sent back the manuscript, she wrote, "We do not get better, only different and older." Development is not linear progression like a temperature chart. It's rather like a circle. The artist, the centre, reaches out to the right, or to the left of the circle. And sometimes, perhaps, he pushes it outward a bit.'

He talked about internationalism in art. Malraux said, shortly before he died, that he hates nationalism because it is a parochial insecurity. But art has to have identity.

Art is not communication, not message. Art is an act of revelation.

He called Duchamp a 'lethal joker, a killer clown'. Duchamp initiated artist as performer. 'Like Gilbert and George, who should have gone to art school a couple of years longer. Like body art. Or Christo's licensed follies. Archbishops and other wealthy people in the eighteenth century had 150 fountains spouting water.'

How should an artist be?

Degas said about Odilon Redon: 'He is a hermit. But he knows the train schedules. That's how artists should be.'

This morning I am painting the first seven-foot canvas since Christmas, telling Maria to take all messages. When someone insisted on speaking to me, it was Bryan Robertson. We were introduced after the lecture yesterday.

'Sorry to disturb you,' he said, 'but I'm only here for one day. I have seen several of your paintings in Perth, in different collections. I was moved. I was touched. What a pity that so little of your art has filtered through to London.'

'I had a letter from the New Art Centre to have an exhibition there.'

'They are excellent. They have integrity and good connections. When you come to London, please contact me. I can put you up in my place. Hotels are forbiddingly expensive.'

From time to time little miracles, like this.

'Not because I want to return the compliment,' I said, 'but your lecture gave me confidence in sanity. When one hears for years that two plus two is five, one starts wondering what's wrong with yourself.'

He laughed. 'There is nothing wrong with you. You just go on painting the way you do.'

Peter is still house hunting.

20 June 1977

Elasco is sold, closed down, moved out, finished. I feel a bit apprehensive when the word 'retirement' comes to mind. We have a few plans, but won't do anything until we come back from overseas.

22 June 1977

Orban and I went to the theatrette at the Art Gallery of NSW to see a film of Gertrude Stein. He visited her studio seventy years ago and would love to see it again.

People sitting in the aisles, on the stairs, on the floor, everywhere.

It was magnificent. Gertrude Stein, buying Matisse when he was rejected from the Salon, and Braque and Delaunay. She couldn't understand what the fuss was all about as she didn't find these early modernists extraordinary at all. People said, she didn't look like the portrait of her by Picasso. 'She will,' Picasso said.

How timeless are matters of art. Whether in literature or painting. I know my vehicle now, more or less. The unstretched canvas, crumpled a bit. The mottled colour. I can get it on the Japanese rice paper too, staining it, using white tempera, covering it with black Indian ink, picking out the whites with the garden hose. When it's dry, it's usually the reverse side which works better. It's more mysterious. So there are actually two paintings. Today, to eliminate one, I brushed plastic paint on the back. I knew that some of the colour would soak through, adding an extra richness to the reverse side. So I used burnt orange on a beige paper, and blue on a grey, then, as I turned it over, I discovered with delight that it looks like a renaissance mural, peeling and mildewed.

No one else is doing anything even remotely similar, I have no way of judging what I do. Whether it's mainstream, or whether the figures would be better if they were immediately discernible. Either I've surpassed Orban, or it's a case of sour grapes (he can't draw figures). He is displeased and says: 'What's the sense of putting figures in when one can't see that they are there?'

10 July 1977

Bodhi Farm

Jancsi and I have come to Surfers Paradise so I can paint Kurt Barry's children. We have a flat in one of the skyscrapers which have grown around the ocean shore. A lovely large flat with a balcony looking out on the sea, but it faces north and I have difficulty with the light.

We're so near to John and Greta. I had a short break from my portrait so we decided to rent a car and go visit Bodhi Farm anyway. Within an hour we were rolling along the coast in a red Ford.

In spite of the rain Bodhi Farm is a truly enchanting place. Greta and John are living in a caravan which has an annex built under a canopy of sail cloth. They cook on gas cylinders. We embraced and admired her roundness and drank tea sitting in a comfortable alcove. There is a huge double bed covered with one of Greta's patchwork quilts. This is where she will have the baby, which is due any day now.

Luckily, a nurse who was a midwife in India for years arrived. She is teaching John how to stitch Greta, if necessary. Surgical needles are prepared, everything is sterilised. I tremble.

They have already built the communal house, called Phoenix. It has hot water (from a waterfall above), a large kitchen capable of baking bread, a carpenter's workshop, a big room and a terrace.

John showed us where they've planted citrus trees, macadamia nuts, avocado trees, paw-paw, sugarcane. He is also in touch with the CSIRO who will send them seeds from South America which are ideally suited to the climate and soil. There are even a few cows supplying the children with milk, and of course fields of potatoes and other vegetables.

I began to lose all my anxieties (like, what do they do for money?) when I saw this huge undertaking. Once a week they take the produce to the market, and also there is a craft shop which sells ceramics, candles, patchworks, weavings, and to which all contribute.

I wish I could see Peter as settled and happy and free.

19 July 1977

Surfers Paradise

The telephone rang, at last. A tired and happy voice said, 'This is Jánoska . . .' I had tears in my eyes before he announced, 'Juci, your grandson was born at 3 a.m.'

Bodhi (my grandson) weighed seven pounds and was born in five hours. The pain was severe. Greta yelled a lot. They both breathed and pushed and worked until the actual birth happened so quickly, John could hardly catch the baby.

Next morning we rented a car, got lost in the mountains, drove through water and fallen trees, and after an hour of panic, we found our way back to Bodhi Farm.

1 September 1977

Germany

We have been to lots of small places. Looked at breathtaking Riemenschneider altars. I sketched a bit the first week. Bus to Wiesbaden, down the Rhine to Koblenz. A beautiful day, sitting on deck in the hazy sunshine, watching the serpentines along the cultivated vineyards. One night in Koblenz, a train to Kassel and Documenta 6. Hardly anything done with a brush.

'The art of the 1970s is not on walls,' says a proclamation. Wandering through a TV garden.

Not difficult to get rooms with baths, but in a crowded place like Kassel, at Documenta time, without bookings, one can't be choosy. This room overlooks the strangest, most surreal yard, filled with tanks. The assistant porter is a retired army officer, Herr Rabenstein, who took a fancy to us and drove us to Wilhelmschloss which has, among other treasures, seventeen Rembrandts. Again, fine old architecture, gutted and replaced with steel and glass, air-conditioned inside and plate-glass views over *Hercules*, ruling the formal garden of hundreds of acres of majestic trees and ponds.

Herr Rabenstein sometimes turns away discreetly to take out his glass eye which he polishes and replaces. We can't even tip him. He bought *us* a book of Kassel, the old town before the bombing. Next day, the Orangerie with an exhibition of drawings on a grand international scale. Impossible to take it in, in one day. Lucky we had one extra morning to see it, before our train left for Köln.

9 September 1977

London

Whole streets being bought up by the wealth of oil.

I went to see Michael Servaes at the New Art Centre. My canvases arrived and we unrolled the paintings on the floor. He placed the gouaches into a portfolio, placing tissue paper inbetween. He looked at *Batur*, said 'ravishing', and though he liked them in reproduction 'they are incomparably more in reality'. The show will be in November next year.

We went to see Graham Sutherland's portrait exhibition. I have learned a lot, though I could never do what he does: six exact sketches which he geometrically enlarges in squares on the canvas. The scaffold is always visible. How he manages spontaneous and penetrating characters with so little instinctiveness is incomprehensible. But the portraits are great. He leaves the top half of the picture almost empty. I tend to place heads near the edge.

I must try profiles. I must try painting on black. He also underpaints, but it's almost stained and the one colour covers the surface. If it's crimson, then background, trousers, chair are all crimson and only the upper body changes colour.

Brett Whiteley's opening. Wendy wore satin breeches and Brett was equally shiny. There were beauties, especially the drawings. The prices were half of what he charged in Sydney. Mine have to be slashed, too.

18 September 1977

Budapest

Staying at the Duna International. I feast my eyes on the Danube, the castle, and the bridges. The place crawls with memories, especially Szentendre, which has been reconstructed and now has a Czóbel museum as well as a Kovács Margit museum. Her ceramics are tremendous.

I saw a woman pushing a pram over the cobblestones and the vision reignited memories of coming from the market with the two babies, watermelons and vegetables.

A new national gallery opened in the castle in Buda. Tremendous. I was astounded to see an exhibition of peasant primitives I never knew about when I lived here.

1 October 1977

Vienna

The first time in Vienna without Gyuszi's schizoid presence, his self-tinted, violet-coloured hair, bulging pockets full of jewels, stuffed pockets full of money. His Tartuffian persona and his Nietzsche-reading self. We went to see his grave. Following the wishes of his will, the grave has the names of my grandmother, my mother and Pista. I was deeply moved and at the same time I felt peace. At last, they too, have a grave.

While the taxi was waiting and a sharp wind blew the dry leaves, Manyi unpacked a sponge and a kitchen towel and started washing the marble stone with detergent. She said she always kept Gyuszi clean.

5 October 1977

Paris

In retrospect, the beautiful things remain. Not that we thought at first that the new Centre Pompidou is beautiful. Jancsi thought it's like a brewery, or Luna Park, or a space rocket. The twentieth century's finale.

We spent a lovely day in my cousin Vera's studio. Her house is timber, tiled with bricks, mattress on the floor, kitchen part of the living area. Plants, mats, sculptures, woven curtains. Essentials. Except for the television and record player, a simple abode.

Her art, which was always in iron, always heavy and hard, is now free. She works on Icarus-type soaring sails. She wrote an extraordinary book, *Massacre de parachet*, which means Holy Ghost, but can also mean free spirit. The pages are sail cloth, slightly crushed. Like my canvases. The pictures are those of several birds, mutilated, caught, pinned in concentric circles, tumbling into death, finally resurrected, taking off, upwards. Vera says, 'It's a monument for your mother.'

12 October 1977

South of France

I only get time to write when we're on the move.

We saw a unique collection in the old Chateau de Cagnes. Forty artists painted one woman, Susanne Solidor. (Picabia, Laurencin, van Dongen, Cocteau, Kisling, Foujita, Dufy, Vértes among others.) The Castle has an open courtyard built around its staircase, a tree growing inside it, with a fine light and a view of Cagnes-sur-Mer.

13 October 1977

Tel Aviv

We spent half the day in Jerusalem with Irénke, Jancsi's niece, and Abraham and took the *cherut* back to Tel Aviv. Today we went to see the ceramic museum, where Ági Yoeli has an exhibition of her great peanut-apple-cat-lion-rose and astronauts. It's a big honour, wonderful for her to be exhibited there.

14 October 1977

Feri Izsák showed us the new cancer research centre, the Beregszász Memorial Centre. Sanyi Vári, who gave most of the money and collected the balance from all of us Beregszászers, wanted the Czechoslavakian name of our town on the building. It gave me another incredibly moving moment. Another memorial for my mother and for our dead. All the books in the library have an Ex Libris in them, with the synagogue and the vineyards of Beregszász. And it's not just a memorial stone. It's an institute which functions and grows and perpetuates the memory of our town which died.

I said I would love to donate a major painting to the Beregszász Centre, if they would accept it.

'Accept it? It would be nice to have a Kaszab Juci painting in this building.'

It should be an evocative painting, like, let's say, my *Magnetic Island*, where water and earth meet clouds and light. Something that could mean what the spectator reads into it. Resurrection?

5 November 1977

Sydney

The weekly Alitalia plane to Sydney departs at the ungodly hour of 2.40 a.m. We have to be at the airport at 12.30 as the search is fierce. That means taxi from Jerusalem at 11.30. At 3 a.m. we were told the plane has been delayed for four hours. On plastic chairs all night, watching the sun come up. Engine trouble in Singapore and another three-hour wait.

Peter, beaming beneath a distinguished beard, met us at the airport.

He told us how he missed us and so was very happy to see us again. He really is sunshine to me.

We then went to see his new house in Paddington. I love it. It has handmade bricks along the wall of the living area, a built-in bookshelf, lovely lamps, curtain rods and a soft, beige, wall-to-wall carpet.

Then on to a meeting in Canberra for the Council for the Order of Australia, with its witty moments. One letter recommended a New Zealander who worked here. 'What has he done for Australia?' one of the members asked in disagreement.

Sir Garfield said, 'He left it.'

The only artist recommended this time is Hal Missingham, for whom an honour is long overdue. We made him an officer.

6 December 1977

Life is really hectic these pre-Christmas days. John Siddeley arrived with his coworker, Gordon Roberts, a talented young sculptor. John has a jewellery exhibition at David Jones Art Gallery, more sculpture than anything else, a group of flowers, called *Fly trap* growing out of an amethyst rock studded with diamonds, which closes as some flowers do at dusk.

I drew John Siddeley in London, enlarged it on canvas with charcoal, made it look (with acrylics) like a giant watercolour and when he arrived I gave him two sittings. It has presence and I hope it will be good enough to show in my London exhibition. I want one or two portraits. After all, that's how I am known there.

15 December 1977

Bernie Leser of *Vogue* magazine came from London, and Leo and Anne Schofield gave a cocktail party in his honour. I bumped into Maggie Tabberer. Five years ago I painted her wearing a Greek national dress.

'This is spooky,' she told me. 'This is the first time since I posed in this dress that I've worn it again. And the first person I meet is you!'

17 December 1977

János, Greta and Bodhi arrived this morning, unexpectedly. Bodhi is the love of my life. His smile is like a beam gilding everything in warm, rich colour. Five months old and wanting to stand up!

1 January 1978

Jancsi is looking for premises to set us up as art dealers. He looks for, and finds, things to worry about. I distract his attention, include him in the morning activities, call him into the studio atmosphere. I remember that he is my friend, and my lover, who never fails to make me feel a fulfilled woman. And that he must not feel superfluous because he does not work.

Magnetic Island was sold in Melbourne to Nauru House, so I am sending *Cascade* to the Beregszász Memorial Centre. Since I returned I have only painted four canvases, all of Jerusalem. But they are good, I think.

I have begun to keep a working diary. In spite of Orban's opinion that one should never know *how* a colour or texture happened, I see that from Delacroix to Braque everybody kept track of *matiére*. With my thin acrylic washes, I sometimes get fantastic passages I might want to use again. My line drawing, *Mother holding a child*, has been reproduced in *The white chrysanthemum: Changing images of Australian motherhood*, an anthology selected by Nancy Keesing.

15 January 1978

A farewell dinner for the Haefligers before they left our shores (which they literally will do on a freighter) for Majorca. I asked them for a list of friends but they wanted it small which suits us.

After the witching hour, Olsen and Haefliger discussed a portrait of Rembrandt's son, Titus. Our giant Rembrandt book open amidst full ashtrays, empty bottles. They conjured Rembrandt into the present. One of the rare moments of this life.

ABC television is researching the program they plan to do on me. They ring Oscar Edwards, Raoul Mellish in Brisbane and Hal Missingham in Perth. They unearthed religious paintings I did in the 1950s. The producer Pat Kavanaugh, who spent an afternoon taping, asked questions like What is absolute truth? and What is absolute goodness? I was out of my depth and told him so. 'Well,' he said, 'think about it.' A hint that they will probably ask me these questions next week when they come.

So last weekend Jancsi and I amused ourselves with this brain sharpener. There is no absolute, we agreed. I rang Rabbi Brasch and asked him. He gave an intelligent but unusable answer about the absolute changing with each generation.

So we narrowed it down. There is no absolute truth, only individual truth. And absolute goodness, if it should exist, would be love for the whole universe. I was better equipped when asked what an artist's style is. Her transforming power, I said.

3 February 1978

On the day of the filming, five trucks arrived hunting for five parking spots, and twenty-five people trampled through the house for seven solid hours.

Some of the crew came again, to film me painting. The program will run for thirty-five minutes, and seven women will be featured in the series. A cabinet minister, a black activist, a nun who is in charge of adoption, an editor, among others.

Margo Lewers is dying of cancer. I went to Emu Plains to visit her. She is a skeleton. Her green nail-varnish made me cry.

26 February 1978

A weekly visit to Andrea who spends her days in bed now, between cocktail parties. In through the 'prowlers" entrance—the back door which is always open. She gives orders. 'Barmaid, let's have a snort.'

Margo Lewers died. I took Gwen, from the Rudy Komon Gallery, with me to Emu Plains for the memorial. About thirty of Margo's friends were eating and drinking in the garden. Bowls of flowers and fruit and the spirit of Margo, however, I felt, being very pleased.

3 March 1978

Bodhi Farm

The house that my János built stands in the beautiful valley. It has a large verandah which has been lovingly padded with chicken wire so Bodhi can't fall over. A handsome staircase leads up to the bedroom, the only room which has walls and windows. Downstairs only bamboo blinds keep out the storms. Three people sleep there while their house is being built.

I watched János scything the long grass. I looked at the grandchild of Anyu of Beregszász, and Apu, the Budapest intellectual, swinging the blade in slow rhythm in the Australian bush, and felt strange and dislocated.

15 March 1978

Sydney

Greta and Bodhi were here for a week. Passport business at the consulate. Oh, the joy and love which permeates the house when Bodhi is here!

An unexpected and rare joy: Peter raced in at the weekend, 'I'm late, I'm late', and told me about some misfortune or other which happened at work. 'Just listen,' I tell myself. 'Just be.'

'Bye, Mum,' he said as he raced out. He then turned and came back. He said, 'I was thinking on the way out what a lovely, wonderful mother you are. And what's the good of thinking it if I don't come back and tell you?'

I sent the seven-foot abstract to Israel for the Beregszász Memorial Centre, months ago. Feri says he didn't understand the picture. But since he has been to Sinai where one sees unreal rock formations and surreal coral reefs, he thinks about our unreal lives, the way we survived the war, the way we created again, and he understood it. I wrote to him that this building is so special for me, I could not think of sending a landscape or some figures on its wall. It had to be a symbol.

24 March 1978

János wants me to book their tickets to London. Filling in forms for John Kampfner, Greta Nelson and Bodhi Seed. The man behind the counter didn't blink an eye.

4 April 1978

The painting which used to be *Village with figures, Bali*, goes through its tenth metamorphosis. First, the figures disappeared, bar one. Then it became a monument which didn't fit. It was such a failure that it didn't matter what I did. So, on that rich, mottled, glimmering and smouldering expanse of colour I painted the two halves of the temple door in dense, smooth, smoky violet. It was the first time since the 1960s that I juxtaposed a texture with a smooth surface. I started to paint a sculpted figure in place of the monument, but left it hollow. At last, it sits. It sings. I have done it again today, on a horizontal, striped Bali scene, so all that movement withdraws, giving pride of place to those obeliskish things.

16 April 1978

The meeting at Government House went as usual with a desperately small section for art (*no* painters), and hundreds of letters on behalf of public servants and community workers. Andrew Grimwade acted as chairman. Sir Garfield Barwick is overseas. Our lunch hosts, the new governor-general, Sir Zelman Cowen and his wife Lady Cowen, active Jews, charming people.

23 April 1978

Tennant Creek

The week in Tennant Creek offered me what I was missing. The subject. And the circumstances in which one can deliver a performance. I was bowled over at the first sight of the Devil's Marbles as we approached it at the end of travelling all day, the sun just disappearing behind the horizon. Twilight lasts an hour in the far north, and there they loomed, like an Yves Tanguy dream, surreal and unbelievably real.

We got up early each morning and Mona drove to the Marbles. We made our camp wherever there was shade. We opened collapsible chairs, squeezed paint on the paper palette, opened the sketchbook and started a new series of landscapes.

Not a human being all week. Only sweet birdsongs and the wonder of this outcrop, where sculptured round, orange giants, balance on top of each other like frozen dancers. There was blinding contrast between light and deep, dark shadows. What with the sun draining colour out of my paper and canvas, how could I help but gain courage? By the time we had a look at the week's results there were twenty-six paintings. Strange and still convincing. I only hope that my delight with them will pass the test of time.

For three or four hours in the mornings, not being cramped inside a car, or rushed by anyone or anything, I observed more sharply and attended each picture with a devotion I haven't felt for years. The marvel of nature seemed to be taking my hand, leading it, and dipping it in strong colours.

A few miles away in the dry, dusty heat, there is a pub at Wauchope (pronounced Walkup). A fan overhead, it has a mural of the Devil's Marbles turning into lollipop. We rent the only available room for a siesta. Jancsi and Mona took the two beds and I (being happy to give my back a hard foundation) took the swag Mona carried in the boot.

We all slept a couple of hours, and ate ice-cream in the pub before driving back to the Marbles where we started all over again, working till about six o'clock. Mona then served Campari and soda on ice. What a joy it was to quench my thirst after a hot and good day surrounded with beauty.

The best of all 'studios' was to be found at the Marbles. When it got too hot, even under the trees, we decided to climb. Mona knew the way. It was like treading over the hide of a prehistoric beast. Through a short spell of jungle, just spooky enough for a whiff of adventure, to a plateau where the Marbles formed cool courtyards with breezes whizzing through. Oh, to sit on a comfortable canvas chair among the giants, a vista of more marbles rolling into the distance. Unforgettable. Some of these formed into images on my painting. Creatures almost.

27 April 1978

Alice Springs

Jancsi was sitting in the sun, while I painted further away. Then I heard him call. It was faint. I could hardly hear. I saw him sitting in a funny position, sideways. I knew something was wrong and I started running. He had fallen and broken his arm.

'I was coming to see how you were doing,' Jancsi said, 'and I stumbled and fell sideways on this rock. I think I've broken my arm.'

We walked to the kiosk where they gave him water and aspirin.

We got in the car, it was noon by then, and I tackled the stony track leading to the highway. Every bump hurt him. We finally reached the brand new, big hospital with all the latest equipment and hardly any staff.

At last, Jancsi was x-rayed and we saw the surgeon. We said we want to do what has to be done in Sydney. Is it risky to wait? Not for twenty-four hours or even forty-eight, for that matter.

We got seats on the next plane, and went straight to St Vincent's.

26 May 1878

I rang the New Art Centre in London to say I wanted an advertisement for my show to appear in *Art International,* and they have to receive the artwork for the September edition *now.* Michael Servaes had good news for me. They won't have changed premises by the time of my show, which will be 5–30 September, and they sold *Bush*, one of the paintings I left in London. Tremendous.

I won't take any commissions. I do not answer the telephone. I don't stop at midday, but work till 4 p.m. when it's getting dark. I hope that will do the trick. Must I work under pressure to get results?

10 July 1978

Jancsi and I had another 'retirement' adjustment to make. He came into the studio, sat behind me, and gave a running commentary. Before I even started, and was squeezing out paint he told me, 'I would take that rock out. It would cut the image with darks. I would ... ' And so it went. 'Tell me, do you want to leave that blue?' I was becoming irritated and inhibited.

'Jancsi, this is like giving birth. I don't know and I don't want to know what I'm going to do in the next minute. The picture has to tell me, not you. Two of us can't paint.'

He was hurt.

'When you worked,' I told him, 'I painted alone. I could hardly wait for you to come home and discuss it. This has not changed.'

20 July 1978

Strange thing: I heard that Charles Blackman was back in Sydney and thought he would be a good subject for me to paint for the Archibald.

I rang one lunchtime. Charles answered. 'And when are you starting my portrait?' he asked.

I was flabbergasted as we had never talked about it.

'How did you know?'

'I am psychic,' said Charles. 'I just walked in the door and I knew it was you ringing.' We made an appointment. I was to go to his studio to do a sketch.

Next day, in his studio, I used one of his paintings for background. A nude, horizontal, with her head upside down, her hair falling in charcoal-line waves. A horse's head. It made the sketch look like a Delacroix, except that Charles, wearing a black beret, sitting in a white cane chair, looked like Rippl Rónay's *Piacsek bácsi*.

I told him Jancsi wanted to open a gallery.

He reached up and took a roll of paintings on paper from the shelf and thrust it onto me. I chose two. There was one, pinned on the wall, where four tiny paintings were painted on one paper. 'You like that one? You might want to cut it into four little ones.'

I went to see Lloyd Rees on a Sunday. He is also going to sit for me, and he gave me a self-portrait as a young man, and an intimate interior called *Sea-breeze* where curtains are blowing in the room. Mrs Scheinberg offered two Szigeti drawings and asked if we want a Haefliger and a Jean Bellette. She also gave us two Ray Crookes, who wouldn't be able to give pictures to us directly. And Oscar wants to give a Henry Moore drawing, a Paolozzi, a Campigli, and a Francoise Gilot, which is a good gimmick for journalists, as Gilot just married Jonas Salk, the man who invented the polio vaccine.

Orban has shingles. Now a show of *his* is coming up at Barry Stern's gallery and Barry wants more of those paintings Orban paints on silver and gold paper.

Orban rang this morning.

'I need you.'

'I would have come anyway.'

'I feel too sick to finish a new painting. Could you do it for me?'

Never did I get a greater compliment than his trust in me. I threw a plastic bag with my own oil paints and palette in the boot. And found this very uncomfortable-looking Italian postcard on his easel. His eyes are getting weak.

I painted an Orban every faker would have been proud of, while he sat beside me with a long stick and pointed at certain spots, 'Don't you think this needs an exclamation mark?'

25 July 1978

I started a portrait of Lloyd Rees. Orban calls him 'my little brother', being only eighty-five. I had the sitting at his place. Rolled up the canvas, stretched it on one of his and, after one sitting, it looks as if this is going to be the Archibald entry. Charles's looks overworked in comparison.

28 August 1978

London

Sydney to London in twenty-four hours still holds a thrill, though ten loos is not enough for nearly 400 passengers. My feet were so swollen I alighted at Heathrow in gold slippers. Taxi to Cadogan Place, which is lovely as can be. A big balcony with a profusion of geraniums, petunias and morning glory.

The gallery is half-asleep in August with a mixed show. Michael Servaes half on holiday. Ethel Chang, the secretary, holding the fort. Nothing has happened as yet, publicity-wise. The invitations have gone out. When I sent Michael the list I warned him things might have changed since 1961—people divorced, died or knighted.

Jacqueline had us to lunch, and John invited us for dinner. They have parted. There is suffering and bitterness. John gave the gallery a typed list of his clients.

30 August 1978

Michael Servaes gave a dinner for me and invited Bryan Robertson and Helen Fesenmaier, a painter from America. Sparkling, witty, worthwhile conversation. Monday is the hanging.

2 September 1978

John Siddeley gave a large cocktail party in 'Judy Cassab's honour'. His new flat is like an artist's handwriting, down to the slanted mirrors around windowframes, mirrors covering the central heating, an ancient camel figure under a Ben Nicholson minimal abstract, facing an equally ancient Egyptian statue of a cat on a slim, high, copper pedestal. Michael and he seem enthusiastic about my paintings. They *do* look better in London than in Sydney. More at home.

Michael told me of a woman who stared in through the window, at the big *Bali*. Finally she came in and asked, 'Would that be a Cassab?' It was Lady Potter. Her portrait by me was auctioned years ago. She tried to buy it back, she said, but the owners wanted $6000 for it. (They bought it for $300.)

15 September 1978

There was a diverse crowd at the opening. Hungarian friends, as well as everyone else. I remember a whirl, turmoil, telegrams, flowers, eight pictures sold at the opening. By 13 September, thirteen pictures sold.

24 September 1978

Spain

The highlights in Barcelona were Gaudi's church and the Picasso Museum. I would never have imagined that the church could permit an artist's unique vision to be erected like this—twelve towers for the twelve apostles. Organic shapes, growing, twisting like trees in a forest, moulding themselves into sculptures and towers like gigantic beehives. And all around on the walls of the construction site are the graffiti, making it more surreal.

It was a long drive to Valencia, and the next day to Alicante. Crowds, crowds, everywhere. The way to Granada is barren, strewn with the ugliness of the industrial age, giant advertising posters dwarfing the dry, dotted hills.

The human race is really out to destroy ourselves. There is beauty of course, but it is of the past.

In Madrid, I unpacked for the first time since London. We went to the Prado twice today. We saw the Goyas in the morning, the Velazquezes in the afternoon. Filling our vessels up to the brim.

25 September 1978

Another day packed with wonder. My second visit to Toledo, but Jancsi's first. Greco's house, the synagogue, the cathedral which is even richer than I remembered. As if it would have sucked in all cathedrals in the world to show them off, with stained-glass windows, marble and ivory carvings, wooden baroque altars, murals, mosaics, organs, copper, gold, silver, plus twenty Grecos, a Raphael, Titians, van Dycks, a Caravaggio. The cathedral was to the senses like an amplified pop concert to the ears.

26 September 1978

Paul Haefliger wrote. 'At the Prado, give my love to Bosch's *Garden of earthly delights*.'

Our life has settled to an almost student routine. I am astonished we can still see and enjoy.

2 October 1978

New York

Jack Lynn arrived in New York the same day as us, and we went on a gallery tour of Greenwich Village. Almost every door opens into incredible gallery spaces. We saw Don Nice's exhibition. The Lynns and I once visited him in Palm Beach. The paintings of native animals, crocodiles and birds now cover the SoHo walls.

Max Hutchinson's gallery in SoHo has an elaborate viewing system. Steel beams built in the ceiling, one can pull a wall out on a leather handle and, by doing so, spotlights go on, bathing the paintings with a glow.

9 October 1978

Hawaii

We are stopping off here for a holiday. Tension and the compulsion to be active starts to abate. On the easychair under the coconut palms, near the turquoise water, I took my sketchpad out for the first time. Not to draw what I see (which is unadulterated kitsch) but to doodle the quick one-line sketches done in the mosque in Cordoba. Human shapes appear, with the help of Henry Moore. What also helped is the fact that he took help, pilfering like Picasso, out of the whole art history. What is unusual is that in a book, published after he was eighty, he frankly admits the sources he owes debt to.

6 November 1978

Sydney

The warmth of arrival. János, Greta and Bodhi are here. But only Peter, my rock, my reliable son, is at the airport with the blonde of the day. He is now manager of Hookers Investment Department.

Some trepidation when János rents a stall at Paddington Market and displays his wares. Indian shirts, incense, massage oil. He takes Bodhi's blue plastic bath, in which Ian gives János a foot massage. Somehow, I have learned to accept him as a farmer in his own environment. But it's different here, in Sydney.

Where is the 'back to nature' call in this?

I look at his prophet's face, the shining intelligence in his eyes and I think, 'What a waste'.

I went out to Lloyd Rees for the second sitting, which is the last. Visit Orban on Thursday, as usual. He had a cataract removed, looks frail, but wants to help hang the show at Jancsi's new gallery.

Oscar gave us a Matisse lithograph, *Mother and child*, a Soulages engraving, a Zao Wou Ki collage. The Warrens came for lunch, bringing two watercolours, Ken Reinhard brought three assemblages to the gallery and Salkauskas two.

A meeting of the Council of the Order of Australia with twice as much material as usual. We gave Arthur Boyd an honour and Brack, and both Frank and Margel Hinder.

Sir Garfield took me to see the High Court building on the way back to the airport. It faces the equally unfinished National Gallery. A bridge will connect the two. After the Opera House, it will be the most significant building in the country.

16 November 1978

Jimmy Gleeson and Frank bring three Gleeson drawing collages over. The Coburns arrive with five, three grey-beige paintings and two silk-screens, lovely in colour. One is *Man throwing a stone, homage to Miró*. The other, *The third day God created the world*, of his creation series. This has only six artist's proofs.

In spite of all this energy being channelled into the gallery, I feel it can only be good for me to achieve closer and more frequent contact with my fellow painters. Often I stayed away from functions because Jancsi would not come. Now it is his business to see other shows, so I see them too.

The same afternoon we went to the Zadors. He gave us three Brett Whiteleys. The two smaller Whiteleys are beautiful, especially the charcoal collage with his poem of the mirrorless prince written in the right upper corner.

I picked up Orban and brought him to the gallery. Not to hang, but to 'place' the exhibition. Isn't it strange, being in the game for forty years, I have never hung a show.

We all learned from him, how not to crowd paintings, how two strongly coloured paintings were placed on two sides of a wall to support the centre. How the Lloyd Rees behaves beside the Guy Warren, how the lower lines of the frames have to be in one line. And mainly: there is no 'elite' room.

The one with the Matisse and the Dubuffet also has an Olszanski and Missingham. And Ilse Tauber takes the place on the same wall as Salkauskas—quite an honourable little painting.

On Monday Mr Cantor comes to actually hang the sixty-four paintings. Nancy Borlase, dear friend, appears on Tuesday to write her review.

I haven't held a brush for three months.

The opening: 400 rented wine glasses, bags of ice emptied into brand new garbage tins, cold flagons of white wine delivered and pushed into the 'cave'.

There must have been 500–700 people between 5 and 8 p.m. We were fully aware that this opening is not so much for art lovers as for all our respective friends, to witness our business venture. As expected, few were sold, five altogether, and cheap ones at that.

My cousin, George Spitzer, bless his heart, bought the major work of the afternoon, Coburn's *Two figures with moon*.

Jancsi's birthday. János and Greta phoned. Peter invited us over for dinner. He prepared a seafood feast with food fetched that day from the fish market. Oysters, smoked salmon, John Dory, Tasmanian scallops, prawns, and champagne to toast Jancsi.

I pray to God every single day to make right whatever we did wrong with my sweet, sensitive and intelligent child. I pray he will find a partner who will share his life.

23 November 1978

The gallery is as dead as a dodo. Jancsi tells with satisfaction, 'We live in such a busy house. When I want to be alone I go to the gallery.'

Brett Whiteley won the Archibald, the Wynne and the Sulman. The portrait wasn't a portrait but I have no quarrel with a good work of art. It's a triptych with a screaming lion, a syringe, and cigarette butts on the left, a self-portrait in shifting planes a la Goya or Bacon, about four linear profiles and a tragic half-mask with a glass eye. The arm is seven-foot long. The right side of the triptych is a clinical, antiseptic, young, smiling Brett, a photograph encased in a perspex box. Coincidentally, I received Beryl Whiteley's Christmas card the same day.

28 December 1978

I started working, mainly repainting bad old pictures. On nights when we are lucky enough not to be invited out, I draw. I like my studio at night. The record player is on and the telephone is quiet. But it's only good for black and white, as the lighting prevents me from using colour. I just wasted one whole evening. I put white poster colour on three drawings and the next morning put the Indian ink over it, then washed it off too soon. No texture, looks almost as it did before I started working on it. In a way, that's why I like this medium. It's unpredictable. Depends on the type of paper I use. Sometimes it stubbornly remains pitch black.

10 January 1979

I paint two good landscapes from a sketch of an erosion at Broken Hill. Vivid yellows, fresh greens, orange and turquoise.

Since Orban had an eye operation and can't see my paintings, his urgings for less contrast and more subdued hues are gone. Perhaps for the best, as other important things prevail. 'Let the painting talk, let it paint.' My brush flows over contours that used to be unyielding. At the same time, some dense passages recreate the textured flatness and contrasts of paintings of the 1960s. Not enough is being done. I still have only a small number of new pictures, and April is not so far away.

18 January 1979

Charles Blackman invited me for lunch, where I met his lover, Genevieve. She's twenty—the same age as his daughter, Christobel.

Charles looks very happy and, as usual, showers gifts on me. A jar of black and a white photographic retouching paint which behaves like nothing else when finishing my Indian ink drawings. And he gives me a sheet of clear plastic out of a big book. It doesn't move or crumple and one can paint on it as on a sheet of glass. I envy him the way he paints, effortlessly it seems, acres upon acres of gardens with cats, and his images of schoolgirls. I labour to get my figure which is still eluding me. His advice was marvellous. 'Paint the figure *first*. Then *paint* the landscape on top of it, flowing over and through it. It *must* in some way loosen up your image.'

10 February 1979

The Christmas show at Gallery One was a disaster. Occasionally a print is sold or the odd New Guinea carving. Perhaps I dramatise, but it certainly gives us food for persecution feelings.

At breakfast, out in the courtyard, I hold Jancsi's hand. I tell him to enjoy the present. The shelter we have in a big city, walled in by the mandarin tree, cacti, and the flowering wisteria—which spreads its green tentacles above the lattice forming an umbrella, giving leafy shade in the rising heat. I tell him to listen to the cicadas, all starting up at the same moment, like under the baton of a tiny conductor.

Orban told me he would like to have an exhibition of his collages if Jancsi wants them. 'Dezsö, you will have to share space with someone as you only have twenty-five.'

'How about sharing it with your drawings? What could be more obvious? Mine are all abstract, yours are all figurative.' His eyes are still handicapping him but, on the insistence of his friends, he started another 'Cathedral' on silver foil with stains, and of course, waited for my remarks.

'Dezsö, the upper right part is excellent, as good as before the operation. The middle could stay empty. The left side and the bottom need work.'

'Would you do it?'

'I would be delighted and honoured.'

The shimmer and ambiguity of the foil, and using the liquid stain vertically are both difficult and strange for me. But I'm a good forger and I almost finished the painting.

Alan Lovell has commissioned me to paint Rupert Murdoch for Dame Elizabeth's seventieth birthday. But Rupert refused to sit, and I refused to paint from a photograph. So, that was wasted time.

10 February 1979

Bodhi Farm

Very sensibly, in 40°C heat everyone on Bodhi Farm walks around in the nude, hence the nude drawings.

I felt odd in clothes.

In *Tolstoy remembered* by his daughter Tatyana: 'The terrible thing for the writer, is that once his characters have been created they begin to live lives of their own, independent of their author's will.' Orban is always telling me, 'Let yourself go. The painting must take over.'

16 February 1979

János has started a company called Effortless Trading. It's designed to get more people at Bodhi Farm off the dole and provide an income for the community.

He's beginning to realise it's far from effortless.

Bookkeeping, accountants, council meetings—the house is stacked with files. They are overwhelmed by the desire for their massage oils, avocado cream and other herbal cosmetic preparations. Everybody was staying up till 4 a.m. hand painting labels. They've decided to spend the money on a printer in order to satisfy the emerging market.

Also, the business needed a telephone. So a few days ago, two Telecom trucks came along with a bulldozer which cut the road in half, laying cables. Yesterday, I had to leave my rented car near the dam and walk all the way in, dodging the powerful machines.

17 March 1979

Sydney

Jancsi told his two partners that he does not wish to continue with the gallery. He feels very relieved and is sleeping much better.

It seems we shall finish our brief career with the exhibition of my drawings and Orban's collages. A 'first' for both of us.

27 April 1979

Of all my teachers, and in all my studies, I have learnt the most from Orban, who repeats endlessly, 'Let yourself go. The picture must take over.'

The taxi truck took the twenty-eight paintings to Rudy's yesterday. I saw them hanging late afternoon. Gwen commented, laughingly, that Charles Moses, said 'Judy turned Stone Age!' In the evening paper there was a small article: 'The artist Judy Cassab is certainly in full command of her marbles. The catalogue for her next exhibition at the Rudy Komon Gallery lists, among twenty-eight paintings and drawings, *The Devil's Marbles II, The Devil's Marbles III, Dusk at the Marbles* and

Oncoming storm over the Marbles, Approaching the Marbles, Details of the Marbles and *Group at the Marbles.*'

And, of course, I am full of doubts.

Meanwhile, I work on old travel sketches. I love tearing paper (instead of neatly cutting it) and using the white of the torn edges. What's more, I tear in a round shape. I used the scaffolding of the lines of the sketch but soon it disappeared and the collage stampeded away with me. And how! There are four ready now, definitely mine but less inhibited and fresher than the paintings.

2 May 1979

For our anniversary, Jancsi sent me red roses, with a note, thanking me for my understanding and love over forty years.

Peter arrived for dinner, with a small parcel which he placed on the dinner table: pâté de foie gras. And a note: 'To my dear mother and father. Congratulations!! Forty years is such a long time. Even longer than my years. There is no such thing as perfection, but you have proved that wrong. With my love, Peter.'

After Peter and Jancsi's toast with the champagne, I said, 'I come from a neurotic family and your father kept me sane.'

Jancsi said, 'I come from a sane family and your mother made me neurotic.'

After dinner, Peter gave us a charcoal drawing by Charles Blackman, *Beauty and the beast.* Witty, generous, unexpected.

The exhibition at Rudy's looks good. Two pictures sold, three reserved. Peter said 'Reserved' means that somebody doesn't want anyone else to buy it. I feel relieved and sleep better. We look at home units. Hookers came today for a valuation of our house.

8 May 1979

I could hardly sleep last night. Greta and Bodhi arrived this morning. We took the base of the couch into the cellar as they always sleep on a mattress on the floor. I bought a little lamp, a heater, filled two vases with flowers. (I was rewarded too. Bodhi said, 'flowers, flowers'.) We blow at each other's noses and Bodhi's sweet laughter rings through the house.

31 May 1979

A letter comes from Ivor Bowden in Canberra. 'The Paris Embassy would welcome a show.' They want it *before* the London one as it's not commercial and thus easier that way. I have to pay transport but they will print a catalogue and posters. They are thinking of around October 1980.

I have far too much on my plate, with three one-man shows in 1979: Rudy's, the drawings in Gallery One, Anne von Bertouch in Newcastle in June (not to mention Brisbane, which was mercifully and wisely postponed by Verlie Just to April 1980, when she heard of the possibility of my overseas trip).

22 June 1979

I have hardly painted at all. It seems pointless at the moment (I dread these thoughts). All the racks are full with unsold (and probably unsellable) black and whites, but framed and perspexed. That 'line', to use a rag trade word, doesn't sell. No portraits either.

5 June 1979

Jancsi found a flat in Ocean Avenue, Double Bay. We drove there and it was a beauty. Next day we bought it. Now we must really work on selling the house.

The Vietnamese boat people, refugees who arrive on the shores of Malaysia, Hong Kong and Darwin by the tens of thousands, seem to me like the new Jews. The fishing boats often perish on their long voyage. People drown by the hundreds, and when they finally arrive, they are unwelcome.

9 August 1979

Outwardly Peter is flamboyant. Only I hear his cry. Up to now, more or less, at least one of my children seems happy. I pray.

31 August 1979

János came a week ago, and, like a dynamo, he works day and night to save the rainforest. Our house is like an army headquarters. When János is not on the phone, then the phone rings for János.

While the forest gets so much attention, Jancsi complains that he doesn't.

4 September 1979

Peter invited us for a Father's Day dinner. János and Greta bought Jancsi a record of Yiddish folk songs. Dinner was delicious. Peter must have cooked all afternoon.

15 September 1979

We are getting to spend a lot of time with Bodhi. We discovered a park we haven't known of in all our years here. Gorgeous palms and a round view of the sea. Also took him to the beach. Greta remarked how important it is for Bodhi to have such grandparents. János is a fantastic father. He does everything a mother can do and has endless patience for play and romping about. His eyes shine when he looks at Bodhi. And Jancsi exudes warmth with the baby. They have a special bond.

27 September 1979

The house is sold, but most of the time I feel tension. When I wake up at night, or sitting in the car, or at breakfast—practically any time I get in touch with my body I find my shoulders are hunched up like a child expecting a blow. I work on this in the afternoon. Sometimes I succeed in making my mind quiet by meditating. Make myself the pure witness. I repeat the magic 'I am', and I stand apart in pure awareness and look at my body. The closest one can get to this in words is, I am what makes perception possible. There is nothing to do. Just be. If one could really change and say, 'It's not my body which has a consciousness. It's a consciousness which has my body.'

14 October 1979

Oscar Edwards' apotheosis is his friendship with Greenberg. For months now every telephone call is about the famous critic arriving in Sydney at the end of October, and that he, Oscar, wants me to come to the dinner of the Dobell Foundation (Greenberg's hosts).

29 December 1979

What a long distance between the dates in my journal.

I opened Orban's ninety-fifth birthday exhibition at Max Taylors. He can hardly see now, but he glues crushed kleenex and drycleaners' plastic on board, paints over it and it's good. Amazing.

We moved. Jancsi worked like a forty year old, the activity lifting his spirit and being altogether very happy in the flat.

We have a telephone-answering machine—just fantastic. A secretary for $20 a month! I intend to switch it on from 9 a.m. till 1 p.m. and have an unbroken painting session every morning. Everything is near, easy, comfortable. The soul moved in with our bodies surprisingly fast.

13 January 1980

I am looking into the 1980s with trepidation. Past civilisations have collapsed through being overrun by barbarians from outside, ours nurtures its own destroyers. Systematically our way of life is being dismantled and our certainties undermined. People accumulate wealth which, thanks to inflation, turns out to be useless paper.

19 January 1980

My good and wise friend, Jancsi, said to me, 'I will help you cut canvases, and prepare the foundations. Don't try to paint pictures. Spoil as many as you want. Don't overwork. The ones which succeed, put aside for Paris.'

After an extended hiatus, I started. We rolled the unprimed canvas over my new studio floor, cut out together, then Jancsi moved into the garage with house painter's brush and gesso, and prepared my canvases.

16 February 1980

I sold eleven paintings at the opening of my one-man show in Hobart. Hundreds of people came, the Lord Mayor, the director of the art gallery, both television channels ran interviews, and the show was on the news. People kept coming, looking, and talking about them.

18 February 1980

When I came back from the hairdresser, I found János, Greta and Bodhi had arrived. I dropped all my plastic shopping bags on the floor to delight in Bodhi's embrace. And even in the small flat, felt like my grandmother in Bergszász, spreading my hen's feathers above them to cover and to love.

I went to Camp Cove with János and Bodhi. I swam and enjoyed watching János swimming with Bodhi on his back like a seal. János even suspended his high nutritional principles, and bought us all ice-cream cones. He said, 'Since we moved to Bodhi Farm, I don't know the meaning of the word anxiety.'

What else can a mother wish for? Everything else is so unimportant.

22 March 1980

Two portraits after a long lull.

Thirty-four paintings left for Brisbane. Next day Verlie Just had a heart attack and is in intensive care. Arnold Just, her husband, rang me. They are worried about me and my show. I told him, 'Tell Verlie to get well and forget about me. It will be all right.'

Raoul Mellish sent me a press-cutting: 'Morley and his portrait'. There is a picture of Robert Morley standing with my painting of him in the Brisbane Gallery.

Since I gave away hundreds of books when we moved, I stopped buying them and now go regularly to the Woollahra library. Jancsi is engrossed in Gore Vidal's *Julian*, and I read Steinbeck's *Pearl*, and borrow fantastic art books like *Picasso's world of children*, Vuillard, Modigliani.

20 March 1980

Brisbane

What an auspicious exhibition this seems to be. There was a printers' strike in Queensland, and also an electricity strike. What is more important however: my attitude is changing. For a long time I have known that without this change I would not be able to produce a work of art that has a figure in it. Jancsi was formidable. 'You have now earned enough for this financial year. Don't waste your time on pleasing pictures. Once again: spoil, spoil, experiment. Leave those five fingers and toes alone. Simplify. Make them awkward. Avoid those elegant *Vogue* figures. It's a dead end.'

In my prayers I now include: 'Give me courage.' In the new, large, floating mottled *Kerosene lamp and landscape* I placed an almost Klee-ish (simple) figure. I draw almost each night till after ten. Jancsi thinks I don't work seriously enough, not enough, my involvement is not enough. Of course, one has to be completely egocentric to do it this way. And I still don't let any of my friends down. Then there is the hairdresser, pedicure, acupuncture. All time consuming. I try. I try.

10 April 1980

The Brisbane show got the usual throng, and five sold, among them, *The Devil's Marbles III*, which is reproduced in *Art and Australia* and also in the catalogue.

Fred Gardiner (my gallery in Toowoomba) drove up the eighty miles for the opening. A surprising number of fellow artists came. Margaret Olley, John Rigby and Jacqueline Hick, who has moved here from Adelaide. And a shadow from the past, the Reverend Felix Arnott, who used to judge the Blake Prize. He is an archbishop now, in a purple vest, and will take up a post next year in Venice.

25 April 1980

Bodhi Farm

Their house has now acquired an Indonesian personality. The open side, where the entrance is, looks like a botanical garden. Walkingstick palms, creepers, sunlight. Bamboo walls, passionfruit ripening. The see-saw in the living room looks like a modern sculpture, and the plate-glass window is covered with a huge mandala.

János, very mellow, said, 'Aren't we blessed to be able to bring up a child in this place?'

Bodhi Farm is the inspiration for all my drawings. I get as many nude couples as I want, and have a number of good new sketches.

25 May 1980

Sydney

The children are here from Bodhi Farm. János is fully occupied talking to politicians about the forests. He is going to Canberra next week.

Bodhi is a delight, and with him and Greta here I feel like my grandmother again.

12 June 1980

Orban left yesterday for London where he has an exhibition at NSW House. At ninety-six he's travelling with his doctor, like a king.

Today I went to the Kletzmayrs' fiftieth wedding anniversary. I remembered how we lived with them for a year in Salzburg, how they babysat János and Peter. Franzi is now a prosperous timber merchant, and Edith an atomic scientist. I took a picture as a present.

28 June 1980

Orban had a grand opening in London. His doctor says he can't keep up with him. Orban, who is nearly a hundred, climbed the Acropolis en route. It surely belongs in the *Guinness book of records*.

I have been invited to become a trustee of the Art Gallery of NSW. Jancsi was very pleased, and I accepted. It means no more Archibald entries for three years, the duration of my term, but that's just as well. The announcement came out yesterday on radio, TV and in the papers. The only other artist on the board is John Olsen—I am pleased, though I don't see how two of us can achieve anything if outvoted by seven laymen. There's Jim Spigelman, whiz kid of the Whitlam government, and Joseph Brender. The president, Charles Lloyd Jones, invited me for lunch yesterday, with Jim Spigelman and Edmund Capon, the director. Capon used to work at the Victoria and Albert Museum in London, and far eastern art is his expertise. While we talked about the rest of the board, not present, Capon remarked about Brender: 'A shopkeeper (teasing Charles), they come in all shapes and sizes.' The two have worked together for years and obviously have a good rapport, while Jim and I, as he remarked, were 'the new boys in school'.

The appointment is a great honour. Again, as in my Australian honours term, they caught three flies with one sweep: a woman, an artist, a migrant.

Ethnic television is making a film of three Hungarian artists. Orban, George Molnar, and me. Frank Heimans, our director, flew to London for Orban's opening, and he suggested I should be filmed in Alice Springs. We are now on a propeller-driven, slow aircraft and I hope I will be able to sketch Lake Eyre, which I missed on the last trip when Jancsi broke his arm. We have five days before the film crew arrives. It's good, perhaps, to interrupt my ceaseless painting and get some perspective about the unfinished pictures. Also, oh wondrous changing vision, I feel I shall see, or look for, different themes in Alice, and when I find them, I shall paint them differently with the new, bolder, impasto approach I discovered in Tasmania.

29 June 1980

All hotels in Alice were booked out for the first five days, so we stayed with Mona. Amazingly there wasn't a jarring note. Mona has two dogs and a parrot. Jancsi was delighted with their company. The garden is full of orange trees loaded with fruit.

Mona has opened an art gallery opposite Mt Gillen in a Spanish-style horseshoe-shaped building, where the collection of the Alice Prize and a diorama are kept.

The television crew arrived on Thursday. Until the day before, we still didn't have permission to enter Rainbow Valley where the film was to be shot. The Kargers (who are the owners of the property) are not on telephone or radio, so we drove a hundred kilometres to see them, and a hundred back again. Rainbow Valley is now fenced in and has a gate with two padlocks. The Kargers want to protect its fragility from tourists. They are happy to share its beauty with us.

Friday morning, Virginia Crippen and Mona came to pick us up in Virginia's four-wheel drive. She has just returned to Alice with her husband from Washington. He is now second-in-command at Pine Gap, the atomic plant.

Frank, our director, started by shooting the long stretch of road. Russell Boyd, the cameraman (who filmed *Picnic at Hanging Rock*) was roped over the hood of our Land Rover and shot us through the windscreen while Kevin, the sound man, crouched behind my seat on the floor, holding the microphone. The turning is not to be seen. Our special instructions were: a milestone with 'K200', a little bridge, a floodway sign and there turn left. They filmed me getting out, opening the gate, and a long day of hard work began. The camera came with me as we compared nature's sculptures to a Henry Moore bone, to a

Jean Arp marble. We had to cross a steep and rather slippery moonscape and I was already worn out by the time I was supposed to choose a subject, set up studio, and paint.

Wednesday Frank wanted to show Orban and George Molnar and myself having coffee at the Cosmopolitan. Thursday they filmed me ringing Orban's bell, coming in, sitting with him and talking about his London show. It all took ages.

The most exciting sketches were done on the plane. I underpainted the paper and used Caran d'Ache pastels to follow the spreading, tear-shaped salt lakes, the winding riverbeds, and the infinite variety of a landscape without perspective. After these, the waiting, unfinished canvases in Ocean Avenue looked timid and lacking contrast.

Today was my first function as trustee. Baron Thiessen-Bornemisza opened his loan exhibition of great masters this afternoon. Tomorrow is my first board meeting.

3 August 1980

The new exhibition at the Art Gallery of NSW, Modern European and American Masters of the Twentieth Century (the Thiessen-Bornemisza collection) is an inspiration. Let the orthodox keep a picture pure (abstract). There is a hand in the Braque cubist woman, while the woman herself disappeared. Tanguy does object-scapes like me. Marino Marini's dancers look like my Devil's Marbles. I find connections everywhere and, mainly, encouragement to be bold. The long years with Orban and his inclination to lessen contrast ('that blue is a hole in the picture, that pink jumps') made me bring the blue forward and glaze the pink back. I am changing this. And I am slashing and splashing oil paint on seductive areas which are a shame to lose, but they must not stand in the way.

I thought I would be shy at the board meeting but, when the director's letter on the proposed exhibition agenda came up, I read out the Act, section 7, point 2, which says '... The Trust shall give particular emphasis to the art of Australia'. I pointed out that there is Pompeii, the Louvre's visiting exhibition and the Chinese porcelain, but there is no mention of new acquisitions (later, Olsen and I agreed that Capon's proposed two-yearly display is not good enough).

However, Sir Tristan Antico, a particularly sharp, matter-of-fact mind, pounced on the 'southern hemisphere' bit, and I thought it ridiculous.

'A misprint,' I said.

'A mistake,' said Charles Lloyd Jones. What is it? South Africa? South

America? We belong to the Pacific region. A subcommittee had to be voted in for acquisitions and loans. They voted in John Olsen and me. When Capon proposed we tackle the backlog after next month's meeting, Olsen said, 'That's an artist's nightmare. Too long a time to be uncertain.' So, we meet on 13 August. I hope we shall pull together.

6 September 1980

Birthdays. I was sixty on 15 August. Unbelievable. And Peter was thirty-three yesterday.

The printer was here, about the Paris catalogue. Thank heavens I have time till the end of January. Lynn will write the foreword when he comes back from his overseas Power Bequest shopping trip. The Alliance Francaise will translate it. I went to the Visual Arts Board to see the international exhibition officer, Katrina Rumley and Nick Waterlow (who is director now) was there. They both praise the publicity man from the Australian embassy, Paul Carpenter. Things start to connect.

25 September 1980

János's arrival these days always coincides with a drama somewhere in the environment. Greta stayed here while father and son camped at Middle Head Beach, protesting about another assault on forest and shore.

There is a danger, I fear, that he is becoming a professional demonstrator. How dull an ordinary job must seem compared to the highs of this?

27 September 1980

All very well to be a trustee, The intrigues and goings on are like politics. Olsen didn't appear, and I was the only painter and person in grave doubt about acquiring a Henry Moore for $180,000 and a Picasso for $400,000. These purchases would deplete the funds and leave hardly any money for Australian art. I said so last month, and when this time, the Moore and Picasso were unanimously accepted I had no choice but to finally agree as I would have been outvoted anyway.

5 October 1980

I want to record our everyday routine. Before 6 p.m. Jancsi holds the little radio to his ear and listens to the stock exchange on which he invests small amounts. Then comes the PM news commentary while I prepare dinner. Jancsi joins me for a drink now, a most civilised habit. After dinner he puts things away and I wash up. Ready for the 7 p.m. news on television. And around 10, when I'm in bed, Jancsi peels an apple or a pear and brings it in with cold soda water for the night. Afternoons I take half an hour or so off, to meditate and pray. I start seeing with the third eye, almost located it. It looks inside. There is a place in my prayers where I tell God I love him, and realise I always have, since my childhood in Beregszász. Then I get a quite vivid picture of myself. I must be twelve or fourteen, a lovely smile and a long chin. I stand under trees, lilacs, on Main Street, with *Nagymama* in her checked scarf, just as in the drawing I did of her at that time. And then come long lines, drawn or painted, to show the movement of a bird and on this end I stand with my grandson. A life, I am thinking, and maybe it's a continuation of another life, loving God, and after I am gone perhaps I will be born to love them again.

However, visual flashes have nothing to do with painting and I wonder why I was born a painter without visual memory. My fantasy only arrives after I made some sort of mark on the empty picture plane. Be it a rock or a landscape, when Jancsi discovers a human face in it, or an animal. 'Can't you *see* it?' he asks, and I get irritable. 'No, I can't.' When finally it emerges, I don't get the impulse to make it stay.

In Lynn's book on Nolan, Kenneth Clark writes that Nolan doesn't have a choice. He is under 'orders'. He plants a face on top of Ayers Rock. So does Chagall, a red angel, or grandfather's clock in the sky, or a face in the cock's feathers. It would be high time, at sixty, to acquire freedom. Will I ever?

Michael Servaes paints a dismal picture in his letters, of London in the 1980s. No sales, terrible economic plight. He is too much a gentleman to say 'postpone the exhibition'. If Paris was not on, I would. But I can't. We may lose a fortune in this venture and I feel like a soul possessed. The only gain in the whole complex situation is the challenge. I press on with the work as never before in my life. Never mind about handicaps.

25 October 1980

We fetched Orban and drove to Cinetel Studios where Frank Heimans
screened the film of the three Hungarian artists for us. Orban has the
lion's share of the film, and so he should. Seven hours of film was cut
down to fifty-five minutes. I tell an anecdote in the Land Rover in
Alice Springs, paint a bit, say a few words in Hungarian, they show two
portraits, a few paintings and one line drawing and that's that.

For yesterday's board meeting, I sent a letter to be put on the agenda.
I wrote:

> I would like to discuss some problems concerning the acquisition policy
> and especially the allocation of funds for the Australian department. It
> seems to me that, as the foundations of the Art Gallery of NSW have been
> firmly based on its Australian collection, the depletion of funds for pur-
> chasing Australian works is not in the best interest of the Gallery. I would
> be sorry to see the repetition of the situation which occurred in the purchase
> of the Bonnard, which resulted in the Gallery's purchasing capacity being
> restricted for about three years. What is happening currently (with the
> acquisition of the Moore and the Picasso) brings us to a similar situation
> for the next twelve months or so.
>
> I would like to quote a passage from the meeting with curators held at
> the Gallery on 24 September 1980, in which it was, albeit reluctantly,
> decided to proceed with these major purchases and hope that some support
> will be forthcoming providing that the Australian department could continue
> with its program to some extent. I confess I felt reluctant too, and later,
> gravely concerned. Of course it is hard for any trustee to say NO to a
> Picasso or a Moore if it is proposed by the gallery staff. Such a situation
> would be prevented if the policy of the gallery indicated that the amount
> allocated for Australian art is inviolate and under no circumstances should
> a situation arise where the funds allocated for Australian works are used
> for other acquisitions, even if a desirable and favourable work of art should
> turn up again, next year.

This memo was received by the trustees in the middle of the meeting.
I only realised later, when reading it through at home, that the sentences
should be exactly in the reverse. That *first* emphasis should be on
Australian art, *then* hope that some support would be forthcoming, for
acquisitions of this magnitude.

At this point, I would like to quote a few lines from the director's
introduction (25 July 1980) where he writes:

'The Art Gallery of NSW could never, except in some highly selective fields, become a mighty storehouse of treasures. We are not a New York Metropolitan Museum of Art. We are not a Louvre or a British Museum and we never can be. Far better that we strive to attain excellence in limited areas of interest.'

The limitations or otherwise imposed by available funds must be consistently borne in mind.

'Areas of specific responsibilities, which are generally determined by the history of the Gallery, its location, and, to some extent, even by its existing collection. It is a perfectly respectable and legitimate principle in the consideration of collecting policies to build on existing strengths. There are certain areas of strength in the Gallery's collections and these, most certainly, influence my thinking in the consideration of future policies.'

'I wholeheartedly agree with this attitude. However, I feel that we are not acting in the spirit in which this policy was proposed. On the contrary, we are neglecting these responsibilities for twelve months to come. And if we have done so already, at least let's make our policy for the future follow those guidelines we are here to protect. I would like to give notice to the following motion: That the allocation of funds for purchasing Australian works for the collection be kept for that purpose and not be reallocated for other proposed allocations.'

When I arrived for the meeting, Charles Lloyd Jones and Edmund Capon took me aside. They explained I am in error: there is no allocation. The curator announces his priorities at the beginning of the financial year and the amount for this year was $113,000. It might be more next year, or less. We only pay half the cost of the Moore this year, therefore $98,000 will be released at once. 'We have made our major purchases,' said Edmund, 'we don't want to make any next year. We may spend *all* our money on Australian art. We can't be dogmatic about things.'

If this is true (with allocation versus curator priority) then I had the wrong information. I stuck my neck out and they chopped it off. The motion was defeated. Olsen didn't appear for the second month running. I had no one to second my motion. It was not a pleasant experience.

9 November 1980

Jeff Smart rang me, just arrived from Italy for his show at Rudy's. He needs to finish two of his paintings and may he use my studio? Gladly.

Jeff had lunch with us, and then took charge of my palette. I just saw him mixing cerulean blue with cadmium red, something I never attempted. How I envy him. His aim has been the same since I first met him thirty years ago. Arrows, posters, radars, trucks, highways, garages, exquisitely painted. My show consists of watercoloury canvases and heavily painted ones (though at least the subject is the Australian landscape), of very good (I think) gouaches of desert shapes from Rainbow Valley, different mother and child and couples on Nepalese rice paper. So late did I realise that perhaps I need a link. And transformed one rock into a figure here and there. Sisyphus's travails. I feel I'd need another year.

Jack Lynn sends us postcards from his overseas travels, each one witty, but the Cézanne card, with the unusual red rock, takes the cake. 'Parisian scholars,' he writes, 'are investigating the view that in 1900 Cézanne was near Alice Springs.'

I sent him a note saying, 'No doubt this is the brain of Ayers Rock, but vegetation must have been abundant in 1900.'

For a mother of a champion of reforestation, I continue painting arid desert shapes, rather unseemingly.

14 December 1980

The expenses for the London and Paris exhibitions will be horrendous. I have to fly over twice. I had photographs and transparencies done this week, the embassy needed one for the invitation card. So did Michael Servaes. *Art International* is due in January with an advertisement.

I went to Charles Blackman's book launching. People queued up to pay $100 for a book. I bought one. His stature as a first-rate artist is more apparent on the pages than in any one-man show. More seductive, more intimate. A few days later I received a letter from his publisher, asking to explore the possibility of a book. We are to meet for coffee in January.

I don't have guilt feelings about Jancsi. I have been a good wife and still am. In every day's sequence, he comes first and he *is* first. He has never hindered my artistic life. On the contrary. He was selfless and gave me freedom. I feel guilt about my children. Had I not have been born a painter, I would have been a better mother.

15 December 1980

A group of citizens have commissioned me to paint Lady Cutler's portrait to be presented to the retiring governor. Lady Cutler, whom I always perceived as mousey, shines with an inner glow. The whole painting is diffused with her light. A yellow-mellow landscape background, open terrace door, transparent white chiffon gown, even the medal can't spoil it. She brought me dozens of rosebuds from the gardens of Government House each sitting. After the presentation, Sir Roden himself telephoned me to say how delighted he is. Half an hour later a bunch of yellow and white carnations were delivered with a two-page letter from Lady Cutler, thanking me.

Jack Lynn and I wrote to my old abode, the secretariat of the Honours of Australia in Canberra, recommending Mona Byrnes for an honour. The Alice Prize and consecutive collection of paintings, the Aboriginal artist's comeback: from gum-tree manufacturing to old symbols, all originated from her. I wrote also to a high court judge and chief minister, and to a member of parliament, asking them to write in too.

Barry Pearce wanted to see the paintings going to Paris. I invited him for a drink. He liked the black paintings (the gouaches) and the sixteen small paintings making up *Images of a flight*. This one is framed now into a suite and much changed. The dramatic red blacks disappeared to make the whole unified, and the tear-drop shapes of the salt lakes appear in each, and in each it's a different shape, size or colour.

25 December 1980

Sixty paintings are done now, for better or worse. I am surfacing from the bottom of a well, and try to shake the loose bits together.

Just finished John Olsen's new book, *My complete graphics*, which is handwritten, and contains drawings—like an illustrated diary. This raises for me the fact that I've never drawn in my journals. I've kept things nicely separated in tight little compartments.

Since I turned sixty I have reviewed my position as an artist. I refuse to go downhill. I feel I'm just starting. No more potboilers. No more charity shows where, when I don't sell, they return the picture with 'but it created great interest'.

10 January 1981

Jack Lynn came over to write the foreword to the catalogue. I'm sure he didn't expect what he found. I left him alone, more or less, to scribble in room after room.

I asked Jack if he would write the book about me that Reed wants to publish. 'Yes' he said. Asked him to pick up any painting out of the show for the Power Collection. He chose half a dozen, none of which will sell. Before he left, when I thanked him on the staircase, he turned and said, 'It's a pleasure to see the work of an old friend come up beyond expectation. It came good. It takes off with a wheeee!' And he rushed out. When I told Jancsi, we both felt enormous relief. Somehow the stamp of approval was marked on the venture. Even though catalogue, printer, translation, freight are still to be done. So are finishing and polishing on some pictures. But God helped me with this show.

24 January 1981

Soon the catalogue goes to the printer—end of this month, and I am painting more desert shapes. Good ones. *Omen, Pilgrim,* are more surreal than any before. Bill Reed, the publisher, was here, and gave me $5000 for transparencies. Above that sum, I'll get it back from royalties. Jancsi is enthusiastic about the book, and proud.

15 February 1981

Greta and Bodhi have been here for a week. János came two days ago. Jancsi comments on how much easier Bodhi has become, not realising it's *him* who is easier. I thank God for every day which passes in harmony. It's the first time also that I have to be nothing else but grandmother, kick the ball, read the story, go to the park with the bike. Bodhi repays, of course, with trust and love. The table is always set, the telephone book on the chair for Bodhi, the toaster out, the fridge full.

20 February 1981

Bodhi can't be cuddled. One has to wait for him to be the initiator. We play. I seem to get involved in the games much more than thirtysomething years ago. 'I am a baby-pitt,' he announces, 'you are a mummy-pitt.' I don't even enquire what a pitt is. His imagination is given free rein, we all participate. Very rarely do János or Greta discipline him—only when he goes around hitting us. A slightly raised, serious warning makes his eyes fill with tears, it's hard not to beg his forgiveness. There are rainy days, unfortunately, and his activity is boundless. Like a small lion cub, used to freedom, no exercising in a cage is sufficient. Today they let him out in the rain without his clothes, like at Bodhi Farm, and hoots of joy filled Ocean Avenue. Then, rubbed down with a towel, glowing, he settles down beside me for a read. By 4 p.m. it's a blessing to have 'Sesame Street' on television, which he watches sitting on our bed.

At 6.30 Clare Dan's reception for the piano competition. I am a director, so off I go and mix with politicians, diplomats, musicians, the press.

Last Monday was selection day, and 800 paintings were paraded before us with only thirty possible for the Archibald and forty for the Wynne. It happens with such speed one's head spins. The good artists were conspicuously absent: no Brett Whiteley, Fred Williams, John Brack, Clifton Pugh. Olsen thinks the prize should not be awarded this year.

It's a headache to say *out* to months of hard work, expensive frames and freights from interstate. I said we have to get used to blood, like doctors.

After this, we come back on our own to choose the five we prefer of those selected for each competition. I kept in mind quality first and contemporariness second, and only those which are not derivative. And how many there are! All those Pollock dribbles, Arp-shaped canvases, vulgar tube colours and bad taste! Many good artists have off periods.

1 March 1981

Stan Edwards, the framer, spent an evening in the studio, drilling loops into all fifty-four frames. Lucky I happened to get this slight information from the Visual Arts Board's Katrina Rumley. It would have been unfortunate to race into hardware stores in Paris and do it at the embassy.

The doorbell. It's Gerard Havekes and Mia, back from his exhibition in Holland. Havekes drinks half a bottle of Hennessy cognac and stays till midnight. However, it was worth it. He has seen my paintings twice before, in the beginning, and didn't like them. No contrast, no strength, no colour. He was so frank, almost rude then, that when he was bowled over this time I had to believe him (and *before* the cognac). 'Nobody can ignore them,' he announced, and 'No one has ever perceived the Australian landscape like this, ancient, mysterious, surreal.' He wants to buy two of them if they come back. The supreme compliment from a fellow artist.

Next morning three hefty fellows start packing. Grace Bros packed the Pompeii show, so I'm not surprised about how excellent they are. Plastic sheet first, then corrugated cardboard. Then, two at a time, they are slipped into shallow boxes. I wrote titles and catalogue numbers on each. I was very exhausted.

Next day Orban day. Can't cancel *him*, he is ninety-seven! At night, dinner with the premier in honour of the former chairman of the trustees, Justice Nagle. All the old trustees meet the new ones. Next day we judge the Archibald and Wynne. Olsen persuades us not to award the prize. The reason that more important artists didn't enter is that last year the standard was so low. Not only is the general standard poor this year but all artists seemed to have been producing a work below their usual standard. When we walked over to the Wynne Prize room, I realised what awesome power one can have over the fate of others.

6 March 1981

Received a printed invitation from Charles Blackman and Genevieve who 'will exchange vows at the sea at dawn. Their hearts and their home is open for their friends from 10 a.m. to sundown'.

For Charles I took the sketch for his portrait, on which the background (his painting) still has the horse's head from Fuseli's nightmare. On a glass door a huge *Herald* poster screamed 'Charles's Wedding'. It was, of course, for Prince Charles, not Blackman, but apt.

4 April 1981

I judged the Lloyd Jones portrait prize for the Easter Show. Two society ladies were assigned to me as 'stewards'. Elimination first, but differing from the Archibald. Here we were not given a list and, except where the style or signature was visible, one didn't know whether it was a man or woman, young or old. I was worried in case I would chuck out say a Dobell.

Then I asked for the list and, yes, I must have chucked out Charles Bush, because he wasn't hanging. I was upset and raced to the rejects to see why I disliked it. One of my stewards came to the rescue and found that Bush had sent in the title but didn't send the picture. Sigh of relief. Jack Lynn asked me two days later: 'Did you give the first prize to X?'

'Yes.'

'Has it been announced already?'

'I think so. Why?'

'Because the rotten bastard wrote a letter to the *Herald*, unpublished, and to the *Australian*, also unpublished, about incompetent, idiot judges of the Archibald, awarding the watercolour prize to something that was neither a landscape nor a watercolour.'

'Well Jack,' I said, 'you could now write a letter too, saying that one of the idiot judges gave him first prize.'

An extraordinary board meeting. The trustees were supposed to decide whether to accept the state government's 2.5 million dollar grant (on a dollar for dollar basis) for a foundation. Or a six million dollar collection, bought from Mr Bowmore. We were told it's a once only chance to acquire Rubens, Rodin, Dufy, Monet etc., plus an Islamic collection.

We didn't really have much of a choice but resolved that two senior independent, expert valuers have to be flown in from England, or America, as dealers are unacceptable, as such. And, that we have to be free to sell what we don't want, even if what we buy in its stead will go under the aegis of the Bowmore collection. I have never set eyes on it, Olsen saw it in Newcastle, and the curators were about to see it.

A Nolan reception at the Art Gallery. Beside his splendid, multipanelled *Riverbend*, a Chinese group of river paintings coinciding with the imminent Chinese exhibition.

7 April 1981

Joanna Capon rang to invite me to their home for dinner in honour of the Chinese exhibition. I looked at the priceless collection of eastern antiquities alternating with Hockney's *Grimm fairytales*, a minor Bruegel (father, son?), a very English racehorse, a shaped canvas lolly-coloured tromp l'oeil. I was amazed to meet scholars from Berlin and Tokyo, the US and New Zealand, flocking to see the exhibition. Some of the scrolls were never unrolled before, not even in China. Eighty guests formed a long queue before the buffet dinner.

Rudy surprised me by announcinng he will come to Paris for the opening of my exhibition.

20 April 1981

Paris

The embassy isn't the least bit attentive. No 'welcome' message in my room. Paul Carpenter wasn't in. I went over, saw the vast, cold expanse of what will be my exhibition space. They search my handbag. My head is stuffed with cottonwool, but I didn't want to sleep during the day, wanting to sleep at night.

Amazingly lonely. I sit on the terrace on the Champs-Elysées with a Campari.

27 April 1981

In the cavernous hall of the embassy, two electricians perched on aluminium scaffolding, pointing the spotlights on the paintings. We worked like ants till 5 p.m. Stella McGowan, secretary to Paul Carpenter, was helping. The famous sliding hooks obeying her more than us. Was glad I had loops on all the frames.

Michael Servaes of my gallery in London arrived to choose the paintings for the London exhibition. After Michael left, Teddy and Zsuzsi took me to the Brasserie Lipp, reminding me of Manet's bar. I must have put on half a stone. Sunday, Teddy ordered an ordinary taxi for the whole day which took us to Vera in Mulleron. It was an enchanted day. Vera has had another book published, extraordinary paper, black and white galaxies and cosmic text. Every 'box' she creates, some filled with wood, some with string, rope, nails, folded canvases, extends outside its frame, bursting out. Just as her sails fly in their exhibition space.

Her rooms are extensions of this environment. In Budapest, she says, she put down plastic foam rubber under canvas on the floor, which not only created an even, white atmosphere, but people walked on something like eiderdown which threw everything out of an ordinary experience. We gave Zsuzsi courage by telling her she is on her own now, not to heed others, not to expect approval and dreading disapproval. This is valid for me, too.

The ambassador, John Rowland, likes my paintings and so does Paul Carpenter. But it doesn't interest me in the least. I have no expectations about this venture in Paris.

Today in the Grand Palais I saw a magnificent Uccello that makes me long to copy for the first time since Bruegel. At the same place, a Pissarro exhibition in its third month. The queue is still a mile long, up the stone balustrade stairs, ten deep, I wait, looking at majestic chestnut trees in blossom. It's bitterly cold. Inside, five rows of windows like a railway station. Pissarro turns my eyes into a strange lens of pointillism. I see the sea of faces around me as he sees—infinitesimal dots. This kind of humble devotion is missing in most twentieth-century painting.

There is also a large Gainsborough show. It teaches me a lot about portraits. Of softness. And he underpaints with a tired pink. It forms the dress, surrounds the brown doorway which is the figure's background.

I have an invitation to the Modigliani exhibition on a Monday when it's closed to the public.

My cousin Vera and I go to the Beaubourg. There is a Bartok centenary debate. The room is packed. People who can't find seats stand on the sides. On the dais are musicologists, Bartokologists, three Hungarians, three French. All this on a cold, rainy, Monday afternoon. I can follow the speakers quite well (especially the ones who have Hungarian accents).

28 April 1981

At the embassy, Stella McGowan and I divided the boxes with catalogue numbers into two piles: those which will return to Sydney, and those which will go to London.

Since the Pompidou Centre was built, a whole new world emerged around it. I went around till night fell, to the Galerie Yvonne Lambert where Judith Reigl (a Hungarian) exhibits. Vera told me she works with oil (or enamel) on unprimed canvas, then soaks the back in an acrylic colour and the painting emerges. Simon Hantai (another Hungarian), she says, crumples canvas, irons it down, doesn't dip or spray but 'hand paints' at the edges of the folded accidents.

I was shown a painter who paints on ribbons. The ribbons are stuck down along a large white wall. 'You can take it home, rolled up in your pocket,' I was told. Another stitches on knitted pullovers and photographs it on the reverse.

30 April 1981

Vera's long list of critics was duly invited by the embassy for a champagne preview at noon on the day of opening. The ambassador, the cultural attaché, Stella, the waiter and I stood around for an hour or more and not one single Parisian critic turned up. Only someone from the German magazine *Spiegel*.

1 May 1981

Oscar Edwards' letters take on frightening proportions. I got twelve letters in Paris, one for every day here, the first one dated a week before my departure. The embassy staff think I am having an affair.

Rudy has an old friend here, his former boss in Prague, a writer and newspaper editor. They took me out yesterday to Charlotte Premier, one of the famous fish restaurants on the Boulevard Clichy. I am paying for it today—spent all night on the loo and am on tea, toast and charcoal all day.

5 May 1981

I spent my second Sunday in Mulleron. This time went by train and Vera picked me up at Orsay Ville. We went to the market first. It's incredible. Such a rich, fresh, wonderful choice in a little village. Hundreds of cheeses and as much seafood, olives, nuts, breads and cakes. I had a contemplative day in the studio while she smeared three-metre poles with black shoe polish, and then polished them with brushes and rags. Meanwhile she cooked the fish with slices of lemon, bay leaves and rosemary in silver foil. It was delicious and light.

Monday was busy. Morning at the exhibition, lunch at the ambassador's. Rudy postponed his trip to Zurich, to be there. It was the same polished table, crystal, silver and gloved waiters as in Canberra's Government House. Rudy went to catch the train. The ambassador drove me home.

2 June 1981

Hong Kong

Jancsi and I arrived in Hong Kong last night starting with a splurge at the Peninsula. A great hotel. Luxury extraordinaire and the top of enjoyment for a Leo. Jancsi feels uneasy in such surroundings, whereas I consider it my birthright. Except for the swarming servants from colonial times, the Peninsula is not oppressive. It's very old and gracious. And Jancsi is travelling backwards to his old, young self, for my sake.

6 June 1981

Casey Pang's invitation to join him on his yacht was a delight. Only on film have I seen such a luxurious boat. All air-conditioned, carpeted, streamlined, with three bedrooms and two bathrooms below, two lounge rooms above and a sundeck on two levels. A crew of four. We sped through the harbour in a rolling mist until we reached the Chinese border, then anchored down in a quiet cove and had hot titbits served with our drinks.

When night fell the boat turned towards Kowloon and moored in a famous fishing village. We walked on planks to a raft where everybody chose live fish, crabs and lobsters, and sat down round a table with more drinks, ginger, thousand-year-old eggs (poisonously dark green), pickled garlic and chilli.

When I couldn't get over the yacht, Jancsi told me there are yacht, yachter, and yachtest.

19 June 1981

Germany

After a *sejour* in Greece and the Greek Islands, I am in Cologne and a casualty of too much art. Each one of my toes aches separately, but it was worth it. Westkunst Art from 1939 to the Present is in the Köln Messe and it could fit the Pompidou into one pocket. Yesterday morning we walked to it through the bridge over the Rhine.

It's bitterly cold and rainy. The queue inside was like folded cottonwool in a plastic bag. It took an hour to get to the ticket counter. After that hardship, we sat in one of the TV rooms not so much to gain wisdom but to rest our feet.

I discovered Hitler's speeches about *Entartete Kunst*, the consequence of which was the exodus of creative artists to New York. In the middle of the main hall, between the excellent bookshop and the cafeteria, was something I took for a Christo, an enormous amorphous shape covered with wrappings. However, it was only hundreds of pillows on which people sat, or lay on their tummies, on their backs, feet dangling, children watching television.

21 June 1981

London

Arrival in London was nightmarish with endless trolleys and tunnels.

4 July 1981

We moved into three different flats in Sloane Gardens. It wasn't quite my cup of tea that the beds were in huge cupboards and had to be pulled out when one wished to be horizontal, which I wish to be several times a day.

Not that there was time for anything. Six days were occupied with my portrait commission, and the exhibition opening which I visited daily. I decided not to worry about who I didn't see. Who wanted to see me, could come to the opening.

The Thorneycrofts were at the opening, Peter stayed close to my side so I had to introduce him to dozens of people. He greeted them with such outgoing charm it was as if he were canvassing at election time. Bernie Leser bought the *Ring*. And, out of the blue, a black, bearded professor from Nigeria walked in from the street, bought three pictures, paid cash, to be delivered to the Savoy next day. Lord and Lady Astor arrived and Robert Morley came, being his most jolly-sinister.

I hadn't known, however, if there would actually be an opening. Michael said he had his nervous breakdown already: the customs were on go-slow and the exhibition was at Heathrow for ten days, not released.

Michael said invitations went out to all the art critics. None turned up while I was in London.

Before we left Sydney Vera Kaldor said: 'Do send an invitation to Ági Sekers.'

'All right, I will.'

'Ring her, try to see her.'

'Vera, why? Ági Sekers has not shown any interest in us for thirty-two years.'

'But now, after Miki's downfall, Miki's death, her tragedy with her children (they kicked Miki out of Sekers Silk) it would be a *mitzvah*.'

Ági came to the gallery the day before the show opened, left a message. So we rang her. It was a time pregnant with confusing emotions, because perhaps no single human being was as good to us or did more for us than Miki. Because of the first London portrait commissions I later painted Hugh Gaitskell (now in the National Portrait Gallery) and Peter Thorneycroft, and then I painted Lady Lloyd Jones on arrival in Sydney. Probably I would have arrived somewhere by other means and ways. But somewhere else. The meeting in St Gilgen with the Sekers changed our life. All this gratitude never had a chance to be expressed. Miki's interest in us became a discontinued line. '*Sein Bedarf in Wohltätigkeit ist gedeckt*', Jancsi said at the time.

On our way to his widow, who lost the man, the castle, the fortune, the collection of Picassos, Dufys, and Matisses, I had a preconceived idea about someone bitter (with reason), beaten, disenchanted, nothing to look forward to. The woman who opened the door of a ground floor, two-bedroom flat was bursting with life, esprit, intelligence, and commonsense. There was no need for pity. She is independent, self-reliant, and spoke about the last years in a detached way.

There were two photographs of Miki. One, as we knew him, in lively conversation, the bonhomie on his face, the success. The other is a thin, tragic face, but noble and intelligent, with enormous eyes.

12 July 1981

Budapest

The new Thermal Hotel is great, a balcony on the Danube overlooking the fabulous old trees on the island. For the first time in my life I am in warm, healing, spring water, then swim in the pool. It makes me feel guilty that someone exactly like me, a friend of Anyu, is in a sterile cell in the Jewish old-age home in Ujpest. It's clean, there are flowers, but it's like a waiting room for death. Vacant eyes, misery, brains gone wrong. Eva's situation is terrible. Her flat is waiting intact, with all the Persian carpets and silver, but she is incapable of living there. She can't cope. Possessions are an added horror. 'The moths will eat the Persian carpets.' She shakes and sobs on our shoulder.

26 July 1981

There are double standards in this city which charges tourists as much as any other city, but where one night in a hotel is the equivalent of two weeks salary for the locals. So, when we moved out of tourist hotels and restaurants territory, we found that buses, even taxis, ordinary eating places, cost next to nothing. But also, that people have given up on quality. There is no incentive or reward for doing anything better, and no punishment either in doing badly. There is no unemployment. Two or three people do the job of one.

9 August 1981

Sydney

I slipped a disc just as we arrived home and Jancsi broke a rib. There was no cleaning lady, and the schnitzel shop closed down. A bit of an anticlimax. Chiropractor, acupuncture, a new cleaner, and slowly the wheel turned.

15 August 1981

I am sixty-one. Incredible.

Had a few heavy days with Jancsi getting laryngitis and coughing, hurting the broken rib. Inhalations with camomile. God forbid for a man to be sick. He feels insulted.

14 September 1981

Lots of portraits looming over the horizon in New Zealand. I said I could come early in October but that isn't easy either as Jack only started writing about my life and, apparently, gets confused with the diaries.

1 November 1981

Joe Brender's partner, Sam Moss, had wanted me to paint Joe's portrait a year ago. 'His birthday is on 7 November,' he said, 'could you do it?'

'I can if he sits.'

'Do me a favour,' Sam said. 'Ring him at the office. Say that you are very embarrassed because Sam already paid you for the portrait. Ask him to cooperate.' To my amazement, it worked. Joe has been twice since then, and made free time for each day next week.

Now, Westfield's sponsorship for the Archibald-Wynne-Sulman has got into difficulties. Westfield wanted to give $100,000 for three years, if it could exhibit the winners in the shopping centres. The Gallery is very poor and the temptation was great. Suggestions varied.

The premier finally agreed that we could do it ourselves, not promising the dollar for dollar help of the state, but hinting at it. When we heard this, the new trustee, Kevin Connor, who is also an artist, and I composed a letter for the board. It was his letter, really, talking about dignity and about Archibald's intention in the will. I only added that it will be counterproductive for the foundation. If we give one business such an immense advertisement for their money, what would others expect? I met the chairman, Charles Lloyd Jones, at the annual Dobell lecture. He smiled at me with glee and said: 'Your letter doesn't worry us any more! Westfield withdrew anyway!' Next day during the sitting Joe said he would put up the money himself, but as a trustee, how would that look?

'Why?' I asked, 'it would be a fantastic example for the other trustees.

Rockefeller is also a trustee for the Metropolitan, that doesn't stop him supporting it.'

The same afternoon at the meeting, Joe gave $100,000 with no conditions. The biggest single grant the Gallery ever received. I said his firm's name should be, of course, on the catalogue. Just as opera sponsors appear in the program.

Tristan Antico recalled that once he sponsored an opera and fifty abusive letters arrived saying he is an Italian, that's why he likes opera and what right has he got to squander shareholders' money? 'We are a private company,' said Joe. I was so proud of him.

5 December 1981

My second year of judging the Archibald. The big prize money drew names we haven't seen for twenty years. Sali Herman sent a portrait of his wife, Wallace Thornton sent in to the Sulman (judged by Mervyn Horton), Lloyd Rees sent an Opera House to the Wynne. Eric Smith's portrait of Rudy Komon was by far the best portrait, no problems. The Wynne was difficult as Eric Smith seemed number one there, too, but competition from Brett Whiteley, Rees, Dunlop, Lynn, Colin Lanceley among others was fierce. As Kevin Connor and I kept coming back day after day the Whiteley lost and Eric Smith gained, Rees became a giant postcard, David Voigt advanced until his and Eric Smith's became like two horses racing neck and neck. We finally weighed the facts. Smith has already won the Archibald and the Art Gallery wants to buy his Wynne, so he has all this.

Besides, Voigt's was the more original work, clouds, horizons, scaffolded into sharp divisions, a bit of pushing the frontiers.

6 December 1981

János has had a professional haircut in order to be acceptable to the Rotary and RSL clubs where he goes to talk about saving rainforests.

24 December 1981

A letter came from Bill Reed saying he had resigned as publisher of Reeds, and that he feels this won't make any difference to my book. Next, a letter from John Reed, the director, saying that if he did not get the completed manuscript before Christmas, the launching won't be in October 1982, as planned. I replied by letter and telephone saying that the manuscript was completed at the end of November. He mentioned that the Blackman book had not even covered printing expenses, and 'we must review the situation'. He is aware a contract exists, but . . .

28 December 1981

It's still Christmas in Sydney and the holiday stretches for me like an endless strudel. Jack gave me a book to read: Robert Rosenblum's *Modern painting and the northern romantic tradition: Friedrich to Rothko*. He quotes from it quite a lot in his writing about my desert paintings. He writes, 'The tradition of the "pathetic fallacy" had consequences that survived long past the deaths of the great romantic landscape painters. Into van Gogh, whose words are no less appropriate to the early tree studies of Piet Mondrian, and later to Rothko.'

14 January 1982

The January issue of *Art International* arrived, in 'London Letter' is a review of my London exhibition by Edward Lucie-Smith. My *Composition with bush* is reproduced.

Raging controversy about the Archibald. On the first page of the *Herald* is a photograph of Rudy and the portrait by Eric Smith. There could be no doubt, he copied the portrait down to the shoelaces, angle of champagne glass, stripes of tie. Only the head seemed to have been painted from life (I hope). Bloomfield, from whom the prize had been taken because he confessed to have painted it from a photograph, wants his prize money back, with interest.

The Hogarth Gallery's Clive Evatt, who was reregistered as a barrister after thirteen years, decided, evidently, to fly back into the public eye on Bloomfield's wings and took up the case. Letters to the editor think that Archibald's will should be refashioned to suit our times. No one seems to even remotely understand the indefinable element that exists between the artist and sitter for which the photograph can't be a substitute.

28 January 1982

Bali

We are back in Bali and it's bliss.

We feel absolutely done in by 9 p.m. and are asleep by ten. We swim, read in deckchairs, watch coconuts being slashed off palms.

Yesterday we rented a taxi and drove to Bengali's rice paddies where I did three sketches—getting a craving for painting.

2 February 1982

We went to Kuta Beach to see Peter's hotel. Long before this, Jancsi, in one of his mellow and wise periods, said to me, 'You know, first I was annoyed at the amount of money Peter sank into this uncertain venture in a strange country. Now I see it as his dream. If it makes him happy, I'm happy.'

12 February 1982

Sydney

The minister for home affairs and the environment, Ian Wilson, rang me from Canberra. Would I be a trustee of the National Gallery (to be opened by the queen later this year)? A salary of $3000, all expenses. I declined. I am a trustee of our Gallery. 'I know,' said the minister, 'but we need you here and you could be more useful on a federal government level than on state.'

'Sorry,' I said.

I'm painting regular hours. The two large gouaches, desert shapes, for the Hungarian exhibition in Budapest are finished and I have three large ones for Rudy. The Greenhill Galleries rang and wrote requesting two exhibitions after Rudy's: in Perth and Adelaide.

13 March 1982

Auckland

I am in Auckland for two commissions. It evokes the old London days of portrait manufacturing. Except I am twenty years older now, and to conserve energy I haven't set a foot outside. Make breakfast, wash dishes, prepare coffee on a tray for the sitter, do my exercises. Paint two hours, make lunch, have a siesta, paint two hours, rest and read, have a bath, go to different people's houses for dinner.

I got two new commissions at the party Lois gave for me. Trish Horrocks and Sir Gordon Tait, admiral and chief of staff, second sea lord of Great Britain. I had to prolong my stay for two days to fit in all three.

At the vice-chancellor's dinner I met Robyn, whose husband is with an expedition sailing in South America 'caused by the male menopause'. I met a well-known endricrinologist who has been in Nepal, researching sherpas' goitres caused by lack of iodine in the water.

18 March 1982

The last day in New Zealand. I had my first free morning. I feel very happy, the three portraits packed, a job well done. Hairdresser, a few galleries with Lois. Found one of my 1964 Paddington pictures going on auction tonight. The reserve is $700. I asked Lois to bid up to $1000, not to let it go cheaper. I can sell it for about $2000 in Sydney.

I am carrying the admiral's decorations in the overnight bag, to paint them onto the portrait, like a still life. Also, Trish's pink frock. Having had to work the full five sittings on the face, I shall get a model to sit in for the sitter. The admiral's decorations drew a loud beep-beep at the airport's x-ray machine, the bag was opened and caused quite a commotion as they admired the Victoria Cross and other trinkets.

20 March 1982

Sydney

Peter had his first big capital gain. He has his eye on a property now in partnership with two of his buyers. Let's hope it goes through. May God bless my son.

27 March 1982

Bloomfield took legal action against the trustees to get his Archibald Prize (with interest). The portrait was painted from a photograph. We read the crown solicitor's letter of 1992 which leaves no doubts that copies are unacceptable. What will happen to Eric Smith's winner this year is dubious. We'll see.

31 March 1982

I went to see Donald Friend in his motel room at Bondi Junction, to do a sketch for a portrait. Like a Russian prince after the revolution, banned from his kingdom of palm groves and beaches and palaces and museums and servants. It was quite tragic to see him in the bedsitter. We talked for an hour, mentioning our friend, Paul Haefliger. This morning, Paul's obituary hit me. He died on Saturday, in Bern, of a heart attack. He was sixty-eight.

3 April 1982

The children have been here for the past week. There are things that disturb me but I won't utter a word. They worry me because I find it incomprehensible that an angelic little boy is not bathed every day and his hair washed every week. A toothbrush is out altogether. Why is this a desirable upbringing?

4 April 1982

I did utter a word. We sat in the living room and János said, 'Some kids grow up bilingual. Bodhi will have grown up in two cultures and will find both natural.'

'I am concerned,' I said, 'that he will be handicapped in our culture if in childhood he isn't automatically taught table manners. Is there a reason why you don't teach him to eat with a fork, brush his teeth and bath daily? Don't you think it necessary for him to learn to say thank you, hello, goodbye?'

According to them it's constant nagging that breeds resentment. These things of which I speak can be acquired anyway, if needed. We'll see.

9 April 1982

When János took Bodhi to Woollahra library to play with the great Lego building blocks, he came back saying what a shame the blocks lack people. 'We will go to the toy shop and buy a fireman, a postman, an astronaut, a workman and a foreman and give them to the library because children much prefer to play with blocks if there are people to go along with them.' So they did.

'What did the librarians say?' I enquired.

'We didn't tell them. We just left the little toy figures.'

Could it be that this kind of example is more valuable than saying hello and goodbye?

12 June 1982

Tonight is the opening of my one-man show at Rudy's. I have worked up to the last minute as usual, enlarged versions of the *Slope*, the *Tilt*, the *Omen*, the *Pilgrimage*, *Desert Shape with triangle* and new gouaches like *Shrine*, *Boulders* and *Grotto*.

When Peter came back from Bali he showed us photos of a girl he met. She is a nurse. Two weeks later Jenny arrived in Sydney and moved into Peter's house. We see very little of them. On Mother's Day they invited us for lunch. Peter surprised me with a kitchen gadget I have longed for, for a long time. If only he turns out one day to be as good a partner as he is a son!

Sali Herman and I have been on TV, talking about trees. The Kandinsky exhibition from the Guggenheim Museum in New York opened in the Art Gallery. Started the portrait of the chief justice, Sir Harry Gibbs. First impression of face, no bones, no lines, outer interests. By the grace of God, the face is, after three sittings, one of the best, most alive, scrutinising, slightly lopsided, intelligent faces for a long time. Only one eyelid droops, the nose is out of angle, the mouth is mobile and curls with fine curves.

To Canberra to see the High Court building and the National Gallery and lunch with the chief justice. I looked at all the other portraits of chief justices, mostly in robes and wigs and decided on the warm timber colour and full regalia. Jim Mollison's assistant, Bruce Dallas, was my guide through the unfinished National Gallery which will be splendid (the Tiepolo ceiling has the face of an air hostess).

Went to see Joy Warren's Solander Gallery (she wants me to exhibit next year). Couldn't resist and bought a storage box of an antelope horn from Lombok in Indonesia, with the Ramayana carved in it. Marina Finlay (whose mother, Marika, was my model before she was born) models for me again and I relish the Sunday mornings I spend painting the figure.

A new phase in my marriage. I am no longer furious with Jancsi for getting old. It's a new love I have for him, mingled with gratitude to God who has kept him healthy, virile, in full possession of his wits. I accept the crankiness as a symptom of age and refuse to be hurt by it. I don't react. I don't answer. I am firm about my independence, even if he accuses me of being a feminist. And I'm steadfast about the studio being my territory.

18 June 1982

Jeff Smart's retrospective last night. An ill-chosen opener, Laurie Brereton, minister for health. Most controversial as he wants to close Crown Street and Sydney Hospitals. Edmund Capon, in his introduction: 'For once he is opening something, not closing.'

Too much is happening again. Two sittings on a new portrait of Rapotec who is now frail and white. Starts well. Visited Donald Friend. He has created a giant book, written by hand, on beautiful watercolour paper. Each page is a delight. Figures, emus, legends, ex librises, Düreresque figures, erotica, talent spilling out richly. There would be five one-man shows in that book, done in the motel at Bondi.

24 June 1982

Rudy doesn't advertise in the *Herald* and people say they didn't know I had an exhibition. Simply not good enough. Just now I have more portrait commissions than usual and *one* brings in more money than a one-man show. And still, I feel very bad about this *good* show not selling, bad timing (Queen's birthday weekend) and no reviews.

The merry-go-round continues. Yesterday I went to Jeff Smart's lecture at the Art Gallery. It was good. I said beside Lou Klepac, with Donald Friend behind me. (His magnificent 'Journal' is now at the curator's office.) In front of me Leslie Walford. ('I couldn't get to Rudy's Saturday opening, and then things just got away.')

28 June 1982

Hal Missingham spent four hours here, we had so much to talk about. Brought a portfolio of sixteen lithographs to show us and some watercolours. Finished a bottle of red and forgave me for being a trustee. Before he came, I drove over to Rudy's where I had an appointment to meet Joe Brender. He didn't turn up. By now I'm not even surprised.

11 July 1982

Surfers Paradise

'Rescue Mission' Surfers Paradise. In our flat (called a suite) in the Iluka. The first morning after a bad night. The sea and the beach stretch in the infinite, they sparkle like a thousand galaxies, in turquoise and apricot. I am settling down for a fortnight's rest.

We visit Bodhi Farm often. János is called by his Hungarian name as there are several Johns on the farm.

We had a picnic in the now famous Terania Creek rainforest which János helped to become a national park.

New South Wales is now leading internationally in the preservation of rainforests and János is involved. Proud as we are of him, ah, to have a son following such a destiny. Single-minded, driven by passion.

Peter tells us he is lonely. There was someone for six months to say good morning to. He has a fish restaurant in the city and works non-stop in two places now.

Peter came to Bodhi Farm with us. Bodhi clings to him in adoration insisting he has two fathers. János is working in the vegetable garden naked as it's raining. Peter plays pick-up-sticks with Bodhi on the floor. Jancsi reads on the terrace. A carpet snake leaps into the wood box near the stove, and a butcher bird flies in for morsels.

I see a need for evaluating the old and the new Peter Kampfner. There is an imbalance, a royal attitude not yet consolidated. As he at last learned to appreciate himself and his qualities, he is swinging too far in the opposite direction. He behaves like a Swiss watch who can't tolerate all those alarm clocks around him. People grow up in leaps and bounds and sometimes leave parts of themselves behind on a lower plane.

Jancsi brought Bodhi his present: a two-wheel pushbike with a real bell. The box of Lego was judged as excessive and was given to the preschool.

The house at Bodhi Farm is lovely with its polished floor. Everyone takes their shoes off before going in, like in a Japanese home. There is a new fireplace in the corner, lovingly and efficiently constructed from a barrel which has been placed on a brick pedestal. Logs of wood burn all day. The wooden platforms have disappeared from underneath couches and beds, so as much as we enjoy the intimacy of the evening and early morning with them, we thought we might have to stay in the Lismore Motel next time. They can't appreciate what age does to us. It is uncomfortable to sit down or get up. My frequent excursions to the loo in the forest were also a bit nightmarish, distinctly lacking in humour this time. First, I put Greta's gumboots on, then opened the umbrella which has three of its metal spikes loose and it flapped noisily, and then there was an enormous spider under the plastic seat.

However, all was not macabre. At four in the afternoon the birthday party started. I kept busy helping Greta cutting sticks of celery. She baked five heart-shaped chocolate cakes. Bodhi wanted pink icing, so Greta boiled some beetroot and coloured the whipped cream with it.

Everybody arrived with quiches, strudels, dips and pastries, and the table groaned with all the food. Soon about thirty people and kids filled the room without pandemonium or irritation of any kind. When five or six boys started to play wildly, they were softly advised to play on the verandah.

Early in the morning we washed half-heartedly in the cold room, and after breakfast, still in the pouring rain we drove back to Surfers Paradise. János was attending a meeting about a demonstration somewhere, and away from their home territory and our own, relationships turn strained. It's a problem where to have dinner with Bodhi's non-existent table manners, their need for vegetarian food and János's principles about simplicity.

1 August 1982

Peter's tests were negative, but he has to go back to hospital next Tuesday for more tests. God knows the spot I have in my soul for that son of mine.

Peter and Jenny arrived at lunchtime. Peter still looks pale and ill, and though obviously relieved and armed with medication, he's still bewildered.

'You inherited it from me,' I said. 'You have to help yourself. You have to live with yourself. You are the only one who can break the vicious cycle. By ignoring the rumble, the nausea, by changing eating habits, by exercising a bit.'

5 August 1982

Peter is having more tests at the hospital. Days and nights of constant prayer. It seems he has inherited his neurotic tummy from his mother. I was his age when I went through a year of illness, weight loss, premonitions of death with physical symptoms like his.

8 August 1982

Perth

I am to ring Jancsi tomorrow to find out how both our sons fared. I have to work on myself daily, seriously, not to drown in guilt.

Golda Meir felt guilt. At the end of her life as prime minister of Israel she was asked if she would change anything she had done with her life. 'I would just stay on a kibbutz.'

With all my warmth I must have been criminally negligent, leaving my children each year for two months. It was not worth it. I would just stay in Sydney.

I posted a letter to Bodhi at the airport. I drew two Batman Bodhis in flight, coloured blue and red.

I didn't realise when I asked Hal Missingham to open my show what that would involve. He and Esther drove the sixty kilometres from Darlington and then sixty kilometres back.

'Today, no exhibition can be catalogued or opened without the artist's track record. So, I think I'll get rid of that one first.'

After that, he adlibbed and said, no one who has seen these paintings will ever look at the desert the same way.

The gallery is an old building, a minute away from the Esplanade where I stay with a view of the river. The exhibition looks really good in different rooms, uncrowded, under Gothic arches. One flight of stairs above is a room with a muslin baldachin as a ceiling, letting the skylight in. Clifton Pugh painted *Leda and the emu* on the main wall, there is 'graffiti' facing it on the other. I contribute by painting Ray Haymans of the university's gallery on it. Salek chose *Omen 3* for the university if other board members agree.

Interview. Visitors. *Tilt* is sold to Philip Low Davies, son of David, whom I painted. Louise arranged a large cocktail party for me at the house of a friend, Rod Kelly, an antique dealer. Spectacular house, exquisite taste, smell of money. Glass walls open on the river, a tropical garden full of orchids, a sculpture dancing on the edge of the pool reflected in the water beside the rippling moon. My giant abstract from the 1960s, *Dust in Derby*, hangs beside Brett Whiteley's giraffe and a Chinese-looking Pugh sits above antiques and soft-cushioned couches. Tulips in one vase, blue irises in the other. Ted, Rod's boyfriend, takes Cocky, the parrot, out of the cage and puts the bird on his shoulder like a falcon. It's faintly medieval. Paris, the cocker spaniel, begs for smoked salmon, Cocky drinks champagne. Rod strokes a huge white cat on his arm as he says, 'Ted was supposed to be a one night stand and stayed for twenty-five years.' Waiter in red pouring drinks, a hundred people, all invited to next day's opening.

Betty Boan, who married Bryan Canny, sent orchids to my hotel. Andrew Mensaros, the only Hungarian to become a cabinet minister, brought me a vase made of blackboy wood. Ken Evans, who works at the gallery, gave me a silver spoon carved as kangaroo paw, in a blue velvet jeweller's box. People are isolated here, and kind.

Excellent reviews the next morning. The final sentence: 'The exhibition is one of expected and sustained authority.'

11 August 1982

Sydney

I wonder how many people are so completely shut off from their childhood as we are. I treasure the memorial I got in Israel which has the synagogue on it, and the names, in Hebrew, of our dead family, killed in Auschwitz.

22 August 1982

I'm reading Peter Matthiessen's book *The snow leopard*, and find it delightful. He walks the Himalayas in search of this rare cat and the dangerous trip becomes a pilgrimage, a luminous journey of the heart. Leaving marks no one else could make, transcending the usual limits of language.

Although I got used to the slow pace of its travel passages, it's the spiritual content I find arresting, particularly when he writes about native American Hopis who avoid all linear constructions, knowing as well as any Buddhist that Everything is Right Here Now.

24 August 1982

I missed the Masterpieces from the Idemitsu Collection opening. I take an almost perverted pleasure in cancelling events, something that used to cause me pain. I have time to read the *Herald*; Frederick Morton's *A nervous splendour*, about the Vienna of 1888, in which Arthur Schnitzler is still a doctor. Hugo Wolff an unsuccessful lieder composer and Freud delaying greatness. Gustav Mahler was struggling to reorganise the

Budapest Opera. Bruckner abided in isolation. Klimt confronted his fresco on the ceiling of the new Court Theatre and called it *Schweinsdreck*.

31 August 1982

It seems Peter is suffering from a lactose deficiency. He is unable to cope with dairy products. I thank God. Peter is very relieved. He will now have to follow a dairy-free diet.

23 September 1982

Working again. I have tremendous difficulty shutting out forty-five years of portrait routine.

3 October 1982

The exhibition in Perth didn't sell well. Only four paintings. Veda Swain, of the Greenhill Galleries in Adelaide, asked me in a letter if I could add a roomful of figurative work for our show. So much for being praised for a 'tough, uncompromising exhibition'. Even *Omen 3* wanted by the university (which I agreed to let go at half-price) wasn't taken. Joy Warren of Canberra's Solander Gallery phoned. She has a landscape exhibition to coincide with the opening of the National Gallery. Could I send one? It was Jancsi's idea to have *Omen 3* flown from Adelaide to Canberra.

Yesterday I did a sketch of George Molnar in his flat above the harbour. I looked at his paintings, which are unique. An amalgam of a cartoon, an illustration, crammed with wit and literary content, and in spite of these things he is *almost* there. Some of them work as paintings, and the humour and caustic view of urban society doesn't detract. Then, sometimes, the literary content is a barrier but it's amazing that anyone can create art like this and get away with it.

Postmodernist. The word suggests that there is no longer any such thing as modernism and that a long series of historic achievements has therefore come to a halt. John Russell writes that modernism is several things in one—a body of work, one that extends from painting and sculpture, through architecture and design to music, dance, poetry and the science of human nature. It is, finally, an environment. Over the last hundred years it has penetrated every department of life in the developed world. What has been left out of modernism—illustration, storytelling, aesthetics, bad manners—is often fundamental to postmodernism. We are left wondering if there is not in the very notion of postmodernism an element of that vindictive philistinism that now permeates so many departments of our life. Is it not likely, we ask ourselves, that postmodernism stands for a dilution, a trivialisation, an end of effort on our part, and an undemanding easiness and smallness?

But creative people move at their own speed. They do not go to pieces when new names are touted. Degas lived through fauvism and cubism. Matisse lived through surrealism. The great artist is the one who makes nonsense of all the labels and seems during a working life to gather within the quintessence of art.

16 October 1982

In Canberra for 'Artist's Day' at the opening of the new National Gallery. A museum built from scratch must have enormous gaps, naturally. Like no Cézanne, Bonnard, Vuillard, old masters, unreachable. But there are two beautiful Monets, one of the waterlilies, for which I would have gladly made the trip. The Americans are given more importance than other contemporaries: Rothko, Gorky, Warhol, Rauschenberg. Brancusi's birds look out onto the sculpture garden where Rodin's *Burghers of Calais* glisten in the rain. It's like a big party at a friend's place. Meeting Rodney Milgate, Clifton Pugh, Frank Hodgkinson, Margaret Olley, Gisella Scheinberg, Rudy (on the same plane) who escapes. Caroline Williams with Georges Mora, years older but a sophisticated Frenchman. Rapotec.

Back home I had my first sitting with Anna Waldman, assistant curator at the Art Gallery of NSW. This has been brewing for months. Ever since she came with Clare Wadworth's eighteen-century portfolio I was inspired by her violently red hair and shocking-pink stockings.

János arrived yesterday. He went with Jancsi to the airport to fetch Greta and Bodhi who are coming home from Minnesota. I took Bodhi to the library. He chose some books. Played with a toy. Packed it back gently when he finished. We went to Rose Bay park. He now climbs everywhere, slips, skips, his old timidity is gone and he has confidence in his body.

'Do you want an ice-cream?'

'I stopped eating shit food.'

The whole day was just sheer joy with him. We then tiptoed in so as not to wake his sleeping parents, snuggled into my bed and read a book. Watched some cartoons.

For some reason I revisited a book of Sutherland's portraits. I pooh-poohed it before, the way he does precise sketches of his sitters, then squares them with a pencil, enlarging it on the canvas and painting it. Not from the sitter but from the sketch. I maintained for forty years that that's anathema to my temperament, that my excitement fizzles out if I have to approach it twice.

Perhaps it was again the material: the vehicle that takes me into the unknown. A few months ago a box of coloured pencils took my fancy. They can be dipped in water and then become aquarelles. And just a week ago George Molnar gave me a pen-brush that behaves like a cross between a felt-pen and a brush. Not needing the old studio light for this, I settled down in the living room where I originally observed Anna, with a trolley, jar of water, book, the pencils. Now the pencils have a virtue. They sing their own little colour tune. I am yellow, they say, I am red, brown, grey, blue. I can't get tonal with them.

Anna has shocking-pink legs in the sketch, she leans forward, hands dangling, carrot hair escaping in ringlets from her chignon. Molnar's brush bounces freely, pencils are pleasantly pure. I squared it in the next day. Squared in my crumpled canvas and enlarged on it. Put it on the floor of the plastic drop sheet, gave it a coat of thin acrylic in grey and a breeze of crimson. When it dried, I gave the couch an ochre-cadmium yellow. When that dried, the ochre got a coat of black which I know will behave in a brisk and porous flight into the wrinkles when settling down. After these preliminaries I started working on it as on my desert gouaches, using thin layers on the oval of the face, semicircle of hair, arms, giving a rhythm of light and dark, getting rid, at last, of my routine portrait handling.

When Anna came for the sitting, the painting was determined, and I drew more than painted the likeness in the face. Anna was stunned. 'It's brilliant,' she said. 'I know,' slipped out, and we both burst out laughing over my 'modesty'. It's a beginning.

19 October 1982

Adelaide

'Come and see my new life,' John Olsen said at my Adelaide opening. He lives, he said, at Aix en Clarendon. I arrived in the middle of the afternoon at what used to be an old rectory. It reminded me of Jancsi and my first home in Podhering, with its thick walls, small windows, a cross between Kaiser Franz Joseph, a peasant cottage and a Moorish castle. The balcony hangs over orchards ('We will build a swimming pool here'), a generous green hill dotted with cows, olive trees, and Noela's new lithographic studio, looking like a restored old building. Then we climbed into his Land Rover for a guided tour of his studios. In the centre of the village they took over an old stone building looking like a church which used to be the school of arts and Masonic Hall.

Fantastic space, like a football field. Noela Hjorth's printing presses occupy the front and create an environment. On one of them sits a headless sculpture with dried twigs sticking up its neck. Behind it, what must have been over a hardware store, four-foot tall, knife fork and spoon in a glass cage. Beautiful paper everywhere and Noela's small etchings really lovely, with bird woman, Dürer's *Icarus*, and above it Kingsford Smith, helicopter, butterfly, Boeing jet, insect, mythology mixed with technology. Looking very private.

John's palette is a huge sheet of glass and very messy. I saw he also puts a medium tone foundation on his canvas, but no painting was to be seen, they're all in Melbourne.

I cooked chicken while Noela went to pick up her ten-year-old daughter from the neighbours (her son is in a chess tournament in Hungary) and we settled down to chopping onions, capsicum and tomato, and cooking asparagus, spinach and hollandaise sauce.

'I am very happy with Noela,' he said. 'With Valerie, there was no balance with the yin and yang. She was vague and helpless and I acquired a macho image. Too masculine. With Noela, a revelation, I can free my feminine self at last! Do you want to see the sketchbooks from the trip to the Kimberleys?'

He went for two and a half months with Vincent Serventy and Mary Durack. The sketchbooks were like Donald Friend's diary: drawings of old stations, baobab trees, Aborigines, emus, kangaroos, rocks, mountains, pubs, pelicans, frogs. Notes beside the sketches. Hundreds of drawings with sepia pen, pencil, pastel, conté, colour pencil. I was really inspired.

23 October 1982

Sydney

I became a member of the Hakoah Club to use its heated indoor pool for my back's sake. I persist, but it's not easy to carve an hour and a half out of my daylight hours. The morning is my prime working time, so I go at lunchtime. This happens to be an unexpected blessing for Jancsi, too, who accompanies me and gets some exercise as well. Hair tucked under a cap I swim ten lengths (for a start) and we both feel virtuous and sporty. Then we have lunch in the bistro. I managed these excursions twice a week, till now. Wondering whether my exhaustion at the end of the day will lessen as I get used to the extra load.

28 October 1982

Wimbledon tennis courts, which have my portrait of Princess Marina, want a portrait of the Duke of Kent. When they asked him who he would like to paint it, he said Judy Cassab. It's absolutely incredible after so many years.

Rudy Komon died. He suffered a stroke and mercifully went quickly. He was a big figure and his loss sucked away tons of air, leaving us gasping. A lucky man. He died as he would have wished it. Living life to the full, at seventy-four still jumping on and off aeroplanes weekly, drinking and eating too much, boisterous, Machiavellian. Suddenly he is no more.

The memorial service at the Queen Street gallery was packed. All his Melbourne artists flew in. Neville Wran, John Brack and Lou Klepac (who taped Rudy) made speeches. Edmund Capon, quoting him with his 'Naturally, you see, bloody barbarians' which no minister of the church would have quoted. A plump Czech housewife who arrived in 1951, the same time as Rudy, told about him fishing in St Mary's in order to have something to eat for Christmas dinner.

7 November 1982

One picture sold in Adelaide. I had a letter from George Patterson's advertising agency offering me $30,000 (to give as scholarship to one or three young artists of my choice) if I go on television for Seppelt wines. Had to refuse, of course.

13 November 1982

My television program aired last Thursday on Channel 0's 'Personally Speaking'. It was very good but I looked a hundred and ten. Sometimes I notice in the mirror what a map life charts on one's face.

22 November 1982

We have possums in the roof and through the studio window. They tracked cadmium yellow oil paint across the floor and onto clips, tubes, brushes and, for good measure, there is Prussian blue all over the windowsill.

I was trapped in a lift at the Cosmopolitan but got home in time for Bill Templeman, the publisher, and Jack Lynn and the first glimpse at our book which looks splendid.

27 November 1982

Lou Klepac brought over Fred Genis, the master printer, to teach me lithography. He wants ten portraits of great Australians for a portfolio. Two enthusiasts, they keep coming here to see how I progress. Fred brought me a lithographic stone on which I drew a view of Jerusalem. Very characteristic of my charcoal drawings. My first try on a plate with the litho crayons was a drawing of Fred and Lou. He printed it and showed me. Then I did a portrait of Jancsi which has likeness, but is timid. Next week I go to Lloyd Rees who will be my first portrait for the book.

I am being catapulted into a new medium, into more work. What a blessing.

John Olsen and Noela came for lunch after her opening at the Stadia.

30 November 1982

Greta told me that János wants to leave Bodhi Farm. He is finding it too confining. He wrote from Tasmania. Greta tells me that János hasn't phoned or written yet. 'He needs to do that at present,' she says. Always loyal. 'Only Bodhi is missing his father.'

6 December 1982

The drawings of Lloyd Rees. On the plate, not so good. It keeps growing and looks too clichéd. The one on the transfer paper with hand to cheek, almost profile, gets nearer the promised land. I avoid tonal effect, scribble doodle in; linear fashion rather. Next day Robert Helpmann came and this time I did better on plate. I discovered the rhythm with which the lithographic pencil sort of hits the aluminium. It's a bit like hitting glue, forms a round dot where I start the line. Need to do ten more before I feel at home there. I'm conscious of '*was liegt, das pickt*'. No erasing possible. No overpainting. The concentration is fierce, and feel drained afterwards. My head trembles on the pillow.

Clare invited me to Ashkenazi's concert. Two Jews, I thought (himself and Mendelssohn) and two Hungarians (Bartok and Kodály), a heady mixture.

24 December 1982

Visiting Andrea in the Buena Vista Hospital. She is there because Dawn, her constant companion and nurse, has to have a holiday. I hear that all private hospitals are bursting at the seams. 'They put a stamp on me,' Andrea said in her rare illuminations, 'and posted me like a parcel. I woke up and didn't know where I was.' An hour later, sipping her coffee which stood on the table untouched for all time. 'Ice cold!' she said, disapproving. Next sip, 'ice cold' again. Our flowers (tribute to the old prima donna) were the only ones in the room. People forget.

11 March 1983

Age shows in unexpected ways. I feel no older than thirty years ago and don't care too much about how old I look. I am the same weight that I always was and give the same care to my body—exercise, swimming and after-dinner walks with Jancsi. I work as much if not more than ever. But there are now limits. Whereas I used to get a second wind, especially after the siesta, I translated my Hungarian diaries at night, played the piano, the guitar, and wrote in my diary, I can't do that now.

And as my days are full, I just realise with dismay that I haven't written since December. It needed a train journey to Newcastle and my fifth exhibition at Anne von Bertouch's to catch up with the last three months.

Lou Klepac who is publishing the portfolio of lithographs, *Great Australians*, used to be the assistant director of the Art Gallery of Western Australia. He now has the Beagle Press, and published portfolios of Donald Friend, Hal Missingham, and a book about Drysdale. An exuberant, handsome man, an enthusiast. Gets tears in his eyes when moved.

Fred is a master printer who worked in Europe and America, and had an exhibition in the Art Gallery of NSW. The Artist and the Printer. Pollock, De Kooning, Rivers, Rauschenberg, Tobey, all of whom he worked with. As soon as one of my drawings is finished, both Lou and Fred race in, it's taken and printed.

I have to go slow because this portfolio can't be launched before my book's launching, which, presumably, will benefit the great Australians. I started the series with Lloyd Rees, did two of Peter Sculthorpe (the composer), two of Sir Robert Helpmann, one of Donald Friend. It marked a return to drawing for drawing alone. I realised the difference between the thin and even (and therefore insensitive) line of a biro and the old-fashioned nib. The line can be as thin as a breeze or, when putting emphasis on it, it swells like a voice, erupts, drips, exclaims. I had grandiose plans to draw every day, but there is lead in my limbs. It will need a painting trip—Alice Springs or elsewhere, with no other activity.

I had a burst of enthusiasm to establish a big album, bound, of good paper, to draw and perhaps write, and stick in the loose drawings of past years. I realised there aren't many of these. I squared them, didn't treasure them. And it also needs time. Only on our weekly visits to Orban do I take ink and pen with the nasty thought of not wasting the day because his hearing is worse and so is his sight and now he rambles. When I start an 'Orban' for him, or finish one, I am his eyes, I thought. This is the end of him as an artist.

But a miracle happened. He complained that he can't see the paper and the line. That he can't see enough contrast. 'Dezsö,' I said, 'you know the black paper you used for thirty years when doing pastels. Try that again.'

I rang up Vitrex and had a dozen sheets delivered to him. That started a new outpouring of small masterpieces like the essence of what he is about. Clouds, shadowy tree forms, the hum of insects, the trembly lines of shrubs, an art disembodied.

I went to see Barry Pearce, curator of the Art Gallery of NSW, told him about the uniqueness of such art by a man who will be a hundred next year. Asked him to go and see the twenty works and give him a small show, possibly to coincide with the launching of his book by Gil Docking. He said the Gallery is booked out for 1984 but Edmund Capon could if he wants to, create space in the vestibule or elsewhere. Next board meeting I brought it up. Edmund said, 'No problem'.

Asher Bilu visited us with his third wife, Luba. He has done something never done before, painted on thin canvas with very thick enamel-like plastic acrylic, an enormous painting—30 metres?—then peeled the canvas off. What remained is visible on both sides, so he hangs it from the ceiling in loops, like a labyrinth through which people can walk.

Calls it *Maze*. Barry Pearce said it would interest Bernice Murphy of *Contemporary Art*. So I rang Bernice to say I saw the photos of this amazing environment and could she go to Melbourne and see it with the view of including it in Perspecta. She saw it. It's too large to fit in Perspecta but she talked to Asher and it will be exhibited in Art Space, a new gallery.

Orban rewarded me with two of the black pastel papers.

I drew nudes each of Marina. I tried the black paper with pastels and some good things happened—mottled as the canvases. Still, I didn't achieve the new figuration that eludes me still. I only came near when I did them on canvas, crumpled, very broadly and simply. Then they have the same style as the landscapes and that's really what I have to pursue.

Molnar's portrait became a companion of Anna Waldman's. One morning he arrived for the sitting with a cartoon he drew of me, painting. 'Judy, inspired,' he wrote. It's delightful. I attack with the brush, legs in a ballet step, hair flying, glasses slipping.

Just saw my exhibition hanging at Anne von Bertouch's mellow, spacious, church-like gallery. She is a wizard. Her grouping is wonderful. She was not mad about the desert shapes at Rudy Komon's (they don't sell easily, for sure), *she* chose the paintings in the studio. And as the recession hit Newcastle even harder than other cities, she wanted inexpensive small work. We chose about half a dozen of those I did for the book's limited edition. The studies of Marina. I thought it will be disjointed, but it isn't. A small head hangs in such a way that the ringlets of hair are a continuation of the desert shapes of the *Shrine*. And right beside the curves of *Reef* hangs *Lovers and arches*, looking as if it would be a plan for *Reef*. *Bush forms* spills over into the small *Palm grove*, and the white curved arm of *Two figures, sitting*. Thus, I learned about myself. Figures and landscapes are not as different as I thought.

Went to Paul Haefliger's posthumous show at the Holdsworth. It was a celebration. *Joi de vivre*, wit, delectable paint. Just when he made it as a painter, he goes and dies. We bought a painting as a final handshake to mark the end of a great friendship. When we took Jean Bellette out for dinner she said, 'Paul is around, nudging my elbow, playing pranks as he always does.'

Paul donated a beautiful Japanese screen to the Art Gallery of NSW, and left them other treasures in his will. Jean sent a Daumier to Sotheby's for auction, has a Cézanne watercolour here, a Rouault in Bern. But no other cash apart from the rent she gets for the flat in Elizabeth Bay.

When we deposited Jean in Edgecliff Road, I went to bed and had a vivid dream about Paul. I woke up with a start. A huge explosive sound. Put the light on. The blind ran up on its own volition. I had to climb on a chair to get the cord which wound itself round on top. Paul, I thought, playing pranks.

At the acquisitions and loans meeting last Wednesday there were two old Australian paintings for us to see. A Tom Roberts, of Circular Quay in the 1800s, a historic as well as artistic find, and a Streeton, of Coogee, at about the same time. The Streeton belongs to Charles Lloyd Jones who wants to auction it at Lawsons. He was expecting to get $120,000 for it. That's the $100,000 he pledged to the foundation. Capon would rather buy the Tom Roberts.

After the meeting I told Capon about Haefliger. That he was a benefactor of the Gallery and he should go to see the exhibition.

23 April 1983

Budapest

Trying to live like a tourist for some of the day. I always wake up grateful for the sight of the Danube, Buda and the bridges. We put our swimming costumes on and the fluffy white bathrobes provided by the Forum Hotel and get into the lift. The swimming pool is patrician. No blue water here—it's sparkling clean, blue-black surrounded with bronze to reach out to the castle and the grand view. We live in the shop window of Budapest, of course, the pearls around Hungary's neck.

27 April 1983

Szentendre was pure nostalgia, once again. Strange that, looking up at the window of our flat, memories don't connect with the sight. Spring is gorgeous. The chestnut trees burst into thousands of candles in the last week and the scent of lilacs brings back Arcadia: childhood and grandmother in Beregszász.

I get more confused with the passing days about the schism, the split, the manifold belongings of my life. Skyscrapers can never give me what the steeples of churches do as I look at them, silhouetted against the curve of the river. I shall always be a European.

I wonder if I have become less compassionate. More callous. Or did old friends become caricatures of themselves? When one is young, the self is cushioned and smoothed by the bloom of youth, by charm, or beauty, or sex, or attraction. By middle age it has half-melted away, leaving the self naked. What clings to that skeleton self is the true, unadulterated nature one is born with and has worked on or neglected. That's why most old people are cantankerous and twisted.

4 May 1983

Vienna

What a treat the new museum of modern art is in the Palais Lichtenstein. Contemporary sculpture in the vestibule—a giant Tinguely machine complete with the bowels of a grand piano. At the cafeteria four white plaster Segal figures sit at tables. This is the enchantment in Europe. Under Tiepolo ceilings, amidst marble columns and antique furniture, white Cupids flying, chandeliers, and baroque carvings are the Picassos, Légers, and all the other well-knowns. I must say that the Chamberlain crushed cars looked poor in it. So do grocers' cardboard boxes under perspex by Rauschenberg, and Warhol's skull.

Dubuffet is returning to what he started out with: art of the child or the insane. Baselitz with two splendid figures in the Schiele tradition. And 6 *Türen* are six nudes upside down. Very juicy painterliness. They don't gain, in my opinion, by hanging by their feet, only confuse.

A beautiful Fautrier, flowers in tissue paper, the paper taking three-quarters of the canvas. Then there is an assemblage cum environment. A wall-size photograph showing two people making love. It transcends into darkness which is a tank, soldiers in battle, death. Underneath are fifteen TV sets in which we discover our two walking images. The text: 'Determine the length of our electronic existence.' When you walk away you cease to exist. Ummm.

6 May 1983

We bought a whole Hungarian salami to take to London as a present. It can only be paid for in foreign currency. Ordinary mortals don't get veal either, that's for the restaurants. True, all my friends have a friendly butcher who can be bribed. Bribery is a fact of life throughout the system. Another fact is that I wouldn't have dared to record this in my diary before leaving the country.

10 May 1983

London

Esmé's flat at Swan Court where we are staying is ideal. The bed was dangerously soft for my back, so I put a mattress down on the floor. The skylight is ideal for a studio.

The day before the first sitting with the Duke of Kent, a detective came to inspect the flat. He showed us his card (police) at the door. Yesterday the duke walked in with a big smile, 'How wonderful to see you again,' he said. 'It's eight years.'

The canvas from Sydney with my mottled underpainting of yellows, ochres, oranges and a warm grey was becoming a presence.

14 May 1983

On the third sitting, after many Your Royal Highnesses in the conversation, the duke said, 'Oh, please (as in for heaven's sake) call me Edward!' The person on the canvas has authority. He worries. He is elegant.

23 May 1983

St Maximine

I had no problems with the way the duke's face was progressing. I got a bit bogged with the grey suit. Painting it at first with rounded, full brushstrokes didn't work with that noble head. As I toned down the spots which 'jumped' it started to come closer to the vibrating background.

Michael Servaes invited us for dinner, and asked, 'Well Judy, when are you having your next London exhibition?'. He seemed to drop me completely after my 1981 show and I was convinced he had given up on me.

'I know you have many commitments,' he went on to say, 'but after two good London shows, I think you have to keep showing.'

My commitments: Perth, Adelaide, Canberra. I am so relieved to be asked. I think I knew for a long time what I wanted, but somehow shirked it, procrastinated. I want the crushed canvases, luminous landscapes and undefined figures. How many have I done the last year? What have I done?

30 May 1983

We are flying from Nice, driving from Avignon. From St Raphael right up on the Corniche to Cannes. No rooms anywhere. By late afternoon I was grateful to be able to place the car inside the courtyard of a pensione and myself on a bed. I feel as if I am in Alice Springs, but it will do for one night.

3 June 1983

Without our overwhelming passion for art, the Riviera wouldn't be what it used to be. Peace only lives aloft. Vehicles zoom so close one is almost sucked into their vortex. A lethal new breed of biker winds in and out of traffic lanes.

11 June 1983

Los Angeles

I kissed the good little Renault goodbye in Nice and checked in at Schiphol airport. It is strange to witness a manmade object chasing the sun. After the clean efficiency of Schiphol, Los Angeles is a nightmare. Nobody gives any information. Home soon.

19 June 1983

Sydney

Diarrhoea plus laryngitis arrived with the precision of a Japanese train, the day I came home. For eight weeks, no cold, no tummy trouble, that's nice. Maybe nature wants me to rest now. It was a holiday, true, but I still drove 1200 kilometres on French roads and painted thirty-four pictures. So, maybe it *was* a strain.

Peter was there to meet us. Greta and Bodhi rang. János has gone to the Solomon Islands. A letter from the premier asking me to serve another term as trustee of the Art Gallery of NSW. I start my second term by not appearing at the board meeting. The television fused, burning out five tubes. The car has a flat battery. A new cleaning lady begins on Tuesday. The place starts having a soul after two strange days. Mountains of mail.

29 June 1983

Greta and Bodhi have come and gone. Bodhi is like an addiction to me. I fill my eyes and soul with the sight of him. I am depressed by the emptiness he leaves behind.

1 July 1983

Andrew Lostia, now nineteen, brought eight-foot canvases to show me. His last year at tech. He is so good, my heart jumped. On Sunday, he came to do my foundations. He earns some money doing it. Good for both of us.

I had a letter from Wimbledon. The duke decided he doesn't want an unveiling ceremony. But everyone admires the portrait.

3 July 1983

János came back from the Solomon Islands. He told Bodhi about children who don't have enough food and clothes. Bodhi has now decided that he only wants the dragon game for his birthday. The money not spent on bigger toys will be spent on clothes for the children in the Solomon Islands.

12 July 1983

The painting I donated to the Art Gallery Foundation (*Dusk at the Marbles*) was auctioned together with a hundred others. Jancsi was worried about my reputation. What if it goes for under $200? It was bought for $1700 by Max Sandow.

20 July 1983

We saw the Whiteley exhibition this afternoon. If I were Capon, I couldn't have denied Brett this show either. Whiteley is a genius. A fifteen-year obsession with van Gogh. On a colour photograph of himself, he painted out the face with the mad eye of Vincent, the cut-off ear and the swirls, and titled it, *Getting quite close*. So he is. Inventive he is too. There are three pairs of Vincent's eyes, which is something I have done for fifty years, but it never occurred to me to handle it this way. I bow before great talent.

25 July 1983

I have always been blessed with being a believer. As I get older, I believe in the power of prayer even stronger than before. I always thank God for all I have been blessed with. Even when I'm in a bad phase in life, after that I am able to see clearly and in proportion.

30 July 1983

Beagle Press's portfolio. After Sutherland, my next subject is Tom Keneally, whose *Gossip from the forest* I read and enjoyed years ago and who, this year, won the most coveted award for fiction, the Booker Prize, for *Schindler's ark*. I bought the book and I'm halfway through. It's marvellous.

1 August 1983

Ninety-two small paintings are finished. I spend more time in the studio now than ever before. No small children to mind, no household to run, no cooking. FM radio is stereophonic and I get tremendous pleasure out of listening to the Vienna Philharmonic or Ashkenazi playing Chopin etudes. I cut my cigarette consumption to five a day—better than to give up completely—it's one of the enjoyments in life. It's with late morning coffee that I smoke the first cigarette and Jancsi comes in. But only for a little while. I have achieved solitude while working.

4 August 1983

Still coughing. Bronchitis taking a long time. When I was a teenager in Beregszász, *Nagymama* tried to cure it with tea of sweet corn. And Máli néni peeped through the door of the salon and said, 'Poor child. I know a person who died of bronchitis.' Apropos death. Kati told me in Budapest that her main prayer now is, 'Please God, let me keep an intact body and a sane mind while I'm alive. And when my time comes, please let me die quickly and easily.' Since then I have made her prayer mine.

When I was about six, I used to implore a doctor friend: 'Bandi, I shall never, never die, shall I?' And he reassured me I never would. Death was unmentionable, unbearable, unspeakable, till middle age. It isn't any more.

Thomas Keneally came for the sitting. He is a pixie, a merry gnome,

electric globes light up his face while he talks. Catching an early plane
to Melbourne didn't make for a satisfactory whole sitting but at least
he returns next week.

Yesterday the first proof of my book arrived from Macmillan's Bill
Reed in Melbourne. I have not seen anything like this before. When I
opened the crate there were twelve sheets of shiny paper with 169
colour reproductions of my paintings. Each was clipped together with
seven other sheets with the same reproductions in yellow, blue, crimson,
black and white, then transposed onto each other until they mixed into
the real thing.

Bill rang me and said, 'Try not to strive for a true colour matching.
Just look at each one as a picture. Sometimes they are more dramatic
than the original. When the book is published, this year or next, depends
on how many you have to reject and send back to Japan.' I was
determined not to find faults in them. Unfortunately there is such a
riot of neon strong reds that it upsets the balance of colour. Also, of all
things, the portraits are often insipid, without contrast, veiled under a
film of magenta or Indian yellow, like a kitsch sequence in a film. I
spent two days sorting out which transparency belongs to which
reproduction. Removing sticky tape, covering two rooms. Like Cinderella
sorting the peas from the lentils.

9 August 1983

Thomas Keneally sat for the lithograph again. I finished it in an hour.
Jancsi came to have coffee with us in the studio and Tom started to
explain the fight of the Irish. While he forgot about me I did a second
drawing, a quick one, in almost profile and almost shadow with only
his nose and bald head in the light. A good drawing. Lou Klepac arrived
to meet Tom. They had a verbal fencing session the likes of which one
doesn't often hear. I wish I had switched the tape recorder on. I thought
of it but it seemed somehow tactless.

8 September 1983

Alice Springs

The magic works again. On my fifth day here I have nine large canvases
and five small ones for the book.

9 September 1983

Rented a four-wheel-drive Toyota. Mona got the gear: sleeping bags, food, table, chairs. We are back at the mushroom, surrounded by the sheep and camel heads, biblical groups, lit in incredible orange. Sand is deep. The flies are bad. Jancsi and I sleep in the Toyota. Mona sleeps under the stars. The desert is flowering in blues and pinks, with masses of yellow mimosa and the constant presence of desert oaks. Behind me is the great lizard, climbing up into burnt-flame sienna. The swallows' nests inside the mushroom are occupied by zebra finches. Surrounding us are shapes of my Paris exhibition. It's 6.30 p.m. We gather firewood, get the fire going, eat steak with a slight flavour of tea-tree.

12 September 1983

Jancsi says his feet had cramp during the night, and that really, eighty is too old to stomp around in deep sand in the dark of the night. It felt like Arctic exploring, except it was hot. The sand was like deep snow and very tiresome to walk in. And walk we did, countless little trips carrying easel, chairs, boards, the roll of canvas, the esky with our food, the fly spray (useless), kleenex, camera, film, cardigans for the extremely cold morning and night, and a lifesaving and indispensable drum of drinking water.

I am afraid that Mona was the work horse. She drove, and heavens, was I glad I didn't. She trusts the car. I wouldn't have. She grew up in the centre, knows where to make a fire, which way the wind blows, which animal's tracks we see crisscrossing our camp, how to load a car, which side of the ancient, prehistoric marble will be lit by the sun at what time.

I photographed about sixty shapes. I find slides useful when time is insufficient and circumstances impossible, as mostly they are. I managed two canvases. Early morning when it was crisp and cool I pinned a yellow underpainting on the board. After a squall sent it flying over the sand, Jancsi assisted by holding the easel firm. Accompanied by his: 'You don't want to learn', 'Don't rape the painting,' and 'Why do you fiddle?' 'Get a big brush and attack!' Flies all over the oil paint, stuck and buzzing, penetrating my ears, eyes, until tears dripped down my sandy cheeks.

16 September 1983

A day's rest after that excursion meant only a short drive out of town. Shopping at Eager Beaver's supermarket, lunching on yogurt, capsicum and radishes, a swim in the icy pool, a sleep in the afternoon. Then out to the old telegraph station. Those cairns of round, red, giant pebbles, hill behind hill in the spotlight of the evening sun.

Next evening we were off in our Falcon to spend a night at Glen Helen Lodge with the prospect of painting in Ormiston Gorge. A new road is built and it's approachable now without a four-wheel drive.

The wind was against me once more. I used three metal clips to hold my paper palette down, and Jancsi held onto the board which wanted to sail away. Sand got in the camera, the biro, and crunched in the sandwiches. When I finished the desperate battle with the elements and the painting, I started to take it off sideways by removing drawing-pins inch by inch.

The lodge has not changed. Three beds and nothing. Communal showers and toilets at the end of what looks like army barracks. No grass grows and no trees offer any shade.

Ormiston was a flop, but on the way back I painted three large canvases of the *Dancing Lubras*. This was a hundred kilometres from Alice. We marked the spot and returned the next day. Another three canvases, back in the afternoon I swim and collapse into bed, shivering. Nineteen canvases, six oils on paper. As I roll them into the parcel, Jancsi remarks that I could become a member of the storemen and packers union.

17 September 1983

Sydney

We returned earlier than planned to spend Yom Kippur at home. We had our chicken yesterday on the plane, not really orthodox. But I lit the candles, and next morning disappeared to conjure fresh coffee, warm poppy loaf, butter and milk to break the fast. I pray and I sleep like a convalescent, on and off all day. It must have been a bloody endurance test. Nobody knows we are here except Judge Raine who collected our mail. A rare luxury, to be at home, incognito.

19 September 1983

I'm catching up with the August board meeting. It *is* very exciting to sit in the centre of things. The Art Gallery of NSW is a recipient of a house and five acres near Bowral on condition it's used as a regional gallery. Because of lack of money to set it up and employ staff, we have to decline the bequest.

I really enjoy the acquisitions of the Asian department as Edmund is a world-renowned expert and I know nothing. This time he wants the *Six immortal poets* by a group of Hokusai pupils. Then *Birds and flowers 1855, Kakemono,* colours on silk by Kiitsu, really good example of the Rimpa school.

We bought a John Walker, whose paintings were the highlight (in my opinion) of the last Sydney Biennale where he showed infantas a la Velazquez without the infanta. This is a triptych and I, with Kevin Connor, had a hell of a time 'selling' the acquisition to Max Sandow who likes Eric Langker. A Mrs Palmer gave us an Arthur Boyd painting, *Nebuchadnezzar on fire falling over a waterfall,* done in the late 1960s when Boyd was in his prime. Patrick White gave us five paintings, among them a Rapotec, three Whiteleys. Haefliger's gift of a painting from the Ming Dynasty in the sixteenth century.

28 September 1983

On the way to visit Andrea, while I was getting the Commodore out of the garage, I fell and broke my arm. One reads about these things— it did happen in slow motion, I slipped and time stopped. The fall was inevitable, my sunglasses were shattered, my watch and bracelet broke. The pain almost made me faint. Jancsi had me in his arms, kissed every inch of my arms, my skin like ice, cold sweat, the hand protruding in a funny angle.

The doctor came, and within half an hour I was in St Vincent's.

My one-man show in Canberra opens day after tomorrow. The Hungarian ambassador phoned, he will pick me up at the airport. Jancsi is coming with me as I can't dress or wash. I phoned Joy Warren today, warning her that I'm arriving with a husband, a sling, and an ambassador. I feel crushed and weak.

21 October 1983

At the board meeting, Max Sandow, who went to China with a group guided by Edmund Capon, told us about the opening of the Australian exhibition in Peking. It was the first time that a 'round-eye' had made a speech in Chinese, and it brought the house down.

I proposed Jim Spigelman as vice-chairman and it was accepted unanimously.

28 October 1983

János and Bodhi came back from Canberra. They both had lice and had to have a long hairwash session with lice killer. A rare event for both. We took Bodhi to the airport, he flew home alone.

Greta wrote. 'One of the few clouds over my world is my relationship with János. I say that not to make you worry, but I do want you to know how things actually are and not pretend all is well when it's not.'

János is changing. He says one of his changes is that he is no longer 'labour oriented'. Others can work the vegetable patch. He saves rainforests. He cares about the planet. In Canberra he rented a video camera and shot about four hours of the anti-uranium demonstration. János spends his days at the Institute of Technology cutting it down to a twenty-minute documentary. He brings friends over. They drink tea, and not being labour oriented he just wants to walk out the door leaving the dishes for me to wash with one hand. I called him in and simply said, 'I don't want to wash your dishes.'

'I'll do it Juci.'

I also said today at breakfast: 'Yesterday at the airport as we waited for you to park the car I saw you from a distance as others might see you. A middle-aged hippie. Your hair is like a mop, your beard too long. I see you taking showers but it doesn't show. You set yourself a huge task and people should be able to take you seriously. It's a typically Jewish characteristic, you know, this chameleon thing. In Hungary, the Jews tried to play noblemen and sang gypsy songs louder than the Hungarians. German Jews had crewcuts, wore pince-nez, square shoulders and were more pedantic than the Germans. In that crowd around Parliament House no one had longer hair and beard or looked sloppier than you.'

He looked thoughtful, not off-handed. 'I shall wear a rubber band around my long hair,' he said.

'Not cut it?'

'Oh no. I want to grow it longer. But it's all right you mentioning it. Once a year.'

With a sidelong glance and a sweet smile.

5 November 1983

It is Jancsi's eight-first birthday. Tomorrow we will have a birthday dinner at the Hakoah Club. Jancsi was glad it's a twosome. We looked at the band and at couples dancing and Jancsi said, 'How beautiful you are. With your decadent, fine face.' So we came to talk of Anyu, and of Ami and Pista and Gyuszi and of Apu—and suddenly I thought—he is my mirror, he is the only witness who knew them all. My only link with a lost world.

11 November 1983

Dr Cass took the plaster off my arm and placed it in the garbage can. Then I had an x-ray. Dr Cass looked at it, said, the position of the bones is good but the bone hasn't knitted properly. Now I have a plastic plaster which is much lighter. Another month. That will make it eleven weeks. I am constantly exhausted and don't sleep well.

20 November 1983

There is a deluge of art books on the market. Orban's is to be launched next month. Lou Klepac brought me his *Drysdale* as a present (I can only read it at a desk it's so heavy). Then, there was Robert Klippel's exhibition and launching at the Art Gallery of NSW. The book is written by James Gleeson. Beautiful but $225 and even heavier than the Drysdale.

27 November 1983

My grandson's first letter, what delight! He made me do what I never did. I used my imagination on a blank white paper. The waterfall cascades down, leaving a white presence out of which only two hands are visible, beating a heart-shaped drum with other small red hearts floating.

The Art Gallery gave a dinner in honour of the departing president of the board, Charles Lloyd Jones, and vice-president Sir Tristan Antico. There were only forty people, all of whom I knew.

At the table, Joe Brender was seated on my left, Edward Obeid, a Lebanese, on my right. They talked eternal friendship across me. One a Jew, one a Lebanese. Ed has nine children, all with dual citizenship.

Today we celebrated Orban's ninety-ninth birthday at Kathy Macarthur's harbourside home in Castlecrag.

3 December 1983

Dr Cass cut the plaster off, but I have to wear a bandage for another two weeks. I marvel at the fragility of bone and muscle and skin. It looks like a dried fish. It's thin where the plaster was and bulbous beyond that. It trembles and the wrist won't move.

I will cancel my show at the Holdsworth. I had to tell Gisella Scheinberg. I went to see her in the gallery while Jancsi waited outside, I said the broken arm was a setback and I would not be ready with the show in April. Also, we planned a trip from then on. Gisella has a wedding next Sunday (her daughter's) and went on crocheting grey yarmulkes with pink edges for the groom's attendants.

'So what', she said, 'if an artist isn't ready, the show can't be on, can it? And Albert wants to travel, too.'

10 December 1983

The first day of the selection of Archibald and Wynne paintings was a marathon, from nine to five. When I came home to pick up Jancsi to go back to the city for Orban's book launching and exhibition, I didn't even bother to change my sweaty clothes. There he sat in his hundredth year, signing the $65 books, going for his life.

This morning there was a twenty-minute segment on television about the Archibald, the board included. 'Thirty seconds for each picture,' announced the wretched woman on the screen. Nigel Thomson said, well, it's $10,000. He will buy better and dearer whisky if he wins. Frank Hodgkinson painted three Thomas Keneallys with three cadmium red pullovers playing billiards on three green tables. Keith Looby's David Combe seems to have great presence, but I don't think he has a chance, after Combe's Royal Commission scandal which accuses him of endangering national security with the KGB. Tuesday we were back working through the rest of the entries. Saturday afternoon I picked my top five and I go back tomorrow. Judgement day on Friday. Thirty seconds a picture, eh?

14 December 1983

As I was walking along the already selected entries in dim light, propped against the wall choosing my five, my first choice for the Wynne is the Juniper. My second is the Rankin, a loose-brushed, freeflowing abstract with reeds and water. The Juniper has a design, which the Rankin lacks.

17 December 1983

At the judging yesterday, Kevin Connor, Denise Hickey (who has a degree in fine arts) and I voted for the Keith Looby. My second choice, Margaret Woodward, came far behind. The head in the right top corner of a ten-foot canvas, the rest is a bourbon-coloured pond. Max Sandow: 'I am not a patriot, but I am a good Australian. Combe can't be placed in the limelight after endangering national security. Besides, the fingers are sausages, the thumbs are badly drawn!' I wanted to tell him about Léger's tubular hands.

The majority voted for Nigel Thomson's Channy Coventry. I am the spokesperson. Michael Gleeson White said: 'Could we ask Judy Cassab to explain, why she feels so strongly against the Nigel Thomson?'

'Firstly,' I said, 'because I'd like us to be a board blazing a trail towards the twenty-first century, not one which is stuck in the nineteenth. I consider this choice a retrogressive step. I don't see a transformation of nature here, only imitation. What one could read into it is its literary content, not form, colour, or presence. Channy had a stroke two years ago and there is this stricken figure in a wheelchair in this clinical surrounding in the empty gallery with empty walls.' We were outvoted. Kevin asked the chairman not to say the choice was unanimous, because it wasn't.

Another unfortunate coincidence. Lawrence Daws, who judged the Sulman Prize, gave it to the same Nigel Thomson for a *copy* of David's famous painting *The death of Marat*. Terence Maloon, in the *Sydney Morning Herald*, amazingly didn't know that it was judged by someone from outside. He wrote: 'I find the jury's interest in this work completely unfathomable. To a conservative jury, old master copies are possibly the acceptable face of popism. Originality, creativity and dash do not seem to have counted much for the judges.'

We have enough to take the blame for, I thought, without having to take it for someone else's judgement. I rang Michael Gleeson White and drew his attention to it, suggesting that he sends a correction into 'letters to the editor'. He sounded cool and guarded, then relieved that this was the reason for my call.

The watercolour prize went to Elwyn Lynn. I liked the picture but it was Kevin who picked it.

24 December 1983

Christmas has always been a violent time for us since we arrived in Australia. Is it our genes missing the snow, fir trees, sleighs, and choir of village children? Instead we get heat, humidity, ruthless honking drivers, drunken traffic, crowded shops, mothers wrestling with turkeys.

26 December 1983

Orban is talking his autobiography onto our tape recorder. He started his recollections at four. The flow of beautifully constructed sentences did not step until the tape clicked off at the end of thirty minutes. I replayed last year's tape and told him what he said so there is no repetition. That time he recalled his arrival in Australia and his first exhibition. 'Next Thursday,' he said, 'bring another tape. I'd like to sing my old cabaret songs.' His voice is hoarse, but his brain is unimpaired. And he wore a white T-shirt with a giant red ninety-nine in front. Old hippie.

30 January 1984

János, Greta and Bodhi stayed with us for two weeks. János used the living room as his office before leaving for the US. The desk sagged under the weight of all the publications. My typewriter gave up the ghost. The overflow soon covered every inch of the floor.

János had a haircut and trimmed his beard. For customs I presume. Bodhi has his ear pierced and wears a small earring. We make no remarks.

Peter was asked by Hookers to lecture about how to negotiate. I was proud.

I am really looking forward to a holiday in Bali.

6 February 1984

Bali

At last we found our rhythm. Late and luxurious breakfast, abundance of tropical fruits. Mangoes, lichees, rangustans, papaya. Rest of the morning at the swimming pool and a dip in the sea.

We now have a car and a driver. He picks us up and I realise slowly what I want. Certainly no temples, no rice terraces, but the same graceful groups I so much enjoyed in New Guinea. Always careful now not to have fingers, toes, features, just brushstrokes, and less of those than a representation needs.

7 February 1984

Our walks take us through this jewel of a garden to the swimming pool where some intoxicated young men cool themselves by diving in. A guitar plays in the fish restaurant. We take the black, polished wooden bridge over the sand to the beach, then on the promenade along the sloshing, lapping waves lit by Indonesian lanterns. The way 'home' is also quite a walk, through the hibiscus court into our frangipani court. Pyramid shapes of the hotel alongside bridges in lush vegetation. There are ceramic saints on both sides wearing fresh red hibiscus in their ears every day.

12 February 1984

It's awesome, but I have fifty-six oil sketches and half a dozen large gouaches in the white stage, not to mention a book of drawings. Considering that I can't use them in the Rainbow Valley series and that I vowed I won't paint ever again for the pleasure of Mrs Brown or Mrs Smith, I don't know why they exist. But they are mine, done in a burst of creation and to hell with consequences. My final aim, in the long run, would be a style of such force that it would tie together the landscape and the figurative. Have not yet been able to achieve it for sixty-three years, will I ever be able to? I think so. The minute that an arm becomes a curve (without an elbow, wrist, shoulder) as well as a chin, a calf and a hip, the elements of picture-making are there.

I liked our second week. After breakfast we swim. We walk through the sand to the ocean where we sit in silky armchairs, watching windsurfers, Mount Agung if it's visible, and spidery-looking catamarans.

The language around us changes every few days. Each afternoon we carry gear into the waiting air-conditioned car. Yesterday we drove to a building site where most of the work is done by women. They carry heavy loads on their heads, arms supporting it, they move, bend, squat and, by now, I only need them as a trigger. I didn't use any Balinese shapes to embellish the scenes.

16 February 1984

Mount Lynton, New Zealand

Just unpacked, packed, and flew to New Zealand to do two portraits. Alistair McGregor is the first. Alistair has 25,000 acres (is that the size of Belgium?) of sheep and cattle. He is invited for the summer to an agricultural conference in Hungary!

I devastated the drawing room. Heavy tables and couches were moved to accommodate my easel, model and me.

The landscape is mind-boggling–emerald and sap, and Prussian blue-black snowcapped mountain peaks. Strategic nets of fences house 130,000 sheep. Cattle wobble flatly in different locations. Deer are separated into special areas. Alistair flies a helicopter above them, shoots a net which catches them and deposits them where he wants them.

20 February 1984

I worked, more or less, all day. It had to be finished in four days. Alistair sat two hours in the morning and again in the afternoon. To achieve my transparencies and textures, I printed the wet oil paint with newspaper, and then painted orangey reds on top of blue-greens. After painting this down, I got almost a more seductive quality than with my crushed canvases. The sliver of blue-green worked as a keyhole in the reds. One looks through it on sky and trees.

I had bad nights, sleepless hours and anxieties, but it's finished today.

I saw around the station, the park is so vast that I didn't see the swimming pool until we reached it. Behind the ancient oaks and poplars is an alley of birches, a circular drive, and a huge vegetable garden.

Lots of horses in the stable, fifty sheepdogs, and a Jaguar, a Volkswagen and Land Rover in the garage. The helicopter lost its tail in a flood rescue operation and is sorely missed.

22 February 1984

Auckland

The stars seem to be less kind on this trip.

23 February 1984

Plodding along. Sometimes I think I chose such a difficult way to earn money. Lady Hellaby's stunning aqua eyes look like fish eyes, the likeness isn't as good as I would wish it to be at the second sitting.

25 February 1984

A really bad day yesterday. The third sitting produced absolute impotence and agony. No likeness that I could see. Nose out of angle. Eyes staring. It looked tortured and had no freshness. I had to pretend all the while that everything was fine. When she left I was shaking. Even the colour was muddy. Where I put dark tone it wouldn't go dark, and the lights were murky. I panicked. How can I hand such a portrait over? And take the money? I spent so much fruitless time over that sitting that the dress and hands were not progressing. After a little while I brought the easel into the bedroom where the mirror is. *Shlepped* in the same table, the palette, the horrid canvas. Put on Dawn's dress, and using myself as model, painted a mouthwatering velvet coat. Even the hands got blocked in.

Then I talked to myself. 'You have been in worse situations,' I was telling myself. 'When Queen Sirikit didn't go so well. And Princess Marina. You have two whole days to get the wretched likeness. Paint over the bloody pupils, start again, you can do it!' I prayed, took a pill and went to sleep. I was up at 5.30 when it was still dark, fretting again. Diarrhoea followed as a matter of course. Somehow, with God's help, it started to come alive today, the fourth sitting, but she is a shining beauty and *that* the portrait is not. But it's a huge relief and I thank God I'm back on the path. One must never never take talent for granted.

26 February 1984

The fifth sitting made it all worthwhile. It's incomprehensible how after fifty years of portrait painting, I could miss the angle of the centre! Even on this last sitting I had to push a nostril into place, and the groove between nose and lips, and this necessitated moving the crease at the corner of the mouth and therefore the line of the cheek had to be narrowed. After I had done all this there was, of course, a goitre, as the neck didn't fit and when that was done, the shoulder had to be drawn. I don't know how I got through it. It's a good portrait now but the agony of it!

10 March 1984

Sydney

Portrait commissions all at once after a six-month hiatus. Rita Lizak, blonde, efficient, manager of Guest Hotel, de facto of Alan David.

Hope my back behaves. Pete Hammerman brought a photo of Bernard, old friend and neighbour of Weeroona Avenue, our first abode. On Friday the television crew drives from the end of Ocean Avenue to the bay. I sit on my field chair, palette on the stone balustrade. They film the underpainting and follow the sketch of hills, roofs, trees, sea.

Neville Wran, the premier, announces elections six months early. He wants the opposition to put up or shut up about corruption. The election date falls a day before he is due to launch our book. He cancelled, which was to be expected, and Sir Robert Helpmann agreed to substitute.

22 March 1984

There are two functions this afternoon. George Olszanski's posthumous exhibition at the Holdsworth, and Shay Docking's book being launched by Edmund Capon at Barry Stern's.

I panic and stay awake all night. Next day the taxi truck takes the paintings to be exhibited at my book launch. As a backdrop, so to speak. Only twenty. They have to be catalogued. Chosen. Prepared.

7 April 1984

There was a queue to the corner of Jersey Road. Six hundred people signed Gisella's visitors' book, but according to her 800 came that day. The limited edition sold out. Nadine Amadio (writer of Charles Blackman's books) wrote a good review in the *Sunday Telegraph*, and after Neville Wran won the election, everybody watched Channel 9's 'Sunday' program. Wran, Peacock, election talk, preceded the profile of me.

All I can remember of the launching is a mosaic of the incredible crowd. The Hungarians turned up, the Australians, the trustees, Edmund Capon, the curators. Helpmann looked elegant in black, said, 'I am not used to being an understudy' which brought the house down. Bill Reed made a speech and Jack spoke to sum it up. Bill, who phoned from Melbourne to invite me for lunch after the launching, disappeared. So, no lunch, which was just as well as Macmillans had an advertisement in the *Australian* with 'Meet the artists at 1 o'clock', so I stayed till 4 p.m. with some cheese and crackers and coffee courtesy of Gisella.

On Monday the alarm clock woke me at six. I am on Channel 9 again, this time with Sue Kellaway and Steven Liebman on 'Today'. Tim Donnelly, Macmillan's Sydney man, drives me to the ABC's 'City Extra', where I am interviewed by Jane Singleton. Then to 2GB. Home for a snack. Back to 2BL to sit in an empty room with earphones, answering a disembodied voice from Melbourne.

2 May 1984

Our forty-fifth anniversary. I bought Jancsi a pure wool dressing-gown, he bought me two pots of cyclamen, and we were very loving.

The plumber comes to quote for a new water heater; we have to wait another week while boiling water keeps running through the wall. He casts a glimpse at the palette. 'You an artist? Well, one day you might be another Pro Hart!'

The judge leaves me his key and his two budgerigars to feed while he goes to Bali.

I buy a new surgical corset as I can hardly walk without it. I feel tired. But painting opens up like a door hitherto closed. I have a few days before the Brisbane portrait. Picked up the large version of *Bitter spring* and sort of go for a walk in it with half-circles of yellows from lemon to orange and browns and blues, and it sings.

10 May 1984

I had an oil sketch on canvas from the Alice trip with two gum trunks, very literary and dull. I changed it with pure mauves, orange and lemon and it turned into a painting. It costs me a great effort but I made myself draw again, after dinner and the walk, projecting the Bali sketches. I do them with brown and Rötl conté and am rewarded as they multiply in the new portfolio.

The other morning as I went to feed the birds I found one of them

ABOVE: *Kerosene lamp*, 1950.
(Art Gallery of NSW)

LEFT: *Salzburg*, 1950.

BELOW: *Still life*, 1954.

The Three Kings, 1954. (Sisters of
Mercy, St Aloysius College, Adelaide)

Warwick Fairfax, 1954.

Hugh Gaitskell, 1957.
(National Portrait Gallery, London)

Stanislaus Rapotec, 1960.
(Art Gallery of NSW)

LEFT: Princess Alexandra, 1961.
BELOW: Self-portrait with Orban, 1960.

Prince
Marir

Queen Sirikit,
1962.

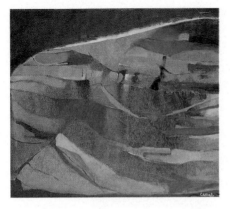

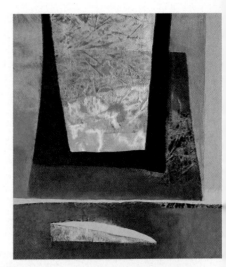

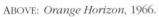

ABOVE: *Orange Horizon,* 1966.
RIGHT: *Retreat,* 1967.
BELOW: *Echoes,* 1967.

ABOVE: Margo Lewers, 1967.

LEFT: Bob King, 1962. (Australian High Commission, London)

BELOW: *Red Desert,* 1972.

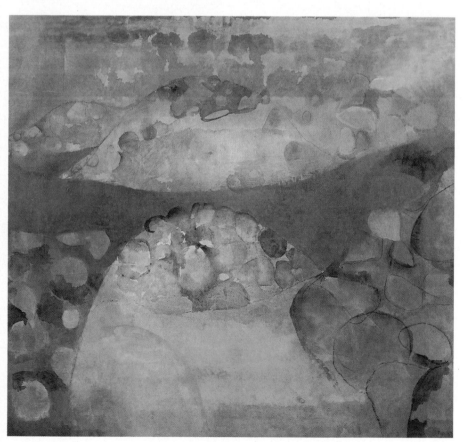

Robert Morley, 1967. (Queensland Art Gallery)

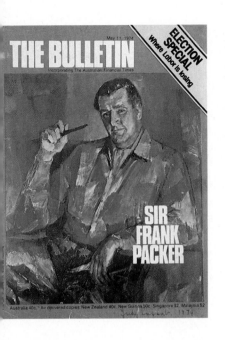

ABOVE: Rudy Komon, 1976.

LEFT: My portrait of Sir Frank Packer on the cover of the *Bulletin*, 1974.

BELOW: *Group*, 1974. (Seymour Centre)

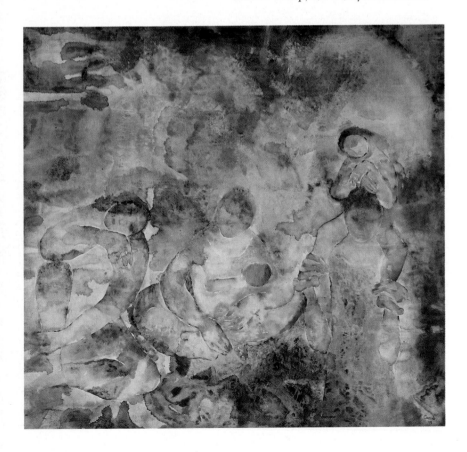

Mother and Child, 1975.

Sir Robert Helpmann, 1975.
(Sydney Opera House)

Dame Joan Sutherland, 1976. (Sydney Opera House)

ABOVE: *Desert Shapes,* The Slope, 1981. BELOW: *Desert Morning,* 1989.

Zenith, 1985.

John Olsen, 1988.

LEFT: Jeff Smart, 1990.
BELOW: *Divided Decision*, 1994. Self-portrait at seventy-four.

ABOVE: *Storm Over Rainbow Valley*, 1993.

BELOW: *The Cave Where the Birds Are Nestling*, 1993.

dead in the cage. It was horrible. I had to take it out and throw it in the garbage, and worried all day about the other being lonely and frightened. Luckily, the judge returned five days early and came up at once to console *me* about *his* loss.

Orban broke his hip without a fall. I was scared that this would be the end of the miracle. But when we saw him last Thursday he sat on top of this new advantage, red beret on his head, a wheelchair and walking crib in attendance, a night nurse and an operation next week. Today, in hospital, he pontificates from the bed, offering Lindt chocolate, a new hearing aid without cord, exercising without pain. The miracle intact.

12 May 1984

This morning, brushing out my hair, I brushed my right eye with the wiry bristles. What other senile indignity? Left the telephone on the gas heater and melted the cord.

2 June 1984

I finished Bernard Hammerman's posthumous portrait, which is painted with love. It came alive, red carnation and all.

Morris West came last week for a lithograph drawing for Lou Klepac's portfolio. He has a painting of mine he bought in the 1950s at a Contemporary Art Society exhibition, which travelled with him to Rome, London and New York. The face could have belonged to an Aussie bloke: strong, coarse. Literature, art, travel, languages, cosmopolitanism had not transformed it into an intellectual map.

Lou gave me a present of two of his books. *Henry Lawson* illustrated by Tassy Drysdale and *The vagabond scholars* in Latin and English, illustrated by Donald Friend. Morris West sparkled at the sight of them.

9 June 1984

I arrived in Canberra to do the lithograph of Judith Wright, the poet. I rang Margo, the healer, who helped my back two years ago and drove there straight from the airport. Again, in the corset. She puts her hands on my spine.

Judith Wright has a military voice snapping you to attention. Very deaf. A box on her chest is buzzing and amplifying her own voice. She also has a cataract in both eyes, but is a young seventy. Lou Klepac arrives. He thinks her eyes in the drawing look like pools of poems, and in the downturn of her lips, he can hear her lisp.

An interesting woman, Wright thinks her readers, mainly school-children, are captives. To build her house near Canberra she sold her Boyds and Blackmans and sent the artists ten per cent of the price.

I did a second drawing in the morning, half-profile, dark shadows, less kind. Jawline is undulating. Chin sags. Didn't remember Degas's *Woman arranging her hair*, charcoal and pastel all black cloud on ochre ground with only some drapery in beige and a breath of red exactly where it should be. Judith said Gauguin was a corrupter, he brought syphilis to the native girls. What about Captain Cook then, I ask. Yes, he too, but at least it was an assignment to navigate, not an ego trip like Gauguin's. She often remarked, when faced with erotic poses, that women were used badly. A feminist point.

11 June 1984

Visiting George Molnar I'm glad to know he made use of my advice for removing a gouache a detail which was ruined. He overpainted it with gesso and could then start on virgin white paper again. I also pointed out that out of almost each of his 'sagas' he can make three separate pictures like the angel with the telegraph pole with wires or the man climbing an industrial staircase leading nowhere.

'I hope I'll have time to do all this,' he said, 'the doctors think I'll be all right but one never knows with cancer.' I pray for him.

16 June 1984

János took Bodhi out of school and to Cairns on the Rainbow bus from whence they sailed in the *Greenpeace* to Cape Tribulation to save the rainforest. Maybe my grandson will be a couple of years late reading and writing, but he sure has a lovely childhood.

26 June 1984

Jim and Alice Spigelman, Kevin and Margaret Connor for lunch last Saturday, before fifty-four paintings left for my exhibition in Brisbane's Town Gallery.

The Rainbow Valley pictures were duly admired. But when the Bali sketches were strewn all over the floor, Kevin said, 'I wouldn't touch these. Here is pure unadulterated talent.'

How I am going to break through with my figurative strain and turn them into major works is another problem.

I saw Dr Glazer as my neck pain refused to vanish. The x-ray showed four vertebrae altered. Wear and tear. I start physiotherapy again.

2 July 1984

Saw a 'Four Corners' promo on television. I yell: 'Look! It's János!' It was only a flash, but my disbelieving eyes caught a glimpse of his wrists in chains. Arrested? Handcuffs?

His letter explained.

> *Hi Juci and Jancsi,*
> *Beautiful winter days at Cape Tribulation, waiting for the bulldozers. We've dug about ten holes six-foot deep in the road where the dozers have to pass. There are steel chains to go with them. When the bulldozers arrive, people jump down the holes, padlock their feet to the chain, and the hole is then filled in up to their necks. The police have to figure out how to get them out so the 'dozers can pass. That's the name of the game.*

Bodhi writes, 'I've dug part of one hole.'

9 July 1984

Brisbane

The morning of the opening of the exhibition at the Town Gallery.

Strange time for an opening, Monday lunchtime. But there were quite a lot of people, the chairman of the board of trustees, the head of the art school, two interviews, one with a lady who brought a feminist pamphlet with her and aimed at getting my support.

No, I don't feel I was discriminated against because I am a woman. Or that it made my lot more difficult. Maybe I worked harder and gave up more of social life but then, that was no sacrifice.

It's not enough to be talented. One has to be obsessed.

Late afternoon, a businesswoman drove in from Surfers (her third visit to the exhibition) to make up her mind which one of the two major works to buy. She agonised and an hour later bought both.

Verlie and Arnold took us for dinner to celebrate. The Fountain Room in the Queensland Art Gallery. It was lovely to look from the old-rose velvet to the white curves of the bridge and its milky reflection in the black ripples of the river.

12 July 1984

Spent a delightful morning in the Queensland Art Gallery.

True, it stabbed me that none of my paintings hang and there is no *Cassab* in the bookshop. But we sat on the terrace of the Gallery having coffee at the water's edge and near the sculptures.

13 July 1984

Noosa

Walking in the national park. It's no rainforest but ancient fig trees seem to tumble down the precipice to the crashing surf below, and accompanying this sound there is birdsong. The path is gentle orange.

For the first time in months I fall asleep in the afternoon while doing my meditation.

14 July 1984

Relentless rain. A steady drizzle, greyness, pea soup and we can't even walk.

János can't make it up to Noosa. Perhaps we will speak before he leaves for the Solomon Islands. Greta chuckles as she doesn't know if I want Bodhi to come to Sydney with her as he has his head shaved.

'Oh no!'

I'm desolate. After the earring, a shaved head. We wished him a happy seventh birthday.

15 July 1984

Instead of having a holiday. What's a holiday? Not only changed surroundings, but rest and enjoyment. I wash dishes at a Noosa sink, make beds. Jancsi locks up doors at night and takes rubbish out. We are mad.

Dr Gertrude Langer gave me a good review. She starts with the fact that I started painting the desert in the late 1950s. 'I consider a group of desert paintings, which make up the bulk of JC's exhibition at the Town Gallery, as among her finest. Most of these are superbly handled gouaches. The experiences turned into art are convincing, as is Cassab's deeper understanding of the message the desert holds for us humans. All is frailty beneath the appearance of permanence and that which is eternal is change.'

The article by Sally Loane annoyed Jancsi as I talked about the war years, small babies versus painting, Szentendre, and the arrival in Australia.

'This has been written a hundred times before,' Jancsi says.

'I can't invent another life, Jancsi.'

In this morning's *Sunday Mail* there is an article by Kate Collins calling me 'the doyenne of Australian art'.

21 July 1984

Sydney

The situation for me, as trustee of the Art Gallery of NSW, is a far cry from what it used to be when I protested against buying the Picasso and the Moore leaving no money for Australian acquisitions. We are buying the Kirchner, a large, expressionist work, as the Foundation's first acquisition, for nearly a million dollars.

It was not me, this time, but Jim Spigelman, who thought we should rather spend this money on five Australian 'old masters' from private collections. Edmund pointed out that the terms of the Foundation were *not* to buy Australian, but European masters. Also, Mervyn Horton left a million dollars for buying contemporary overseas paintings, which, in the future, might mean the works of people like Mark Rothko or Lichtenstein.

At yesterday's board meeting, it was recommended that we buy a Kossoff (from Fischer Fine Art in London) for $10,000. We all had difficulties but finally accepted: an Imants Tillers (all Apollonian) and a Dale Frank (all Dionysian) because of their track record. Being invited to the Venice Biennale and the Guggenheim cannot be ignored.

In my opinion, neither will have staying power. Tom Wolfe's *The painted world* applies here. A lot of bloody profound writing tries to confuse the viewer. Without it, the picture is reduced to a horror comic. *It* says: 'This painting explores a number of themes which crop up in his [Dale's] work continuously. There is the ocean symbolising the energy of nature and at the same time suggesting tides within the human body. What seems to be landscape becomes internal space, which doubles as a womb. The record (gramophone) applied to the painting as the moon becomes a black hole in the surface which seems to act as a vortex for all the forces in the image.'

We bought a second studio in Paris and talked about this one's availability to art historians and curators as well.

22 July 1984

In the *Sun-Herald* this morning there was a photograph of Mac Nicholson, Beja's father. He is now an alderman in Lismore. He said it's no longer enough for members of the alternative society to grow their own food, but they must form rural communities.

Beja's mother, Subana, leaves for India tomorrow. So Beja will stay with us and fly with Greta and Bodhi to Bodhi Farm to live with Mac.

Bodhi and Beja hit a balloon with ping-pong bats, watch television, play cards, and melt wax off candles into glasses of water.

The washing machine turns. Greta makes sandwiches for the morning. They're booked on a 6.40 a.m. plane.

János didn't ring from Brisbane before leaving for the Solomon Islands.

I am deeply saddened for Bodhi, who looks like ET, the extraterrestrial, with a head like a billiard ball.

27 July 1984

I sat in the Commodore this morning in a long queue trying to get petrol. I listened to Haydn on the radio while Sydney unleashed its tropical rain. Heater and rain-wipers were on. The trees were glorious, some even looked European, turning rusty gold.

Earlier, I gave a new desert shape a second coat of gouache. It's all yellow, sienna and black.

Lunch at the Art Gallery on Bill Wright's invitation with Kevin Connor to meet the new curator of contemporary art, Tony Bond.

I do enjoy belonging to this policy-making body, and of course, hit it off with Tony Bond at once, knowing every single topic he brought up, like Kaldor's New York show of Australian painters, and why they succeeded where good artists before them failed.

11 August 1984

Acquisitions and loans meeting and there, among them, hangs my old *Kerosene lamp*. It was bought at auction by Lou Klepac who donated it to the Art Gallery. Barry Pearce's description:

Curatorial department: Australian
Submission: Judy Cassab, born 1920
  Kerosene Lamp 1950
  Oil on board
  Reproduced: Elwyn Lynn, pl. 1–8 (colour)
  Provenance: Mr Richard Crebbin
  Gift. Lou Klepac, Sydney
  Condition: Excellent
  Relevance: Amongst the small group of paintings representing this artist in the collection, including landscapes and portraits of notable Australian artists, the earliest is the *Old Stove* of 1954.
  The small work offered was painted in the year before Ms Cassab and her family migrated to Australia from Vienna where they had stayed for a short period after leaving Hungary. It is therefore of some historic significance to her career, and would represent her earliest work in the collection.
  At the same time there is a sense of poetic transformation in this painting, so deceptively casual and underplayed in its handling, that exemplifies the artist's special sensibilities that were soon to blossom in a new country.

Orban said, 'I hope nothing will go wrong this time with the exhibition the Art Gallery is putting on for my hundredth birthday.'

I told Edmund about these false expectations, and he said (before Michael Gleeson White, the chairman and Kevin Connor), 'Christ! We were to give him one last year and didn't! Perhaps we could put up a small show in the smoking room.' I told him that the National Gallery in Budapest extended the show there for a month because it was so successful. I hope all will be well.

Lou Klepac really was very enthusiastic about one of my new Rainbow Valley paintings I titled *Above and below*. Also, about one I thought unfinished. I overpainted a transparent orange on a charcoal drawing, with some black and red shapes. He thinks this represents absolutely my essence, and I should do a series, and could he bring Barry Pearce along, as the curator should be informed.

They came last Friday and Barry was every bit as taken with these latest works as Lou. I sat and listened and learned from their descriptions of my painting, what has made these so much better than the work of the previous two or three years. It's not contrived, Lou said, it's an outpouring of expression—not of the landscape as depicted in other landscape paintings—but an inner landscape, merging with the antiquity, and myth and mystery of this land. It looks like no one else but me and is the culmination, Barry Pearce said, of decades of searching, and I am home now.

22 August 1984

Kevin Connor said at last Friday's board meeting: 'I propose that all artists who reach a hundred should have an exhibition and celebration.' (So it's not always me who nags about Orban.) 'Judy can curate it,' said Edmund, and I will, with the help of Anna Waldman who is writing about Orban, anyway.

We still had no answer from the premier's department about the launching of Lou Klepac's portfolio.

Peter decided he wants to attend meditation classes. I rang Ruth Komon, a serious yogi. She gave me the name of a teacher and invited us to watch a video of Sydney's meditation activities. When we arrived at the house in Watsons Bay, I noted (to myself) that never, in our twenty-year association, did Rudy invite us home. The walls were sagging with paintings. No Cassab.

Ruth offered $50,000 as a start, to the Art Gallery of NSW, for a Rudy Komon Memorial Fund.

I go to openings sometimes as a gesture of loyalty. Yesterday it was Roy Dalgarno, from Melbourne, one of the old guard. We have never met but as Gwen introduced us he embraced me in a bear hug, white beard overflowing. His paintings and lithographs of miners remind me of Hungary's Domanovsky.

Am struggling with two Bali figure compositions, trying to get them nearer to the look of the desert shapes.

24 August 1984

Took an overbusy and unsuccessful old gouache on paper, desert painting in mauves and beiges, and with Marina modelling, turned the horizontal vertical and eliminated bit by bit, like a sculptor chipping away the stone to free the figure hiding inside. It became a spiritual creation and with the momentum, I attacked an existing figure painting—a nasty self-portrait—and changed that in the same way. I brush a shadow across the middle of the face, arms, body, leaving the light on the edges which makes it an illumination.

Orban can hardly work now. To fill the long hours, I took one of his old paintings from the Budapest catalogue, transformed it into a pastel on black paper: an Orban trademark. I would make an excellent forger.

By the time we returned a week later, he smudged almost all of it under a layer of thick grey pastel. Still, it had *some* form left which I freed with the aid of a sharp long blade, scratching greys off. Then started a new one on which he can 'work' next week.

Lou dropped in, bringing me a lovely Käthe Kollwitz lithograph signed and framed for my birthday. Jancsi sent me splendid orchids. Still, it was a melancholy day, my sixty-fourth. After next year I shall be heading downhill towards seventy.

26 August 1984

The Lynns, Jack, Lily and Victoria took me on a gallery tour. It's the first time that Victoria (wasn't it just recently that they brought her in a basket?) drove me. It was somewhat consoling that Lynn's daughter has a punk hairdo, shorn at the temples like a boy, glued in front so it defies gravity and stands up like a porcupine's thorns. Edmund Capon's daughter from his first marriage looks even weirder as the same coiffure is bleached to straw and sits on puppy fat.

Jack is the art critic for the *Australian* again and goes outside the establishment, where I, to my eternal shame, have never been. The Mori Gallery in Leichhardt, Yuill Crowley (Pyrmont), where Imants Tillers shows a copy of a Baselitz—even the copy looks Kokoschka-Schiele—consisting of 165 canvas boards. The press release, quoting New York's *Village Voice*, extols the virtues of second-hand 'received images' and not using brush but fingers. What's more, the large copy harbours several substrata of other borrowed images, Lilliputian ones nestling in the clawing paint.' Then to the Irving Sculpture Gallery in Glebe.

1 September 1984

'Kirchner's *Three bathers*,' writes Elwyn Lynn, 'is but one example of the timeliness of this purchase but, above all, what we have now is no mere example of expressionism, but a work that takes its place amongst the best of Klee, Nolde and Beckmann.'

It feels gratifying to have had a part in the Kirchner decision.

About meditation. Le Shan wrote: 'We meditate to find, to recover, to come back to something of ourselves we once dimly and unknowingly had and have lost without knowing what it was or where or when we lost it.'

Krishnamurti teaches: 'There is nowhere to go. You are already there. Wander by the seashore and let this meditative quality come upon you. If it does, don't pursue it. What you pursue will be the memory of what it was, and what was is the death of what is. Or when you wander among the hills, let everything tell you the beauty and the pain of life, so that you awaken to your own sorrow and to the ending of it.'

And: 'What matters is not what our parents did to us but what we do with what our parents did to us.'

8 September 1984

How short-lived was my euphoria at the success of a few new paintings. The Bali figures I thought rather good didn't fare well with Lou Klepac. He said. 'The heads look like emu eggs in the landscape.'

Barbara Blackman is interviewing artists on tape for the National Library. We had five two-hour sessions. Being blind she handles a multitude of unlabelled cassettes with great exactness. She leads the questions in a direction which places lives of individuals into historical perspective. We both enjoy sudden highlighting from my diaries where past happenings become the present.

22 September 1984

I have just reached a stage where I accept that my children are middle-aged men and that they don't 'belong' to me. I try to feel more detached and to accept that they have their own karma.

Greta brought me tapes of the retreat with Vimala Thakar, the Indian guru who came to lecture at Bodhi Farm. During my afternoon's meditation, I switch the recorder on and listen and smile because in the background there is nothing but birdsong. I understand, perhaps, an iota more than before. That is arriving after deep relaxation to a silent and empty and vast place within us. Most feel a fear of this unknown place resembling death. This is the place within us which releases a healing power. I have touched it. I know it's there.

23 September 1984

This morning the premier, Neville Wran, launched my portfolio, *Ten Australian portraits*. I was able to introduce 'Greta, my daughter-in-law', my son, Peter Kampfner, and my son, John Seed, both of whom he met before. Jill came with him. Mary Fairfax turned up, and Edmund Capon

made it back from Melbourne and a directors' conference. Seven of my
ten sitters turned up.

Morris West bought the portfolio, as did Thomas Keneally's wife for
his birthday, in spite of the faulty spelling of his name (with two Ns),
which is embarrassing, as it's visible in every bookshop.

The woman who bought my two major paintings at the Brisbane
show, Win Schubert, phoned. She wants a portfolio and is opening an
art gallery in Surfers Paradise. She would like to buy a few paintings.

Peter Sculthorpe brought his mother, leading her across Holdsworth
Street where his house is, by the hand. Robert Helpmann, Donald
Friend, Lloyd Rees and Rosemary Dobson came.

Wran suggested a libretto for a new opera—a script by Morris West
and Keneally, Sutherland will be the soprano, Helpmann the choreog-
rapher. Dobson and Wright will write special verses, and Nolan, Friend
and Rees will do the stage decor.

'I don't say,' Wran continued 'that Judy flatters her sitters, but certainly
there is no malice in the portraits.'

22 October 1984

Surfers Paradise

Ten days gone. The first five were sunny, we lazed and read at the pool,
swam and sat in the spa, lunched in our room, slept, walked, drank
Scotch, watched the news, went out for dinner. The next five days were
cold, grey bleak.

10 November 1984

Sydney

Had a hard week with three openings to attend. One was Jeff Smart's
at Irvings. The small paintings were all sold, most of the larger ones as
well. People seem to want to buy contemporary art that they can 'read'.

Next day I took Jack and Lily to James Gleeson's show at Watters.

And then, Philip Guston at the Art Gallery of NSW with the Picasso
in the basement. An embarrassment of riches. I knew his abstracts. This
is figurative. Obsessed by feet, hairy arms, spiders, one teapot on an
eight-foot canvas. Bold, free, large brushstrokes.

Next day I moved my easel to the end of the second studio to be
able to become braver with large areas. I have taken an old Rainbow

Valley oil on paper I did about a year ago and which I judged worthless, and painted a head and shoulder on it incorporating the blues and pinks and yellows of its base. This sun-drenched head grew into a key picture, almost a breakthrough. I lost the contours of the face and it melts into the land. For once, eyes and mouth are done exactly the same as other shapes. Now, this head is helping me to take steps forward in the Bali groups.

9 December 1984

Orban had two parties on his hundredth birthday: one at the Glenview Motel where he proudly stood with only one walking-stick. Mollison came over from Canberra, Nevin Hurst from Hobart, the Lynns, Rapotec and Max Taylor sat with us. Speeches, the reading of the queen's telegram.

Dezsö looked blissfully happy though he couldn't see or hear.

Same at the Art Gallery of NSW where the Orban Award was announced. Wran spoke beautifully of Orban. Capon said, 'Such small exhibitions are getting to be a habit with us.'

They are making a film on him, and he raised his beret for the camera with panache.

23 December 1984

We judged the Archibald and Wynne prizes. Keith Looby's Max Gillies impersonating Bob Hawke was clearly a winning picture, in spite of some objections. We didn't get away, however, with giving the Wynne to Ann Thomson's major work. We were outvoted, in favour of a gentle, minor Brett Whiteley. All this tension, however, was nothing compared to the fact that Arthur Boyd judged the Sulman Prize (won by Tim Storrier with a bull's carcass) accepting forty works instead of the twenty-three he was told could fit in the room.

Our superb Wynne landscapes (culled cruelly by Kevin who bullied me this time) were just as squashed as last year because Arthur pilfered our space. Some had to be hung two-deep, among them a Nigel Thomson, *Children's rites*, where eight and ten-year-olds, all naked, dance in a circle around a man, tied to a pole, *naked* with a huge erection. All photographically correct.

By the time we arrived at the board meeting preceding the announcement of the winners, the Nigel Thomson painting (already printed in the catalogue) was taken off the wall, awaiting the trustees' decision. Although censorship in art is abhorrent, I couldn't defend this painting with its sado-masochistic connotations connected to child pornography.

Out of nine trustees, who did Nigel Thomson ring the next day? Me. I told him it was a board decision and as a member of that board I have no personal opinion. I patiently held the receiver while he told me he is off on a lecture tour overseas, to Budapest too. Won't they be surprised when they hear of this? I suggested that he also show them a photograph of the painting in question.

26 December 1984

First time in twelve years, the four of us had Christmas dinner together.

János arrived with his new love, Kavi, and her daughter, Anki.

After dinner Peter improvised on the piano, János played his guitar. We had an hour-long concert.

A joint went round. No tension. Sweet nostalgia.

In the afternoon I seized a canvas on which I painted a foundation a long time ago, waiting for the right subject. There is a square in the oblong, broken blues on mottled pale turquoise, a rich ultramarine disc, deep brown-green underneath. It was obviously waiting for this still life. I painted it in three hours and it's good, I think. I squared in the original sketch, enlarged it on the foundation, used the oil on paper I did in the morning, and it fell into place. Then, today, I brought the pale ground lower down, changed the ultramarine disc to the shadow of the leaves. The 1920 Preston metamorphosed into a Cassab, glass vase so brittle and beautiful, leaves so dramatic, I just saw the direction the Bali figures could take.

Reinforced by the second sighting of the Passmore show.

9 January 1985

I'm using crumpled canvases again, underpaint them in translucent clear colours and then treat it horizontally as watercolours. I finally reached the conclusion that my first, intuitive session is my best—when the canvas has life, when it still breathes. The idea that to earn the 'reward'— money, fame, or good reviews—one must toil because it can't be easy, is irrelevant. I have toiled for fifty years. I want to pick the flowers now.

20 January 1985

I set myself a rigorous workload. Draw with charcoal in the evenings, on either canvas or Arches paper. Next morning I work with acrylics on the table or with gouache on the paper. Willing to discard those which are not showing promise rather than flog them to death. It helps me produce, suddenly. I only hope they are as good as I think they are. All else becomes an additional strain.

Lou Klepac dropped in to have a look at my paintings. A fresh and expert eye is welcome. He thinks that some don't have enough subject matter, others have too much and crowd the canvas. He admired the gouaches ('Cassab written all over them') but not the large canvases which I now see as confused and muddy.

18 February 1985

Three of us at Sydney University, talking about The Making of a Painting. Alan Gamble talked about the making of etchings and lithographs. Lloyd Rees reminisced about the 1920s, and Melba and Lionel Lindsay. I talked about the portrait and demonstrated with Lloyd as my sitter. There were 300 in the audience, situated in such a way that they were facing the windows and therefore, so was I. The dais was small, I couldn't step back. Lloyd had to sit lower than I to get any light at all. The microphone was on my left and I tried speaking about what I was doing. The canvas was quite large, with an acrylic base of blues and greens. I painted the head and I finished it in thirty minutes. One of those incredible instances where God paints the picture.

6 March 1985

Hiroshige exhibition at the Art Gallery of NSW. The fifty-three stages of the Tokaido. Delightful details one would like to dissect with a magnifying glass.

A huge pop art show opened last week with most of my pet hates: Lichtenstein and Warhol. But Robert Rauschenberg, Larry Rivers, Jasper Johns and Kitaj are all good artists, and the 1960s revisited is useful and exciting.

24 March 1985

Andrea died. For so long a chore, now she leaves a gaping void.

I paint and listen to the radio. It's the centenary year of Handel and Bach, and glorious baroque surrounds me. East Germany, the homely sister of the glittering west (a war bride locked in a loveless marriage with a former neighbour) must find cultural solace and pride in its heroes. 1983 was the 500th anniversary of Martin Luther's birth. Goethe and Wagner's lives intersect. Bach's music (considered outdated in his time) has even been sent into space aboard *Voyager* I and II as an example of the best that human culture has to offer.

13 April 1985

My exhibition at the Holdsworth is being hung. Gisella phoned and I went over.

I found Arthur Boyd, giving an interview to Channel 10's 'Good Morning Australia'. Arthur came towards me with arms outstretched, embraced me with great force and warmth, and took me to one picture and then another and another. Excited and obviously sincere, he said, 'There are not many painters nowadays who give so much delight. This one is iridescent!' He leaned quite close to the surface and asked, 'How do you do it?'

'What I admire most,' he continued, 'is that in spite of the rich secondary pleasure, there is no concoction. No cuisine. No repetition. Each is different.' I can't tell how marvellous it was to hear these things from Arthur Boyd.

Barry Pearce phoned. Could I come with him to see the exhibition? He would like to buy *Leaping* for the Gallery. *Leaping* is the gouache that Lou Klepac discovered. He actually stopped me going further as he thought the charcoal drawing behind the thin veil of orange was very beautiful. He brought Barry to the studio to see it. I know (being on the board) that there is no money for any acquisitions this year. So I told him to set his own price. I am not really interested in the money. I feel a bit embarrassed because I'm a trustee. I told him so. But he said: 'That's irrelevant. The painting stands on its own merit.'

'That right bottom corner with the deep reds and the black.' Barry said, 'I would feel proud if I could have painted that corner.'

Arthur Boyd left for England, but when he comes back would I come to Shoalhaven? I could paint him and he would paint me.

I am now planning the Portraits of the Artworld exhibition for the bicentenary year. I detected (with a pang) that Tucker has beaten me to it: Gisella showed me a catalogue of his portraits of artists.

14 April 1985

We were invited to the Wrans for lunch. Jancsi has shingles, so I went. Vincent Serventy was there, John Coburn, John Player, director of the Conservatorium. Lunch didn't start till 2.30. Jill and Neville served it. She worked hard through the meal which lasted till 5.30. With champagne and wines and the loosening of tongues it grew into a memorable afternoon, with the Wrans relating a visit to the iron ore mines near Wittenoom, with Lang Hancock. Hancock's Learjet was kept in a shed with walls which didn't touch the floor. Why? So when there is a flood the water gushes under and out of the building.

'I had bladder trouble at that time,' said Neville, 'just before the surgery which wrecked my vocal chords. So the first priority was the loo. The loo, Hancock said, is out here, but be careful because poisonous snakes come out at night. After spending the most uncomfortable night of my life, Hancock flew us to the mines in a small plane which he piloted himself. I'm a nervous traveller at the best of times and this flight was a nightmare. He peered above his spectacles at the instruments, a difficult task in his jockey cap, and meanwhile he shaved with an electric shaver so each time he was on a downstroke he loosened his grip on the steering and the plane went into a dive.'

The Wrans' paintings are the right mixture of antique and modern, Fred Williams, Clifton Pugh, a good Ray Crooke and an excellent Aubusson copy of the unicorn tapestry in the New York Metropolitan Museum.

29 April 1985

Lismore

We arrived on the afternoon flight. János, Greta and Bodhi were loving and warm. They showered in our motel room—a rare luxury for them, as is television for Bodhi.

We went to a new club: Boheme. 'Our kind of people.' The musicians don't get paid. The cash register is a tin cup. I brought my sketchbooks as wonder of wonders, János wanted me to do some drawings. He took his place in the band, played the guitar and sang. Bodhi joined him, singing songs about the rainforest and funny ones like 'Eat meat, you bastards, the country's going broke'.

Bodhi asked me for a pencil, and the sketches I started of guitars and fingers on clarinets become a joint effort with genuine Dubuffet faces.

No loitering when János is around. We wake at 6.30 on Saturday morning, and eat breakfast together in our room. They have spent the night in János's office at the Rainforest Information Centre in Lismore. They now have a computer so the Word reaches masses of people.

'As you look at me now,' Janos says with eyes as clear and innocent as when he was six years old, 'I am where I want to be, doing what I want to do.'

5 May 1985

My exhibition was very successful. Marvellous reviews, a lot of feedback. Two paintings reserved for the new Parliament House, Canberra. Nine sold, altogether.

Lou sent me a letter with Xerox copies of Tintoretto charcoal drawings of figures. 'They are,' he writes, 'like the drawings of desert shapes in Judy Cassab's paintings.' I rang him and told him to choose any painting. Jancsi and I want him to have one. He has been an inspiration over the last two years.

12 May 1985

Arthur Boyd's exhibition, which follows mine, is sensational. I was especially smitten with the way he fuses a half-picture of landscape with a lower half of figures. It breaks every rule, and it's a remarkable affirmation.

Woollahra Council named a Raoul Wallenberg Garden with Anna Cohn's sculpture. I had no idea that it would be such a devastating emotional upheaval for me. The garden was cordoned off and there were about 1000 people to pay tribute to one of the heroic figures of the Second World War, the Swedish diplomat who saved the lives of 100,000 Jews in Hungary. He disappeared after going to meet the advancing Russians, and rumours are he is held captive in a gulag. But more than the memories which sprang up fresh and bleeding, it was a poem which tore me apart.

Written by a child in the ghetto, it was delivered by a five-year-old girl. In a high voice she recited it without fault. It was about a butterfly kissing a flower. A yellow butterfly. 'I know it's the last butterfly. Butterflies don't come into the ghetto.'

19 May 1985

Peter left for a two-week holiday in Bali. We are going there too, in about ten days time. When my mind strays to all the things that can go wrong with Peter's restaurant, or his dog, Cain, I try to realise that my caring days should be over. That I am at an age when children care for elderly parents.

10 June 1985

Bali

We have been in Bali for ten days and I have done fifty-two small paintings. Jancsi thinks I have *such* good raw material that most of the figures must not be touched. Good news.

Bali is paradise. We even went sailing in one of the native catamarans. Two Balinese boys carried more than sailed us in the low tide over the coral reefs until we reached depth and became airborne, noiseless above the swell. We walk every day at sunset, an hour barefoot in the sand.

The best paintings are about movement. Women coming out from the river, mining sand, loading it in baskets on their heads, carrying it up the hill and dumping it. Repetitious movement, easy for me to capture.

16 June 1985

Sydney

Claude Monet's Painter of Light exhibition opens this week at the Art Gallery of NSW. Terence Maloon writes that Monet was riddled with anxiety. Monet wanted to see the way a newborn child sees. He advised a young artist: 'When you go out to paint, try to forget what objects you have before you. Merely think, here is a little square of blue, here an oblong of pink, here a streak of yellow, and paint the exact colour and shape.' He said he wished he had been born blind and then suddenly gained his sight so he wouldn't have known what the objects were.

9 July 1985

My Victorian catalogue looks splendid, *Floating rock* occupies front and back (and also the poster). It has a foreword and acknowledgements by David Ellis, and an introduction by Elwyn Lynn, which he did not show me. I was bowled over by it.

Peter has just been told he's the highest earner for Hooker's in this last financial year!

3 August 1985

I have finished a portrait of Collin Bull, chairman of Johnson and Johnson, started one of the headmaster of Trinity Grammar School, Rod West.

The *Sydney Morning Herald* interviewed me for an article in their *Good Weekend* magazine about portraits.

4 August 1985

A donors' weekend at the National Gallery in Canberra. Donors' names engraved and unveiled. So there I am in stone.

Among the new acquisitions is a Cézanne, *An afternoon in Naples* (1877), the last year he exhibited with the impressionists before he left for Aix-en-Provence. A Seurat, a delectable Derain, *Horseman in a landscape* (1905), which could be a Kandinsky. And a Sonia Delaunay.

A beautiful exhibition of one of the world's great master printers, Ken Tyler, with the collaboration of artists like Rauschenberg, Jasper Johns, Motherwell and Frankenthaler.

Next morning we were taken to Drill Hall at the university, a new venue for the National Gallery's modern art. German and Italian neo-expressionists dubbed by critics anxious to classify them. There are apocalyptic visions, a reaction probably to depersonalised abstraction which dominated the art world for two decades. I liked an Immendorf (aggressive and politically directed), feel hostile to Baselitz since he turned perfectly realistic figures upside down. Drawings by Martin Disler are crude and unaesthetic with titles like *Endless modern licking of crashing globe by black doggies time-bomb*.

I would have dismissed the eclectic and seemingly badly-drawn oil paintings of the Italian Enzo Cucchi and Mimmo Paladino, if I had not discovered beautiful and poetic drawings and watercolours, suggestive of myths, religion, and memory. 'A return to the tradition of figurative art may be under way,' says the catalogue. 'If this development is sustained, abstraction may come to be viewed as a critical breakthrough, but not a permanent condition, in the evolution of art.'

Jim Mollison, chatting with viewers, talked about the complete neglect of teaching drawing for two decades.

I received a letter, posted in Budapest, addressed to: 'Judy Cassab, paintress, Sydney, Australia.' In it were old postcards of Beregszász. One of them was dated 1938, had the name of the main square still in Czech as '*Masaryková námĕsty*' but the stamp on it says in Hungarian: '*Beregszász visszatért*' (Beregszász returned). It's the square I crossed as a schoolgirl every morning going to the *gimnázium* amidst oxen, horses, geese and poultry. There is a chemist shop of Ili Rottman (now Kalina, of Sydney) and where Évi Ságh lived, my classmate whose uncle, Sanyi, married my mother.

The sender, Sándor Weiss, writes that he saw my paintings in a Hungarian magazine. He remembers me as a young girl, 'pretty and talented and at that time already, the pride of our small town', and hopes he can give me pleasure by sending these photographs. One of them is of the synagogue. He lost his parents and sister in Auschwitz. He escaped to Soviet Russia wanting to fight the Germans, but was interned instead in Siberia for seven years. He doesn't expect a reply, and doesn't ask for anything. He sent all these treasures to a stranger in Australia like sailors send letters in bottles on the sea.

I sent him a drawing and my thanks.

11 August 1985

Next week I'll be sixty-five years old. I am very fortunate. I am an artist and still working to full capacity. I draw out the rituals of the morning. Lovingly look after my flowering plants, polyanthus, primula and violets on the sill of the kitchen window, cyclamen in the living room.

I spend more time preparing Jancsi's shirts and clothes, and my personal toiletries. I also make a resolution. In my prayers I asked God's forgiveness for grave mistakes I made when the children were small. Because I cannot really forgive myself for leaving them for weeks when I worked in London. If God forgives me, it's up to me to forgive myself. So I threw the guilt off. I don't wish to be responsible now for the young woman who made the errors. God help me.

15 August 1985

What a birthday present!

Peter sold the restaurant today, and János bought a house in Lismore, in his own name, taking responsibility for owning something for the first time.

I'm on my knees.

24 August 1985

János is in town and staying with Peter. János arrived this morning saying that they stayed up until 2 a.m., just talking. For the second night in a row.

2 October 1985

All at once so many portrait commissions; they will have to stretch out into December. Renata Ratzer. Diminutive flute player and teacher who sat down on the floor immediately with legs tucked under. When I asked her to hold the flute, the painting was ready for me. What I did not foresee was that it turned into a renaissance pageboy. Even her eyes are of that period and the face looks as if illuminated from within.

Renata was born in Russia, lived in Persia, loved her old father so much that since his death she has not been able to write any poetry. But at her last sitting, she brought me flowers, a cheque and a poem which ended with the line: 'He came to greet me from your brush today, gentle and welcoming behind my eyes.'

16 October 1985

Surfers Paradise

Jancsi wanted to show me O'Reilly's at Lamington National Park where he and János spent a few days last year. We went on a tourist bus and had a wonderful day in the rainforest. I discovered the bowerbird: a collector of blue. Blue what? Blue anything. Bits of shiny blue plastic from an Arnotts biscuit wrapping, children's toys winking from under strangler figs surrounding the nest.

In the mornings we go for our celestial walks on the beach treading on clouds' reflections. A brisk hour later a swim in our heated pool. Doing my exercises on the lawn.

We stay in the Paradise Centre on the twenty-third floor. I refuse to see the plastic palms, the kitsch on the walls, and mainly, the acres of mirrors.

23 October 1985

Sydney

I started a portrait of Susie Carleton. Susie has a restaurant in Macquarie Street and a pub in Balmain, described in one of the magazines as the closest thing here to a literary 'salon'. A writer, Frank Moorhouse, got together the money to give her a portrait for her fortieth birthday. When I heard, I decided to paint it for less than half-price. She is full of the joys of life, intelligent, bubbling overweight, curly blonde character.

I did a larger-than-life portrait of Kevin Connor in one sitting. His gentle, brooding personality is all there, besides the likeness. I painted the face on dark blue-green mottled acrylic veils and what with the urgency of brushstrokes, there is a face no one else could have painted.

14 December 1985

The Archibald and Wynne selection was a marathon, with 1000 entries.

Laurie Short had to retire on his seventieth birthday 'into constitutional senility' as he put it. Dr Denise Hickey is dying of cancer. She is so brave; rang up to say she regained the use of her voice temporarily and will come in a wheelchair, to see us and the exhibition.

Only Michael Gleeson White supported us two artists, as others seem to think that being a trustee automatically bestows expertise. As Kevin said: 'It's the difference between people who spent their whole life in Afghanistan, and a tourist visiting it.'

21 December 1985

At the last board meeting of this year, a new scandal popped up. Someone found the original rules of the bequest for the Sulman Prize and gave it to Kevin. It clearly states that the prize has to be judged by 'a professional artist'. By then, Ray Kidd, the wine merchant, had already awarded the Sulman.

Although there were precedents in the past, when Mervyn Horton, James Fairfax and Patrick McCaughey judged it, we can't *knowingly* go against the rules. Jim Spigelman found a legal way out.

Pugh, after years of mediocre entries, sent in a small masterpiece, a portrait of John Perceval. Gentle, sensitive, to be compared with a Schiele. It was my number one. A week earlier, Terence Maloon prophesied in the *Herald* that Guy Warren is the 'sure winner' with a portrait of Flugelman. This time Kevin and I didn't agree. He found Perceval insipid. The Dunlop, a fine painting of an interior complete with jars, bottles, basket, curtains, windows, table, carpet and a small figure, was everybody's second choice. Guy Warren won.

25 December 1985

I sent Greta some of the photographs I took of Bodhi before he went to India. In her letter she writes. 'Oh, Bodhi. I have forgotten how beautiful you are.'

János writes from an ashram near Ahmadabad:

> *Yesterday when we arrived, there were all these wild monkeys and we started playing with them in the garden till Kaiser came out shooing them away from eating the garden all up. (She has a beautiful vegetable garden as well as roses, and big silky oaks tower over it all.) So anyway she got some bungers and skyrockets to scare them away for a moment or two and then Bodhi was into it, preparing crackers for the next onslaught as they leaped about the trees and roof.*

This morning Barbara Leser came to have a look at Bernie's portrait which is practically finished after two sittings. After the experiences with the one-sitting artist's portraits I woke up to the truth of it: after two sittings I start spoiling the work as I make the likeness more photographic. I am old enough now to charge as much as I do without justifying it with sweat.

17 January 1986

I tried painting Jancsi, in one sitting. Not good enough. I told him: 'Jancsi, of *you*, I have to paint a more psychological portrait.'
He said, 'Psycho, perhaps. But logical?'

19 January 1986

Mona is here from Alice Springs. Brought a portfolio of Aboriginal paintings. Told us she sold a Namatjira for $5000, unframed. Jancsi remarked: 'The person who bought it was framed.'

We watched television, switched the channel to something else and it was the monkeys at Mount Abu, in India.

15 February 1986

At a subcommittee meeting we decided to submit a proposal to commemorate Dr Denise Hickey (who died in December) by naming one of the Paris studios after her. She always helped young students. I vaguely sense that she knows about it and feels pleased.

22 February 1986

A one-sitting portrait of Jack Lynn. Perhaps the best so far, it evolved (against my intention) into a larger than life-size presence. It grew by magic—so stunning after the first hour that Jancsi wanted me to stop without blocking Lynn's head. I did add that shock of hair though.

The first acquisitions and loans meeting of the year. Meeting the curator of contemporary art, Tony Bond, with Kevin Connor for coffee first. There were two things to discuss. He wants to spend the Horton Bequest money on a Kiefer which he saw in the artist's studio.

We resolved at the board meeting that Tony should go overseas next month and either grab it or drop it. Also, he should look around as one can't possibly know in Sydney what the art scene is like overseas. We always wait until the artist's price increases tenfold by which time we can't afford the paintings.

The Heidelberg school, our own brand of impressionism, is, to most minds, a historical rather than a visual attraction. Like Conder's *Circular Quay* (1888) or Streeton's *Railway station*. His *National game*, however, is only 9 x 5 inches and is a gem, with its brilliant light. Delightful show.

Next day Kevin and I invite Barry Pearce for lunch, before the board meeting. He wants us to buy Pugh's Perceval which missed winning the Archibald despite my intense efforts.

Barry complains that curators in NSW are the lowest paid in the country. Kevin (who is a lecturer himself) realises that Barry, for his expertise and endless hours of dedication, earns $10,000 less than a part-time lecturer. We bring it up at the meeting as 'the trustees are concerned we shall lose our best people'. Jim Spigelman wants to take the matter before the industrial court.

23 February 1986

Kitaj writes in his catalogue: 'I made a startling discovery ... There seems to be no representation of the crucifixion itself in art for hundreds of years after the event.' Anyway I thought why wait 400 years after our (Jewish) passion? The appearance of the chimney form in some of my pictures is my own very primitive attempt at an equivalent symbol, like the cross, both, after all having contained the human remains in death.

In one painting called *Germania (the tunnel)* he has a self-portrait splattered with blood and black arrows. A naked woman, ensnared within an evil chimney shape. Behind these figures is a borrowed corridor from van Gogh's San Remy asylum. It evokes the gas chambers.

In a review of this exhibition, Peter Fuller writes that other Jews, especially other Jewish painters, recoil with embarrassment.

The conventional wisdom has long been that the Jewish experience in the Third Reich was so extreme and horrific that no painting can ever encompass it. Fuller quotes Jaroslav Pelikau's book *Jesus through the centuries*. A historian who believes that theology is too important to be left to theologians. He points out that Chagall clearly perceived Jesus as first and foremost a Jew, rabbi and prophet.

In my view, Kitaj's intention is a magnificent failure because it takes more than iconography to depict the universal. There I stand humiliated. For I cannot say I found my art in my own backyard. I have never tried to approach the great tragedy of my life in visual ways—the chimney through which my mother, my grandmother, Jancsi's mother and his brother perished in Auschwitz. And when my cousin, Vera Szekely, showed me her book where birds are the symbols, and the soul remains free-flying heavenwards without chimneys—that comes closer to how I would express it if I could.

I have no backyard. I have appropriated one country's backyard in my Alice Springs and Rainbow Valley paintings, and the figures from another country, Bali.

Apart from the inevitability of depicting oneself in every brushstroke I do this by formal means: colour and form. Meaning is the enigma— open and free to the interpretation of the spectator.

Long letters from Bodhi in India about 'a new Asterix my dad bought me and a book called *Around the world in 80 days* and another called *20,000 leagues under the sea*. (Verne, eh? Strange. He is discovering a writer from my childhood.) Also: 'You'll have to help me with lots of letters when I come back to write to all my friends.'

János writes '... Vandana's father is a retired army commander aged seventy-six and looking so much like you, Jancsi, amazing. You would have made an excellent Indian. He is in spirit, a sort of Hindu Hungarian. So, anyway, feeling very much at home in India again. We are sitting under some flowering eucalyptus and I'm chewing a bit of Australia in my mouth, a twig from the big young trees. Bodhi and I wonder what Mum is doing?'

25 February 1986

Feldenkrais will start its first formal training program this year. A disappointment, surely, to Greta whose annual workshops in the Feldenkrais method now will be invalid. She has to start from the beginning if she wants to become a practitioner. And that's all she wants. I feel compassion and love for her.

27 February 1986

Drove out to Kevin Connor for lunch, and to see new paintings. Always an inspiration although he seems to feel just as isolated and unsure as I do. But there was an interior of his studio—two ordinary armchairs in front of the balcony and the view, painted of course with the expressionist verve one expects—and so beautiful! Why don't I look in my own backyard?

I started (and finished) a portrait of Ken Reinhard, for my series. They are getting better as I go. He looks like an Antarctic explorer in an anorak. He remarked that it's 'genius' the way the greens and aquas come through while the flesh has substance.

8 March 1986

Greta picked up János and Bodhi from the airport. Love and tears and laughter flowed. Bodhi has begun collecting stamps.

János has now done all the interviews for the film he is coproducing. Footage arrived from Germany and England. He will stay in Sydney to work on the film with Jenny Kendall and Paul Tate (the director), and they all move into Peter's house. They have already sold the film to the ABC, who will also distribute it internationally.

I did a one-sitting portrait of János. His face is superimposed on a glowing orangey earth colour, letting it come through. He wears his rainbow T-shirt with 'Earth first' printed on it. János, who never takes any notice of my paintings, went quite mad with enthusiasm— photographing me, himself and Jancsi with the portrait.

9 March 1986

I painted Orban again. This one is quite small, his face owl-like, his hands folded on his lap over the blanket on his knees. Suddenly he said, sarcastically, 'Good to have friends like Juci, who paints. While *I* haven't painted a picture for months.'

Went to Lady Beale yesterday, to paint Darling Point from her window. Chose foundations, took a canvas. There was a giant fig tree I never intended to paint, and it forced itself on the canvas.

15 March 1986

Surfers Paradise

János rang from Lismore. He is holding a public lecture at the Environment Centre and wanted us to attend. So we took the bus to Lismore, and after checking into the motel János took us to Wotherspoon Lane where his house is.

Knowing János's abodes (like the rainforest bus), I was delightfully surprised by the house. The most magnificent hall came to be under the existing building when the builders lifted the structure above flood level.

Friends polished the floor and there is a huge French window leading into the garden. There is a ping-pong table in the middle of the room and oversized cushions on the floor. It looks like the meditation centre at Bodhi Farm.

He sold the Hills hoist which 'made the garden look suburban'. The kitchen stove will share this fate. 'I want an old-fashioned wood stove.' It's his life.

29 March 1986

Canberra

Jancsi and I took an Art Gallery Society bus to Canberra to see the New York Metropolitan's Modern Masters. We had lunch at the Lanyon homestead to see Nolan's gallery, and I'm so glad I saw it. What an inventive, rich talent he had!

The exhibition in the National Gallery was worth the trip. Picasso's Gertrude Stein is a modern icon, and in that room is a most beautiful Modigliani portrait of Jeanne Hebuterne, mother of his son. A black and red portrait of Soutine, and Picasso's classic *Women in white*. Chagall's *Market place, Vitebsk,* of 1917 is most unChagallish but close to the bone, portraying a street which could be in Beregszász. I have never painted anything of my childhood town. There are five wonderful Bonnards, an early *Saint Tropez* (1911) with a dreamlike quality, figures dematerialised by the sunlight. A wall of tiny Klees, each with borders which formed an important feature.

Among the Americans, I only like Georgia O'Keeffe who liked mountains and deserts and skeletal shapes, as I do.

5 April 1986

Sydney

Jeff Smart's annual descent on Sydney was so rushed this time (he exhibits in Melbourne) that we were invited to a crowded cocktail party. Jeff flitted among his collectors like a tycoon. Margaret Olley and I were the only practising artists there.

27 April 1986

Lou Klepac has become, for me, a knowledgeable enthusiast who takes the trouble and time to provide an outside eye. I'm hovering (as always) on the thin border between nature and transformation of nature. Unsure of what I'm doing with my figures. Approaching them from every which way towards the goal winking at the end of the tunnel.

Projecting one-line drawings at night, onto hardboard, using white acrylic. Next morning, black Indian ink. Too black. The hose uncontrollable. Nasty struggle with palette, knife, needle, blade, then, in desperation, white paint. Another way, good white grainy Arches paper.

Too hard on the edges. Too much black washes off, leaving not much more than the exposed contours. Then I remembered the grey Ingres papers Oscar gave me last year. That worked. It's more absorbent, so the white, as well as the black clings to the pores so the stream of water handles like a brush.

Lou shrugs. 'You are too talented to resort to tricks,' he says. 'I know, I know, it gives you the mottled surface you want. And the figures are wafting mysteriously out of the accidents . . . '

I protested, because this technique is my trademark.

'It's your charcoal drawing which is your trademark,' Lou says.

We grab last year's unsuccessful gouache figures out of one of the portfolios. He points at skies and background where the charcoal line still shows. The figures are thickly covered. 'Not at all what should happen. Try more charcoal, less body paint. Rather, thin washes.'

I decide to try.

Is it exposure, perhaps, to the bending Bali woman, to the swinging sandminers, which changes Lou's appreciation of them? Or are they better than they used to be? *On the terrace* has a sitting and a standing figure with rice paddies behind them. The latter are floating indigo shapes, almost hairy, on lemon yellow and emerald green.

Lou sways side to side, enchanted with one part of the painting. 'But the standing figure is levitating. Perhaps you should bring her feet lower and also the head, as the invisible line of the composition between the two heads is too steep.' Absolutely.

I gave Lou's portrait two more sittings and gave it to him. On the last sitting, he suggested that for the portrait exhibition in 1988, to make it look more varied, but also to widen my range, I should paint tiny ones as well. 'You know, like the Macchiaioli.' The word means oil spots. Degas, who lived in Naples, exported the style—an ancestor of impressionism.

There and then I painted a profile of him about 8 x 10 inches. It works. Did a study of Marina exactly the same.

Lou brought up the idea that a portrait exhibition, going back four decades, should not be shown in a commercial gallery. He mentioned it to the curator of the S.H. Ervin Gallery (where Nolan's Burke and Wills paintings were shown) and she was enthusiastic. Barry Pearce also thinks so. We'll see.

3 May 1986

Edmund Capon's first sitting. Talks about the public school he went to more spartan than Eton, his consequent rebellion against the class system that made him join the communist party. His flash of destiny. At eleven, he first saw the photo of the Great Wall of China in a geography book.

10 May 1986

Greta writes in one of her letters:

> *I haven't seen much of János since your visit, so last weekend Jane and I listened to one of his tapes and that way I felt in communion with him. He does some wonderful things—that tape is one of them.*
>
> *So everything is just fine. Underneath superficial turmoils and dramas life seems quite solid and sane. I hope it is the same with you.*

The fact is Greta and János are separated. But somehow it's different for them. Though she lives at Bodhi Farm and he in Lismore, they are friends. And they share Bodhi. It doesn't affect me as deeply as it would have ten years ago.

Do all mothers grieve so often and so much and so deeply? If so, it's one of life's more cruel tricks. Not to be able to forget or dissociate from fragile, small, infinitely adored, tenderly nurtured creatures, the way they were.

18 May 1986

Lou Klepac, in conjunction with the Eddie Glastra Gallery, wants five major works for Ansett's Hayman Island suites. I'm painting new landscapes from old slides onto old canvas because the existing paintings are 'too abstract'.

I am onto the fourth landscape. As they flow and the brushes get larger, so do the areas of colour. I tackle them with less inhibition. I care less about how they fit in and almost not at all about whether they will like them.

I painted Gisella Scheinberg into the series. Again, Kokoschkaesque. The pale square of fleshy face is placed upon a burgundy red. 'My' background, the crumpled washes of acrylic, are playing into reds and pinks with a bit of blue, and a red pullover shows under the bulky beige cardigan. A Jewish mother who stepped out of her class and became a personality.

I finished Edmund Capon.

We spent a long time at the Biennale. Nick Waterlow's grandest effort transported Kassel and Venice into two floors of the Art Gallery, and Piers 2 and 3 at Walsh Bay. Current issues are concerned with whether art needs to be original any longer. Some say it never was, every image or gesture having been seen before. Only now, copying becomes 'appropriation'.

Many might feel that it's all fun behind the pseudo-philosophising. A cartoonist gets the title page of the catalogue. His Japanese counterpart has Hokusai to pilfer. There is a fetish of borrowing worldwide. So is there annihilation, a lot reaching towards the certainty of Malevich's black square.

The pier is in itself a splendid happening. The warehouse's blackened timber walls support all that nonsense which congregates here, coming from Germany, England, the USA and Japan, copying Oldenburg with corrugated cardboard hoovers and pianos. Our Ken Unsworth has a grand piano levitating precariously, in the company of equally floating rocks. There is a boat, hanging before the open warehouse door with a real (as in still being used) boat in the bay, only our boat has two busts of bronze and some potatoes for good measure. There are mounds of rice. There is a hill of floodlit salt, highlighting its crystal quality.

I'm glad I'm not young.

At Channy Coventry's there is a phenomenal Roger Kemp exhibition. Channy said he came back from the Biennale wanting to cut his throat, but was revived by the authority of these works.

Keith Looby also has an imposing show at Ray Hughes.

1 June 1986

Nora Torok is doing a survey for the Jewish Centre on Ageing. When she phoned for an appointment, I only consented because she is the daughter of old friends.

Ageing? Me?

The questions (Have you phoned anybody since last Monday? Have you been anywhere since last week?) made me realise there are people who are lonely, or handicapped, poor, sick. How fortunate we are. There are domestic help, handymen, delivered kosher meals (from the Wolper

Jewish Hospital), nursing aids, personal support visits, post-hospital care, and help with shopping and transport, where needed.

Brett Whiteley came to sit for a portrait. Told me he was still a schoolboy at Cranbrook when he and his mother saw a painting of mine and bought it for eighteen guineas. Is my son John still sculpting? No, he is a conservationist. Changed his name to John Seed. 'John Seed of the Daintree?' asked Brett.

In two hours we had a renaissance portrait.

'Where am I from?' asked Brett.

'From the Netherlands, I'd say.' The eyes are old, hooded. A face which changed from boyish to tragic. He was fascinated by the pigment, the stained appearance of the canvas. It's raw sienna and it comes through the face and also the white renaissance shirt. All that's missing, he said, is the ledge at the bottom. I remembered it from Giovanni Bellini. Took a rag with turps and rubbed the ledge across. He took the rag from me, dipped it in turps again and rubbed some more. Then with a side look, he touched the rosette on the painting and added a pinpoint highlight with his finger.

He embraced me, happy with his painted self.

19 June 1986

A splendid Ann Thomson show at Coventry's. When asked if she is an abstract or figurative painter she said, 'Yes'.

Michael Taylor at Rex Irwin's brings ecstasy to our eyes; thin paint is traversed with torrents of rich paint with flashes of delicious colour shining through.

21 June 1986

Last weekend Peter relaxed at home with his door open. Cain is allowed out, and uncharacteristically, disappeared. Peter found him early the next morning in the front foliage. His paws bleeding and his toenails cut with either an axe or pliers. God knows how he came home. Wash, iodine, bandages.

I was so depressed I couldn't work.

14 July 1986

Lismore

The floor of János's house is covered with the carpet from Peter's restaurant. Only the initiated know that this is why the fish pattern is woven in lighter grey. The house is a new community. Downstairs, in the studio, T-shirts are being printed (Earth first), volunteers silk-screening, typing, addressing envelopes, computing. Barefoot helpers go in and out. I think some stay and sleep on the cushions. János sleeps in a caravan at the end of the garden.

Next morning we drive to Bodhi Farm. The new community building there is a far cry from that first primitive structure where we OMMMed, holding hands before lunch. This is an octagonal pavilion with a round skylight. The wood is polished to perfection.

29 July 1986

Sydney

Elwyn Lynn was 'sacked' (his word) as editor of Art and Australia, when his three-year contract expired. He had doubled the circulation from five to ten thousand. I wrote to Sam Ure Smith standing up for my friend.

13 August 1986

Since the treasurer, Paul Keating, brought in the fringe-benefits tax (an administrational nightmare!) I have a logbook in the car. Each time I drive to galleries or anything connected with my 'business', for Christ's sake, I fill it in. People interviewed on TV mostly agree that instead of making tracks they fill in forms.

I heard from Lily, with dismay, that Lou is the new editor of Art and Australia. A test of divided loyalty? How on earth can I advertise my next exhibition? How can I not?

17 August 1986

My sixty-sixth birthday. I feel thirty-three, spoiled rotten, more than when I was young.

A parcel, delivered by courier, contained the poster I have done for the ABC (a line drawing of mother, father *and* child) with a note 'from all of us at ABC publicity, Happy birthday'.

21 August 1986

Orban's 'minder', Marika, went to Europe for six weeks, and his children put him in a private hospital in Chatswood.

Today, when we arrived, his room was empty. I put down the pot of cyclamen and went to look for him, finding him coming out of the toilet on his own. He was bent very low and could hardly shuffle with his four-pronged walking-stick. Don't know how on earth he could pull his trousers down without falling. I helped him back to the room, and with a nurse, out into the sunny garden.

It's like death's waiting room, sleeping in chairs. Lucky he is almost blind and can't realise how dark and small his room is.

He seems to survive on a surge of triumph that he is still alive.

23 August 1986

For many years I prayed that God would create a niche that János would fit into. I think he has found it with the rainforest work, his own house and with the film.

I pray that God will find a niche for Peter too.

3 September 1986

Alice Springs

The town looks like Darling Harbour under construction. Ugly developments have made it nearly unrecognisable. We are resting.

6 September 1986

Wallara Ranch

Dinner at communal tables, just like at Hill End twenty-five years ago, even the menu of roast beef, peas and carrots is the same.

After the rain, there are hundreds of miles of wild flowers, carpeting the red soil with tender silver-green and blinding yellow. Wattles are in riotous bloom and everything is gentle and furtive. The absolute remoteness and emptiness of this vista, and the incredible light in which everything is bathed, made me think that the transition from this life must be like this light.

It's healing the soul.

We walked through the creek bed over smooth large stones, white sand, red rocks, ferns and snowy gums, sitting on some concave seats for painting. I have oils by now.

7 September 1986

Mona arrived. We are going to the Kings Canyon. Wake-up call 5.30, breakfast in the dark and to the bus to join the tour. The overnight bag is as light as I could make it, only the basic colours.

I was sitting in the Lost City among round boulders, a mountain each, scaly like a fish's skin, in red and black. I had a pullover and a heavy coat, sat on a stone, fighting the wind and pouring out four paintings.

10 September 1986

Alice Springs

We set off in two vehicles for a day in Rainbow Valley. I ponder the fact that some of the world's most magnificent and spiritual places in this country have to be reached by hundreds and thousands of (sometimes) dreary miles on corrugated dusty, sandy, stony roads.

We left our rented Mitsubishi, a useless city car, off the Alice Springs–Adelaide highway and packed our gear into Mona's four-wheel drive.

Jancsi and I, Mona and Mina (the dog) drove towards my treasure trove, this time amidst a profusion of wild flowers. The mushroom, our beloved picnic cave with the birds' nests, surrounded us with shade and a cool breeze, and the presence of something unseen.

The day flowed as Mona and I painted. Jancsi read Morris West's new book. Mina had her own supply of water in a thermos and ran back frequently to lap it up in the cave. Sandwiches, cool drinks, a stretch on the incredible red and fine sand, burrowing hollows for our bodies.

As we started photographing I felt I saw all the intricate shapes for the first time. It will be intriguing to see the slides. If I'm right, the rains and winds have sculpted and changed them, perhaps the light caused variations, or my vision perceives them in other ways.

I know I wanted to contain much less in the frame, simpler images.

As the sun slanted deeper and the shadows became longer and more velvety, my excitement grew.

Obviously this is not a landscape one can 'paint', record with patient brush. It's not a landscape at all. It is a surreal miracle of found objects and I felt so fortunate to have been led there.

Eighty photographs later, I thought of this place as Mona's enduring gift to me.

Mona took us to Ewaninga where the oldest Aboriginal carvings are. She feels I should see them. Lovingly placed steel plaques lead the viewer. Long, long before Julius Caesar and the Egyptian hieroglyphs these images were chiselled with sharp stones into red rock.

There are concentric circles, primitive renderings of alligators with fern-like faces, Olsenish tracks over landmarks, probably mapping waterholes.

I became intrigued by the tunnels the ants dig. They suck a glue-like moisture out of spinifex and build fantastic 'highways'. I held a broken-up piece in my hand, it hardens to a cement-like substance and looks like macaroni. Out of the same substance they erect eight-foot-tall ant hills, surely a greater edifice to skilled engineering than the pyramids. The 'highways' crisscross vast distances, and we watch an army of workers getting on with it.

Mona's new house is a rambling, flat-roofed, terraced building, with Cocky the parrot, who greeted us with the old 'Hello Cocky', and four wild parrots chatter from the tree. There is a birdbath facing the terrace.

11 September 1986

280 kilometres today. Painted three oils in Ormiston Gorge.

I'm too close to them now, but I think I might be approaching my aim, in which landscape and figure are the same spirit. There were bathers at the Gorge, and I placed them before the rocks, on the sand-dunes, or at the old Telegraph Station. There is even a figure doing a cartwheel. I am thinking more of brushstrokes than rocks, of which way the stroke works in the painting than which way it appears in nature.

12 September 1986

Today at Simpson's Gap too, there are figures embedded in the paint. I now have twenty-four little paintings.

We felt happy in the Heavitree Gap motel. It's built around a quadrangle and each side looks at the magnificent rocks. At night, they are floodlit and wallabies hop close. They look at us looking at them.

7 October 1986

Sydney

Orban died. Fittingly, his funeral is on Thursday. What a gap he leaves.

7 November 1986

Canberra

Luncheon for the president of Israel, Chaim Herzog, given by Bob Hawke at Parliament House, Canberra. I arrived on the morning flight, wanting to see an exhibition at the university's Drill Hall, but was captured by Syd and Billie Einfeld.

We got into a taxi. Driver's name was Shlomo Cohen. 'You must be Jewish,' said Billie. Not only that, but an Israeli who used to be sports commentator on Tel Aviv television.

Hawke and the leader of the opposition, John Howard, spoke first, then Herzog who is Irish born. The food was kosher. Joe Brender gave me a 'lift' back to Sydney on his private jet.

Gratifying. Hawke introduced me to Herzog: as 'One of our most famous painters in Australia'.

14 November 1986

Sydney

I saw a magnificent Josl Bergner show at the Holdsworth. He lives in Israel now and the themes of the exhibition seem about Hassidic tales, myths, Jewish legends. Orthodox Jews as angels, as birds, as predators in ancient bastions, very strange and surreal and beautiful.

Gisella wants to donate the largest work to the Art Gallery of NSW, but would they accept it? I said I would speak to Barry.

Meanwhile I painted Bob Juniper (whose exhibition at the Holdsworth is also masterly). He sits in a black Anzac hat and a pale blue denim jacket, black and white striped shirt. The picture appeared in two hours like magic. A good one.

Emmet Costello, a Jesuit priest whose mother I once painted, arrived with twelve new tapes for me. I have two shelves full with these marvellous gifts. I take the Schubert Impromptus into the car and listen while I drive. I didn't realise that I know almost all of them intimately as Anyu played them all through my childhood.

16 November 1986

Sydney

János is getting a worldwide response to his rainforest information magazine.

30 November 1986

Each morning I take one of the original small oils on paper and varnish it, and some go through transformations. From these transformed ones I then tackle the large version. Without fear and inhibitions, it is slashed, changed, refreshed, mostly in one session, then put aside to rest, à la Delacroix. (The last brushstroke is always done by God.)

I went to the B'nai B'rith's 'Paint-in' which I took upon myself to oversee. Senior citizens and kids with texta colours scribbled all over a huge white board. Three Orban students, Mary Indyk, Maadi Einfeld and Judy Auerbach were my handmaidens. Maadi had the brilliant idea to bring three paper cut outs which, when unfolded, formed mandalas. We glued them on, painted over stencils, tore the paper off, and that kicked the board to life. After an hour, we instructed our enthusiasts to stop painting, and then we erased what was superfluous with white paint. Wonder of wonders, a celebratory hymn appeared on the board, so successful, they will print postcards of it. It's called *Painting for peace*.

21 December 1986

A strange and difficult Archibald and Wynne. There was nothing that jumped at me. And in such a flat year, where the just-all-right ones blushed on a plateau, Clifton Pugh didn't send in, or Margaret Woodward, who might have won this time. The same artists turn up year after year with monotonous regularity; but we try to inject more variety into the final selection.

I had to compromise in a major way when I agreed to give the Archibald Prize to Davida Allen. This one was less vulgar and crude than is her usual work and, I must say, in her portrait of her father-in-law (hosing the garden) every Australian teenager can recognise the face of authority and disapproval. It was the boldest choice since Dobell won with Joshua Smith, but apart from the usual 'my six year old could paint that' comments, not too many people will have their sensibilities ruffled.

Rosemary Madigan won the Wynne Prize with a sculpture, a sandstone torso. The first time in thirty-three years it hasn't been won by a landscape.

Albert Tucker judged the Sulman and split the prize. Nigel Thomson is menacing enough to counterbalance the anecdotal expressions on the faces of the insane, and Wendy Sharpe (just out of art school). Tucker has a cantankerous disrespect for reputation or track record, which somehow wouldn't matter if he had respect for quality.

A long day that was, what with the final judging, the board meeting, the press announcement, then the opening.

27 December 1986

As I have more than twenty small paintings for the exhibition and perhaps ten very large ones, I felt I needed an inbetween size. At the moment these seem to flow easily. I do the drawing with charcoal at night, either on white ground or on my mottled grounds. Next morning I work mostly horizontally on the table, using acrylic like oil paint for the first time.

I had a lunch party for Andrew Sibley who came from Melbourne with Irena, the Lynns (back from Paris), Rapotec, and Charles Blackman who brought Diana Davidson, the printer. It was good to have old friends. But although I started cooking three days ahead, I rushed to and fro like the pendulum of a clock, missing most of the conversation.

10 January 1987

János phoned to say that Bodhi is on the train. He's coming to visit Janaka and Francesca and would I meet him at the station. Bodhi arrives barefoot, punk haircut, with a guitar. Big hug. I love him. On the way to Francesca Bodhi tells me that they (himself, Janaka and Brett) are busking. They are making money playing guitar and singing on the street. I find it hard to take.

A few days later Greta, Peter and I went to fetch him for dinner. His punk hair has been tinted pink. Jancsi calls him his pink punk, fondly, but insists he wears shoes. He borrows a pair of Janaka's. Bewildering.

According to Greta 'he's doing his own thing'. At ten? He doesn't phone. Why? Greta says he is afraid to see us because he has now shaved the sides of his head. On his last day he phoned saying that he'd like to come over. He says, 'Juc, one day when you have time, would you paint my portrait?' He brought his guitar, sits on the floor barelegged and strums and sings rainforest songs, and that's how I paint him. The angelic boy face under the punk dome.

15 January 1987

Greta showed us a video of her dance theatre, held at the Channon. I just wasn't prepared for what I saw. Though the tape itself was a bit dark, it would have been quite at home in any art gallery. Greta chose the projected backdrops, she designed the costumes which were lovingly hand painted by the cast, and selected the electronic music. She also choreographed this avant-garde performance. It has all my admiration.

16 January 1987

Gisella Scheinberg was here to see pictures for the exhibition, and put the prices on the paintings. They are somewhat higher than two years ago but less than others of my standing. Maybe this is right. Kevin doubled his and didn't sell. We don't collect Cassabs, says Jancsi.

I measure each one for the catalogue. Gisella writes the measurements down.

Lou enthused. We'll see.

My back is better with thrice-weekly treatments but tires too quickly.

31 January 1987

János phoned Greta to tell her he is disappointed that Bodhi chose to visit Francesca, Janaka and Brett, rather than go bushwalking with him.

For Christ's sake, are they right? Isn't a ten year old told what not to do?

Greta picked up Bodhi at the station. The two sides of his beautiful head were shorn bald, the long ponytail has grown longer, and the top is now forced upwards with gel. The hair is a neon-strength, shocking pink. A colour which does not exist in nature. Greta found that he has lice in this work of art, so we proceeded with an anti-lice spray.

Dropping Jancsi at the Hakoah Club, we went to Woolworths where shocked shoppers stared at Bodhi. One of the employees (who obviously didn't connect me with my grandson) muttered to another: 'What a gross thing to do to a kid.'

For twenty-five years I have asked God to make normal men out of my sons. I now add the same prayer for Bodhi, in whom I fear the streak is perpetuated.

2 February 1987

The truck took the paintings to the framer.

I hugged Jancsi this morning as the truck was leaving. Thanking him for all his help. Giving him credit for his immaculate perceptions.

Sitting before the next picture that's meant already for the Melbourne show in August, I think of the story of Hershele.

Hershele was the village idiot in Munkács. As he shuffled along Main Street, before the Csillag coffee house, the children taunted, vexed, annoyed, teased, sickened, molested and plagued him until they achieved their goal. He screamed. One day, the adults explained to the children about the misfortune of Hershele and they stopped their torture. Hershele was suspicious, bewildered and frightened. He ran after the children, saying: 'Why don't you cry "Hershele"?'

That's how I feel. Getting used to adverse criticism.

5 February 1987

Canberra

Packed my evening gown into an overnight bag and caught the afternoon plane to Canberra for the Murdoch dinner.

Stayed at the Canberra International by necessity, because the Ansett coaches only picked up guests from there and the Lakeside. Recognised my Leo nature feeling totally at home in luxury. In the atrium of the tropical garden and the non-motel, non-impersonal room.

'Cavan' is an hour and a half from Canberra, through rolling hills and yellow grass, gums, stones, cattle, sheep. It's a rambling old house. Anna and Rupert Murdoch greeted the arriving guests, passing us to an army of waiters with trays of champagne and Pims and flies.

With the exception of Tim Storrier there are no artists among the 250, but all the well-known faces from television and politics are visible. The prime minister and Hazel Hawke, Punch Sulzberger, chairman and publisher of the *New York Times*, and John Howard, the Wrans, James Mollison, the Capons.

We are in a huge tent, worthy of the Shah of Iran.

I glimpse Rolf Harris, John Spender, Paul Keating, senators, Adele Weiss, Dame Leonie Kramer. White orchids and bush flowers fill the six-foot-long glass tubes across the tent.

Rupert and Hawke made speeches.

Later at home Jancsi said that it's like Genghis Khan vanquishing the government, and everybody bows, worships, pays court and genuflects.

8 February 1987

Sydney

Lovely Sunday evening at home. After our walk on the beach with seagulls, a boxer and a schnauzer, listened to a fantastic concert from Monte Carlo with Yehudi Menuhin, Itzhak Perlman, Jessye Norman, and Peter Ustinov as presenter, Rodriguez on the guitar.

Reading a book about Max Beckmann.

1 March 1987

I listed forty-seven portraits for a retrospective exhibition, without effort. That's not including this year's work in which I hope to paint more portraits of the art world.

I enlarged one of the oil sketches of Marea Gazzard in a landscape of her sculptures. It will be good when her body has the same weight and chunkiness as the pots.

Robert Morley came to sit for me. It's been about fifteen years since the last portrait. 'One of the great advantages of old age,' he said 'is deafness.'

8 March 1987

We booked a trip, 21 April, to Vienna, then Budapest. I cross my fingers.

14 March 1987

I am badly shaken. Judge Raine is dead.

As we went on our evening walk, Jancsi said he had not collected his *Herald* for two days. I went upstairs to get his key. We had each other's keys. I asked Rodney Moses, another neighbour, to come in with me. We switched the lights on. Nothing. Then we proceeded to the bedroom. He was in his bed. Dead.

16 April 1987

My exhibition at the Holdsworth had one review: Jack Lynn's. The *Herald* didn't bother, but what the heck. I sold twenty-two paintings, and hundreds of people came to see it and it was a triumph.

17 April 1987

János and Bodhi came to Sydney for the preview of his film *Earth first* which was screened at the Chauvel cinema. It's a wonderful film. János gave a talk before it began. His beard has disappeared, perhaps because Inji, his new girlfriend, doesn't like it. János asked me to do a few line drawings of them. Bodhi came every day with János, and consequently we spent a lot of time together. He and Janaka drew and painted for hours in the studio.

A few days later Greta arrived.

Why am I so sad that they parted? They are a haven to each other, and such good friends.

13 May 1987

London

First day we went to see the new Turner wing at the Tate, what a treat. And today, to the rambling National Gallery, with our newly-found old-aged wisdom.

We looked at a small exhibition, Bodyline, where Perugino hangs with Degas's pastel nude, Correggio with Cranach, Rubens with Piero della Francesca. My choice is a great Filippino Lippi with a madonna which melts into the white sky. Then the impressionists. Jancsi thought Cézanne's *Avenue at Chantilly* is like a prayer. One then comes to a sunken room where the giant Monet *Waterlilies* painting is gently concave, and standing before it, it envelops one like a Rothko. Pulsating with lilacs which turn invisibly into green.

The Art from Europe exhibition is a big bore, pretentious and mostly without quality.

The only thing of interest is a Marlene Dumas with larger than life-size heads. There are also balaclavas in boxes under glass like precious antiquities. Why in a museum? We revisit a quiet Balthus, a Derain which seems ahead of its time, a Rothko room with tremendous floating images.

Our Kirchner is better than theirs. First day, Peter Thorneycroft sent his driver to take us to his exhibition of watercolours. It was a sell-out. He has become a minor master from the hesitant amateur I used to teach thirty years ago.

18 May 1987

On a free evening we went to Soho, which four years ago crawled with prostitutes, sex shops and blue movies, and is now clean as a whistle. Converted to Chinatown it is all restaurants and shops.

Edmund Capon's introduction brought me to the National Portrait Gallery's Dr John Hayes. I want to make a gift of the new Robert Morley portrait or the Brett Whiteley (if he is eligible as an Australian), and left the reproductions with him. He has to consult trustees as we do. The Gaitskell hangs in a prominent position. It is much admired and they sell postcards of it.

Since Michael Servaes died I don't have a gallery in London. I rang André Kalman, where I held my first two shows in 1959 and 1961, and who parted company with me when I started my abstract phase. I told him I would be ready for him now, showed him photos of my March exhibition and he gladly took me on. Not with a one-man show, however, he can't be bothered with openings or critics any more. But he chose the ones he likes and if I send him three or four paintings, they will take their place on the wall with the Sutherlands, Moores, Lawrys, and Hitchens, etc. A foothold.

26 May 1987

Paris

The Arctic air has followed us from London. Grey sky, a drizzle. The hotel Macmahon is on one of the avenues radiating out from the Etoile. We have a balcony overlooking the Avenue Macmahon, good beds, bath, loo, minibar, television, looking as French as Matisse with shutters.

Vera Székely, my cousin, burst into the hotel looking boyish in a black leather jacket, trousers and high red boots, and reminisced about events fifty years ago. She drove us along the boulevards. We walked on St Germain, saw an Albers exhibition at the Galerie Denis René.

First morning the Musée d'Orsay, a mega-monster railway station converted to house the nineteenth century and all of the Jeu de Paume.

We went to the Printemps, Expo Australia. Lloyd Rees's exhibition lent dignity to the diorama of a red Ayers Rock pavilion with stuffed koalas and kangaroos.

The Musée Picasso, a hidden palace. Walked from St Sebastian de Froissant for twenty minutes, but what bliss! Outpouring of genius, little time for *belle peinture*. It hits you in the guts anyway. Mural collage, *Femmes a ses toilettes*, tatty, white cut-out sculptures, shop soiled and for that very reason, human, warm and approachable. A great place. Lunches always in the musées, to yawn and rest and go on and on.

The Pompidou took all day. Special exhibition on the ground floor was of Jean Charles Blais who is thirty. Like a *Plakatreisser* in reverse he sticks 10.8-metre sheets of paper on each other in layers and tears it in every direction, with the edges curling and sometimes shaped into half-moons or triangles. There are torsos without heads or feet. As he uses tins of paint with huge brushes, the richness of texture is achieved by the demolition. An impressive talent.

Another special exhibition includes John Flannagan who sculpts ten-foot rabbits. One was called *Nijinsky hare*. Enzo Cucchi and Clemente (known from Canberra). Gilbert and George frame slick photos expensively; over each giant assemblage, in large letters is FUCK, CUNT, QUEER and COMMUNISM. Nothing to do with the content of the photos.

We went to the Musée d'Art Moderne. As we went round, commenting about that Pascin, this Soutine, in Hungarian, a museum guard spoke to us in Hungarian. She is a poet, Esther Forrai, a friend of Krisztina Passuth (who wrote a book of Moholy Nagy, and one of Orban) who is the librarian of the museum. We all had lunch together. Krisztina said: 'Remember, twenty years ago I was approaching you the same way, at the Venice Biennale.'

4 June 1987

New York

To the Museum of Modern Art to see the new exhibition, Berlin Art 1961–87. In the rebuilding of the postwar years, Berlin sought to restore the cultural and artistic freedom of earlier days. Then, in 1961, the wall divided the city, rendering West Berlin a virtual island.

So emerged a highly charged, socially involved art that has since become a major current. Young artists turned to the human figure to express the despair and isolation of their situation. Baselitz and Schönebeck, students at the Hochschule für bildende Künste, organised an exhibition and published a manifesto: *Pandemonium*. Baselitz is perhaps best known now for the upside-down imagery of paintings. Hödicke came through strongly and Markus Lupertz. His work in the Dithyramb series refers to a Dionysian hymn, in a wild, irregular way. It was Nietzsche's term for the turning point between shapelessness and form, that point for an artist between the abstract and the figurative. These invented objects assume an almost mystical quality.

8 June 1987

The Metropolitan Museum has a new Rockefeller wing with fantastic wood sculptures from Papua New Guinea lit to perfection, in memory of his son who died there.

I met Georgette Klinger for the first time. She is a new Helena Rubinstein with beauty salons in all major cities. Just voted woman of the year by the industry. She was Gyöngyi Eckstein in Munkács. Jancsi knew her when she was sixteen.

15 June 1987

Los Angeles

The Los Angeles County Museum is exhibiting Treasures of the Holy Land. Ancient art from the Museum of Jerusalem. Antiques covering all archeological periods from the eleventh millennium BC to the end of the Byzantine period in the seventh century AD.

There is Avant-Garde in the Eighties. At its entrance is a splendid sculpture by Kiefer, the *Book*. It has two wings, angel, or eagle, spanning eight metres. Made of lead, steel and tin.

The new Museum of Contemporary Art is downtown. Do we want to sit on a bus for one hour there and one hour back? Of course we do. And *was* it worthwhile! My only regret, we could only see one of the buildings. We ran out of time. It's the most magnificent space for modern art anywhere, including New York.

What it contains is a different matter. It goes on quantity rather than the excellence of individual work. On the other hand, it's a good thing to show a whole room of each artist, usually with one or more early works. How clumsy and mediocre Pollock still was in 1944. His *Enchanted forest* of 1947 already shows the inventor in full flight. One has to keep in mind the scale of the building which is enormous—leaving more than usual museum space for all its artists.

17 June 1987

Also visited the Paul Getty Museum. While we had lunch on the terrace I suddenly saw Annette Olszanski who is on a museum tour with the Art Gallery of NSW Society.

23 June 1987

Honolulu

As this God-given gift of a journey draws to its conclusion I want to emphasise one of the most important yields of our distance from home.

In spite of all old-age idiosyncrasies we were as close as two humans can get. I have always said that, living with Jancsi, I never knew the meaning of the word loneliness, that I have never been bored with him. Perhaps another aspect of our closeness is that this relationship has allowed all the young ages in oneself to find compatible partners.

7 July 1987

Sydney

It took a week to work through the mountain of mail and wait for my soul to arrive in Ocean Avenue.

26 July 1987

Kevin Connor's term as trustee is over and John Firth-Smith joins the board. Very tall and soft and mild. Lou says 'he has no teeth'. Neither have I for that matter. But he is a good artist and I have little doubt that our judgements about quality will work.

Colin Lanceley's project show opened at the Art Gallery of NSW. He started as one of the Annandale imitation realists, street-scavenging poetry as Schwitters did in 1920. It's interesting to follow his progress:

he made the picture plane more sculptural in the 1960s, with antennae emerging from its rippled sides, a bouquet of shapes. It's an exultant exhibition.

I painted Anna Murdoch in two sittings. She said she was thrilled that she looks 'like a writer, not like someone's wife!' I took Dame Elizabeth through some galleries with Anna. To the Bonython, to the Art Gallery of NSW to see the Lanceley show, then to the Liverpool Street Holdsworth which is a space for unknown, young and experimental art—like her own sculpture centre in Melbourne. Anna saw a silk-screen painting which she bought for 'Cavan', their country home near Canberra. We went on to see the Lynn show but instead of buying a painting, Dame Elizabeth bought a wonderful sculpture from the fellow exhibitor, Fabian, a neglected, old and excellent sculptor.

9 August 1987

Melbourne

My show with David Ellis. The gallery is in a back lane and hard to find. There is a train strike, but about a hundred people turned up. I sold eleven paintings at the opening. Dame Elizabeth was the first to arrive and the last to leave, taking us to dinner. Conversation lasted till 11.30. She then drove me to the Regency Hotel and went home to the farm at Langwarrin.

She also bought *Bending figures*, one of the major works.

Clifton Pugh came, Louis Kahan and Charles Bush.

Next day David took me to see Tapestry Workshop, Dame Elizabeth's baby. It was a first and great experience with Boyd's forest painting being enlarged to about twenty metres for the new Parliament House. Eight weavers working on it among a 'palette' of exquisite coloured wool.

19 August 1987

Imre Klein, a classmate from Beregszász, wrote me a five-page letter from Israel. He wants to compile an anthology, a book of our town with old photographs and memories from us all. Somebody sent in a photo, which he enclosed. I see myself with three girls from our class, in white dresses, shoes, and hats surrounded by Czechoslovakian soldiers.

The venue is the courtyard of your high school at the unveiling of the flag of the Betar Zionist movement. Please do a painting for the cover which would convey somehow that we used to exist. Unfortunately, a short history of Beregszász was published by the Russians. Not even the Nazis (or the Japanese) falsified history so shamelessly. If somebody were to see this book in fifty years, they will read only about communist strikers who tried to fight for social equality in factories founded by no one. Not a Jewish name to be found. In the Second World War, 6000 'citizens' perished. There were no Jews, no industrialists or merchants or intellectuals. We had no merit because we didn't exist. My book should convince readers of the opposite.

When I read the letter, I wondered what I could paint about Beregszász. Jancsi picked up a 1985 painting, painted for no particular reason, a crowd climbing an invisible staircase.

'You have done this,' Jancsi said, 'for this book.' So I had.

I placed the synagogue into the left bottom corner, tilting and aflame, and some other buildings I remembered. The martyrs rise above the town.

5 September 1987

János wanted us to come to Sydney University to hear him talk.

Neville Wran is giving the keynote address followed by John Seed.

'Threat to Rainforests,' A worldwide perspective of rainforest destruction. János is an authority in his field, polished, intelligent.

6 September 1987

Last time János had a dinner-suit on was at his matriculation, I think. He didn't come home from the seminar and I felt the usual anxiety. Lo and behold, he arrived at 6.30 with a rented suit and we were festive at Peter's fortieth birthday dinner. Bodhi had a velvet black tie on his jumpsuit.

Leighton came from New Zealand. Henry Feiner was there. He is an architect now. And Van Cooney, also from school. From the glamour set: Anne Landa came, and Yvonne, resplendent in white fox, Sandra Leveson, the host's partner in black velvet with sequins. After the crush at cocktails, we were seated at long tables. Peter invited Abe and Doreen Saffron, who hangs on by his nails before a jail sentence, and seated them at our table.

We all thought it was decent of Peter to stick by his friend. As Leighton pointed out in his speech, 'The best bookie is here tonight, the best horse trainer, the best artist, the best accountant and the best restaurateur in Sydney.'

7 September 1987

Bodhi went to visit Janaka. I am the hen who sits on the ducks' eggs while the ducks are in the water leaving the hen desperate on the shore. Bodhi bought a skateboard with his own money.

Greta left for her first Feldenkrais workshop.

János gave me instructions. He is buying a second-hand car and he has no time to see it because he has to prepare a press release for tomorrow's action against the Malaysian government's destruction of rainforests. If the NRMA rings, I must write down all the problems ... oil smoke, worn piston rings, old battery, old fan-belt, an oil leak in the gearbox, something wrong with the universal joints on the tail shaft, no reverse lights, clutch needs adjusting, gearshift needs lubricating ...

8 September 1987

Opening of Orban's exhibition at the Holdsworth. All paintings so well known to us, we only spend half an hour.

Tom Orban, when congratulated on his son's success in Vancouver: 'It's my fate. I used to be the son of my father, now I am the father of my son.'

21 September 1987

Ayers Rock

I first saw Ayers Rock twenty-eight years ago. Now it is Uluru National Park. I remember the shed I used to stay in, the bunk on which I slept, and how at the end of our stay the plane took our sheets to Alice Springs to be washed. There is an underground lake now (an aquifer) from which an oasis has been created.

The Yulara Sheraton, with a sparkling swimming pool, which in spite of 2000 solar panels is too cold for us. Sixty spectacular sails overhead to deflect the heat and encourage a gentle breeze.

Mount Olga is Katatjuta now. A corrugated, deeply swaying, sandy track leads to it.

Went into Kantju Gorge walking track, saw caves with madonna-like formations Dubuffet would have been proud of, and of course, the fantastic birds' nests on the ceiling of the caves. My studio was the rented Ford Falcon.

24 October 1987

Sydney

One would despair if one was younger about glorification of Perspecta, a bicentennial exhibition at the Art Gallery of NSW. Everyone in it has done better. Ken Unsworth's installation of one white plaster head in an empty room with a windblown curtain; John Nixon's scythe attached to his ovals, most of them adorned with Malevich's cross. Elwyn Lynn writes this morning, that not only is the style minimal, the quality is minimal, too. About the catalogue: 'It has some of the finest claptrap, pseudo-profundity and balderdash gathered in the cause of obfuscation.'

No wonder painters like me are out of curatorial fashion at home. I admire Jack's courage in writing against the Perspecta, even though Victoria is the assistant curator.

27 October 1987

Robert Klippel and Rosemary Madigan live in Balmain, and I drove out on Saturday afternoon to do an oil sketch of them together.

Bob has extended his body image into his house, his shell.

Discarded old washing machines clutter the yard—presumably his raw material for sculpture. Inside, there is room after room of dishevelment and jumble, or so it seemed to my alien eyes. The house is full of sculptures, hundreds of them on tabletops, windowsills and drums, in cardboard boxes, on pillars, a perplexity, a network of an artist's mind.

I chose a bay window as background with the water shimmering through. Bob sits on the left smoking his pipe. There is a typical Klippel machine sculpture beside him. Rosemary sits on a window seat, chin cupped in hand, lavender blue skirt. Beside her I have put a small torso.

Klippel and Madigan, on the six-foot canvas are half-size, something I haven't done before.

On Sunday I did an oil sketch of Margaret Olley amidst her still lifes.

I had Ann Thomson's first sitting, in a red hat.

30 November 1987

Margaret Olley's first sitting yesterday went like a charm. She raised one hand to her face and I caught it like a butterfly with thick brushstrokes. The apples are overgrown and too red, waiting for my tonal judgement.

Bob Klippel and Rosemary Madigan came on Saturday to pick up the marble torso, and Bob seemed to be impressed by the large composition. He liked Channy's portrait, said: 'The eyes are amazing, as if surprised and desperate about the injustice of the stroke.'

A new commission. John Neild, who has multiple sclerosis and is in a wheelchair. I did a sketch of him and got acquainted. He is a beautiful man with fine bones, white hair. He rests his head on a cushion as he has lost the ability to move it. The hands rest on a checked rug over his knees. I did the sketch on the terrace with a green-yellow lawn and shrubs in the background.

Ann Thomson's second and final sitting this afternoon. Hazel eyes under the red hat. Good. Before she left she sat down at the piano and played a lovely sonata for me. I played a Hungarian folk song.

Clare took me to see Gordon Chater in the *Rocky Horror Show* before he sits tomorrow morning.

5 December 1987

I asked Gordon Chater why it is necessary to make the sound so loud? It is, I said, like eating curry ceaselessly. How does one enjoy subtle tastes?

Teenagers were uttering piercing screams and howls at hermaphrodites on stage. Men were touching each other's pricks, women making advances to each other but crisscrossing the act to the opposite sex as well and not taking it seriously either. He thinks it's a catharsis and a laundry for repressed emotion.

6 December 1987

I have prayed for decades for my children who seemed to lose their way. It was only recently that I realised that János has actually found his. Although different to what I expected, my wish was granted.

And Peter, who for many long years has talked about being miscast in his role of businessman. A sensitive soul in a cut-throat game. The other night he mentioned in passing that a big corporation tried to head-hunt him. 'I'm not for sale,' he told them. 'I do what I like to do and I like where I am.'

8 December 1987

My last Archibald and Wynne judging, and about time. Seven years. A record number of entries. The first day took ten hours.

An attendant gave me a press-cutting which said: 'Paddington artist Stephen Wesley Gorton startled the NSWAG last week when he submitted his entry for the Archibald Prize. Its title? *Nude self-portrait with erection.*'

Mr Gorton runs an art school, now showing an exhibition of his erotic works. 'It is a self-portrait of me at my best,' he said. 'I must say I am exhausted after it. It took a lot out of me.'

Louis James' landscape was rejected yesterday, but today I scratched it back with all ten nails.

My greatest joy was that Andrew Lostia, the boy whom I have helped since he was fifteen, rewarded me with a convincing portrait of staring eyes and was accepted. So was Caroline Williams with a portrait of Charles Blackman as Alice, with two rabbits. Bravo, Caroline.

19 December 1987

The Archibald is drawing strangely hybrid performances from artists who submit work that differs from what they do the rest of the year.

I was as surprised as anyone when we voted Bill Robinson the winner. His cows proliferate on the walls of the Ray Hughes Gallery and who fits the mould here in a slightly larrikin way. His equestrian self-portrait is mocking even to the horse which focuses on the viewer.

25 December 1987

János and Inji arrived yesterday in the early morning. He phoned the night before saying that they are hitchhiking to Sydney so maybe they'll arrive in the wee hours. Which is why in the wee hours we didn't sleep, and tottered like zombies all the next day.

Greta and Bodhi went over to Paddington before ringing that they wanted to be picked up, so János fetched them.

Peter came for Christmas dinner which we ordered from the Chinese vegetarian. It was festive nonetheless.

Peter bought Bodhi a Walkman and a tiny shiny torch. We gave him a remote control car and new tubes of gouaches. He gave us all self-made pottery jars.

3 January 1988

Bodhi has been 'discovered' playing at Paddington market by some talent scout, and with Janaka, they have been offered a job at Darling Harbour during the Sydney Festival. Bodhi is shorn at the sides again, and his blond top is an angry magenta.

10 January 1988

Unexpectedly Peter announced that he thinks he is getting married.
I almost choked.
Who is she? When did it happen?
It turns out that Peter met a young South African woman, Rene Reznick, in my studio. When a friend of Rene's visited her from London, Peter fell in love. Her name is Shayne, and she's from Zimbabwe.
'We feel we are right for each other. We feel comfortable together.'
Shayne works for a property development company in London, and she can possibly transfer to Sydney. She is thirty-one.
'I'll bring her over on Wednesday night.'

Peter came around seven with Shayne. I still can't believe it. It's a miracle. Bachelors at forty rarely change their minds. Shayne is what we call special. She is warm and intelligent, and beautiful and sophisticated as well.
I will pray that the short spark (less than three weeks) will grow into a large flame.

15 January 1988

Bali

We are settled in our room in the Bali Beach Hotel waiting for my cousin Zsuzsi and her husband Teddy.
Our friend, Chevy, the taxi driver, has a new Toyota minibus, ideal for when Zsuzsi and Teddy arrive.
We swim, we sleep, I start to feel on holiday.

21 January 1988

We went to meet them at the airport, and we saw Teddy being pushed in a wheelchair by a Garuda steward. 'He had a heart-attack,' said Jancsi.

'Maybe he broke a leg,' I offered.

Zsuzsi said with her wide-open, innocent gaze,' We always travel with a wheelchair. One doesn't have to stand for hours in the queue before customs, or worry about porters.'

Interconnecting rooms are important because Teddy snores.

Chevy is like a mother to us, bringing bottled springwater on trips, carrying our gear, finding our models. He bought four collapsible chairs for us.

On our last day he invited us to his house. He is a friend and this was an honour.

29 January 1988

Sydney

I was awarded a high honour, Officer in the Australian Order, *and* in the bicentennial year. A truly uplifting, unforgettable day. We were invited to the Opera House forecourt in the morning, saw splendid costumes, a choir of 200, the Sydney Symphony Orchestra with Joan Carden, Prince Charles and Princess Diana, all the heads of state, every state governor, and all the ministers. The tall ships came in majestically. (Anne von Bertouch started the trip on one of them in England nine months ago.) Helicopters and planes in formation. Jancsi was with me.

In the evening I took Peter to the premier's reception in the new overseas passenger terminal. We went by ferry and the sparkle, the thousands of small craft, the tall ships and the red sun setting on the Opera House were indescribable.

There were eighteen telephone messages, telegrams, letters, flowers.

A sitting with Richard Bonynge. That handsome head, done in one hour.

Next day Olsen came in a Spanish hat. I was delighted. Jancsi argued passionately against it. An act of bravery then, to paint the hat. His hands are locked near his chest. That's bad, Jancsi said. I don't know how I still finished up with such a good painting.

4 March 1988

Joan Sutherland was not finished in *one* sitting, but it was a fabulous beginning and it was good to see her again.

John Olsen took us and Annette Olszanski to dinner in the garden of an Italian restaurant in Paddington. When she was Annette Shaw, in Haefliger's time, they (the Shaws) became Olsen's patrons. They sent him to Paris, for the first time. Not only did he remember this, decades later, but freshly divorced and lonely, he burnt a vivid flame all evening for Annette, touching and a bit sad to witness.

6 March 1988

The morning of the opening.

Philip Krass, the framer, asked me how I slept. I said. 'At five this morning I was counting sheep.'

'We counted paintings,' he said, 'and they are all there.'

Joan Sutherland and Richard Bonynge saw the show the day before the opening as they are leaving Sydney. She bought hers. She bought his.

At six the doors were opened and people poured inside. From then on I was signing books like crazy.

At seven, Morris West was introduced by Max Kelly of the National Trust. Morris said: 'Judy is in every sense of the word an artist. She has mastered the full grammar of her craft. She is endowed with that special vision which enables her to look beyond.'

Morris has taken up painting and he came through our door with one under his armpit, the rest rolled up in the other hand. Like a schoolboy to the teacher. He said that after his double bypass, painting saved his sanity.

'It gave my brain a terrible shock to have been separated from my heart. I couldn't write a word for weeks.'

9 March 1988

I wrote to Morris West ... 'Your warmth seemed to me like those tile stoves of my childhood on which one could lean for comfort. If I have a gift for friendship, it is minuscule compared to yours. I thank you for an unforgettable and truly great experience.'

11 March 1988

Dinah Dysart lent me the tape of Morris West's opening speech. I popped it into my recorder, pushed the button, and erased the speech.

One owes the gods a sacrifice, says Lou.

1 April 1988

While the portrait exhibition was on at the S.H. Ervin Gallery and life was throwing more curved balls than usual, my refuge was Heddy Varga's pool.

Afternoons, hot and shaky, I dropped by, went through the white courtyard where János's mandala hangs, through the garden where geraniums spill over stone walls, into the pool room. The water is heated, not a soul to be seen, so clear that the reflection of tall palms forms a picture across which I swim.

Juliska is a different haven. Cold coffee with ice-cream floating in it, and lively conversation with my old friend.

When the Hermitage exhibition was opened by the prime minister, he referred to Edmund Capon as Ed Campion.

2GB wants me to do an interview with Gough Whitlam, who will talk about my exhibition of portraits. I rang him offering to guide him through the show. He arrived on Saturday afternoon, strolling in in shirt sleeves and spent an hour there with me. He pointed at *Portrait of John Kampfner*. 'Does he know about us meeting here?'

'Yes. He knows of our rendezvous. Does Margaret know?'

'No, no, she does not.' In a mock whisper.

Sunday is my last day at the Ervin Gallery and there is talk of it going to the National Library in Canberra next year, and possibly to other university galleries.

4 April 1988

Shayne tells me Peter has delegated her to organise the wedding. She also arranges for a carpet cleaner, cares for Cain, empties drawers, sorts out the debris of bachelor life. It seems too good to be true. I pinch myself and pray.

6 April 1988

Went out with Peter and Shayne for dinner at a pub in Paddington. They talked about Bali, and about working painfully and hard on their relationship (my heart sank) but came up full of hope and resolution. To take brisk walks together. For more positive thinking. For reading aloud to each other.

13 April 1988

Shayne is growing more and more like a daughter to us. Strange how her name is so similar to János's first wife, Shan. Jancsi kept calling her Shan, until I sang him the German song *'Bei mir bist Du Scheen'*!

20 April 1988

Palm Cove

Visiting Ray Crooke was like seeing Czóbel in Szentendre. Same gaze roaming far away from us. A whole first floor rented because the 'workshop' became too small.

We looked through literally stacks of neatly piled empty canvases, all underpainted in different shades of foundation. Spotless beige, or brown, or blue or green. He is having a show in Brisbane later this year and also one at Agnews in London.

We drove to Yorkey's Knob. Nothing exists of what I used to paint there. No swamps, reeds or mangroves. Only suburban flatness with a surprising look of a Corniche on the heights, rich people's villas hidden in lush tropical parks with stunning views.

23 April 1988

Distinctively North Queensland clouds every day. Soft as velvet, grey and smoky pink, lazy shrouds sitting on the peaks of black-green mountains covered in rainforests.

I think of János often when these sights surround me. Particularly of his radio interview with Caroline Jones where he said that the rainforest is so supremely intelligent that 'it enlists the help of even people like me in its drive for survival'.

We found a little gallery. The owner obviously doesn't follow 'market' prices as we saw a good Ray Crooke for $750 and bought it.

25 April 1988

Driving along the coastline towards Mossman, on the right side there is a group of rocks we call the burghers of Calais. Rodin would have recognised them.

I am rather pleased with the way we ignore the weather. After breakfast we go off even if it's pouring with rain—which happens every day. Sometimes I work with the motor running, the windscreen wipers clearing my view, the air-conditioner keeping the temperature bearable. A lot of help for an old painter!

I have fourteen oils on paper. Many of them done at Yorkey's Knob on a small tongue of a peninsula, hiding a little beach with amazing rocks. Figures quite often appear by themselves now. They are not at all contrived, as sometimes I only recognise them after the act.

We drove to Mossman Gorge and had our first meeting with the Daintree. A young man who obviously works there came out of the forest, bucket, gumboots, gloves. 'It's an easy track,' he assured us. 'And let's hope this will be world heritage status next week.' We told him, our son, John Seed, would also like it.

He dropped the bucket and clapped his gloved hands in wonder. 'You are John Seed's parents!' he exclaimed. 'He is the greatest!'

The rainforest was like the inside of a cathedral. We walked on a hanging bridge over a waterfall and saw the 'pool'. A crystal-clear lake with smooth round rocks the size of houses. We saw cassowaries, which looked like feathered camels.

Jancsi said, 'I don't know too many eighty-five year olds who are like me. It's due to you. You keep me young. Your creativity radiates and your life force is contagious.'

1 May 1988

Sydney

Rene Rivkin bought the old Rudy Komon gallery. We went to see it after our return. An excellent Nolan, an effeminate Dobell of Bob King, Dickerson when he was still a young artist, I could go on about Baldessin, and the superb Fred Williams, etc.

My portrait of Rudy is on the cover of the catalogue, and it is sold to someone in Queensland.

All those years, the value of that epoch, is lost on the media.

5 May 1988

The queen is opening Darling Harbour. Invitation, car sticker, rigmarole, and will Judy Cassab accept the invitation to dinner on the royal yacht *Britannia*. Now, that sounded fascinating.

8 May 1988

Britannia and the queen's dinner was a magic happening. To my amazement I found that there were only fifty-six guests invited. That means that, including spouses or partners, the number of invitees was only twenty-eight. Harry Seidler was there: I thought 'Architect'. Don Burrows: 'Jazz'. Victor Chang: 'Heart surgeon'. And so I was obviously chosen as 'Artist'.

I couldn't believe it. Why me? Jancsi declined, but suggested I take Peter.

The new premier, Nick Greiner, was seated in the centre on the queen's left. I was rather proud of him when, the day before, at the Darling Harbour opening, he said: 'When her Majesty first visited Sydney in 1954 I was a small boy, a child of European immigrants.' Later he said, 'I would like to pay tribute to my predecessors whose vision made Darling Harbour possible'. Clever boy. Sir James Rowland with his wife, the chief justice, two archbishops, and that was it at the main table. I was seated beside Rear Admiral John Garnier, a stunningly good-looking aristocrat and captain of the royal yacht, *Britannia*.

21 May 1988

'I dream a lot' said Jancsi, 'and you know, you are always there. Not always visibly so, but there nevertheless.'

And in the car on the way to the club he said, 'When I am not angry with you, I feel such love for you.' And he laughs at that 'cantankerous old man', absent at the moment.

1 June 1988

Adele Weiss asked me to be photographed for *Vogue* in a Weiss design. Jancsi, amazingly, thought I ought to do it.

So this morning a French make-up man with a pigtail arrived; Jenny Garber from Weiss with a navy skirt and a striped smock and earrings from Michael, Richard the photographer, his assistant, and Amanda Jones from *Vogue*.

5 June 1988

Peter mentioned that he has bought a site to build a house for him and Shayne. They have an architect who will supervise the building while they are away on their round-the-world trip. They are leaving at the end of the month.

11 June 1988

John Caldwell picked me up for Beth Mayne's funeral in a Rose Bay church. Sheila McDonald's studio days came back as a flash. Beth had her Studio Shop in Sheila's building in Darlinghurst, and I was one of her painters for thirty years. The church was packed.

The speaker was a priest who lunched at the Studio Shop three times a week. 'Something,' he said, 'I have to get used not to do.' He is a poet and always read his poems to Beth. The last one was a prophecy, without either of them knowing. He recited the poem. Beautifully simple. One could feel a wave lifting the souls of the crowd, a very powerful emotion.

1 July 1988

I project either a Rainbow Valley shape or a Bali painting on good, acid-free paper, and do a charcoal drawing of it. I bought an excellent fixative, and before going to bed, spray it, hold my breath, open windows and close the doors of the studio. Next evening I might do the same theme again with charcoal on Arches watercolour paper. Next day I do a watercolour, more like a wash.

The day after, I project it on canvas, quite large, and start horizontally with acrylics. Both the charcoals and the acrylics are very personal statements.

The bridge at Mengwi is first, a small original oil on paper, charcoal drawing, large canvas. *Crossing the bridge* the same, very watery canvas, flooded with light.

12 July 1988

Greta and Bodhi arrived last week and stayed for five days. Bodhi will be eleven in two days time. Incredible. We went to the Powerhouse Museum, played Monopoly, went for dinner and watched TV together. He is beautiful, warm and sensitive, and hugs us a lot. We take him to the Chinese restaurant where he eats with chopsticks as well and a fork and spoon—like a prince. I love him so much.

16 July 1988

Started Margaret Whitlam's portrait in her flat. Talk about conditions! I have painted in wind, red dust, with flies, with 300 people behind me. This time it was with no space to step back, no proper light. But it's a good beginning and she is sitting again next Monday.

27 July 1988

Surfers Paradise

Clare's piano competition went fabulously. Harold Schonberg, former music critic of the *New York Times* and author of several books, was one of the eleven judges. Clare commissioned me to paint him and he sat twice. It was delightful. 'I envy you' he said. 'You are composer *and* interpreter, while composers *need* an interpreter.'

31 July 1988

We walk for an hour in the mornings. I feel new and fresh, stepping where the waves sweep footprints away. This I see. What I don't want I don't see.

I don't want to hear the blaring loudspeakers selling barbies and beer.

Although Expo has a lot of this, it also has redeeming virtues. We spent a whole day there. Sculptures by Pomodoro, Tinguely, Moore, Archipenko and Chadwick. A robot in a glass pyramid with a welcome greeting in fifty languages. All is festive. Water, sound, light and motion merge with steel, bronze and wood.

10 August 1988

Sydney

Jeff Smart's letter from Arezzo:

> Dear Judy,
> The book of your portraits arrived this morning and I have devoured it so eagerly and happily. Besides liking your painting, it is wonderful to have so many friends there. I am amazed at your talent! You have, like Cézanne, made a picture of a portrait.
> I read all your diary excerpts, of course, got a lump in my throat with 1955 Archibald Prize and the greengrocer and the bank teller. How lucky we are that you went to Australia and not USA or Canada—you have enriched the country. I like all the portraits and the one of Dr Coombs is magnificent.
> At the moment I'm working on a study for a portrait of Clive James. The figure is a stand-in, and the '5' is going to change to a '4', better angle and his age is forty-seven.
> Cézanne. Last week Hermes and I drove up to Provence to stay with James Fairfax who has rented a house north of Brignaly but you can see Mount St Victoire in the distance. The house was very like the Jus de Bouffan and it was so interesting to live almost as Cézanne must have lived.
> The landscape is not as diverse as Tuscany but the pine woods and rocks are evocative.
> In the garden in the morning the pines make a gentle SOUGHING sound in the breeze, unlike the tougher Italian pines. We have bought some young tougher trees in the hope we'll have that sound one day (?).
> I have a beautiful new piano.
> I am just mad about No. 30 of Schumann's album. Thought of you so much when I played it five minutes ago. Do go and try it, and I'm certain I'll pick you up.
> The new book on Picasso, by Mrs Huffington is truly vile. She is a wretch even if he is such a horrible man. For example, 'Cubism was not yet born, but Picasso was pregnant with it.' Ugh. The recent portrait of Jancsi is very good. Love mine. Best love to J and to you. Jeffrey.'

PS Picassos, which I missed in Paris (and London) in April, from what I've seen, it is all bad stuff. He started producing amazing things in the late 1890s and it went on until 1939–40 with the Night fisherman at Antibes and I'd also include Woman combing her hair, but that was it.

*You can say, at least forty years of a lot of good stuff. The falling off, to
my mind, due to his arrogance and total lack of self-criticism. People are
really frightened to say 'decadent' because it savours of Nazi fascist usage—
but decadent it certainly is and I crown Marcel Duchamp as King of
Decadence.*

18 August 1988

János flew in from two and a half months of workshops and lectures,
and making music and T-shirts—and sending all the money he earned
to Ecuador.

I baked a cake to celebrate his arrival.

János stormed in. We had breakfast, but since this trip, he no longer
eats eggs, milk or butter. He has become a 'pure' vegetarian. The cake
stays untouched.

22 August 1988

A letter from the curator of the Monash University Gallery, Jenepher
Dunan:

*Dear JC, It was a pleasure to meet you and your husband last Friday. I
very much appreciated the opportunity to talk to you about those post-days
in Sydney painting with Michael Kmit and other artists.*

*I am now writing to confirm our request for loan of your painting by
George Olszanski which will be an interesting inclusion in the Body and
Soul show. We would also like to include your own portrait. At the same
time we would like to invite you to open the exhibition. Your personal
knowledge of Kmit and the context in which he painted, as well as your
own career as an artist, would most appropriately inform such an occasion
and I do hope you will consider a trip to Melbourne for this purpose.*

*Monash University will provide your return air tickets and overnight
accommodation.*

*The exhibition will focus on the works of Michael Kmit in acknowledge-
ment of the millennium of Christianity, neo-Byzantine will be included in
the show together with still-life tradition.*

*The other artists in the show are Asher Bilu, Lawrence Daws, Brian
Dunlop, Leonard French, Donald Friend, Peter Kaiser, Michael Kitching,
Alun Leach-Jones, Elwyn Lynn, Justin O'Brien, Desiderius Orban,*

Ignacio Marmol and Fred Williams. It is going to be an extraordinarily interesting show.

You will recall that I was planning to invite Elwyn Lynn to open the exhibition but he will be in Queensland during that week. We believe that you are the next most appropriate person and hope that you will agree with our conviction.

1 October 1988

Nine paintings have been sold in the first week of my Canberra exhibition. *Leaning figures* was bought by Ingrid Murphy, widow of Lionel, the high court judge, one small *Crossing*, by Laurie Oakes, a well-known journalist.

Last night Bodhi was on television on 'Newsworld' as part of a band of buskers. Janaka has his punk hair á la cocks comb in rainbow colours. Mercifully, Bodhi looks just beautiful in a brown hat but has, alas, a long blond ponytail trailing down his back, and earrings.

Today I went with Greta to see him performing at Paddington market. A professional. About fifty young people sit round the band, clapping and hooting after each ecological number while the basket fills with money.

2 October 1988

Eva Klug's visit to Sydney prompted me to go see Terra Australis, at last.

The Furthest Shore is indeed the most complex exhibition both in terms of its loans and its concept. Australia as an idea, long before settlement. As a symbol of a place beyond the known world. Terra Incognita. The Great Southland. Terra Australis.

Reality enters and departs, the mermaid is depicted on the same level as other water creatures. The monsters have either one eye in their forehead or a giant foot the wrong way round. It is from the word 'Anti-Pod' that 'Antipodean' originates. Exhibits came from Holland and East Germany, Vienna and France. Under a drawing of a tiger lily I read: 'By Engelbert Kaemfner. German 1651–1716.'

5 October 1988

The moths have invaded Sydney. Black and hairy, they are not pleasant. But being parents of a conservationist somehow rubs off. We couldn't kill an insect now. We hunt them down and carefully hold them in a Kleenex, and then drop them out to the trees.

8 October 1988

Tiger lilies meet at this juncture in my life. The material I designed for John Kaldor twenty-five years ago is now a Chinese scroll and hangs in our bedroom, adding its antique blues to the blues of the armchair and a Bali triptych.

9 October 1988

According to their itinerary, Peter and Shayne are now sailing down the Nile on a boat. Their wedding invitations are printed, so I put them in the pre-addressed envelopes and I will mail the overseas ones on Monday.

16 October 1988

Peter and Shayne came home today. János was lecturing in Katoomba and spent the night here with Stella, his American girlfriend.

I pray every day for patience and for finding the right attitude.

19 November 1988

Last Sunday we gave a cocktail party in Peter and Shayne's honour. We invited all those old friends who knew him as a child.

22 November 1988

Peter's wedding to Shayne was such a perfect, wonderful happening that the joy spills over for many days after.

Leon Fink was the host at Bilsons. Wonderful flower arrangements everywhere. Champagne flowed together with the backdrop of the Opera House and the Harbour Bridge. Mea Havekes was the marriage celebrant.

Storm clouds were gathering as the bride arrived. Anyway, Peter was waiting with Leighton, his best man, the orchestra played Vivaldi,

Shayne appeared on the arm of Jonathan (her brother who came from London), both blond and tall and beautiful. She had a tearose-coloured silk gown and flowers in her hair.

I was very moved during the ceremony, but when Mea introduced Mr and Mrs Peter Kampfner, I cried, it was such a miracle.

János even had a dinner suit, but wore an Earth first T-shirt with a bow-tie underneath. He has grown his beard again. It's quite grey now. Bodhi arrived without Greta who had her dance group all week.

12 December 1988

Jack Lynn is quite bent after his accident. He had a bad fall from the first floor of Rudy Komon's Gallery. Lily helped him by physically carrying buckets of cement for his Wynne Prize entry. He needs such heaviness for the texture without which (he thinks) he wouldn't be Elwyn Lynn.

I visit almost every Saturday or Sunday on my way back from the Hakoah Club, staying no more than thirty minutes as he is weary.

The best news for years: the Art Gallery of NSW is giving him a small retrospective in 1990 or so. And Sydney University is going to give him an honorary doctorate. All long overdue.

Kevin asked me to see his Archibald entry: a self-portrait. I drove out to his Newtown studio and stood before a magnificent canvas of a Connor garden in which what looks like a dwarf stands. No likeness I told him. Offered to touch it into recognisability but he declined with a smile.

Yesterday was the opening of the new wing of the Art Gallery. I watched its birth like a midwife for so many years.

The Archibald, Wynne and Sulman are exhibited for all to see before the prize announcements.

Edmund brought in a new crowd pleaser: a people's prize for the Archibald. 'It would be a real disaster to win that,' Kevin said. However, Ray Hughes, who has Keith Looby in his stable, printed how to vote cards, his favourite in the race.

18 December 1988

Elwyn Lynn won the Wynne Prize. Not even Lily could possibly be happier than I was.

I dream that now, with this $10,000 prize and stardom, the fickle public will begin to buy.

There is the usual scandal about the Archibald. Vladas Meskenas has a defamation writ pending against Edmund Capon who called his portrait of Rene Rivkin terrible.

Fred Cress won the prize.

Sidney Nolan who entered a portrait of Arthur Boyd became ineligible (also courtesy of Meskenas) because he isn't a resident.

My portrait exhibition opened in the National Library in Canberra. Nugget Coombs, my friend, made such a lovely speech. He even said that during the sittings, 'I was falling a little bit in love with her'.

26 December 1988

I admire in Charles what is lacking in me. His rainforest changes into a Gothic facade like that of Chartres, with a rose window made of flowers. Energy and the life force are the quality pervading all these new creations, at the expense of all the old Blackman icons: tenderness, child, love, cats, grief and loss.

He says he loved Debussy's *Engulfed cathedral*, and as a result, had painted cathedrals beneath the sea like stones. He says the light shimmers through the green water to a soft, secret gloom, like an imaginary place of the psyche. The underwater cathedral is the key to his rainforests.

When Charles gathers pictorial images on the spot, he calls them his 'poetic Kodakchromes'.

14 January 1989

I work every day. The seven large works for David Ellis's show in March are almost finished.

18 January 1989

Bodhi rang me yesterday for Greta's phone number. János has gone to Tasmania where there is an action. I feel anger. Greta has Bodhi most of the time. In the one month that she studies Feldenkrais, János shouldn't abandon Bodhi.

Is János paying back for my absences when he was Bodhi's age?

5 February 1989

The Readers Digest's collection in the Art Gallery.

Monet's *Waterlilies* of 1918 is a multilayered ambivalent masterpiece in which the surface of the pond disappears behind reflections of the sky and of unseen trees. Height and depth become confused, and at the same time the wonderful brushstrokes remind me that all the spatial illustrations are also a flat, painted canvas. The canvas becomes the pool.

Matisse's *Anemones and mirror* was my second choice, with its rich black blind mirror—a bold transformation bringing out the bright hues of flowers.

25 February 1989

Thirty-six paintings arrived in Melbourne.

The Count Schönborn died. I felt apprehensive for Jancsi. His past has been so tightly connected to the six foot five, handsome man.

13 March 1989

János wanted us to come and visit. 'See how the trees have grown.' Jancsi didn't want to go, so I went for one night. I flew to Ballina. János picked me up and took me to Wotherspoon Street. Janaka's mother, Francesca, is in charge of what seems to be an ashram. The man she lives with, Konrad, does the cooking, naked but for a leopard-spotted silk loincloth. A most beautiful body. Long blond hair. The dinner is high-class vegetarian.

The rainforest van, by now, looks like all János's cars. Battered and littered, but responding to its master's touch. The land is full of trees in riotous magenta bloom. The smell is unmistakeable. Molasses grass and lantana, a pungent rich green odour.

Bodhi sleeps in the motel with me. In the morning bacon and eggs (what? rebellion?), but I don't take any notice.

We have lunch in Byron Bay where Greta's boyfriend, Warwick, greets us with his two-year-old son, Harry, perched on his shoulder. I had the privilege of treating Bodhi to new shorts, T-shirt and jacket.

János (with his helpers) planted 150 trees between his house and the river.

Bodhi writes short stories about extraterrestrials and a talking toothbrush.

24 March 1989

Limbo. Without painting—like a boat without an anchor. Mixed feelings about the trip to Paris. Anxiety. Will the studio be warm enough? Take down our winter clothing.

János is due to arrive today. He is leaving for Scotland and Ireland the day after us. Farewell parties abound.

6 April 1989

Paris

We were delayed in Rome because visibility in Paris was zero. At last we flew in. I couldn't believe it, there was snow everywhere, falling in large cottonwool flakes.

It's a lovely studio, but spartan. The saving grace is that it's well heated. No one to help us with the luggage. So we *shlepped* it to the door which has a copper plate: Art Gallery of NSW.

There was clean linen, but the beds were not made. Not one towel and no toilet paper. Tiny hanging space and five miserable wire hangers.

Our first outing was to a department store where we bought the essentials. Then we went out again to buy provisions to stock up our little fridge. No jet lag, no swollen feet.

Next day we bought the art materials. Without much French, it was a lengthy and frustrating exercise. Then, at last, off by Metro to see the Gauguin exhibition. We arrived at the Grand Palais in the drizzling rain, and joined the queue. We stood there, arm in arm, under the umbrella, for two and a half hours. It was torture, but turning back? Never.

Saw graphic works from the Washington National Gallery and paintings I have never seen from the Pushkin Museum in Moscow. Monotypes in aquarelle. Those small, sad self-portraits.

7 April 1989

The sun came out today, and it was lovely to realise we are in Paris.

I love every inch of the Picasso Museum. Its washed-out sand-coloured stone, its nooks and corners, slopes and domed courtyard, and the outpouring of creative genius.

We have discovered how close we are. It's only a short walk across the Pont Marie to a boulangerie, a charcuterie and, alas, the world's best ice-cream.

9 April 1989

We seem to be extra careful with each other, not in a repressed way, but rather as if we find each other's uniqueness illuminated. There is a wealth of tenderness showered on each other.

Stella from the Australian embassy and Marcel who was chef at Claridges came to take us into the country. Marcel carried a big box with champagne glasses. Stella gave us bath towels, plates, tea-towels, place mats and a tablecloth with napkins. And a vase which will be part of a still life I want to start tomorrow with Paris through the window.

We drove towards Giverny, had lunch in a truck bistro which had pink linen table settings and elegant glasses.

There was a long queue before Monet's house, so we left, and Stella drove to Gisors which has a cathedral which was rebuilt in 1124 after war destroyed it. Incredible height and beauty.

11 April 1989

Yesterday I painted two still lifes: a vase of flowers with Pont Marie through the window, and Parisian houses, and trees.

Are we old? Yes.

When one is old one recognises quality. Nothing less will do! There is, of course, as much rubbish in Paris as elsewhere.

14 April 1989

A touristy day, we walked to Notre Dame and inside all its naves, caves and saw a puppet show of Crucifixion. My cousin, Vera, brought a board for one of our beds, an act of friendship *shlepping* it up. She also brought me a treasured book by Gitta Malasz *Talking with angels* which I haven't been able to get in an English translation. I stop Christina Stead's *The man who loved children* to share *Angels* with Vera whose life is interwoven with it.

On rue Pont du Phillipe she guided me into a recycled-paper shop where I bought a kilo of paper. I shall keep two sheets each of green, rose and off-white, and take the roll to Mulleron to Vera on Sunday. She brought me a bedside lamp, too.

Next week an exhibition of my beloved Bohemian teacher's work, Dénes Diener, is opening, and Veronique gave us an invitation. Thirty years after his death his son has arranged it.

15 April 1989

Sightseeing on a double-decker bus. The sun shone and Paris smiled and the chestnut trees are a riot of blooms. We got off near the opera, had a big lunch with white wine in a brasserie, then sat on the terrace of the Café de la Paix with a disgustingly huge ice-cream *avec crème Chantilly.* (Sounds so much more than whipped cream.)

Jancsi carried my sketch materials all day, but nothing happened. I was on holiday.

There are lots of musicians in the Cité; trumpets from one room mingle with violins from another. For some reason, a room with a piano has a glass door. Behind the curtain I see the silhouette of a fat black lady singing chromatic scales.

23 April 1989

The cotton duck I bought behaves differently from canvas, but there, pinned on the wall, are two mysterious-looking paintings. Much simpler than the oils on paper. The drawings also gain character as I create juxtapositions between old architecture and the space age pipes of the Pompidou.

We discovered the Marais, where we live, the old Jewish quarter which looks like the French version of Mea Shearim in Jerusalem.

On Friday night we stumbled upon a phenomenon on the rue des Rosiers: a kosher restaurant, behind a delicatessen with every conceiveable traditional speciality from *kreplach* to *sholet.* It looked like a nightclub, red leather upholstery and candles (I rejoiced about the candles on Friday night). On the wall there is a version of Chagall's Vitebsk paintings, naive but obviously done with integrity. The place was packed.

The Cité was fumigated for pests. They invaded our studio too early in the morning so we were not prepared. Next night we both had violent diarrhoea, probably a bit of poisoning. We are fasting. And now, humble rice is boiling on the cooker for our first dinner.

1 May 1989

We used our Eurorail pass for the first time and took a trip to Orleans. Had a sunny, warm and peaceful day walking in the old town. The mood of somnambulists, as if time had stopped still.

Our fiftieth wedding anniversary was a very happy occasion.

János rang us from Findhorn in Scotland. He remembered. We got a telegram from Peter and Shayne. They phoned a little later. We felt cosseted and warmed.

We booked dinner at La Coupole and celebrated with a bottle of Moet Chandon, eating duck á l'orange.

4 May 1989

Chambord

We went to Orleans for the second time with our gear in two overnight bags. Rented an automatic Peugot.

I was not prepared for the stunning sight in Chambord. A renaissance building in the midst of forests and fields. It's one of the magic visions of this world. When I got over the intricacies and irregularities of the strange building, I did a picture of a row of typically French trees. I remember those trees from Maisons-Lafitte. They trim them so that there are knees, elbows, shoulders, swollen arthritic joints out of which sprout the finest, lightest green tapestry, forming a halo over their top.

As usual, my second try is always the more relaxed and painterly.

I secured a room for the following day in the Hotel St Michel at Chambord, and so we woke happy.

The fog was quite dense as it often is in Europe and so we drove on to Blois, to see one more three-star chateau. We drove into a jewel of a town, reminiscent of Salzburg. The Loire was on our right and when I saw a lovely theme, I climbed up the side and snuggled to a halt near an old, low wall. The perfect studio.

Painted three that morning, unconscious, as I am when gathering raw material, of the virtues or failings of that effort. Drained and trembling and happy.

We had lunch at Chambord, went to our hotel room; a huge suite with a bedroom on the left and a little sitting room on the right. I laid out my tools on the table.

Towards evening we took a very long walk around the castle. It must be as big as Versailles. The crowds on buses have departed and we became one of those nineteenth-century types who populate Proust's novels. At the elaborate dinner, waitresses carried loaded silver vessels, steaming, and served with fork and spoon in one hand.

It's still quite light here at 9.45, so we went to see the river, the elaborate moats, the ducks and black reflections of poplars.

7 May 1989

Paris

At last, we got into the Louvre. We passed it, truth to be told, with no intention to queue. There was no queue.

As soon as we were inside the pyramid, we felt absolutely certain that this solution was the one and only right one. It's a light and friendly place. The Louvre has reached into the twentieth century.

I enlarged one of the Ned Kelly-like funnels of the Pompidou on canvas, with a view of Paris, and another canvas is the giant clock of the Musée d'Orsay.

We returned to the Musée Rodin where I painted *Balzac* and the *Thinker*.

We spent the next day in Monet's house in Giverny and it was quite a strange experience. Wherever I chose to enclose an inch of a square, there was a Monet painting. My cousin Vera says that not only was Monet the father of lyrical abstraction, 'think of the waterlilies', but he was also the predecessor of all those artists who transform earth and sand and pack the coast like Christo. Monet created a fantastic palette out of the colours of flowers. In his will there are strict regulations as to where which colour should be planted in his garden.

17 May 1989

London

I go to the Crane Kalman Gallery to deliver four Australian paintings he wrote to me about for a future Australian exhibition. Mr Kalman is busy with a client. Jenny, the secretary, asks if I would like tea or coffee.

Forty-five minutes later I try to behave as if I'm not angry that André thinks his time is more important than mine. (We had an appointment.) Anyway, I left *Rainbow Valley* and *Rocks and waters* (on canvas) and *Stormy Bay with yellow sky*, and its sister (oil on paper).

31 May 1989

Budapest

János is here to spend two days with us. He is not interested in castles and museums. He wants to see the house where we lived when he was born.

The Fürst Sándor ucca is narrower than it used to be. When we step in the hallway, an old lady asks if we are looking for someone. I tell her we used to live here forty-four years ago. She invites us in. We accept gratefully.

There is an intimate and sudden recognition. Did we really sleep in that dark hall? All we ever looked at through the window of the living room were the windows of the opposite flat.

János didn't remember anything except the smell.

5 June 1989

Zurich

Zurich is freezing. We took the train to Basel. Both the Museum für Gegenwartskunst and the Kunsthalle exhibited Julian Schnabel, who is a con. He paints over old maps, preferably upside down, paints over the Holbein, towelling, velvet. *Letter to my wife* has plum house painter's brushstrokes with banana yellows. In the museum we saw Paladinos, Cucchis and Clementes.

The Schnabels in the Kunsthalle are white letterings over twenty foot of soiled and cut and bruised linen. The paintings spell and isolate the names of saints, mystics, and royal ecclesiasts. They are from the *Recognitions* by William Gaddis.

7 June 1989

Paris

Derelicts are an integral part of this city. On the corner of the rue Rivoli near Metro St Paul, there is an old alcoholic who sleeps on the pavement every night. The policeman doesn't give him a glance. He lies on the ventilation bands of the Metro, with the warm air serving as his blanket. Inside the underground are young men sitting on the floor, their stories written on the cement. A form of begging. Lots of excellent musicians play there, waiting for coins.

13 June 1989

Exciting turn of events in painting. The two oils on black pastel paper, done on the steps of the playground of the Pompidou, are turning surreal. It's the globe, hovering in mid-air which can't be mistaken for the moon or the sun. The Tinguely machine splashing in the water and the four Ned Kellys menacing on the left. Then I did the edge of the building, stairs all black and white horizontal spanners, Parisian buildings on the left, and a clown figure in the water. The globe hovers, balancing the composition.

Three Clavé exhibitions opened simultaneously. I love Clavé. Have a book of his work twenty years ago. Figures, still lifes. This one is purified, settled and illuminated with light. Less colour, but it isn't missed. It's renewed creation, all of it abstract. And I wasn't bored as with so much else. I was excited and wanted to rush home and paint.

15 June 1989

The Place des Vosges doesn't lend itself to contemporariness, but I'm painting Paris in these three months. It's a rhythm of burnt orange and butter stripes, and a variety of windows with and without shutters, curtains, black holes, white blinds. Then back to Pompidou where the light is different in the mornings and I ran out of black paper.

16 June 1989

My friend Ági Whyte came from London to see us. She has been back to Beregszász, our childhood Atlantis, with a rabbi and a television crew. Brought me photos of our house which is now a children's nursery. There is a photo of a little Jewish boy of about six. He is the only Jewish child in Beregszász, and 5000 years of sorrow and worry is written on his face.

12 July 1989

Sydney

I have two large paintings started since arriving. Both are of the Pompidou courtyard. Inky blue. The houses are brokenly textured.

14 July 1989

I painted a portrait of Shayne for their new house. Almost threw it in on the second sitting, but it improved on the third. I wonder if it is more difficult because she is family, or is it because I always have difficulty with great beauties?

29 July 1989

To the Moet Chandon art prize opening. Elisabeth Kruger is the winner, with a strip of cloudy sky and ornate frame and brocade wallpaper. I don't know. Champagne flowed. My two big paintings still hang beside Olsen and Lloyd Rees.

Barry Pearce told us that Donald Friend is dying. He asked for the easel and wanted to draw, couldn't, wept. Barry wonders whether, with the grand prospect of the retrospective, he hasn't helped Donald linger. I am sure that is it.

15 August 1989

On my sixty-ninth birthday we sit on Balmoral Beach on our way to Kevin and Margaret Connor for lunch. His birthday is also on 15 August.

Jancsi sent me three cyclamens in a basket. I still adore this day. I am still celebrated with embraces and kisses and his 'I'm glad you have been born'. Seagulls keep us company. We are early as usual.

20 August 1989

I draw every night we don't go out. Preparing for a watercolour. Using one of the forty drawings from Paris, I positively wallow in inspiration. Never expected old painted-to-death Paris to yield so much.

27 August 1989

At Spigelmans for Sunday lunch, with Kevin and Margaret Connor. Kevin's survey shows open at the Art Gallery of NSW this week, coinciding with the book written by Barry Pearce. 'He interrupted it,' said Kevin 'when Lloyd Rees was dying and he had to finish his book. Then, Donald was dying so he raced off to finish *his* catalogue. I told him if it goes on like this, *I* will be dead before *they* are!'

I went to Donald's wake, organised by Stuart Purves who has just opened his Australian Galleries in Sydney.

Gisella went to see Donald every day through his long illness, she brought soup and drove him to doctors, was dropped like a hot coal. Stuart got the eighty paintings Donald painted with the hand not affected by the stroke.

I brought my 1975 portrait up from the garage. *Donald Friend in Bali.* I will have it framed, and include it in my Brisbane exhibition. My memorial.

Lots of portrait commissions. I'm painting the vice-chancellor of the University of Technology on Verlie Just's recommendation.

7 September 1989

I have a cataract in one of my eyes. My vision has slightly deteriorated. I go see the specialist who calls it an 'insignificant' cataract. He asked me if there is a history of blindness in the family. I couldn't tell him that they all died young.

I decide to include in my daily prayers the burning desire I have to be able to paint as long as I live. Sixty-nine is too young to start having eye troubles, but I can't imagine I'd want to live without painting.

13 September 1989

Surfers Paradise

A flat in the Beachcomber. The rooms are bliss. One wall of the living room is glass looking out on the ocean, so is the second wall. The third is also glass but looking out on the river and the mountains.

This is our third day and I haven't written or drawn anything yet. Flopping lazy I am, only the hours marching barefoot are active.

14 September 1989

János spent a day with us after five and a half months of touring and lecturing. Greta, who is also here for her Feldenkrais course, asked him: 'Aren't you sick and tired of it?'

'I love it. I could actually do it for another year, but what I want now is to leave the office to the others. I want to stay quietly on Bodhi Farm and write my new book.'

'It would do us a great honour,' Greta said, 'to have you working on Bodhi Farm.'

While we are on holiday, Warwick will stay with Greta in our flat.

18 September 1989

Somehow we have moulded into each other's character so thoroughly in fifty years, that I, the spendthrift, generous, luxury-loving Leo, took over some of the puritanical traits from Jancsi. He, the saver, the man who only likes simple places, suggested as we prepared for my portrait trip to Brisbane 'Let's go in a limousine.' And so we travelled in imperial comfort in one of those long things which accommodate seven.

25 September 1989

Brisbane

Verlie Just looks like a true eccentric with a brown jersey scarf entwined in strands of hair. She always wears caftanesque garb the likes of which you are not likely to see anywhere. It may even have been patchwork, quilted out of flowery, dotted, striped, wallpapery bits of silk. On top of all that hung long necklaces of amber.

The opening flowed with champagne and (in exact opposition to Sydney shows) all the artists of the gallery.

I went to the Queensland Art Gallery and saw a Japanese exhibition which took my breath away. Japanese Ways, Western Means. It's as contemporary as the Documenta, but better. Because, for instance, a raw wooden bench with one wing and three apples sitting on it could be crude and 'anti-art' to correspond with its utter senselessness. However, the seat of the bench is polished to delight a lover of sculpture. The wing belongs to a golden angel, just lifting the bench into the transcendental. And the silver apples jumped off a Cézanne still life.

The same respect for *matière* everywhere, and the sophistication belongs to minds civilised a few thousand years longer than ours.

9 October 1989

Sydney

Donald Friend's posthumous exhibition at the Australian Galleries.

Only a few artists in history have persevered as he has, with handicaps in old age. His painting hand was paralysed, and somehow he learned to use the other unskilled hand. And his composition and colour triumphed. In the best of them, a dignity emerges that was missing before.

15 October 1989

In spite of Lou's opposition to my Indian ink and white tempera gouaches ('Because the eye gets tired looking—it's like a print although I know it's an original') I slowly add to their number. Each paints itself in a different and always surprising way.

One needs perseverance. I do the drawing at night, from one of the Parisian drawings. Paint white tempera in different densities. Next morning I cover it with black and also vary the thickness of the flow.

Opposite our flat's entrance in the courtyard where cars park, there is a long hose coiled on the tap. I unravel some of it, carry it to a tree growing above the brick wall, place it gently in a fork of a branch nozzle down into the shrubs. Turn the tap. While the water sprinkles I lift up the drawing which is clipped on masonite and lean it away from the gushing water. It's too steep an elevation for me to climb so I go out on to Ocean Avenue and walk left until I can re-enter the place under the trees. I free the hose, hit my head in branches, but feel rewarded. Under the liquid 'brush' the window of the Musée Picasso reveals itself as do the sculptured head and the old houses opposite.

I have done the same theme on the handmade pink thick French-Japanese paper. There I made the charcoal alternate with white acrylic, then glazed it with a warm yellow ochre.

11 November 1989

I received an honour from Israel along with twenty others in the Town Hall. The ambassador of Israel placed a medal around my neck, 'for her contribution to progressive Judaism'.

How much more is in store for our generation, living in historic times?

'Freedom: the wall crumbles' shout the headlines as Berlin is united after twenty-eight years.

18 November 1989

I went to see the German expressionists at the Art Gallery of NSW for the umpteenth time.

Jancsi chose to read the newspapers, sitting in the blue velvet armchair at the open window. The jacaranda trees are in full bloom, and somehow Jancsi seems happier in his eighty-eighth year than at any other time in Australia.

Our half-century leaves us with the wonder of what a relationship is capable of.

28 November 1989

The jacaranda nods before the bathroom window. I see it again from the kitchen. It's flaky, and like millions of cushions all gentle and lilac. The streets have patches of violet carpet where the flowers descend like snow.

30 November 1989

We fell in love with Josl Bergner's painting, *Hora*, at the Holdsworth and incredibly, bought it.

We accumulated some money, but not enough to buy bricks and mortar. Jancsi was thinking of buying shares. But we always tell those who want a painting that it's a better investment than shares. The value goes up and one gets joy by looking at it. So now we have proved it. It's an expressionist work, a merging of mouthwatering brushstrokes, Jewish air, humour, transformed humans.

János arrived a day early for his 'gig' at the Bondi Pavilion. After driving all night he spent two hours on the phone, did an interview for the

ABC and slept all afternoon. He is now a middle-aged hippie, still barefoot in thongs, long hair and T-shirt. His tracksuit trousers are full of holes. All this energy, this brilliant talent in the lifestyle of a circus tent.

16 December 1989

Bryan Westwood won the Archibald Prize with his portrait of Elwyn Lynn. It's a compelling presence and an excellent likeness, but for all that, photographic realism.

I rejoice, though, for Jack's sake who is thrown up into the public's eye.

Olsen entered all three competitions and won the Sulman, judged by Kevin Connor.

23 December 1989

Jack and Lily brought me all the photos Bryan Westwood used for Jack's portrait. Slowly I begin to be a convert to this aid so many painters use. He photographed Jack in segments.

First he intended a double portrait with Lily, and there is Lily's hand on Jack's shoulder. Jack's hand on Lily's arm. Jack's hand on his belt. Lily's feet. Jack's feet. And the photography is perfect.

I'll try.

24 December 1989

Josl Bergner's Hora is hanging beside Blackman's Alice. A great wall.

26 December 1989

My eagle flew in on his way to New Zealand. Five of them came in the rainforest van. He is growing into a kind of cult figure. One of the girls told me: 'Thank you for raising such a magnificent son.' Three of them stayed overnight on Peter and Shayne's living-room carpet.

12 January 1990

Warwick phoned from Lismore. Greta's mother died. Although she has been expecting it, when the news came it was an amputation. We embraced her. I cried with her.

28 January 1990

The *Christian Science Monitor* dubs John Seed 'the town crier of the global village'.

3 February 1990

János rang from Byron Bay. He sounded marvellous. Top of the world. He is working on his book with Joanna Macey and Patrick. Three computers are ticking. 'Bodhi loves high school. He'll ring you to tell you all his good news.'

21 February 1990

Bali

The magic never fails. Spicy humid cloudy heat envelops me, the sound of Indonesian music. Chevy, our friend the taxi driver, took us to Ubud today where at the Cafe Lotus we asked after Ian van Wieringen.

We met him in Double Bay with a blindingly beautiful young girl. He was looking depraved but dashing. Hearing about our plans he invited us to his house in Bali.

It is a villa high up on the mountain overlooking the Ayung River and the rice paddies. There is an intricately-shaped lily pond at the entrance and exquisite stone carved reliefs, old ones, from temples hang on the walls. Noel, the mother of his daughter, took us to her house.

While Noel was barefoot, in a T-shirt and shorts, the nanny stepped out of Proust's childhood, in starched snow-white linen.

Soon I was painting a mythical bird (of wood) with the curve of the river and rice terraces, continuing the theme of a sculpture as foreground. Another is a strangely awkward primitive pair embracing, as still life in the landscape.

23 February 1990

Turkeys are strutting in our courtyard with fandango Spanish skirts.

Back in Sayan terrace I painted a *garuda* before the winding river, but I want to change him into a Nike at home. The second still life is a dwarf frangipani in a pot and a sculpted head.

26 February 1990

A day trip to Batur lacked the magic and excitement I remembered. I didn't take the tubes out, but did draw. Pencils sharpened eight at a time so the line may be sharp and black and blurred and thick and thin.

We have our swim when the sun isn't fierce, and the clouds darken to blue charcoal. Today we swam in the rain.

8 March 1990

Sydney

Tackling two huge (for me) canvases of Pompidou rafters and cathedral. Calling one *Barred Pompidou and cathedral* and the other *Pompidou cruciform and cathedral*.

After the absence I know exactly what to do.

9 March 1990

Brett Whiteley has one exhibition at the Australian Galleries and another of his Paris drawings at the Art Gallery of NSW.

Is it that Australia can't stand tall poppies? Unkind reviews abound. Today, Christopher Allen writes among other things that the media promotion of the romantic genius is out of proportion to his real abilities.

To me he is near genius and I don't doubt Brett will become more humble with age.

14 April 1990

Bodhi has shot up and is now my height. A beautiful boy, outside and inside. The only remaining sign of hippieness is a tiny earring. His hair is short and blond, and he brushes his teeth in the evening without being told.

23 April 1990

Just like my János to catch a plane at 6.20 a.m. It means a wake-up call at five and a taxi at 5.30. At 5.10 a.m. as I crawled out, János was in his usual spot on the floor in the corridor. The computer was attached to the telephone socket and humming. His eyes shone. 'Isn't it fantastic?

During the night three letters arrived from America,' he said.

Bodhi, methodical and efficient like Greta, packed his rucksack, then lovingly laced his Reebok shoes we bought in Bondi Junction.

22 May 1990

Charles Blackman rang and told me Victoria had a baby boy.

'His name is Axiom. It means perfect truth in Greek.' He came to the Holdsworth with his grown-up sons, August and Barnaby, and they spent a long time with the paintings. Charles said: 'Judy, I admire them. Especially the light, which seems to radiate from within.'

(Twelve paintings are sold, and two reserved.)

29 June 1990

Darwin

We came a day before leaving for Kakadu so we spent the morning at the Museum and Art Gallery of the Northern Territory, quite lovely with small Blackmans, medium quality Olsens, lots of Frank Hodgkinsons. The Aboriginal bark paintings of Arnhem Land are outstanding, the Streeton poor. There is a huge Wendy Stavrianos so good it should hang in a large city. It's a forest on canvas, in black and white, and the trunks of trees are rolls of canvas with apertures cut and sewn. I liked it very much.

Loafing on wide empty avenues. Our window opens on a woolly, soft, pink sea. The tropical philodendrons in the hotel atrium fall seven floors down like green waterfalls.

Today we joined the group. We wear badges with our names on. We are all old.

30 June 1990

Rum Jungle

Sketchbooks for pencil drawings, watercolour pad, and oil foundations are in a striped plastic Sportsgirl bag. In a yellow Pathfinder overnight bag are oil paint, aquarelles, pastels, brushes and palette.

Visit to the aquarium where we stopped for half an hour. I drew the sloping pier, people frozen in movements—bending, kneeling, throwing bread.

Outside I sat on a tree trunk to draw the stranded skeleton of a boat on the land. We stop again at the Pink Buffalo to 'buy those last minute souvenirs' and to guess at the length of the buffalo horn.

Jancsi remarked that the ratio of females is four to one. So few men. I said, the rest already killed theirs.

We stay at the Rum Jungle Motel overnight, a name loaded with foreboding. Dale has bagpipe music on the recorder. Maybe he had a Scottish father.

1 July 1990

Kakadu

On the road from Rum Jungle there are soft furry barrels on the fields. These are bales of hay. What? No more haystacks? Monet would be heartbroken.

A hat was lost. And a stubby. A sign. 'Emu Export.'

Stopped at War Memorial cemetery. No idea if they lost their life in the Japanese bomb attack on Darwin or in Papua New Guinea. McGormack, twenty-two years. Webster, twenty. Also Li Wong and Wu Chi Ming.

The second day now, the landscape is sheer monotony.

Lunch at Fogg Dam. At least there are rainbow honeyeaters sitting on waterlilies. The male guards the chicks, flies with them under his wings.

2 July 1990

At Ubiri Rock I had oil foundations and oil pastels. That's where the famous rock paintings of the Aborigines date back to around 25,000 years. The ten pieces of oil pastels were the best choice not only for quick progress but one skips over underlying texture and colour. I had one precious hour for two sketches.

Used 400ASA film to take photographs with my camera which has a zoom lens. The combination of both will be a help for eventual large oils.

In the afternoon we cruised Yellow Water, the wetland which is home to millions of birds. Herons, ibis, brolga, pelicans, kingfishers with azure jackets and orange breasts, and the jabiru, known as the black-necked stork. The egret is one of the most striking with the lily trotter which walks on the lotus leaves.

3 July 1990

Katherine

Nourlangie Rock. Used my last two rosy foundations, it will be hard to do these caves in green or blue without the power of oil paint.

The side of the Arnhem escarpment could have been a highlight for several paintings but this is a coach tour. One pees on time and has the cup of tea and hopes for another wonder at the tail end of another monotonous landscape of hostile gums, burnt halfway from the ground.

The giants are missing. This is the proletariat. Struggling palms only reach up to the knees of tree trunks. Their lower skirt is like a long dried-out mop. There is no curve. The earth is not red.

5 July 1990

Lake Argyle

On the boat on Lake Argyle, larger than Sydney Harbour. The dam controls the floods and droughts of the Ord River.

A pelican, blinding white on ancient red rocks which haven't seen water since they were part of the bottom of the sea 500 million years ago. Drowned trees stick up their top branches, full of egrets, crocodiles look bloated.

On a small triangular island a spider is weaving a golden web. It's such a strong web, fishermen could use it for a line.

Sunlight illuminated Ayers Rock's little brother, Elephant Rock. It's magic.

7 July 1990

Kununurra

As we sat in the Slingair ten-seater plane, taking off towards the Bungle Bungles it must have been 120 degrees. I fanned us with the leaflet, thinking, how could you take a man on such an irresponsible adventure? The pilot looked back at me smiling, to say air-conditioning will be all right in a little while. I thought as it lurched and it bumped, what are you doing above the inland sea? Tidal waves of panic threatened to engulf me.

Then it was five minutes to the Bungle Bungles. I opened the sketchbook and the box with the oil pastels. And while the pilot banked right and left and my stomach was left higher than my body I picked up the oldest landscape on earth. The Kimberleys are 2500 million years old. The Bungle Bungles, relatively young features, are only 350 million years old.

14 July 1990

Sydney

Bodhi's thirteenth birthday. I wanted to go to Lismore, and I surprised myself by thinking that if he were Jewish, this would be his *bar mitzvah*.

My globetrotting offspring, Peter and Shayne, flew to Tahiti for a week.

2 August 1990

It has been a long break from my Artist and Friends portraits. Finally I went to John Firth-Smith's studio to do a sketch. He is six foot seven with a little boy's smile and short-cropped hair. An explosive abstract strength bursting into ovals and maritime shapes. I imagined him in one of his ovals.

He bought a dilapidated factory and a National Trust house beside it. Bought old and tall palm trees from a demolition site and had them transplanted with cranes. Inside there are cases full of tubes, several great tables littered with an artist's paraphernalia for collage, for printing. Three mandolins (he plays them). Space as huge as he is.

15 August 1990

I am seventy today. Feeling thirty-five. Jancsi's red roses had a card: 'El nem múló szerelemmel' which means 'With love that never dies.'

I started Rex Irwin's portrait. Had two sittings with Elizabeth Evatt. She has fine and handsome features and lets herself go. Hair grey. A great career. Her husband, also a judge, lives in London. No, they are not divorced.

23 August 1990

Jancsi's memory is formidable. He remembers even the smallest details of eighty years ago. The thing he tends to forget is where he put his spectacles.

Lou Klepac said this morning the painting of Kakadu opened a new door. He brought me two 'dummies' (books of glorious white pages, for diaries and a new working journal), and two copper plates for etchings. The proofs of the two previous ones look splendid. One is a soft-ground *St Paul's Cathedral*, the other is *Renoir bust and shadow*. The first etching, *Beam of Pompidou across cathedral*, is hand-coloured and resting in its portfolio.

4 September 1990

The first outburst of Rex Irwin's portrait looked good enough to eat. Never mind about the likeness, whispered a conceited devil in my head. I always get *that*.

Rex—a distant English manner, polite acquaintance until now— became a warm confidant.

He gave me the pages (from *his* journal?) about sitting for a portrait for Sam Fullbrook in 1983. About the first sitting: '... at this early stage it is wonderful—hope the finished picture fulfils its early promise. It is shaping up to be as good a Fullbrook as I had ever seen ... It must be entered in the Archibald—cannot fail to win. Will leave the pedestrian boardroom pictures and the very unsuper-realists for dead ... One seems almost incidental. In a way one is, as Sam's portraits are firstly good pictures, secondly likenesses of people. Just as it should be.'

It continues in June 1987: 'Aged eighteen months since we started but luckily being a Fullbrook it will not show. Sam has just rubbed out my face. Sam and Giacometti seem to have the same problem. I remember James Lord telling me that Giacometti was reworking his face for months. I must try to get the book James wrote about the portrait.'

I lent Rex a copy of Lord's book about Giacometti painting him.

After the second sitting of Rex went desperately wrong, I rubbed out his face. On the third sitting of the face, Rex brought me a present: Richard Ellman's *Oscar Wilde*.

13 September 1990

Christo retrospective at the Art Gallery of NSW. Sponsored, twenty-one years after he wrapped Little Bay, by John Kaldor. Christo's 'temporary monuments' have been conceived for places never associated with art before.

In Bulgaria, he absorbed enough Marxist theory to question how works of art in the west were limited as commodities within the capitalist economy. He has resurrected the monument which he associates with pre-capitalist culture, in the form most characteristic of consumer capitalism—the package.

The documentation of the project, photos, films, collages, drawings, all play an important role. They belong to the work of art.

24 September 1990

Gordon Darling, former chairman of the National Gallery, came to see me. He wants to create a national portrait gallery, wants an even number of artists, sport heroes, scientists, businessmen, etc. Wants the portraits of champions at the time of their Olympic triumphs, from photos. I said I would do it if they also sit. Eyes don't change and I get life in the picture.

I finished my third Kakadu. I have done all of them, up to now, from my own sketches, and they change into something new and lyrical. But I also did two small canvases from my photos of the cave paintings. For the first time in my life.

Juniper's new exhibition swarms with mimi figures. I feel as if I'd intrude into *their* culture. But I have been in Australia for forty years. The greater part of my life. I would rather dip for inspiration into something as ancient as this than something contemporary.

7 October 1990

Greta and Warwick arrived, and I lent them my car. It's good to see Greta happy with Warwick. They laugh a lot together.

9 October 1990

Surfers Paradise

We have the same flat as last year's happy place for our holiday. On our first morning it rained so we went to our coffee house, sat inside, and watched the umbrellas cry.

Soon we were walking on the incomparable sand under smoky clouds. Jancsi said, '*Olyan mint a nullásliszt.*' I haven't heard that word for forty-five years. It's a very fine flour that our grandmothers used for making strudel pastry.

We think of past things more often since we are old.

15 October 1990

We went to Springbrook and stopped on the way at Lyrebird Ridge Pottery, where we saw ceramic plates, vases, and bowls decorated by Joe Furlonger and William Robinson.

Joe Furlonger won the Moet Chandon prize three years ago. Errol Barnes, the potter and owner of the place, beamed at me as he recognised my face. He introduced us to a tall lanky man in his early thirties. That was Joe Furlonger. He lives nearby at Palm Beach, and works one day a week on pottery. Not since Vallauris have I seen such splendid ceramics. Bill Robinson (whom I know from his equestrian self-portrait which won the Archibald Prize when I was a trustee) also lives close, in the mounains. His ceramics are pure Robinson with his tunnel-vision bursting trees into the sky.

19 October 1990

Bodhi Farm

All is changed. Greta lives with Warwick, and his two boys stay every second week. János has mud bricks drying. He is going to build Bodhi a room.

I am resting with Jancsi on the living-room cushions while Peter and János argue about dole bludgers, taxes and the environment. 'Would I reach you easier if I wore shoes and a proper suit?'

A proud new loo is built in a rocky outcrop. Human waste will turn into compost in two years.

Greta's lunch on the terrace gives Peter faith in vegetarian food.

Marinated tofu in olive oil, soya sauce and garlic, with a salad I watch her pick in the vegetable garden.

Peter drives us back to the Gold Coast on dark curving roads in half the time I would take.

'János could have turned into a guru for other causes. Judaism, communism, anything. Perhaps I envy him. He is not regimented and works on what he loves.'

'It's the same with artists,' I said. 'Society can't forgive dedication, obsession and love for one's profession.'

4 November 1990

Sydney

My plan now is to do with Sydney what I have done with Paris. I just realised how many times my eyes perceived and my subconscious recorded things. Juxtapositions like Henry Moore's sculpture outside the Art Gallery of NSW with a crane and the harbour. Also one of the skyscrapers on the corner of Bridge and George Streets, where a small cupola was reflected in the mirror windows, looking like a Vasarély gone wrong.

Not the best of times to embark on a huge undertaking.

Rex's portrait is a good likeness now, but the head is tired from all the work and sweat. The rest of the painting is fresh and contemporary. If only I could solve it.

I think I shall have enough time to embark on new adventures in painting as commissions are unlikely in such a recession.

10 November 1990

Jack has started to paint a self-portrait for the Archibald but is quite unable to achieve a likeness. Do I think I can help him?

I arrived with some tubes of acrylics (he continues with water-based paints and materials) fully aware that the excellent, quick portrait of Elwyn Lynn I conjured onto the square of white in the field of yellow-orange will be cracked and buried under cement, straw, and rivers of a Lynn texture.

14 November 1990

Trafford Whitelock, my friend who stood by me in my lonely London years, is now himself lonely in a retirement village in Jersey Road. Sick too.

I included him in something which I also enjoy. I drove him on two Sunday afternoons to the Rocks. He likes to photograph old buildings. I find old stairs with shadows, or a terrace house with a balcony staring at an industrial tower. I take photos too, but also managed one pencil drawing and a quick pastel.

We took him to Jeff Smart's opening at the Australian Galleries. Jeff left Rex Irwin and went to Stuart Purves whose Melbourne gallery he has exhibited in for many years. Traffi told us after the opening where he met Morris West, Margaret Olley, Ron Robertson-Swann, Kevin Connor and many of his 'old chums': 'I almost felt human again.'

I asked Jeff if he would consider sitting for a second portrait. It's a gamble, ten days before the Archibald, but I will risk it.

2 December 1990

Woollahra Art Removals took both Rex Irwin and Jeff's portraits. My first Archibald entries in nine years. I know only one can hang.

Did an oil sketch of Martin Sharp in Victoria Road. His grandparents' house, he said. He lives in a Luna Park metamorphosed into Kienholz, with three dogs and a passion for the music of Tiny Tim. Finishing the sketch for his portrait I exclaimed: 'I forgot my camera!' He lent me his Polaroid which promptly became an object of my desire. A replica of my painting would materialise in two minutes instead of two weeks—if I'm quick. Often I forget the impetus which makes me take the snapshot.

13 December 1990

Since I left the Art Gallery board, the rules have changed. Previously, the Archibald was hermetically sealed and never ever could a photograph of any of the entries appear.

Yesterday the *Herald* stated: 'Archibald field stumps bookies. A mixture of proven performers and dark horses dominate the field of thirty-one for this year's $20,000 Archibald Prize, to be announced on Friday. The former include past winners Davida Allen (1986) Judy Cassab (1960,

1967) Fred Cress (1988) Kevin Connor (1975, 1977) Eric Smith (1970, 1981, 1982) and Wes Walters (1979).'

The *Herald*'s bookmaker, Darren Knight of the Ray Hughes Gallery, complains that it is a very difficult year to frame odds.

However, he has nominated the Cassab portrait of Jeffrey Smart as the 4–1 favourite. Cassab is a former trustee of the Art Gallery of NSW, and according to Knight, 'will certainly be carrying a lot of the conservative money'.

I have been invited by the volunteer guides, along with the other artists, to talk about their paintings. I hang beside Davida Allen whose picture is five times the size of my entry and in primary colours.

14 December 1990

I heard on the radio that Geoffrey Proud won the Archibald with his portrait of the writer Dorothy Hewett.

Soon after, Lou rang. You know who won the Archibald? Windsor and Newton! That's meant to be your consolation prize.'

23 December 1990

Untimely scorchers. There hasn't been such a hot December for thirty years. Jancsi and I spend weekend mornings at Juliska's pool. There is someone who will never be lonely. It's open house. Everybody likes to come.

9 January 1991

Louis Kahan and his wife, Lilly, are in Sydney and I have had two sittings with him already, a great pleasure as he is like a slim owl, sits on my yellow bar stool ('I feel better if I don't recline') and conversation is, of course, about painting. He never seems to have considered that chiaroscuro is sucking contemporariness out of a portrait, and is surprised that I transformed the use of it into a rhythm of light and dark, playing an almost equally important part on both sides of the face.

19 January 1991

War broke out in the Persian Gulf this week. For five months, the world waited for Saddam Hussein to withdraw from Kuwait.

Dinah Dysart of the National Trust's S.H. Ervin Gallery brought

Dawn Fraser for a sketching session. I am to paint her—in public—a week hence, in connection with the Holmes á Court collection's Images of Women exhibition.

After years of meeting at art gallery openings, Yasuko Myer invited me for lunch to their home in Elizabeth Bay. The first surprise was that I had to take my shoes off and leave them in a small entrance full of shoes, slippers, umbrellas and boots.

Ken Myer, whom I painted thirty years ago, is now seventy, and as charming and dashing as a prince. Yasuko, who is twenty-four years younger and about four foot to his six, cooked in the kitchen. While we waited, Ken took me on a tour of the flat which has a lovely view over the bay. One bedroom is full of trays of peaches and plums from their property in the country. The other has golf and tennis paraphernalia, hats, swimsuits and suitcases. Yasuko's office has a fax and computer.

They showed me her kimonos after lunch, gingerly lifting trays onto the beds, opening ribbons, folding back tissue paper looking exotic with brushed ink writing. All kimonos were hand painted, and hand stitched with flowers and giant butterflies in pure silk-thread embroidery.

Ken said, 'If you want to paint Yasuko in a kimono, I would think this green obi would be lovely on a yellow base.'

I will go back in February when her mother, who will help Yasuko dress, will be in Sydney.

3 February 1991

John Schiffer, another Jancsi, died yesterday and the world seems poorer for it. Owner of 21, our second dining room, he grew into one of the city's most colourful characters.

6 February 1991

Yasuko's mother dressed her in a yellow kimono and green obi.

I have an oil sketch and one quickie I couldn't resist, showing the back of the obi, with reds and blues, and her in profile.

10 February 1991

Lots of correspondence lately about Beregszász. Lenke sent a press cutting of the inhabitants voting to re-establish the Hungarian name, instead of the Czech-Russian, Berehovo-Beregobo.

12 February 1991

We try to eat early and catch the incredible light on the bay. Taking bread and rice for the birds, we sit on one of the children's castles and feel sheer delight feeding them. One of the seagulls has a number tag: 669. There are the shy ones which stay on the periphery. I aim my food in their direction.

I have almost finished *St Paul's Cathedral, Paris*. Drew *Caryatid with Eiffel Tower* on canvas with charcoal and sent the *Botanical Gardens with Opera House and bridge* to be stretched.

This morning Marina posed for another nude.

14 February 1991

I think the last time we had lunch at Charles Blackman's place he had another wife and two daughters. Today we arrived not knowing it's Valentine's day. Charles embraced us, wearing a singlet. It's thirty-four degrees and the wind is scorching.

There was a watercolour on the table. He placed it in Jancsi's hand and said: 'That's for you, Jancsi. For your wisdom and your goodness and your friendship.' We were stunned.

'No one else would get away with this,' Charles said, 'but I do.'

Before anyone else arrived, Charles said: 'This is a hard day for me. You remember Rapotec's wife? She wasn't well. So I gave her this studio to live in while I was in Queensland. She bought me two great books of German masters, which I found on the floor, before the door. And you know, the breeze picked up a little yellow piece of paper, a note she wrote me, and it blew away across the rooftops. Next day she killed herself.'

His eyes were full of tears.

'I couldn't forgive myself, all those years. Maybe, if I would have read the note I could have saved her.'

26 February 1991

Greta wrote:

> Besides the multitude of things already in our lives, Warwick and I have decided to get married. I don't imagine you will be especially surprised by this. He is 'that sort' of person, which in turn brings out 'that sort' of feeling in me. So here we go.

So if nothing disastrous happens to prevent it, we will get married on 6 March, with our kids present and five other couples only. All of these couples we feel represent successful relationships. Then we will go to Ballina for a dinner together, and Warwick and I will have a little two-day holiday. I am sorry that János has commitments in the Blue Mountains and can't look after Bodhi, but I will find someone he wants to stay with.

I hope you can feel positive about this event—it's strange these complicated relationships that we juggle with in our lives.

Many people avoid ones that do not fit into the prescribed order and limits, and you have never been like this. Your willingness to engage in original relationships that come into your lives has always been one of the wonderful things about you.

Of course, we all wish that János and my relationship might have lasted and our family remained intact. It didn't. I hope my present and future happiness means good things for you and János and Bodhi, as well as Warwick's children, as much as for ourselves. You are very precious to me.

All my love,
Greta

3 March 1991

Lynn's retrospective was splendid. Lily confessed later she was very nervous about how many people would turn up. The crowd catapulted us back into the 1960s. A bit wrinkled and tottery, some of us, and not seen together for decades.

Jack stood there during the speeches, a head smaller than his old height, the corners of his mouth deeply etched downwards, blinking under the assault of so much adulation.

'The happiest day of my life,' Lily said.

5 March 1991

To Melbourne for Ken Myer's birthday. It was at a place which looked like Schloss Belvedere. Two secretaries took the guests' entre-cards, and then we proceeded down an avenue of trees to the smiling Ken and radiant Yasuko. A garden party for 300. I saw Dame Elizabeth Murdoch, Sheila Scotter, Max Sandow, the Capons, Freddy and Caroline Storch (collectors), and Leonard French (after twenty years). There were round tables with yellow tablecloths and white umbrellas. An orchestra dressed in renaissance costume walked among us, playing guitar and flutes on the grass. We made our way to the barbecue tent, where the food was served, and a large wheelbarrow full of rolls and loaves. After that, we loitered around the abundant fruit pavilion. Then, as we got closer to where the speeches were being held, we bumped into a patisserie.

I collapsed into bed in the hotel after all that food and champagne.

Invited to dinner at Andrew and Irena Sibley's. He wants to paint my portrait for the Archibald Prize and I accepted. Interested in how others go about it. He wants childhood photos and to read my curriculum vitae. Comes to Sydney in June to do it.

24 March 1991

Ilse Tauber died. I visited her every week at St Luke's Hospital, watching her wasting away. Her daughter came from Holland and took the ashes to Europe.

George Barber died of a heart attack.

Jean Bellette died in Majorca.

29 March 1991

Bodhi Farm

At Bodhi Farm, Bodhi showed us his architectural drawings, and spoke about how, at fourteen, he is playing basketball in the under-sixteens' team.

He waited modestly till we asked him to play the guitar. He now has a teacher, and reads music. I was astounded as I remembered a kind of pop strumming from his busking days, and now I was hearing a young musician with a love for pure sound and an ambition to play scales smoothly.

Greta brought her flute and they improvised together. I did two drawings of them playing.

1 April 1991

Surfers Paradise

Yearly renewed delight in the world's shiniest beach in the light of the Elysium above, where charcoal purple cumulus clouds move like prancing horses.

The edge of white surf turns into crystal-clear ripples on the virgin sand under my feet. I look at Jancsi by my side, and the miracle of him striding steadily into the wind like a young man fills me with childish gratitude.

Upstairs we put swimsuits on, take our books and settle down at the swimming pool on the fourth floor, among the skyscrapers, and swim.

6 April 1991

The sea is sliding and shifting today, looking like platinum broken into a million diamonds. And on the crest of a wave a surfer is poised in his trajectory like Pegasus in orbit.

I see myself from Beregszász, in my old age, stepping out in the shimmery sand, barefoot, in a T-shirt, feeling young and privileged.

13 April 1991

Sydney

Ken Myer came to Yasuko's last sitting yesterday and enthused about the painting. She looks like an Oriental regal child in the kimono. The background turned smoky orange, and the blues on the sides appear in the obi. He wants his portrait painted.

The Australian Medical Association commissioned the portrait of Bruce Shepherd who is a colourful figure, and I'm delighted.

David Ellis rang to ask if he could have the Artists and Friends exhibition in July. Jancsi and I think this is good. Melbourne hasn't seen it and I am happy to let them out from the garage where they sleep.

14 April 1991

Jack's exhibition was on for two whole months and not one review. Finally, Christopher Allen wrote a stinker which I won't bother to quote.

'He had two months to write the review,' said Jack. 'He chose to publish it on the day of his wedding and disappeared for his honeymoon in France, like a hit-and-run driver.'

28 April 1991

Bruce Shepherd is almost finished after two sittings. Even Jancsi exclaimed 'Amazing!' when he saw it. Shepherd has two deaf children. 'We were a genetic disaster,' he said. His daughter has married a hearing man and they have a hearing child.

3 May 1991

It requires more effort now to reach out-of-the-way galleries. But we made it to Joe Furlonger's show at Ray Hughes. An impressive outburst from the young winner of a Moet Chandon Prize that took him to France, and brought him back with Matisse's *joi de vivre*, pink figures and Picassoish black outlines. He says it's no shame to lean on those. The figures discover anxiety but also play.

Ray takes us over to his house across the lane which used to be Rudy Komon's wine store. Acres of sculpture, puppets, cubism, Persian rugs as tablecloths, giant canvases diminished by the height of the room. 'Look at the garden,' he says. 'That used to be Rudy's room but the roof leaked so I took it off.'

He lives upstairs in a further clutter of art works. Only when his small son returned from primary school did I realise that the suitcase crammed with toys is not another exhibit. Darren, his assistant, remarked: 'A thin line between the two.' Annette Hughes takes us to the ceramic room with Furlonger's vases and pots which we saw in Springbrook last year.

Ray took twenty of his artists to the last Venice Biennale, exhibiting them unofficially at Galleria San Vidal. Louis Nowra wrote in the catalogue (translated in Italian to *'Oltre il Recinto del Dingo'*.):

'There is a fence longer than the great wall of China and it stretches across the centre of Australia. It has only one purpose and that is to keep out the dingo, Australia's wild dog, because once inside, the dingo kills the cattle and sheep. The dog is cunning. Even when used by the Aborigine for thousands of years the dingo remained independent.

'The artists in this show remind me of the dingo, fiercely independent, who are breaking through the dingo fence into rich pastures where plump, well-fed animals graze, believing they are still safe ... It is becoming obvious that it is the New World and the bottom of the world that have purpose and energy and it has become a positive bonus to be an outsider and on the margin when the centre has become dispirited.'

11 May 1991

It was Lou's idea to come and talk to Jancsi while I paint a portrait of him. The first sitting showed Jancsi in a sombre mood, though in animated conversation in which he always raises the centre of his forehead so his eyebrows run to the corners of his eyes and he half-closes his eyes while doing this.

Both Jancsi and Lou warned me after this sitting, not to touch the face. 'Only the head, Judy. That big brain of Jancsi's needs a wider skull. Also, please, emphasise his ears. It's the symbol of wisdom. The jacket is too smart!'

So on the second sitting I painted the jacket over into a wine red pullover.

I finished Bruce Shepherd's portrait today and seven people came at noon to look at it! Dr Peter Arnold and his wife Shirley who brought chilled champagne; Bruce's girlfriend, Janice; a surgeon from Adelaide with his wife, carrying an esky with two more bottles of champagne. Finally, his daughter Penny came with Jack, the grandchild who can't walk yet but pointed at the picture, 'Papa'.

12 May 1991

Received a letter from the Art Gallery about an exhibition: Two Hundred Years of Australian Painting, Japan, to be shown at the Museums of Modern and Western Art in Tokyo and Kyoto. This gallery is coordinating the tour of 120 paintings, which includes works from twenty-five galleries and private collections.

26 May 1991

Nick and Romy Waterlow gave a reunion dinner for the Louis Jameses, the Lynns and us. How young and lovely they were twenty-six years ago when I first met them. They have aged beautifully, like good wine.

Romy is the towering personality, the earth mother, the rare, devoted dedicated human being. Although she inherited money from her father, she works as a social worker in a hospital for AIDS patients. Cooked excellent food for eight of us after a gruelling day, and her eyes shine like beacons in the candlelight.

Nick is more balanced and happy than he ever was, teaching at the Alexander Mackie College.

7 June 1991

David Ellis came from Melbourne for the day to choose twenty-four portraits for my Artists and Friends exhibition. I will also show six (*his* number) oil on paper studies, which have never been seen before. Hell of a job in Joyce's garage, but he does the lifting and sorting out. Who will put the bubble plastic back on? But, so what.

I serve quiche (he is a vegetarian), cake, coffee, wine, then Jancsi and I drive him around the Paddington galleries, finally depositing him at Martin Sharp's old mansion in Victoria Road. He was mad about Sharp's portrait with the van Gogh and Luna Park which forced me to carry the yellows and blues into the face. It's six o'clock before I start washing dishes.

Some day!

10 June 1991

János spent three whole days with us. We were filled in, overwhelmed and amazed that we created this extraordinary human.

He takes off this persona like a jacket to be father to Bodhi, to tease and tickle and wrestle and roar with laughter.

16 June 1991

Ken Myer at seventy has the physique of a film star and a strikingly handsome aristocratic face, aquiline nose, wise twinkling cornflower-blue eyes and a curve in his upper lip like Cupid's bow.

On our first sitting (after thirty years) he is telling me that Yasuko's forebears were samurai. Wives of samurai were left to defend the home. 'You know that even now, when we walk at night at the Cross and a shadow approaches, Yasuko steps in front of me, shielding me with her body.' I find this touching as he is very tall and she is as small as a child.

Telling me that the Art Gallery of NSW is getting the Guggenheim exhibition—the only state in Australia to do so. Edmund Capon and Frank Lowy, chairman of the trustees, are going to the opening in Japan.

18 June 1991

János writes long letters from Kyoto and Hiroshima about the interest in his 'Council of All Beings'.

At our Monday dinners I enjoy Peter as raconteur, and gaze at Shayne's great beauty. A masterpiece of a nose and chin. Skin gently rippling over the dimple in the centre. Beauty is as great a gift as a talent or a voice.

22 June 1991

There are days when my Jancsi becomes cantankerous. He said, 'Why is Panni putting my slippers in two different places under the bed? Why are you throwing papers over the hearing aid?'

I am silent. We eat breakfast.

When I feel the force of the beam, I look up and there are those eyes full of love, at the edge of tears as he says, 'I just realised I haven't said a good word to you yet.' Both of us burst out laughing.

Elizabeth Evatt's portrait was being unveiled at Newcastle University. I went to Anne von Bertouch for lunch.

When I received the fee for Evatt's portrait, I sent Anne (who had nothing to do with it) a thousand dollars. I wrote that, though this wasn't done under the aegis of her gallery, Newcastle is her territory and I'd like her to have it.

She thanked me and said she bought a painting by a young artist, Susan Davies, who is overseas for the first time in her life, travelling in Florence on a shoe string. Then, she donated the painting to the university. When I was a young artist so many helped me so often, it's only fair for me to pay back.

The ceremonies took from 5 p.m. to almost midnight. First the unveiling, speeches, then dinner for eighty. Elizabeth, beside me, says she feels she is at the Last Supper.

23 June 1991

János and Bodhi are here, en route to the Snowy. They have hired a caravan in Jindabyne, and I will lend them my car for the week.

1 July 1991

Ita magazine sent Bunty Turner to do a profile. The photographer, Stuart, has photographed me before for *Mode*.

I chose my *St Paul's Cathedral, Paris*, as the backdrop. He was fascinated by my painting table (from Budapest, with forty years of crusted paint), and made it the foreground. I'm stuck between without glasses, out of vanity. He suggested I sketch him as he takes my photograph. I did just that without my spectacles and then gave it to him.

7 July 1991

The Melbourne exhibition looks great. David decided to leave Yasuko's portrait out. We had a short collision about that and she now hangs beside Thomas Keneally. Then he proceeded to price the portrait like the landscapes, according to size. Can't do that!

'Why? Do you consider them better than the landscapes?'

'Yes. There are many who do good landscapes but very few good portraitists.' So, finally peace.

Went to see Wolseley at the Australian Galleries. Delicious, sensitive, an immersion in butterfly wings. Prices around the six-figure mark and lots sold.

After only three lithographs of Famous Australians sold at my opening, my feet hurt and I couldn't help thinking: what for?

14 July 1991

Lyall Ellis rang to tell me huge throngs of people are going through the gallery. 'We never had such crowds before.'

Andrew Sibley came to Sydney last week to paint my portrait. Amazing how different artists can be. He did four pencil drawings of me on Tuesday morning staying until the afternoon. He won't show them to me, but I couldn't help glimpsing that they were faithful renderings of likeness, not at all Sibleyish in style.

'If the subject would be in the room while I actually paint the portrait,' he said, 'I would die!'

He also took about twenty-four photos, slides, not prints which, he said, he can project on the canvas.

I am just starting to use the photograph, but only when I have almost finished the portrait.

Packing for Alice Springs became a task. I'm fretting about what I will forget. And there are so many things to think of like paint, brushes, palette, foundations, canvases, scissors, spare spectacles and all the medicines for our blood pressure and digestion.

15 July 1991

Alice Springs

Mona at the airport in her four-wheel drive. Her life has changed. Des, her husband who once lived happily with a great dane in Adelaide is now eighty-six. He gave up driving, buried the dog. Mona's dog, Mina, just died. The two graves are in the garden and the humans live together again.

From Heavitree Gap Motel she drove us to town to rent a car and stock up. Back at the motel, as we opened the glass door on the shimmering hill in the late afternoon sun, little wallabies came and sat close by.

Our first visit to Araluen Art Gallery. A show of Aboriginal women's painting, pottery and craft. In the Namatjira room Jancsi and I both headed like a bullet towards a small watercolour of a kangaroo. It was dated 1937. Before he had 'tuition'.

Lunch at White Gums Park with Mona and Des. A bit past Simpson's Gap where the road turns into Honeymoon Gap. It didn't exist on our last trip.

At White Gums they didn't know how good food should taste: I had a cracked-wheat biscuit stuffed with spinach, and, for heaven's sake, lentils drowning in yoghurt. Jancsi's fettuccine had olives, the Greek salad was julienned, and the fetta cheese crumbled until it was like wilting coleslaw.

When we got home I couldn't find the key to our room. I had locked it inside. I was downhearted by the incident until Jancsi hugged me, told me he adores me, and said we must take care of each other and not be impatient with our weaknesses.

Then we fed the wallabies. Seven tiny kangaroos tiptoed close to Jancsi's feet begging with paws outstretched.

18 July 1991

Glen Helen

The new bitumen highway now stretches right up to Glen Helen. The lodge belongs to Sandra, Di and Jill. Mindy, the chef, is the daughter of a Sydney GP. She did four years of architecture and discovered that all she wanted to do was cook. Awards and diplomas litter the wall of a huge lounge-cum-bar.

They went through three disasters: fire, when the lodge burned down; water, when it was almost flooded; and death. We remembered reading about the truck driver who killed five people in Ayers Rock by driving through the wall of the pub. It belonged to Di and Sandra.

After the siesta we drove up the hill, parking off the road. Then we settled on Mona's collapsible chairs facing the miraculous formations glowing red in the middle distance.

I brought twelve pieces of canvas prepared for this trip, painted two of them just by casting my eyes on two consecutive details of the rock face.

Coming home I bumped into Mandy Martin. We know her work. Strong, talented work, mainly of industrial buildings, factories, chimneys. This year she won the Alice Prize which, besides the prize money, offers six weeks as artist-in-residence in a house near Aralumla. She is around thirty-five, good-looking, black ringlets blowing around her shoulders, tall, with an open, dimpled smile.

Right before the motel room the river shimmers along the bulrushes, apple-green, and a heron is whiter than the silver of the moon in the still blue sky. The rock wall gets more and more cadmium red, and Mandy paints over the oilstick with red watercolours using a narrow horizontal long paper. When I said I liked it, she ran into her room, brought out four more, all in a day's work.

I felt better at once about having done three in one afternoon.

On the first evening in Glen Helen we invited Mona for dinner to Cloudy's restaurant. A great log fire was burning in the old-fashioned room. Sandra appeared with the waiter bringing a bucket with a bottle of champagne and a letter for me. It was from Beryl Foster, my old friend, Cloudy's daughter.

The parchment paper had a red wax stamp. In it was a photocopy of a drawing I did of Cloudy in 1959. 'To our dear friends,' writes Beryl, 'This is the Cloudy who smiled at you thirty-three years ago in her little home in Gap Road. In our hearts we will be with you when you raise your glasses.'

Sandra said the camels are on safari, only Oscar is at home, bedded down in the truck with a sore foot. However, modern times are here also, with a helicopter taking tourists for joy rides above the gorge and the top of Mount Sonda.

This morning we drove to Ormiston Gorge. There is a lot we have to carry for quite a distance over pebbles and large stones. I painted the red and white colours of the rock wall and its reflection on bluish-grey water with lemon-yellow shimmer. On the other canvas, Jancsi suggested

I include the shadow of the branches of a tree on the green water.

I am now very aware that the more I work that creative first outpour, the less it will be a Cassab, the more it'll be a realistic description of place. This is especially true of the mottled pieces of canvases which already have my 'trademark'.

At 5 p.m. the camels arrived, silhouetted on the hill, a cinema scene. I did two sketches and took snapshots.

19 July 1991

I love the place more and more each day. We decided to stay here until the day of our flight.

We sit at trestle tables on the terrace soaking in the fabulous sights. One could paint Ormiston for a lifetime.

No overpainting now, just putting it down with gusto.

Afternoon we walked along the river until, to my delight, the Glen Helen group of rocks appeared, and they were magical. I really enjoy impasto. This painting came out well and it cries for enlargement.

20 July 1991

There is no television, no newspaper, no post office, no radio, no telephone in the rooms. This is the outback. No one stays here longer than two days. Most bus tours stay only one.

22 July 1991

My world took a turn suddenly. I heard the rain during the night drumming on the corrugated-iron roof. Now rain is a great rarity in these desert parts, about three inches a year. It all came down yesterday.

26 July 1991

I rang David Ellis as it's the last day before the exhibition in Melbourne closes. A review in the *Age*, one on radio, and the Olsen portrait was sold, hurrah!

The wind was cruel this morning in Ormiston. After I moored down the palette with two stones, anchored the canvas with four clips and started, Jancsi proposed we should leave as one can't stay in a hurricane. I asked him, 'Who is the one who taught me never to turn back when beginning something?', and soldiered on. Not as excellent as some (a

Yehudi Menuhin is *Er nicht*) but I can make them so in the studio.

The staff is interested in my paintings. Helen the waitress and Mindy the cook come to see them, and Steven and Pat from the kitchen also.

After resting, I found a new subject in Glen Helen Gorge. No wind, total absorption.

28 July 1991

The wind still blows but I moved into a small cave and needed less stones to keep objects from flying around. Today, I photographed the twenty-four paintings in the sun for future enlarging.

I am so grateful to have a body of work again.

29 July 1991

Yesterday we walked to the 'mysterious city', and I painted the next part of its triptych. Jancsi insisted on a figure of Christ in the rock, so I did it to please him, but even he said that it looked better on its side, when the literary meaning disappears.

We were told to be in the lounge at six. It's a surprise. Dress warmly. By now the paintings are already packed. We walked to the edge of the Finke River where it turns into a lake between the sides of the gorge. Two black swans came, and white and grey egrets. The river stones are polished to silvery smoothness.

The surprise was a helicopter flight to the top of the dreaming serpent. We were introduced to David, the pilot, whose blond ponytail hangs under his pilot cap. No doors, only three seats (with seatbelts) behind the pilot. Off we swirled in the glass bubble as in a fairytale.

I was scared stiff as I wondered if he would make it over that rock wall. Then we hovered above the whole fantastic land and gently touched down. He made another trip to bring Jill and Mandy, iced champagne was conjured from a basket. Such generosity. We watched the sun setting over the well-known shapes in glowing hues. The breeze was caressing and the helicopter sat like an extraterrestrial looking at us with its insect eye.

This morning we paid our bill, our car was checked for oil and water, our esky stocked with lunch and beer. All three girls waved us on our way.

Mandy Martin was expecting us for lunch but we stopped at Simpson's Gap for a walk. The drive was divine as well. Such a fine new road exclusively for us. Not another vehicle in sight for a hundred kilometres.

Mandy met us on the path, with another young woman artist, Judy Holding, with her daughter Isabelle.

We were enthusiastic about Mandy's work. There is a change towards an almost Auerbachesque impasto. She uses enormous tubes of oil paint, squeezing what looks like half a tube out at a time, and since a palette would be obviously insufficient, she uses small trays to mix all that paint.

11 August 1991

Sydney

A dinner at Parliament House with Joan Sutherland and Richard Bonynge as the guests of honour. I sat with Adam and Helen Bonynge, their children. When it was time for me to leave, Joan unexpectedly bent and kissed my hand. I was flabbergasted. There was nothing else to do but kiss hers! She said, 'Such a hand one must kiss.'

14 August 1991

Mandy Martin and her husband, Robert Boynes, came for dinner, before the opening of his exhibition at the Macquarie Galleries. She brought me the long narrow painting I admired, where her old theme of industrial subjects first merged with the landscape.

8 September 1991

Richard Wherrett's portrait nearly finished. Blond streaks in greying hair and a gold earring in his left ear, eyes are bedroom-sleepy, the face intelligent. T-shirt, denims, and a deeper, almost Prussian-blue raincoat with the collar turned up. I just had to paint two vertical slabs of red into the background.

Yasuko Myer, returning to Sydney, came up to take the small sketch of her in profile with her back turned showing the obi which I gave them as a souvenir.

Suddenly, many commissions: a doctor's portrait for George V Hospital booked for November. I started Sister Bernice of the St Vincent's Hospital (commissioned also by doctors). Then there is tall, slim, fiftyish, elegant Ragnar Pahlman, originally from Stockholm. I start this portrait next week.

Out of the blue, Professor Emeritus Robinson rang, commissioning his wife's portrait on her seventieth birthday.

Meanwhile I am enlarging the second Glen Helen painting and I finished all the canvases which are glued on wood.

Watching Stuart Challender who is dying of AIDS, conducting. At the end, when somehow (because he can hardly walk) he came on the stage, we all gave a standing ovation. I thought, what heroism and how right he is because isn't it better to die on the podium, so to speak, than in a hospital bed?

4 October 1991

Sister Bernice's portrait is finished. She brought two friends to the last sitting. Leith Meyerson, president of the Blind Institute, and a younger nun. She told us how when after decades of only having a small hand mirror she saw herself for the first time in a shop window's mirror, she didn't know who it was. She had never seen herself before.

12 October 1991

Second year of sending in for the Blue Mountains Grammar School's Kedumba Art Award.

Jeff Plummer was inviting exhibiting artists to stay at the five-star Hotel Fairmont with enough tempting meals and a pleasant holiday, to get Kevin Connor to judge, Hendrik Kolenberg to open and James Gleeson, Guy Warren, John Coburn, Reinis Zusters and Reg Livermore to come.

A painting prize worth $7000 automatically shuts out those first-rate artists who wouldn't sell a major painting for this money. 'Make it a drawing prize,' Kevin advised, and also suggested asking the curator of drawings of the Art Gallery of NSW to provide a list of artists to invite.

So, miracle of miracles, Leura is now an exhibition place of—Kolenberg said—national importance. It fairly glows on the walls of two elegant exhibition halls attracting Senbergs, who shared the prize with Gleeson, Dunlop, Gilliland, Caldwell, Coburn, Shay Docking, George Haynes of Perth, Jan Riske of New York, Michael Shannon, Guy Warren and me.

21 October 1991

Shayne gave me my first lesson on her computer. Being hopeless with gadgets, I had a healthy respect for this word processor. It will be really useful not to have to repeat the same information in my extended correspondence. I write to Argentina, Brazil, California and Budapest. I also write to Paris, Hong Kong, Prague and London.

I will inherit this computer from Shayne soon because she has bought a more sophisticated system for her office.

3 November 1991

I've been excited for weeks. János flew in from San Francisco yesterday, and Bodhi arrived a little later.

János arrived with El-Ana and about twenty pieces of luggage. 'Travelling light,' he said as he staggered up and down the stairs.

El-Ana slept all afternoon, but János wanted to go to the airport with me to fetch Bodhi. It gave me rare and treasured time to talk to my son. His influence, especially in the USA is growing. And after decades of single-mindedness, he bought lots of books to read: psychology, philosophy, even literature. He wants to be on the coast, possibly in a caravan without a telephone, to write his new book. *Thinking like a mountain* is being translated into Russian and Japanese.

Bodhi arrived with a smile of pure bliss as he hugged János. Sitting in the back seat, I listened to Bodhi's school results—which are fine, and how his knee is getting better, he is swimming a lot and he's taken up guitar lessons again.

We had a lovely night celebrating Jancsi's birthday. Greta sent a touching tribute. Bodhi gave him a comfortable set of earphones for his favourite small radio, and Peter bought two sports shirts.

Peter made a toast, and Jancsi toasted me, and then János decided to watch the world rugby from England. So they carried the television into the living room.

4 November 1991

At three o'clock Marina came. Since she returned from her Paris *sejour* she doesn't know what to do with her life. Except, she showed me twenty-five small, naive, colour-pencil drawings, which are delightful and talented. We went to the Holdsworth where Gisella is exhibiting fifty unseen Donald Friends which she has completely forgotten for twenty years. He used to sell her batches of watercolours in Bali, and took the paintings to show her.

Gisella liked Marina's paintings and will give her an exhibition in the right wing. We were stunned.

28 November 1991

We spent twelve days in Surfers Paradise. Same place, same blissful beach walks and long hours of reading. Reading Potok's *The gift of Asher Lev*. Few readers get the same rewards as I do, knowing enough about Hassidim with black coats, earlocks, tallis and twilem on the streets of Munkács where I married Jancsi. While simultaneously knowing about art and the incredible resistance of the Hassids to graven images. Asher Lev's awe of possessing such a gift, which at its core may have the befouling sediment of the pagan, the allure of centaurs, satyrs, naiads, dryads, or worse yet, the demonic world of the 'other side', the destroyer.

The motto from Rainer Maria Rilke. 'Surely all art is the result of having been in danger, of having gone through an experience all the way to the end, to where no one can go any further.'

I went to a panel discussion at the Alexander Mackie College, about the accompanying Baldessin exhibition.

Imants Tillers was showing some interesting copperplates on which he started an etching which Baldessin finished, or the other way round.

7 December 1991

Rabbi Fox asked me to open a children's exhibition at the Emanuel School. It was easier than I thought, and a delight. The teachers are creative and so was the show. Then a small children's orchestra of violins played Mozart, another group formed a choir, I made a speech, all this plein-air in the sunset, reinforced with spotlights.

We chose a guided tour for our first viewing of the new Museum of Contemporary Art. The early session was led by the curator, Bernice Murphy. To our great amazement, she gave Elwyn Lynn the most incredible kudos, raising his fourteen years as curator of the Power Bequest and buyer of the museum's backbone, to the high level it deserves and which was denied him for decades.

In the evening we went to George Molnar's opening at the Institute of Architects in Potts Point, in an old gracious house called 'Tusculum'. He is one of those gifted and charming people who is his own worst enemy. He didn't invite anyone from the Art Gallery ('They never bought any of my stuff') and didn't notify the press.

Forty-six wonderful watercolours bursting with wit, hardly any sales, prices sliced to half of what they used to be at the Holdsworth.

Two titles: *Ned Kelly at Gallipoli rescues Mrs Frazer from the swan, and Unauthorised birth of Venus at Nielson Park.*

15 December 1991

Lunch at the S.H. Ervin Gallery, organised by Lou under the title Pens and Pencils. The under-fifties are pencils. No need to emphasise that the pens were the majority. Frank and Margel Hinder and Nora Heysen, all in their eighties. We were served excellent bread, ham, cheeses and white wine.

25 December 1991

Because of the spirit of goodwill, drivers are more aggressive, pedestrians more careless and everyone more social than normal. I haven't painted for three weeks.

There are pleasant happenings too. Like Sister Bernice of St Vincent's Clinic, whose portrait was unveiled last week, unexpectedly delivered a huge Christmas cake, resplendent with gold-dusted Christmas tree and bearded Santa Claus.

I made a big decision prompted by Bernie Leser's suggestion. Jancsi feels, and strangely the same thought surfaced in me just now, that the time has come to do something about my journals. I used to think, when I'm old. Well, seventy-one is old enough. It will take years, I suppose.

Before approaching a suitable literary person, to edit it and add the technique I lack, I am editing it. That is, I censor those things which are either repetitive (smoked salmon for birthdays—boring to others), what János and Peter said in Salzburg in 1950, or too private (quarrels with Jancsi).

Even so, I have to get the children's permission when the time comes, about their teenage rebellions and agonies, and our family meetings.

4 January 1992

Bodhi rang to report that he swam in the creek with Clay and they met a platypus. It wasn't frightened but frolicked around them. Bodhi said over the phone, 'Would you like to hear me playing the guitar?'

I was serenaded.

János sent us his diary of the Amazon expedition.

19 January 1992

After a year of illnesses, Jack and Lily Lynn came for lunch. I kept visiting regularly on weekends and after I looked at his Wynne and Sulman Prize entries he expressed a wish to see mine.

Joshua Smith, he said, is a great portrait. He was genuinely surprised about the Wynne Prize painting, *In Ormiston Gorge*. Declared it daring (because of the burgundy sky and the deep sap-green water) and liked it. I then showed him the other two enlargements of the same size, the personage which appeared unintentionally and which we called Balzac. And the one which looks a bit like two figures.

Now he really was enthusiastic about those and said, 'Both should go in the Sulman.'

'But they are not "genre"!'

'Who cares! They are "Subject". Call this one (Balzac) *The spirit of the gorge* and the double figure *Gemini*.'

Since the blessed routine days are back, lighting up steamy January, I have painted a large *Glen Helen Gorge* and almost finished a *Snake dreaming*. Painted a watercolour on the bumpy Paris paper of *Monet's house from the garden*, thinking of four Parisian shows this year. Hobart, Canberra, Newcastle, and Win Schubert's gallery in the Marina Mirage on the Gold Coast. Unlikely as it is that I'll sell anything during this terrible depression, but the devil doesn't sleep.

Anyway, *Monet's house from the garden* turned out to be such a beautiful transformation of the original oil, that I'm really pleased.

2 February 1992

Jancsi and I went to see Paul Atroshenko's exhibition at the Holdsworth. In the room to the right, Marina's show hangs. I was surprised to see how much better the Sydney paintings look than I remembered. As we crossed the main room, I saw Jack Lynn sitting there, writing.

As we talked, I mentioned Marina, my friend and my model for the last decade. A talented child who surprised me with those excellent naive paintings of Paris, after an acting career.

9 February 1992

All of Marina's thirty paintings sold. Jack mentioned her in his review. Max Taylor included her in Delmar's pastel exhibition.

Stuck on the side of our fridge is the Toulouse-Lautrec calendar I bought at the Brisbane exhibition. Since at every meal I feast my eyes, as well as my stomach, with wonderful posters, I realise what a waste it is to have a pedestrian calendar.

Jack phoned about a month ago: The Melbourne *Age* has János on the cover of the colour supplement, titled, 'Green guerillas'.

14 February 1992

The *Herald*'s Peter Cochrane had me on his Archibald betting list. I was on the shortlist. (But Bryan Westwood won it with his portrait of Paul Keating, the prime minister.)

I painted Ormiston Gorge on a medium-size canvas with acrylics on the studio table, Kiri Te Kanawa's voice singing out the haunting sweetness of a Richard Strauss lieder that Anyu used to sing. At eleven, I knew I hadn't won as nobody rang me. Only Louis James (who hasn't telephoned me for ten years) to say he liked my Joshua very much.

When Westwood first won with Elwyn Lynn's portrait, realist as it was, I had no doubts it had a terrific presence, a powerful tension. I don't like the Keating portrait.

7 April 1992

Hobart

We flew to Tasmania for my one-man show at the Freeman Gallery in Hobart, which turned into a gem of a holiday, starting with the first breath of fresh, dry, unpolluted air. I almost forgot how it tasted after the Sydney miasma.

An East West Airlines deal took us to the Sheraton Hotel, with a room which overlooked the harbour and all the fishing boats.

In the art gallery we met old friends in different guises. A small red and green *Still life with lamp* by Elwyn Lynn (1955), Moya Dyring's *Fishing nets, Concarneau*, Kmit's *Signature*. A magnificent blue Nolan we thought was Antarctica, but it was Greece in the 1950s, with unexpected black scribbles rushing up the hill.

'Look,' I said to Jancsi, 'what a beautiful Drysdale!' It was Donald

Friend's *Hill End* (1950) obviously painted together with his friend, Tassy.

Margaret Olley's interior of David Strachan's house; Westwood with a Hopperesque street (1973), Jeff Smart's *Car park attendants* (1965), where a ferriswheel and red-yellow electric bulbs are surrealistic but the figures suffer from orange neglect. Masterly old works of Lloyd Rees, and beside them the lemony apple-green of his old-age style. An Orban from 1935, magnificent on black ground.

Lou Klepac and Hendrik phoned the curator, Christa Johannes, who took us for coffee on the wharf. She came originally from Riga, went to Canada with her parents at sixteen, married a marine biologist who chose to live and work in Australia.

Christa worked in Perth first with Lou and Hendrik, and followed Hendrik (who is like a brother) to the Tasmanian Art Gallery. My two paintings, she said, are not hung at the moment because of rebuilding.

Jancsi and I loved our first two days here. The city has a special character, like a Danish whaling village. We overlook a rectangle with a sandstone warehouse, the Drunken Admiral Fish Restaurant.

Jill Freeman asked me weeks ago to send ten paintings besides the Paris ones (which have to be sent on to Canberra) which she can keep in stock. I can't blame her for hanging them in corridors and backrooms and selling them!

The opening was crowded, festive, above the means of most—not one sold. Lucky that Jill acted against my expressed wishes (hanging the small other works) as *Darling Point with island*, a small nude, *Girl in black hat*, and *Botanical Garden* were sold. So, possibly, the freight and our trip is covered.

9 April 1992

Painted some flowers in the window, with ships.

Mia's house was a huge surprise. Her Greek parents bought a property in Tinderbox, a village in the mountain, on the river. Mia learned from Gerard Havekes with whom she lived for many years.

She created a small kingdom, an offspring of *his*—a happening of immense charm and beauty. I had no idea she had learned his craft so well. She is now creating sculpture and pottery, tiles like Gerard's, having three kilns, hundreds of shallow shelves, an abundance of found objects à la Moore, from fish bones to ship ropes. One such long rope (as thick as a thigh), dyed orange, is slung and woven in and on the gutter, another is on the terrace holding a huge church bell. One sculpture sits on the railing over the Derwent River. A winged nude is on the oversized, low, bronze table.

23 April 1992

The opening of the Henry Moore exhibition, more thrilling even than the Guggenheim. I saw drawings I have never seen before, looking like Egyptian friezes or sarcophagi.

12 May 1992

My Paris Paintings opened in Canberra's Solander Gallery. Six paintings sold on the first day. Unexpected pleasure. A big, enthusiastic crowd. Among them Ken Back, the vice-chancellor of Townsville University whose daughter was once married to Greta's Warwick. He told a friend at the exhibition, 'We are sort of relatives, you know. I was the former father-in-law of the stepfather of Judy's grandson.'

A siesta in the Pavilion, and dinner at Ian Templeman, a director of the National Library.

1 June 1992

Back from San Francisco, János has breakfast with us in the kitchen. 'You know my friend from Esprit who is such a supporter? He has a mansion in San Francisco with three Francis Bacons, each the size of your kitchen. He will be away in November and has offered me the use of his house.'

Jancsi said, 'Take a Bacon'.

'Dad, how can you say that? You know I'm a vegetarian!'

He told Bodhi over the phone. 'I have decided not to travel at all next year.'

'You said that last year.'

6 June 1992

Anna Cohn, the sculptor, who told me she keeps a 'Cassab file', sent me a press-cutting from when we both exhibited at the New Australians Cultural Association in the Education Department Galleries. I was thirty, didn't tint my hair, had no double chin, stood before my picture of Franzi and Edith Kletzmayr painted in Salzburg in national costumes with a harmonica and flute. It stirs up memories. But it made me smile as I read: 'One of the women, Miss Judy Cassab, treats painting as a business and has a studio ... She is the only woman to have a painting highly commended ... '

When, of course, any reasonable person knew that painting is only a hobby.

18 June 1992

Clare Dan, in the midst of the usual turmoil of her four-yearly Sydney international piano competition, gave a scholarship to a seventeen-year-old schoolboy, Gidon Mead, arranged a concert at his school. Clare seems at last, to receive the accolades she deserves. She helped, after all, to put Australia on the musical map.

Brett Whiteley died. Sudden shockwaves through the country. He was fifty-three. Wendy, in spite of the torrid divorce, is sobbing with shock, anger and love. Theirs was an intense relationship. She knew it could happen at any time but hoped it wouldn't. Heroin is a destroyer. It has a power and a life of its own.

He said, 'I go cold turkey, I vomit, retch, get cramps for three days; it's hideous.' Then he announced that *this* time he was off it for good. 'But then I get some overwhelming problem, I reach for that short-term chemical solution. It's strange how an addictive personality like myself, born with a gift, has this compulsion to test the gift, challenge it, push it to the edge, to see if it is still there and you are in control.'

He was magnetic, infuriating and lovable.

Colin Lanceley, his friend, after saying he drew like an angel, says, 'He has often tried to correct the world, wearing his heart on his sleeve. Such works have been the target of some of our more jaundiced art critics, and, of course, he was too successful in the marketplace to have favour with the commissars.'

In 1979 Brett hand wrote his own biographical notes for an exhibition. The notes included: 'Whiteley is a noted draftsman, which in his eyes means he can damage the integrity of a piece of white paper properly. He imagines he will die sometime in his fifties.'

23 June 1992

My childhood friend, Évi Ságh, now Kershaw, sent me a catalogue of a Japanese exhibition in Japan. My *Desert shape* was chosen by the Japanese curator. I find it amazing that the only witness should be a Beregszászer on a visit from America.

George and Carol Molnar invited me over after a long hiatus, and he showed me fifty new watercolours. Among them are memories of childhood. There is the tiled stove and one feels the tactile warm, glittery sensation of it. Another round stove lived in bathrooms, filled with water. He remembers the loo, it's majolica pattern and the chain. Lamps out of Tiffany, his parents' bedroom as he, at age three, disturbs them, and father's stretched-out arm, bans him, finger pointing. Every object on mother's dressing-table is detailed, as well as the way father's underpants and starched shirt are placed on the chair. He has another series, the muses, in his inimitable manner.

30 June 1992

David Edwards is here for Margery's exhibition at the Holdsworth. His whole life revolves around building her a memorial. I was amazed by what such determination can do, as he has placed her paintings in a dozen museums in the USA, among them the Metropolitan!

He has the look of someone possessed.

14 July 1992

Gene Sherman came to choose a Paris drawing which will become a lithograph printed by Fred Genis, to accompany a Paris exhibition she has planned with the Alliance Francaise. She has Frank Hodgkinson's Paris, Charles Blackman's, Brett Whiteley's and mine for the big exhibition.

Brett's Paris paintings were exhibited at the Australian Galleries in Melbourne. Charles is in hospital, Fred Genis couldn't sell his house in Kenthurst and has already started to move his studio to Glebe, can't work now.

Gene decided to postpone till next year.

János has installed a world network in our living room, receiving mail on his computer from all over the globe, no idea by what sorcery. The filing system was the floor, three different black boxes were wired to power points.

He said, 'Dad, I'll be in Siberia, I won't be here on your ninetieth birthday.'

Jancsi replied, 'I hope I'll be.'

18 July 1992

Channel 2 sent a taxi to pick me up and deposit me at the Gore Hill studio. Peter Ross of 'Sunday Afternoon' told me that he knows I consider the war years ancient history, but he would like to ask me about the time when Jancsi wore the yellow star and I wasn't supposed to greet him on the street.

He planned the past to form the first part, and the second part, the Australian years. It took eighteen minutes.

26 July 1992

The Peter Ross 'Sunday Afternoon' was a pleasure. One hour of the finals of Clare's piano competition, then Monet, then eighteen minutes of me, then Mantegna.

The feedback was astounding. Telephone call from Mr Andrews, headmaster of Sydney High when Johnny and Peter were schoolboys. Twenty-eight years later he rang!

Next day, János took a plane an hour earlier than planned, to have more time to spend with us. Consequently, his overseas luggage didn't arrive with him. One ponders, will it be posted from Amsterdam or will it travel to Siberia?

29 July 1992

Long letter from Jack who's at the Cité International des Arts in Paris. In it a Matisse postcard *Le boudoir*. He writes on the back: 'I think that here Matisse catches some of your lighter moods.'

He writes a long, witty account of events in galleries, and of Bastille Day, about practice-playing at the Cité which forces them to wear earplugs. The atelier has a new shower, toilet and heater!

They met Victoria and Ross in Kassel. 'Since then we have compared notes. Ah, the young. They see everything and remember lots more.'

A Lynn article in the *Australian* of the Kassel Documenta. The photograph is of dog turds on white tiles, which I first read as *Capogrossi*.

17 August 1992

Peter and Shayne took us to Lucio's for my seventy-second birthday. Jancsi said, 'This year is your favourite, number nine. Seven and two.'

'Yours is also nine,' I said. 'You will be ninety.'

Suddenly Peter exclaimed, 'Goodness! I'll be forty-five, that's also nine!' And Shayne, amazed. 'And I'll be thirty-six.'

When I first heard over the radio that a small plane crashed in Alaska and Ken Myer died, my first thought was, I hope Yasuko died with him. Since I painted them both so recently, I knew she had left her whole world for him, and loved him to the exclusion of everything and everyone. We were devastated. He also cut through barriers when he left his family to marry a young Japanese woman. It was love at first sight. Nobody else mattered.

The Kedumba Art Award was on again, and I went to Leura as a guest of the Grammar School and the Fairmont resort. This year Jan Senbergs judged it (he won it last year) and awarded it to John Wolseley. I might have done the same, not only because it was one of four or five equally good works on paper, but thinking that this comes into the school's collection, it was the only major work. Title: *Of the morphology of sand-dunes, Aranda (Simpson) Desert*.

We had a letter from János in Vladivostok. He has an assistant, a greenie called Sergei, who said if he could find $16 a month, he could quit his job and become a full-time activist.

24 August 1992

Surfers Paradise

The Esplanade has changed into a kind of resort; brick-shaped pavement with intarsia of wooden frames; cheerful yellow benches placed onto jutting wooden terraces above the sea. Between sea and Esplanade are islands of fenced-in sand, like an apology to the magnificent sweep of beach, an appeasement for separating it from the shore. It acts as a windbreaker, I think, and as a sieve to keep the walkway clean of sand and help the struggling plants withstand salt and sand.

There are youngsters whizzing by on rollerskates, cyclists dodging thoroughbred dogs, holidaymakers careful to wear the proper gear. Hundreds of Japanese tourists, and mainly, geriatrics who retired to this spot of sun with its European coffee-house way of life.

27 August 1992

Bettina McAulay invited us to visit her at the Queensland Art Gallery to see Uncommon Australians where my portraits of Joan Sutherland and Frank Packer are included.

Win drove us in her wine-red Jaguar, twice as fast as anything on the road. She made me a proposition: to buy *Beam of Pompidou across cathedral* for a token price and donate it to the Queensland Gallery. Bettina has admired it. I gladly consented, simply because it's a wonderful alternative to putting it in its grave in the garage where its size makes it a nuisance. Bettina was happy, took us to Doug Hall, the director— suave, cheeky, young, with bold socks.

This is a lovely gallery where I see hitherto unknown works like those of Trevor Nickolls, an Aboriginal artist doing a Baselitz with three figures upside down.

28 August 1992

Win and Agnes have a tiny flat below their house where Hugh Sawrey is a guest. I knew his pictures as one knows Pro Hart's. He paints horses in the outback under windmills in the evening glow. We met him at the champagne breakfast, he wanted to show us his studio. He is a bushie who doesn't pretend to be anything else, but oh! How much more one earns when one pleases bad taste than by plying a boring trade!

Damien Hackett invited us to view the Gold Coast Art Prize. It was a brash, uncouth, talented young exhibition of collage, assemblage and reliefs, judged by Rosalie Gascoigne, an artist of integrity and high standing, working mainly with letters of the alphabet, on crates, materials and such. She made a bee-line towards me with outstretched hands saying 'I know who *you* are! I know you from television and magazine articles.' She didn't say she knew me from my paintings.

6 September 1992

Jancsi tries to persuade me that I am doing too much.

'Those letters to classmates you haven't seen for fifty years. Fan mail which you answer. You visit people in hospital you have never been friends with.'

I try to explain that's why we are human beings. That I feel I am more fortunate than them.

Jancsi replies, 'The whole aim of this conversation is to *keep* you more fortunate.'

János writes from Khabarovsk. 'All day a constant stream of young Russians, thirsty for spirit. A bit intense with sixty people booked for the Council of All Beings, *before* I announced it on the radio, they're hungry for the earth.'

8 September 1992

Edmund Capon's secretary, Margaret, rang to invite me to a memorial service being held in the Art Gallery for Ken and Yasuko Myer. Joanna Capon took over to ask me if I had a sketch for the portrait of Yasuko. 'Yes, I have, in the kimono. Another sketch is hanging in their flat.'

'I know. But I would like to buy this one for the Gallery. Could you bring it with you? Edmund is in St Vincent's Hospital after an operation for a pinched nerve in his neck, but he will be here, and Yasuko's parents came from Japan. They have donated Yasuko's kimonos to the Gallery.'

A very select group, about thirty people, came into the Asian wing and sat on chairs in a semicircle amongst ikebana arrangements and the latest Japanese screens and scrolls Ken and Yasuko donated. Ken's son spoke about how he became a family man after he married Yasuko. She kept the family together.

Edmund walked to the microphone very carefully, a plaster collar protecting the wound. It was a warm and moving oration, and I could just see Yasuko and Ken when Edmund talked about a Chinese train journey they made together.

I looked at the yellow kimono crucified on the wall, which they so lovingly showed me when I first came to the flat, which her mother's ministrations built on her for the sketching and which she unpacked with such care.

17 October 1992

Gene Sherman and the Alliance Francaise Parisian exhibition is proceeding.

Yves Corbel, director of the Alliance, chose my *Max Ernst on Pompidou Terrace* with the old Parisian houses for the lithograph.

In Fred's Glebe Point Studio I was given a metal plate and chalks, tuss, a pen, brushes. I gridded my drawing to enlarge it, and did the black version on the first day. The three other colours were yellow for the sky, red for the houses and pale blue for the part of the sky, part of figures and terrace, so yellow and blue got over each other, red over the yellow houses and over the blue ground creating mauve. Each colour had a different plate on which Fred traced my drawing. I then gave tone with water and tuss and blobs, creating my mottled surface.

1 November 1992

Robert Hughes is in town to deliver the Qantas lecture for the Australian National Gallery's tenth birthday. He privately said he would like to be reincarnated as a rat in the Prado. At which the prime minister said, 'I'm quite happy to be a rat in Canberra.'

9 November 1992

Jancsi's ninetieth birthday was amazing. Lots of books. The astonishing thing was that he wasn't 'insulted' by all the celebrations! János rang from America.

16 November 1992

Surfers Paradise

Ten days in our birdcage above the waters.

Jancsi cautioned me again to take on less, to mind my years.

I painted Bunny McConnell in four consecutive days. I dread this because the 'observer' is left out. I was lucky, it's good.

22 November 1992

Sydney

The Jewish Holocaust Museum opened. I am one of the survivors. Instead of going to the opening after flying from Surfers, we had soup and pancakes at 21. Eva Klug arrived from the museum and said, 'Judy has such a big photograph there.'

'I am not impressed,' Jancsi said, 'I have the original.'

On Friday, Bob Raymond took me to Avalon to be filmed painting a portrait of Sali Herman. I chose a foundation: blue and umber floating shapes with ivory in the top centre.

Sali wore a blue and umber shirt. His egg-shaped skull was the ivory.

He is lucky in old age. His eyes are good, his mind alert and he still works. Gout has forced him into a wheelchair, but that doesn't bother him.

When we finished the portrait he called. 'Tell Ned to bring the Rolls Royce!' That's the wheelchair.

He is with his son Ted, his daughter-in-law Dawn (who takes care of Sali), his grandson and his wife and child.

I worked in the studio, lit by a skylight. Great good luck gave a red walking-stick into Sali's hand so the position of the hands, one above the other, grabbing the walking-stick shows determination.

'This is magic,' I heard the cameraman say.

13 December 1992

This morning I saw a possum before the open bathroom window. It climbed the pine tree without effort. How many cities in the world make such sightings possible?

Marina who came regularly all through the year with her paintings (besides going to the Willoughby Art Centre) met Lou who finds her talented. He talks to her in his usual intense way and when we discussed the way she should be guided through the maze, Lou said: 'We are different, Judy. I am Freud. You are Mother Teresa.'

3 January 1993

Exactly a year ago when the Lesers invited us to the Ritz-Carlton for dinner, Bernie suggested I should do something about my journals.

The Lesers arrived for their Christmas holidays. As Bernie was 'godfather', I gave Barbara all the volumes to take out to Palm Beach.

Bernie rang to tell me, we are both professionals. 'As you would not praise a painting of a friend if it is a bad painting,' he told me, 'I would not praise the writing of a friend if I did not like it.'

17 January 1993

János, Bodhi and his friend Adam are here. Bodhi is nearly six foot, gangling, loose-limbed, a beautiful child. I am in my grandma role. Chocolate torte and other culinary outpourings for the three days of their stay.

I can't disperse this love into normal slots, it's concentrated for occasions.

I started the portrait of Woolworths chairman, Paul Simons, who bid for it at the Smith Family auction. He is Welsh, came here during the Second World War with the navy, fell in love with his future wife and stayed. He told me about the cancer they fought together. She died two years ago.

Death is very much in the forefront. Sidney Nolan died. Frank Hinder died. But there are also untimely deaths. Nureyev was only fifty-four. He had AIDS.

'All lives are irreplaceable,' says an article, 'but the death of an artist leaves a void that echoes beyond the circle of loved ones. There is the art work that will never be made, the lessons not passed onto a new generation. A single death creates a chain reaction.'

26 January 1993

Guilt-driven visit to the Art Gallery of NSW where Tony Bond's Biennale is shown. Also a separate show of Kiefer, Richter, Polke, Beuys. Four big names but that's all. Kiefer has a huge room with an installation, honouring great women. How does he honour them? By making iron beds with crinkled soiled sheets of lead, and in the middle a pool of blood. Urine?

Beuys has bleached photos of Greta Garbo on dark magenta paint. Sigmar Polke presents us with an experiment. He collected atomic stones. He credits the countries where he collected them, put the stones on photo negatives and waited for the radiation. With all this blurb, what we have are uninteresting, unaesthetic, boring, white blobs in black surrounds.

The Biennale proper has practically no paintings. The standard of the objects low. Exception: Dokupil. Three good paintings, spare and abstract but to fit in, he finds it necessary to tell us that one was done with burnt candle wax and two with smearing orange halves on muslin.

As we wandered in the expanse I saw one of my guard friends, sitting strangely enough, in a perspex box.

'Why are you in this box?' I asked him.

'I am an exhibit,' he said.

31 January 1993

Paul Simons's last sitting. He appeared with a great bunch of roses. Tom Harvey, of Woolworths, came to see it, as well as Paul's daughter,

Margaret Krempff (like Kampfner going topsy-turvy) and her baby, Sheena.

Camparis, sodas, apple juice, nuts. Half an hour later the Smith Family's Susan Hall and Bob Turner. All liked it. Paul commissioned me to paint Margaret. My good deed rewarded!

Daryl Hill rang. He wants to screen the Sali Herman film for us. The film is excellent, but the cameraman likes to distort. Sali is ninety-five, but I am twenty-three years younger. I look as old as he does. My teeth are dark and crooked. Not that I care.

János was up to the third version of arrival with Eshana. Originally they were due on Saturday morning. He changed it to Friday morning. They now will arrive on Sunday morning.

I have told Jancsi he should always do what is pleasant for him. 'Greet them, and settle down in your favourite armchair with Saturday's papers and the radio. Or have brunch first. Whatever you like.'

He was the life and soul of the party.

15 February 1993

My Rolls Royce of an easel arrived from Italy. At the switch of a button it lifts the painting up and down, or tilts it. It rolls softly and glows with the discreet polish of good furniture.

19 February 1993

Shayne and Peter talked of the days of the workshop. János's back is sore again and Eshana remarked, 'It's usually at the workshop when it happens.'

Shayne said affectionately, 'Of course. He carries the whole workshop. He carries the planet on his back.'

25 February 1993

Paul Simons's daughter came with seven-month-old Sheena for the first sitting. I sketched them together with some speed as Sheena, of course, slithered, stretched, cried, fed, laughed, crawled. Yellow blobs alternated with blue, a plump baby hand appeared on Margaret's chest, a fat thigh at her mother's waist. Then I took the camera. Sheena's face is now enchanting, and I am amazed why I have spurned such a useful device all my life.

Thirty-five paintings of Ormiston and Glen Helen and some of Kakadu were picked up by Philip Krass of Cyril Framing, the same day as the opening of Marina Finlay's second exhibition.

That morning, Morris West, whom she met in my studio, rang her to say both he and Joy will be there, and 'Please, put a red dot on the painting you would like me to have.'

What kindness!

I prepared Marina for weeks not to be too disappointed if she doesn't sell much. 'Last year was a sell-out,' I said, 'because they were very cheap, because all of your mother's friends bought, but I told you then, the public is fickle. Nobody sells in this recession.'

There I was, eating my words with a huge grin as twenty-three paintings were sold.

Now that my exhibition is finished, I invited my girlfriends for Sunday afternoon coffee again. I realise how old we have become. Juliska is eighty-two, starts to look frail and her habit of finishing one's sentences has become more pronounced. However, she is wise, quick-witted, curious, well-informed and devours books.

Nelly is my age, but gave up on herself. Márton is in hospital with pneumonia so she didn't come. Gréti Pallai is nearing ninety, stopped playing bridge and driving the car. Emma, at seventy-six, is young, still creating top cuisine and she loves spending money. Vera Kaldor is also keeping young by being active and interested.

26 February 1993

Bowral

At Jancsi's insistence, we are having a blessed and much-needed break at Bowral. I haven't driven that far in years and had a bit of secret apprehension about how my back will behave, and how I'll find my way on the new highways, and how I'll cope with speed.

After this morning's magic walk in the park with ducks and geese, and of course, remembering Monet's garden, I said, 'I'm really happy to have come for these five days, after the trauma of the drive ...'

'It's not trauma now,' he said. 'It's a *Traum*.' (Dream, in German.)

27 February 1993

We swam in the pool before breakfast, and drove to Kangaroo Valley yesterday, down hairpin curves into sweltering heat, escaping up the mountain again to Fitzroy Falls. I discovered an enchanting lake at the bottom of the park of the Heritage Hotel and spent mornings doing small pastels of swirls in the water and exotic plants.

2 March 1993

We drove home on the coast, through Wollongong and had lunch on the Bulli Pass. Not only was the landscape spectacularly beautiful, through winding forest roads, but I regained confidence as I realised I can drive as well as twenty years ago, and the tension was gone.

3 March 1993

Sydney

With Betty Riddell at Morris West's testimonial dinner. 'At the end of a long career,' Mollie Missen writes in our program, 'it seems utterly appropriate that it is he who has elected to break the mould that has served him so well, and sign off with a flourish.' She writes that his appeal lies in the way he opens windows on the world, and that he is one of the illuminators. And that, what really pleases his readers is placing themselves into the hands of a decent, compassionate man, who helps them make better sense of the modern world.

Morris's speech was spellbinding, like hearing short stories read aloud.

When I got home, after listening to the outpouring, Jancsi said, 'I am so happy you were there. The only thing that makes me even happier is that you came home.'

12 March 1993

We are on an exclusive diet of election. Radio, television, newspapers, at breakfast, lunch and dinner. It has taken Jancsi over completely. But it's marvellous that he can be so interested.

I finished the Louis Kahan painting for the Archibald and two Rainbow Valley gouaches for the new Dobell Prize for drawing. Am hoping and praying that I might have achieved the old-age style I so admired in old masters like Hokusai or Monet or Turner. Looser, more transparent.

14 March 1993

Labor won the election. With one million unemployed, and a huge foreign debt, Keating triumphed over Hewson, who couldn't sell the people his goods and services tax. I'm glad it's over because Jancsi became a radioholic.

Last week was Lou Klepac's first 'Masterclass' interview and I was his subject. It was advertised, and by the time we woke up, the Art Gallery venue Lou chose was booked out.

31 March 1993

A slap. My portrait of Louis Kahan was rejected from the Archibald. A humbling experience.

I'm hanging in the, apparently outstanding, inaugural Dobell Prize for drawing, with *Desert alp, Rainbow Valley*.

S.H. Ervin Gallery asked my permission to hang the Louis Kahan in their 'alternative Archibald' which is the '*Salon des Refusés*'. The name was changed this year to the Rival Show. Manet's *Déjeuner sur L'Herbe* was there in 1863, as was Whistler.

Charles Blackman rang me a few days ago reporting that, in preparation for his retrospective this year, a film is being made of him. 'Judy, it will be opened by Zelman Cowen. An apt choice, don't you think? Jews have been my spiritual parents. Like Georges Mora, like Jancsi. We were filming in the Botanical Gardens. I drew the Opera House. Japanese tourists surrounded me. A lovely honeymoon couple came, so I drew a geisha in the sky above the Opera House. She was so delighted, I tore the page out and gave it to her. 'Wedding present,' I said. It was all being recorded. I like painting near the sea, Judy. Claude Debussy composed his *Sunken cathedral* above Atlantis where, at a certain tide the spires rise.'

3 April 1993

Garry Shead won the Archibald Prize and Kevin Connor the Dobell Drawing Prize, and I am delighted about how delighted I am for both. Garry has been a runner-up for nine years. His Hungarian wife Judit, a sculptor, lived in poverty and unable to do her own work. The sight of Garry's sixty-four teeth and the huge cheque last night was a joy to behold.

Not knowing their address I rang the Spigelmans who are great friends of theirs. Garry and Judit were there, and I congratulated them.

I also rang Kevin and rejoiced with him.

Both film-makers, Bob Raymond and Daryl Hill, telephoned. They can't make the opening of my show this afternoon as they are going to a wedding. Daryl said Sali Herman passed away yesterday.

Friday morning unexpectedly, Robert Walker came up with Robert Juniper who was rejected from the Archibald as well as the Wynne. Juniper wonders whether to do this over again. The freight costs him five hundred dollars one way, and his airfare as much. He looked splendid in black with the usual hat, and I offered to do an oil sketch.

11 April 1993

In one hour, the 'Macchiaioli' of Juniper emerged like Hosanna from the general gloom.

The opening of my solo show at the Holdsworth was a swinging party, full of artists, sprinkled with Hungarians. Buyers were hiding. It's been open for a week now, and there are two small sales, not enough for half the frames. No reviews. Good feedback from artists. George Molnar rang to say I am the best colourist in the country. Kevin thought it's my best show to date.

Lou turned the Pens and Pencils, a meeting of some artists at the S.H. Ervin Gallery, into a monthly lunch. Nora Heysen, always so shy, asked me to sit for a double portrait with Margaret Woodward. Both of us consented.

John Dowie, the Adelaide sculptor who did an excellent head of Lou, read us funny memoirs like when Ivor Hele's portrait of a general (who escaped from Singapore, leaving his troops behind) was found with its painted throat cut.

The Alliance Francaise and Dr Gene Sherman opened the exhibition Paris–Sydney at the former Macquarie Galleries in Clarence Street. Thirteen of my Paris paintings hang with Frank Hodgkinson's, Blackman's and three Whiteleys Gene borrowed from Perth and Melbourne. The rest are under probate with a court case around the corner. Arkie, Brett's daughter, is contesting his last will. Beryl is very unhappy.

My *Place des Vosges* was bought by the owner of Darcy's restaurant. Six hundred people made it awfully crowded, the French ambassador opened the exhibition. Gene gave dinner for forty in her Goodhope Gallery afterwards.

14 April 1993

All that can possibly go wrong with my painting-self went wrong this time. Out of thirty-five, only two little paintings sold in ten days. The one that sold first was the one printed on the Melbourne invitation card. Lyall won't rejoice. I try to ask the buyer to lend it for the show.

The Saturday, one week after the opening, Elwyn Lynn writes about the Archibald for the second time. I hoped, understandably, that the review I saw him write on opening day will appear, albeit only days before the closing date.

Lily rang me last night. The *Australian* can only publish Sydney reviews every fortnight as advertisers need the space. Shit. I know I have had a good and long run and shouldn't complain. I don't. But I woke up at 4.45 a.m. with anxiety. What can one do about that?

22 April 1993

Nora Heysen saw a photo of Margaret Woodward and myself. She liked the composition. We are both wearing white, and the tablecloth is white. There flowed a tremendous current in my studio with the three of us, women, painters, interested in the portrait. Alas, I am the one who is standing, but for art I have to make that sacrifice. Nora is in her eighties. Her beauty comes through still, I used to think her unfriendly, but it's all shyness.

The drawing she did of us is an artist's drawing. She was the first woman to win the Archibald in 1937. I was the second.

Yesterday was a marathon. Moriah School asked Anna Cohn, Maadi Einfeld and me to talk to twelve-year-old children about art. I thought that's what I was going for, but no. In the headmistress's office four chairs were placed round and tea prepared. It was to work out who is going to do what in June. She actually wanted us to teach once a week, but we declined.

I had an hour's siesta afterwards, dressed and went to the Alliance 'do' for the Art Gallery Society. Frank Hodgkinson and I talked about Paris experiences and our paintings. Blackman didn't come.

3 May 1993

We celebrated our fifty-fourth wedding anniversary. We booked at Darcy's whose owner, Attilio Marinangeli, bought my *Place des Vosges*. It hangs well-lit, and we were ushered to a special nook at a window with a palm tree and creepers. After a splendid meal and being fussed over, Attilio brought a small Taramisu cake with a burning candle, 'Happy Anniversary' written on it in chocolate.

Sali Herman's memorial at the Art Gallery of NSW. Nice speeches by Edmund and Barry Pearce. I sat with Van Hodgkinson, Frank's first wife.

On Saturday my exhibition opened at the former David Ellis, now Lyall Burton Galleries.

The small irritations continued, an Elwyn Lynn review appeared in the *Australian* three days after it was finished at the Holdsworth. I'm glad I have it for my scrapbook, and Lyall pinned it up for my show. Further, several people complained that Lyall's invitation didn't have an address or telephone number. We looked and found that some did, some didn't as the printer haphazardly cut the cards at the wrong spot. However, the support of artists was gratifying.

12 May 1993

I watch myself ageing. Not so much wrinkle-wise, as that doesn't disturb me, but everything I used to do efficiently and fast has slowed down, requires more effort, and something or other gets neglected in the process. We used to be a hospitable house. Now Jancsi is disturbed by visitors and usually stays in his armchair in the bedroom.

20 May 1993

Surfers Paradise

It's the lap of luxury, in the Marriott Resort. From the window of the sixteenth floor one sees the beach on the right, surfers, a cumulus of rain clouds with a blinding streak of silver. Directly below the lagoon fed by a waterfall. Over the Japanese bridge, the pool, a gazebo, the walkway on the shore of the river where a red and white boat just docked.

János and Peter rang from Cape Tribulation. Shayne and Eshana are also there.

26 May 1993

A week loitered by. I feel rested, not grasping why dialling a number in Sydney or writing a letter was like lifting weights. Jancsi is a source of love and warmth. Sometimes the beam of his eyes makes me look at him and he says, 'I love you.'

Today, as we left the water and waded through sand towards the promenade, our footprints merged with those of the seagulls and look powdered softly as if with an airbrush.

We sit down on the wooden bench, clean our bare feet which feel like schnitzels, with a towel. Undo the knot of the laces of our Reeboks which we hang over our shoulders when we walk.

1 June 1993

Peter had an unused plane ticket. Hearing that János, Greta and Bodhi arrive on Monday, he arrived Friday.

They arrived, after Bodhi's maths exam. Greta and Bodhi surfed, her body still perfect. In the hotel we all swim. Father and son jump in and race. They have fun under the waterfall.

2 June 1993

Our last walk, grey clouds under our feet, the surf foaming over them.

6 June 1993

Sydney

I was waiting for Jancsi to bring dinner from the Hakoah when the telephone rang. A nurse told me that my husband was hit by a car and is in the emergency ward of St Vincent's Hospital. I took a taxi, and found Jancsi in a wheelchair in the corridor. 'I'm sorry, Jucókám,' he said, 'it was my fault. I was crossing New South Head Road while the Don't Walk sign was blinking. A taxi came up the hill and hit me. The driver brought me here.'

We waited for an hour in a cubicle to get a bed. Undressing him was agonising. An hour more to be x-rayed. An hour to have the x-rays read. An hour until the doctor told us that his right shoulder and right leg are broken. Another hour's wait for a bed in the orthopaedic wing on the sixteenth floor. The registrar, on our request, phoned Dr Cass. He is overseas. Dr R. will operate on him, next morning.

When I got home at midnight I rang Peter and Shayne whose birthday party was in full swing. I couldn't sleep for hours, my heart hammering in my chest like a terrified bird. Had to ring János next morning, before his departure to the US. Peter drove me to the hospital at 8 a.m. We were told the operation on the shoulder will take about an hour, the leg an hour, and he will be in recovery another hour.

I went home and cancelled all my engagements for the week.

At noon Jancsi was wheeled in, Peter, Shayne and I were stroking and kissing him. A bit later János walked in with Bodhi. Jancsi's drugged glance lit up in recognition but his pain was extreme and we all cried. Bodhi's eyes were red. János and Bodhi slept at Ocean Avenue and came to hospital with me in the morning. We found Jancsi sitting up in bed, bright as a button. He said, 'Even in my pain I felt that love you radiated. The beam concentrated on me and made me feel much better.'

'A miracle,' János said, and we got all teary again.

11 June 1993

Jancsi had a blood transfusion yesterday. I asked for the vascular professor, McGrath, because Jancsi was anxious about the leg with the blocked veins which was the one he broke. He looks very miserable and doesn't want visitors.

SBS came this morning for a longstanding appointment for their program 'Vox Populi'. Amanda Hickey told me she is interviewing a sample of the immigrant artists whom *Art and Australia* has done a special edition of.

12 June 1993

Jancsi hasn't slept for three nights. He was lifted into an armchair near the window where he was cold. I brought in his cashmere cardigan. 'My feet are cold.' I got sheepskin slippers but they fell off.

One learns. It's better to go home evenings, not to Medi, not to Ili. It's better not to accept all the food that's now overflowing in the fridge. Jancsi eats little and I take the rest home. I'm too exhausted to eat. Almost.

15 June 1993

Bottles of urine are on tables beside the beds. I do a drawing of Jancsi every day, and watercolours of rooftops.

17 June 1993

Sister Bernice invited me for coffee today. She said, 'Why don't you come over to St Vincent's Private? We have an orthopaedic wing also, with all the equipment and manpower.' Jancsi said he wants to sleep on it.

Peter and Shayne come twice every day, without fail. Sometimes three times. Great support.

21 June 1993

Sunday afternoon as I returned, Jancsi told me he will move to St Vincent's Private. I packed the miserable belongings into two plastic bags. Maya and George came just then, escorting me through one hospital into the other. Desk, filling out forms.

Jancsi has a corner room with a view from the ninth floor over Sydney. He grew more and more tense, I saw fear in his eyes. 'I think,' I said, 'you should have a special nurse for a couple of nights until you are used to the new place.' To my amazement he agreed.

Today Jancsi sat in the chair, still enjoying the pushbuttons. Even the curtains can be drawn with a button. He enjoyed an excellent lunch, like in a good hotel. Ready for bed. Really tired. When someone wheeled a chair in, taking him for an x-ray, I went home to rest.

22 June 1993

Peter remarked it is better to suffer in luxury.

Leon Fink, Peter's friend, came with a girlfriend, and Jancsi sparkled at his wry humour. Keeping his frustration exclusively for me.

26 June 1993

I snatch time to do a small pastel of the church in Victoria Street. I still draw Jancsi daily. Then, start anew with the round of massage. When lunch comes I help him eat, cutting everything into small bites so he can use a spoon with his left hand.

After lunch I bumped into the doctor in the corridor. He was in a rush, as always, but said, 'I hear you want a physician to see him.'

'That's right. My husband has a dry mouth, a blocked nose, and wants someone to look at the whole man, not only a part.'

'Oh. He wants someone to cure him, eh? To put the clock back.'

I didn't reply. Better if that sentence echoes back in his own head.

Tubi brings homemade honeycake. Gréti made him fish soup which turns into aspic when cold. The response of friends is tremendous, cards every day. I answer them as they arrive. I do anything that has to be done in the 'lunch break'. Shopping for food for János and Bodhi's imminent arrival.

I put the timer on for half an hour, and pray.

Yesterday Nelly fell and broke her leg and wrist. The stars are unkind. I offer Juliska lifts to St Vincent's Hospital when she cares to join.

27 June 1993

János arrived from the US this morning, before my usual call to the hospital. Nicola, the nurse rang me. 'Your husband asked me to call you. I've been trying for the last half an hour but it's engaged.'

'My son is here.'

'Your husband is not well. He didn't sleep last night. He is running a temperature, has a sore throat, didn't have breakfast, he has given up. He wants you to come. Here he is.'

'Juc,' Jancsi said hoarsely, 'come in now.'

'Jancsi, of course I'm coming. I haven't showered yet.'

'Don't shower. Come now!'

János and I arrived in record time to a distressed Jancsi who was awake since 2 a.m. He breathed like someone drowning, saved in the last minute. Then, like a miracle, Dr Cass walked in. I kissed him. Told him it is he we wanted but he was overseas.

'Yes,' he said, 'I had a lovely time in Paris with my wife.'

Proceeded to find out all complaints, medications, shone a torch in his throat, listened. I told him we want him to take over from the other doctor. He said he doesn't see why not. But I have to talk to him.

I hope he will be pleased to get rid of such a neurotic Jewish family. János listened to me not wanting to overdose Jancsi.

'Do what he wants,' János admonished me. 'If he wants an overdose, give it to him. Give him control over his own life. He is ninety. He has every right to do what he wants.' Wanting to bring Jancsi marijuana which would keep him happy, but hospital rules forbid smoking. So we stay with Valium.

Now, reassured, he sleeps all morning and I am fretting about the night to come.

29 June 1993

We have a special for the nights. János and Bodhi kissed him this morning on their way to Thredbo and skiing. I rang Dr Cass's secretary to say that since I told the doctor I would like Cass to take over, we fell between two stools. Neither turned up.

We had a breakthrough yesterday. Dr Cass took over. He simply said it usually takes six weeks for bones to knit and 'in about two and a half weeks we try to mobilise you'.

He talked to Peter and me, a sweet warm man after the chill.

I also called Peter Klug (son of my friend Eva) whose speciality is insomnia. This combination of well-known humane healers did us both a lot of good. All the doctors add: 'And what about you? You can't do this for too long or you will also get ill.'

7 July 1993

The x-ray showed that the shoulder collapsed. Dr Cass told Jancsi it is important to regain the use of the arm. It needs another operation.

I spent eight hours in hospital, but set limits when he wants me to stay till nine. I say *no*. It hurts.

Peter always escorts me down to the bowels of the building to the car. Last night they came home with me to share a drink. Peter made warm buttered toast. I receive more affection from all my children than I can ever remember.

Shayne and Peter are off to France and England this afternoon.

8 July 1993

Today, waiting to be wheeled to the operating theatre Jancsi said, 'This misfortune was perhaps necessary and important. It made me realise how wonderful Peter and Shayne are. Without it I might not have known Peter's real qualities, so generous and giving his time and his person. He is a jewel. A noble diamond. Always there with his big heart. A treasure.'

'I was a fortunate man,' he continued 'to have found you. You are a magnificent woman. Your good nature was so often mishandled by me and you never thought of revenge.'

Then, when they wheeled him back to his room, the agony started again. We were back to square one, I thought. Cass gave him a 'brand new shoulder' I was told, and Jancsi raved about why I let him live.

Jancsi told me he doesn't want to have this arm. I should take the bandages off. 'Let's take a taxi and go home,' he said.

It was 2 p.m. when I got home to rest. Jancsi rang at three to come at once. I took a special from one to four so he isn't alone. But I went.

In the evening I told him I can't sit ten hours on a chair, and if I break down I won't be able to come.

At home tons of messages on the recorder. I'm heating up the osso bucco Tubi sent over with her grand-daughter, Caroline. It's ten o'clock by the time I have dinner.

11 July 1993

Jancsi and I are almost back to 'normal', that is as he was before the second operation.

Bandi, Dr Kennedy, said to him today, 'Oh no, Jancsi, you obviously bang on that door up there in vain. They sent you back saying it's too early.' Which brought an old Jancsi smile to his sad face. For me, he only produces moans and groans.

12 July 1993

János rings us in the hospital daily, talks to Jancsi. Yesterday, he rang me in the morning, at home. 'I am so thankful, Juc,' he said 'at the way you built your life around Jancsi now. It is a lesson to me and to Bodhi that in this day and age, people still care like this for each other.'

13 July 1993

Cain died this morning, Marie told me tonight, crying. I am so sad, so sad.

17 July 1993

János was here for twenty-four hours to see Jancsi, leaving Bodhi alone for the first time, as Greta and Warwick are still in America. Yesterday, Dr Cass took the plaster off his leg and the bandage off his chest. He exchanged the plaster for a splint of some steel and rubber and plastic. The knee is left free, and every couple of days it will allow him to bend it more.

18 July 1993

I found him all melting honey this afternoon. Does he need to torture me in order to feel good? So it seems this morning. He asked me to help him from the bed to the chair, without the splint. I explained that I can't do what two nurses have done for six weeks. Besides, the splint has to be on at all times, Dr Cass said, except in bed.

I became the enemy once more. He argued, fought, wore me out. Made me responsible that the physiotherapist was late.

'Go to the desk (imperiously). Tell them to page her, otherwise I'll be worn out sitting in this chair with the splint on before I even begin.' By then I wasn't only crying, I was shaking too and couldn't stop. Like a leaking tap needing plumbing.

That's enough, I told myself. Set limits. If he behaves with you like this, walk out of the room.

22 July 1993

All evening it was: 'Ah, if I could only die. Call the doctor. I need something strong. An injection. My mouth is dry. (Apple juice, mouthwash, lemon-glycerine swab.) Perhaps a cold compress on my head. A toothpick. Massage my knee. I am afraid of the night.'

Then, the old Jancsi looked over the shoulder of this cranky, complaining tyrant and said, 'Juc, you have to be strong.'

'I *am* strong.'

'You have to be strong to put up with me.'

30 July 1993

St Vincent's Private is secretly named the Jesus Hilton. Of which Jancsi has had enough. 'I haven't drawn a breath of fresh air for six weeks,' he complained.

Then, suddenly, a bed became available at the War Memorial Rehabilitation Hospital.

My day started an hour early as the ambulance is a law unto itself, said the nurse, and they come as they please. I packed, took Fritzi's red cyclamen home and bought a tracksuit which is recommended for the gym.

I went to the opening of Surrealism last night. Marina picked me up, still from St Vincent's and deposited me back at 7.30 to give Jancsi a goodnight kiss. I didn't see the exhibition, only the crowd. Well-loved, well-known artists' faces.

31 July 1993

Unmitigated misery at the War Memorial Hospital. On a weekend it's the same 'neglect' as at St Vincent's, minus the luxuries. The unfulfilled promise of delivering the product. Old-fashioned Victorian cluster of buildings overshadowed by some high-tech discs on Birrell Street. It looms like a golem of a Christmas tree above the plaster statues at the edge of the lawn seriously considering parked cars. Upstairs a different car park of wheelchairs.

A nurse took Jancsi for a stroll. A walk means endless straps around the splint for his broken leg, pulling him up into a walking-frame. In the corridor, bent, crippled, shuffling geriatrics do the same.

A terrace which would be nice in summer is icy now, and Jancsi shivers in the tracksuit, so back we go. Dick Carter, the man in the bed next to Jancsi, is half-blind and half-deaf. Still, Jancsi is not alone in the room. In St Vincent's we had a special night nurse for all those weeks.

1 August 1993

'Ah, Mum, I'm so glad you called.' Peter sounded genuinely relieved in London, especially when hearing about Jancsi's walks to the dining room for his meals, and about feeding himself.

When they heard that János flies in again this week, Shayne exclaimed, 'Good heavens! And Jancsi isn't even a rainforest tree!'

'But almost,' I said.

4 August 1993

The gym is cavernous. White grandmothers lie on huge beds, with various contraptions pulling extremities up and down.

Jancsi did two and a half hours yesterday and two hours this afternoon. It isn't strenuous but still hard work. For instance, a rope through a wire mesh above his head holds two handles, both of which he grabs. The good arm pulls down and the injured arm goes up, then, pulls up the good arm. I suppose it really teaches the brain to signal the muscles which are now wrapped around steel instead of bone. It means also that therapy starts at 9.30 a.m., goes on till lunch, then a siesta. All of which requires my absence.

I was standing in the middle of our flat yesterday, utterly bewildered. It seems that *my* brain also has to grasp the fact that I can paint again, or edit my journals for half a day. I have done none of these.

This morning I slept till eight. Felt like a convalescent.

Sent *Renoir bust and shadow* to Sister Iris Parker, head sister on the ninth floor, to hang it there. Sister Bernice, who put me in touch with all of these people, and who gave me countless parking tickets, gets an original, *Water's edge, Bali.*

10 August 1993

Giant strides every day now. First, Jancsi was sent upstairs from the gym on his own. Walking in the frame to the lift, into it, out of it, walking to his room, to his chair. sitting down all independently. After this, going to the toilet on his own, after being lifted by two nurses for two months.

Today he was taught to walk with a four-pronged stick.

I finished a group of five small oil paintings on paper, for Anne von Bertouch's Collector's Choice.

13 August 1993

I had a visitor. The occupational therapist brought Jancsi home to see how he manages the stairs. She told both of us not to forget that 'The good leg goes to heaven, The bad leg goes to hell.'

Walking upstairs, use the good leg, down, use the bad leg. We looked at the shower recess, it needs a rail. The wall at the loo needs a rail too. We can borrow a wooden seat over the bathtub, a sturdy stool for the shower, a higher seat for the toilet bowl.

I served coffee, the orchids in the garden went mad and exploded into six stems of lilac blooms. Jancsi would have stayed if only he could have.

20 August 1993

Jancsi is home. I gave the hospital an aquatint, *Mother and child*, framed. János and Eshana were here for three days. The day before Jancsi's release, her parents, John and Jane Bragg, came for lunch. I couldn't believe my eyes. In walked a tall, lovely lady who resembled Shan, János's first wife.

Peter and Shayne returned that night from England, and came over to have a Scotch with me.

Next morning they also came to the hospital. I got a letter of the medical history, a letter to the district nurse, the x-rays, the stool, and the bathroom equipment. We removed all the Persian carpets on which one can stumble.

Jancsi walked upstairs beautifully, sat down in his favourite blue armchair in the bedroom, surrounded by both young couples, and we radiated love and happiness.

Eshana told us she will be Doctor Bragg in one more year, doctor of philosophy of ecology. Shayne asked, 'And you, János? What plans do you have?'

'I retire,' he said, 'and let Eshana support me in the manner I am accustomed to!'

I made scrambled eggs for the six of us.

Jancsi tries to do as much for himself as possible. The broken arm learned to do some writing, he can cut food with a knife, undo most buttons but he can't take his shoes and socks off, or the splint. It takes us about an hour to settle for the night, with a chair pulled between bed and armchair to support him when he stands up.

1 September 1993

Regimented life in Ocean Avenue. Monday and Wednesday the War Memorial Hospital bus picks up Jancsi and takes him for physiotherapy.

I shop for lunch and dinner, then race home as he is brought back at eleven.

On other mornings Sister Vi Duffy takes over, bless her. She seats him on the wooden seat over the bathtub and showers him, dries, dresses him, takes him for a walk. While I paint Sarah Indyk's portrait.

4 September 1993

I am painting the Brisbane commission. Kym Syvier, having the thumbnail photo enlarged. She died of an aneurism at twenty-eight. Marina sat in Kym's summer blouse tying a knot across her waist as she liked to do, with her beads and the dark glasses hooked in the buttonhole. Leaning forward slightly, in jeans. I use a magnifier to see the other snapshots of her, a mosaic of features hoping for the best.

For equilibrium, I worked on two of my hospital sketches.

14 September 1993

At last an important verdict: Dr McGrath listened to the blood in the bad leg, even Jancsi and I heard it on the machine sounding good, even surf on the beach.

'You can tick this one off your worries,' he said.

20 September 1993

The three months' hiatus must have seemed only longer for Nora Heysen who had her weekly portrait painting sessions with Margaret Woodward and me interrupted. As she is eighty-three and has trouble with her retina, this decision was a great renewal of the creative flow. Last week we kick-started it again.

While I am posing, my hands on Margaret's shoulder, I also scrutinise Nora, whose wrinkles can hardly spoil the beauty of her features, particularly her large blue eyes. Wearing a painter's apron, grey hair in a ponytail, tied by a ribbon, she looks almost girlish, being a silhouette against the light. Her palette is shiny, its surface like silk. After work she polishes it with a medium like French polish on an antique desk. The palette was given to her for her fifteenth birthday by Dame Nellie Melba.

Her father, who sent her to art school, made her milk the cows early mornings. When she returned after school she did the separating. She loved it, the smell, the farm atmosphere.

Lou, the minder of neglected artists, gave a retrospective exhibition for her bringing her forward and up from the past. She talks about events as 'before the resurrection' and 'after the resurrection of Lou'.

23 September 1993

One of János's frequent visits. Long, rewarding talks. Stalking up and down he describes his two homes in Wotherspoon Street, being by now in the middle of a forest. They have planted so many native saplings between them and the river that the whole cheap suburb has become upgraded. The drunks don't like it any more 'since the hippies moved in'.

Young people know about the Rainforest Information Centre from

Europe to the US. They appear in Lismore to offer their labour to the saving of rainforests.

How many live in 13 Wotherspoon Street? They come and go. About eleven. No, they don't pay rent. It's explained to them that donations are accepted for the rainforest. All contribute something.

Steve is a landscape gardener. 'You should see our garden. Everyone can pick any vegetables. Evenings we have communal meals. Steve made a wishing-well in the garden. Children can't fall in as they could into a fish pond.'

'Everyone's responsibility. It's a matter of honour to keep the house clean. And Eshana and I have the attic, the whole length of the house, overlooking garden, forest and river. She has her filing cabinet, I have mine. We have our computers. And if I am gone for six months everyone takes care of it.

'We spend the greater length of time in our "bus" at Bodhi Farm. The terrace, which is bigger than your living room, is completely fenced and walled in by mosquito nets. The tent-roof keeps it dry. How can I describe waking at five thirty to the thrill of so many birds? The yellow robin which uses the birdbath and then puffs himself up like a ball. I leave Eshana asleep in bed, go outside to light a fire in the open, and put the percolator on. Real coffee. We are completely surrounded by the forest, nobody can see us.'

24 September 1993

This morning Sydney has been declared the winner of the Olympic bid. The young people stayed up all night at Circular Quay for this moment.

As it happens János drove Jancsi and me to Homebush yesterday, which is the Olympics site. Bulldozers work full-time, and now it will be even fuller.

Bodhi was playing basketball for Lismore School and we sat in the Olympic stadium to watch him in the championships. Jancsi negotiated the steep steps downwards with splint and stick, and we were rewarded with radiant smiles and hugs.

The end is not really the end ...

I still keep a written record. My marriage remains a constant source of strength, nourishment and inspiration.

My art work is so intrinsically interwoven in the fabric of my being that I cannot conceive of any sort of existence without it. I pray that I will never have to.

And so my life will continue until God chooses to paint the last brushstroke.

This is a horoscope my mother had done for me in Vienna when I was about nine years old. I didn't see it until I was seventeen, by which time, of course, I was already a painter. I lost sight of the horoscope during the upheaval of the war and it wasn't until our last move fifteen years ago that I found it again. My family and I were amazed by the accuracy of its predictions.

The fifth house is the dominant house in this horoscope. It contains love, children (including spiritual children), art, and love of life. The field also indicates a person who is a central figure. She creates something outstanding.

The ruler of the fifth is Mercury. Mercury rules the intellect, as well as the hands. Leo is strongly represented and is the fifth sign of the circle, therefore a good connection.

Cancer-Leo signs in the second field (Capricorn) already point at a painter. It also shows that art is connected with financial benefits. It is interesting that in the beginning much pastel or gentle tones (Cancer) will be used, later comes stronger, more individual colour. The contact of Mercury with Venus for the development of her art is important. The strong contact between Venus and Pluto in the first field leaves an opportunity for practising this art. The sun in Leo, in the sign of painting, provides the talent to achieve. Neptune in Leo reinforces this talent, giving colour-richness, fantasy and something fascinating and bewitching.

However, Jupiter in Leo (good luck and success) is the crown in this talent. Jupiter guarantees success, as Jupiter is well-connected with the ascendant (the person herself). This is the pinnacle of the horoscope, which points to achievement in vocation. The work, therefore, is certain to set high standards of professionalism. A true artist.

The moon in Virgo indicates contact with the public and with criticism. (Virgo is an intellectual, critical sign.) Criticism by and large is favourable as Venus also stands in this sign. Contact with the public will be strongly activated by good contact with Mars (activity, power, energy) at the same time connecting with work (the sixth house). The combination of Venus, Saturn and the moon in Virgo gives the work a deep philosophical content. The sometimes too pleasing aspect of Venus and the Moon is being stretched firm by Saturn. The danger of the work becoming kitsch is prevented. The same situation acts on the psyche as a real resistance to express the depth of creativeness. The moon's influence makes it possible for the public to feel and realise this depth.

All this happens in the fourth field. This means that the home situation will be such as to make the possibility strong to grow and unfold.

When one thinks of the strong influence of the moon on art, and takes into account that the moon rules the second field (finance), one can presume that through good contact with Mars and Saturn, financial advantages and a regular income can be expected.

The profession stands in Pisces, an emotional, passive, moody sign. Uranus in this sign brings ideas in the profession which are eccentric and unconventional. This takes place in the twelfth house sign—inside the home or studio.

Normally, Uranus in the tenth field (profession) would indicate an adventurous career, something extraordinary. This sense for adventure will be fulfilled completely through the opposition with Venus.

The work is in the sign of Scorpio, a water sign and therefore very advantageous within the tenth field, the vocation.

Mars in the water sign in the sixth field is known to produce in painting the so-called dry technique, that is use of colours without too much medium. The type of work mostly preferred will be portraits because Mars, ruler of the head, rules the work field. The real striving will be getting under the surface (Scorpio).

In the house of realised ambitions, in Capricorn, is good luck. Above all else it shows that the art of painting has completely fulfilled this person.

The character is volatile but not as much by mood changes as by the impatient desire to break through and become somebody.

There is a somewhat nervous searching for new possibilities which may lead to irritability. However there is a tendency to live in harmony with family and a readiness to give in. Clashes—if they arise—are to be smoothed out.

Illnesses will appear in the abdomen, in the digestive tract. Also frequent colds with bronchial inflammations. There is great resilience and fast recoveries.

She will love journeys and travel. Will change her country later in life.

The abundance of planets in Leo is typical of a ruling nature, generous thinking, an open mind, a fighting spirit, independence and dignity. A good sign for artists and satisfaction in work.

Sun position: upbringing and intellect combine in creating a personal effort of work on herself. There is generosity, open hospitality. Very great life force. Ascendant: twin. Mobility. Many sidedness.

Position in Mars: great work capacity but also frequent states of exhaustion.

Pluto in the first field: abundance, creativity, originality.

All planets: emotional. Led to decisions by emotions.

Marriage: will be with a man much older than herself. Will marry very young.

Index

Abakanowitz, Magdalena, 255
ABC television, 278–9, 358
Abeles, Sir Peter, 225, 250
Aborigines, 119–20
abstract, 28, 51, 65, 71–2, 75, 88, 118, 155, 167
Adelaide Art Gallery, 58
Adelaide Festival (1962), 144–5
Agnews (London gallery), 115, 157
Akis (New Guinean artist), 220
Alexander Mackie College, 470
Alexandra, Princess, 108, 109, 114, 115, 122, 125, 138, 156–7, 176–7
Alice Prize, 307, 464
Allen, Christopher, 457
Allen, Davida, 396–7, 452
Alliance Francaise, 477, 481, 489, 490
Alvarez, A., 185
Amadio, Nadine, 357
Anderson, Sir Colin, 104, 107
Andrea, 48, 49, 50, 56, 63, 88, 143, 168, 193, 194, 216, 218, 251, 258, 279, 336, 373
Annand, Douglas, 246
Annigoni, Pietro, 84
Antico, Sir Tristan, 301, 319, 350
Antipodeans, 155
Araluen Art Gallery, 463
Arcades, 104–5
Archibald Prize: (1937), 490; (1953), 50; (1955), 60, 61; (1956), 64; (1957), 73–4; (1961), 123, 128; (1964), 161; (1968), 181; (1969), 189; (1972), 207; (1974), 230; (1975), 242; (1976), 252; (1977), 263; (1979), 283, 284, 289; (1980), 322; (1981), 309, 310; (1982), 319, 320; (1984), 351–2; (1985), 370; (1986), 380; (1987), 396–7; (1988), 411; (1989), 425, 426; (1990), 440; (1991), 450, 451–2; (1992), 456, 473; (1993), 487, 488, 490
Argus Gallery (Melbourne), 143, 152
Arias, Dr, 114–15
Arnold, Dr Peter, 459
Arnold, Shirley, 459
Arnott, Reverend Felix, 298
Art Advisory Board, 145, 152, 179
Art and Australia, 298, 391, 493

Art Gallery Foundation, 343
Art Gallery of NSW (*see also* Archibald Prize; Sulman Prize; Wynne Prize); JC's first visit (1951), 42; JC wins *Women's Weekly* prize (1955), 64; tapestry exhibition (1956), 66; buys painting from JC (1956), 67; library, 75; neglects Rapotec, 129; buys another painting from JC (1967), 179; Missingham retires (1971), 205; Lynns' visit (1973), 229; JC refuses to lecture (1974), 242; Orban retrospective (1975), 251; Abakanowitz exhibition (1976), 255; Biennale (1976), 260; Trustees, 299; Modern European and American Masters exhibition (1980), 301; Trustees, 301–2, 304–5, 311; Westfield proposes sponsorship (1981), 318–19; Bowral bequest, 348; Klippel exhibition (1983), 350; Lloyd Jones dinner (1983), 350; buys Kirchner (1984), 363; Rudy Komon Memorial Fund, 366; Guston exhibition (1984), 369; Orban Award, 370; Hiroshige exhibition (1985), 372; Monet exhibition (1985), 376; Lanceley show (1987), 405; Perspecta exhibition (1987), 409; Lynn retrospective proposed, 425; Readers Digest collection (1988), 426–7; German expressionists (1989), 439; Whiteley exhibition (1990), 442; Christo retrospective (1990), 448; Guggenheim exhibition (1991), 460; Myer memorial (1992), 481; Biennale (1993), 484; Herman's memorial (1993), 491
Art Gallery Society, 211, 490
Art International, 306, 320
Artists and Friends exhibition (1991), 457, 460
Askin, Robert, 189
Aspden, David, 206
Astor, Gavin, Lord, 163, 182, 316
Astor, Irene, Lady, 163, 316
Atroshenko, Paul, 472
Auerbach, Judy, 396
Austen, Sir John, 254
Australia Council, 255
Australian, 490, 491
Australian Consolidated Industries, 254